Travels

in
Persia, Afghanistan, Turkistan, and Beloochistan

HAJI MIRZA AGHASSI, Prime Minister of Persia under the late Mahmood Shah.
From a drawing by a Persian Artist.

FRONTISPIECE.

Travels

in

Persia, Afghanistan, Turkistan, and Beloochistan

with

Historical Notices of the Countries Lying Between

Russia and India

by

J P Ferrier

Formerly of the Chasseurs D'Afrique, and
Late Adjutant-General of the Persian Army

Edited by H D Seymour, MP

Manas Publications

New Delhi - 110 002 (India)

MANAS PUBLICATIONS
(Publishers, Distributors, Importers & Exporters)
4858, Prahlad Street,
24, Ansari Road, Darya Ganj,
New Delhi - 110 002 (INDIA)
Ph.: 23260783, 23265523 (O); 27131660(R)
Fax: 011- 23272766
E-mail: manaspublications@vsnl.com

First Published, 1857
Reproduced, 2005

ISBN 81-7049-265-3
Rs. 795/-

Printed in India at
Nice Printing Press, Delhi
and Published by Mrs. Suman Lata for
Manas Publications, 4858, Prahlad Street,
24, Ansari Road, Daryaganj,
New Delhi 110002 (INDIA)

Dedicated

TO MY ANCIENT COMRADES,

OF

THE 2ND REGIMENT OF CARABINEERS

AND

THE 1ST REGIMENT OF CHASSEURS D'AFRIQUE.

J. P. FERRIER.

Pondicherry, 1856.

PREFACE.

THE Travels presented in this volume to the public contain, it is believed, the latest accounts by an European of the countries of Central Asia. A part of the route is wholly new, and has never before been described. The author, M. Ferrier, is a French officer at present holding a government appointment at Pondicherry, who, born of respectable parents, enlisted as a private soldier, and served with distinction in Africa, where he gained the rank of "First Adjutant-Major."

In remembrance of these campaigns he has dedicated his book to his ancient comrades of the Carabineers and Chasseurs d'Afrique. About sixteen years ago M. Ferrier was selected, with other French officers, to go to Persia to drill and organize the Persian army—the English detachment,* which had been previously employed on that duty, having left the country, when diplomatic relations with the government of the Shah were suspended in 1839. M. Ferrier served in Persia for many years, and received the honorary rank of Adjutant-General of the Persian army.

He at length got into trouble from his known opposition to Russian interests, and, as he believes, through the intrigues of the Russian ambassador, was removed from his post. He returned to France in 1843, visiting

* Several of the officers belonging to this detachment subsequently rose into notice. Sir Justin Sheil held for ten years the important post of Minister in Persia; Colonel Farrant was Chargé d'Affaires at Teheran during a period of great difficulty; Major D'Arcy Todd was Envoy to Herat during the Afghan war; and Sir Henry Rawlinson, after successively filling the posts of Political Agent at Candahar and in Turkish Arabia, has been recently appointed to the East India Direction.

on his way all the Russian provinces to the south of the Caucasus.

M. Guizot was then first Minister in France, pursuing a temporizing peace policy, so that M. Ferrier entirely failed to get his alleged complaints against the Persian government attended to. After waiting several years in France in vain attempts to obtain the assistance of the government, he again, in 1845, turned his steps eastwards, determined to seek his fortunes in Lahore, where several of his countrymen were serving under the Regency which had succeeded the death of Runjeet Singh and the murder of Shere Singh. He staid a short time in Bagdad, and then set out upon his journey for Lahore, through Persia and Afghanistan.

At this point the following Narrative begins. It details with spirit and liveliness his journey through Persia till he reached the territories of Yar Mohamed; and here the more important part of the book commences, because henceforward the countries through which he passed are little known. There is probably no part of the world, not excepting the interior of Africa, which is so dangerous and inaccessible to the European traveller as Afghanistan and the countries of Central Asia. It is curious to read a Frenchman's account of Herat seven years after the celebrated siege, and four years after our evacuation of Afghanistan. It is satisfactory to find from an impartial witness the respect in which the English name is still held in these countries, and the grateful remembrance which the people entertain of the many acts of benevolence and kindness performed by our distinguished countrymen while there.

The graphic account of the interviews of M. Ferrier with that shameless politician, but most able ruler, Yar Mohamed, will also be found characteristic and instructive.

From Herat M. Ferrier tried to penetrate to Lahore by Balkh and Cabul, and here takes us over ground only partially known. Baffled in his attempt to pass, when at no great distance from Cabul, he strikes through the Hazarah country to the west by a route which no Afghan dare travel, and where no European had hitherto set foot, till he nearly reached the ancient town of Gour. Here he was again stopped, and sent back to Herat.

After resting from his labours, although warned of the danger of attempting it, he now set out to try and reach India through Southern Afghanistan, by Girishk and Candahar, and it is only wonderful, after reading his perilous adventures, to find that he was enabled to return alive from these inhospitable lands.

This part of the journey is particularly interesting, because he fell in here with many traces of the previous English occupation. He passed the post-houses we had erected: he met the chiefs who had either harrassed us in our misfortunes, or stood boldly by us in time of danger. His life was probably saved at Girishk by one whose good-will we had gained; and at Candahar he saw the unburied remains of one of our surest and best friends, slaughtered in his own garden, in tardy vengeance for the assistance he had rendered us during the Afghan war.

M. Ferrier's account of the grand river Helmund, which disappears in the Lake Seistan; his description of the country of Seistan, and of the wild Belooches, is clear and ably written, interspersed as the Narrative always is with exciting personal adventure, and traits of the character of the natives, such as could only be obtained by one who travelled alone, and like a native himself.

These parts of Candahar and Seistan are particularly interesting to us, because, since the port of Kurrachee in Sinde was improved and the fair established about four years ago, considerable traffic has sprung up with these countries; and it is probable that in a few years our intercourse with them will be much increased. It is said that of late years they have been principally supplied with English manufactures by way of Petersburg, since steam-communication has been established on the Volga and the Caspian, and even, I believe, the Aral Sea.* If such be really the case, there can be no doubt that Kurrachee may offer a successful competition, as it is on the coast of the countries to be supplied; and the longer sea-voyage from England would be cheaper than the route through Russia, which requires tedious land-carriage and a constant change of the means of transport. The probable reason that the Russian has hitherto had an advantage is, that there has been no port on the coast of Beloochistan or Sinde, and English merchandise could only penetrate into Central Asia from the south, either by the Persian Gulf, Bombay, or Calcutta. The Talpoor dynasty in Sinde, which preceded our occupation of the province, shut up the mouths of the Indus and the ports of Sinde against commerce, as the surest means, in their opinion, of preserving their country against annexation; consequently the large commerce which once flourished there is only just beginning again to spring up. The establishment of the port of Kurrachee; the rail which is being now laid down from that point to Koltree on the Indus; steam-navigation on the Indus; the railroad from Moultan to Lahore, which must be made in a few years; the projected railroad across Mesopotamia, corresponding with a line of steamers from the Persian Gulf to Kurrachee; and the roads across the Himalaya Mountains, opening routes into Thibet and China, must

* See Mr. Andrews's work on the Sinde railway.

gradually draw down to the ports of Sinde a large portion of the commerce of the great Asiatic table-land.

Some of the first countries to be influenced are Beloochistan and Afghanistan; and therefore every information concerning them, as to their productions, population, and the temper of the people and their rulers, is a subject of great and increasing interest. It is in these countries of Central Asia that we shall have for some years to come to fight a pacific battle with Russia; a battle which friends may fight, in which the struggle will not exhaust but invigorate the combatants; where the object of contention is as to who shall bring to the nations of Asia the manufactures of the civilised world? who shall stimulate them most to send in return the productions of their own fertile countries?

I had the pleasure of meeting M. Ferrier in 1846, at Teheran, soon after he had returned from his dangerous adventures. The next time I saw him was at Pondicherry, in 1854, when he showed me his MSS., and I offered to take charge of, and try to get an English publisher for a translation of them. They formed two volumes, of which the first, containing the Narrative, is now presented to the public; the second, a History of the Afghans, with Traditions collected in the Country, will follow, should the first be well received.

The excellent translation of them is due to the labours of Captain Jesse, who has bestowed great care upon it. I have been greatly assisted in revising the volume for the press by Sir Henry Rawlinson, whose great proficiency in ancient and modern Eastern lore, and special acquaintance with Afghanistan from having been political agent at Candahar during the Afghan war, made his assistance invaluable. My warmest thanks are due to him for having been good enough to look over the work of an unscientific, but very observant traveller, and for having enabled me, from his communications, to furnish the notes marked "Ed."

Sir John Login, who was surgeon to the British Mission at Herat, under Major Todd, and is now the guardian of the Maharajah Duleep Singh, most kindly looked over the part relating to Herat, with which he is so well acquainted, and the notes marked "L.", as well as an Appendix, are contributions from his stores of knowledge.

These competent witnesses declare M. Ferrier's Work to be, in their opinion, most accurate and faithful.

Extracts from the MSS. were read at the meeting of the British Association at Liverpool, in 1854, and Sir Roderick Murchison, in his observations upon them, said that he considered the work a valuable addition to our knowledge of the important countries of which it treats.

I do not hold myself responsible for the opinions expressed by the Author, especially upon political subjects; neither do I profess an agreement with some of them. They are given from a French point of view, differing from that generally taken in England, but are always expressed in most friendly terms towards our countrymen, doing them ample justice. It appears to me always desirable, in order to form a correct judgment, to hear the statements of others, even though we may be inclined to disagree with them.

I now commit the book to the candid judgment of the reader, believing that it shows acute observation, conscientious care, and considerable reading; which latter accomplishment is surprising when we consider the active life of the Author, and his few opportunities for consulting books.—The Editor.

CONTENTS.

CHAPTER I.

CHAPTER II.

CHAPTER III.

CHAPTER IV.

CHAPTER V.

CHAPTER VI.

CHAPTER VII.

CHAPTER VIII.

CHAPTER XII.

CHAPTER XIII.

CHAPTER XIV.

CHAPTER XV.

CHAPTER XVI.

CHAPTER XVII.

CHAPTER XVIII.

CHAPTER XIX.

CHAPTER XX.

CHAPTER XXI.

CHAPTER XXII.

CHAPTER XXIII.

CHAPTER XXIV.

CHAPTER XXV.

CHAPTER XXVI.

CHAPTER XXVII.

CHAPTER XXVIII.

CHAPTER XXIX.

CHAPTER XXX.

CHAPTER XXXI.

APPENDICES.

NOTE.—Certain Appendices are referred to in the body of the Work, which there has not been time to prepare for insertion.—ED.

ILLUSTRATIONS.

H. D. Seymour del. 1846.

VIEW OF BAGDAD, AND THE BRIDGE OF BOATS ACROSS THE TIGRIS, TAKEN FROM SULEIMAN MIRZA'S HOUSE.

The large ruin in front is now pulled down.

Page 1

CARAVAN JOURNEYS.

CHAPTER I.

The author leaves Bagdad — Object of his journey — Necessity for concealment — Scene with his servant's creditors — Nasséli Florès — Fortifications of Bagdad — Bakubáh — The caravan — The author's costume — The necessity for wearing it — Mollah Ali — Sheraban — Description of the jovial Mollah — His opinion of his countrymen — Appearance of the country — Kuzil Robat — Ancient walls — Kanaki — The Mollah's opinion of Mussulman pilgrims — His lòve of brandy and sausages — The private and Caravanserai Shah — The bazaar at Kanaki — Bandit population — Advantages of an Eastern dress — Caravan travelling — Kind feeling of the Mollah — Adam's forks preferred to silver ones — Marauders — Kusra Shireen — The Mollah all courage — The Bilbers appear — The Mollah all fears — The attack — The Mollah found where he should not have been — Description of Kusra Shireen — Ruins near it — The legend connected with them — The site of the ancient Oppidam.

In the spring of the year 1845, after a stay of sixteen months at Bagdad, I decided upon trying my fortune beyond Persia, in the countries yet imperfectly known of Central Asia. I did not conceal from myself the risk I was about to run in undertaking a journey which the majority of Orientals with whom I had conversed respecting it considered as likely to end fatally for me. To justify their apprehensions, they referred to the recent deaths of Stoddart and Conolly, setting before me the most fearful pictures of the cruelty of the Afghans, who, having recently escaped from the short-lived dominion of the British rule, were wholly devoid of pity for all Europeans on whom they could lay their hands. I saw nothing, however, in these representations to induce me to alter my determination, and feeling prepared for whatever might happen, and sure that my resolution would not fail me, I said to myself, like the Mahomedans, "What is written, is written: we cannot struggle against destiny; may mine be accomplished."

Fearing that my intention to pass through the states of Mohamed Shah, the King of Persia, might become known, and thus create serious difficulties and even dangers (for I had been obliged to leave that country by order of the government, in consequence of intrigues against me), I gave out that I was returning to France by Mosul, and obtained from Nejib Pasha, the governor of Bagdad, a *boyourdi*, or passport, to travel in that direction. Having divested myself of my European habiliments, and assumed a light Arab costume, I addressed myself to a man attached to a caravan, with whom I agreed to hire his mules for one tomaun* as far as Kermanshah, and quitted Bagdad at sundown on the 1st of April, 1845.

I had scarcely left the gates of the city ere I met with my first annoyance. For more than a year I had had in my service an Armenian named Ivan, whom I had previously known at Teheran; he was a strong fellow, sharp and intelligent, but a consummate scoundrel, and an unparalleled boaster. This fellow had travelled amongst the Turcomans with the unfortunate Nasséli Florès, who was assassinated by the Emir of Bokhara; he had also visited Herat and some of the neighbouring provinces, and it was this that induced me to keep him in my service, although I was aware that he was a dangerous man, a wrangler, obstinate, and a greedy thief. However, as I should have found the same vices in any other Persian servant, though perhaps in a less degree, but without his useful qualities, I gave up the idea of dismissing him, which I had thought of doing, persuaded that if he did not kill me himself, he would certainly not let any one else do so.

I was on the point of leaving the city by the gate of Mosul, and in the act of mounting a half-laden mule, when, as I have said, my troubles commenced, for Ivan introduced me to half-a-dozen of his creditors, who declared they would not allow him to leave till he had paid their bills, amounting to five tomauns. I sent them all to the devil, and left Ivan to settle with them; but as he was in possession of the secret of my journey, which I could not conceal from him, he took for granted I should not dare to be very hard upon him, and that on no account would I leave him in Bagdad, where he might divulge my projects. This was indeed the fact, but I did not wish to appear to give way at the first specimen of his knavery, so I mounted my beast, and left, pursued by the disappointed creditors, one of whom hung on by my bridle,

* Ten shillings.

another by my pack, while a third seized the tail of the innocent beast I rode, stopped me short, and reduced me to the sad necessity of letting fall a shower of blows upon them to rid myself of their importunities. Grumbling and growling they speedily withdrew, and I was not sorry to hear them bestowing upon Ivan, and with usury, the drubbing they had received from me. But before he could come up to entreat me to help him out of this dilemma, half his beard was gone, and thinking he had received sufficient punishment I made terms with his creditors, he giving them up a gun, and I advancing him two and a half tomauns. We now started by a magnificent Eastern moonlight, and crossed the desert plains, which on all sides surround the city of the Caliphs: some ruins, and a village half-way to Bakubáh, were the only objects that attracted my attention. A journey of nine hours brought us at day-break to the left bank of the Dialla, on which were ruins and over a considerable extent of ground.

The fortifications of Bagdad have been built with so little judgment, and are so much out of repair, that it would be impossible to defend the city against any serious attack. Its real defence on the side of Persia is on the Dialla; and here again there is another disadvantage—the right bank of the river, by which the enemy would advance, is higher than the left, by five and twenty or thirty feet, and is covered with gardens filled with trees which would much facilitate the approach to and passage of the river: though it is true the besieged might occupy these gardens themselves, still the absence of a bridge, by which to retreat in case they were beaten, would oblige them to use great caution in adopting that kind of defence.

Bakubáh is a small town, with a bazaar and mosque; it was formerly of great importance, being the point where several much frequented roads meet; but bloody wars and Mussulman apathy have brought it to a state of decay from which there is little chance of its ever recovering. There are now not more than seven or eight hundred houses. The town is surrounded by numerous gardens, in which the palm, orange, lemon, pomegranate, and mulberry trees flourish, and the immediate neighbourhood produces crops of all kinds of grain.

The caravan I joined had been assembling in small parties at Bakubáh for several days, and the detachment to which I belonged was the last. For this they waited before they set out to travel through the country between Bakubáh and Karúnd, the first station within the Persian frontier, for there were four dangerous spots to pass. Nothing now prevented our departure, and I was glad enough, as delay might create difficulties, and I was anxious to leave Turkey before any arose at Bagdad. Persia, it is true, might be still more insecure; but then I had a better chance of eluding those who were ill-disposed towards me, by changing, according to circumstances, the direction of my route.

Our caravan was composed of more than seven hundred persons, the greater portion being Persian pilgrims returning from the holy city of Kérbelah, and amongst them were the Princess Fakhret Doulet, aunt of the Shah of Persia, some princes, her brothers, and other lords attached to the court of Teheran. I recognized many who had not the same advantage with me, so much had my Arab dress, and a long beard dyed black after the Persian manner, disguised me. Speaking Persian as well as they did, I passed unnoticed in the crowd as a Greek merchant from Mosul. Prudence induced me to keep the strictest incognito, as I was entering Persia without leave, and without any definite object; and the intrigues of my enemies, and particularly the most implacable one, Mirza Abul Hassan Khan, the foreign minister, might misrepresent my motives to the Shah, and place me in a false and very unpleasant situation. Persia is a despotic country, where steel and poison play a great part, so that I took care in travelling to preserve my simple name of Yusuf, and to conceal myself as much as possible.

Though only the 2nd of April, the heat was intense; the centigrade thermometer stood at 35° in the tent, and the flies and musquitos left us no peace.

I had resolved to isolate myself as much as possible from the rest of the caravan, in order to avoid indiscreet questions, although I could not resist the polite advances that were made me by five or six of the pilgrims, amongst whom was a certain Mollah Ali, quite a modern Rabelais. Short, fat, with an open rubicund face, and a most sociable disposition, it was always his turn to speak; he knew a little of every thing, and was listened to with pleasure, even when he undertook to sing his own praises, which was not seldom, but he did this in a manner so droll and so witty, that it was impossible to resist the uproarious laugh which his eccentric sallies always provoked. From the first he declared he would be my friend, and from that moment he never ceased doing his utmost to prove to me the sincerity of his impromptu affection; always gay and original, I passed many a happy day in his company.

Sheraban, April 3rd—seven parasangs*—ten hours—a level road—and the country much intersected by canals, for the purposes of irrigation.—There were many villages on both sides of us, but the beautiful crops, still standing, were much injured by clouds of locusts. The day had scarcely dawned when I was made somewhat uneasy by recognizing the prince Timour Mirza,† whom I had known at Bagdad, and who accompanied as far as the frontier his aunt, the Princess Fakhret Doulet. This prince had been exiled from Persia ever since his father, Ferman Ferman, formerly Governor of the province of Fars, had aspired to the crown. He eyed me closely, but without being able to recollect me in my humble attire; his manner, however, showed that he suspected some mystery, for he followed me perseveringly, until I eluded him in the crowd, where I found my new friend, Mollah Ali, whose cheerful gossip soon made me forget my fears.

This singular follower of Islam was one of the most extraordinary of Mussulmans: superstitious, and orthodox to the very roots of his hair, with his countrymen, to whom he never ceased preaching, and always reprimanded sharply for any religious short comings, when alone with me he set no bounds to his toleration and self-indulgence. "Look at these sons of the infernal regions" *pidar sukhta*, he used to say; "at each moment they invoke the

---

* A *parasang* is about three miles and a half, more or less in different districts.

† Timour Mirza was one of the Persian princes who were in England some years ago, and who have lived ever since at Bagdad on small pensions from the English Government. Timour means 'Lion' in Arabic, and this prince is worthy of the name, for his courage is celebrated. He has had frequent mêlées with the Arabs, who come sometimes up to the gates of Bagdad. On one occasion, in 1846, he was surprised by a party while out hawking. At first, the Arabs knowing him, would only have taken some plunder, until one of their number approaching the prince too familiarly, was struck by him. The Arabs, irritated, made a general attack, in which Timour fell, bravely fighting, and was carried into Bagdad for dead from a spear-wound through his lungs, from which he however recovered. The Arabs have a great superstition about killing or wounding any person of a chief's family, and in their own quarrels the chiefs are generally shut up in a tent while the tribe fights. The attack on Timour Mirza, they thought, brought ill luck upon them; their sheep and camels died; disease attacked their families, and, for a long time afterwards, they used to send in deputations to the prince to induce him to remove the fancied curse from them.—ED.

name of God, of Ali, and the holy Imaums, and yet they never cease to disobey their commands. What hypocrites! pretending poverty, but having their clothes lined with gold ducats all the while, and don't give me an obolus in spite of all the pains I take to keep them in the right way, and make the good seed grow in their hearts. As to promises, they have storehouses of these that are never empty. In the morning, when we arrive at our halting place, I often have to cook my pillau myself, and, without any respect for my sacred character, they allow my hands to be degraded by the low labours of the kitchen, instead of assisting and feeding me. Ah! you Younàns * are much more humanized; all men are your brothers, and yet these dogs look upon you as impure; but I, though I am a Mussulman, am far from sharing this stupid notion, and to prove it to you, I come to-night to settle myself with you in a retired corner, and we'll mess together—what say you? do you agree?"

The intention of the Mollah was very evident. He wished to hang upon my hooks. But his amiable character, and metaphorical language, so thoroughly pleased and amused me, that I accepted his proposition, and from that night we chummed together, to the great despair of Ivan, who had to receive his reiterated orders, which he dared not disobey.

There are from two hundred and fifty to three hundred houses in Sheraban, and many of them are crowned by five or six nests of storks. I never saw so many of these birds as in this place.

Kúzil Robát, April 4th — four parasangs — six hours.—We travelled during an hour and a half through the plain, gradually rising, and then crossed a mountain of sand and gravel, the western side of which was covered with immense rounded blocks of stone. It took us an hour and a half to pass this mountain, when we descended into a plain, pretty well watered, with here and there some fine pastures.

On arriving at Kúzil Robát, my friend the Mollah very nearly broke his neck by a fall; he and his mule rolled one over the other, until they were brought up by a stinking marsh, in which some wild ducks were dabbling, that flew off with loud cries. Thinking this accident a warning from heaven not to go through

* The Persian name for the Greek subjects of the Sultan.

the village, Mollah Ali insisted on going round it to arrive at our encampment, and I went with him, as it gave me an opportunity of seeing the walls. These were made of thick layers of earth, placed one on the other, and hardened; they appeared very ancient, and were of considerable extent. On the eastern side we remarked a gate built of burnt bricks like those at Babylon, and these certainly dated before Islamism had become the religion of this country. Kúzil Robát contains four hundred and fifty houses.

Kanaki, April 5th—four parasangs—six hours—across a plain varied by low hills.

A caravan of Mussulman pilgrims is very dull society for a Christian traveller; for amongst them he is always sure to meet with the greatest fanatics. "These dogs," as their countryman Mollah Ali called them, although covered with vermin and smelling of rancid butter enough to suffocate one, used to run out of the way to let me pass, keeping to windward as if the air were tainted by my Christian presence. Even by paying heavily, I could not have obtained the smallest service from the crowd of beggars, almost naked, who followed the caravan on foot: from these ragamuffins I endured the greatest insults, which I was obliged to put up with. The pilgrims deafen one with the repetition of their pious vociferations, for the sole purpose of impressing their hearers with a great idea of their holiness, which it is quite allowable to question. They regularly recite the five prayers prescribed by the Koran, and every time the appointed hour comes round, the caravan stops until they have finished. I was the only person who did not join in their devotions; for my rascal Ivan, although a Christian, accommodated himself to the customs of all nations: he prayed to Jesus with his co-religionists, to Mahomet with the Mussulmans, to the divine fire with the Ghebers—in short was never embarrassed by any creed, as he was conversant with the external forms of all religions, and practised them alternately, according to the company in which he found himself. Standing therefore as I did aloof at the hours of prayer, many an angry scowl was cast upon me, and many unpleasant remarks were directed against me; but the consideration with which Mollah Ali treated me, and the tenacity with which he defended me, had a certain effect upon these fanatics, for they were afraid of incurring his displeasure by molesting me. My friend failed not to let me understand by the most direct allusions, made in the most flowery terms, how happy

I ought to think myself in the enjoyment of his protection under the circumstances, and how proper it would be if I comforted his stomach after such speeches with a glass of wine or brandy—a request that I willingly acceded to: the Mollah even ate one of my pork sausages, swearing by Allah, that at Bagdad, where I bought mine, they were all made of beef, and "even if they were made of pork," he added in a low tone, "the sin would not be such a wonderful sin to eat one on a journey, where the privations are so great." He then confidentially owned to me that he could not understand why the Prophet had forbidden this innocent food, and commented on the Koran, in such a manner as to make light of his transgression.

Kanaki is a small town of a thousand houses; the entrance to it is by a paved street, which crosses the town, and terminates at a fine bridge of burnt brick of nine arches, leading to the suburb situated on the right bank of the Dialla, where there is a splendid caravanserai: the caravanserai-shâh is open to travellers gratis; in those which are the property of individuals, the traveller pays a trifling sum to the *dalan-dar*, or porter, for admittance. The caravanserai-shâh at Kanaki is in the centre of a square surrounded by low booths which form the bazaar. Here are always to be found crowds of the pillaging population of the neighbourhood, both Arabs and Kurds: the Jaf elbows the Sindjavi; the Bilber finds himself by the side of the Bachtiyári and the Lour;* and this assemblage of types of races so different is very strange and picturesque. Ferocity, and instincts the most uncultivated and energetic, were depicted on almost every countenance. Every one

* The Jaf are a very large tribe, dependent on Turkey, and numbering about 25,000 families, who inhabit in winter the plains of Sulimaniah and Zohab, and in summer migrate to the mountains of Ardelan. They are the most warlike and unruly of all the Kurdish tribes.

The Sindjavi are a tribe of Kurds depending upon Persia, who alternately inhabit the mountains of Kermanshah and the plains upon the Turkish frontier. They do not number more than 2000 families.

Bachtiyári. The name of a great Persian tribe inhabiting the mountains between Shuster and Ispahan. They are named Πατισχορεις by Strabo, and Patiskhuris in the cuneiform inscriptions. Their manners and language have scarcely changed since the days of Cyrus. They retained their independence till about 1840, when they were conquered and decimated by the Persian Government, and their chiefs kept in perpetual imprisonment at Teheran.

The Lour is the inhabitant of the province of Luristán, a Persian province joining the pashalik of Bagdad on the East, and extending to the Bachtiyári mountains.—Consult Baron de Bode's Travels in Luristan, London, about 1844; and Sir H. Rawlinson's Memoir, Trans. Geogr. Soc. 1839, from which an extract is given.—See App. A.

was armed to the teeth, and the majority of them come here rather to find out what opportunity is likely to present itself of plundering a caravan than for any honest purpose: perhaps there is not a greater set of vagabonds on the face of the earth. I cannot help, however, admiring the air of dignity with which these men wear their wretched rags, that contrast so strangely with the richness and beauty of their arms: one bandit, whose clothes would not have sold literally for sixpence, had a gun of great value; the long damascened rifle barrel was of the finest workmanship, but the lock was bad; both the lock and barrel were fixed to the stock by bands of silver, ornamented with gold and precious stones. Some fine lances, which I also saw, were made of a long, hard, and flexible reed, but they did not seem to me very handy. At Kanaki it would be imprudent to go for a moment unarmed, or to lose sight of one's baggage; for men, women, and children crowd round travellers with one single object, that of robbing them; they rarely retire without having got something, and if they are superior in number, raise a shout at a signal agreed upon, rush upon their victims, and strip them in open day. A pleasant occurrence of this kind had taken place about eight months before, after which Nejib Pasha of Bagdad detached 400 Albanians to protect the bazaar, and though they were strong enough to prevent robberies, they winked at them on receiving a proper consideration.

I had now worn my simple Arab shirt for several days, and quickly discovered its advantages over an European dress, for it contributed to my security and ease, and saved me many a tomaun. Our European clothes, tight, in bad taste, and, as an Oriental considers them, indecent, if they have by chance the merit of procuring a certain consideration on the part of Persian functionaries, do most decidedly attract the insults of the children and lower orders, and make the wearer a mark for every kind of extortion. For economy also there is nothing like an Arab robe: it costs five shillings, and will last for two or three years: we may with good reason take an example from the simplicity of Oriental habits, and repress among ourselves an excessive luxury in dress. Never, I must confess, did I feel more at my ease than in my simple shirt of coarse linen, mounted on my mule, which carried all that was necessary for my wants. Without being quite as lightly clothed as Diogenes, the reforms in my wardrobe had been considerable; the same mule carried my whole equipment, a simple saucepan, a small iron stove, and a felt carpet, which, doubled in two, served me for a bed and covering. Ivan was not so easily accommodated, and seemed humiliated to serve a master who made such a sorry figure. He revolted at the idea of riding a mule for which I paid only half price, because, besides his precious person, it carried two bales of American cotton. On arriving at Kanaki he bought a horse with some tomauns of which he had cheated me, and began to play the gentleman, even with Mollah Ali, whom he no longer obeyed without much remonstrance. Luckily my friend was good natured, and made the best of everything. Each day, on reaching our encampment, he was the first to dig a cooking place, and prepared our simple pillau; when it was ready we each attacked it with our fingers, without the aid of either spoons or forks, and after two or three days I acquitted myself as well as if I had eaten in this manner all my life. Really, whatever European etiquette may teach us, this Eastern fashion has its advantages, and now that I am once more amongst people who consider their civilisation superior to that of the Persians, I often regret being obliged to use a pointed instrument, for I enjoyed certain dishes much more when I carried them to my mouth with the assistance of my fingers.

We were on the watch the whole night we passed at Kanaki: but in spite of our vigilance the marauders contrived to steal several beasts and their loads. Our pleasure was great when at sunrise we left this inhospitable place.

Kusra Shireen, April 6th—five parasangs—six hours.—The country for the first four parasangs wild and undulating, the last cultivated and irrigated from the waters of the Dialla. Two days before we reached this, a brigade of Persian cavalry cantoned at Serpeul, under the orders of the Sertip Shah Abbas Khan, had a bloody engagement with the nomadic Bilbers on the road we had to pass; killing several of them, and making many prisoners. The general opinion, therefore, was that the defeated Bilbers would revenge themselves on the first caravan that came their way, and before leaving Kanaki every one looked to his arms. "What is written, is written," however, being the Persian motto, the caravan, as on other days, divided itself into small detachments, which followed one another at considerable intervals, consoling themselves with the words *Khooda Kerim*, God is merciful. Observing our scattered line of march, I begged Mollah Ali to exert his influence and rally round us a hundred men, but my eccentric companion answered me only by a look at once dignified and droll. His eye kindled, his nostrils distended, and assuming a warlike air, he put himself in the attitude for throwing the "jereed," and thus apostrophised me: "What have you to fear, as long as you are with me? Are you ignorant that my reputation extends over every Mussulman country, and who is the dog that dare to expose himself to the edge of my sabre? Cease your fears, my friend: whatever happens, trust in me." Notwithstanding this assurance, I kept close to some armed horsemen, who were with the women and the loaded mules, the detachments in front and rear being out of sight. Suddenly Ivan called out, "*Sahib, duzd amadest!*" Master, here are the robbers! At this exclamation Mollah Ali looked round, with a quivering lip, and seeing no one, said, "*Merdké*, Oh man, why disturb the calm we were enjoying? may God forbid it! *Khooda né Kouned!* keep your visions to yourself, hold your stupid tongue, and cease to agitate our minds." But Ivan persisted, and he was correct, for he showed us the heads of men looking over the tops of some little hillocks on our right. Our scouts immediately galloped to the front, the women and children offering invocations to Allah, and all the Imaums were sent to the rear; in an instant the mules were unpacked, the bales of merchandise ranged in a circle to serve as a breastwork, and we waited the attack. When our scouts thought our defensive dispositions sufficiently complete, they retreated in good order, and joined us. The Bilbers, about three hundred in number, followed them, but at a respectful distance, firing out of shot, which we answered by a shower of balls, that likewise fell short: both parties continued this amusement for three quarters of an hour, until the Shah's aunt came up with her brothers and numerous escort, when the brigands dispersed in all directions. Mollah Ali, who had disappeared at the beginning of the fray, was, after some minutes' search, discovered under the litter of one of the women, ensconced between two bales of English cloth. Frightfully pale, and his tongue and throat so dry he could not speak, the holy man was some time before he recovered. I watched him afterwards as he walked amongst the various groups of pilgrims, relating his adventures, and heard him frequently pronouncing a pompous eulogy on his own valour.

Kusra Shireen, a small village of twenty-eight houses, with a caravanserai-shâh in pretty good condition, is situated on the side of a mountain, at the foot of which flows the Dialla. This is an abominable place, and the inhabitants, a rascally set, form part of the rabble who lie in wait for travellers at Kanaki. Provisions sell here at an exorbitant price, that is to say, when there are any; for generally there is nothing to be had, and it is prudent always to lay in a stock at the preceding stage. In the rare times of plenty there are only eggs, sour milk, bad black bread, and barley and straw, which the inhabitants purchase in other places and re-sell to travellers; Kusra Shireen produces nothing but flints, which cover the ground six inches deep.

This village is situated at the western extremity of a large town in ruins, and the enceinte, which is clearly to be traced, forms a long square of at least a league in length on the shortest front. Numerous portions of wall and remains of edifices, which must once have been very magnificent, are still standing; many of these were built of enormous blocks of hewn stone, and this must have been a very important city, for the ruins extend over a distance of twelve miles. The Persians, who delight only in the marvellous, have not failed to write a host of legends on this locality, most of them in honour of the beautiful Shireen and her lover Ferhad, the famous sculptor, to whom they attribute the most gigantic works. They say this amorous artist cut an aqueduct in the living rock, five parasangs in length, the ruins of which are still visible, extending from the foot of the mountains to the town, and filled it with milk for his favourite courser, which was lodged in the palace of his beloved. Shireen, who is such a favourite with Persian authors, lived in the beginning of the seventh century, and was the favourite of the Sassanide king, Khosroo Purviz, but she nevertheless responded to the advances of the sculptor Ferhad. Khosroo was not ignorant of the fact, and promised Ferhad to yield him the object of his love if he could bring into the plain the abundant waters which flowed from the mountains, and were lost amongst them, or at their base. Ferhad immediately set to work, and this labour, which all supposed impossible, was accomplished with complete success by the artist, and nearly terminated, when the King, foreseeing that he would lose his beautiful mistress, sent a messenger to Ferhad to inform him of her death. The unhappy man was at that moment on the summit of a precipice, and in his despair cast himself into the abyss at his feet, and terminated his existence. As for the beautiful Shireen, although the poets say that she passionately loved Ferhad, yet they make her poison herself some time after, not for him, but partly for grief at the death of Khosroo, and partly to escape from the unhallowed love of his son and successor Sirsez. All the ancient monuments in Persia, of which the origin is unknown, are exclusively attributed by the Persians either to Ferhad or to Roostem.

It is not necessary that I should give the Persian version of the origin of Kusra Shireen. No doubt it had been built many ages when Ferhad lived; it is indeed impossible to attribute its construction to the Persians at all, because they never used hewn stone. In the most ancient times, as now, they always employed brick dried in the sun, and occasionally burnt brick, and this is the reason we find no vestige of the monuments that originally existed in the great Persian cities, the very sites of which are now an object of doubt among the learned. If I may be allowed to hazard an opinion, I should say that the ruins of Kusra Shireen might be those of the city of Oppidam, which is placed by ancient authors in the Zagros mountains, between Opis and Ecbatana, and was founded by a colony of Bœotians, who followed Xerxes into Persia.

CHAPTER II.

Serpeul — Attack on the Jafs — Attacked by the Jafs — Persian honour — Shah Abbas Khan — His vile conduct to the foregoing tribe — Official malversations — Karund — Mountain road — The Sindjavis — Conduct of the Princess — Scene of confusion — Iliate apathy — Mollah Ali's opinion of these nomads — Relation of Mahomedan sects to one another — The pass of Karund — Arrival at that town — The inhabitants — Revolt of the Karundians — Reason for this — Horrible treachery — Crime committed with impunity — Haroonabad — Mahed-asht — Kermanshah — Mohamed Ali Mirza — Abbas Mirza — Kurdish troops — Decay of Kermanshah — Persian army — Emir Mohib Ali Khan — Bad administration — Flocks of the Kurds — Horses of the province — Carpets — Cakes of Manna — Revenues — Tak-el-Bostan — Ivan's villany — Bêsitoon — The Kerkha river — Extensive ruins — Inscriptions — The Persian caravan — Kungawar — Mount Nahavend — Fortress of Kungawar — Battle here in 641 A.D. — Fine pastures — The site of ancient Ecbatana — Arrian — The tomb of Hephæstion.

SERPEUL, April 7th—four parasangs—five and a-half hours.—Before leaving Kusra Shireen we fell into fresh difficulties, which were nearly ending in a more tragic manner than those of the previous day. The Sertip Shah Abbas Khan, commanding the Persian cavalry quartered at Serpeul, had made an expedition in the month of March against the Jafs. This tribe inhabited a territory, the possession of which had been previously claimed by the Shah of Persia and the Sultan; but as the Persians occupied it in force, they remained in possession and enjoyed the revenues. The present attack on the Jafs was made on account of some pretended depredations which the latter had committed, and their refusal to pay tribute. The Persian cavalry fell suddenly upon their camp, sabring the Jafs, and pillaging everything they could lay their hands on. Thus surprised, they had only time to leap on their horses and secure the safety of their women and children, abandoning to the assailants their tents and flocks, and leaving in their hands the bodies of seven men killed upon the spot. They were, however, able to carry off the greater part of their wounded, and only seventeen were taken into Serpeul by Shah Abbas Khan with the rich booty he had captured. We heard this at Kusra Shireen, and as the Jafs were in the neighbourhood, many of the pilgrims with myself thought it prudent to retire within the walls of the caravanserai; but the Princess Fakhret Doulet, believing herself sufficiently safe under the protection of her numerous suite, and the near neighbourhood of the Persian cavalry, did not think it necessary to adopt this precaution, but pitched her tents on the banks of the river. This imprudence was nearly costing her dear. It was by the greatest chance that in the middle of the night she received information that Mohamed Beg, the chief of the Jafs, was advancing with six hundred horsemen to carry her off; and she and her escort had scarcely rejoined us in the caravanserai, and barricaded the door, when the Jafs appeared, crowning the eminences which commanded our retreat. A fusillade immediately opened upon us, but as harmless in its results as that of the day before with the Bilbers: it continued till day-break without any one being either killed or wounded. Ibrahim Pasha, Governor of Zohab, who was with the Princess, was then sent out to parley with Mohamed Beg, when they came to the following terms:—Mohamed Beg engaged to escort the Princess and her suite as far as Serpeul, on condition that when she reached that town she would intercede with Shah Abbas Khan for the restoration of the Jaf prisoners, and all the property and flocks he had carried off. Mohamed Beg executed his engagement faithfully, and conducted us to Serpeul, but the Princess was no sooner in safety than she showed herself far less sensitive to the value of a promise than the Jaf chief, for she shut herself up in her tent, refused to receive him, and told him if he did not instantly retire, she would order Shah Abbas Khan to make him.

The Persians are famous for treachery, and this is well known; but I am bound to say, in justice to those who formed our caravan, that they were indignant at the base conduct of the Princess, and declared loudly that Shah Abbas Khan had invented the delinquencies of the poor Jafs, because he wanted an excuse for plundering them, and to make the Shah believe that he was a brave, zealous, and intelligent officer. The pilgrims assured me that the Jafs, far from pillaging any caravans, contributed, on the contrary, to the safety of the road; for, occupying as they did the contested ground between Persia and Turkey, they had a positive interest in expelling from this district all desperadoes, and putting down disturbances which might otherwise compromise them. The tribute had been faithfully and regularly paid, but as Shah Abbas Khan wished to double it for his own benefit, they had refused his unjust demand. Such was the lawless transaction that took place at Serpeul, and such are of daily occurrence in all parts of the Persian empire. With so bad a system, how can this country recover from its present state of impoverishment and decay? The subordinate officers pillage and divide the fruits of their peculations with the ministers who retain them in their places, because they profit by their iniquity. The most unfortunate portion of the Persian population, namely, the labouring classes, are always the most ill-treated, and their complaints never reach the foot of the throne until they have been so transformed and falsified as to draw upon them fresh persecutions instead of procuring the justice they seek. Finding it impossible to obtain this, they take the matter into their own hands when opportunity offers, and the thousand miseries which they bear in silence become at length so insupportable that many a bloody episode is the result. Nevertheless the Shah thinks his people happy. Unfortunate Persia! wretched Persians!

The road from Kusra Shireen to Serpeul is undulating, the surface arid and stony. The caravanserai-shâh, at the latter place, is bad, and occupied by a detachment of Persian cavalry who refused to admit us within its precincts; a dozen huts are built against it, and in these provisions are sold; the river Dialla flows near the caravanserai, which is spanned by a bridge that gives its name to the place. I was now on the Persian territory.

Karund, April 8th—seven parasangs—eleven hours and a-half. After three hours' travelling through meadows, in a valley watered by several streams, we left on our right the high mountains of Louristan, covered with tufts of trees and still capped with snow. Our road lay across some others on our left: the oak, lime, beech, and elm were thinly scattered on their summits amongst various kinds of wild fruit trees and brushwood. The road, though not particularly steep, is very difficult, on account of the many blocks of fallen rock, and the flints which cover it so thickly,—it was with infinite difficulty the horses picked their way. Besides these impediments an accidental circumstance considerably delayed our progress.

The road from the base to the summit of the mountain was crowded with beasts of burden and flocks belonging to the tribe of Sindjavis; they were migrating from the plain, which becomes arid in summer, to settle for a time in the mountain pastures. Their baggage and four thousand tents were carried by camels, horses, oxen, mules and asses, which barred our way at every step. The Princess and the Persians paused not at these obstacles, but breaking their way through the multitude, upset everything before them. Their shouts, the lamentations of the Sindjavis, the screams and tears of the women and children, the bellowing of oxen, neighing of horses, braying of asses, barking of dogs, bleating of sheep and goats, and crowing of cocks, gave a most strange character to the scene. This avalanche of Persians, clashing with the heterogeneous mass, threw many of the laden animals over the precipice, and it was piteous to see the young lambs, kids and calves, attached to some of the loads, dashed to pieces as they rolled down the ravine. I could not comprehend the resignation of these unfortunate Iliates, who, strong enough to have overpowered us in the twinkling of an eye, submitted to the destruction of their property without daring to utter a word of remonstrance. This, however, they did, and called down the blessings of heaven upon the royal lady and her ill-conditioned escort.

I could not refrain from expressing my sentiments on this subject to Mollah Ali, who had scarcely recovered his powers of speech, so much had terror impaired it at the time we were attacked by the Bilbers. His native air, however, and the variety of scenes presented to us in the midst of the Sindjavi migration, had restored him to his normal condition. "How," he replied, "can you pity these brutes? they can only be compared to the beasts of the forest,—they are quite as savage. These nations are Mussulman only in name; they say no prayers, they perform no ablutions, they do not fast, and they refuse tithe to the Mollahs. I am convinced that to exterminate them would be an act infinitely pleasing to God and to the Prophet. I grant you that the women might be spared to supply the harems, where they would learn something good. To think otherwise of these miscreants would be to provoke the wrath of Heaven." And there is no doubt that the opinions of my friend the Mollah were held by every Persian in our caravan; the Sindjavis being looked upon as belonging to a sect that is only nominally Mussulman, which is sufficient to put them out of the pale of the law in the opinion of these fanatic pilgrims. In those countries in which Islamism is divided into various sects, the state of the people in relation to each other is almost inconceivable: they are all irreconcilable enemies, though they occasionally fraternize.

In spite of the obstacles we encountered, three quarters of an hour brought us to the top of the mountain, and the first step of the ascent to the great table-land of Central Asia was accomplished. Thence we traversed a country, sometimes undulating, but more frequently level, by a defile much wooded, and very fatiguing to our animals on account of the stones which covered the road. In the middle of the defile we came to a caravanserai-shâh, at the extremity of the forest; beyond it the valley expands to the width of about two miles, and contains extensive pastures, on which the nomadic tribes pitch their innumerable tents during the summer months: here and there might also be observed a few villages.*

Having left the forest, we pursued our way for two hours and a half along the valley, when we arrived at Karund, a large town of eleven hundred houses. Here we found a caravanserai-shâh surrounded with gardens. The inhabitants of this place are *Ali illahi*, worshippers of Ali, whom they consider as God; they eat

* Since I wrote this journal the Persians have bound themselves by the treaty of Erzeroom, in 1848, to restore Zohab and Serpûl to the Turks. The mountain of Karund, the most natural boundary between the two states, has been pointed out by the special commissioners as the frontier to be recognised in future by both nations; but, in my opinion, this division will only complicate the question, instead of setting it at rest, and for this simple reason:—This border is inhabited by a nomadic population, who are unable to maintain their flocks unless they can, for the five coldest months of the year, resort to the pastures of the plain which has been ceded to the Turks: during the seven hot months it is indispensable they should remove to the pasturage of the mountains to replace that which is dried up in the plain. The district, therefore, will probably be deserted, it being a physical impossibility that the tribes should maintain their flocks when deprived of the right of moving from one country to the other; or else this right ought to be conceded to them, and then Turks and Persians will equally seek to levy tolls upon these Iliates, which will give rise to interminable differences. The Persians under Mahomed Ali Mirza undertook the government of the plain, simply to put an end to such feuds; and, though taking it from them might to a certain extent satisfy the Sultan's self-love, it will most surely create endless difficulties for his government.

For a trifling expense the Shah might fortify the pass of Karund, and his frontier on that side would then be very difficult to attack; but Persian money is seldom spent for the purposes of public utility, and these important works will no more be executed by Nasser Eddin Shah than they were by his late father Mahmoud Shah.

pork, drink fermented liquors, never pray, never fast in Rhamazan, and are cruel and savage in their habits. Although almost always in revolt against Persia, it is scarcely possible to subdue them: therefore these feuds are compromised, and never thoroughly repressed by force; if this is resorted to, they immediately abandon their dwellings and take refuge in the mountains, where a Persian army cannot follow them. The tax levied upon the people of Karund is very trifling, though their territory is rich; the tribute was reduced in 1842, in consequence of a revolt which recalls the memory of the Sicilian Vespers, and caused the greatest sensation in Teheran. I was there when the news arrived, and the following is the account that was then given of the event.*

A young man of Karund having prevailed upon a girl belonging to a neighbouring village to leave her father's roof and live with him, afterwards refused to pay the indemnity customary in such cases, to induce the parent to give up his right to his daughter. On this he made a complaint to Hadji Khan Sheki, of the tribe of Shirvan, Governor of Kermanshah, who sent some *farraches*, revenue officers, to receive the indemnity; but the inhabitants of Karund attacked them, and in the end drove them out of the village. This was followed by another visit from a stronger party of farraches, but the second expedition fared no better than the first. Hadji Khan then marched against the

* The following is Colonel Rawlinson's account of the singular religion of the Ali Illahi sect:—"This faith," he says, "bears evident marks of Judaism, singularly amalgamated with Sabæan, Christian, and Mahometan legends. The tomb of Baba Yadgar, in the Pass of Zardah, is their holy place; and this at the time of the Arab invasion of Persia was regarded as the abode of Elias. The Ali-Illahis believe in a succession of incarnations of the Godhead, amounting to 1001; Benjamin, Moses, Elias, David, Jesus Christ, Ali and his tutor Salman, a joint development, the Imam Hossein, and the Haftan (the seven bodies) are considered the chief of their incarnations: the Haftan were seven Pirs, or spiritual guides, who lived in the early ages of Islam, and each, worshipped as the Deity, is an object of adoration in some particular part of Kurdistan. Baba Yadgar was one of these. The whole of the incarnations are thus regarded as one and the same person, the bodily form of the divine manifestation having alone changed; but the most perfect development is supposed to have taken place in the persons of Benjamin, David, and Ali. The Spanish Jew, Benjamin of Tudela, seems to have considered the whole of these Ali-Illahis as Jews; and it is possible that in his time their faith may have been less corrupted. . . . Amaria also, where the false Messias David Elias appeared, with whose story the English reader is now familiar, was certainly in the district of Holwan."—*Journal of Royal Geographical Society*, vol. ix. p. 36.—Ed.

rebels with five hundred men and four pieces of cannon, not only to punish them for this breach of custom, but also to collect the arrears of tribute, which had been of several years' standing. This occurred in the depth of winter; and as the Karundians could not, without danger of being frozen, avail themselves of their usual retreats, they adopted a different system. When the governor approached the city they went out in a body to meet him, entreated his pardon, and promised that if it were granted, they would pay thrice the sum demanded of them; Hadji Khan, glad to conclude the affair without bloodshed, granted their request and entered the town. He was lodged in one of the best houses with a suite of ten persons; his soldiers were dispersed amongst the inhabitants, who showed them every possible kindness, and wearied with their hard day's march through the snow, soon sunk into profound slumber. At midnight a single shot was fired: it was the signal agreed upon by the Karundians to fall upon and slaughter their unsuspecting victims, and they did so. The governor, who had not retired to rest, alarmed his attendants and had time to barricade the house ere the rebels reached it: for ten hours he defended it successfully; for his people never threw away a shot, and each time a piece was discharged one of the Karundians bit the dust. Seeing themselves thus decimated without obtaining any result, they determined to set fire to the besieged house, which being partly built of wood as well as the houses near it, was soon in flames.

Hadji Khan, however, was resolved to die the death of a soldier, and had no idea of remaining there to be burned without revenge. Supported by his ten devoted followers, he rushed out of the house like an infuriated lion, and fell upon his brutal assailants; but his heroic courage availed him not against the fearful odds—he was surrounded, and, after a desperate struggle, fell to rise no more. The Persian Government displayed its usual feebleness by forbearing in any way to punish these cut-throats: they were pardoned, and the amount of their tribute reduced. It is thus that the certainty of impunity relaxes all the ties of obedience in Persia: there is no medium there; and when useless severity is not employed, the most dangerous weakness is exhibited.

I heard afterwards that the Persian Government had good reasons for not punishing the Karundians, for though the foregoing report of Hadji Mirza Aghassi,* the Prime Minister (who was in the habit of constantly deceiving the Shâh), was entirely false, it was nevertheless this report which was inserted in the Persian archives by the *tevarik-neuvis*, historian, of the Kajars, to serve hereafter as an historical document, connected with the reigning dynasty; and for that reason I have left it in my journal. This incident is a striking proof how necessary it is to receive Persian statements with caution, even in books on the most important subjects: venality or fear, or both, so often lead to the distortion of facts, that it is very unusual to find an author who has the courage to tell the truth; neither is it easy to ascertain it. There is no free press in the country; communication with different and distant places is exceedingly bad, or there is none at all; and the despotism of the Government will not suffer any event to be made known, but in the manner, and at the time, that best suits its own purposes, so that the verification of any report is extremely difficult, if not hopeless. There were not five persons in Teheran who knew within the year how the massacre of the Karundians really happened, nor did I, until some time had elapsed. Hadji Khan Sheki had no complaint to make against the Karundians other than that they were unwilling to pay their taxes, and this determined him to march against them with 800 men, of whom 300 were Gooláms,† of Turkish origin: these he

---

* This remarkable man, whose portrait forms the frontispiece, was a native of Erivan, and, consequently, a Russian subject. He was tutor to the late Mohammed Shah, and when the pupil ascended the throne the tutor became his prime minister, and remained so till his death. He was a man of ability, but rapacious and cruel; the great offices of state and governorships of provinces were always sold by him, and, as the purchasers were sure of a very short tenure, they were allowed to oppress the people in a fearful manner. The army was nearly nominal, as the men lived in their villages and the officers pocketed their pay. The Russians were naturally paramount under such a minister, who used, when anything displeased him, to say, "I am not a Persian, I am a Russian; and if the king does not want me, I will order my mule and ride back to my native place, Erivan." During all the time of his ministry, English influence was reduced to the lowest ebb.—ED.

† Gholam means properly slave, and the term is now applied to a kind of inferior civil officer or policeman, answering to a "cavass" in Turkey; several of these are attached to each European embassy in Persia. The Shah has also a number attached to his person who are called Golami Shah: these form a kind of body-guard.

The Russians use their Gholams only for posting purposes, to accompany members of the embassy, and have a body of Cossacks for escort. The English Gholams are used for escort and also for posting purposes, as the regular native Indian cavalry who used to form the escort of the English ambassador was discontinued during the mission of Sir Gore Ouseley, which lasted from 1812 to 1818.—ED.

took into the village, leaving the 500 Kermansháh infantry in a caravanserai and huts amongst the gardens, at about a cannon shot from the place. Many of the inhabitants, foreseeing there would be bloodshed, sent their wives and daughters into the mountains, though in the depth of winter; others, less prudent or less fearful, kept them at home. From the time of his arrival Hadji Khan manifested every intention to act with severity, and at once levied the tax and demanded provisions for his troops. The tax upon the inhabitants, which he had already heavily increased, became doubly vexatious, owing to the avidity of his subalterns, each of whom played the tyrant over the master of the house in which he was quartered, who dared not offer the slightest resistance, though they also savagely ill-treated the women.

As for the governor, he sent some of his servants to seize and carry off one of the most beautiful girls in the village, but when they arrived at the house they found her father there: indignant and exasperated, he defended his child and wounded the foremost soldier, but his comrades coming up, they seized the unhappy man and carried him before the Khan, who, with his own dagger, gave him more than twenty wounds, and afterwards swore by the beard of the Shah that he would, as soon as day broke, strangle half the people in the village. The old man vainly begged forgiveness; the monster continued inexorable; and the Karundians, driven to despair, rushed to the public square, and there, by an oath, to break which would, in their opinion, expose them to eternal condemnation, swore to fight their ruthless enemies to the last gasp. They then dispersed, fell upon the drunken and sleeping Gooláms, and slaughtered them like sheep. The governor, warned of the fact, barricaded himself in his quarters, and died as related by the infamous Hadji Mirza Ághassi.

As to the troops in the caravanserai, they belonged to the same province as the Karundians, and did not disguise their sympathy in their cause, so that when ordered to advance to the support of their rascally chief, they marched up so slowly as entirely to secure the victory to the unhappy townspeople. These troops returned to Kermanshah without having received the smallest insult, while of the Turks not one ever left the place. The people who are designated Turks by the Persians, are those subjects of the Shah who inhabit the province of Azerbaiján, because they all speak the Turkish language: they are abhorred in the other provinces where Persian is spoken; less, however, on account of the difference of language, than because they furnish the greater number of the soldiers in the regular army. They tyrannize over and outrage the population in every way wherever they are quartered.

The people whom Europeans call Turks, and who are governed by the Sultan, receive in Persia, and all other parts of Asia, the name of Osmanlis.

When I was at Karúnd the centigrade thermometer marked but 16 degrees of heat in the shade; at Bakubáh, eight days before, it indicated 35.

Haroon-abad, April 9th—four parasangs—seven hours. An easy road along the valley, varied occasionally by low wooded hills. This village is situated nearly at the rise of one of the sources of the river Kerah: its population inhabit it only in the summer; in the winter they resort to the plain to escape the intense cold. About sixty houses and a caravanserai-shâh constitute the village of Haroon-abad.

Mahed-asht, April 10th—five parasangs—seven hours and a half. For the first three quarters of an hour the road, which was level and good, crossed the plain of Karund; afterwards turning suddenly to the east it led into the mountains, and was for the next hour very steep; it then came out upon a superb plain, in which stood Mahed-asht, a village of eighty houses; by it flows a little river in which are found an amazing number of tortoises: there are many villages amongst the rich pastures of this plain.

Kermansháh, April 11th—three parasangs—five hours wending our way through valleys and mountains to the foot of those against which the town stands. Numbers of gardens line the gorge which lies west of the city. The walls are in ruins, and the moat much encumbered with their *débris*, so that it is now an open town. Under Feth Ali Shah, it was the capital of a large province, and the residence of his eldest son Mohamed Ali Mirza, Governor-General of Persian Kurdistan. This prince was the son of a Georgian slave, and for that reason his father determined to deprive him of his right to the crown at his death, and transfer it to his second son Abbas Mirza, Governor of Azerbaiján, whose mother was of the royal tribe of Kájars.* But Mohamed Ali

* The Kájars are the tribe to which the reigning family of Persia belong. They are one of the seven Turkish tribes which supported Shah Ismail, one

Mirza protested against his father's decision, and declared in a solemn audience at Teheran, in the presence of all his brothers, that after his parent's death the sword alone should decide between him and Abbas Mirza. Having said this, he mounted his horse and returned to Kermanshah, where he devoted himself to the organisation of such an army as should enable him to execute his threat and render his claim triumphant.*

The Kurds, who serve in considerable numbers in Mohamed Ali Mirza's army, are a warlike race, and possessed of every quality that belongs to a good soldier. They were trained by excellent French officers, such as Messrs. Court and Devaux, and would well bear comparison with the troops of Abbas Mirza, who were trained by English officers sent to him by the East India Company. †

The province of Kermansháh benefited much by the disunion between the royal brothers, for Mohamed Ali, feeling the necessity of attaching the population to his interests, administered the affairs of his government in a truly paternal manner. His charities had enriched the town, and the people lived in the enjoyment of plenty. Unhappily they were driven out of it by the tyranny of his suc-

---

of the first kings of the Suffávean dynasty, about A. D. 1500, when he raised the sect of the Shiahs to importance, and made their belief the national religion of Persia. "Shiah" means sect in Persia, and the name given them as a reproach he took as a title. The only material point of faith in which they differ from the Sunnis is their belief that Ali, the companion, son-in-law, and nephew of Mahomet, ought to have immediately succeeded the Prophet instead of Aboubekr, Omar, and Osman. The greater number of the ancestors of Shah Ismail had been "Soofis" or philosophical deists, and Malcolm supposes that he raised the sect of Ali because he thought it necessary that holy raptures in which the devotional men of his time and family indulged, should have some object more comprehensible to the mass of his countrymen than the abstract contemplation of the Deity. The names of the other Turkish tribes who supported Shah Ismail were Oostajâloo, Shâmloo, Nikâlloo, Bâhârloo, Zûlkudder, and Affshâr.

Aga Mohammed Khan, 1794, was the first monarch of the Kájar dynasty, and at that time the tribe were principally settled in the neighbourhood of Astrabad, where they still remain.—See Malcolm's History of Persia.—ED.

* But fate, which delights in foiling the cleverest combinations, annihilated the hopes of these two, in many respects worthy, princes. They both died before their father,—Mohamed Ali Mirza of cholera, as he was on the point of possessing himself of Bagdad; Abbas Mirza of a mysterious disorder, just at the moment of his victorious entry into Herat.

† The English officers principally employed in disciplining the Persian troops under Abbas Mirza were Sir Henry Lindsay Bethune, Capt. Christie, Major Hart, and Colonel Shee. The two first have left an enduring reputation through the country, and a few years ago the traveller was still often asked in the villages of Georgia and Armenia whether Lindsay Sahib was still alive and well. —ED.

cessors, who considered nothing but their personal interests. Now the splendid bazaars of Kermansháh are deserted; nine tenths of the shops are shut; and if some unlucky fellow, imagining the possibility of gaining a trifling profit, exposes a few goods, his venture rapidly disappears under the hands of an undisciplined soldiery, who give themselves up to every description of excess, certain that they do so with impunity. The terror they inspire is such, that when the inhabitants quarrel amongst themselves they dare not apply to the ordinary tribunals, being forced by the *serbas*, soldiers of the Persian infantry, to make them the arbiters of their differences. It is needless to say that there is no appeal from their decision, and that they generally end like the fable of the lawyer, the oyster, and the two clients.

The Emir Mohib Ali Khan, Governor of the province of Kermansháh, is the General whose ignorance and cowardice so often caused the failure of the Persian arms under the walls of Herat, in 1838; but he belongs to the family of Makoo, who are patronised by the first minister, and thus it is that in the eyes of the Shah his vices are transformed into virtues, that he has attained one of the highest military appointments, and governs one of the finest provinces of Persia. The evil would not be quite unbearable if this personage contented himself with taking double, or even three times the amount of taxes due from the inhabitants, but he has completely stripped them. The misery is frightful wherever his jurisdiction extends: the peasantry have hardly bread to eat, and when they complain of their grievances at Court and endeavour to obtain justice, they are treated as rebels, condemned to be bastinadoed, and Mohib Ali Khan remains their governor.*

This bad policy has produced its fruits: three-fourths of the population have emigrated; the townspeople to Azerbaiján, and

* M. Ferrier's account is but too true. When I was at Kermansháh, in 1846, I witnessed the most distressing spectacle I ever beheld. The province was fearfully oppressed by this fiend in human shape, Mohib Ali Khan, who had bought its government from Hadji Mirza Agassi. He had coolly seized what every man possessed, and had driven away their flocks and herds to his own estates at Makoo near Ararat. The people were picking grass in the fields to eat, and the children were naked and emaciated, except the stomach which was unnaturally swollen —a half-starved child is a horrible sight. In one street I passed through in the town, the people were lying on each side at the last gasp of death from starvation. I never shall forget one whole family, father, mother, and several children, lying together in a heap, unable to move from inanition. I wrote an account of this state of things to the English embassy, at Teheran, but I believe no effort of any kind was made to check the atrocities committed. —ED.

the nomads to Turkey. A great diminution in the revenue of the province has been the result; but Mohib Ali Khan gives himself very little uneasiness about that, and levies from those who remain as great an amount as they formerly paid, including in short the sum previously obtained from those who have escaped from his exactions. This state of things is the more unhappy because Kermansháh is a peculiarly productive part of Persia. The mountains are as much so as the plains, and on these pastures hundreds of thousands of sheep can be reared. The Kurds of these mountains in a great degree supply the capital, whither each spring they take as many as 70,000 sheep. A great number also go to Turkey, and everything indicates that it is to the latter country that the nomads of Kermansháh will eventually send the whole of their flocks destined for sale. The horses of this province are esteemed, and have much Arab blood; but their form is more developed, the neck is strong, chest full, and they are as well adapted for draught as for the saddle.

The carpets* of Kermansháh are a manufacture which adds much to the wealth of the province: none can be more rich, soft, and beautiful; the patterns are in perfect taste, and the colours most brilliant; but these are not their only merits, for they are cheap and very durable. These carpets are made in the villages, and in the tents of the nomadic tribes, generally by the women and the children. Here there is no complicated machinery: four stakes fixed in the ground, which serve to twist the woollen thread, form the simple mechanism employed in weaving these beautiful carpets. Manna,† *guzengébine*, abounds in the province of Kermansháh; the Persians mix it with flour and sugar, and make it into little cakes; these they consider great dainties, and export them to all

---

* Persian carpets are justly celebrated for the beauty of the patterns, the fineness of the wool, and the durability of the colours—vegetable dyes—green not made elsewhere, conjecture saffron and indigo. Some of them fetch high prices, as 6*l.* or 8*l.* for one 2 yds. square, in the country itself. The finest are made at Senna, and there is a famous manufacture carried on at Ferahoún, near Teheran, which belonged to the late Sirdar Baba Khan. Carpets of any size can be made there. The finest carpets of all used to be made at Herat, and there are some splendid ones in the Chehil Minar, at Ispahan, one of which is 140 feet long and 70 feet wide. Large numbers were exported to England through Trebizonde before the late war, and they were sold nearly as cheap in London as in Persia, owing probably to the course of trade.—ED.

† It is a deposit by a green fly on the back of the leaf of the dwarf oak. It is very accurately described by Diodorus Siculus.—ED.

parts of Asia. The revenues of the province of Kermansháh, which now only consists of five districts, amount to—from the taxes 60,000 tomauns, from the customs 13,000 tomauns, making a total of about 35,000*l.*

At Kermansháh I left the caravan with which I had travelled from Bagdad. The Princess Fakhret Doulet continued her way to Senna to visit one of her sisters, and the other pilgrims took each the road that led to his own home. My friend Mollah Ali also left, to my great advantage on the score of provisions in general, and brandy and sausages in particular. Nevertheless I could not refrain from regretting his cheerful society and satirical jokes, which made him almost necessary as a travelling companion, after having once enjoyed them. He went on to Bouroojird, his country, and I never saw him again.

I had scarcely entered the caravanserai at Kermansháh when I found a caravan ready to leave for Hamadan. Accordingly I hired mules at the rate of five *sahebkrans* each,* and as it was still early I mounted a horse, which in half an hour carried me to the magnificent bas-reliefs at Tak-el-Bostan, one parasang and a half from the town. These are splendid works of art, and well worthy of a visit; but their history has been commented upon by so many authors, and amongst them by Sir John Malcolm, who has given so detailed and learned a description of them, that, confessing my incompetence on this subject, I must refer such of my readers as may desire to have an exact description of the sculptures of Tak-el-Bostan to the work of that admirable historian of the East. I would merely mention that these bas-reliefs were executed by command of Baharam IV., the Varanos IV. of Roman history, who lived at the commencement of the fifth century, and who, as it is said, was the founder of Kermansháh.

I remained here during the 12th, and was attacked early in the morning by violent bowel complaint, which reduced me in less than an hour to such a deplorable state of weakness that I found it impossible to stand. I attributed this indisposition to two cakes of manna that I had eaten the previous evening; but I discovered subsequently, and without the least room for doubt, that my illness was the result of poison, which my servant had happily without effect mixed with my food—I had only escaped death because

* A *sahebkran* about equals in value one shilling.

the dose was too small. This poison is made from a plant of an ashy white colour, found in the mountains of Kurdistan; the powder, to which the leaves are reduced after they have been dried in the sun, is tasteless. Taken even in a very small dose, it will sometimes to a person of lymphatic temperament cause immediate death. In the first instance a slight colic is felt, and this is succeeded by excessive weakness, which goes on gradually increasing till life is extinct; sometimes its effects are prolonged for several years. It is said that amongst the women of the harems particularly this subtle agent is frequently used. As during the succeeding days I took only light chicken broth, which was made in my own presence, my gentleman did not find a second opportunity of practising upon my unfortunate stomach; not that he was any way disinclined, for at Hamadan he boasted publicly of the attempt he had made upon my life. Seeing that I carefully concealed my identity in Persia, he hoped to get rid of me without much noise, and seize what little property I had; for probably no one would have cared to inquire what became of me, and if at a later period any investigations had been made there would have been nothing to prove the guilt of Ivan.

Besitoon, April 13th—six parasangs—nine hours by an easy and level road, leaving on our right, at a great distance, the mountains of Louristan still covered with snow, and having very close to us on our left those of Kurdistan, which consist of masses of naked rock, without one inch of alluvial soil. When I left Kermanshâh, I was so extremely weak that I was obliged to be lifted on my mule, and had I not been strapped to the pack I should certainly have fallen twenty times before we arrived at the next halt. At an hour's ride from Kermanshâh, we crossed the Kerkha, sometimes called the Kerah, by a handsome brick bridge, also the Kara-su, which falls into the Shat-ul-Arab,* and is presumed to be the Gyndes of the ancients. Near the bridge is a caravanserai-shâh in ruins. Four hours' march from here the mountains gradually approach each other, and form a defile, at the entrance of which were strewed large blocks of marble, and amongst these were the capitals of columns sculptured in an artistic manner —they had doubtless ornamented an edifice, the foundations of

* Literally, "river of the Arabs:" applied to the united streams of the Tigris and Euphrates below Korna.—ED.

which, composed of courses of hewn stone, are still, though level with the ground, easily distinguished; from their dimensions it may be concluded that they are the remains of a temple or some other small structure. Besitoon is a little village of eighteen houses with a caravanserai-shâh. The rocky mountains at the foot of which it stands are covered with bas-reliefs, which the Persians attribute to the chisel of their famous sculptor Ferhad. A description of them is to be found in Sir John Malcolm's 'Persia.'* Enormous marble capitals of columns are also to be seen at Besitoon: they are of the most finished workmanship; one of the largest bas-reliefs against the mountain side, and about the height of a man, has been disfigured by Fatteh Ali Shâh. These ancient bas-reliefs, and the cuneiform characters on them, have been defaced by his orders, and the latter replaced by an inscription highly eulogistic of that sovereign; those which are at a higher

* The following is a summary of Sir H. Rawlinson's account of the geography of Besitoon:—" D'Anville first suggested the identity of this place with the Baghistane of the Greeks, and there are good grounds from the ancient notices of this place for supposing him to be correct. Etymologically considered the evidence is even more striking. Baghistane signifies the Place of Gardens, and the name appears to have been given from the famous pleasure-grounds, ascribed traditionally to Semiramis. Bostan has the same signification, and is only a contraction of the former word; and the great range of mountains bounding the plain of Kirmanshah, and called by the geographers Jabali Besitoon, preserve, in the Tak-i-Bostan at one extremity, the title which, at the other, has been corrupted into Besitoon. The descriptive evidence now remains. The precipitous rock, 17 stadia high, facing the garden, the large spring gushing out from the foot of the precipice and watering the adjoining plain, and the smoothening the lower part of the rock, all convey an accurate idea of the present appearance of Besitoon; but what are we to say of the sculptures of Semiramis, and the inscription in Syriac characters, which have wholly disappeared. There are now only two tablets at Besitoon—the one nearly destroyed, which contains a mutilated Greek inscription, declaring it to be the work of Gotarzes; the other a Persepolitan sculpture, adorned with nearly 1000 lines of cuneiform writing, exhibiting the religious vows of Darius Hystaspes, after his return from the destruction of Babylon, on the revolt of its Udpati, or Governor Nebukadnazzar, the son of Nebunit. We have no reason to suppose that either of these can represent the sculptures ascribed to Semiramis; yet besides Ctesias, Isidore also mentions the statue and pillar of Semiramis at Baptane. To solve all difficulties it may perhaps be admitted that the sculpture did really exist in the lower part of the rock, scarped by the Assyrian Queen; and that Khosroo Parviz, when he was preparing to make the scarped surface the back wall of his palace, and for that purpose began to excavate deeper in the mountain, destroyed the sculptures, and removed all further trace of them. With regard to the pillar of Semiramis, it is very curious that an Oriental writer of the 15th century should describe the rock of Besitoon from his own observation, as though it were sculptured in the form of a minareh, or minaret. Certainly nothing of the kind now remains. The ruined buildings of Besitoon, like those of the neighbourhood, are of the Sassanian age."—*Journal of Royal Geographical Society*, vol. ix. p. 114.

elevation on the rock owe their preservation to the difficulty there would be in reaching them. The little river Garmi-ab, one of the affluents of the Kara-su, passes by Besitoon, and fertilizes all the district through which it runs; this is covered with beautiful meadows and numerous villages surrounded by magnificent orchards, which have procured for it the name of Baghistan, country of gardens, which it is known to have borne from the earliest ages.

Sannah, April 14th—four parasangs—six hours and a half. The road runs through beautiful valleys covered with pasture, well watered, and rich cultivation, in the middle of which are seen numerous prosperous villages. Sannah contains five hundred houses, surrounded by fruitful gardens of immense size. There is no caravanserai-shâh here, but my muleteer procured me a good lodging in the house of one of the inhabitants. The Persian caravaniers are the best in Asia, and the worst are those of Arab origin; nothing can equal the idleness, carelessness, ignorance, and coarseness of the latter. The caravan I joined at Kermansháh was less numerous than the one with which I travelled from Bagdad; it consisted only of twenty beasts of burden, a circumstance much to my satisfaction. Notwithstanding the desire I felt to travel alone, I could not remember without regret my jovial friend Mollah Ali: my new companions were but poor substitutes for him—they consisted of six stupid muleteers, though good fellows on the whole; my rascal Ivan and two Mollahs followed, accompanied by a subaltern of some sort, who played the part of their factotum. The Mollahs, like my friend Ali, wore white turbans, a close gown, and long beards; but what a difference between them and him! These fellows were dirty, and stunk like Capuchins: their eyes always sought either earth or heaven, never turning in any other direction, except obliquely; and their expression indicated as much bigotry as hypocrisy. Morally and physically they seemed to me equally ugly. Luckily they always avoided my impure person, an insult of which I took advantage by invariably keeping to windward, and thus my infidel breath was, to their great disgust, wafted to them.

Kungawár, April 15th—four parasangs—six hours and a half—across valleys, plains, and mountains, covered with a vegetation as luxuriant as that we travelled through yesterday.—After four hours' journey we arrived at a declivity, from which we suddenly came in view of Mount Nahavend, with its dazzling coronet of snow. The town, which gives the name to this mountain, is on the other side of its summit. In ancient times this was a strong and very important place, often mentioned in Persian annals, and is about fifteen leagues south-west from Hamadan. It was at Nahavend,* in 641 A.D. (Hejira 21), that the celebrated battle was fought, in which the troops of the Caliph Omar, commanded by the Arab chief Noman, who was there slain, defeated the Persians in the reign of Yezdijerd, one of the Sassanide princes. This monarch, shortly after his defeat, was killed by a miller of Merv, with whom he had taken refuge. The dynasty of the Sassanides had reigned in Persia 415 years; it became extinct with Yezdijerd, and Persia then fell under the dominion of the Caliphs, who compelled the population to embrace Islamism. The Turks having seized upon Nahavend, Shah Abbas retook it in 1602, when he destroyed the fortifications; from that time it has been gradually falling into decay, and has now only one thousand houses. Bouroojird, another town situated a little more to the south-east, is the capital of a small government which bears its name, and contains about 12,000 souls, amongst whom are many fanatical Syuds, Mollahs, and others — the governor is usually a prince of the blood. Here are the finest pastures in Persia, for which reason the Shâh has always some cavalry cantoned here. A quarter of an hour from Kungawár we crossed a small river by a brick bridge of four arches, and, after a slight ascent, arrived at the town of Bouroojird. This is situated at the back of a mountain, which shelters from the north a remarkably beautiful plain, on the pastures of which are reared numerous and excellent horses of Arab blood. The caravanserai-shâh at Kungawár is in ruins. A mosque here is supposed by some travellers to have been a temple of the ancient Ghebers;† the foundations of the interior wall are built of enormous blocks of granite, and rise six feet above the ground; these are surmounted by broken columns, also of granite, but partly concealed by clay and stones, with

---

* The town of Nahavend is built just at the foot of the north-east range of hills, upon some craggy points. In the centre of the town rises the citadel, a most imposing-looking structure, and really of some strength. It crowns the top of the highest of the craggy points upon which the place is built, and is supported by immensely solid mud walls from without, rising at least 100 feet high.—ED.

† For Ghebers, and the emigration of a portion of them to India, see Appendices.

which the inhabitants have endeavoured to repair a portion of the walls. Other antique remains, particularly columns, are scattered here and there over the mountain, and in the ruined fortress which crowns an eminence at the back of the town. All the materials that could be moved have been used in the construction of modern buildings.

Surrounded by these numerous proofs of the grandeur of the edifices of bygone centuries, which the ruins at Kungawár presented to me, the various opinions respecting the position of the ancient Ecbatana were recalled to my mind. Reading Arrian again attentively, I felt that I might now be standing on the site of that city, and for these reasons:—Though the majority of writers suppose Hamadan to be the ancient Ecbatana, that modern city contains no monuments or ruins which can justify this opinion, and those who have sought to establish the identity of the position of the two towns support their assertions by conjecture only, destitute of real proof. That Hamadan should have been as it were transported from Ecbatana twelve parasangs farther east, may appear possible, for we see a similar instance with regard to Persepolis, reproduced in the town of Shiraz, which has arisen twelve parasangs more to the south. But here the point that we have to prove is the spot on which stood the palace of Déiokès, and I cannot for a moment conceive that it ever occupied the little hill, now known by the name of Musella, outside the town of Hamadan; whereas the eminence on which stands the old fortress of Kungawár was, by its extent and its commanding situation, far more likely to have been chosen as the site of the palace of the Median king. However, this proof would not have appeared to me conclusive, if Arrian had not furnished us with another corroborative of mine.

CHAPTER III.

Sahadabad — Walled villages — Fanatical Mollahs — Hamadan — Highwaymen — Small respect for the Church — Effects of poison — A French homœopathist — How treated by his General — Mode of punishment — Historical associations of Hamadan — The tombs of Esther and Mordecai — Description of Hamadan — Inhabitants — Prince Khan Lar Mirza — Sertip Ferz Ullah Khan — An united family — The author meets an old acquaintance — A visit to Ferz Ullah Khan — Persian morality — An importunate Seid — The author robbed — Caravanier's reason for not commencing a journey on a Thursday — Veracity of muleteers — Persian servants — Bibikabad — Zereh — Noovaran — Flourishing villages — Rich country — Appropriation of public revenues — — Persian superstition — Tame fish.

SAHADABAD, April 16th--six parasangs—seven hours and three quarters, by an easy road, through a plain, in which were villages, cultivation, and meadows, as on the preceding days. About half way, the river, or rather a marsh, is crossed by a brick bridge of eight arches; there is also a watercourse on this side of Sahadabad. This is a large town of eight hundred hearths; there are also bazaars: it extends one parasang in length, at the foot of the Elwund the road divides it into two parts, and it is surrounded on all sides by innumerable walled orchards. From Karund to Sahadabad the walled villages, situated on the crests of eminences, or rather artificial mounds, are very numerous; the practice of enclosing them has existed in Persia from time immemorial, and became general during the civil wars of the last century. The supreme authority was so badly maintained, and passed from hand to hand so rapidly, that the Persian Khans cared little for it; they were pretty nearly absolute in their own fiefs, and their principal occupation was to pillage each other. As a sudden onslaught was their usual system of attack, these walls became necessary for defence, and to give them a chance of living in comparative security.

In the course of this stage I witnessed the most charming effects of the mirage, but unfortunately I was in a condition too subdued to enjoy them, for the poison which the scoundrel Ivan had given me at Kermansháh had reduced me to a pitiable state. The two Mollahs, my travelling companions, were little disposed to show me any compassion; on the contrary they cursed me, because the passers by, ignorant that I was not a Mussulman, and observing my cloth coat cut Persian fashion, with which I had replaced my Arab shirt since I had been ill, salaamed me, rather than themselves, who cut a most shabby figure under their tattered and filthy clothes. One of these priests, a fat, sullen looking fellow, who was always muttering texts of the Koran, and apostrophizing God and the Prophet, as we entered every village, or when travellers passed, was silent when there was no one to hear him. On entering Sahadabad he was half suffocated with passion to see that his mummery was little heeded, while I received many a salute. Afraid to make a direct attack upon me, he turned in a rage towards Ivan and said, "Servant of the damned, how is it that your infidel master monopolizes the salaams, and leaves so few for me, a true believer?" and then raising his eyes to heaven, exclaimed "O God, *Ya Khooda*, what dirt have I eaten in travelling with this son of perdition!"

Hamadan, April 17th—six parasangs—ten hours.—The road crosses the mountains of Elwund. Leaving at midnight, we wound round the most elevated peak of this chain to reach the pass, and once at the summit, could distinguish, by the light of the moon, the mountains of Loristan and the country through which we had travelled the preceding days picturesquely spread out behind us. The ascent was difficult, and took us two hours. Descending on the other side, our road lay through the bed of a torrent now nearly dry, in which were rolling stones and pieces of rock that brought the mules on their knees at every step. One must live in Persia, where the life of a man is so little thought of, even one's own, to expose oneself to the chances of a broken neck on such roads. The governor of the province, Khan Lar Mirza, a brother of the Shah, had placed a few soldiers in an old caravanserai which stands in the defile, about four hours from the pass; but being neither paid nor fed, they left their post and retired each to his home, without any one troubling himself about their desertion—this spot is now the resort of the brigands whose robberies they were sent to repress, and the government takes no further notice of them. I learned at Hamadan that these fellows had established themselves there with the governor's knowledge, who shared the spoils which they levied upon travellers. I had been warned that we should meet the rogues, but was told they were honest in their way, and that we should get out of their clutches without any very great damage to our purses. And so it proved, for on our arrival at the caravanserai we found a dozen of them there, and were desired to halt; they were all armed, and could have cleared us out completely, for the gun I carried was the only one amongst us. However, they behaved very well, and driving men and beasts together, counted us all, and levied a contribution upon us at the rate of three shillings a head. Happy to be let off at this price, I paid my quota without murmuring, for which I received the compliments of the individual who appeared to be the chief and Demosthenes of the band. But the fat Mollah was not disposed to pay, and obstinately refused to satisfy the demands of these gentlemen who impudently styled themselves the *rah-dars* or guardians of the road. He invoked Ali, and a thousand other such sanctities, and reminded them of his sacred calling, offered them indulgences, talked to them of the mercy of God, of Paradise, of Hell, and a host of other things of the same kind, in which the rah-dars seemed to put very little faith. At length the Mollah was so obstinate that they laid him on his back, emptied his pockets, and dismissed him with a shout. I now thought he was rid of them, but the captain having spied his large turban, and fancied it would with advantage replace his own worn out sash, seized it and the money that was hidden within its folds, without further parley, leaving the unfortunate servant of the Prophet bald and half clothed, and in a state of despair which gave them very little concern. I did not laugh, but I must confess to my shame that I felt uncommonly inclined to do so.

We were two hours and a half descending the mountain before we caught a glimpse of Hamadan.* This town is not seen until the traveller has reached the last ridge of the range; from that

* It is impossible to conceive a more charming situation, a country better suited to live happily in, than Hamadan and its neighbourhood. The country is undulating, the soil rich, the water good, the climate singularly clear, healthy, and bracing; with picturesque mountains at hand for retirement during the heats of summer. I shall never forget the observation of the postmaster as I rode out of Hamadan, on the way to Kermanshâh, one lovely morning in May: "Ah! sir," he said, "the air is well, the trees are well, our horses are well; it is only poor Iran (Persia) that is sick."

Very sick she has been a long time, and if her regeneration be effected, it will be by the middle classes of the highly gifted Persian nation, who are fully aware of their present melancholy condition, and are not corrupted in their morals like the nobles.—ED.

point its aspect is picturesque. Its position is happily chosen; the approach to it is through a richly cultivated country, and numerous plantations and gardens, which are watered by the streams that descend from the glaciers of Elwund. It was time that I should reach the town, for I could then scarcely keep on my mule. I resolved on leaving Hamadan as soon as a caravan was ready, but the pitiable state of my health forced me to remain a few days to recruit. I was frequently obliged to lie down, and even then fainted away; the fruitless efforts that I made to vomit left scarcely any life in me, and, though I had swallowed only milk and broth for several days, I felt as if I had a fire in my intestines. These symptoms led me to suspect that I was the victim of my rascally servant, but I could not prove it; besides, I wished to preserve my incognito as long as I remained in Persia, and in the mean time I had the consolation of knowing that I could leave him behind me here.

There was at this period a French homœopathic doctor residing at Hamadan, who paid me several visits, and whose treatment, though it did not cure me, enabled me to continue my journey. My countryman was attached to a battalion of infantry, recruited amongst the tribe of Kara-guzloo in this province, and had been robbed, under most atrocious circumstances, two months before; the villains bound him, and, with a dagger at his throat, obliged him to tell where his money was concealed. His wife, an Armenian of Hamadan, they thrust into a kind of oven, in which the ashes were still alive. His own general, who was in his debt for arrears of pay, was the thief, and these arrears M. Jacquet had pressed him for, when he took this mode of providing the money for the purpose—plundering the poor fellow of his twenty years' savings, and that too from a man who had cured him of a disease which the Persian doctors thought must end fatally. But gratitude is not a Persian virtue: such conduct in a Sertip* is not uncommon, and, according to the standard of morals in that country, scarcely a crime, especially as the sufferer was an infidel; on the contrary, such a deed would be considered as rather pleasing in the eyes of God than otherwise. M. Jacquet subsequently applied to the French Ambassador at Teheran for redress,

* Sertip comes from "ser," head, and "tip," a clump of spears.—Compare "tope," clump of trees; "tépé," a heap of earth. Sanscrit root.—ED.

who replied that his position at the court of the Shah was rather doubtful, and that he had better temporize, so that, to obtain relief, he was driven to seek the assistance of the Russian Ambassador, Count de Medem, who brought the affair to a satisfactory conclusion.* I was at Hamadan when an officer came there, with orders from the Persian government to make due inquiry into this matter, who, with the consent of Prince Khan Lar Mirza, hamstrung an individual suspected of having participated in the theft. He died under the punishment, but not before he had pointed out the real criminal, swearing upon the Koran that the Sertip Ferz Ullah Khan had ordered certain parties to commit the robbery. To punish such a chief seemed impossible to the Persian government, but the representations of Monsieur de Medem obliged them to indemnify the doctor.

Persian writers attribute the foundation of Hamadan to Jemshid, a king of the Pichdadian dynasty; it has many times been the capital of Persia. There are not any monuments or ruins in it that could be looked upon as having belonged to Ecbatana, which, as we know, was the town of Déiokès, called by the Persians Kay Kobad, and by the Jews Arphaxad. Jemshid reigned 700 years B.C. A little towards the east, and out of the town, is a small eminence, now called Musella, said by various authors to have been the spot on which stood the palace of the Median kings. I have already remarked that I do not agree in that opinion, and for the reasons I have stated. There are no traces of a royal palace; pieces of pottery, and portions of fortifications constructed of sun-dried bricks, are the only remains that I observed.

In the centre of Hamadan is the tomb of Ali Ben Sina, and not far from it are those of Esther and Mordecai,† which are held in

* Both in Persia and Turkey the best advocates with the respective governments are always the Russians. They understand the Oriental character better than ourselves, and do not get deceived as we do. As the central government is very weak in these countries, it is extremely difficult to get any promise executed. The Russians are well aware of this fact, and watch every affair of theirs, until what they want has actually been done; while we are contented to gain a concession on paper, which will never be carried into effect. —ED.

† These tombs are most singular and interesting to visit. The traveller, unless told, would never know they were tombs. You enter by a low door, and the tombs occupy the whole of the internal space to the ceiling, leaving only a very narrow passage for walking round the huge stove-like looking construction in the middle. Literally, not an inch is left on the whitewashed walls on which the Jewish pilgrims of a thousand years have not inscribed their names.—ED.

great veneration by the Jews of this town, and kept in a perfect state of repair. On the dome over these tombs is an inscription, of which the following is a translation :—

> " On Thursday the 15th of the month of Adar, in the year of the creation of the world 4474, the building of this temple over the tombs of Mordecai and Esther was finished by the hands of the two benevolent brothers Elias and Samuel, sons of the late Ismaël of Kachan."

It is now, therefore, nearly eleven centuries and a half since this monument was constructed. The tombs are made of a rather hard black wood, which has suffered little from the effects of time. They are covered with Hebrew inscriptions, still very legible, of which Sir John Malcolm has given the following translation: " At that time there was in the palace of Suza a certain Jew, of the name of Mordecai : he was the son of Jaïr of Shimei, who was the son of Kish, a Benjamite, for Mordecai the Jew was the second of that name under the King Ahasuerus, a man much distinguished among the Jews, and enjoying great consideration amongst his own people, anxious for their welfare, and seeking to promote the peace of all Asia."

The bazaars of Hamadan are very beautiful and spacious and always crowded ; numerous caravanserais are close at hand ; there are also many mosques and public baths. This town is of great commercial importance, and has a population of 50,000 souls. Its manufactures in copper are in repute. Several streams of water descending from the mountains, and passing near the town, contain gold, which the inhabitants, particularly the Jews, collect in skins by washing, but in a clumsy manner. They earn about a shilling a day, but with a better system could no doubt gain more. Many streets in Hamadan, and certainly several parts of the town, are closed by great gates which are open only from sunrise to sunset. This is an excellent custom, and adds much to the security of the honest portion of the inhabitants in troublous times, or for the purposes of police. The vicinity of Hamadan to the mountains of Elwund is an advantage, on account of the numerous fresh and cool streams which temper the heats of summer ; but it has also a disadvantage, for the summits of this range constantly attract a dense mass of clouds, which prevents the air from circulating freely in the town, where the atmosphere is heavy and unhealthy. I was informed of there being some hot springs at the foot of the hills about one parasang from the town, and near them a bas-relief of the Sassanide epoch, but my state of health prevented me from visiting either.

The plain which surrounds this town is covered with villages, the cultivation good, and cheapness and abundance are the result. The population of the province of Hamadan may be divided into three distinct classes—military, religious, and mixed. The first consists of the tribe* of Kara-guzloo, one of the most brave and warlike in Persia, and a branch of that of Sham-loo, which was brought from Syria, in Media, by Tamerlane—this class is more numerous than the other two. The second is composed of an infinity of Syuds and Mollahs, who seem to have a marked predilection for this province, most of the villages in which have been given to them in fief by the government. The third class, the smallest, consists of merchants, tradesmen, workmen, and agricultural labourers. Though quite an exceptional case in Persia, the Shah has appointed a separate officer over each of these classes, fearing to put too much power in the hands of one person by intrusting to him all three. Prince Khan Lar Mirza is governor of the town, and the villages inhabited by mixed tribes. Hadji Mirza Ibrahim, a person of considerable influence, and a native of Hamadan, is at the head of the Syuds and Mollahs, *et hoc genus omne*, and the Sertip Ferz Ullah Khan, who plundered my countryman, is the chief of the tribe Kara-guzloo and commandant of the military force of the province. The latter consists of three regiments of infantry, commanded by his nephews Mahmood Khan, Ali Khan, and Reschid Khan; the first is married to a sister, and the second to an aunt, of Mohamed Shah. The apple of discord was thrown into the Sertip's family with the princesses of the blood, for these, being powerful at court, take every opportunity of placing their husbands in opposition to their uncle, each hoping thereby that some successful intrigue may procure for hers the command of the tribe. It was not without design that the Shah

* Persia resembles the Highlands of Scotland, in being divided among tribes, the chiefs of which command great respect. Persia is a thoroughly aristocratic country, where high birth and polished manners are much considered. In this point it differs much from Turkey and even Russia, where the feeling is thoroughly democratic; that is to say, Turks and Russians cannot feel or understand why, because the father has been distinguished, the son should be respected.—ED.

gave these princesses in marriage to the Khans of Kara-guzloo, that tribe being one of those whose opposition he has most reason to fear; it has never joined in any foreign intrigue, and he showed his judgment in connecting himself with its chiefs.

A few days sufficed to improve my health, and I profited by this to pay a visit to my countryman M. Jacquet, who lived at the village of Chevereen, about a parasang from the town. On the road I met Colonel Mahmood Khan, which annoyed me not a little, for we had been acquainted a long time, and I thought he might inform the authorities of my whereabouts. Deceived however by my beard and the change in my dress, he did not recognise me, though, nevertheless, he fancied he had seen me before. The same evening on my return I met him again, but this time the vagabond Ivan, who was in front of me and drunk, from the potations in which he had indulged at Chevereen, betrayed my incognito, and, when we met, the colonel reproached me for doubting his friendship, and made me promise to breakfast with him at his house at Chevereen on the following morning. Accordingly I went, and met there his brother Aman Ullah Khan, whom I had known several years, and his cousins Shefi Khan and Metel Khan. These young men are the chiefs of their tribe, agreeable and intelligent, and as brave as Roostem. Shefi Khan especially is considered a remarkable man amongst his countrymen. On the following day Mahmood Khan introduced me to his uncle Ferz Ullah Khan as an European traveller on his way to Teheran, but without mentioning my name or the object of my journey. The Sertip was a man of from forty to forty-two years of age, sickly, morose, and careworn-looking, but affecting great politeness and suavity of manner. Like his nephews he has the reputation of being brave and resolute; I found him very intelligent, and his remarks on the advantages and disadvantages of European and Persian civilization, and the comparisons he made between them, surprised me. But what astonished me more was to hear him the next minute saying the very contrary to another visitor, and appearing as narrow-minded and ignorant as any of his countrymen. When his acquaintance left, I expressed my astonishment at so sudden a change in his sentiments. "Pigeon with pigeon, falcon with falcon," he replied: "with you I was sincere; to hold the same language with a Persian would be to play the dupe. It is not that we are deficient in intelligence, but in morality. In Persia a straightforward and honest man passes for a fool, whereas roguery is taken for intelligence." Such is the opinion which Persians entertain of themselves, though few would avow it as frankly as Ferz Ullah Khan—as to my own opinion I can but confirm his.

On arriving this day at the Sertip's house, I found several Syuds with him, who were doing their best to talk him out of some money, and, unless one has witnessed the fact, it is impossible to conceive the impudence of these descendants of the Prophet; they are the veriest bloodsuckers of the people, who are obliged to keep them at their own expense. Nothing can equal their arrogance, but so sacred is their origin in the eyes of Mussulmans, that, generally speaking, they are afraid to refuse their demands, intolerable as they may be. One of these Syuds was disgustingly dirty and the most uncivilised ignorant brute I had yet seen. Presuming on his descent as a Syud, he took his seat above the Khan, whom he menaced with all the wrath of Heaven if he did not give him ten tomauns, which he required, to pay for finishing the building of his house. When breakfast came, he, without ceremony, plunged his filthy hands into the same dish with the Khan, who seemed by no means pleased to have him as a guest, and especially to be obliged to eat with him; but he was a Syud, and the Sertip resigned himself, though unwillingly, to the observance of established customs. Breakfast over, the holy man pocketed the ten tomauns, and was, I thought, going to retire. The saying, however, that the more you have the more you want, was never better illustrated, for the rogue was not yet satisfied; he wanted a cloak for himself, some linen for his sons' pantaloons, and five quintals of corn for bread. When he heard these accumulated demands the Khan could no longer suppress his anger, and launched out with such a volley of the vernacular, that I feared for a moment the illustrious blood of the Prophet would scarcely protect his descendant from a hearty application of the stick, in addition to the other donations. At length the Sertip cooled down, but he was evidently annoyed that this scene should have occurred in my presence, and, to put an end to it, said to the sacred beggar, "Enlist, and I will then take care of you and your family, otherwise don't come here any more and annoy me with demands which I certainly shall not satisfy." The Syud seemed to lay these hard words very little to heart, for he quietly turned to me and said, "Sahib, you must have a very bad opinion of us Persians, to see how cruelly they treat the descendants of their holy Prophet. In your country how do they look upon the clergy?" "Why, like dogs," said the Khan, giving me no time to reply. "It appears that the constellations are not favourable to-day," said the Syud rising; "I shall return to-morrow." "Go to the devil," muttered the Sertip between his teeth, as he accompanied his agreeable guest towards the door, adding, when he had disappeared, "So long as we submit to the moral influence of these fellows we shall continue to eat dirt."

I had determined, as a matter of prudence, not to discharge Ivan till the day of my departure; but, having discovered that he had robbed me of ten tomauns, I started him at once, and engaged another Armenian, of the name of Melkom, in his place. Determined to be revenged, he went to the governor and gave information of my being in the town, the object of my journey, and my anxiety to keep it secret; but Mahmood Khan stood my friend, otherwise, disagreeable consequences might have ensued. Nevertheless I thought it as well to leave as soon as possible, and requested the muleteer of whom I had hired my beasts to hasten his departure; but this was not so easy, for he was in no hurry, and, on one pretence or other, always broke his word. The other travellers had not joined, the hour was not propitious, or he was detained by some official; but on the 24th, being fairly tired with his humbug, I demanded the return of my deposit upon the mules. But he had still one more excuse, and that I could not but admit was imperative; he was obliged by the law of the Prophet to sleep with his wife on Thursday night, the non-compliance with which would enable her to claim a divorce; to object therefore was impossible, and I waited accordingly till Friday evening. What a book is the Koran! it legislates equally for the conduct of the sovereign, and the most minute details of domestic life; every thing is anticipated, indicated; this possibly precautionary measure of the Prophet's was intended to mitigate the effects of polygamy.

Europeans in Persia should be on their guard against the lies and shuffling of the muleteers, who always swear by everything holy and unholy that they will start without fail at a fixed hour, and, as they seize upon the traveller's baggage, it is nine chances to one that he is put to much unnecessary inconvenience in the interval, for leave they never do at the appointed time. The best mode of proceeding is never to pay anything in advance until the first stage is accomplished, and to keep your baggage to the last moment in your own possession. As to servants in Persia, they are the concentrated essence of idleness and dishonesty. With them time counts for nothing; "what is not done to-day can be done to-morrow," is their motto; if you complain they have neglected your affairs, they tell you that they have their own to attend to; and in an European establishment I verily believe three-fifths of the household expenses go into the pockets of these knaves. In spite of this, domestic service is, in Persia, considered a most honourable occupation. The Shah is the servant of God, and is in his turn served by his nobles, who, in like manner, are served by others, and so on to the lowest step of the social ladder. The nature of the occupation is not considered important; a cook and a public functionary are much upon a par. Our caravan was at length marshalled and ready to leave, and we started for

Bibik-abad, April 26th—distant seven parasangs—nine hours and a half, by an easy road, through a well-cultivated country, over which were scattered many villages. Bibik-abad contains four hundred houses, and is situated in the middle of a vast and rich plain. A heavy storm of thunder, lightning, and rain broke a short distance ahead of us to-day, and was the first exception to the fine weather we had all the way from Bagdad. I resumed my Arab dress before leaving Bibik-abad.

Zereh, April 27th—five parasangs—seven hours and a half—country well irrigated. We travelled during the night, and my mule nearly tumbled into a dry well. Zereh is a little village of two hundred and fifty houses, and near a stream of very good water, a rare thing in Persia.

Noovaran, April 28th—nine parasangs—twelve hours—for the first three by a level road across a plain; the remainder through the mountains, by a stony and bad one, the soil for the most part arid, except near Noovaran. This place is situated in a valley near a small river; on its banks are many large and handsome villages; a few are inhabited by Armenian Christians. Noovaran contains from eight to nine hundred hearths, and is surrounded by vineyards and orchards, which are exceedingly productive, and a source of great profit to the villagers. The Shah gave this splendid village in fief to his brother-in-law, the Sirdar Khan,

Baba Khan;* it is to be remarked that twelve or fifteen Persian nobles, the prime minister being at their head, have practised upon the easy disposition of their sovereign to monopolize the most fruitful parts of Persia. The same thing may be said of the customs: the revenues from the former of these sources are not intended simply for their own personal benefit, but to pay and feed the troops, and to maintain in complete efficiency the public establishments of the country. This Sirdar has, for instance, the command of 10,000, the half of whose pay he appropriates to himself. At the end of each year, although the revenues in his hands far exceed the payments for which he is responsible, he always contrives to make it appear that the government is several thousand tomauns in his debt.†

The heat this day was intense, but towards evening a storm of rain burst over us, and, though it drenched me to the skin, delivered us from myriads of flies, which generally settle on the animals and baggage, and, but for such storms, would travel from one end of Asia to the other. I saw at Noovaran a large fishpond, so full that it was impossible to plunge one's hand in without touching a fish. They were each about two pounds in weight, and so tame that they came and fed out of my hand. Expressing my great surprise at their being in such numbers, a bystander accounted for it as follows: "You must know that once upon a time the inhabitants of Noovaran committed some great crime, when the genii turned them into fish;" and, said he, "were any one to eat them he would certainly die." When I told him that I fully intended to have one for dinner, great was his consternation, but he was somewhat pacified when I boasted that I was possessed of a talisman; nevertheless, when he saw me actually devour, with good appetite, one of the finny criminals, he retired, evidently with the firm conviction that I was a sorcerer or something of the kind.‡

* Everything has been resumed by the present Shah, probably to be thrown away even on less deserving favourites.

† This system explains the demand of several millions of francs which Baba Khan made upon the Persian treasury at the death of Mohamed Shah in 1848. His successor Nasser Eddin Shah then played, it is true, the bankrupt with his officers, but he dared not do this to Baba Khan, because in his character of Russian subject it was not advisable to meddle with him.

‡ A few years after, when I was at Ispahan, I had an attack very like cholera after having eaten the *roe* of the same kind of fish, of which I had not partaken at Noovaran. It was perhaps in ignorance of the fact that the roe was poisonous that the story had its origin, and the choleraic effects upon the people and their love of the marvellous were turned to account by some shrewd Mollah to serve the purposes of mystification.

CHAPTER IV.

Shemereen — Koshgek — The peak of Demavend — Khanabad — Rabat Kerim — Irrigation — Modes of travelling in Persia — A royal Firman — Travelling on horseback — With a Mehmendar — His mode of proceeding — Travelling with a caravan — The Djilo-dar — The Persian and his ass — Mules and muleteers — Persian rule of faith — Ab-dookh — Caravanserais — Teheran — View approaching the city — Melancholy reflections — Blighted prospects — General Sémineau — Doctor Jacquet's indiscretion — Village of Shah Abdul Azim — The author discharges his servant — The consequences — Joins a caravan of pilgrims on their way to Meshed.

SHEMEREEN, April 29th—three parasangs—five hours and a half—across the mountains, and by a good road. Villages, orchards, and cultivation succeed each other almost without intermission; the vine and the walnut are in greater numbers than any other trees. Shemereen contains one hundred and fifty hearths, and is situated on the side of a mountain. The great heat and the storm of the preceding day were followed on this by a keen wind.

Koshgek, April 30th—five parasangs—seven hours and a half—across the mountains by an easy road: an uncultivated country, with a scanty population for the first part; in the last two parasangs a few pretty villages lie right and left of the road. The peak of Demavend is distinctly to be seen two hours before arriving at this halt, distant forty-five parasangs. A few years before I had seen it at Kohrood, a village on the road to Ispahan, distant fifty-four parasangs or eighty-one leagues. Koshgek is a village of a hundred and fifty houses. The inhabitants are of the Beijat tribe of nomads.

Khanabad, May 1st—six parasangs—nine hours—through a plain. A few villages are seen in the distance, and the tents of wandering tribes. Khanabad has two hundred hearths. The water here is very brackish.

Rabat Kerim, May 2nd—eight parasangs—twelve hours—through an extensive plain with hills here and there; on the last that we crossed is a ruined caravanserai of stone, built by Shah Abbas. This spot is a favourite haunt of the tribe Shah Sevends, who frequent these plains, and sometimes pillage the caravans. Rabat Kerim is a large village of nine hundred houses: there is a caravanserai-shah, the only habitable one between Hamadan and this place. The water of the river Kerech, which is excellent, irrigates the soil in the neighbourhood. It has been mentioned that the water at Khanabad is very brackish. This is frequently the case in some parts of Persia, where the privations of Eastern travelling are very great.

Those who have plenty of money and can afford to be robbed, and are disposed to submit with patience to such treatment, may travel in comparative comfort. If the object is to proceed rapidly, that is to say thirty or forty leagues a day, a royal firman, or an order from a governor-general, is necessary to obtain post-horses.* These are kept only on the great roads which lead to the capitals of provinces. If the traveller rides his own horses he may accomplish about ten or twelve leagues a day; mules can be hired anywhere, and the muleteers are always ready to accompany the traveller in any direction or to any distance: in this manner ten leagues will be an average day's journey.

Sometimes, and by special permission, rarely granted, the government authorizes ministers, nobles, and strangers of importance to take the private horses of the villagers, if there are none at the post; but this plan is very expensive. The various towns near the frontiers, from which there are roads to the capital, and on which post-horses are stationed, are Khoi, Resht, Astrabad, Meshed, Kerman, Shiraz, and Kermansháh. At the post-stations the proper number of horses, as a matter of course, is not kept up, and a bribe is necessary to bring out the few wretched Rozinantes they have.

Foreign ambassadors, and European travellers of distinction,

* Travelling in Persia by post is very agreeable and cheap. An order is easily obtained by a European traveller to use the post-horses kept up by the government, for which nothing is charged, and a backsheeh of a couple of crowns or shillings, contents the "suriji" at the end of the stage, generally from 20 to 30 miles long. Sometimes the horses are very bad, but generally they are quick little Persian riding horses, that canter pleasantly through the long plains. I remember once on riding from Tabreez to Teheran, that at the last stage from Teheran, there were no horses in the post-house, and those which had just brought us 30 miles carried us easily the same day into the capital, another 30 miles; so that we reached the gates just before they were closed at sunset. Col. Rawlinson once rode 100 miles on the same post-horses, waiting of course to bait at the different stages, and was run away with for the last 5 miles.—ED.

are generally favoured by the government with the attendance of a *mehmendar*, whose rank varies according to that of the person he is appointed to travel with. The English and Russians have in their treaties determined the rank of the mehmendars who are to accompany their ambassadors. This officer is responsible for all losses, accidents, and vexations that may happen to the person confided to his care; he rides forward to prepare all things necessary for his comfort and accommodation, which, by the terms of the firman, every village at which the party halts is obliged to provide gratis. On his arrival at a town or village the mehmendar sends for the mayor, the *Ket-Khoda*, to whom he briefly gives his orders to furnish the articles required, and, by way of commencement, instals himself in the best house in the place; he then proceeds to the mosque or principal square, where he takes his seat with his *kalioun*, or water-pipe, and is soon surrounded by the crowd of persons who have been invited to supply his wants. These individuals assure him emphatically that they are wholly unable to provide him with anything; they have neither wood, sheep, butter, bread, &c., and that they are poor devils not worth a copper. The mehmendar deigns not to reply, but gravely smokes his kalioun, gravely listens to all they say, and gravely smokes again; for all the world he would not let his pipe go out. In Persia this is a very serious affair, to which great importance is attached. But no sooner has the last whiff of smoke floated away from his lips than he slowly rises from his carpet, and begins to lay vigorously about him with his stick on the refractory supplicants, who make off with cries and curses upon those who thus unjustly despoil them of their goods. Should unnecessary delay take place, the stick of the mehmendar is again put in requisition which rarely fails to produce the desired effect. The quantity of provisions thus forcibly levied is generally much greater than can be consumed; in this case the mehmendar sells the remainder and pockets the amount.

No greater misery can be conceived than that of travelling with a caravan, the désagrémens of which are many and various. The ordinary muleteers are the greatest liars upon earth, and annoy you in every possible way. The *djilo-dar*, he who has or holds the bridle, or chief muleteer, is a very different character. He is generally an intelligent honest man, is familiar with the roads, the towns, villages, and habits of the various tribes of the countries through which he journeys. Merchants often place large sums of money in his hands for transit, and I have never known one of them betray his trust. His horses or mules are usually sound and in good condition, and it often happens that a djilo-dar owns from thirty to fifty of each. The lower orders travel on asses, on which they place enormous loads. It is true that when they arrive at a halt they take the greatest possible care of them; not only do they feed them well, but curry-comb them, wash them, shampoo their legs, twist and pull their noses, ears, and tails, and talk and pray for them—no father can have more affection for his child than a Persian has for his ass. Once in motion, the caravan breaks into small parties of ten or twelve persons; that of the djilo-dar is at the head of the column, and there, in front of all, he puts his best beast, to set an example to the rest by her steady and sustained pace. This mule is always gaily caparisoned, the harness covered with embroidery and other varieties of decoration, in addition to the bells which give notice of the approach of the caravan. After these detachments comes the merchandize, also carried by mules, and those travellers who have only half, nay, sometimes only a third of an ass, for there is often a triple partnership, ride and tie—the foot passengers bring up the rear. All halts and hours of march are determined by the djilo-dar. If there is no caravanserai, he selects the camping-ground, and the goods are ranged under his orders, in a circle or a square, round which the travellers sleep; the space within is reserved for the horses and mules, which are tethered to a long pole. The djilo-dar is, as he well need be, an active fellow, for he has sometimes to look after five or six hundred mules, their burdens and their drivers, who are ten thousand times more troublesome than their beasts. When the halt is made, he announces the hour of departure for that day or the next morning; he also regulates the pace, or stops the caravan, by various cries, which are passed from mouth to mouth along the road.

When a caravan is attacked by robbers, the Persian muleteers, if armed and having the advantage of position and numbers, generally defend themselves with spirit; but if there is any doubt as to the probable result, they think only of their mules, cut the harness, throw off the loads, and, leaving the merchandize to its fate, gallop off as hard as they can go. It is curious, but, when these scenes take place, the mules seem instinctively to scent the danger, and show it by their energy and rapid strides, in singular contrast to their usually quiet and regular pace. A caravan of mules or horses, on an ordinarily paved road, will carry from four to five hundredweight, and with that burden will get over one parasang in an hour and a half, but in the desert, for instance between Meshed and Bokhara, or in the mountains, as in the Mazanderan, the distance travelled will not be so great in the same time. Delays not unfrequently occur, for the Persian muleteer is most exact in his observance of the exterior forms of his religion, which, however, is rather a proof of his hypocrisy than his morality, for I am convinced that, generally speaking, he more often prays to God to help him to cheat and pilfer his customers than to entreat his assistance in keeping him in the right path. But be this as it may, it is curious to see them, at the hour of prayer, running in front of the caravan to go through these forms. Sometimes there is no water with which to perform their ablutions. In that case a handful of earth serves the purpose of purification —dirt, not water! With this they rub their faces and hands, and, reciting their *namaz* like so many parrots, and in a language which they don't understand, resume their journey. With them, as with us, faith and forms can alone save them. When the latter are strictly performed, and they rigidly observe the fast of the Rhamazan, they think they have a right to commit every species of rascality and crime, and without being in any way called upon to give an account either in this world or the next. This does not apply to muleteers only, but it may be said to be the Persian rule of faith: everything for their creed and nothing for morals.

Provisions are to be obtained at almost every village; but if they are at a great distance from one another, or it is at the period of the year when the Persians keep their horses on green food, that is, between May and July, the caravan rarely encamps near the towns, and then the djilo-dar gives notice, and the traveller lays in a stock. Poultry, eggs, and milk are to be had in most villages; but rice for the pillau, the best and most nutritious food in Persia, is not always to be met with. *Ab-dookh*, a favourite dish with the Persians, and very refreshing, is not at all suited to the stomach of an European, and should be carefully avoided. The caravanserai-shahs are handsome buildings, but the filthy habits of the Persians make them very disagreeable.

Teheran, May 3rd—six parasangs—nine hours—by a level road, but frequently traversed by the runs of water which irrigate the country. The villages are numerous on both sides of the road. The rascal Ivan had so completely divulged my projects at Hamadan that the muleteers of our caravan knew that I was going to Herat. I also discovered that the fellow had given my servant Melkom a letter, addressed to the Russian Minister at the capital, informing him of my arrival. As the Count de Medem was one of my persecutors, it was fortunate for me that I had an opportunity of laying hands upon the letter, and destroying it. I had intended, on reaching Teheran, to hire a lodging in the city, but subsequent reflection induced me to change my mind, for I did not wish to be seen, or to give umbrage to the French Ambassador. He thought my presence might embarrass him; and though the manner in which he had supported my claims upon the Persian Government, as well as the result of such support, were far from satisfactory to me, it was not a sufficient reason for my complicating the matter further. He had acted in the interests of France, and it had always been my practice to make my own subservient to those of my country.

We arrived at Teheran as the first rays of the sun tinged, with softened crimson hues, the village of Shimeran, picturesquely situated at the foot of the Elboorz, and in the foreground the Kasr Kajar, or Palace of the Kajars, with its splendid sycamores, under the protecting shade of which I had frequently walked, and endeavoured to escape the many annoyances I experienced in the city. The harvest, an abundant one, was being gathered in; peasants on horses, mules, and asses, with various productions, fruit, and vegetables, were already on their way to market; and the great messenger of day, suddenly emerging in dazzling brilliancy from behind the bold outline of the peak of Demavend, threw over this springtide picture a bright and cheerful character, in striking contrast with the anxiety and sadness that oppressed me. Melancholy, indeed, were the reflections which memory suggested to my mind as I approached the city of the Shah. A high military rank and the favours of the Sovereign had been conferred upon me, but in endeavouring to serve France I had lost both the one and the other; and instead of receiving, as I ought to have done, the support of those who then directed the councils of my country, I was neglected and abandoned to my fate. Now I entered Teheran in disguise, my face half concealed by a bandage, to make my incognito complete. Fortune is truly an inconstant jade, and intense is the folly of those who put any faith in her favours. Deeply agitated and dejected, my heart for a few minutes gave way to grief, and my mind dwelt upon my blighted prospects; but this soon passed, my courage gained the ascendant, and I had need to preserve it intact to assist and support me in the great struggle with adversity in which I was about to engage.

On reaching the outskirts I put up at a caravanserai, south of the city, and outside the gate of the Shah Abdul Azim. There, despite my precautions, I was recognised as an European, but, thanks to the state of my wardrobe and the poverty of my baggage, I escaped all inquisitive inquiries, and directly I had taken possession of my filthy apartment I wrote a note to General Semineau, one of my friends, to inform him of my arrival, and requested him to send me a few books and some other things I was in want of. The General, regardless of the consequences a visit to me might bring upon him, was soon at my side, and the information I obtained from him determined me to leave Teheran as soon as possible. Doctor Jacquet had written to a friend there, and mentioned my arrival at Hamadan, adding, luckily, that I had taken the road to Tabreez. The Government knew, perhaps, that I had gone in some other direction. Desirous, however, that they should lose all trace of me, and a caravan starting from Meshed, I agreed with the djilo-dar of it, and at once made a bargain with him for two mules, at the rate of twenty-five *krauns** each. Accordingly, on the following day we left Teheran, and proceeded to the rendezvous at the large village of Shah Abdul Azim, situated about a parasang and a half from the city. Here are bazaars, baths, a caravanserai-shah, and a royal residence. The streets are large and planted with trees, and a spring of good water flows through them; there is also a handsome mosque, named after the Imaum who is buried within its precincts. This adds much to the prosperity of the place, for the tomb is visited by pilgrims from all parts of Persia; every Friday the pious portion of the inhabitants of Teheran come here to offer up their prayers. The village of Shah Abdul Azim is built

* A *kraun* equals in value a shilling.

amongst the ruins of the ancient city of Rhages, or Rhé, of which I have already made mention when referring to Arrian's Expedition of Alexander.

The last traces of civilization were left behind me in the Persian capital, and I now took my solitary way towards those distant and inhospitable countries in which my acquaintance had prophesied I should find my last resting-place. I approached them, however, without alarm or uneasiness, well convinced that, with tact and management, I should avoid the catastrophe which they had predicted. In a little inventory I made of my effects this evening I found fresh evidence of Ivan's rascality, and I felt not a little pleased to think he was no longer with me; for, had he remained in my service, he would, without doubt, have taken the first opportunity of making away with me, or at least with what little property I had. The Armenian who replaced him had only engaged to accompany me as far as Teheran; and as in the few hours I remained there it was impossible to find another servant in whom I could place confidence, and I was afraid to engage one who might play the spy, I made up my mind to go without; but, if I had known the sufferings to which, on the grounds of policy as well as economy, I exposed myself, I would never have adopted this step. I think it doubtful whether any European ever travelled through these regions without a servant of some kind or other; Asia is not the country to make these experiments in.* Here there are no hotels or taverns; the traveller must carry with him his bed, provisions, cooking-utensils, and sometimes even wood and water. He must load his mule, cook his dinner, clean his saucepan and gridiron, and do other menial offices, which, though of temporary inconvenience, exposes one to the loss of that consideration which in Eastern countries is of the greatest importance. Without this the traveller is exposed to ill-treatment of every kind, and without the least reason but simply because he is deprived of all protection, and because, being a Christian, he is an impure being in the eyes of Shiah Mussulmans

* This remark is generally correct; but some of the members of the Herat mission have a pleasing recollection of having been surprised, while seated round their fireside, in the "gloaming" of an October evening, by the appearance among them of an English traveller (Mr. Mitford), on his way to Bombay! Although ignorant of the Persian language, and speaking only "a little Barbary Arabic," he had travelled from Hamadan to Herat, for the greater part of the way without any servant—his whole baggage, I believe, being carried under his saddle-flaps, about the safety of which he appeared very solicitous.—L.

—an unclean dog, who may not even use their drinking-cup, or touch their food, or any other thing that they have. To tyrannise over the infidel is, in short, a duty, and to suffer all this was my fate, and God knows what I endured at their hands. Nevertheless the European traveller will find a Mussulman servant preferable to an Armenian; the Armenians, being Christians, more readily fall into our habits, but, accustomed to be tyrannised over and insulted, they are timid, and dare not stand up for their own rights or their master's. Irrespective of this, they are great rogues, liars, and cowards, and in their quality of co-religionists think they have a right to rob an European, when they would not dare do so to a Mussulman. The latter are not over-scrupulous, but they are less dirty and more handy; the knowledge that they are Mussulmans renders them proud and determined, and they know how to make themselves respected.

The reader is not to suppose by what I have just stated that Europeans are habitually badly treated in Persia; this opinion applies to the few who are unprotected, isolated, and of an humble grade in life, and especially those who travel with a caravan composed of pilgrims, amongst whom, of course, the greatest fanatics in the country are to be found. The European who has a good establishment and the protection of the Government will have every attention paid him, and be treated perhaps with more respect than he would be at home.

The caravan with which I had to travel to Meshed consisted of five hundred mules, and three hundred and fifty pilgrims on their way to the tomb of the Imaum Reza, and I did not fancy the society of these pious folk, but resignation was necessary, and to that I made up my mind.

CHAPTER V.

Hissar-emir — The ruins of Rhages — El Boorj — Antique coins — Tomb of Bibee Sherabanon — Legend connected with this lady — Plain of Verameen, rich and fertile — Eywanee-Keij — Irrigation — Vultures — Description of a caravan of pilgrims — How collected — The Chief Syud — Abject reverence for him — His evening sermon — Fanatical brutality — Kishlak — Defile of Sirdaree — Military position — Kohi-tuz or salt mountains — Position of the Caspian Straits — Erroneously laid down — Arrian's description of the site — Deh-nemuck — Ferooz-koh — District of Ich — Aredan — Bricks of salt — Lasjird — Military position — Fortifications — Semnoon — Description of the town — Its ancient history — Effects of irrigation — Rear-guard of Bessus — Arrian — Scene in the kebab-shop — Advantages and disadvantages of wearing a native dress — The constellation of happy import — The lame Dervish — Monsieur Ferrier taken before the Governor — The satisfactory result.

HISSAR-EMIR, May 4th—four parasangs—five hours—by a good and level road, frequently intersected by watercourses. We left Shah Abdul Azim at twilight, passing through the extensive ruins of Rhages, now called Rhé, originally one of the largest and most ancient cities of Persia. These remains are in the plain, and cover a surface of six parasangs in circuit. This was the site of the town; the fortress was more to the north, and on a detached mountain, a spur of the Elboorz, called by the Persians El Boorj, The Tower. Two brick towers, in pretty good preservation, a few slight bas-reliefs, and the foundations of buildings, particularly those of the walls of the city, the time of which is still clearly indicated, are all that remain to point out the position of the ancient Rhages. The materials are constantly used in the erection of modern buildings at Teheran, and are conveyed there by the peasants of the neighbourhood. In turning up the ground for these bricks they frequently find gold and silver coins and other objects of antiquity, for which they realise a good price.

Much, however, of the space on which Rhages was situated, is now occupied by villages and cultivation; in passing through them we had on our left a ramification from the chain of the Elboorz, and on the side of the last range that stretches into the plain is the tomb of Bibee Sherabanon, wife of the Imaum Hussein. Pursued by the troops of Yezid, this heroine, mounted on her famous horse the fleet Zul-Jenah, and assisted by a miracle, viz. the opening and closing of the mountain on which is the tomb of the Imaum, escaped unhurt. Beyond the ruins we skirted on our right the fertile plain of Verameen, on which are many villages; the productions of the rich and well-watered soil that surrounds them supply the markets of Teheran. The river Jajerood, which descends from the mountains of Mazanderan, is lost in the irrigation of this plain; and the Persian noble who holds land in it is considered fortunate, the estates being rarely sold, and only when a proprietor is in great distress. The district of Verameen took its name from a city now in ruins, evidently built of materials brought from Rhages,* distant only two parasangs. On our left was seen the majestic peak of Demavend, covered with long lines of eternal snows. Hissar-emir was the property of the late Prime Minister Haji Mirza Aghassi. We camped at about twenty minutes' walk from the watering-place, and I could not prevail upon any Mussulman to fetch me any water, though several were in rags and without bread. To touch my pot would have been impure, and not even the reward I offered would tempt them.

Eywanee-Keij, or *Heivanak*, May 5th—seven parasangs—ten hours, the first half of which was by a level road much intersected, as of late, with watercourses from the Jajerood, which flows

* After the death of Alexander the Great, Persia, as well as Syria, fell to the lot of Seleucus Nicator, who established the dynasty of the Seleucidæ. Antiochus Soter succeeded Seleucus Nicator, and in the reign of his successor, Antiochus Theos, Arsaces, a Scythian, who came from the north of the Sea of Azoff, induced the Persians to throw off the Greek yoke, founded the Parthian empire, and made Rhages his capital. This was likewise the period of the foundation of the Bactrian kingdom by Theodotus the governor of it, who finding himself cut off from Syria by the Persian revolution, declared his independence. Arsaces is called Asteh by Eastern writers, and is said to have been a descendant of the ancient Persian kings. When he gained the kingdom it is said he promised to exact no tribute and merely to consider himself as the head of a confederacy of princes, united for the double object of maintaining their independence and freeing Persia from a foreign yoke. This is the commencement of that era of Persian history called by Eastern writers, Mulook-u-Tuaif, or commonwealth of tribes.

In A. D. 906, Rhages was taken by Ismail, founder of the Samanee dynasty. It ceased now to be a seat of empire, and in A. D. 967, became the capital of the house of Shemgur, a race of petty princes who maintained a kind of independence, while the dynasties of Saman and Dilemee divided the empire of Persia. In A. D. 1027, Rhages was the last conquest of Mahmood, of Ghuzni.—Smith's Bio. Dic.; Malcolm's Hist. of Persia.—ED.

about a parasang and a half east from Hissar-emir. The system of irrigation is in Persia attended to with great care, and the water here is distributed equally amongst all the villages of the plain of Verameen. A mountain-gorge, covered with bushes, is passed about two hours from Heivanak; the vultures are to be seen in it in myriads, and short would be the existence of any animal that enters this pass; he would not be alive two minutes, and in an hour his skeleton would be as white and picked as clean as if it had been exposed to the sun for ten years. I have given in the preceding pages some account of a caravan of traders, I will now briefly describe a caravan of pilgrims.

A Syud, and not a *djilo-dar*, is in this case the head-man, and is blindly obeyed in everything. For two months previously to his intended departure this descendant of the Prophet scours the towns and villages, inviting the faithful to join his green standard, and undertake a pilgrimage to the holy places. A sufficient number being collected, he passes them in review, and, raising the wind from each to the extent of four or five sahebkrans a head, promises to conduct them in safety to all the shrines held sacred by pious Mussulmans; these are Meshed, Shah Abdul Azim, Koom, Kerbelah, Sammarah, Kazemen, and Mecca. He promises also to halt at the best and cheapest stations, to preserve them from the effects of the evil eye, the temptations of the devil, the machinations of bad genii, to consult the stars, to leave on propitious days—in a word, he promises to make this pilgrimage the happiest and most acceptable to God that ever was made. Each pilgrim thinks himself specially favoured if he is allowed to perform gratis any service for the chief Syud, and during the whole journey this individual is the object of the most delicate attention. A tent is always at his disposal to shade him from the heat or protect him from the rain; some drive the flies from him, others water the parched earth around the spot on which he sits; his clothes are washed, his dinner cooked; each pilgrim is, in short, delighted if by any act, however menial, he can hope through him to propitiate the Prophet, and obtain a blessing from heaven. To be allowed to kiss the Syud's hand, or the hem of his garment, is all the remuneration they expect, and this he grants with the coldness of ascetic pride, appearing to consider that the kind offices which he continually receives are nothing more than what is due to his meritorious and holy life.

As to our sainted chief, he was puffed up with the self-importance of his sect. In the evening, after he had eaten the dinner prepared for him gratis while he was asleep, instead of allowing those to rest who had not obtained one wink during the day's journey, he preached a sermon, the subject of which was taken from the life of one of the Imaums, and marvellous were the details. The Persian language is well adapted to flights of poetry, sallies of buffoonery, is emphatic and exaggerative, all of which is highly exciting to Persian ears. A tale indifferently well told, though most improbable in fact, will interest a Persian audience intensely; and if in a sermon the Syud thoroughly understands his business, and arranges his subject skilfully, developing it by degrees, and in a way to rouse little by little the emotions of his hearers, which he will easily do by dexterously throwing in the marvellous and the sentimental, he reaches the climax; his voice falters, he is overcome with feigned emotion, and a deluge of tears is seen to flow down the cheeks of his audience. His own are always at his command; if he is telling a tale, he is sure to shed them at the proper moment; for example, when his hero sprains his ankle, or wants to smoke and there is no kalioon; but if he is dying of thirst, or falls into the hands of his enemy, oh! then the groans and lamentations are past belief; the men cry like calves, the women like does, and the children bawl loud enough to make a deaf man hear; and the unfortunate victim who, like myself, is condemned to listen to all this trash, has no resource but to stop his ears, or resign himself to be kept awake by these scenes of desolating grief. The tale or sermon finished, the Syud proposes a cheer for the Prophet, and, after that, one for Ali, the same for Hussein, for Hassan, for Abbas, for the sainted Imaums (and there is a long list), and, lastly, one for himself, the Syud. These exhibitions sometimes last two hours, and when it is over and one is revelling in the delightful idea of getting a short nap, the inhuman brute the very next minute calls out, with the voice of a Stentor, "Load the mules, and let us be going." This is enough to drive one mad, for a night on horseback is certain to be the result, and when one cannot sleep during the day, which was my case, it is downright torture.

The pilgrimages made by Persians to the holy places of Islam are frequently as much for fashion's sake as to save their souls, or from a motive of hypocrisy, not conviction; the title of Haji is conferred only by the pilgrimage to Mecca, and this gives consequence and consideration to the greatest scoundrel; in the eyes of his countrymen he is a reformed man, he is approached with respect, the chief seat is his. The Haji is in fact held in general esteem, but in this, as in all external forms of their faith, the Persians sacrifice the substance for the shadow: hundreds of them undertake a pilgrimage without a stiver in their pockets, and without being much embarrassed by that fact, for their wants are on the smallest possible scale, and they beg from house to house, or tent to tent, and this with success, for the Mahometan religion is, with respect to charity, truly edifying. It enjoins it as a great duty, and a Mussulman not only always gives, but, if rich, with a simplicity and kindness of manner that enhances the value of the gift, and not in that spirit of ostentation so frequently seen in Europe, where the columns of a newspaper silently but surely publish an act in the performance of which vanity should have no place.

A social feeling pervades all the members of a caravan: they have their food in common; the noble, the tradesman, the peasant, and the *fakeer* sit in the same circle and eat out of the same dish, and this without the least possibility of offence being given or pride being wounded; it is sufficient that they are Mussulmans and pilgrims. On such occasions there is every liberty of speech; if a stranger appears in the circle, and offers a remark, he is instantly requested to take a seat; if he refuses, he is requested to retire, for a Persian detests to see a man standing who is not his servant or his inferior, and always imagines that an individual who objects to converse or refuses to be questioned must be a spy or a criminal. Pilgrims who have luckily a little spare cash carry with them a few goods which they think will sell well at the holy places, and with the gains they realize return to their own country with a similar venture.

The village of Eywanee-Keij contains about four hundred hearths, with a caravanserai-shah half in ruins; the soil is rich, well watered, and highly cultivated: the harvest had commenced: the heat was excessive, the centigrade thermometer being 38 degrees in the shade. I was seized with an attack of fever at this halt, and no one offered, or rather every one refused, to let me share the corner of a tent. Exposed to the burning rays of the sun, covered with perspiration and flies, and forsaken by every one, I entreated some pilgrims to give me a little water, but in reply they only abused me, as on the preceding evening; at last, and for a shilling, one of them filled my *tumla* from his vase: this done, he turned to his companion and said, "But Abbas the Most High has ordered us never to give water to these infidels of Christians, and I fear I have sinned." "That is true," replied the other; "but we Persians are so humane, *murvet-darestini*. You have sinned. Make him swear to become a Mussulman, and do not give him the water till he has professed the faith of Islam." Hearing this, I made an attempt to seize the jug, but unluckily upset it: sufficient, however, remained to quench my intolerable thirst. At length Heaven took pity upon my helpless state, and, a wretched peasant making a pilgrimage to Meshed on foot happening to pass near me, he agreed to serve me on condition that I allowed him to cook his meals apart and respected his creed. I eagerly accepted his terms, and, though badly attended, I was glad indeed to make so good a bargain, and be relieved from the necessity of asking for assistance at the hands of the fanatics my fellow-travellers.

Kishlak, May 6th—seven parasangs—ten hours, the two first by a plain, the third through the defile of Sirdaree, an opening across the chain of a vast spur, separated from the Elboorz, which, gradually descending into the plain, runs for four or five parasangs in a south-easterly direction. A salt desert about ten parasangs in length separates this spur from Siah-Koh, which, notwithstanding this interruption, seems to be a continuation of the same range. The defile of Sirdaree presents an excellent defensive position, more especially at its entrance and exit; at the latter it is only a pistol-shot in width; but it might be easily turned, the only difficulty in doing so being the want of water, which would have to be carried for one day's consumption, and in going direct from the district of Verameen to that of Khar, passing by Eywanee-Keij. A small stream of brackish water runs the whole length of the defile, in the direction of Khar. In this little valley, about a quarter of a parasang in length, from eight to nine hundred yards in width, and in the centre of the pass, are the ruins of a caravanserai; great quantities of salt are found in the mountains on either side of it; hence the name of Kohi-tuz: the first word is the Persian for mountains, the second is Turkish, and signifies salt.

All doubts may I think be set aside as to the site of the Caspian Straits: in my opinion they are to be found in the pass of Sirdaree. I resided near them for twelve years, during which time I made numerous excursions into the surrounding country, especially amongst the mountains of Demavend and Firooz-Koh, and had ample opportunity of carefully considering the subject. Many persons still consider those mountains as the real Caspian Straits. By reading Arrian with a little attention, they might convince themselves of the error into which they have fallen. Here follow some explanations, which may I hope facilitate their researches. It would be a mistake to take Teheran as a starting-point from which to reach the straits. It is from Rhages the traveller should start; this town then extended up to the villages of Khatoon-abad and Hissar-emir, a fact which is sufficiently indicated by the numerous ruins. These villages are on the direct road to Bactria, and their distance from Tingi-sirdaree is eight parasangs or one stage. Emerging from the defile, the traveller enters the fertile plain of Khar; this is succeeded by a desert twelve parasangs in length, at the extremity of which is Lasjird: about midway is a hamlet called Deh-nemuck, or the Salt Village, which gives its name to the desert. Let us compare this description—I can vouch for its accuracy—with the words of Arrian, and see if there is not complete conformity between them.

"He" (Alexander) "marched with his army against the Parthians" (this warlike nation was not established in Mazanderan, but in the plains at the foot of the mountains of this province), "and encamped the first day near the Caspian Straits" (that is to say the eight parasangs which separate Rhages from this pass of Sirdaree), "which he entered the day after, and came into a fruitful country; and as he was resolved there to lay in forage for his army, because he had heard that the inner parts of the country were uncultivated and waste" (that of Deh-nemuck), "he despatched Cænus with his horse and some of his foot to gather in stores for that purpose." . . . . . And farther on Arrian says, "Alexander, hearing this" (the news of the captivity of Darius), "imagined there was now more need of expedition than ever; wherefore, taking with him only his auxiliary forces, his light horse and his stoutest and best-marching troops of foot, he set out without waiting for the return of Cænus. . . . . Those who accompanied him carried only their arms and two days' provisions," that is, the two stages of Deh-nemuck and Lasjird, at which point you leave the desert. Why therefore seek for the Caspian Straits in the mountains of Mazanderan, when they are so clearly pointed out by the historian of Alexander? Bessus did not direct his flight towards Zadracarta, but towards Hecatompylos, to reach Bactria;

and when Arrian, in addition to this, writes that Artabazes, disapproving of the crime of Bessus, retired into the mountains, he clearly infers that the Persians moved through this plain.

Kishlak is a village of about one hundred houses; the water here is brackish, thermometer in the shade 39 degrees of centigrade; thirty villages are seen from hence, forming the district of Khar. The country here, as well as at Verameen, supplies Teheran with grain.

Deh-nemuck, May 7th—six parasangs—eight hours—by a level and easy road, except in spring and winter, when it is much cut up, for the soil is a stiff clay; half way, after heavy rains, the road is sometimes impassable. The caravans are then obliged to take the upper road, which skirts the foot of the mountains of Khali-bar; this is longer by one parasang, and covered with the stones swept on to it by the mountain torrents, consequently difficult and sometimes dangerous; nevertheless it is preferable to the lower road and its quagmires. The gorge through which the river here flows is the only way by which a direct communication is kept up with the district of Itch, on account of the great natural difficulties in the mountains. The chief town of that district is Firooz-Koh. No laden mule can cross the mountains in any other direction, hence the word Khali-bar, without a load. The district of Itch is in repute for its excellent pasturage; it supplies Teheran with large numbers of cattle, deer, wild boar, and goats. Half way to Deh-nemuck is Aredan, a fortified village, and near it are three villages on the border of the salt desert. There are about one hundred and fifty houses within the *enceinte* of Aredan; the inhabitants collect the salt which surrounds them. The ground is covered with a thick crust: this is cut into the form of bricks, and sold at Teheran. In Mazanderan, Khorassan, and the Tartar states, the soil, though largely impregnated with salt, is, if not encrusted with a compact layer, susceptible of cultivation; there were proofs of this at Deh-nemuck. There is a large brick reservoir near the caravanserai-shah there, in which the rain-water is caught; this is the only water the villagers have to drink.

Lasjird, May 8th—seven parasangs—eight hours—across the desert, and gradually ascending one of the least elevated ranges of the Elboorz. The soil is gravelly, and the plain in two or three places traversed by deep ravines or beds of torrents, and these are crossed by bridges in pretty good repair. The mountains over which we travelled are impregnated with salt; at their most elevated point, and at one hour from Lasjird, they are scarped, and would be easily defended with a small force, but, as at the pass at Sirdaree, the position might be turned. Beyond this is a fine table-land, in the centre of which is Lasjird, surrounded by productive gardens. Between this stage and Herat a number of small towers may be seen close to every village or inhabited spot, they are loopholed at the top, one single hole, only large enough to creep through, being left in the lower half; these towers will hold eight or ten persons, and are places of refuge and defence for the peasants when attacked by the Turcomans. These gentry are always on horseback, but armed only with lances, and, as the villagers never go out without their fire-arms, they keep these land pirates in check; they also place videttes in some larger towns which crown the adjacent eminences, the watchmen in which give notice of the approach of these marauders. Lasjird, and other villages in the neighbourhood, have been partially fortified for the same reason. There are the remains of a fortification at two hundred paces from Lasjird, the walls of which are about twenty-four feet in height; it would hold a garrison of 2000 men. There are a caravanserai-shah at this place, a reservoir of rain-water, and a brackish stream.

Semnoon, May 9th—five parasangs—seven hours and three quarters—by a good road, a clay soil for the first half, the last gravelly and strong. On the right and about midway is the village of Seurktab, red water, built in a circle like Lasjird; it contains one hundred and twenty families. Semnoon is an ancient town, situated on the foot of the Elboorz chain; we were half an hour traversing the ruins in its vicinity, both on entering and leaving it. The Persians called Semnoon, Darab, or Darius, after their ancient king. It formed part of the country of Kom or Komus, which signifies in the Persian language, sand, from the nature of the soil. Kom was a dependence of Tabarastan, but they were both frequently united to Khorassan, especially at the period when that large province had its own kings. Since the Kajar dynasty ascended the Persian throne, the Komus, though considered a part of Irak, has had its own governor, whose jurisdiction extends beyond the little town of Damghan.

Formerly Semnoon was fortified, but the walls have fallen into the ditch; the palace, commenced in the reign of Futteh Ali Shah, is in the same condition. There are here 1100 inhabited houses, bazaars, public baths, caravanserais, and a handsome mosque; avenues of trees adorn the streets, and an excellent stream of water flows through them from the neighbouring mountains; in the spring these are dammed up at the north of the town, and when the drought of summer sets in the country is irrigated by the supply from these reservoirs. Previously to their construction, in 1825, the crops were not sufficient to supply the inhabitants with grain for three months; now, thanks to these wise precautions, they have more than sufficient for their wants.

Semnoon appears to me to be the spot where Alexander came up with and cut to pieces the rear-guard of Bessus, on the fifth day after he left Rhages. Arrian's words confirm the opinion I have already expressed, that the Macedonians marched through the plain; he says, "Alexander, having gathered up those whom he was forced to leave behind, marched into Hyrcania (Mazanderan), situated on the left hand of the way that leads to Bactria; which road is bounded on one side by a chain of mountains, high and inaccessible; but on the other is a spacious plain, extending itself even to the great sea." . . . . . . And a little further on in the same book he writes—"Alexander, having therefore passed over the first mountains, encamped." . . . . . This was, therefore, the first time that he went into the mountains after he left Rhages; he had till then followed the plain, which he could not have done had he reached the Caspian Straits from the side of Firooz-koh; and as all the country south of the mountains of Hyrcania, through which runs the road Alexander followed so far on his way to Bactria, is a plain, and that it was not until after he had attacked the rear-guard of Bessus that he entered the mountains, there can be no doubt as to the route of the Macedonian hero; with Arrian as a guide, we can trace his march from day to day.

Our caravan encamped amongst the ruins of a caravanserai-shah outside Semnoon. In the afternoon I went into the town to get something to eat; and being a perfect stranger there, the inhabitants could not, under my Eastern garb, suspect me of being an European. I therefore entered a cookshop in a retired bazaar, where I thought there was no probability of meeting any of my travelling companions. Here I installed myself without ceremony or uneasiness, in delightful proximity to the savoury kebabs, and close to three or four native lovers of good cheer, drinking out of their cup, and accepting those civilities which at a meal are never offered by a Mussulman to a Christian. Emboldened by my success, and thinking it would check any suspicion that might arise, I made myself quite at home, and even rather played the important; but I had scarcely finished my kebabs when I was horrified by catching sight of the chief Seid of the caravan, who suddenly made his appearance in front of the shop. Seeing me there, he could not control his indignation, and apostrophized the *kebabji* thus: "Think you, oh man, that God's blessing will rest upon one whose house is open to infidels?" At these words, and the sight of a descendant of the Prophet, all the kebab-eaters started to their feet, turned anxiously to one another, and seemed to inquire what could have brought down upon them such a rebuke. Keeping my seat, and continuing to devour my food with the appetite of a man who had eaten nothing for twenty-four hours, I was immediately recognised as the infidel thus charitably held up to public opprobrium. "Spit upon his beard!" cried one. "Belabour him with your shoe!" said another. This brought me at once upon my legs; and, seizing my stick in a manner that meant fighting, I in my turn repaid their abuse with interest. I knew the Persians, and their way of reasoning. If they are insulted or beaten by any one they do not know, they argue thus: "If this fellow illtreats me, perhaps he has the right to do so; if he has not, why his father, brother, or friend may, which is all the same; it will be more prudent to be quiet." Upon this principle they put up with any abuse without remonstrance; and frightened either at my menacing attitude, or my assertion that I was a Georgian, and would complain to the Russian minister at Teheran, they soon decamped, and I was left face to face with the kebabji, who was not long in taking his cue.

"What do these rascals want?" said he. "What do they mean by interfering with my business? Four fellows who have spent only eight *shahis*, fivepence, whereas you, sir, have expended twenty-two: what have they to say? do these vipers wish to ruin me? Let them go to the devil! I am your very humble servant; this shop, agha, is yours, and everything in it; do with it as you will. Pray God preserve and plenteously reward you!" I knew what this compliment meant in the mouth of a Persian; and after giving him a *backshish*, I started back immediately to the camp.

There can be no doubt that this attack, and many of the vexations I encountered after leaving Bagdad, were owing to the humble dress I wore; but if this was a reason for my not receiving any attention or consideration, I at least escaped from the restraint which an European garb would have entailed upon me; in my Arab dress I was free as air, and, if my travelling companions had not been pilgrims, the journey, though without doubt personally uncomfortable, and accompanied with many hardships, would have been exempt from the annoyances I endured from their bigoted fanaticism. I suffered no loss of dignity by the menial offices I performed, which would certainly have been the case in a frock-coat. I could converse freely with every one, and unrestrained by etiquette; and the last, though perhaps not the least advantage, I could go to the bazaar and purchase what I required. Here the wretched figure I cut was a positive benefit; the tradesman looked for small gains from me, and always asked the real price for his goods. It was then that I discovered how nicely I had formerly been cheated by Ivan and others of his class, and subsequently found the value of the experience I then gained.

To travel under the protection of a Royal firman, with a retinue of servants, horses, &c., would have been no doubt more easy and agreeable; but the most observant traveller must not then expect to see thoroughly into Persian character; he cannot hope to understand the people, their idiosyncracy, and detect the duplicity veiled by their exaggerated politeness and servility. Without apparently protection of any kind, far away from the great towns and roads usually visited and travelled by Europeans, and thrown amongst them on a footing of inferiority, I saw them in their true colours, and my complete knowledge of the language enabled me to comprehend and appreciate the real value of their words, their opinions, and their actions, much better than if I had made my inquiries through the medium of a dragoman, who very often does not even take the trouble simply to translate with accuracy. Of the Travels which have been written on Persia and Central Asia, only two, or at the utmost three, give a true and faithful picture of those countries.

Troops of beggars are to be seen at Semnoon, who live on the donations they wheedle out of passing pilgrims, and some of them had not at all the air of that fraternity. One of them—a great fellow, decently dressed, and full of complimentary speeches, which I returned—informed me that he had for some considerable time projected a pilgrimage to Meshed, but that the want of funds prevented him from realising his intention. In making this admission, the expression of his face evidently indicated a desire to treat me with a flood of tears—these, however, would not come, not even a dozen; and so, rejecting at once the pathetic style, he addressed me, in the most animated manner, as follows:—"Yesterday I discovered in the heavens a constellation of most happy import to me, and a dream last night confirmed me in this hope. The Prophet appeared to me, and said, 'Go to-morrow to the camp of the caravan, and you will there see a stranger who will give you the means of visiting the tomb of the sainted Reza.' You must be the stranger: give, therefore, agha, of your abundance, in the name of the Prophet and this fortunate conjunction of the stars—in the name of the holy Imaums and all the saints of Islam, give, I beseech you!" For a long time I may say I was an emblem of moderation and patience, calling in vain his attention to my appearance, so completely the reverse of rich; but his importunities continued until human nature could stand it no longer, and I bade him begone in a manner which plainly proved to him the little faith I had either in astronomy or dreams. Other rascals tried the same game, but with no better result. At length a lame Dervish, to whom I had given a copper in the morning, again asked an alms, and I offered him another shahi; this, however, he refused, declaring he would have a sahebkran or nothing, and in spite of my obduracy, persisted in his insolent demands, bellowing like a bull, twisting his body into a thousand contortions, and appealing to the pilgrims, who were standing by with approving looks. "Look," said he, "the infidel is deaf to my rights—a fellow who has the misfortune not to be a Mussulman, and ought to be too glad to feed the faithful." And then, seizing a stone, he pummelled his skinny chest with it till blood flowed. When I saw this, I regretted that I had not saved myself this scene for the value of a sahebkran; but, disgusted with cheating and tyranny in any shape, I would not appear to give in. It was evident there was a combination to insult, if not to maltreat me. "Give the Dervish his rights!" cried one of the foremost of the crowd; "he holds them from God, like the Shah." But my blood was up, and, come what might, I determined to settle these pilgrims for good; so, rushing from my room, I said, in a firm and commanding tone —"You are a vile race! When dying with thirst the other day, I asked you for water, and you refused to give me a drop—refused even to lend me a cup, for I am in your eyes an infidel, and impure; but when it comes to smoking my kalioon after me, or eating the remains of my pillau, you hold out your dirty hands to me—I am no longer an infidel—my impurity vanishes. Your mummery and hypocrisy don't impose upon me. Because you see me badly dressed, you think that I am powerless. Don't think I intend to be victimised by you: go and eat dirt, *go-mikhoured.* I'll have your fathers' ashes burnt, and break the head of the first man who comes near me—not one shahi shall your rascally Dervish get."

This address cooled their ardour; but, as my bad luck would have it, who should appear on the scene but my evil genius, the chief Syud of our caravan, who insisted upon a long explanation, and, had not a *daroga*, a police officer, arrived, I do not know what would have been the consequence. This official, on the look-out for a bribe or a fine, gave orders for my immediate arrest; and this order would probably have been roughly executed, had I not claimed the protection of Soliman Khan, the governor of the town, and before him I was speedily brought, surrounded by all the tag, rag, and bobtail of the place. We had been acquainted with one another for years; but he could not recognise me under my disguise. Directly, however, I made myself known, and told him the object of my journey, he received me with great kindness, seated me by his side, and, to the great astonishment of all, sharply admonished the daroga, dismissed the pilgrims from his presence, and ordered his men to drive the Dervish out of the town. As to the Syud, the Khan informed him that strangers were not to be molested in his government, and that he should hold him responsible for my good treatment for the future, and made me remain and dine with him. From this moment I was well treated; and, though ignorant of my real history, my companions saw clearly that I was not what I appeared to be.

CHAPTER VI.

Aheeiyon — Goocheh — Damghan — Description of it — Position of Hecatompylos — Persian legend — History of the Parthians — Opinion of the Kazee of Herat — District of Komus — Decline of Damghan — Arab minarets of burnt brick — Citadel — Shah Rokh — Deh-mollah — Whirlwind — Effects of it — Meimandoos — Attention of Soliman Khan — The merchant arrested — Persian justice — Shah-rood — Description of this town — Important place — Manufactures here — Bostam — Fertility of this district — Good horses — Shah-rood and Bostam coveted by Russia — Hecatompylos — The pilgrim pilferer — Scene in consequence — The French botanist — Privations — Meyomeed — Turcomans — Miyane Dasht — Abbasabad — Georgian colony — Muzeenoon — Attacked by the Turcomans — Russian and Persian slaves at Khiva — Horrible fate of General Bekevitch — Atrocities of the Khivians — Mouravieff's account of them.

AHEEIYON, May 10th—six parasangs—nine hours and a half—a sandy road across a plain during the first three parasangs, the last three hilly and stony; the highest point commands several gorges, and would be a good military post. The Turcomans sometimes lie in wait for caravans at this spot. The country is deserted and sterile. Aheeiyon is a caravanserai-shah. There is a reservoir of water and a few shepherds' huts.

Goocheh, May 11th—six parasangs—seven hours and a half. The road, which is at first stony, becomes sandy, and descends towards the plain of Damghan. There is a caravanserai-shah; but, as at the last stage, bad black bread is the only thing to be had in the way of food.

Damghan, May 12th—six parasangs—eight hours—the road tolerable—villages numerous: that of Doulet-abad is considered one of the finest in Persia; surrounded by a triple wall, it has within its enceinte a palace, a mosque, baths, and large stables. In the reign of Feth Ali Shah, one of his sons, and governor of the district, resided in this fortress. There is a good stream of excellent water here.

Judging by the extensive ruins, Damghan must originally have been a place of considerable importance. European travellers who have studied the ancient history of Persia are of opinion that this was the site of Hecatompylos, the capital of the Parthians. Without rejecting that opinion, I may be permitted to offer the following conjectures, the result of observations I formed upon the spot, and which appear to me equally probable. As to the Persians, they are never at a loss to account for the origin of ruins or towns, for with their inventive faculties they make up any history they like, and fabulous indeed are their traditions. One is not wanting for Damghan :—"There was," says the legend, "a silver palace, in which was held captive a beautiful princess; this lady was enamoured of a handsome prince, who very politely ran off with and married her, and subsequently built a city round the palace; and this," says the legend, "was called Sheri-gumuch, or the Silver-town." The first word is Persian, signifying town; the second Turkish, silver.

It need scarcely be remarked that there is nothing in this tale which can be connected with the history of Hecatompylos.* "That town had a hundred gates." Now, in this instance, and in figurative language, the expression means a town in which a great many roads meet. Is that the case at Damghan? Certainly not; for, excepting that which leads from Irak to Khorassan, and that is a bridle-road, there is only one other, very difficult and very little frequented, that leads to it, viz. the road which descends from the mountains of Mazanderan by the gorge through which runs the river of Damghan. But if, on the contrary, we place ourselves at the spot on which are situated Shah-rood and Bostam, eleven parasangs more to the eastward, the site of Hecatompylos is determined by the natural features of the country. There is to be seen a large table-land enclosed between the mountains, furrowed by deep gorges, from which issue on to it on all sides many roads coming from the most important towns of the north and south of Persia, such as Kachan, Koom, Teheran, Firooz-koh, Saree, Astrabad, Goorgan, Boojoord, Koochan, Meshed, Toorcheez, Toon, and Tubbus.

---

* Hecatompylos was one of the capitals of the Arsacidan princes. When Alexander the Great invaded Parthia it was an important town; and in the second century had either ceased to exist, or changed its name.

According to Strabo (xi. p. 514), it was 1960 stadia (about 224 miles) from the Pylæ Caspiæ, or Caspian Gates, and, as may be inferred from the passage, in the direction of India, eastward; while Ptolemy places it in the same parallel of latitude as Rhodes. Again, Pliny makes the same distance only 133 Roman, or about 122 English, miles. The writer of the excellent article on this town in Smith's 'Geog. Dict.,' where many authorities are collected, agrees with Mr. Ferrier in thinking that Damghan is not the site of the ancient town, which he thinks ought to be sought near Jah Jirm. Col. Rawlinson is of opinion that there are strong grounds for supposing it to be marked by the ruins of Kumis, which are distant 15 miles south-west from Damghan.—Smith's 'Geog. Dict.,' art. 'Hecatompylos.'—ED.

It is true that there are scarcely more ruins here than at Damghan, but one must not forget the perishable material with which the Persians, from the earliest times, have built their houses; it is only in Media and Kars that are found a few edifices, constructed with hewn stone, which have defied the hand of Time. To the eastward of these two provinces the royal palaces of the Persian kings were constructed of sun-dried bricks, which will scarcely stand the rain and tempests of a couple of centuries. It is not, therefore, extraordinary that little remains of Hecatompylos, which, after all, was, according to the writings of the ancients, a vast encampment of nomadic tribes, and not a large and well-built city. On this hypothesis, the space on which the tents of the Parthians were pitched could very well extend from Shah-rood and Bostam to beyond Damghan, a distance of twelve parasangs. Rhages and Persepolis in ancient days, and Teheran in modern times, offer examples of the same dimensions. However, this has little to do with the question now under consideration, but that which I wish to establish is that the position of Hecatompylos cannot be reasonably assigned to any other spot than the one now occupied by Shah-rood and Bostam, as being one of the extremities of the capital of the ancient Parthians.

As to the history of that nation, it would be still more difficult to determine the question. During my long residence in Persia I made every effort, but unsuccessfully, to discover from whence the Parthian tribes came, and what had become of them. My researches in Eastern authors were also fruitless, for they make no mention of them. I also frequently interrogated the Turcomans, the Afghans, and Uzbeks, but without effect. The Kazee of Herat, Mohamed Hassan, had a notion, which I mention, but do not admit, that the word Parthians, used by the Romans to designate the Persians, was only a corruption of the Parses or Perses, by which name they were known to the Greeks from the earliest ages.

Damghan was the chief place of the district of Komus, and, as I have already said, a dependence of Tabaristan, anciently forming part of Mazanderan.* This province belonged alternately to Media

* Mazanderan is a province of Persia, lying on the southern shore of the Caspian Sea. It is very mountainous and rich, and the mountains are, with the exception of those in Georgia, the only ones in Persia covered with forests, principally composed of the *azad derakht* or Persian teak-tree, admirably adapted for ship-building. This fact made Peter the Great and Catharine II. so anxious to obtain possession of Mazanderan, and the neighbouring province of Ghilan;

and Khorassan, and the position of Damghan, on the extreme frontier of these two countries, frequently rendered it an object of contention between the little tyrants amongst whom Persia was so frequently divided. It is not, therefore, surprising that, after so many vicissitudes, Damghan should be the shadow of what it once was. Several succeeding sovereigns repaired its falling edifices, and Shah Abbas the Great rebuilt the city, as well as the interior enceinte now existing. This is one parasang in extent, and contained 15,000 houses; a heap of ruins here and there attest the fact.

At the present time there are only about three hundred inhabited houses; large portions of cultivated land and many gardens occupy much of the ground on which houses formerly stood. The troubles that followed after the death of Nadir Shah were the cause which led to the decline of Damghan, and it received its last blow when Prince Abbas Mirza, attracted by the salubrity of its air and the abundance and fertility of its soil, encamped his army of 30,000 men here for three months in 1832, previously to his departure for the siege of Herat. Everything was devastated by the Persian troops; with them it is all one and the same thing; friends and enemies are alike pillaged. Fragments of a mosque in burnt brick, built by the Arabs with considerable art and taste, still remain; the modern Persians have disfigured it by repairing its crumbling walls with mud and straw. Two elegant and lofty minarets, also built by the Arabs, have been respected by these ruthless destroyers, and, though a small cupola which graced the top of one of them has fallen, they are very interesting specimens of Eastern architecture.

The streets of Damghan are planted on each side with the jujub-tree. The citadel is on the western side; it crowns an artificial mound of earth, and commands both the city and the country. The wall of the town and several forts in connexion with it are in ruins at several points. When in a good state of

---

and indeed they were ceded to Peter by treaty at one moment, although he was afterwards obliged to relinquish them. Down to the present time the Russians have never ceased their efforts to gain even a small *pied à terre* in this neighbourhood; and they have now succeeded in obtaining and fortifying the small island of Ashounada close to the shore in the neighbourhood of Asterabad.

In fabulous times Mazanderan is said to have been conquered by Roostum, who is said to have killed there a number of elephants, an animal now unknown in Persia.—See Malcolm's 'Hist. of Persia.'—ED.

repair these works were quite strong enough to resist the attacks of an Asiatic army. The unfortunate Shah Rokh,* grandson of Nadir Shah, committed suicide in the citadel of Damghan, at the age of sixty-four; and it is said he was induced to commit this act by the injuries and sufferings resulting from the horrible tortures he was put to by Agha Mohamed Khan Kajar, to force him to give up the diamonds he inherited from his grandfather.

Deh-mollah, May 13th—seven parasangs—nine hours—by a level road, but of no solidity, the soil being for the most part of clay. Villages are numerous on both sides. The rain came down in torrents as we left Damghan, and this had been the case since we quitted Teheran. Every year, from the commencement of May to the end of September, the wind blows from the north-west with a force that can scarcely be imagined; at times it is impossible to sit one's horse, or even stand; it levels the tents, scatters the baggage, raising up dense columns of dust which at times completely obscure the atmosphere. The violence of one of these whirlwinds, on leaving the town, was such that some *kedgeves*, a kind of close litter, in which a few women were travelling, were blown off the mules, and five or six pilgrims fell into a *kariz*, dry well; these are in great numbers all along the road on this stage. Fortunately this disaster caused only the death of one horse and the loss of some garments, but, owing to the dust, we suffered from inflamed eyes during the remainder of the journey. This was so thick that the greatest confusion prevailed, the muleteers could not see two paces in front of them, and an hour elapsed before the caravan was again on its march.

At two hours and a half from the town we arrived at the small eminence of Meïmandoos, also called Boorj-meyoos, fortified by Nadir Shah,† at the time when, merely a general under the Shah

* Malcolm, ii. 290.

† Little remained of Persia in the feeble grasp of Shah Tamasp when, in the year 1726, Nadir Shah, after a life of vicissitudes, found himself at the head of a band of robbers in Khorassan, at the age of about thirty-five. The genius of this man alone quickly changed the aspect of affairs, and Persia, from being trodden under foot by all, became, during his lifetime, a formidable empire, and enjoyed once again the glory, such as it is, of being a conquering nation. The first exploit of Nadir Shah was the conquest of Meshed, and the rescue of all Eastern Persia from the Afghans; the next was his victory at Hamadan over the Turks, and their expulsion from Azerbijan and the other western provinces of Persia.

While he was besieging Erivan he received the news that the Afghans had again invaded Persia: so he turned round, beat them, and took Herat and Ferrah. He forced the Russians to

Thamasp, he fought his first battle with the Afghans, then masters of Persia, and commanded by Mir Eshreff. These fortifications are now entirely destroyed. A little beyond the hill, and in front of the village of Naim-abad, we came up to the camp of Soliman Khan, whose kind intervention had been so useful to me at Semnoon. Though it was past midnight, he was up, and occupied in re-pitching his tents, some of which had been blown to ribands by the storm. His reception of me was as courteous and considerate as at our first meeting, and this he proved by

---

abandon, by treaty, all conquests on the Caspian Sea, preparatory to his attack on Turkey, and then dethroned his imbecile sovereign Shah Tamasp, whom he had first taken the pains thoroughly to discredit. He failed in an attack on Bagdad, but was successful in Georgia and Armenia, taking the cities of Gengah, Tiflis, Kars, and Erivan, the former possessions of Persia in those parts. He then concluded peace with the Sultan.

The veil he had hitherto used was now thrown aside; the infant sovereign of Persia was reported to be dead, and Nadir summoned all the notables of the kingdom, to the number of 100,000, to meet him in the plain of Mourgan, to choose a new king. "Shah Tamasp," said he, "and Shah Abbas were your kings, and the princes of the blood are the heirs to the throne. Choose one of them for your sovereign, or some other person whom you know to be great and virtuous. It is enough for me that I have restored the throne to its glory, and delivered my country from the Afghans, Turks, and Russians." He then retired, that their deliberations might seem free, and was soon recalled to hear their unanimous request, that he who had saved the country would accept the throne. He refused this offer, solemnly protesting that the idea of ascending it had never entered into his imagination. The same scene was acted every day for a month, until Nadir, apparently subdued by their solicitations, agreed to comply with their wishes; but, in return for what he called such a sacrifice, he required his countrymen to abandon their national religion, and become of the Sooni instead of the Shiah sect of Musselmen. They consented, and he was crowned with splendour. He now immediately devoted himself to immense military preparations to carry out the vast schemes of conquest which he had formed. He first subdued the Bakhtiyari and put Teheran in safety; he then marched 80,000 men and took Candahar and Cabul; sending kind and flattering letters to the Tatar chiefs beyond the Oxus, whose country he did not want, telling them that he would never invade the rightful inheritance of the descendants of Gengis Khan and the high Turcoman families. He thus secured his rear; and affecting indignation and necessity, advanced to the attack of India, because the emperor of Delhi had not answered his letter requiring the reddition of certain Afghan chiefs. In a rapid and successful march he passed through Lahore, beat the Emperor Mahomed Shah, and entered Delhi in 1739. The inhabitants were respected, till, on a report of his death, they rose upon his troops. He then at last gave orders for a general massacre. While it raged, Nadir sat alone and gloomy in a mosque, where Mohammed Shah found him, and entreated him to spare his people. "The emperor of India should never sue in vain," replied Nadir, who gave orders for the carnage to cease; so great was his discipline and power over his troops, that he was immediately obeyed. After restoring the emperor to his throne, he returned to Persia, conquering on the way Scinde, Balkh, Bokhara, and Khaurism or Khiva. Meshed was his new capital, whence he made expeditions against the Lesghins and Turks: becoming gloomy and cruel during the last six years of his life, he was murdered in 1747.—Malcolm's 'Persia,' vol. ii.—ED.

asking me to a repast which he had prepared expressly for me before my arrival. Having taken tea with him, I rejoined in haste the caravan, and at break of day we reached Deh-mollah, a village of two hundred and fifty houses, surrounded by highly-cultivated grounds and gardens irrigated by a brackish stream. This was not drinkable, and we were therefore obliged to push on to the caravanserai-shah, about a mile in advance of Deh-mollah, where there is an excellent stream of water. Like many others in Persia, this caravanserai was loopholed, and capable of being defended against any sudden attack, for there is no possibility of forcing an entrance except by the door, and this is generally made of thick hard wood, covered with nails and clamped with iron. Many of these resting-places are indeed almost fortresses, and unless supplies failed, or artillery was brought up, a garrison of thirty determined men would be able to hold out against a large force. In the small mountain-range, one parasang south of Deh-mollah, are mines of gold and copper.

We had scarcely been an hour at this place when an official arrived with a royal firman, or order, to arrest one of our party and conduct him to Teheran. I felt myself change colour at this announcement, for I felt as if I was the person of whom the messenger was in search; but this was not so; the officer was in quest of a merchant accused of having left the capital without settling with his creditors. Meshed, to which he was going, is a sanctuary open and inviolable even to the greatest criminals, for within its precincts is the tomb of the holy Imaum Reza, and pursuit had been made in the hope of seizing the merchant before he could reach that city. As the unfortunate man was in our caravan, I hurried off to the camp of my acquaintance Soliman Khan, to whom he clearly showed he was the victim of an intrigue. This functionary, however, dared not oppose the orders of the Shah, but all that lay in his power he would do, and this consisted in his accepting a present from the unhappy merchant of one hundred tomauns (about 50*l.*), which he paid him down in hard cash on the spot, for permission to let his wife and son continue their journey, while he was taken back, as rapidly as post-horses would carry him, to Teheran. On my return to the capital, some months after, I made inquiries, and found that the merchant was an honest fellow, and did not owe a single shahi to any one—he was well known at Teheran, and his intention to leave also. Some false bills of exchange were produced by one of his enemies after he had left, and upon these he was arrested and brought back to the capital, where he had to spend some money before he established his innocence; for in Persia right generally belongs to him who has the longest purse. The words justice and equity are always in every man's mouth, but in reality signify nothing. The clergy, who are the judges in matters of religion, are as venal as the functionaries who execute the civil law. False swearing and evidence and false documents are common; they are admitted if the party in whose favour they are advanced can or will pay the judge a larger sum than his adversary; but should such testimony be refused, nothing results,—perjury is not a crime in Persia.

Shah-rood, May 14th—four parasangs—five hours—by a level road, sandy and stony at intervals, and skirting on our left the mountains that separated us from Mazanderan. Villages were to be seen on our right, and a herd of deer that scampered off at our approach. Shah-rood contains about nine hundred houses, an ill-constructed citadel, bazaars with thatched roofs, two or three caravanserais, and baths. The soil in the neighbourhood of the town is well irrigated by a small river of excellent water, and, as well as an immense breadth of garden-ground, is well cultivated. This town, being situated half-way on the road between Teheran and Meshed, and the point at which all those of Mazanderan and Upper Khorassan meet, is a place of great commercial and strategical importance. It has been for some years the entrepôt for every kind of merchandise, and especially for the rice of Mazanderan. The manufacture of boots and shoes is the most celebrated in Persia, not only for the elegance of the workmanship, but the quality of the leather. The population is a mixture of the natives of Mazanderan, Khorassan, and Turkistan, but the latter are the most numerous. The climate is temperate and healthy.

Bostam, situated about a parasang more to the north, is renowned for the great fertility of its soil, delicious air, beautiful streams of water, and excellent horses. It is here we begin to meet with the breeders of that race of Turcoman horses so much esteemed by the Persians. The cotton goods of this locality are also held in great repute. Bostam is the chief place of the district commencing at Deh-mollah and terminating at Abbas-abad. Thirty-eight villages, all rich and fertile, are within its limits.

Formerly this district was the last dependency of the Little Komus towards the east. If the Russians ever take Mazanderan, which is very probable—for they have, in the first place, coveted it for a long time; and in the second, because no one can prevent them—Shah-rood and Bostam will be most important positions for them; and when fortified, will form a tête-du-pont against the Persians. The governor of Bostam is a namesake of Soliman Khan's. Every caravanserai and halting-place between Damghan and Shah-rood is infested with a species of bug, called *sheb-gez*, the bite of which, if it does not kill, causes a severe illness.*

When I described Damghan I gave my reasons for thinking that Shah-rood must be, if not the centre, at least one of the extremities of the city of Hecatompylos, and a careful examination of the neighbourhood confirmed me more and more in this opinion. It was here that the principal road from Hyrcania débouched, and this was probably the one followed by Alexander when he left the country of the Parthians, and marched to Zadracarta. It would be difficult to assign any other, for one or two roads, situated on this side Shah-rood, leading from the plain of Mazanderan, are almost impassable in the present day; and as in the time of Alexander the principal mountain-range was covered with thick forests, now arid and naked, these roads must then have been still less so.

But to return from these historical investigations to my personal narrative - not a very agreeable subject—I can say, and with truth, that during the whole of my long residence in the East I never travelled with such an insupportable set of companions as those with whom I journeyed between Teheran and Meshed—they were downright Anthropophagi. After leaving Semnoon I was treated with respect, for they feared Soliman Khan; but directly we were out of his government they again showed a disposition to molest me; and a scene which occurred on the road this day confirmed me in that opinion. In the afternoon I heard a great clamouring of voices in the distance, which made me for a moment think of the Turcomans, but in a few minutes the brawlers

* The extraordinarily venomous bite of this animal is well known, and has been remarked by many travellers. See 'Modern Traveller,' Persia—note on Meani, by Dr. Campbell.

approached my encampment, and I found myself surrounded and insolently interrogated by a crowd of the pilgrims, at the head of whom was the chief Syud. "See," said this worthy descendant of the Prophet, dragging a drunken fellow to the front, "see the effects of your infidel habits; the Koran forbids the use of fermented liquors at all times, and you give a bottle of brandy to a Mussulman pilgrim. Shame upon you! are we to eat your dirt?"

"I admit, Syud," I replied, "that I drink brandy, but my religion does not forbid it; and I cannot acknowledge your right to prevent me from doing so, any more than we Christians have a right to interfere with you for having several wives. Every faith has its fasts and festivals; keep your own and leave me mine. It is true that I have some brandy in my trunk, but I have never given any to this drunkard; and to prove this I will show you the bottle."—We instantly looked, but no brandy was there; the fellow had stolen it and several other things in the trunk besides. The Syud, seeing this, believed, and, applying the stick to the rascal's back, he confessed the crime. The blows were now redoubled, and I was not inclined to interfere in mitigation of punishment, nor were they, though he entreated by the Prophet, by the bowels of Omar, to be released. This rascal, Ali Mohamed, of Shiraz, was one of those who had shown the greatest hostility towards me since leaving Teheran.

The many persecutions and sufferings I met with on this journey reminded me of those experienced by Monsieur Aucher Eloi, one of my countrymen, for the space of two years—they ill-treated him in every possible way, not so much because he was an infidel as because he was a botanist. When the Persians see an European scrambling up a mountain-side in search of some diminutive plant they believe this to be a mere excuse; his real object, they say, is to have an interview with the devil at the top, who points out those which will enable him to discover the philosopher's stone, by which they suppose all Europeans obtain their riches. They considered Monsieur Aucher a being who associated with demons, and consequently a fit and proper object to be tormented.

But it is not only the fanaticism of the people that renders travelling in Asia disagreeable, the hardships arising from bad roads, broken-down horses, bad water, food, and shelter, and the fear of being robbed, as well as other physical wants, are to be added: these augment in number as the wanderer approaches central Asia and recedes from the great roads traversed by Europeans. In Turkey in Asia and in the west of Persia the resources may be considered as being excellent and on a scale of comparative comfort, and there is perfect security from molestation; but in some parts of Khorassan, and to the eastward of this province, one is sometimes taught lessons of frugality which almost amount to extremity; and I have endured privations in these countries which, though a soldier's life had inured me to some, were enough to shake the strongest constitution. I felt, nevertheless, a certain degree of pleasure in this kind of life: the freedom of action purchased by such dangers and privations is of an exciting character, and ennobles a man; the mind is more vigorous than usual; he thinks more rapidly and more justly in the midst of these deserts, and the traveller is soon accustomed to look misery and misfortunes in the face when they are shared with equanimity by every one around him.

As the stage from Shah-rood was ten parasangs, we travelled two in three hours the same evening. After the first we passed on our left the large village of Budusht, and, then turning east, encamped for an hour near the ruins of another large village. Here there was a small stream and a few shepherds, and while the mules were eating their barley, one of the violent storms of wind and rain, so common in these countries, broke over us.

Meyomeed, May 15th—ten parasangs—fourteen hours—by a level and sandy road across a desert; half way is a reservoir of water; the caravanserai-shah in front of it is in ruins. One parasang beyond the reservoir, and on a slight eminence, amongst some hills, is a small fortress recently constructed; in this, besides a few peasants sent here by the Prime Minister to cultivate the land in its immediate neighbourhood, four artillerymen are quartered with their field-pieces. This fort was built to protect the country against the depredations of the Yamoods, Turcomans, and Goklans, who infest the road between Shah-rood and Nishapoor. These rascals not only attack and plunder the caravans, but even the villages, sometimes destroying them utterly, and carrying off the inhabitants to the desert, where they sell them to the Uzbeks of Khiva or Bokhara. Meyomeed is a village of three hundred houses, which, with their gardens, extend along the banks of a brook for about half a parasang; the water is tolerable, and there is a good caravanserai-shah, but in the summer, travellers prefer halting under the trees in the public square. This village is situated at the foot of a pointed and precipitous rock, which the inhabitants have never ascended, believing it to be the abode of evil genii.

Miyane-Dasht, also called *Ferrash-abad*, May 16th—six parasangs—seven hours and a half—the first part across a range of stony hills stretching from the peak of Miyane; the last part over a sandy plain. The ground, for three parasangs, was irregular and much cut up, with now and then some brushwood and brambles, a capital cover for the Turcomans, who sometimes lie in ambush here; we therefore closed our ranks ready for an attack, but arrived without any casualty at the next halt, near a caravanserai-shah, which had been transformed into a barrack and arsenal for some artillerymen and a few pieces of cannon. Miyane-Dasht is a hamlet of twenty-three houses, newly built, and inhabited. The village is surrounded by a wall and dry ditch on three sides, the fourth being connected with the caravanserai; the water is in small quantity and bad, there is no cultivation; the two or three gardens which the inhabitants have are at the foot of some mountains in the distance, where there is a small stream; it takes two hours to reach them. These gardens are not sufficient to supply the wants of these few families, who purchase their barley and straw elsewhere, and resell them at a large profit.

Abbasabad, May 17th—five parasangs—six hours and a half—the first parasang through a plain, the remainder by a sandy road winding through some low hills. As the locality was said to be dangerous, we were off early, lighted by the moon till sunrise. When a Persian sets out upon a journey he says, "God is merciful;" and if he is taken prisoner by a Turcoman he exclaims, "It was my fate." But this time the pilgrims got off with the fright, and we arrived in safety at Abbasabad.

This village stands on an eminence, and consists of forty-five houses surrounded by a mud wall. We found the inhabitants in a state of consternation, for the Turcomans had attacked them on the previous evening, and carried off two men and six women. Shah Abbas the Great, anxious to make the road to Meshed safe, and have the country near it cultivated, built at every five parasangs a caravanserai-shah, or a village, in which he settled one hundred and forty-three families accustomed to the military service: there are now only thirty-two. Abbasabad was one of these villages.

The inhabitants were originally Georgians and Christians, but, with few exceptions, became subsequently Mahomedans, and only eight or ten preserve their ancient faith: as they have constantly intermarried, they still retain the Georgian type. They pay no taxes, and the Shah continues to allow them annually a hundred tomauns, which Shah Abbas granted to them in perpetuity. Travellers are obliged to pay for everything they may provide, even though furnished with a firman. But they are, nevertheless, in a miserable plight, and refrain from improving their condition, because they are afraid of being taxed to such an extent as to neutralise any benefits that might arise from their exertions; and though they could bring their land into cultivation by turning a good stream, they prefer living from hand to mouth, and buying their provisions at Shah-rood or Subzavar, and selling them at a large profit to the passing caravans. Another village of Georgians was founded by Shah Abbas, an hour's distance north-east, but the inhabitants have been all carried into slavery by the Turcomans.

Muzeenoon, May 18th—seven parasangs—eight hours and a half—by a level sandy road, but much impregnated with salt. We were aware, by the account of the attack on the last village, that the Turcomans were on the road, but, most of us being armed with muskets, and they only with lances and bows and arrows, and our numbers being much the same, we left at sunrise, pretty confident in our strength. Feeling our way, we, after about an hour's march, discovered them lying in wait for the caravan at a place called Sertsheshnie, a spring; and before they had time to advance, we sent them a volley, to which they replied by a flight of arrows that fell short, falling back upon Pul-Ebrishim, where thirty more of their party were posted. Here, thinking to frighten us, they raised a loud shout; and a few of them seeming disposed to move upon our flank, we gave them another volley, which did not do much mischief, the distance being too great; we managed however to kill one horse, and his rider, who fell with him, rising from the ground, pointed to the least honourable part of his person, and then, jumping lightly up behind one of his comrades, they all, to our great satisfaction, disappeared in the twinkling of an eye.

These Turcomans are, and with reason, a great terror to travellers and the inhabitants of villages liable to their incursions, for, if armed with similar weapons only, the Persians always take to their heels. This want of courage is partly explained by their apprehension of the fate that awaits them if they are taken prisoners by these barbarians, who sell them to the Uzbeks, a race as cruel as themselves.

An European who visited Khiva in 1819 has given us some dreadful details regarding the treatment of the Russian and Persian slaves he saw in that khanat, to the amazing number of 30,000: some of them who would not embrace Islamism were buried alive, the Khivians declaring that they put them to death in this horrible manner because it was not fit that the earth should be sullied with their impure and infidel blood. I believe there never has been a greater example of atrocity committed by any nation than that which put an end to the life of the Russian General Bekevitch, made prisoner by the Uzbeks in an expedition sent against Khiva in 1717: he was flayed alive from the knees upwards. These wretches thought a speedy death too good for their victims, and always invented the most refined and lingering tortures to accomplish their diabolical purpose. The following is the account given of the fate of these unfortunate men by General Mouraviev * after he returned from his dangerous embassy to the court of Khiva:—

"The captives, who are under the absolute control of their owner, have to endure every torture that he can invent: they do not always kill them when they are in fault, but gratify their revenge by cutting off their ears, putting out an eye, or stab them with their knives in a part which is not mortal. This consideration for their lives is owing merely to the fear of losing a slave as a matter of property; the torture inflicted, the master sends him again to his work, scarcely giving the man time to dress his wounds; the excessive labour under which they too often sink is almost worse than death.

"These punishments are generally inflicted if a slave attempts to abscond; at the second attempt he is nailed by the ear to the street-door of his master's house, and remains in this state for

* The conqueror of Kars, who published an account of his embassy to Khiva in 1819-20. 1 vol. 8vo. Paris, 1823.

three days, exposed to the insults of the passers-by, and without food; the wretched man, already emaciated and feeble, frequently dies on the spot of cold and hunger. To escape is almost an impossibility, for Khiva is surrounded by vast steppes, on which water is exceedingly scarce, and the fugitive would certainly perish. It is by no means a rare thing for a slave to destroy himself, to escape from his dreadful sufferings."

CHAPTER VII.

Turcoman preparations for a foray — Mode of training their horses — Singular kind of forage — Forced marches — Arrangements before attacking a caravan — Wretched fate of the prisoners — Turcoman cruelty — Reprisals — Turcoman mode of fighting — Monsieur Ferrier's opinion of the Turcoman as a soldier — The comical consequences of a defeat — Honour amongst thieves — Geographical position of the Turcomans — The Khirgah — The three principal tribes — Their origin and similarity to the Uzbeks — Mental and physical characteristics of the Turcomans — The women, and their value as wives — A Turcoman excuse for kidnapping the Persians — Turcoman religion — The way to reduce these hordes — Mode adopted by Shah Abbas — Simple fare of these tribes — Their treatment of horses — The steppes of Turcomania — The breed of horses — Introduction of Arab blood by Tamerlane and Nadir Shah — Breed of the Hazarahs and Uzbeks — Extraordinary journeys performed by the Turcoman horses — The price of them in the steppes — Cavalry horses in France — Bad system of breeding there — The veterinary art in Turcomania — Diseases of horses.

THE majority of the thirty thousand unfortunate creatures who were in the khanat of Khiva in Mouraviev's time had been sold into slavery by the Turcomans, and I shall in this chapter give a brief history of these accomplished man-stealers, with some account of the manner in which, by the agency of their admirable horses, they are enabled to carry on their inhuman traffic. The rapidity with which the Turcomans accomplish great distances on their pillaging excursions is really inconceivable. The following is the manner in which they prepare for them:—when a chief is determined upon making a foray, he plants his lance, surmounted by his colours, into the ground in front of his tent, and a crier invites all good Mussulmans, in the name of his Prophet, to range themselves under his banner, and join in the raid upon the Persian infidels. His wishes however are no law to any of the tribe, for the Turcoman enjoys the most perfect liberty, and those only who have confidence in their chief ride up and strike their lances into the ground near his, the signal that the volunteer has decided to follow his fortunes. When the chief thinks that he has assembled a sufficient number of men to insure the success of the expedition, he names that day month as the day of departure, this time being required for each man to get his horse into that high state of condition without which he could not support the extraordinary fatigue and hardships he has to undergo.

During this month the forage of a horse for twenty-four hours consists of six pounds of hay or clover-hay and about three pounds of barley, or one half the ordinary quantity of corn. This reduces the animal considerably in flesh, which is the object in view, the first step in his training; his pace improves under it, and he is thus prepared for the strengthening and somewhat singular food which he is subsequently to have.

The horse is then put to his full speed for half an hour every day, and is not fed until some considerable time after he comes in: very little water is given him, and if he is eager to drink it is a sign that he ought to fast a little longer; but this training never exceeds a month. The thirty days having elapsed, the Turcomans take the field, each of them with two horses; the one, the charger, which has been trained in the manner described; the other, a *yaboo*, or inferior animal used for burden, which the Turcoman mounts on leaving his *aoul*, encampment, and which carries him to the Persian territory; the other follows him without saddle or bridle, and never strays from the party, for both have been accustomed to follow their master like dogs from the time they were foals. The first day's march seldom exceeds three parasangs; the second, four; the third, five; and the fourth, six. When they arrive at this point the Turcomans change the forage of the charger, and substitute four pounds and a quarter of barley-flour, two pounds of maize-flour, and two pounds of raw sheep's-tail fat chopped very fine, all well mixed and kneaded together: this is one day's ration, without either straw or hay. The horses are very fond of this food, which is given them in balls, and puts them in tiptop condition, and after having been fed in this manner for four days the animal is capable of supporting the longest forced marches. Then, and not till then, their masters mount them, and prepare for the work of pillage.

Previously to this, however, they look out for some hiding-place fortified by Nature, which will furnish them with a secure retreat under adverse eventualities. While they are quietly resting themselves and their horses here, three or four are detached from the band to ascertain, if possible, whether any caravans are likely to pass. Sometimes these scouts will join the *kafila* in the guise of inoffensive travellers, and as they go along take very good care to find out the nature and value of the merchandize, the number of armed men, &c., and then suddenly disappear and convey this information to their companions. Though the Turcomans do not run much risk in such *reconnaissances*, they prefer, for prudence sake, to obtain this information from Persians living in the frontier villages, with whom they are frequently in communication, and pay accordingly—these vagabonds, who, without an idea of pity, thus deliver up their unfortunate countrymen to these bandits, explore the roads and give intelligence, which is generally but too accurate. During the time thus occupied in reconnoitring, the main body of the Turcomans that remain concealed are not inactive ; the majority scour the immediate neighbourhood in small parties of five or six, and, as their numbers do not attract attention, they frequently manage to carry off some of the peasants working in the fields: this is the ordinary prelude to operations on a large scale. In the evening they rejoin their friends to hear the news from their scouts, and deliberate upon their plans for the morrow.

When the attack is at length decided upon, half a dozen men are selected by the chief to remain with the provisions and *yaboos ;* the rest, mounted on their best horses, gallop quickly to the appointed spot, whether village or caravan, on either of which they fall like a whirlwind, and, like it, devastate and finally sweep up and carry off everything, including men, women, and children, that comes in their way ; in a few minutes all is over. Incendiarism is not unfrequently their last act ; and, leaving the flames and smoke to tell the tale of desolation to the distant villages, they fly with their booty, and gain the spot where they left their horses, putting from thirty to forty parasangs behind them without drawing bit ; and in an incredibly short space of time reach their encampment. Their horses, accustomed to these long and rapid journeys, accomplish them without knocking up ; but this is not the case with the unhappy persons who have been kidnapped : these, if few in number, are generally taken up behind their captors, or, if more numerous, they tie them on the horses they have stolen, and drive them before them until the animals drop with fatigue. The unhappy prisoners they carried are then attached by a long cord to the saddle-bow of their brutal tormentors, who drag them along, sometimes walking, sometimes running, according to the pace at which their own horses are going at the time. Woe to them who slacken their pace! for directly any show symptoms of fatigue, the head of the Turcoman's lance pricks and forces them on to further exertion; and should nature give way entirely, and they fall, they are killed without remorse. Of one hundred Persians thus carried off and obliged to march with their captors, scarcely a third reach Turkistan, or, at any rate, the spot from whence the party set out on their villanous expedition. A Turcoman's sensibility is never awakened to suffering, no matter how terrible—the sentiment of pity is unknown to them; a Persian is in their eyes simply a mercantile and marketable commodity, and not worth taking care of after it has been injured—they are merciless by habit and by calculation. A prisoner who could make his escape would never forget the treatment he had received at their hands, and would certainly take his revenge by giving information at the first military post he came to. In killing his captive, therefore, a Turcoman looks upon the act as one of proper foresight and a necessary precaution; in their *aouls* they give their prisoners the smallest possible quantity of food—just enough, in short, to keep life and soul together, so that they may never be strong enough to entertain a hope of effecting their escape.

In consequence of the mutual understanding which exists between the Turcomans and the Kurdish chiefs employed by the Persian government to guard the frontier, the former are rarely interfered with in their expeditions. It sometimes happens, however, that the inhabitants of the border villages, who are the most liable to be attacked, and have also their own spies, receive intelligence of their enemies' movements, and, assembling in arms, lie in wait for them as they pass through some defile or other difficult ground, and exterminate the whole band without pity; but these reprisals are unfortunately of rare occurrence, and will never be more numerous until they are loyally seconded by the regular troops.

In spite of the impudent manner in which the Turcomans thus enter the Persian territory, sometimes to a distance of from sixty to eighty parasangs, it should be remembered that they contrive to do this by gliding between the villages at night and unperceived. The stealthy and sudden nature of their attack is the reason of their success; this is, no doubt, a very useful military quality, but after having seen them fight it is impossible to have any high opinion of their courage. They will expose themselves to unseen dangers for the chance of taking their enemy unawares, but let them meet their enemy face to face, let their adversaries send a volley about their ears, they will not stand a minute. They never fall upon a caravan unless they are superior in numbers and the travellers appear disinclined to fight; but immediately there is the least appearance of resistance, they rarely attack in earnest: on such occasions they are right careful of their skins, hanging, though at a respectable distance, on their flanks, to cut off the stragglers or some portion of the baggage; but directly there is a chance of their losing any men they soon make off. The Turcomans are the best mounted robbers in the world, but will never make good soldiers; nevertheless there are Turcoman chiefs who have some regard for their reputation, and are ashamed to return empty-handed to their *aouls*, and expose themselves to the jeers of the old men and the reproaches of their wives. The latter on such occasions present them with their petticoats as a mark of contempt, and, disgusted with their want of success, worry and endeavour to make them start again; but the Turcoman ladies, as in more civilized countries, do not always carry their point, and succeed in making themselves obeyed. Under any circumstances nothing will induce a Turcoman to attack more than three times; he then retires to his encampment, completely convinced that Providence declares against him. Should a family lose one of its members in the first or second attempt, they are not obliged to furnish another man, nevertheless they preserve all their rights and participate in the booty; this is sold to the Uzbeks, who visit the encampments two or three times a year. These speculators pay of course with ready money or articles in barter. A boy about ten years of age will fetch about forty tomauns; a man of thirty, twenty-five; and of forty, twenty, &c. &c.

The Turcomans inhabit the countries which lie between the eastern shore of the Caspian and the river Moorghab; this is the extreme length of their territory. There are some encampments of them beyond this river, but they are very few in number. In breadth they may be said to occupy the country from the line formed by the Goorghan and the prolongation of the Elboorz chain (north of Boojoord, Deregez, Koochan, and Meshed) up to the deserts of Khiva and Bokhara, and they are sure to be met with where the soil is fertile and well watered. A tribe or two here and there may also be seen on the banks of the Oxus. It is a rare occurrence to find them living in villages; when this happens they have been forced to do so by the sovereign who has subdued them. These people have been accustomed, from the most remote ages, to dwell in tents, which enables them to wander about with their flocks with greater facility. This mode of life is also a means of escaping from the Persian dominion, of which they have always been, and to this day remain, the most determined enemies.

The wants of a Turcoman are few in number,—a tent, called a *khirgah*, shelters the whole family, and this is of a superior manufacture to anything of the kind made by the nomadic tribes of Persia. They can make these khirgahs warmer than the best-built houses—a matter of some consequence to them, seeing how severe the winters are in the country they inhabit. The khirgah is conical in form, the frame-work being made of laths of hard wood interlaced one with the other, which can be opened or folded up at pleasure, according as they wish to camp or decamp ; a camel, or at most two, is able to carry this tent. Thick felts are stretched either entirely or partially across this frame-work, according as the Turcoman may wish to avoid the burning rays of the sun or protect himself from the rain or cold : they are very commodious, and of all sizes, and a high price is given for them by some of the Persian nobles. The Turcomans, whose principal occupation consists in making *chap-aouls*, raids, upon the Persians, belong to the three following tribes :—

1. The Yamoods, settled beyond the river Attrak, near the shores of the Caspian Sea, and between this and Khiva, consisting of 25,000 tents or families.

2. The Goklans, on the banks of the Goorghan and the Attrak, consisting of 12,000 families.

3. The Tekies, who are separated from the Kurds by a chain of mountains which extend from the sources of the Goorghan and the Attrak near Sharaks, consisting of 35,000 families.

These three tribes have become intimately united from having been a long time near neighbours ; many family alliances also have taken place between them, and they give one another a mutual support when they are attacked either by the Shah of Persia or the Uzbek chiefs. The Tekien tribe, by the position it occupies in the middle of the steppes, is the best protected ; these are but little known to strangers, who would run a great chance of dying of hunger and thirst if they attempted to traverse them without a guide ; it is to them the Goklans retire when pursued by the

Persians, an occurrence which generally takes place every year, but without much success, for they fly at the approach of the enemy, and advance again when he has left. The presence of the Shah's troops in this country can have no good result until some forts have been built and permanently garrisoned, and the troops are paid and officered as soldiers should be. Other tribes of these nomads, and numerous, also inhabit the countries beyond those I have already named, and I will mention them as I approach their territory.

The Turcomans belong to the great Turkish family,* of this I have not the slightest doubt; and between them and the Uzbeks I see only a difference of tribe and nothing more: the types are similar; the face is flat, large, and pointed at the chin; the beard is sandy or light, thin, and irregular; the head often too small for a body exhibiting considerable development of muscle; the face is pierced with two small holes, the form of which recalls the eyes of a Chinese. These tribes speak the same language, have the same disposition, the same tastes, the same ferocity, the same hatred for and the same desire to pillage the Persians; in a word, everything conspires to keep them united. There is, however, one striking difference—the Turcomans lead a wandering life, and the Uzbeks † live in villages; the more regular life to which in con-

* "The Turcomans are a nation of Turk race, which, in the 11th and 12th centuries, overran Boukharia, Northern Asia, and, on the westward of the Caspian Sea, Armenia, Southern Georgia, Shirvan, and Daghistan. They lead a nomade life, and compose the principal part of the population of these countries, where they are called Tarekameh, Turkmens, and Kizilbashi. To explain the name of Turcomans, the Persians relate, that the Turk tribes, at the time of their invasion of Khorassan, had married the women of the country, and that to their descendants were given the name of Turcomans, which means, 'like the Turks.' This specious etymology appears very paradoxical, since the hordes of this people, who speak Turkish, and have remained beyond the Jihon, also call themselves Turcomans. I think the name is rather derived from *Turk* and *Coman*, and that it was given to that part of the Coman nation which remained on the east of the Caspian Sea, under the domination of the Turks of the Altai, while another part, which was independent, came and established itself in the vast plains to the westward of that sea, and to the north of the Sea of Azof, and who afterwards pushed forwards into Hungary."—Note by M. Klaproth, 'Voyage de Mouraviev,' p. 394.

† "Mouraviev supposes Uzbek to be derived from '*Uz*,' his or himself, and '*bek*,' master; thus meaning master of himself, or independent. Klaproth derives it from the people called 'Ouz,' or 'Gouz,' by the Arab historians. These were the same as the Ouigour, a Turkish tribe which formerly inhabited the countries to the south of the 'Celestial Mountain,' that is, Little Boukharia. At the commencement of the 16th century, the Uzbeks passed the Sihoun or Jaxartes, proceeding westward. Everywhere they spread terror and desolation. They are at present masters of Balkh, Khaurism, or Khiva, Bokhara, Ferganah, and some countries

sequence of this the Uzbek is accustomed has brought out some contrasting points between them ; but the difference is not so great as to lead one to believe that they are not people having a common origin. It is all very fine seeking, or endeavouring to create, new etymologies or theories, which can only serve as the text of long dissertations that cannot destroy or modify the facts : Turcoman or Uzbek, Uzbek or Turcoman, there will never be any more difference between them than there is in Europe between the country and the town, that is to say, the peasant and the citizen.

The Turcoman is coarse, his manners rude as the country in which he lives, and he is insensible to pain and sorrow for himself as well as for others. The cold and insensible temperament of this people is in singular contrast to the amorous nature of the nations that surround them, and without doubt it is to this cause that we may attribute the little attention they bestow upon their wives. They have for them almost a feeling of contempt ; allowing them full liberty to do as they please, they trouble themselves very little about what licences they indulge in ; and, if I may judge by the conduct of those who were, to the number of a thousand, brought prisoners to Teheran as hostages, these ladies are not particularly distinguished by their severity of manners : they are never veiled. The principal thing that interests the Turcoman with reference to the qualifications of his wife is, that she should diligently attend to the work of the house, or rather tent, and the superintendence of the crops and flocks ; he cares little for anything else. As to occupation, the men are perfectly ignorant of the meaning of the word, unless it is in some manner connected with their expeditions, and they pass the greatest portion of their time in unmitigated idleness.

In religion they are Sunnite Mussulmans, whereas the Persians are of the sect of Shiahs, and this in their opinion justifies the right they have arrogated to themselves of seizing the latter and selling them into slavery ; indeed they consider this a very meritorious act, and agreeable to God, for directly they have them in their possession they make orthodox Mussulmans of them. I think it not impossible that the Turcomans hold this language, feeling

---

in the neighbourhood of Mount Belout Dagh. The Uzbek tribes who inhabit Khiva are the Ouigour-Naiman, Kangli-Kipchak, Kiat-Konkrad, and Noikious-Mangood."—Klaproth's Note, Mouraviev's Bokhara, p. 395.

that they cannot offer any other excuse for carrying on the infamous traffic of man-stealing. They are Mahomedans in name only, and are certainly quite as much sinners in the fact as in the form ; the majority amongst them do not know a prayer, and never say one ; fasting, ablutions, and purifications, and meats forbidden by the Koran, with the other precepts of that holy book, are matters to which they pay not the slightest attention. Their Mollahs are few in number, and as ignorant as themselves.

If the Persian government were itself more moral and enlightened—if the Shah and his ministers ever devoted themselves to the organization of a good government, and keeping their army in an efficient state, the disorders and villanous practices of the Turcomans would be soon put down. To do this it would only be necessary to occupy three passes in a mountainous district through which they march from their steppes. This done, four or five columns of cavalry, supported by a few light howitzers and fieldpieces, should be formed in *échelon* on the frontier bordering their territory. These guns ought to be served by men who know the country thoroughly, so that they could hasten to any point at which they might be required, even into the very *aouls* of the Turcomans. A tax might then be levied upon them which would pay the troops thus employed. By these means the state would insure the peace and security of one of Persia's finest provinces without any expense, and bring a misguided people to understand those feelings of humanity and civilization which, though only partially understood in Persia as compared with Europe, are far more so than amongst the Turcomans. Unhappily there is little hope that such a plan would be adopted by the government of the Shah: provided gold flows into his treasury, little does he care whether his people are pillaged or not, or that eight or ten of his principal nobles eat up the revenues of the country. The Turcomans have pillaged, and will go on pillaging ; no one prevents them. The worst of it is, the small Persian chieftains charged with the defence of the frontier districts almost always have an understanding with these rascals, who pay them a portion of their ill-gotten plunder on condition of their leaving the passes open for them, or being at the moment of the foray conveniently out of the way. The Khans of Boojoord, Deregez, and Koochan, who command in the Kurdish colonies, may be cited as amongst the chiefs whose avarice produces such deplorable results.

Shah Abbas the Great, whose wisdom and foresight enabled him to do so much good in the course of his reign, hoped to be able to repress the Turcomans, by opposing to them a warlike people strangers to the province; with this view he removed several thousand families from Kurdistan, where they were always in a state of anarchy, and settled them to the north of Khorassan, between Astrabad and Meshed, with orders to protect that frontier. All went on well during the life of Shah Abbas, and even as long as the Suffavean dynasty lasted; but during the long wars which followed upon the invasion of the Afghans, the Kurds and Turcomans feeling that separately they were not strong enough to protect themselves from the arbitrary power of the many ambitious chiefs who disputed amongst themselves the possession of Persia, united to resist them. This they did successfully; and from that time each tribe or district in Kurdistan formed itself into a small independent state, and joined the Turcomans in carrying off the Persians and plundering the caravans. It was only in 1832, when their fortresses were besieged by the Prince Royal Abbas Mirza, that the Kurds felt themselves compelled to return to their duty and pay their tribute to Persia; but since the death of that estimable prince, which occurred in the following year, their submission has become only nominal, and they have frequently joined the Turcomans in their old depredations.

The defiles, which are supposed to be guarded by the Kurds, ought to be held by the Persian regular troops, and they are so well fortified by nature that a small force would suffice for that purpose: the Turcomans would then not even attempt the passage. The impunity with which they commit their crimes is an encouragement to these bandits: when they hear of any preparations being made to attack them, their expeditions cease for a time, and they promise amendment and remain quiet; but this is only to lull the vigilance of the Persians, and when they fancy they are not thinking about them the Turcomans recommence their exploits. The conduct of the government is in this respect most deplorable; for two or three years they leave them to plunder and pillage to their hearts' content, and, when the clamorous complaints of the people at length reach Teheran, they despatch to the spot a few thousand serbas; but while this is going on and the soldiers are demolishing the *aouls*, the tribe retire *en masse* into the territory of the Tekies, where, in the heart of their steppes, it is impossible for the troops to follow them. Having, therefore, but half accomplished their duty, they are obliged to retire, dragging with them as hostages the women and children of the few families they have succeeded in capturing. As a matter of course, the tribe which fled at their approach now returns, and plunders the caravans with greater ardour than ever. In these encounters they soon make up their own losses, for they rarely consist of more than a few tents, felts, and kitchen utensils. As to money, a Turcoman never has any with him; he buries it in some secure spot known only to himself, and this is his resource should fortune turn the wheel against him. Giving up part of the spoil to the border chief he knows to be an infallible means of ingratiating himself, and through this means recovers his wife and children, if indeed he feels interested about them. Thus it will be seen that in the most adverse cases the Turcomans' loss is far less than that of the Persians.

As to the value of a Turcoman's wardrobe, it is little indeed; a long and wide dress of woollen and cotton, trousers and shirt of coarse linen, and a sheepskin cap, will serve him for several years. Maize, a little corn, millet, and some milk satisfy all his internal wants. Those who live after this fashion are in Europe considered in a state of poverty; there are, nevertheless, several millions of individuals in Asia who do so, and I can affirm are perfectly contented with their lot. Comparing this state of things with our European habits, I have often asked myself if it is really happiness that we procure for ourselves by pampering our appetites and tastes with innumerable kickshaws, ever-changing fashions, and a passion for displaying the most refined luxuries. After such reflections I arrived at the conclusion that, if the condition of Asiatics was susceptible of amelioration, that of the European would allow of some retrenchment of these superfluities, which become wants simply from the habit of using them—exciting vanity, selfishness, and every bad passion, and provoking those revolutions which lead to the shedding of blood, without improving the real condition of man.

The Turcomans would never venture to advance so far over the Persian border to make their forays if they did not possess so fine a breed of horses, on which they bestow more care than upon their wives and children—it is more than tenderness, it is an absorbing passion, which they feel for that noble animal; it is a sin in their eyes to maltreat him, and he who commits that crime incurs the reproaches of the whole tribe. A horse is to the Turcoman what a ship is to the pirate, it carries himself and his fortunes. In his saddle he is in his fortress; in truth, it is on horseback that he fights: there is no instance of a tribe having ever voluntarily retired within the walls of a town to defend themselves from their enemy. To this feeling, and their wild mode of warfare, they owe their security quite as much as to the clumsy system pursued by the Persians in endeavouring to reduce them to obedience.

The steppes of Turcomania are very favourable to the development of the equine race; the pasturage and artificial grasses grow in dry soils, having no other nourishment than the winter snows. The fodder thus produced is much more sweet and nutritious than that of our more moist and temperate climate. It produces in their horses a higher temperature and better condition of the blood, as well as a peculiar elasticity and strength of nerve and muscle perfectly wonderful. Green food is produced on these steppes only in the spring; at that season the Turcomans refrain from making any expeditions, and this state of abnegation continues to the end of July. During this period they have time to gather in their crops, and their animals rest those limbs which have so well done their duty the previous season. From the month of August up to the winter they are kept on dry food: this consists of seven pounds of barley per diem, mixed with dry chopped straw, lucerne, *sainfoin*, or clover-hay, unless a *chap-aoul* is coming off, in which case the horse is put upon half forage, as I have already mentioned.

The Turcoman horses are a modification of the Arab breed, and as good in every respect as the famous horses of the desert. They differ, however, in respect to height, and their form is more developed; but I must admit that their outline is not so pleasing to the eye. Their neck is long, straight, and proudly curved, is almost always slender, but terminated by too long a head. The chest is generally narrow, and the legs rather long and slender to carry a large but well-proportioned carcase, though occasionally a little too long. It is a tradition in this country that the Turcoman and Arab horses were crossed at a very remote period: but breeding on a very large scale took place when the first sectarian followers of Islam conquered Persia. Tamerlane that prince of irregular cavalry commanders, introduced new blood by dispersing amongst the tribes 4200 mares, which he had selected in Arabia from the very best breeds. After this, Nadir Shah renewed this cross with 600 mares, which he confided exclusively to the Tekiens. The horses of this tribe are now held in the highest estimation in all Turcomania, especially those from the district of Akhal. The next in reputation after the Tekien horses are those of Mero-Shah Jehan, the horses of the Yamoods and the Goklans, and the race of the Moorghab, of the Hazarahs, the Uzbeks of Meimana, Shibberghan, &c. &c. &c.

The extraordinary distances which some of these horses will travel at a stretch is scarcely to be credited. I have heard a Turcoman relate most marvellous stories of their powers of endurance: for instance, that he has known a horse go two hundred leagues (six hundred miles) in six, or even five days. As to my own knowledge, I can affirm that I saw one of these animals—the property of Habib Ullah Khan, general-in-chief of the artillery—go from Teheran to Tabreez, return, and again reach Tabreez, in twelve days; the distance is ninety-four parasangs, or about one hundred and forty leagues (or four hundred and twenty miles). But from this three days must be deducted; the horse having been allowed twenty-four hours' rest after each journey.*

When a Turcoman horse has given great proofs of strength and endurance in a *chap-aoul*, he never leaves the tribe except by force of arms. With the exception of the Shah of Persia, and more particularly Assaf Doulet, Governor-General of Khorassan, and a few Uzbek princes, there are few persons in Asia who possess the real and best-bred horses of the Turcoman breed. They have not been sold to them, but have been wrung from the chiefs of

---

* In the interesting little work by General Daumas on the Horses of the Sahara, are a number of curious notes and answers by Abd el Kadr. On being asked how many days the Arab horse can march without resting or being injured, he answers, that if the horse has as much barley as he can eat, he will perform 16 parasangs (64 miles) a-day for three or four months, without a single day's rest.—p. 404. He also states that he has known a horse go from Tlemsen to Mascara in a single day, a distance of about 50 parasangs (200 miles). After such a journey he says the horse ought to be spared the next day. General Daumas relates several anecdotes within his own knowledge, of Arab horses having gone distances of 70 and 80 leagues, from 170 to 200 miles, in 24 hours.—p. 58. See Les Chevaux du Sahara, Paris, 1854, 1 vol.—ED.

tribes as presents, or taken in some sudden onslaught. The reader will understand the value a Turcoman sets upon a horse that he has bred, when I state that the second best of the best breed, which they will occasionally consent to sell, cannot be purchased for less than from 120*l.* to 160*l.* A useful and excellent horse may, however, be had, of inferior breed, for 40*l.* to 48*l.* Fourteen guineas will purchase an ordinary animal, which would, however, in Europe be thought not a bad sort of horse, and certainly worth three or four times its value in Turkistan.

The manner in which Eastern nations manage their best-bred horses has proved to me how many prejudices we have to conquer in France on this subject. The old routine, scientific words and works, artistically, or perhaps I ought to say veterinarily arranged, and the saws of the knowing ones, are always in opposition to reason. Our horses are brought up like young ladies, in a stable hermetically closed, leaving it neither when it rains or snows; the least indisposition alarms the owner, and he calls in the doctor. They are scarcely worked, and up to four years old are almost treated like children at nurse. The result of this is that they have no stamina, and knock up on the very first occasion they are required to do hard work. If we were at war, and our cavalry took the field—I mean composed of horses bred in France—I feel convinced that two-thirds of them would be ineffective one month after the opening of the campaign. The prizes which the government give at the various races they have established for the amusement of the Parisian public, and in the departments, only serve to divert the breeders from the object they really ought to keep in view, namely, that of developing the physical power of the animal before looking for speed. This is a quality useful only on the race-course, where the effect is no doubt striking and pleasing. The consequence is, that breeders, instead of looking out for stallions of great substance and good constitution, uniting the best possible conditions of strength and endurance, prefer those which promise to give length of body and limb, and consequently of stride, to the detriment of the former important qualities. Speed for a given time is all that is thought of; and a breeder is of course indifferent when he knows he will be well paid for yearlings and two-year olds of this description. Everything is sacrificed to this English custom, and we suffer accordingly.

Eastern nations, on the contrary, hold to ideas that we despise; the selection of an entire horse with them is a most important affair; and he is not allowed to cover a mare until he has shown most incontestable proofs of vigour. The question of his speed never influences their opinion. As soon as the foal is two years and a half old they begin to work him in proportion to his strength, and thus prevent him from acquiring vicious habits which might subsequently become incurable. It is quite a mistake to suppose that the work the colt or filly does at so early an age is weakening; we might with as much reason say that lads ought not to work.

A Turcoman horse never sees a stable; he is always picketed in the open air, and clothed with felt rugs. Those which are sold to a person living in a town are kept in stables during the winter; but tied with head-and-heel ropes in the court-yard or fields when the sun has a little warmth. With the exception of the period they are at grass, they are well exercised every day, and will work well for twenty, ay, and twenty-five years. These famous animals resist cold as well as heat; they are accustomed to drink at all times, even when covered with perspiration—but in this case they take care to give them a gallop afterwards; without this precaution they might have inflammation, and the Turcomans assert that if they did not adopt it, the skin where the saddle had been would puff up like a bladder.

In their treatment of diseased horses custom takes the place of science in the East; and on this subject it must be confessed they are far behind us in knowledge. Nevertheless, they succeed at times better than might be expected. For example, when a horse is in the first stage of glanders, they give him daily six pounds of *sainfoin* hay and six pounds of camel's milk, mixed with a pound of powdered sulphur. I have seen a cure performed in fifteen days under this treatment. Young horses are frequently subject to a loss of appetite; and to cure this they make an incision, and remove a kind of cartilage which grows in the upper part of the nostril; they also remove windgalls by an operation which seemed to me easy enough, but which would be more neatly done by our veterinary surgeons. For elephantiasis and dropsy in the legs they employ boll ammoniac diluted with vinegar, and bleed in all four legs. Horses in Asia are subject to a disease which I have never seen in Europe; the Persians call it *nakhoshi yaman* (bad or wicked disease). This is a fearful cholic, which blows the skin of the horse out all over in the form of knobs, and the animal dies in three or four hours. When opened, the flesh is found to be perforated with numerous small holes, and the intestines mortified. This disease appears to be the result of a complete obstruction of the bowels; the horse suffers the greatest agonies—I have seen them stand on end, making the most horrible contortions, and having all the appearance of being attacked by hydrophobia.*

---

* This disease appears to resemble the influenza which of late years has been very prevalent among horses in England.—ED.

CHAPTER VIII.

Extensive ruins near Muzeenoon — Alayar Khan — Ancient caravanserai — Mehr — Large herds of deer — Villages — Subzawar — Arab town — Prosperous appearance of Subzawar — Invaded by the Afghans in 1721 — The author hires a new servant — Zaffouroonee — Aridity and fertility — Ruined caravanserai — The largest in Persia — Cufic characters — Legend respecting the builder — The merchant and his saffron — Nishapoor — Description of the town — History of it — Turquoise-mines in the neighbourhood — Visit to the Governor-General of Khorassan — Courteous reception by Assaf Doulet — Persian politics — Mohamed Hassan Khan — A present from the Governor — Amazement of the pilgrims — Turning the tables — Derrood — Beauty of the country — Picturesque village — Turgoveh — Mountain road — The Mollah and the trout — Mountain scenery — Splendid view — Jugkerk —Gipsies.

BUT to return from this digression to the events of my journey, and the Turcomans at Pul-Ebrishim. After witnessing their rapid flight we continued our march without further accident. Three parts out of four of this stage was a deserted country, and beyond Pul-Ebrishim we came to two fortified towns garrisoned by Persian troops, quartered here to protect the road. They were reduced to a fourth of their numbers when we passed, and kept themselves carefully shut up within their walls for fear of the Turcomans, whom it was their duty to look after. Their comrades, receiving neither rations nor pay, had decamped, and those who were left would not be long in doing the same. When distant about a quarter of an hour from our halt we were assailed by a furious wind, and a dust-spout so thick that I could not see the horse's ears I rode. During this time we traversed extensive ruins in front of Muzeenoon, amongst which I remarked a pretty mosque, large baths, and several handsome houses, which required but little to make them habitable; indeed this is the case with the greater part of these ruins; they seem rather abandoned than destroyed. Not long ago they formed part of a prosperous town, Musnedabad, governed by Alayar Khan, an independent chief, who, at the commencement of the reign of Futteh Ali Shah, commanded the road between Teheran and Meshed; no caravan could pass without paying him a heavy tax, that is to say, when he did not pillage them altogether. Troops were at length sent against him, the town was taken, the citadel razed, and the Khan strangled.

Muzeenoon, a large walled village not far from hence, received the population of this ruined town; it contains about four hundred houses and a public bath, and is a dependence of the rich district of Subzawar. We entered here the province of Khorassan. Our encampment was between two caravanserai-shahs, on a large esplanade. One of these, still habitable, was built by Shah Abbas, the other by the Caliph Mamoon, son of Haroun-el-Raschid, and was destroyed by Tamerlane. It must have been a remarkable edifice in its time, and constructed with great solidity and good taste. The exterior wall, built of burnt bricks, is still standing, but the interior is in ruins—the façade is covered with Cufic inscriptions and arabesques, in a good state of preservation.

Mehr, May 19th—five parasangs—six hours and a half—by a level, easy, and sandy road. Large herds of deer were seen on the plain; the mountains situated on our left, and at about a parasang distant, were covered with handsome villages and rich plots of cultivation rising one above the other. Before arriving at our next station we passed through the pretty village of Sootkar, near which there are several streams of excellent water flowing from the mountains. Caravans often halt here in preference to Mehr, especially in coming from Subzawar, provisions being abundant and at hand; whereas, at Mehr, the caravanserai is a long cannon-shot from the village. Mehr has about two hundred and eighty houses; water runs through most of the streets, and they are shaded by plane-trees of large size; it is one of the most picturesque villages on the road between Teheran and Meshed.

Subzawar, May 20th—nine parasangs—eleven hours and a half—situated in a plain, by a good but sandy road. There is a caravanserai-shah near a village. Half way, some other villages are on the left, two hours before arriving at Subzawar. Extensive ruins are to be seen from hence between the road and the foot of the mountains; they are the remains of an Arab town. I observed here some tombs built with a hard cement, composed of gravel, sand, and lime, which has resisted the action of time and the elements. A minaret similar to those at Damghan, and isolated from any other building, stands in the centre of this scene of desolation, as if keeping watch and ward over the wreck of time. These ruins extend even as far as Subzawar, and are said by the

Persians to be the remains of Khosroo-gird, a large city. On the left, and about half a parasang from the road, there is still a village of the same name.

The little modern town of Subzawar is full of life, and, on entering it, one soon remarks, by the air of ease and contentment expressed on the countenances of the inhabitants, that the administrative power here is of a paternal character, very different from that which is seen in other provinces of Persia. Subzawar is the chief town of a rich district; in its environs are handsome villages and well-cultivated land which stretches beyond the horizon, a sight of rare occurrence in Persia. It was the first time I had witnessed such a scene, and this is the best proof of the efficient and benevolent rule of the governor-general Assaf Doulet. The town contains about twelve hundred houses, caravanserais, mosques, and clean and well-constructed bazaars roofed in, which cross the town from one side to the other. The citadel is on an artificial mound north of the town; the walls are in earth, high and thick, but with only one four-pounder, a Russian gun, to defend them. There is an outside wall and dry ditch, which could be filled with water from the streams which flow here in great abundance from the mountains. This spot is more free from the Turcomans than the villages we recently passed, in consequence of the great circuit they would have to make.

Subzawar was, during the invasion of the Afghans in 1721, the theatre of some sanguinary combats. The troops of Mir Mahmood Ghilzye disputed the possession of it with those of Mir Mahmood Sistanee, into whose hands it fell, but only for a brief period, for it was soon taken by the famous Nadir Shah, who raised it a little from the ruined state to which so many wars, one after another, had reduced it; but it is only within the last ten years that it has recovered its ancient prosperity. Hussein Khan, a son of Assaf Doulet, and consequently cousin-german of the Shah, whose sister he married, is governor of Subzawar.

The pilgrim whose services I had engaged at Eywanee Keij, although a good sort of fellow, was nevertheless obliged, to please his countrymen, to play the part of a fanatic to me, which I determined to put an end to, and have a servant, if possible, who was not a pilgrim. I thought I had found what I wanted in an individual by name Saduk, whom I met with at Subzawar, and thought I recognised as having been a servant to the English embassy at Teheran. But I made a mistake, for I learnt subsequently that the rogue was a *lootee*,* named Ismael, who had fled from the capital for some malpractices; in short, he was here to get out of the way. The fellow, seeing me so well disposed towards him, took good care not to undeceive me, and I hired him as my servant. This was a sad mistake, and, as the reader will see further on, cost me half my property, and the consequences might have been even worse.

Zaffouroonee, May 21st—six parasangs—eight hours—by a level road, at times sandy, and sometimes in clay soil. We journeyed during the first half of this stage through villages, rich cultivation, well irrigated, and numerous ruins; the last half was a desert. This halt was at a wretched village, protected by a mud wall, containing forty-four inhabited houses; a ruined caravanserai-shah, the largest in Persia, is in front of it. Tradition says that in former days there were 1700 rooms within its walls, also baths, a mosque, and handsome gardens. I suspect that tradition is, in this case, somewhat of a romancer—not an uncommon thing—though the ruins that surround it certainly occupy a considerable space. The Cufic characters and arabesques upon various parts of the building denote its Arabic origin, but the Persians, in their love for the marvellous, give it the following.

A Persian, they say, finding an immense treasure on this spot, made a vow to employ it in good works, and the first was the construction of this caravanserai. The foundations were just finished, when a merchant, with three *kharvars*—nearly a ton—of saffron, came that way. He had left Khorassan with this purchase, and travelled to Bagdad, in the hope of disposing of it on advantageous terms; but trade was bad; he saw in perspective a certain loss, and when he arrived in the city of the Caliphs he thought it preferable to return to his own country with his merchandise, and wait for better times. Halting at Zaffouroonee, the rich man saw and addressed him thus: "Friend, what makes thee look so sad?" "Sad," replied the merchant, "I have enough to make me sad," and related the history of the bootless errand he had been on. "Oh, is that the cause of your grief? Here, men," said he to his masons, "shoot the saffron on the ground, and mix it with the mortar." This was done, and he

* The designation in Persia for a good-for-nothing fellow, a thief, &c.

paid the astonished merchant three kharvars of precious stones for his three kharvars of saffron. This is a good specimen of a Persian tale, and, absurd as it is, it finds believers amongst them, even the educated. To seem to doubt its truth might bring one into trouble. "See," said a pilgrim, turning to his companions, and taking up a brick, "they have quite the colour and smell of saffron." There was no arguing with them after this, especially as the bricks were as red as cochineal.

Nishapoor, May 22nd—eleven parasangs—fourteen hours, the first two through a plain, the road even and solid; the three next over a chain of mountains which cross the plain obliquely; they divide the districts of Subzawar and Nishapoor. The road follows the sinuosities of this chain, having for the most part a scarped wall on either side, and the neighbouring heights, if fortified at points judiciously chosen, would render the passage of this defile extremely difficult. To turn it, it would be necessary to go to the left, and march a distance of sixteen parasangs through a desert country, without water. There are two caravanserai-shahs in ruins at two and a half hours from one another on this stage. Ten hours' march brought us to the large village of Hassanabad, also in ruins and uninhabited; some horses of Assaf Doulet's were feeding on the pastures that surround it. The soil is clay, and in winter the road is almost impassable.

After a fatiguing march of four more hours we reacned the small but pleasant town of Nishapoor, prettily situated amidst gardens and villages grouped near to one another, and in a vast plain at one time irrigated by 12,000 watercourses coming from the Kariz; at the present time the greater number of them are dry; there is nevertheless amazing fertility. The climate is delicious, but, owing to the high mountains to the north, about a parasang from the town, is rather cold in winter. These mountains, like a vast amphitheatre, almost encircle the plain, and many villages lie in the gorges and on the slopes; the cultivation is carried up to the very summits, and numerous springs gush from their sides and run in silvery streams into the plain. The water of the one we passed near Nishapoor, called Shooreh-rod, is rather brackish. The fruits of this district are considered the best in Khorassan; silk and cotton and large quantities of grain are amongst its productions.

Nishapoor was in former times one of the richest and largest cities in Persia, and one of the four royal cities of Khorassan. European authors inform us that it was founded by Shah-poor, the second of the Sassanide kings;* hence its name, to which was added *neï* or *nee*, signifying a reed both in ancient and modern Persian, and this, says tradition, because the plain in which Nishapoor was situated was then covered with reeds. But in the opinion of Persian historians the city was of much more ancient date. Its founder was, they say, Tahmurat III., King of the Pish-Dadian dynasty. It then bore the name of Aber-chehr, or the Upper Town, and was taken and destroyed by Alexander the Great. Shahpoor restored it, and, to perpetuate the fact, gave it his name, and erected an immense statue, which remained standing until the first invasion of the country by the Mussulmans, who in their zeal destroyed it.

Nishapoor also suffered greatly from the invasion of the Arabs, and it would have utterly perished had it not been subsequently rebuilt and repeopled, first by the Taherides and afterwards by the Soffarides. Mahmood the Ghaznevide, who, later still, and in the reign of Sebek-tagy, his father, was governor of Khorassan, fixed his residence at Nishapoor, which contributed much to its prosperity.

Toghrul Beg, the first Sultan of the dynasty of the Seljookides, also resided here, and his princely liberality restored it to its former splendour; but in the year 1153 (Hejira 548), and in the reign of the Sultan Sanjar, one of the same dynasty, the Turcomans took and ravaged it so completely that, in the words of the Persian historian Khagani, when the inhabitants, who had fled at the approach of these hordes, returned after their departure, it was impossible to recognise, amidst the mass of ruins, the position in which their houses once stood. Nevertheless, such was the fertility of the country, that, with the assistance of the princes of Khaurizm, into whose hands it fell after the Seljookides, Nishapoor rose once more, like a phœnix, from its ashes.

But the disasters which attended the fate of this unfortunate city were not yet over; for in 1220 (Hejira 617) Kooli Khan, son of Ghengis Khan, besieged and took it. This monster was

* About the year A.D. 250.

even more savage than the Turcomans, for he not only made it a heap of ruins, but massacred the inhabitants and the people of the adjoining territory to the number of two millions. From this period Nishapoor became the sport of fortune in every possible way, reviving and perishing in turn, and has never regained its ancient position and prosperity. Placed on the extreme frontier of Persia, on the side of Tartary, the Mongols, the Turcomans, and the Uzbeks sacked and plundered it almost from year to year. Towards the commencement of the eighteenth century it was little more than one vast ruin, and remained in this deplorable state until after the death of Nadir Shah. In 1752 (Hejira 1166), after having stood a six months' siege by Ahmed Shah, King of the Afghans, it was, to some extent, restored by Abbas Kooli Khan, chief of the Beiyat tribe, who declared himself ruler over this district.

At the present day it contains a population of only 8000 souls. The citadel is in ruins, and the wall of the town, in earth, with a dry ditch, is in a bad state of repair; the bazaars, caravanserais, baths, and a mosque, are on a moderate scale; the handsomest caravanserai is outside the walls, on the road to Meshed. The city of Nishapoor having been brought thus low, it may be readily imagined the country in its environs has suffered in proportion; but the villages and the cultivation which still remain sufficiently prove that not even all this misery could induce the population wholly to retire from this valley, for in no other part of Persia would they have found such another fertile spot. Mohamed Zeman Khan, one of the youngest sons of Assaf Doulet, is now governor of the district, but under the superintendence of his *Nazir*, or lieutenant.

One of the greatest inconveniences that arise in travelling with a caravan is the impossibility of leaving it for a few hours to visit any interesting object which may be at a little distance from the road. I suffered in this way many disappointments, and particularly at Nishapoor, for it was from thence only I could visit the turquoise-mines in the neighbourhood. Fatigued, however, by a long stage of fourteen hours, I was not able to start immediately upon another of sixteen to gratify my curiosity; moreover, I was most anxious to see the Governor General of Khorassan, who happened to be here. The information I obtained respecting the turquoise-mines was therefore by hearsay, and consequently very imperfect.*

---

* After my return from Afghanistan I saw by accident the following account of them in the 'Révue d'Orient.' This paper is from the pen of M. Alexandre Chodsko, and the following is the substance of what he writes:—

"These celebrated mines are near the village of Madene, and the only ones known in the world. This village is about thirty-two English miles from Nishapoor; the road to it is for the first five miles across a plain of great extent, covered with villages, gardens, well-cultivated fields marvellously productive, owing to the many streams which flow from the Benaloo Koh and other mountains near. Approaching these the country changes, and we found ourselves riding through hills of sand and a reddish clay devoid of all vegetation; their sterile appearance was accounted for by the traces of efflorescent salts, which were seen in large quantities, and would prevent any cultivation.

"Salt abounds in this locality, and we passed the principal mine, Dooletaly, about six miles from Madene. This is an enormous rock, covered on its exterior surface with a thin layer of red clay, similar to that I have already mentioned. Nothing can be imagined more simple than the mode of working out the salt: the miner's mattock is the only instrument used. These mines are the property of the government, who lease them to the highest bidder. At present the rent is only 150 tomauns yearly. A good workman can extract about 800 lbs. a-day. The salt is beautifully white, and of a fine grain.

"The road which led to the turquoise-mines—the principal object of our excursion—ran through some high and naked rocks, which, by their dark colour, seemed to be of porphyry: I think, however, they were of a hard, compact, calcareous nature, strongly stained, as I did not see any rocks of another system. At their highest elevation they had a metallic appearance, which made me think that iron was the colouring matter; but, not being sufficiently learned in geology, I could not positively determine this. In the middle of this rocky and broken ground we came, at length, in sight of two villages, one on the crest of a hill, the other in a pretty valley. Beneath they were fortified by a loopholed wall, and inhabited by about 150 families, who emigrated here from Badakshan under the protection of one of the last of the Persian kings. These colonists speak bad Persian, and have quite forgotten their own language: they show considerable tact and intelligence in working the mines.

"The turquoises are divided into two classes, according to the positions in which they are found. The first, called *sengui*, or stony, are those which are incrusted in the matrix, and which must be removed by a blow of the pick or hammer; the second are found in washing the alluvial deposits, and are called *khaki*, or earthy: the former are of a deep blue; the latter, though larger, from being paler and spotted with white, are of less value. If we are to believe the miners, no turquoises have been found except in this group of rocks. The Persian government never makes any explorations on its own account, and is content to lease the mines at an annual rent of five hundred tomauns. I understood that the most valuable stones are found amongst the *débris* of the old workings and at the bottom of shafts long since abandoned. Excavations have been made one above the other, but for the most part near the base of the mountain. Here are to be seen galleries, tunnels, and shafts, the largest of which are thus designated: Abdoorryzak, Shahi-perdar, Kharydji, Kemeri-Khaki, and Goor Sefid.

"Having given a largesse to the miners to strike a few blows with their picks in honour of the happy planet of the traveller, *Bé-taleï-saheb*, we were permitted to enter the first of these mines to witness the operations. These were simple enough; the mattock was again the only instrument, but it was very skilfully used, and, when a layer of rock was detached, great precautions were taken to remove it without disturbing the turquoises which might be met with. These are not found in the hollow of an eagle-stone, like the amethyst, but are seen as if incrusted or glued in the matrix to the number of

As it must have been well known that I passed through Teheran, I had little doubt that, if the Persian government intended to molest me on my journey, it would not have waited until I reached Nishapoor to carry such intention into effect; and, under this impression, I resolved to throw off the incognito I had preserved since leaving Bagdad, which had caused me many very unpleasant scenes and much suffering, as well as debarred me from receiving that attention which I should otherwise have met with. But in doing this, I wished to give the act a certain degree of *éclat*, not being at all unwilling to show my fellow-travellers the pilgrims that they had, by their scandalous behaviour, subjected themselves to the chances of unpleasant retaliation, or, in the words of a Persian, *Feder et mi souzoomm*, "see their fathers burnt."

---

from twenty-five to thirty, and more or less near one another. Each of these stones is enveloped in a thin calcareous covering, white on the side adhering next to the turquoise, but brown on that next to the matrix. How is it that the colouring substance has stopped precisely at the exterior, and that it has not injured the purity of the turquoise? But I will rather relate what I saw, and not undertake to explain; I will simply state that one finds on the side of this very mountain of Benaloo Koh indications of the carbonate of copper both blue and green, as are the best varieties of malachite.

"We were not very successful in our researches, but the best turquoises are found, with the exception I have before stated, in this mine Abdourryzak; those of Kharyji follow.

"We next examined the washings in the valley. These are to the south of the village. The rock is not met with here, and the soil is composed of clay, gravel, sand, and rounded stones, evidently an alluvial deposit. Here I was again obliged to try the influence of my planet, after which several sieves were filled with the soil and gravel in question taken from a shaft just opened: these were carried to a running stream close at hand, and the earthy substances washed from them, and, the stones being turned over, the turquoises were soon recognised by their azure tint. Of these we found a pretty good number and of fair size, but they were unfortunately of a pale colour, and therefore of little value. The workmen called them by the name of Tâzè-madene, or of the new mine, to distinguish them from those of a deeper colour found in the old workings.

"These worthies affirmed that turquoises are similar to cherries, inasmuch as both one and the other acquire their colour as they ripen; and they added that, although a cherry comes to perfect maturity in one season by the vivifying rays of the sun, a turquoise requires a thousand to obtain the same result. The miners here do not enjoy a great reputation for honesty, and very fine turquoises are said to take their way to Nishapoor instead of into the pockets of the owners of the mines, being sometimes transferred for a consideration to parties who visit the mines. But here the uninitiated may be taken in, for the miners keep them for some time in a wet cloth, which deepens their colour; and the purchaser does not find how pale the stone is until he has parted with his money. I was informed that turquoises of immense size are sometimes found in the washings. Futteh Ali Shah, the predecessor of the present monarch, had one made into a drinking-cup; and it is well known that there was a turquoise in the treasury of Venice which weighed several pounds. A nobleman's harness in Khorassan is frequently ornamented with small turquoises, but these are, of course, of comparatively little value."

Assaf Doulet was, as I have before remarked, at Nishapoor when we arrived, and I hastened to send him the commissions I held from Mohamed Shah, so that he might know who I was; and at the same time I requested permission to pay my respects to him. In return I received a favourable and courteous reply, and at the appointed hour one of his *pishkhetmets*, followed by eight farraches, came to the caravanserai as an honorary escort to conduct me to his house. I went in full uniform, and found the Governor transacting business with some of the official personages of the district, whom he dismissed on my arrival.

Assaf Doulet received me in the *bala khaneh*, for thus is named the first and only story built above the ground-floor in Persian houses; it looked upon a large garden full of roses, the perfume of which scented the atmosphere. The Governor, simply dressed in a woollen robe and a sheepskin cap, sat near a window in a corner of the room. His attitude was that of a man who knew the importance of his own position, but not in the least partaking of that vain pompous air which Persian noblemen love to assume when they receive their inferiors. He seemed already bowed down by the weight of years; but his intelligent countenance had preserved all the vivacity and freshness of youth. His reception was of the most gracious kind; and tea and the *kalioon* having been brought in, he inquired kindly after my health, and then asked the news of the capital. Aware of his antipathy for the Persian Prime Minister, I threw aside all reserve, and made him acquainted with many facts that I thought would interest him. I also informed him of the intrigues which led to the dismissal of the French officers at the Persian court, and the resolution I had come to of taking service under one of the princes of Central Asia. The Governor heard me with attention, and encouraged me to persevere in my plans, assuring me that the dangers of the journey of which I spoke had been much exaggerated. "Everything depends," said he, "upon the chiefs of Herat and Kandahar, from whom, however, you have nothing to fear if you present yourself before them in your real character of a French officer"—he also advised me at once to throw off my disguise, and avert the suspicions to which it might naturally give rise.

Coming back again to the conversation which we had had with reference to his own country, he testified his great regret to see it so badly governed; also that his nephew Mohamed Shah should adopt without examination the absurd theories of his Prime Minister. Of this individual he spoke in terms that were anything but complimentary; and in order to give me an idea of the footing on which they mutually stood, he mentioned, with many an expressive epithet, some of the ill-natured tricks they had played off upon each other.

After having taken my leave of Assaf Doulet, I paid a visit to his favourite son Mohamed Hassan Khan, more generally known by the name of Salar, which is the Persian term for General-in-Chief—a rank given him by Futteh Ali Shah when the young Khan was yet in his cradle. As I reached the door, he was on the point of mounting his horse, on his way to Koochan, of which district he is the Governor, and I had therefore only time to exchange a few complimentary words with him. He seemed to be about five-and-thirty years of age, rather handsome, and, like his cousin Mohamed Shah, his manners were frank and open; but though he made every effort to conceal it, he had all the self-sufficient, consequential air of a Persian noble. With this little exception, he was irreproachably polite. Hassan Khan is much beloved by the population of Khorassan, and for a good reason—he possesses a virtue very rarely seen in his family: he is generous, and liberally rewards those who serve him; the unfortunate never apply to him in vain. This is an excellent way of making partizans and friends in Persia; and Salar has a good many.

Returning to my caravanserai, I found there one of my old acquaintances of Tabreez, Mirza Mohamed Noori, formerly *intendant* of Prince Karaman-Mirza, after whose death he entered the service of Assaf Doulet. He had been sent with several presents for me from the Governor-General—sweetmeats, fruits, and sherbets, &c. &c. Attentions of this kind are highly appreciated by the Persians, more particularly when they emanate from a person of high official rank and power. The pilgrims of our caravan, who had hitherto known me only as a miserable Greek or Armenian, were amazed when they saw me leaving the caravanserai in the full uniform of a general-officer; they were still more so when they heard that I had been received at a private audience by the Governor General, and saw the presents which the Mirza brought. Every one now was most anxious to visit the despised *feringhee*; compliments, flattery, the very lowest adulations, were showered upon me in profusion, but I elbowed the vagabonds as they deserved, and, adopting the arrogant tone which is usual in Persia when a superior addresses an inferior, I no longer allowed those who had shown me even the least ill treatment to remain seated in my presence; in fact I behaved myself to them as a pasha with three tails would have done, under similar circumstances, in the fifteenth century.

This little indulgence to my pride was I thought pardonable, considering the gross insults I had endured; and the punishment was small compared with what it might have been, for one word to Assaf Doulet, and they would all have had the stick. My visitors were not in the least surprised or disconcerted at the arrogance I manifested; in their eyes it was my right, and I used it—what more natural? They thus held me in greater esteem; but they came to my servant, who, treating them all the while as the scum of the earth, deigned nevertheless to speak to them, and show a little more sociability of feeling than I did. "Who would have thought," said one, "that this European under his Arab rags, for which I would not have given two *shahis*, was a general?" "I told you," said another, "that he had all the polished manner of a noble, and you were very wrong to insult him." "We must admit," replied a third, "these Europeans are very queer people. With us, if a man has twenty tomauns he knows what he is, has his servants, and lives in all the luxury and state that such a fortune justifies; but here is this *feringhee*, whom we now see covered with gold embroidery and wearing a decoration set in diamonds, has lived amongst us from Teheran to this place like a poor devil without one shahi. Why it's abominable, improper, perfidious, dishonest, and contrary to all rule; exposes people to very disagreeable mistakes and dangerous misunderstandings. Every one ought to be made to travel in the manner befitting his rank, and not to dissimulate after this fashion." Those amongst them who had treated me with every species of indignity, and felt that they were the most culpable, begged Saduk to intercede for them, and endeavour to calm my resentment—some had a suit in hand, and wished me to say a word for them to the Governor. My servant promised everything to those who made him presents, and told the others who did not, to call again. He knew the Persian system to a hair; but they had no more cause to congratulate themselves on his intervention than I had subsequently on his fidelity.

The muleteers also underwent the same transformation as the

pilgrims, and came in the evening to know at what hour I would start. Profiting, therefore, by the new position I had assumed, I declared, to the great annoyance of the chief Syud, who now only played the second violin, that I should rescind the order for the night-march, and leave the next morning at daybreak; and this was carried into effect.

Derrood, May 23rd—five parasangs—six hours and a half—by a level and sandy road, through gardens, villages, and cultivation admirably irrigated. These succeeded one another so rapidly, that this stage seemed as if we had taken the road for the mere pleasure of making a morning excursion. Never had I before seen in Persia such rich and luxuriant vegetation; and, as the eye revelled in contemplation over it, I could quite understand without difficulty the predilection which the sovereigns, to whose violent and selfish deeds I have had occasion to refer, had for Nishapoor. After a march of five hours and a half in the plain we passed on our left Kademgah, the halting-place for travellers who intend to reach Meshed by Sherifabad, and entered the great mountain-range upon our left. This road is shorter by three parasangs than the other, but rough and steep; and after having toiled along for an hour we arrived at Derrood.

This is a large village of four hundred houses, situated in a most picturesque position at the extremity of a gorge, enclosed by beautiful gardens and a multitude of aged plane and other trees, whose spreading foliage affords a most delightful shade—abundant and excellent water flows on every side. It is really one of the most delicious spots that can be conceived. Derrood pays a tax of one thousand tomauns to the state.

Turgoveh, May 24th—six parasangs—ten hours—across a mountain and by the roughest and most precipitous road I ever travelled in Persia. The ground was covered by stones and rounded boulders, the path winding through a narrow defile, and we ascended every now and then steps worn in the rock by the continual passing to and fro of the caravans. The melting snows and mountain torrents flowed across two-thirds of the road both ascending and descending. In these clear and limpid streams were numbers of excellent trout, and these are, singular to say, the property of the defunct Imaum Reza. His claim to them was clearly established some forty-five years ago, and in the following manner. One of the chief mollahs of Meshed, who had the good taste to be passionately fond of trout, was in the habit of sending here every two or three days for a dish, but they began to get scarce, and on making inquiries he found that there were many persons in Meshed who were as fond of trout as himself. His stomach became alarmed; how was he to control the taste of his townsmen? A thought struck him; he dreamt that the Imaum Reza appeared to him and signified that the streams and trout were his, and that in future mollahs alone were to eat them. This gratifying dream he immediately made public, and since then the rivulets of Derrood have been the sacred preserves of the mollahs of Meshed.

But to return from this little digression to the road we were travelling: this in many places and near the water was bordered with trees, under whose shade we rode for a considerable distance; the effect of this cool green foliage against the bare sides of the precipitous rocks which enclosed them on either side was very picturesque, especially when looking upwards we could descry several herds of deer and troops of active goats feeding on some of the highest and least accessible of their summits. The trees observable in the greatest numbers in this mountain-range are the poplar, willow, ash, and plane, but there were many other kinds of which I know nothing. The seedless barberry and the green rhubarb, in Persian *rivas*, were seen here in great quantities. After three hours' march we came to the last ascent. Here the trees and water disappeared and their shade was replaced by that of a little caravanserai of stone, roughly built, very *à propos* as a place of repose after the difficulties we had encountered, as well as to prepare for the much steeper acclivities we still had to surmount. In point of fact, the last range, though not so elevated, was so fatiguing by reason of the extreme steepness of the road, being nearly perpendicular, that it took us with all our efforts one hour to reach the summit.

I had never at that time, and have never since, seen such a road in the course of my travels. The laden mules at one time refused to advance, and we were obliged to relieve them of half their loads and return again for the rest; had we not done so they would never have reached the top: women and children were every one carried up, and the men, thoroughly worn out, fell down by the roadside completely exhausted. It was May, and the sun in Persia during this month, already very powerful in the plains, was scarcely felt at this height, on which it was so icy cold that we could scarcely keep ourselves in motion. It was this, probably, which prevented me from enjoying as much as I should otherwise have done the majestic scenery that surrounded us on every side.

In the centre of a vast plain, situated between the mountain-range on which we stood and another more to the north, which separates Khorassan from Turkistan, we saw, though eight parasangs distant from us, the great and holy city of Meshed. The cupola and lofty golden minarets, rising from the mosque which covers the tomb of the Imaum Reza, stood out in brilliant relief against the cloudless heavens, lighted up as they were under the dazzling beams of the midday sun. The green band of verdure which we had to traverse in our descent from this elevated region lay picturesquely unrolled at our feet, and with my glass I could see crowds of the faithful entering and leaving the blessed city of God. As to our pilgrims, they were in ecstacies, in spite of their great fatigues, and in a delirium of pleasure when they distinctly saw the mosque within whose walls reposed the remains of their venerated Imaum; they ceased not for a long time to cry "Yah, Ali! Yah, Imaum Reza!" and then, after reciting their *Namaz*, each of them rent a piece off his garment, and hung it to the nearest bush, as an offering to their adored and holy saint. I was, till then, utterly unable to comprehend why all the bushes in this desert spot were hung with myriads of rags, of every colour, flapping in the breeze; but the chief Syud, who was civil enough after I threw off my Arab shirt, explained to me that, the eye of the Imaum being always on the top of this mountain, the shreds which are left there by those who hold him in reverence remind him of what he ought to do in their behalf with Mahomet, Ali, and other holy personages, who are to propitiate the Almighty in their favour.

Close to and around these bushes, hung with these rags and tatters, were heaps of stones, to which every pilgrim added some from the loose ones about; the chief Syud could not give me a reason for this, but said that it was customary. These cairns are frequently seen in Persia by the roadside; sometimes they seem to mark a path or a resting-place, but I fancy that, generally speaking, they are thrown up by the passing traveller without any object whatsoever. Perhaps the custom may have originated in this. Mahomet, when flying from Medina to Mecca for refuge, threw stones at, and poured forth some terrible imprecations against, that city; and as every act of the Prophet has been made a rule of faith and practice, hence possibly this habit of heaping stones by the wayside.

We were six hours in descending the mountain, and without meeting with any serious difficulty. At the foot of the first ridge we came to a little *châlet*, the occupant of which sold his goats'-milk and bread to passing travellers. At this spot springs of water and trees again appear, and in greater quantity and numbers than at Derrood. After a march of five hours and a half from the spot at which we commenced our descent, we arrived at the fine village of Jugkerk, embosomed in gardens. The inhabitants have left in front of their houses, and under the shade of large clumps of trees, very commodious spots of ground, admirably adapted for the caravans that frequently encamp here, especially in coming from Meshed; but as ours wished to reach the city early on the following morning, we moved forward an hour more, and halted at Turgoveh, also a flourishing village and of eight hundred houses. Here, however, our stay was not a happy one, for we found a troop of gipsies had taken possession of the great square, and we were obliged to encamp on a piece of ground strewed with dung and alive with fleas, bugs, and other insects, which bit and stung us most horribly.

The gipsies in Persia are what you see them everywhere else; they lead a wandering life; each band is independent; they preserve their own ideas of caste as a peculiar people, and with them the dirtiest habits, live upon next to nothing, and detest a regular life and a fixed place of abode. There are more than 15,000 families of gipsies dispersed over the various provinces of Persia, paying a heavy tax to the government. They are all under the orders and supervision of the Shater-bashee, who exercises the most absolute powers of administration over them. The tax they pay is a kind of *kharaj*, or price of blood, which is never levied either on Christians or Jews: it is to this fact that they owe the name of *Kooli*, slave, one of the epithets by which they are designated. They are likewise called *Fal-sen*, or, as we should render it, fortune-tellers; also by the name of *kal-bir-bend*, or sieve-makers, because this is their principal occupation—these their wives sell from door to door. Their faces are, in defiance of all Eastern customs, uncovered: they are tall, robust, and of a bronzed complexion; their white teeth are not concealed;

and no matter to whose lips their own are pressed, neither husband, father, nor brother seems to care the least about it. The names of Zingari, Gitano, Brinjarries, Ambadies, and Gipsies, &c., by which the race of Bohemians are known in other countries, are never heard in Persia. Those encamped so near us at Tergoveh were members of the fraternity of tumblers, who performed the usual gymnastic feats, and enchanted the delighted pilgrims with their tricks and the good fortunes they promised them: this was, however, not done without lightening their pockets.

As night fell I suddenly heard my servant Saduk making a great uproar, accusing the gipsies of having stolen his knapsack, which, he said, contained many valuable articles, worth at least twenty tomauns, and which he had left safe a few minutes before. "Son of a dog," said he, "how could you think of robbing a man whose master received a present of sweetmeats from Assaf Doulet, the Governor of Khorassan? You will certainly die under the stick for this abominable act. Listen to me, race of vipers! May your fathers be cursed and burnt, if you do not, within the next hour, deliver up the stolen goods!" But for this animated address I should not have believed Saduk had been robbed; but his indignation seemed so sincere that I felt ashamed of my suspicions, and was fool enough to offer to make good his loss. The real fact was, the rascal took his knapsack to a friend's house in Turgoveh, a *lootee*, like himself, in the hope perhaps of moving my compassion, and, as I learnt afterwards, of being in light marching order when he found an opportunity to rob me and decamp, which he subsequently did.

CHAPTER IX.

The city of Meshed — Gold and silver mines — The pilgrim's reason why they are not worked — Altercation with the custom-house officer — The general's visitors — Afghan manners — Mohamed Wali Khan — Agreeable acquaintances — Hospitality of the Persians — The author robbed — The ancient Thous — History of Meshed — Its commercial importance — Population — Persecution of the Jews in 1839 — Burial-grounds — The Khiabane — Commerce of Meshed — Carpets — Stone-quarries — The great mosque — The Hindoo's justification for entering it — Dr. Wolf — Stoddart and Conolly — The author advised not to proceed — Reasons for not taking that advice — Fight between the townspeople and the troops — Escorted out of the town — Leaves Meshed.

MESHED, May 25th—four parasangs—four hours and a half—by a level and sandy road. At half an hour beyond Turgoveh we crossed what appeared to be the bed of a large river, which had been dry for many years. The sides of the perpendicular rocks through which it once flowed had been worn away by the action of the water; a mere streamlet trickled through it. The plain in which Meshed is situated is naked and uncultivated; this may be attributed to the repeated incursions of the Turcomans, the Uzbeks, and the Afghans. It is covered with numerous small towns, similar to those I described at Lasjird, and intended for the same purpose. The sterility is confined to the plain; for, at the foot of the mountains which surround the city, the villages are numerous, and the cultivation rich and fertile, the crops being sufficient to supply the wants of the inhabitants of Meshed.

Before entering Meshed, on the side of Derrood, two small eminences called the Koh-i-tellah-nogreh (the gold and silver mountains) are left on the right. These metals are said to be found in them in tolerably large quantities. Those who have worked them up to this time have not, however, covered their expenses, and the following is the reason given by the Persians: they say the mines were very productive in the olden times, and the ores that are still raised are of more than ordinary richness; but the deceased Imaum Reza, to whom they belonged, indignant at seeing himself pillaged, changes the gold and silver into earth directly the ores are thrown into the furnace. This was a pilgrim's tale to me, and, like that of the trout, all in favour of the priesthood. Subsequent inquiries respecting these mines convinced me that they were not profitable to work, in consequence of the ignorance of the Persians in metallurgical operations, and also the want of fuel and water-power, which must be brought from a great distance, and at a great expense.

I had scarcely entered the holy city of Meshed before I was engaged in an altercation with a custom-house officer. Contrary to usage, and the privileges which Europeans enjoy in this country, they required me to pay the *baj*—a tax levied on all travellers; and he would not let go the bridle of my mule until my stick had made acquaintance with his back—an argument always highly to the taste of a Persian—which put an end to the affair. I heard that I was not the only European who had been treated after this fashion, and that the native merchants were nicely mulcted by the head of the department, a protégé of Assaf Doulet's, who, if complaints had been made to him, would not in this instance have acted with his usual decision, in dismissing the official. Making our way through several handsome streets, in which crowds of people were passing to and fro, I took up my quarters in the large and well-built caravanserai of the Imaum Jumeh, situated on the *Khiabane*, avenue.

My arrival at Meshed was an event, for a European is rarely seen there; and in less than two hours the incident was known in every part of the town. The first person who honoured me with a visit was Mollah Mehdi, *vaghè-ul-nager*, correspondent, or, more literally rendered, news-writer, to the British Minister at Teheran. He came to volunteer his services, which I gladly accepted. After the Mollah a host of people made their appearance—Hindoos, Afghans, Uzbeks, Turcomans, and Belooches. Some of these, thinking I was an Englishman, came with the intention of finding out, if possible, what object I had in coming to Meshed; some with the ulterior view of immediately forwarding the information to the government in whose employ they were, others to offer their assistance to England, and a few to complain that they had not been sufficiently recompensed. It was rather hard work to see them all, to talk to half a dozen at once, listen to their numerous and absurd demands, and reply to the same; but they could tell me much I wished to know respecting Central Asia, and so I played the Persian to admiration, and I flatter myself they were enchanted at my extreme politeness.

The excessive love of etiquette and ceremony so rigidly observed by the Persians is in singular contrast to the brusque manners of their neighbours the Afghans. The latter think any conversation insupportable which is constrained, and they speak their mind in terms which we should consider exceedingly rude, if not insulting; but they are quite ready to be paid in kind. If they try to deceive a European, or act with dissimulation, their schemes are so badly planned that they are sure to be found out. They visit without knowing one another, accost you without ceremony, and are your intimates in five minutes; not to adopt the same line with them would be to expose oneself to suspicion, and it was from knowing how to accommodate myself to their humour that I was enabled to make a few friends amongst them, from whom I learned much of what I have written, and, through their kind assistance, was enabled to leave Afghanistan alive.

The day after my arrival at Meshed I paid a visit to Mohamed Wali Khan, the nephew and lieutenant of Assaf Doulet, and governor of the town in his absence. This was the same nobleman who, four years before, was made prisoner by the Turcomans and taken to Khiva; he owed his delivery to Mr. Thompson, of the British Embassy, who went to Khiva in 1842 and effected his release. As the heat was already great, Mohamed Khan received me in a garden situated in the *enceinte* of the town, and towards evening. Arm-chairs and carpets had been placed for us amidst a mass of roses and jessamine in full flower, round and through which ran numerous little rills of fresh and limpid water. Having taken our seats, plates of fruit, and sweetmeats, and bowls of sherbet were put before us, also tea, and the grateful kalioon. The Khan evidently did his best to make himself agreeable; and I saw that he wished I should retain a good opinion of him, which I felt quite disposed to do. He has the reputation of being one of the bravest men in Khorassan, is by no means wanting in capacity, or, like most Persians, in conceit either; he knew everything, especially the geography of Europe, but five minutes after betrayed his intense ignorance of that of his own country. He did not, in fact, know the position of Mohamra—a small town situated to the south-east of Bussora, the possession of which had been a subject of contention between the Turks and Persians for the last thirty years. I did not think it wise to enlighten him; for vanity is the weak point of every son of Irak, and it would have been bad policy to wound his.

My two first days at Meshed were passed most agreeably in

receiving and paying visits; and I can assure the reader I thought myself amply repaid for all the tribulations I had endured on my journey from Bagdad to Nishapoor. But I ought to say that the vile conduct of the pilgrims, my companions, was quite an exception to that of persons generally to Europeans. The Persian nobleman is kind and hospitable, and more tolerant than many Christians. While at Meshed I made the acquaintance of all those persons whom it was desirable to know; from them I received the very best treatment, and it is my pleasing duty to mention the names of the following in particular: Mohamed Hussein, the chief of the merchants—a man remarkable as well by the qualities of his heart, the amenity of his manners, and his liberal and tolerant spirit, as his high position and the influence he has in the councils of Assaf Doulet. I also mention, and with great pleasure, the cordial reception I met with from Abdul Ali Khan, colonel commandant of the artillery of Khorassan; also the Imaum Jumeh, one of the heads of the Persian hierarchy, an amiable man, learned and polite; I shall not easily forget the very kind manner in which he made me always welcome. It was to Mollah Mehdi, the English agent, that I was indebted for these acquaintances, and for many other little services which one is so glad to accept when travelling alone in these distant countries. The mollah had originally been the chief of the Jews, at Meshed; but, as will be seen further on, was obliged, as well as his co-religionists, to embrace Islamism in 1839.*

A most unpleasant and unfortunate affair, the result of the incredibly imprudent confidence I placed in my servant, Saduk, ushered in the 27th of May. When I got up on the morning of that day I found the door of my room locked on the outside, and I was at least an hour hallooing and knocking before the servant of the caravanserai heard me, and came and opened the door. Saduk was absent, I thought, perhaps, early to the bath, and, fearing that some one might enter my room while I was asleep and steal some things, had locked the door. Noon came, but with it no Saduk; my suspicions were roused; I called the roll of my effects, and examined my baggage, and was at once convinced that

* It is very pleasing to see that Mollah Mehdi continues his good offices to European travellers. There are few Englishmen who have been in Khorassan who have not had cause to be grateful for his services. I fear that they have been but poorly rewarded.—L.

he had started with a pair of my pistols and a pretty round sum of money; the attack upon the gipsies at Turgoveh and his pretended loss of his knapsack were explained. Fortunately I had only the evening before removed part of my cash from the trunk, and fastened it round my waist. So much for this rascal, whom I had treated with every kindness.

Meshed is considered by some writers to have been the ancient Thous, the primitive name of which was Sapleï; but this is an error, its origin dates back only a thousand years. The Persian historians assert that Jemshid, the fifth king of the Pish-Dadian dynasty, was the founder of Thous: its ruins are still to be seen six parasangs from Meshed. The importance which the latter city has acquired is entirely owing to the fact that the Imaum Reza, the fifth in descent from Ali, was buried here; his memory was revered, and his tomb became in the eyes of the faithful a sacred object—a few houses for the use of pilgrims were built around it, and these, as they increased in number, formed the suburb of Senabad. Time went on, mosques and other edifices followed. Persian kings and rich pilgrims endowed it with many costly gifts; and Meshed acquired such regal dimensions that the ancient Thous declined, was eventually deserted by its inhabitants, and became a city of the past.

But like all great eastern cities, Meshed had its vicissitudes and fearful calamities, in which the lust of conquest was never softened by a feeling of humanity, or victory restrained by the hand of mercy. In 1587 (Héjira 996), the Usbek Tartars, under Abd-ul Moomnee Khan, sacked and pillaged the town, and put three-fourths of the population to the sword; and it did not rise from its ashes until ten years afterwards, at which period Shah Abbas the Great united it to Persia. Nadir Shah made it one of the four royal cities of the kingdom of Khorassan; and it retained that title under his grandson, Shah Rokh Mirza, who was in the city when it was besieged by the Afghans and his revolted subjects. This attack was not successful, and Shah Rokh retained possession of the province until he was deprived of it by Agha Mohamed Khan, founder of the dynasty of the Kajars. From this date Meshed has always belonged to Persia, and generally been the residence of the Governors General of Khorassan. It is now a flourishing and important place. This prosperity may be attributed to two circumstances,—its commerce, and the sacred character it enjoys amongst Persian Mussulmans: to the former, because, being situated on the extreme frontier of the Tatar and Afghan states, it is the great entrepôt of all the merchandise and productions exported and imported from and to those countries;* to the latter, because of the crowds of pilgrims which come here from all parts of Asia. Fifty thousand are said to be the annual average number of these itinerant disciples of Islam; and during their stay in the city they leave behind in alms, in contributions to the mollahs, and the necessary expenses of living, considerable sums of money. Since the emigration of the population of Merv and Sharaks, Herat and Kandahar, the number of resident inhabitants may be fixed at 60,000, and 30,000 pilgrims and strangers, who bow the knee at the tomb of the Imaum Reza.

There are also in the town about 600 persons of Jewish origin,

---

* The bazaars of Meshed are frequented by merchants from Yezd and the southern parts of Persia, who trade with Bombay. During the siege of Herat, and for some time afterwards, Eldred Pottinger had great difficulty in procuring money there to meet the expenditure authorized by our government. His bills on Bombay were only cashed by the Hindoo bankers (from Shikarpore) at a discount of 25 per cent.; and even for a year after the arrival of the Mission, Major Todd could only get his public bills cashed at a discount of 16 per cent. Yar Mohamed had also, at the instigation of the Hindoo bankers, on finding that the Mission had only brought Indian coins, depreciated their value in the bazaar, and raised that of the "Bajoglee" (the Belgian ducat, which, strange to say, is universally current there to the exclusion of almost all other gold coins), thus adding to our embarrassment. Thinking that a better market might be obtained for our bills at Meshed, Dr. Login obtained some on his private risk from the Envoy, and sent them to Mollah Mehdi, and Mohamed Hoosein, at Meshed, to be negotiated by the Yezd merchants. The experiment was most successful; and he had the satisfaction of making over the money to the treasury at 16 per cent. premium on the bills, instead of 16 per cent. discount.

There were, however, other circumstances which greatly facilitated our financial arrangements at this time. The communication between Kandahar and Herat had been made so safe, by posting horsemen along the road for the protection of travellers, that the trade between these cities increased immensely. The communication with Meshed had also been rendered less precarious, and large kafilâs with merchants arrived almost every week. To counteract the difficulty with respect to the comparative value of the ducat, as it was generally considered at Herat to be a *Russian* coin, sovereigns were procured from the treasury at Candahar, through Major (now Sir Henry) Rawlinson, and, on the plea that it would be an insult to the *Dowlut Injlees* to depreciate their coinage below that of Russia, they were issued from our treasury at a rate corresponding to the enhanced value of the ducat. As this happened to be the exact value of 2 Herat tomauns (3 Herat Rs. being equal to 1 Cos. rupee), they were readily received in circulation under the name of "Do' Tomaunees" or "Sooltanees," and as such are, no doubt, pretty well known at Herat to this day.

On seeing a large sum of money paid from our treasury to Yar Mohamed for the release of the Cazee of Herat, it was some consolation to know that he had received it in sovereigns at the rate of 1*l*. 6*s*. 8*d*. each!!—L.

who, since 1839, as I have already remarked, are Mussulmans in form, but not in heart: life is dear, and to save theirs they adopted the faith of Mahomet. The story of this forced conversion is as follows:—A Jewish woman having consulted a Mussulman doctor for an abscess she had on her hand, this empiric ordered her to open a dog recently born, and to keep her hand for one hour in the bowels. The good old lady did as she was bid; unfortunately, however, this was done on the day of the *Koorban Beiram*, the festival of the victim, the most remarkable of Mahomedan holidays: a sheep is killed in every Mussulman family on that day, and eaten with great rejoicings. This act of the Jewess having come to the ears of some fanatical Mussulmans, they propagated all kinds of lies in connexion with the circumstance; they asserted that the unfortunate dog had been killed in the presence of an assembly of Jews, and that in doing this they intended to cast ridicule upon the Mahomedan religion. These statements lost nothing in the telling; and at length the town was in a state of ferment and agitation, the soldiers of the garrison hurried to the Jews' quarter, pillaged it, and killed several of the wretched inhabitants. The remainder were pursued like wild beasts, and, receiving no protection from the officers of the local government, they, to save their lives, embraced a faith which they abhorred. During the time they were paralysed by these scenes the Imaum Jumeh and other mollahs, as well as some noblemen of Meshed, seized the prettiest Jewesses and married them.

Assaf Doulet, usually reputed so just, did not take the measures he should have done to repress these disorders, nor affect even to inquire into them until it was too late; and some persons went so far as to say that he secretly promoted this disgraceful and brutal piece of tyranny. This was not proved; but it is well known that his hatred of the Armenians and Jews was intense; which gave a certain amount of credibility to the report. Fanaticism, however, was not the only motive which roused the Mussulman population to the commission of these crimes. They were jealous of the Jews, and vexed to see them wealthy, and the most profitable commercial operations in their hands; they also imagined that their houses were full of treasure; these they pillaged, and carried off everything, even to the doors and windows. From the period at which this took place the Jews of Meshed have never set their feet within the walls of their synagogues; on the contrary, they make a point of going every day to the mosque of the Imaum Reza, in order that their conversion may not appear hypocritical, which would, without doubt, subject them to fresh persecutions. They have also pledged themselves to send their children to the mollahs to study the Koran, and never to teach them the Hebrew language. Those who emigrated to Herat have openly returned to their ancient faith, for which they would certainly suffer if they were to revisit Meshed. The Jews of this town appeared in every way superior to those generally met with in Asia. They have not, perhaps, the same astuteness, but they have not the same servile air. They are ready to be of service, polite, and certainly more loyal than what one generally expects, or, indeed, sometimes finds in persons of that nation.*

Meshed is surrounded by a dry ditch and mud wall, about four miles and a half in circumference, incapable of resisting any regular siege. The citadel, situated on the S. E. side, is in a bad state of repair; the construction is on the same plan as all other Persian fortresses, an oblong, with large towers at the angles, and smaller ones at intervals, connected by curtains. Within the enceinte of the town are numerous cemeteries of immense extent, far exceeding the requirements of the resident population. The explanation of this is, that hundreds of devotees, whose bodies are brought from a considerable distance round Meshed, are buried here, in order that their remains may be nearer those of the

---

* There were only a few families of Jews at Herat on the arrival of the Mission, but they are settled in great numbers in different parts of Eastern Persia and Turkistan. Major Eldred Pottinger had shown much kindness to them, and they were very well affected towards us. As they communicate with each other in the *Hebrew* character, though in the Persian language, Dr. Login was induced to get an old Rabbi at Herat to transcribe a little tract for circulation among them; and as they appeared to be much pleased with this, he employed him to transcribe a part of Martin's Persian Testament in a similar way. The transcript into the Hebrew character was not completed when we left Herat, and he took it on to Kabul, where he met the son of the old Rabbi, who had just brought a letter from Colonel Stoddart at Bokhara. He engaged him to complete the work, leaving him in charge of his friend (now Major) Dawes, of the horse artillery on his departure for India. The Jew accompanied Dawes to Jellalabad, and finished the transcript during the siege of that place. The first kafila which passed through the Khyber after General Pollock opened it, brought it to Peshawur, whence it was forwarded to Dr. Login at Luknow. On looking over a book of Sketches published by Mrs. Colin Mackenzie, since his arrival in England, Dr. Login had the gratification of learning, after a lapse of *thirteen* years, that the poor Jew, who had been employed under Major Dawes, had, while so engaged, been led to inquire into the truth of the Gospel, and died a Christian at Bombay.—L.

Imaum Reza, in whose good company they hope one day to journey to Heaven, and enter the Mussulman paradise. Besides these open spots there are some gardens to the west of the town; but these are being cleared away to make room for houses, which are rising on all sides.*

There is only one remarkable building in Meshed,—the mosque in which is the tomb of the Imaum Reza. This is situated in the centre of the town, and divides the Khiabane into two parts. The Khiabane is a magnificent promenade, extending from one end of the city to the other, that is to say, from the gate of Herat to that of Koochan; a large stream of running water flows along its whole length, shaded on either side by fine plane-trees. Retail shops line each side of the avenue. The merchants meet in very handsome caravanserais, of recent construction, and in the bazaars, which, though roofed in, are narrow and of small extent, quite unworthy of such a city.

This Khiabane is the general rendezvous of the population of Meshed; to it also resort all strangers, and the crowds of people assembled between the hours of eleven and two are so great that it is difficult to thread one's way amongst them. The noise and bustle are then indescribable; fruit, sherbets, and other refreshments, with all kinds of Eastern productions, are spread out on the banks of the stream, frequently under the very feet of the ever-passing and crowding people, who jostle and take little heed of the remonstrances of the owners of the wares. To these may be added the clamours to buy, with all the chaffering that takes place when a bargain is being driven in the East. The result of all this is a loud hum, that may be heard at some distance from the animated and picturesque tide of human life.

The commerce of Meshed is, in some respects, important, with reference to the surrounding and distant countries. Sugars, which are brought from the refineries of Yezd, form a considerable article of trade. These, as well as every kind of silk and cotton goods, glass, porcelain, and delf, brought from Teheran, but of European manufacture, are forwarded to Central Asia; and from hence the merchants receive in return Kashmir shawls, black lamb-

* The foregoing was written in 1844; since then the Shah having dismissed and exiled Assaf Doulet, his son Salar revolted, and after a resistance of three years was taken and strangled. Meshed suffered greatly by these occurrences, and it will be many years before it recovers them.

skins from Bokhara, assafœtida, camels'-hair cloth called *barek;* fur cloaks made at Kabul, camels from Khiva, and Turcoman horses, which are for the most part disposed of in Persia. There is also a large sale of articles manufactured in the province of Meshed. Of these the first in importance are its magnificent carpets, perhaps unequalled for colour, wear, and beauty in the world; shawls of a Kashmir pattern, called in Persian *Meshedees.* These are held in greater estimation than those of Kerman. The felts, light silk goods—the produce of the silk in the north, should also be mentioned; and arms, particularly swords, which have a great reputation.

The quarries in the mountains, a parasang south of the city, furnish the material for another branch of local manufacture—a stone of a blackish tint, somewhat resembling plaster, but much harder. This is an excellent substitute for delf or glass, and is made into many articles of first necessity, such as cooking-pots, vases and jugs of every pattern and shape, tea-cups, tea-pots, sugar-basins, and salt-cellars. Assafœtida is also a production of Khorassan.

The principal mosque of Meshed is an imposing edifice, not only from its size, but the rich and costly materials of which it is constructed. The building is divided into two parts; the first into a large square court, in the form of a caravanserai, with two stories of small apartments looking into it, and here the pilgrims are lodged gratis. This court is paved with large flagstones, the walls being covered with enamelled bricks, or rather varnished; the blue ground of these brings out in strong relief sentences of the Koran, which, in gold and white and from the base to the summit, ornament this magnificent place of worship. Shah Abbas the Great was the founder of this portion of the building; and Nadir Shah subsequently restored it.

The second division consists of the mosque, the work of Goher Shah of Timour origin; it covers the tomb of the Imaum Reza, which is in marble, and decorated with arabesques of most admirable workmanship; a massive silver railing, surmounted by gold ornaments, surrounds it; and a large cupola and two minarets, remarkable for their bold conception as well as elegant form, rise above this monument: these are externally, from halfway up to the top, covered with rich gilding, and when the burning rays of an Eastern sun are shed upon them they dazzle with their brilliancy the eyes of the spectator.

Some of my Meshed cicerones assured me that the tomb of the famous Caliph Haroon-al-Raschid was next to that of the Imaum Reza, but it would have been the height of imprudence on my part to verify the fact; I was therefore obliged to be satisfied with promenading the quadrangles of the edifice, the mosque being open only to the faithful, who would lay violent hands upon any infidel they might find within its precincts.

Some years since, a Hindoo, led by curiosity, penetrated into the sanctuary, and they were on the point of maltreating him, when he demanded to be taken before the *mutévelli*, a public officer, of whom, as a British subject, he claimed protection. This dreaded name produced its effect, and he consented to listen to the following justification. "Why do you," said he, "reproach me with a crime for having entered this building—because I am impure? What is the use of such reasoning?—Did God create men from two kinds of dust? I don't believe a word of it. We are all fashioned in the same mould, and of the same material; and, if you think otherwise, I can prove that you are wrong. Let one of you cut his finger, I will do the same: if milk flows from my wound, and blood from a Mussulman's, you will then have reason on your side, and you may kill me; but if blood should also come from my finger, why should you affirm that your blood is purer than mine?" No one felt inclined to try this test, and our Indian was allowed to go quietly about his business. It would not, however, have been prudent to speculate upon his good luck, and I adopted the opinion which I would recommend to others who are not Mussulmans—namely, to abstain from making their bow to the tomb of the Imaum Reza.* The revenues arising from the legacies and

* The ordinary position of Hindoos towards their Christian masters, in respect to caste and purity, was reversed in Afghanistan. At Herat, and beyond the Indus generally, Christians—as people of the Book—were freely admitted to eat with Mussulmen, so long as they abstained from the forbidden food; and we were often asked why we allowed unclean Kaffirs like Hindoos, to be freely admitted into our houses.

When travelling between Candahar and Cabul we were met by a few horsemen of one of our irregular cavalry regiments, Mussulmen from India. Our servants, Afghans and Pharsevâns, to show their hospitality, offered them a kalian which had just been smoked by Major Todd. The Indian Mussulmen asked if they intended to insult them, by offering a pipe which had been smoked by a Kafir: whereupon our people retorted, that the Indian Mussulmen were Kafirs, in following the customs of Hindoos; and a battle royal would have ensued, had we not interfered.—L.

donations of pious Mussulmans are immense, and furnish the means of relieving each day the wants of indigent pilgrims who have no other means of subsistence; the trustees of these revenues also lend a portion of them at the rate of 25 per cent.

When I was at Meshed, one heard a great deal of gossip respecting the journey which had been recently made to Bokhara by the Rev. Dr. Wolf, with a view of obtaining the release of Colonel Stoddart and Captain Conolly, believed to have been assassinated by the Emir of that city two years before. I shall not enter here into the details relative to the captivity of these two officers, having already given them in another manuscript, entitled 'Researches into the History of the Afghans,' and will simply say a few words respecting Dr. Wolf. On his return to England that gentleman published a work, that I have never read, but which I have been generally assured was a most eccentric production; and I can have no difficulty in believing this after what I have heard of the author—in the first place from one or two of his servants who were subsequently in my employment, and afterwards from several Persians, Usbeks, and even Englishmen, who, be it said, were little disposed in his favour. My opinion, therefore, of the Doctor is partly based on what his countrymen said of him, and coincides with that of the Asiatics. It was known to many persons—and those who do not know it I will inform—that after his return to Teheran from Bokhara the Doctor refused to cash some bills which he had given to a Persian, Abdul Samut Khan, the commandant of the artillery at Bokhara, amounting to 60,000 francs. This refusal was interpreted in various ways at Meshed: some said the bills had been extorted from him by Samut Khan, with whom he had settled all his accounts before he left Bokhara; others said that he ought to have paid the money. For my part I believe that the honour of the Doctor was free from the slightest imputation. Having frankly said this, I think I am entitled to be believed when I mention faults that may, it is true, hurt his *amour propre*, but the correctness of which it would be impossible to deny. I have, however, no desire to lessen the credit due to the zeal the reverend gentleman showed in his endeavours to ascertain the fate of these unfortunate Englishmen; but his devotion would have appeared more praiseworthy to me if Christian charity and benevolence had alone directed his conduct. Vanity, quite as much as an impulse of the heart, was, I believe, the motive that induced him to take this perilous journey, the dangers of which he did not seem to appreciate; thus proving that in his preceding peregrinations in Central Asia he had only seen men and things through the prismatic illusions which continually deceived his judgment. The mission which he had undertaken was not suited to his organization; timid beyond all belief, he never had the least idea that he staked his life in going to Bokhara, and up to the time he arrived there manifested a sense of security so eccentric that it bordered upon craziness; letters that I have read of his, certainly not a great many, confirmed me in that opinion. Dr. Wolf was born in Germany, of Jewish parents, and on arriving at the age of reason went to Rome and abjured his faith, and became a Roman Catholic; but he gave himself such licence in the practice and teaching of his new religion that his superiors were obliged to place an interdict upon his doings, and he would have been in some scrape if the English, who made a martyr of him, had not taken him under their protection. The Doctor then became a Protestant, but he did not show any increase of common sense after this fresh change of faith.

His first *contretemps* on his arrival at Meshed was to find himself face to face with several Mollahs, to whom in 1832 he had prophesied that our Saviour would in 1840 return to this earth, when all the human race would embrace the English Protestant religion—a prophecy which had not been realised. The Doctor has the assurance to believe that he is inspired; that with the Bible in his hand and a smile on his lips he can at once convert any Mussulman or the most hardened idolator—that he has only to speak, and the individuals he addresses are at once converted to the true faith. Thus it is evident that no man could be so little suited for this dangerous expedition. Nevertheless, singular to say, he undertook it, and for what?—the hope of acquiring apostolic renown and passing for a prophet. The *selamliks*, bows, and benedictions he talks of having received on his entering Bokhara, existed only in his own fertile imagination. The little children, instead of kissing the hem of his robe, abused and threw stones at him. This increased his fears, and he endeavoured to propitiate all who came near him with money and presents: it was this that induced him to give the bills to Samut Khan for 6000 *tellahs*.

The first day of the Doctor's reception by the Emir Nasser

Ullah Khan he was in such a state of alarm that he did not seem to know where he was; he could not recognize the persons near him; his language was incoherent and he trembled violently. The Emir observed this and had pity upon him. "Take this wretched man home," he said to the master of the ceremonies, "he is incapable of conversing, and the terror he manifests distresses me." At this time the Khan had no idea of putting him to death, but he subsequently changed his mind, and would have carried his intentions into effect had not the Shah of Persia, at the pressing solicitations of Colonel Sheil induced the Emir to alter his resolution. The Doctor's fears were, I will venture to say, not without reason, of the most intense kind until he reached the Persian territory.

In my opinion, Dr. Wolf's safety might have been much more assured had he been furnished with letters from his Government for the Emir of Bokhara. The Khan was, on a former occasion, indignant at being requested to treat with the representative of a company of merchants at Calcutta, and not direct with the English Government. "He had had," he said, "communications with the Emperor of Russia, one of the greatest Christian potentates, and why not with the Queen of England?" The Emir is stated to have made this refusal of the English Government to treat with him direct, a pretence for putting Stoddart and Conolly to death. This susceptibility on the part of the Government, in acting upon the notion that it would degrade the sovereign to correspond with a barbarian, was absurd and out of place, and cost the lives of two brave and intelligent officers, who had devoted themselves to their country, and deserved a better fate. The Bokharians, Persians, and Afghans I met in Meshed, who had known Stoddart and Conolly, were agreed in thinking that the former was a brave, energetic, resolute man, but violent and of an irascible temper;*

* Mr. Khanikof, who was sent by the Emperor of Russia to endeavour to release Stoddart before Conolly's arrival, told me that there never was a man so unfit to deal with Asiatics as Col. Stoddart. He was a fine, gallant, chivalrous, highly accomplished English gentleman, but very imperious and touchy. He lived in Khanikof's house for four months, and might have left Bokhara, but he would not owe a favour to the Emperor of Russia, and thought that his own government ought to have delivered him. When Conolly came, he left Khanikof to live with him, and from that time Khanikof told me he thought their fate was sealed. Khanikof left, our disasters at Kabul occurred, and the Emir no longer feared to act according to his inclinations.

Stoddart had treated him, very injudiciously, with contemptuous haughtiness. Khanikof told me that he was once sent for with him to the and that to this unfortunate infirmity of temperament his death may be attributed as much as to the refusal of his Government to write to the Emir. Of Conolly, they spoke as a judicious, conciliating, prudent, and gentle individual, perfectly organized and by nature adapted to negotiate with Asiatics; they looked upon his death as a fatality, and attributed it to the imperious and unbending character of his companion.

The melancholy fate of these gallant soldiers was often referred to by my friends at Meshed when I spoke of continuing my journey to Afghanistan; they assured me that my project would certainly terminate fatally. Some advised me to retrace my steps; others, who really took an interest in my proceedings, entreated me to forbear, and the majority, who cared little whether I took their advice or not, said, "You will certainly have your throat cut; for the occupation of Afghanistan by the English, and their subsequent disasters, have caused such an irritation in the minds of the inhabitants that the presence of one single European is capable of rousing their indignation and leading them to acts of violence. Their neighbours the Persians, who are connected with them by more than one link, but whom they erroneously believe to be devoted to English interests, cannot enter Afghanistan without exposing their lives." These arguments were, it is true, calculated to restrain me; but when I reflected on all the fatigues, privations, and dangers I had undergone since I left France, and the possibility of being arrested in Persia, I determined to continue my journey. To shrink from perils which I had foreseen before I left Bagdad seemed to be the height of puerility and cowardice. With prudence, courage, and perseverance, a man almost always attains his object; and though I could not manage to reach the Punjaub, I am still persuaded that there is no country in Asia inaccessible to a European who speaks the language fluently, and is acquainted with the customs and religion of the inhabitants of the territory through which he desires to travel. The principal thing is to

---

Emir, who told him of reports that the English army had been destroyed at Kabul. Stoddart fiercely retorted upon him — "That is a lie! such things could not happen to the English." The Emir ordered him back to his house without answering, the confirmation of the report came afterwards, and left the Emir free to gratify his cruel revenge. Mr. Khanikof is a distinguished Oriental scholar, of mild, agreeable manners, and great judgment and sagacity. He has a high reputation among his countrymen, and now fills the important post of Consul General at Tabreez.—ED.

know how to conform oneself to their habits and modes of thought, to adopt that pliability of disposition which is necessary to meet and counteract their duplicity of character; these, with a stout heart and patient perseverance, would triumph over everything; and if I failed in Afghanistan, it was because I was the first European who had made an attempt to enter the country subsequently to the English disasters at Kabul. Hatred and distrust were still paramount, and overcame every precaution; nevertheless I made my way through many provinces, and was only stopped at Kandahar. I risked my head, it is true, but after all I brought it back on my shoulders; and if there was any necessity or reason for again undertaking the same journey, I should not, in spite of the dangers I underwent, hesitate a moment. Having no interest, and seeing no advantage—on the contrary, dangers—in travelling in my European dress, I decided upon leaving it in my trunk, and adopting an Afghan costume; nevertheless I resolved, though in this disguise, to avow myself a European to all the chiefs of those countries through which I passed; concealing the circumstance, however, as much as possible from the inhabitants in general, less from the fear of any danger that might happen to me, than to avoid the annoyance resulting from their insufferable curiosity and their cool and unceremonious manners.* It was Providence that suggested this determination, for if I had acted otherwise I should have been infallibly known by many persons at Herat who had seen me at Meshed, and it would thus have been very difficult to have removed any suspicion which Yar Mahomed Khan, chief of that principality, might have conceived against me.

The servant I hired at Meshed was a native of Herat, and well recommended. I would not engage another Persian; for besides their habitual villany, he would have created as much suspicion as myself; whereas, in taking an Afghan servant, I appeared to trust myself to their good faith. I had also the advantage of learning many things concerning the country which I should never have learnt from a Persian. There was, however, one disadvantage that operated against me in my character of European,

* The advice given by M. Ferrier is most judicious. By wearing a turban, or kujar-cap, and a common chogah over ordinary clothes, Europeans avoid much annoyance. By the officers of the Herat Mission no attempt was made to conceal from the chiefs that they were Englishmen, when travelling in any quarter.—L.

and which I had suffered from ever since we left Nishapoor. I was obliged to pay much dearer for everything I purchased, and this drained my resources, which I could little afford. It was precisely the same in Afghanistan. When the English have once overrun a country in Asia, it is unapproachable for any one else.* The natives, having seen them throw their money about in such profusion, when recompensing the most trifling services, or submitting to pay most exorbitant prices for articles of food of a nominal value, consider that they have acquired a right to rob any European travelling through their country; and I was on several occasions very nearly getting into scrapes in my endeavours to avoid their unreasonable exactions.

Before leaving Meshed I called upon Mohamed Wali Khan, who had the courtesy to give me a letter of recommendation to Sheik Jami, governor of Toorbut, of which the following is a translation :—

"May the most high, the most puissant, and most valorous Azi Abdul Rahim Khan enjoy perfect health. Then I have the honour to inform his high wisdom that at the present moment the most high, the General Ferrier Sahib, the companion of honour, the possessor of courage, and the cream of Christians, has been sent on a mission to Herat; therefore, as he is on his way to that country, you will protect and take care of this very distinguished person, so that he may be enabled to travel in a proper and dignified manner. I beg that you will always inform me in your letters of the state of your health, and that of affairs in general."

On my arrival at Meshed I made an arrangement with a camel-caravanier *en route* for Herat, and hired two of his camels; one to carry my baggage, for which I was to pay one tomaun, and the other, with a litter on either side, for my servant and myself, at the rate of one tomaun and a half. The 28th of May was the day irrevocably fixed for our departure; but at the very moment they were going to load our beasts, a sanguinary conflict arose between the soldiers of a battalion of Kurds of the tribe of Gourān,

* Instances have occurred in which Russians, and other Europeans, have personated Englishmen in Khorassan, by refusing "soorsaut," and paying handsomely. Our excellent friend, Mollah Mehdi, mentioned in page 119, was on one occasion a heavy loser by having been so imposed upon. For the credit of the national character in those quarters his losses should be made good to him.—L.

garrisoned here, and the inhabitants of the town, who have the reputation of being the most warlike citizens in Persia. The fight took place just in front of our caravanserai; and at the first outbreak a panic seized the pilgrims and the peaceable portion of the inhabitants, who fled in every direction; the itinerant shopkeepers and vendors of small wares followed them, and the Khiabane was soon cleared of every one but the combatants, who worked away without interruption the whole day with sticks, swords, and poniards, to their hearts' content. The cries and orders of the authorities on both sides were totally disregarded, and they were utterly powerless to stop the bloody fray. The number of killed and wounded was very great. I saw all this from a window of the caravanserai, the doors of which were closed and locked; and here we were compelled to remain, trusting that there would be a cessation of hostilities on the morrow; but in this we were disappointed; the belligerent parties remained on the ground all night, and at daybreak renewed the attack with greater fury than on the preceding day. Towards nine o'clock, however, our caravanier, Hassan Obereh, espied from my window a *vekil*, a sergeant, with whom he was acquainted; and this man, being informed of our embarrassing position, ordered fifty soldiers to escort us to a caravanserai a little beyond the Herat gate. Here we arrived without hinderance, and waited for Hassan Obereh, who was not so fortunate; for in his endeavours to join us he unwittingly got into the *mêlée*, and received a sound thrashing.

CHAPTER X.

Turokh — Shock of an Earthquake —Sangbut — The offensive Camel — Toll on Women — Hedireh — Variety of Partridges — Mahmoodabad — Tamerlane the Destroyer — The sedentary Dervish — Fertile district of Shehr-noon — Hazarah horses — Toorbut-ishak-Khan — Toorsheez — Toorbut Sheik Jamee — Kariz — Celebrated melons — Wild asses a delicacy — Kussan — The Army of Ahmed Shah annihilated — The Heri-rood — Geographical error — Consequences of turning a stream — Pay of a Sirdar — Environs of Kussan — Forest of Shevesh — Game — Rosanuck — Gorian — Shekwan — Anticipated reception by Yar Mohamed.

TUROKH, May 29th—two parasangs—three hours—by an easy road, that brought us to some ruins, amongst which we encamped. In the centre of them was a large square edifice, constructed of burnt bricks, in pretty good repair, and covering the tomb of some holy personage. A clear stream ran past, and turned a small mill. In the village, at ten minutes' walk from hence, no provisions were to be obtained. I met there Deen Mohamed Khan, cousin-german of the chief of Herat, and commander of the Afghans in the service of Assaf Doulet, but had only time to exchange a few civil words with him. The south wind had since the morning blown with extreme violence, raising clouds of dust; the atmosphere was heavy and suffocating; and about four hours before sunset the shock of an earthquake was felt. Hassan Obereh was immediately of opinion that the site we occupied was not of happy omen, and at once decamped.

Sangbut, May 30th—four parasangs—eight hours—by a road the greater portion of which was undulating and, though not level, easy. On this journey it was equally the same to me whether I travelled day or night; for, extended in my litter, I could not only rest but even sleep, which was impossible on horseback. There was, to be sure, some little annoyance when the road was hilly, in having one's head lower than one's feet; but after a time I became habituated to this. A much greater inconvenience was that of being to leeward of the camel's breath, to avoid the disagreeable smell of which it was necessary to tie a handkerchief under the nose. A camel is far preferable to a horse or mule for locomotion; the pace is, no doubt, a little slower, but the fatigue infinitely less.*

Sangbut is a caravanserai-shah, which Assaf Doulet gave Prince Mohamed Yussoof,† an Afghan prince of the Suddozye tribe, for his private residence and that of his followers; so that there is no room for travellers who, winter and summer, must encamp in the open air. About ten minutes from it are the ruins of an ancient town, the materials of which the Shah-Zadeh had during the last two or three years cleared away by the emigrants who joined him from Herat. There is now a large village well inhabited. The Khan's position is well chosen for levying contributions on the passing traveller. Having been ordered by Assaf Doulet to keep an eye on the caravans, and especially to prevent the Afghan and Parsivan women, who had for some years been settled in Meshed, from returning to Herat—and knowing full well that the men would not leave without them—he has turned these orders to his own account. Those who would not pay for permission to cross the frontier he sent back to Meshed; whereas those who satisfied his demands were permitted to pass. There were five women with our caravan, who, having paid the toll, were allowed to continue their journey; but on setting out, a fresh contribution was demanded, which they refused to give. For two hours the women's tongues were going, and to no purpose. At last my patience was exhausted; and after having shown my letter of recommendation from Mohamed Wali Khan, I drove the rascally claimants away, and threatened to write to Meshed, and represent their venal conduct to Assaf Doulet. This had its effect; and taking advantage of the diversion thus created, I put my camel at the head of the column, which defiled victoriously in front of them, who, though little satisfied, were afraid to offer any further resistance.

Hedireh, May 31st—six parasangs—ten hours—the first three by a flat and easy road. At Shek-ab it becomes undulating: here we halted for several hours near a stone building in ruins, called, with more pomposity than truth, a caravanserai, and

* In the event of another campaign in the East, and an advance from the coast, we shall soon find out the advantages of camel conveyance for our sick and wounded.—L.

† Shahzadeh Mohamed Yussuf, the present ruler of Herat, is, by education and character, far superior to any of the Suddozye Princes of Kamran's family. He was much respected at Herat, and on very friendly terms with the officers of the Mission.—L.

which serves in bad weather as a refuge for the wild asses which are numerous in this neighbourhood. A variety of the partridge also abounds here; it is called in Persian *siahsine* (black-breast); the neck and belly are covered with feathers of that colour, the rest of the body approaching to a very pale yellow: their flesh is tough and without flavour; and to eat them they must be well boiled. These birds are to be seen by myriads at Shek-ab, in the dry bed of a river, similar in every respect to the one I crossed three hours before we reached Meshed. At ten o'clock in the morning we were again afoot, and slept that night in the uninhabited and almost ruined caravanserai of Hedireh, which we reached after crossing some mountains. There is here a small rivulet, but no village; a few shepherds were seen in its environs.

Mahmoodabad, June 1st—eight parasangs—thirteen hours—through a plain, and for the first part by a firm road; the last argillaceous and easily cut up after rain. This plain is a desert; but there are many ruins, intersected by watercourses on each side of the road, which indicate its former fertility. These ruins, once large and flourishing villages, were destroyed by the Turcomans and Hazarahs, a nomadic tribe, occupying the country on the borders of the Moorghab river. At two parasangs from Hedireh is the *ab-ambar*, reservoir of water, of Haouz-bibee, by the side of which we halted to rest our camels; and, six parasangs further, encamped at the small fortified town of Mahmoodabad, situated on an eminence, and defended by two four-pounders. The approach to it is through a muddy stream which flows at its foot. This is a good military position.

On the right of the road, and in front of Mahmoodabad, the plain is covered with ruins, as well as a small hill, which appeared to have been once fortified. The Persians assert that this was once the site of the large and populous city of Linger, devastated by Tamerlane. There is a square and rather handsome building close to the road, under which repose the remains of an Imaum and nephew of the Imaum Reza of Meshed. There is nothing remarkable about this tomb. It occupies the centre of the edifice, in the exterior wall of which are small chambers to shelter travellers. An old sedentary dervish performs the part of *cicerone*, and makes something out of everybody,—from the caravaniers who halt near the tomb, and purchase a few provisions from him at a high price, and from the Turcomans and Hazarahs, whose spy he is, and who lie in ambush near here when there is a chance of plunder or of carrying off the unhappy pilgrims.

In a direct line S.W. from Mahmoodabad are three fertile districts which produce a handsome revenue to the Governor-General of Khorassan. The first, of which the chief town is situated four parasangs from Mahmoodabad, and called Shehr-noon, the New Town, is inhabited by 2000 families of Hazarahs, who have recently emigrated from Herat to Persia. These Hazarahs are encamped at the foot of the mountains, where there is good pasturage; and here they breed and graze a considerable number of excellent horses, with some of which they pay their contributions to the government. Shehr-noon is taxed at the rate of fifty horses every year; some of these will fetch from one hundred and sixty to two hundred tomauns, 80*l.* to 100*l.*; and none are accepted under the value of twenty-five tomauns. These Hazarahs are also obliged to arm and equip, and have in readiness for service, one thousand cavalry.

The second district is that of Toorbut-ishak-Khan: the town of this name contains 3000 houses, inhabited by the warlike Persian tribe of Garaï. This place is walled and surrounded by a ditch, and there are bazaars, but not roofed, mosques and caravanserais; there are more than 200 villages in the district of Toorbut. The productions are opium, silk, tobacco, and fruits. At sixteen parasangs from Toorbut-ishak-Khan is the third district, that of Toorcheez. The chief town, also walled, has 2000 houses; the inhabitants are Persians; there are four villages dependent on it, but a considerable population of nomadic Belooches, who number about 8000 tents, and have very large flocks. The productions are the same as those in the district of Toorbut-ishak-Khan, but less in quantity.

Toorbut Sheikh Jamee, June 2nd—four parasangs—seven hours—through a plain and by a good road. This little town, of eight hundred houses, is the chief place of a district situated on the extreme frontier towards Herat, and surrounded by gardens and cultivation. About 2300 families of Iliates are encamped near the mountains situated at two parasangs south of Toorbut, and, like the Hazarahs of Shehr-noon, they pay their taxes in horses. The final word in the name of this town is taken from that of the famous poet Jamee, author of the Beharistan, who lived in the 15th century, and was held in great repute for his sanctity and erudition in theology; people still flock from all parts to his tomb, which is believed to work miracles, and the prayers offered there are said to be particularly effective in making barren women fruitful. There is a caravanserai-shah outside Toorbut Sheikh Jamee.

Kariz, June 3rd—nine parasangs—thirteen hours—through a plain, by a level, sandy but good road. At the fourth parasang are the ruins of Abbasabad, a caravanserai-shah, and near it is a small rivulet. Kariz is a little walled village of sixty houses, furnishing no accommodation; we encamped, therefore, at ten minutes in advance of it, and near a caravanserai-shah partly in ruins. The melons of this locality were in ancient days considered the best in Asia, and were reserved for the courts of Teheran, Kabul, and Delhi: but the village having been destroyed at the close of the last century, and consequently deserted, the seed was lost, or degenerated from change of soil. Kariz has recently been repeopled by Hazarahs, who are taking pains to re-establish the reputation of its melons—judging by the two I ate, they have not yet succeeded. This is the last village in Persia on the side of Herat; extensive ruins surround it and denote a country once largely populated. The wind, from which we had so constantly suffered between Teheran and Meshed, had increased in violence since our leaving the latter city; it blew almost always from the north-west, and continued from sunrise to sunset; at night it was scarcely felt: less hot than the simoom, it caused almost as much lassitude, and brought on a slow fever with violent pains in the head. It is almost impossible to imagine the immense quantities of game we saw between Hedireh and Kariz, particularly near Mahmoodabad; the deer were feeding in herds of several hundreds, and at no great distance from one another, they were not frightened at our approach, and frequently remained within gun-shot. This was not the case with the wild asses, which were quite as numerous, but much more scared: they fled at the least noise, and with a speed for which I was not prepared; when wounded, a single sportsman has great difficulty in taking them; they kick, bite, and make a tremendous resistance. Their flesh is more delicate than Persian beef, and the Afghans consider it a great delicacy. Every variety of partridge is met with on these plains, and also the heath-cock. The royal tiger is sometimes seen, but the panther, hyena, wolf, jackal, and fox are common.

Kussan, June 4th—five parasangs—nine hours—still through a plain and by an easy road. At the third parasang are the ruins of Kaffir-Kaleh, the fortress of the infidel, situated on a high artificial mound. Near it is another fort of more recent construction, also in the same state; a caravanserai-shah, one of the handsomest in Persia, close to it, is also half in ruins. In former times these buildings were erected at every second parasang on the road between Meshed and Herat; the greater number have been destroyed or fallen down, and their foundations are alone visible. Kaffir-Kaleh was the scene of memorable events: first, the annihilation by cold, in 1752, of the army under Ahmed Shah Suddozye; secondly, the battle fought here thirty years ago by Hassan Ali Mirza, Governor-General of Khorassan and son of Futteh Ali Shah, King of Persia, and Futteh Khan, Grand Vizier of Mahmood Khan, King of the Afghans. Kussan, the first halting place in the province of Herat, is situated two parasangs beyond Kaffir-Kaleh.

We encamped at fifteen minutes from this fortress, and on the borders of the river Heri-rood, the only stream to which this designation can be applied between this and Kermansháh. The clear and limpid waters of the Heri are pleasant, though aperient; fish are few in number. The position of this river is not always well laid down on the maps. Of very considerable size at the first part of its course, in the centre of the Paropamisus, several leagues above Sir-jangal, it is increased in volume as far as Obeh by numerous streams, which descend from the mountains north and south of it. From here it gradually diminishes, the water being taken from it by the canals for the purposes of irrigation. After leaving Herat the body of water is again increased by some large streams below Kussan, and as it enters the Persian territory it divides into two branches, the smallest of which flows in the direction of Meshed; the other, four times more considerable, runs, without being turned to any account, to within a short distance of Sarukhs, where it is lost in the steppes. The plains which it traverses, and which it would fertilize, are far from being sterile; but whoever attempts to settle there is carried off by the Turcomans or the Hazarahs, and in consequence of this the country has become quite deserted. The inhabitants told me that the Heri-rood, eighty years ago, instead of flowing north-west, turned abruptly to the north after having passed Kussan, and fell into the Moorghab.

We may be allowed to give credit to this assertion, for these abrupt changes in the course of a river are frequently seen in Central Asia,—not in consequence of natural causes, but the united manual labour of whole tribes, who, wishing to settle themselves on a more advantageous site, turn the course of the river in order that it may flow through their new locality. The wide and deep beds of rivers, which are dry and continually met with through the whole of Khorassan, have had their origin in such undertakings; and this is proved by the bloody wars that have taken place, and continue to take place even in our day, between the various tribes in these countries, on the occasion of their turning a stream or river. Here it is impossible to calculate upon rain; the contributions of the heavens are rare, for rain falls only in winter and at the commencement of spring. To remove the water from a tract of country, therefore, is to take away from its inhabitants the means of subsistence; the crops dry up and produce no grain, the meadows share the same fate, and the cattle perish for want of food—trees at length wither, and the result is the fearful calamity of famine.

It is an error to suppose that the Heri-rood flowed south in former days, and fell into the Lake Seistan. This geographical mistake may possibly have originated in the fact that a small river, also flowing from the Paropamisus, is called in the latter part of its course the Haroot-rood, which is sometimes corrupted into Heri-rood; it continues its course between the Khash-rood and the mountains as far as the Seistan Lake. But the two rivers are not in any way connected, though they rise very near each other; besides, the mountains that bound the plains and the valleys to the south, by which the Heri-rood passes, prevent it from taking the direction in question.*

Kussan is nothing but one vast ruin, and within its walls there are now only four hundred inhabited houses. The wall of the enceinte is open at several points, and its desolate appearance agrees with the tradition that the town has been rebuilt and de-

* My own observations agree with this statement. I had, however, no opportunity of tracing the course of the Heri-rood to any distance. An accurate survey of the Herat Valley, and also of the country between Herat and Candahar, was made by the late Colonel Edward Sanders, assisted by Sir Richmond Shakespear and Captain North; and the late Captain Edward Conolly gave some geographical information in the report of his journey from Herat to Girishk *viâ* Seistan, published in the Asiatic Journal of Bengal for 1841. There is also a very correct account of the road between Kandahar and Herat to be found in Arthur Conolly's Journal, published in 1834.—L.

stroyed many times; certain it is that the materials of which the citadel was constructed are very ancient—the burnt bricks, of a fine grain, being as hard as stone. The ditch that surrounds it is wide, deep, and in good repair, and always full of water; the foundations and a large proportion of the gates are of hewn stone, and were apparently constructed two or three thousand years ago. The garrison consists of one hundred and fifty Heratian soldiers, commanded by the Sirdar Dad Khan, cousin of Yar Mohamed Khan: he is also governor of the district, and farms it of the government; this induces him to commit all kinds of extortion, of which the people loudly complain. Besides the tax upon the cultivated lands, he takes also that on travellers, and in the most rigorous manner—which is not to be wondered at, for his pay and allowances are only thirty tomauns (15*l.*) a-year. Europeans in Persia are exempt from this tax; but in Herat they were not so considerate, and I was obliged to pay it. Four sahibkrans are charged for a laden camel, two for a horse or a mule, and one for an ass, also laden. It was in the citadel of Kussan that Shah Kamran, the last Suddozye king of Herat, was strangled.*

If the town has a melancholy and desolate appearance, the same cannot be said of its environs, which are extremely picturesque; the banks of the Heri-rood are admirably wooded for a distance of twelve parasangs, both with copse and trees of large growth. This tract is known as the forest of Shevesh, from a little village at the entrance to it and about two parasangs east of Kussan. The tamarisk rises above every other tree, and is the kind generally met with in Central Asia, more especially by the side of a river. That part of the forest which extends in a radius of two parasangs round Kussan has been preserved as the hunting-ground of the chiefs of Herat, and the game is collected here in prodigious quantities. Pheasants, black-cock, hares, grey partridges, and the very small kind called in Persian *tuyou*, are in abundance; also boars, deer, and the wild ass; carnivorous animals are also in great numbers, who here find ample rations.

* I had understood that Shah Kamran had been killed in the citadel at Herat (his body having been found one morning at the foot of the tower in which he generally slept)—but M. Ferrier's statement may be the correct one. He had not been out of the citadel for eighteen months before the arrival of the British mission, and he was only induced to ride out, for the benefit of his health, at Dr. Login's suggestion. During our stay at Herat, he never rode out without asking Dr. Login to accompany him. One reason he gave for not showing himself in public was, that the vizier had not allowed him a proper retinue.—L.

Kussan has a trade by barter with Khaff-rooye, a Persian town, fifteen parasangs distant, to the south-west of it; it has a good citadel, which was built by the Sirdar Taymoori Kalesh Khan, who was killed under the walls of Herat by the Shah Kamran. The nephew of this Sirdar, Dost Mohamed Khan, is now governor of the district, in the name of the Shah of Persia. Khaff-rooye was anciently called Ferhad.

Rosanuck, June 5th—five parasangs—eight hours—through a plain, by a smooth and solid road. At starting we skirted the forest to the village of Shevesh. This is situated on a kind of promontory, the elevated point of which rises from the Heri-rood. We did not halt here, but pushed on to the ruined caravanserai-shah of Rosanuck. There is no house here, nor accommodation for travellers, and the nearest villages are distant three-quarters of an hour. The fortress of Gorian is two parasangs south of Rosanuck, and can be seen from hence distinctly with the naked eye; the walls and towers of the enceinte alone remain. The citadel was demolished in 1844 by Yar Mohamed, to court the favour of the Persian monarch; and to disguise his real reason from the Afghans, he told them that he had acted thus because with so many towns to defend his forces would be too much divided, and that he intended for the future to concentrate his troops in Herat, which being well fortified would then be able to resist all attacks. In the environs of Gorian are numerous and rich villages, forming the district of Baruabat, the productions of which partly supply the population of Herat. Gorian is considered by European writers to be the ancient Foosheng. This is possible; and I think Gorian succeeded that city, but not on the same site. It occupied the spot on which is a village of that name, situated half-way between Gorian and Herat, and inclining a little to the south.

Shekwan-mimizak, June 6th—four parasangs—six hours—by a good road of sand and gravel. At this halt are two villages which join one another; they are both walled and surrounded with a ditch, and contain about one hundred houses each. I heard here that my arrival had been expected for several days past at Herat, and that I was the subject of much conversation there. The Heratians, to whom every European is an Englishman, remembered, and not without a certain degree of satisfaction, the large sums of money which the authorities of that nation had spent in their town between 1839 and 1841, and they would no doubt have been glad enough to see them return.* Yar Mohamed Khan entertained, perhaps, the same sentiments, though for a different reason; for if the sympathies of Persia were not with him, he felt the necessity of again looking to the British Government for support. But whether this idea was correct or otherwise I cannot say, I was informed that he intended to give me a handsome reception; for having heard that I had visited the Governor-General of Khorassan in uniform, he imagined I was a person of some consequence. Several battalions had been ordered to hold themselves in readiness to receive me at the entrance of the city, and divers chiefs were to meet me with complimentary speeches at half a parasang from the town. This was not by any means agreeable news to me, for I was not in a position, nor indeed had I any right, to receive such honours; nor could I afford to do so, for they are dearly purchased in Asia. Besides, they might have thought that I was on some diplomatic mission; and how could I make a public entrance, hanging on one side of a camel and my servant on the other, with one solitary baggage camel in the rear? My position was indeed embarrassing; and, with a view of withdrawing from the distinguished marks of respect that were in store for me, I requested Hassan Obereh to leave at an earlier hour than usual, so that by arriving at Herat at break of day the troops would not be on the ground. Hassan, however, required great pressing, for he knew the reception I was to have, and had been ordered not to arrive before ten o'clock; moreover, he wished to have his share in it; but in the end he acceded.

* No doubt the greater number remembered with satisfaction the large sums of money expended there by Englishmen; but not a few, I feel persuaded, had a grateful recollection of other favours received at their hands.—L.

CHAPTER XI.

Herat — Early reception — The officer on guard — The Sertip Lal Khan — His daring feat at the siege of Herat — Monsieur Ferrier is sent to his house — Orders of Yar Mohamed — Visit from the Doctors — Their mode of treatment — Cyanate of Mercury — The Bayaderes and the wine cup — Visit to Yar Mohamed Khan — His reception of the author — Persists in taking him for an Englishman — Result of the conference — Policy of Yar Mohamed with the English — Asiatic characteristics — The Khan's engineering tactics at the siege — Yar Mohamed's policy — His confidants — His power — Protection to the Eimaks — Probable result of this — The Vizier's administration of justice — Security of the public roads — Taxation at Herat — Measures taken for the Khan's personal safety—His origin and rise to power—His son Syud Mohamed Khan — Competitors for the throne — Mirza Nejef Khan — Other Sirdars.

HERAT, June 8th—six parasangs—nine hours and a half—by a good road of sand and gravel. Four hours before arriving at the city, and on the left, at the foot of the mountains, are vast ruins, which continue without interruption up to it: amongst them are the remains of edifices and mausoleums, interspersed with gardens and numerous fine trees. That which I had hoped occurred: we arrived in the suburb of Musella and Thaleh-bengui before the day broke, and waited in the ruins of a magnificent mosque for the first indications of dawn. We then remounted our camels, and after having traversed a street, the crumbling houses in which exhibited the effects of the siege in 1838, we debouched upon a large esplanade, and were suddenly brought in front of the dismantled towers and battered walls of Herat. Favoured by my Afghan disguise I passed the town-gate in my litter without being recognized as a European. The officer, however, seemed much surprised that the caravan had arrived so early, and demanded of Hassan whether he had left me very far behind. The latter replied by pointing to me perched on my camel: at this the Heratian warrior appeared astounded, and at once gave way to cries and lamentations. "By Allah," said he, "I am a lost man; our most high and excellent Vezir will cut my head off—my orders were to send a naïb to a point two hours' distance from the town to tell this European to defer his entrance until a happy constellation had been observed in the heavens; and after that I was to fire a gun to give notice of his approach. In my ignorance of this early arrival I have done neither the one nor the other: I am a ruined man." The despair of this unfortunate fellow was enough to melt a stone. I tried to re-assure him, and promised to speak to Yar Mohamed in his favour; this seemed to console him a little, and he lost no time in firing the gun and performing thus much of his instructions—soldiers were likewise sent off in all directions to announce my arrival. As to myself, he held me in conversation at the gate for twenty minutes, to gain time. Profiting, however, by a momentary absence on his part I proceeded onwards; but camels always move slowly in a town, and before mine had gone five hundred yards I saw the soldiers running towards me on every side, some of them only half dressed, and one or two in little more than that uniform which Dame Nature had given them at their birth, and which my sudden and unexpected appearance probably justified in their eyes. One of them, who had thrown his jacket over a very short shirt not much longer than the jacket, had forgotten his *sir-jameh* trowsers; and as the wind somewhat disturbed his upper garments, he reminded me of the Tahitian islander and Madame Pritchard under similar circumstances, the satisfaction demanded by her husband for the impropriety being however backed by the guns of the British fleet. But I had no navy at my disposal, and besides I was not so susceptible as Queen Pomare's protector; neither was the soldier much distressed, and, pulling my camel by the bridle, he made room for himself amongst my escort, which, jostling and gaining an accession of numbers at every step, amounted to three or four hundred men before I reached the bazaars. Officers of various grades made many complimentary speeches as they came up; and after they had promenaded nearly all over the town I was conducted to a lodging, which had been expressly prepared for my reception at the house of the Sertip Lal Mohamed Khan. This was done by order of the Vezir Sahib, the only title assumed by Yar Mohamed Khan, the independent chief of Herat.

My host, the Sertip, was of Kandaharian origin, and by birth of the same tribe, Ali Kiouzye, as Yar Mohamed Khan; his family had been for a long time attached to that of the chief.

The father of the Sertip had been master of the ceremonies to the father of the Vezir Sahib, Abdullah Khan, formerly governor of Kashmir. The fidelity with which this family served every one by whom they were employed induced Yar Mohamed to place him near his person; and he subsequently gave him two or three of the most important appointments in his government; amongst them those of *Kaleh-begi* and that of *Mir-sheb*, commandant of the fortress and minister of police. It happened, however, that during the siege of 1838 the Vezir entertained some doubts of the fidelity of his lieutenant; but as his supposed defection was only a rumour of the bazaar, Yar Mohamed merely wrote to him, with a request that he would explain himself in reference to these injurious reports. The Kaleh-begi answered that he could only reply to the communication by his actions, and that he would feel obliged if the Vezir would dispense with his presence at court until his conduct had clearly proved what his intentions were. The Sertip did not leave his master long in doubt, and the same evening distinguished himself by one of the most clever and daring feats performed during the siege. The place had at that time been for several days invested by the Persian troops, and the *Shahaghi* battalions under the command of the Sertip Hadji Khan, were in observation at the gate of Meshed. This duty, according to their custom, was very carelessly performed, and Lal Mohamed Khan knowing it ordered a hundred unarmed men to walk into the trenches at dusk, say they were deserters, and claim the hospitality of the Persian soldiers—the order was executed, and they were received as anticipated. Towards midnight the troops went to sleep, when, at a given signal from without, the Afghans threw themselves upon the piled arms and rushed upon the slumberers with the bayonet. At the same moment Lal Mohamed Khan made a sortie from the town, and by these combined movements put the Persians completely to the rout; the besieged killing 360 men, and taking a captain of artillery prisoner, with two guns, which they brought back with them in triumph.* This brilliant affair, and the many proofs of

* Although the Sertip Lal Mohamed behaved with conspicuous gallantry during the siege, the Heratees were indebted to Pottinger for the success of the sortie in which they carried off the Persian gun from the works. The second was taken on a different occasion.

Pottinger was as remarkable for his candour in making known his mistakes, courage and fidelity which Lal Mohamed gave during the siege, procured him the unbounded confidence of the Vezir; and he is now his right hand. His brothers, one of whom is a colonel, and two others captains, are also highly esteemed by Yar Mohamed.

I considered it a great honour to be lodged in the house of such a man; but the Vezir in giving me these good quarters had much less regard for my personal consideration than to ascertain with accuracy the object that brought me to Herat; and what could I do or say which could escape the surveillance of the head of the police and his officers? The original intention was to have given me apartments in the royal palace, Char-bagh, situated in the centre of the town; but the apprehension that I might be too much at liberty, and could with greater ease enter into some intrigue, had led them to alter the plan.* My apartment at the Sertip's house consisted of one little room on the first floor; it looked out upon the court, in which when I arrived fifteen soldiers were quartered, and here they remained till I took my departure—the sabre of my entertainer was hooked on one stand of the piled arms, as a compliment to me. In witnessing these arrangements, and the kind and courteous manner in which I was addressed, I thought that the detachment stationed in the court was intended as a mark of respect to my rank; but the active surveillance kept up, and of which I saw I was the object, soon convinced me that I was only a prisoner honourably treated. I presented myself at Herat as a Frenchman; and I thought I had sufficiently proved the fact, by exhibiting the firmans I had received from Mohamed Shah; but I was not believed, they per-

as for his modesty in alluding to his services. Although he had faithfully reported to government that he had kicked Yar Mohamed's brother out of his house, for giving him the lie, (which led Lord Auckland to declare him unfit to be our representative at Herat,) he had said nothing of his conduct in driving back the Persians at the last assault, when the city was almost in their hands. It was only after the mission under D'Arcy Todd had arrived, and Pottinger had left the place, that his boldness and gallantry became fully known, and his successor had the duty —which to his generous spirit was, I am sure, a most pleasing one—of reporting his heroic deeds to Government.

Pottinger was one of those men who do not shine on paper, and who should never be asked to give a reason for their acts.—L.

* The Char-bagh had been the residence of Shahzadah Hajee Ferozeoodeen, for some time ruler of Herat. The buildings were in a most dilapidated state on the arrival of the mission, but were repaired and put in order by Major D'Arcy Todd. Hajee Ferozeoodeen was the grandfather of the Shahzadah Mahomed Yussuf, the present ruler of Herat.—L.

sisted in considering me an Englishman charged with a secret mission to Afghanistan, and it was in vain that I denied this strange idea—nothing would convince the Heratians. They thought I wished to conceal my identity; they knew, they said, how clever Europeans were in carrying on their schemes, and that Eldred Pottinger, when he came to Herat to assist in the defence of the city against the Persians, had, for several months previously to his declaring himself, passed for an Indian doctor of Mussulman extraction.* Yar Mohamed Khan had given orders that I should not be lost sight of for an instant, and that all I said should be reported to him; but he did not put too great a restraint upon my liberty, and I was always treated with the greatest deference and attention, supplied with plenty of food, and allowed to visit, with an escort, anything I wished to see in the town. I was also permitted to call upon the principal inhabitants, though not indiscriminately. I saw only those whom the Vezir Saheb permitted me to know; and they were individuals from whom he had nothing to fear. Yar Mohamed encouraged these visits, in the hope that I might drop something in conversation, or give them some opportunity of penetrating my designs; but in spite of the traps that were laid for me I always told the same story, namely, that my intention was to go to India, to take service in that country. However, these repetitions were of little use; for almost to the very last the Afghans persisted in thinking that I had some secret political mission.

A few hours after my arrival the Sertip Lal Mohamed, accompanied by a staff with very unpleasant physiognomies, came to see me. He appeared to be about forty or forty-five years of age, with a countenance of the true Tartar type, but having, in spite of this, a mild and benevolent expression. The first interview was passed in the interchange of mutual civilities; after which he retired to convey my compliments to the Vezir Sahib, and attend to his official duties, leaving with me his mirza, writer,

* Pottinger, in the disguise of an Indian Mussulman, lived for a few days in a "serai" at Herat before he was recognised as an European. I remember him mentioning, that he was walking in the bazaar, when he was touched on the arm by a person, who whispered to him in Hindustanee, "You are an Englishman," and made himself known as Hakeem Mohamed Hoosein. He had accompanied Arthur Conolly to Calcutta, and after being educated there, under Mr. Tytler, at the native medical institution, had returned to Herat to practise as a hakeem. He at once offered his services to Pottinger, and was most useful to him.—L.

and his brother the Sultan, Captain, Mohamed, to prevent me, as he said, from feeling lonely; his real object in giving me the advantage of their society being, that they might observe my every movement. They were, in short, spies, and never left me a single moment, whether in the house or out of it.

The Sertip's visit was followed by those of several men of rank; after them came the *Hakim bashee*, doctors, who hold a high rank in the society of Herat.* Amongst them were Mirza Asker, Mirza Mohamed Hussein, Goolam Kader Khan, and Agha Hussein, the ancient adviser of the Shah Kamran. As in their eyes every European must be a doctor, the conversation never ceased running on the healing art, of which they considered themselves such distinguished professors; each in turn was anxious to give me a high opinion of his talent, and I was condemned to listen to a long and absurd display of Afghan erudition. They also brought with them some of their drugs, in order that I might give them some notion of the manner in which certain chemical preparations which they had received from British India should be employed, as they were ignorant of their effects. They had, they said, up to that time given these medicines in progressive doses, until they ascertained the cases to which they were applicable. How many of their unfortunate patients had been killed by this system I dared not ask; but Mirza Asker filled up the blank by pulling from his pocket a bottle of the cyanate of mercury, requesting to know what devil of a salt this could be? "It has been of no use to me," he added, "for of one hundred patients that I have given it to, only one was cured—all the rest died."

Having finished with medicine, alchemy had its turn, for some of these idiots spend all they possess in their search after the philosopher's stone. They are convinced that the English have found it, and attribute their riches to that discovery. They imagine all European gold coins are at the outset only bits of iron, rubbed with a certain preparation, and then placed in devil's water from some well or spring, which metamorphoses it into gold. The doctors entreated me to initiate them into the secret; but I could only in

* The influence which the "Hakeem Sahib" has generally exercised in the British embassy at Teheran, and the employment of such men as Jukes, Campbell, M'Neill, Riach, Bell, Lord, and others, in various important duties in those countries, has naturally led the chiefs of Herat to suppose that "physicians" occupy a higher place in the councils of the English than is accorded to them, and they attribute much of the prosperity of the English nation to their "hikmut."—L.

a most learned discourse refer them to humanity, civilization, political economy, and the rights of man, assuring them that it was only to these and our principles of order and justice that we owed the riches they envied us. This they would not believe, and from that moment conceived the highest opinion of my diplomatic talents, admiring the cleverness with which I eluded their pressing and repeated inquiries.

The first few days of my stay at Herat were spent in thus receiving and returning visits. I had requested almost immediately after my arrival to be allowed to present my respects to Yar Mohamed; but upon the pretext of a feigned indisposition he delayed my reception from day to day. In thus adjourning it he hoped before seeing me to learn the object of the political mission with which I was charged; and my obstinacy in persisting in my first statement only confirmed him in the belief that I was a shrewd, cunning fellow, and *busior pookhte*, well cooked. In spite of this the Sertip did everything that lay in his power to make my semi-captivity as little irksome as possible; he often came himself to know whether his servants had attended to the orders he had given, and sometimes breakfasted with me—his conversation on these occasions furnished me with valuable information, which would have been particularly useful to me if I had been what he supposed—a *diplomate* in disguise. Though the Sertip's education had only been very limited, his opinions and reflections were generally correct, and bore the impress of great good sense; he was exceedingly good-natured, and his manners pleasing, and I saw that he wished to make himself agreeable, and sought to make it appear that he was sorry he was under the necessity of watching me. His brother and secretary often sounded me to know whether I would accept this or that present which he proposed to make me; but as I was well assured, in spite of his agreeable qualities, he was acting only upon the true Afghan feeling—that he who gives an egg expects an ox in return—I always repelled any advances that were made me of this kind, and accepted only his breakfasts, dinners, and a few melons which he occasionally sent me. I could refuse them without scruple, if not as his guest at least as his prisoner, and I never departed from this system during the whole time I was in Afghanistan. I never received and never gave; I purchased everything I required, and was always moderate in my expenses, in order not to excite the cupidity of the Afghans, whose natural and national propensity is to lay hands upon other people's property.

A PERSIAN GENTLEMAN. From a drawing by a Persian Artist

Page 151.

Sometimes the Sertip passed the evening with me, and brought with him some *bayadères*, whose dances were frequently prolonged into the night—these ladies were accompanied by a band of musicians, and the wine-cup circled with rapidity amongst them. The Sertip wished to include me in the libations, and seemed surprised that I showed so little inclination for them; but wine I had always eschewed since I had resided in hot climates, and for the best reason, namely, to avoid the inevitable consequences—broken health. The Sertip could not understand this self-denial in an European, for I only quaffed two cups of his wine during my stay, and it was not particularly good.* A Mussulman thinks more of strength than flavour, for his only idea in connection with drinking is to get drunk; the one has no attraction for him unless it is followed by the other, and, generally speaking, I found that the precepts of the Koran on this subject were very little attended to in these countries—if a man has the means of indulging himself, he gets drunk every night. No one may make wine at Herat; but the use of it is not altogether forbidden. To be positively authorised to drink it, a medical certificate is necessary, and this is readily given by the doctors, to whom the infirmity requiring this genial medicine is a source of revenue. The Sertip was the more chagrined at my abstemious habits, as he no doubt expected that I should in my cups let him into all my secrets; he tried this game several times without the least success, and I declined his pressing solicitations in so decided a manner, that he at length desisted.

Failing to accomplish his purpose with the assistance of Bacchus,

---

* The Afghans at Herat cannot understand the self-denial of Christians in declining to drink, when wine is not prohibited to them by their religion.

Shortly after our arrival at Herat, in walking across the garden one dark night, after dinner, without waiting for the lantern, on my return from the envoy's to my own residence, I struck my foot against the ledge of the "houz" (cistern surrounding the fountain), which happened to have been nearly emptied that day for the purpose of being cleaned out, and fell to the depth of nearly 8 feet, receiving a severe concussion. It was at once supposed by all the people of Herat that I had been drunk on the occasion, although by habit almost a "*tea-totaller*;" and all the kind condolences with which I was honoured by Shah Kamran and his family, and Yar Mohamed and his chiefs, were evidently offered under this impression. Nujoo Khan, the "*top-chee bashee*," himself a noted toper, wished me quietly, in confidence, to acknowledge that I had taken ("kudre-zeadah") a drop too much; and it was not until my habits were better known that I was exonerated from the suspicion. About a year afterwards, happening to go up to the citadel to the king, I found him drinking some Shirâz wine, which he also desired the "*athar bashee*," after I had been seated, to offer to me; and on observing that I had merely tasted it, the Shah said, with a knowing look, "Don't be afraid of it, there is no *houz* here!"—L.

he endeavoured to do so through the seductive influences of the bayadères. Those engaged by the Sertip for my amusement were ordered to captivate, and if possible enthral, the young Feringhee; but I must not raise the drop-scene of these ballets, and will merely add that his orders were executed to the letter.* The music to which they danced was not inharmonious or devoid of a certain merit; but the principal instrument, a small viol, being monotonous in the literal sense of that word, and the tone wiry, it was far from agreeable—the other instruments were much more pleasing to the ear. The tunes were varied and the execution good; and I should have listened with more attention to this part of the performance had it not served as an accompaniment to the voices of twelve herculean Afghans, who made themselves hoarse in their attempts to produce the most distressing sounds that can be conceived, he who howled the loudest being evidently considered the best singer.

Six days having elapsed since my arrival, and the physician Goolam Khader Khan, performing also the functions of astrologer, having observed a happy constellation, Yar Mohamed sent to say he was ready to receive me. His house was not a hundred yards from that of the Sertip, and I could easily have walked there, but this would have been an indignity to the great personage I was about to visit. I mounted, therefore, a splendid Turcoman horse, richly caparisoned, which the Sertip had ordered out for me, and escorted by a detachment of infantry and about thirty farraches, we commenced our formal march to the house of the Vezir Sahib. This was remarkable only for its great size. Within the exterior door was a large square court, and in the centre of this a reservoir of dirty water; small chambers opened into this court from either side, and the whole appearance gave one an idea of a caravanserai. In this square the newly-enrolled recruits are drilled under the eyes of the Vezir. When I entered the quadrangle it was full of troops, Afghans, Usbeks, and Parsivans, who were loitering about gossiping on the events of the day. My uniform having attracted general attention, I was soon surrounded by the crowd;

* It may be stated here, that had the same high sense of their responsibilities as Christian Englishmen, and the same anxiety not to compromise the dignity and character of their countrymen in the estimation of the rude people with whom they had been, for the first time, brought in contact, been uniformly shown by European officers at Caubul and Candahar, as at Herat, we might, humanly speaking, have been spared a very humiliating chapter in the history of Afghanistan. —L.

but the soldiers and farraches made a lane for me to pass through, and after going through various apartments and passages, in which were numerous scribes and petitioners, I arrived at the great audience-chamber, called the *Divan Khaneh*, which had not anything more remarkable about it than any other portion of the edifice. Yar Mohamed received me, attended only by a few of his officers. Nadzoo Khan, the head of the Ordnance department, the Serdar Hussein Khan, Hazarah, Feïz Mohamed Khan, Ishik Aghassi, master of the ceremonies, the Athar Bashee,* chief physician, Agha Hussein, and the Sertip, Lal Mohamed Khan, being the only individuals who had obtained permission to be present at this interview. Directly I appeared at the entrance of the Divan Khaneh, the Vezir rose, advanced three steps towards me, and taking my hand shook it heartily; he then resumed his seat, and made me take one by his side. The Vezir was tall, his features hard but expressive, and strongly marked. Though sixty years of age, if not more, he had the appearance of a man of fifty; his dress was made of Kashmir shawls; but, unlike his subjects who wear the turban, he had adopted the black lambskin cap of the Persians. I was informed that this head-gear was intended as a compliment to the Shah of Persia. A stranger cannot please a Persian more than by wearing this head-dress; hats and caps they hold in abhorrence, considering them as the distinctive badge of European nations, and of that power which has so frequently humiliated them. Officers in the Persian service may, without annoyance or inconvenience, wear their European dress; but if they wish to make themselves popular, they will certainly change their hat or cap for the black lambskin; and this, as a matter of taste, is certainly much to be preferred to either.† In giving up the turban, the cunning Vezir wished it to be believed that he was devoted to the dynasty of the Kajars.

The affable manners of the Khan soon put me at my ease, and after we had smoked a kalioon tea was served, a cup of which he took himself from the *pich-khetmet* and offered it to me; in fact,

* The Athar Bashee was for many years the most trusted servant of Shah Kamran, and to him the people of Herat, especially the Parsivans, were much indebted for his influence in protecting them against the occasional fury of the king and the tyranny of Yar Mohamed. He was much respected, and was supposed to have been the only man of consequence at Herat who had not been engaged in slave-dealing. —L.

† I have seen Yar Mohamed wear such a cap when he had no wish to pay a compliment to the Persian king. The lambskin-cap is generally worn by Jumsheedees, Hazarahs, and other *Soonee* tribes in the neighbourhood, but of a smaller size and different shape from the Kajar cap.—L.

he treated me with so much consideration that I really felt confused. Politeness is carried to a great extent in Eastern courts; but the rules of etiquette are also exceedingly rigid, and invariably observed, and if these are occasionally departed from with Europeans, it must be confessed that it is due to the English, who have shown that they know how to make themselves respected in these countries: the youngest ensign in the service of the East India Company receives the most distinguished honours when he passes through the principalities of Central Asia that border on their territory. After a mutual interchange of compliments, Yar Mohamed launched into politics. "You are an Englishman," said he, abruptly; "I know it, why therefore concealment? Come now, tell me what are your intentions? If I have been to blame with your Government, I have a right to complain of their conduct to me—let bygones be bygones. There is something to be said on both sides; our political relations can again be renewed, and on a friendly footing, and I will be as sincere as you can have a right to expect; the duplicity that I formerly practised to Pottinger and Todd Sahebs ought not to lower me in your opinion: they excited the anger of that old drunkard the Shah Kamran against me; my life was at stake, and it was high time that I should defend it. I was in a state of continual alarm, but this has ceased since his death; at the present time all authority is centered in me—the Afghans are devoted to me, and I have got rid of the Persians: speak to me, then, without reserve, and if your alliance can be useful to me, mine may be of service to you."

I felt so embarrassed that I scarcely knew how to reply to this sudden expression of his opinion, given too with a tone of assurance which proved his profound conviction of my being an Englishman. The Vezir saw by my countenance that I did not feel very comfortable, for he made an observation to that effect. The feeling was, however, transient; I declared that I was not an Englishman, I protested most energetically against the supposition that I had any political intentions, mischievous or otherwise; and that the surveillance with which he had surrounded me was unjustifiable. This produced excuses on his part; he dwelt on the difficulties of his position, on the conduct of the English who had previously been at Herat—it was not, he said, of a nature calculated to tranquillize him respecting the intentions of those who might come after them; and, getting by degrees more and more excited, he continued as follows:—"I knew too well the projects of the English to be sincere with them, their influence would have become far too deep-rooted at Herat to have suited me; they left, it is true, a good deal of money in the province, but not that I might profit by it. I feigned to be their dupe, but I never was. When I went out on horseback with Major Todd I used to help him on his horse, allowed him to ride in front of me to gratify his vanity, but I filled my coffers at his expense; when he ceased to be generous I ceased to serve him; he wished to upset me, but I sent him out of Herat, and he is now little esteemed by his superiors. Such is this world—everything is written in the book of fate; if fortune has decided in my favour, it is because God willed it so. All your armies and gold cannot contend against the will of Heaven. If you have arrived here with different views from your predecessors, speak frankly, we will be friends; pay me well, and I will be your very humble and devoted servant; but if your business here is to intrigue, I shall not permit it. Not one hair of your head will be hurt, you may even remain here if you like, but treated as you have been up to this time; you are also equally at liberty to leave Herat: decide." *

It took me at least an hour of denials and protestations to convince Yar Mohamed that I was not an Englishman; and the conversation, which to my great regret, had at one time become more animated than was agreeable, settled down into a more kindly spirit—the Vezir's suspicions were moderated, and Eastern politics

* The account given by M. Ferrier of his interview with Yar Mohamed is very interesting, and I have no doubt most accurate. He appears thoroughly to have understood and appreciated the character of the Vezir.

Yar Mohamed was quite right in supposing that the influence of the English at Herat would have become far too deep-rooted to have suited him. Even at the time that the mission left the city, I believe that it would have been quite possible for us to have retained our position there in spite of him, had it been considered expedient to have risked a collision. It did not accord with his policy that any of his subjects should be protected, by the presence of the mission, against the oppression of his soldiers, or that, under the superintendence of British officers, money should be expended in opening canals, repairing roads, giving advances to cultivators and manufacturers, and restoring the country to the state of comparative prosperity which had existed before the invasion of the Persians.

I have little doubt that, had the arrangement made by Eldred Pottinger been continued, of making payment directly from the British Treasury, instead of through Yar Mohamed, we might have held possession of Herat throughout all the subsequent reverses in Afghanistan. The estimation in which English officers were held by the people of Herat is confirmed by Wolf in his account of his journey to Bokhara; and even Yar Mohamed can scarcely have entertained any *acrimonious* feeling towards them, although he may have considered himself fortunate in getting rid of their influence.

From my personal knowledge of the present ruler, Shahzadah-Mahomed Yussuf, I am satisfied that he will be at any time ready to enter into friendly relations with us.—L.

dismissed. The power, wealth, and intelligence of the different European states were then discussed, and the arts and sciences, railways, balloons, and finally the electric telegraph. The opinions enunciated by the Vezir, so far as they were connected with subjects which he could understand, were characterised by great good sense; and I came to the conclusion that instruction alone was required to have made him a very superior man. But on many subjects he was deplorably ignorant; and, like the generality of Asiatics, full of illusions which could not be dispelled. The Khan has numerous mines of iron, lead, silver, and even auriferous copper, and is burning to work them; and I need scarcely say they would increase his revenues. He would also like to have mills for spinning and weaving wool, silk, and cotton, with European machinery—to have a manufactory of arms, a cannon foundry, &c.; but he would like to have all this Afghan fashion, that is to say, without the necessary outlay. The Vezir has also the Eastern caprice of supposing that everything can be done in the least possible time; that one man ought to have a knowledge of everything, be able to undertake twenty different kinds of employment, and find in the province of Herat, where there is nothing, the means for carrying out all his projects.

The Khan appeared to take a great interest in everything connected with the military profession, and put a number of questions to me on this subject which showed considerable judgment; he spoke also, and at great length, of the defence he made against the Persians, and attributed their want of success to the cowardice and treason of their chiefs. He mentioned, however, in high terms the bravery of the troops, and furnished me with much curious information respecting the siege; his mode of ascertaining the direction in which the besiegers were carrying the galleries of their mines to reach the ditch of the place was very ingenious. Plates were filled with as much small seed as they would hold, and placed upon the ground in those spots under which it was presumed the sappers were at work; and, in spite of all their precautions, the least concussion or blow from a spade or pick brought down a few grains from the heap, and discovered their position.

My interview with Yar Mohamed lasted three hours, and though at times a certain tinge of acrimonious feeling was observable, originating in the fixed idea that I was an Englishman, I nevertheless left his house satisfied with my reception; for I could plainly perceive that, in spite of this, there was a kind feeling for a stranger, to whom he was anxious to show hospitality. It was difficult to believe that he was the man who had strangled his sovereign, who had ordered the execution of so many unhappy beings, and sold his subjects by hundreds to the Turcomans, including even the princesses of the blood—such, however, was the sad truth. During the lifetime of the Shah Kamran, Yar Mohamed had carefully removed from office nearly all those who had taken umbrage at the position he had acquired ; but, after the death of the Shah, completed the work by admitting Afghans only to places of public trust devoted for a length of time to his interests, or men of his own tribe. He was wily enough to make it appear that his officers were the cause of many severe acts, and testified great anxiety to do justice to the sufferers directly a complaint was brought before him ; and there was policy in this, for he was desirous of destroying that unanimity, so hostile to the sovereign, which usually exists between the turbulent Afghans and their subaltern chiefs, and to uphold one against the other. This system answered admirably, inasmuch as he showed great impartiality in settling the differences which arose between them, and his sovereignty is now perfectly established in Herat. The dynasty of the Suddozyes, the Kamran branch, dethroned by him in 1842, has not the least chance, at any rate during the Vezir's lifetime, of returning to power.* Four individuals shared the confidence of Yar Mohamed when I was at Herat: Feiz Mohamed Khan, Sertip Lal Mohamed, Najoo Khan, and Mirza Nejef Khan.†

* Since Yar Mohamed's death in 1852, his son Syud Mohamed Khan has held the government of Herat on a very uneasy tenure, both on account of his weak personal character, and of the difficulties bequeathed him by his father. His first care was to send a number of the Heratian nobles, including Najoo Khan, ostensibly on a mission to the Shah, but in reality as prisoners, having previously arranged with the Persian government that they should be detained or otherwise got rid of. The Persian government accordingly made away with Najoo Khan and some others, and would probably have destroyed the whole party had not the British government interfered and procured their release. Of those released a few remained in the service of the Shah, but the majority sought refuge at Candahar, passing through Bagdad to Mecca, and thence returning through Beloochistan to their own country.

Mohamed Youssouf Shahzadah, who has been recently invited by the inhabitants to assume the government of Herat, and who now reigns there, belongs to the ancient Suddozye family, being a grandson of Hajji Feroze, who was brother to Shah Zamaun, Shah Mahmoud, and Shah Shooja, who was placed on the throne of Cabul by the English in 1839. Yar Mohamed was minister to the Suddozye prince, Shah Kamran, and, as before related, murdered his master, and usurped the throne.—ED.

† The first was killed in 1847, in an encounter with the Hazarahs; the second died, and Najoo Khan lost the Vezir's friendship in consequence of some intrigues with the Chiefs of Kandahar, to whose tribe he belonged. There was, therefore, up to the time of Yar Mohamed's death, only one person of any importance at Herat except

The Mirza is of the ancient Parsivan race, or Parsi-zebán, as we should say in Persian, that is to say, the people who governed the country before the Afghans. Under his advice and protection a great number of Eïmaks,* such, for instance, as the Taymoonis and the Jemshidees, have come or have been forced to reside at Herat, where they live contented and happy; the Vezir treats them with the same consideration as the Afghans, who are much fewer in number all over the principality. But it may be doubted whether there is not some imprudence in thus augmenting day by day the subjugated race; they will submit to the yoke during Yar Mohamed's life, because he is just to them; but after his death, should they become discontented, they will, if possible, exterminate their conquerors; and the Afghans, who have only held Herat about a century, may possibly be under the necessity of taking refuge in Kandahar, the land of their birth. They are of the Sunnite sect of Mussulmans, whereas a large majority of the Parsivans are Shiahs, and for this reason they are and ever will be irreconcilable enemies.

From the peasant to the highest functionary every one has ready access to Yar Mohamed; he gives up six hours of every day to hear the complaints and listen to the petitions of his subjects, and deals out prompt, equitable, and severe justice to all.† Every one can travel through any part of his territory without fear of molestation, and the measures he has taken for the suppression of robbers have been so terrible that not one is to be found at the present time. This extraordinary security of the public roads of Herat is a fact unique of its kind amongst the numerous provinces of Central Asia, for the most part infested with thieves and bandits. The Heratians, who never before enjoyed such security for life and property, offer up many a fervent prayer that the Vezir may long reign over them. He is reproached only with having created new taxes, increased the old ones, and monopolised all the revenues; even the cobblers of Herat are laid under contribution, and there is no public establishment that does not pay something to the State—that is, himself. But the Vezir knows how to pluck the fowl without making it cry out too loud;

himself, his minister Nejef Khan, in whom he placed the greatest confidence.—ED.

* Of the Parsivan race, with this difference, that the Parsivans live in towns, and the Eïmaks are nomads and live in tents.—ED.

† This was a very wise measure. There is nothing so popular with Easterns as an open durbar, where all, from the highest to the lowest, may see the face of their sovereign.—ED.

he has taken lessons on this subject from the English, by which he has largely profited. His love of gold is certainly great; nevertheless he is not avaricious with those who serve him faithfully, and I have always heard his officers bear testimony to his generosity; but he is mean and miserly to the last degree with those from whom he expects nothing.

Since he dethroned Shah Kamran he has looked carefully to his personal safety; night and day six hundred men guard his house, though thirty would be sufficient: when he leaves the city at least a thousand men accompany him, and a native of India, a Mussulman, who enjoys his confidence, sleeps every night across the door of his bedroom. This man, who is a sergeant and drills his troops, also brings him his morning and evening meal, and in dishes that are closed with a padlock. The Sertip Lal Mohamed Khan, or his brother, always sleeps at his house armed at all points, and a saddled horse is kept in readiness for any emergency—every precaution, in short, is taken, and in most minute detail, to meet any adverse circumstances which might arise.

The family of Yar Mohamed had no political existence until his uncle, Atta Mohamed, became governor of Kashmir; he is the most remarkable man who has figured in his tribe up to the present time, and has on every occasion shown a courage, talent, and administrative capabilities which justify us in placing him in the first rank amongst the sovereigns of Afghanistan. It would have been fortunate for others had he been born to the high position he has attained, for he was under the necessity of acting as many an Eastern potentate has done in arriving at the possession of supreme power. If Yar Mohamed has performed many splendid actions, he may also be reproached with many crimes,—which is much to be regretted, for there is in this chief more than enough material to make one great man.*

On leaving the Vezir I took my way to the citadel, the commandant of which was Syud Mohamed Khan, the Vezir's eldest son, a handsome young fellow, of from twenty to twenty-two years of age, with agreeable manners. I found him surrounded by the principal chiefs of Herat, who paid assiduous court to him, in the hope of obtaining through his influence some favours of his

* Sir John M'Neill was also much struck with him, when he spent many hours with him at a midnight interview during the siege of Herat. He calls him "certainly one of the most remarkable men of his age and country."—See Persian Blue Book, 1838, p. 90.—ED.

father, whom he will probably succeed. Unfortunately, however, Mohamed Khan has not had the tact to win the sympathies of the Afghans, who for the most part think him a proud, haughty, and presumptuous man, incapable of directing the affairs of the country. It may, therefore, be expected that at his father's death a number of rivals will be found to dispute with him the sovereign power; and perhaps, for it is a circumstance frequently seen in Eastern affairs, he may find his brothers amongst his adversaries: there are two, both very young, but they promise even now to have all the energy and intelligence of their father. It is true that Yar Mohamed has endeavoured to strengthen the position of his eldest son, by marrying him to one of the daughters of the family actually reigning in Kabul; but when it is remembered how little the ties of blood are respected in Afghanistan, it must be admitted that his connection with Dost Mohamed may not prevent the fall of his son-in-law, to which contingency he will be decidedly exposed at his father's decease. His best chance of success will be in the support of Persia and the Parsivans; with that it is not improbable he will be able to defy all opposition. The reception I met with from the young chief was sufficiently polite; but his conversation convinced me that the Afghans were not wrong in the estimate they had formed of his capacity.* He showed me a splendid elephant, with which he amused himself from morning to night: it was a present from his brother-in-law, Mohamed Akbar Khan, to his betrothed wife, Bobodjan, the eldest daughter of Yar Mohamed.

My visit to Syud Mohamed being finished, I went to the house of the minister, Mirza Nejef Khan. His brother, Mirza Mir Ali, one of the richest merchants in Meshed, and whose acquaintance I had made during my short stay in that town, had recommended me to him in a manner which ensured me a kind and cordial reception; and in this my hopes were fully realised. The Mirza Nejef Khan is a young man for a minister, and appeared to me not more than thirty years of age; I found him lively, witty, and intelligent, and quite equal to the duties of the high

---

* The officers of the mission had formed a similar estimate of Syud Mohamed's capacity. During one of his visits at the Char-bhag, he expressed a wish to learn English, upon which a wag of the party offered to teach him a sentence, and under the impression that it was merely an ordinary English salutation, like "khoosh amedeed," taught him to say, "You are a spoon!" Full of the importance of the acquisition, although somewhat doubtful of the exact meaning, on meeting his father on his return home, he accosted him by saying, 'Agir-be-adebi na bashud" (if it be not disrespectful), "You are a spoon!"—L.

office entrusted to him. His bravery is equally well spoken of; but of this I had no opportunity of judging. I also saw the Sirdars Dad Khan, Shiriam Khan, Sultan Mohamed Khan,* Goolam Khan, and Emir Khan, all of them cousins-german of Yar Mohamed.† Suyd Elias and Suyd Futteh Shah, the two principal merchants in Herat, were most polite and attentive to me.‡

* This chief, in 1841, took refuge at Candahar from his cousin Yar Mohamed, and was of great service to the English during the subsequent troubles in the country, raising a considerable body of Alikozye horsemen, for such service as was required of them.—ED.

† Those who knew Sirdar Futteh Khan will regret extremely to miss his name out of this list. His loyalty and faithfulness to the English mission were in bright contrast to the treachery of other members of Yar Mohamed's family, and to his services we were largely indebted.—L.

‡ The following extract of a letter from Sir John M'Neill to Viscount Palmerston, dated Meshed, June 25, 1838, will serve to show the importance of Herat:—

"The key of all Afghanistan towards the north is Herat; and though I can have no right to press my personal opinions upon your lordship after having already stated them, and although I must necessarily be ignorant of the many important considerations not immediately connected with this question which must influence the policy of her Majesty's Government, still I cannot refrain from saying a few words more regarding the importance of preserving the independence of Herat.

"I have already informed your lordship publicly, that the country between the frontiers of Persia and India is far more productive than I had imagined it to be; and I can assure your lordship that there is no impediment, either from the physical features of the country or from the deficiency of supplies, to the march of a large army from the frontiers of Georgia to Kandahar, or, as I believe, to the Indus.

"Count Simonich being lame from a wound, drove his carriage from Teheran to Herat, and could drive it to Kandahar; and the Shah's army has now for nearly seven months subsisted almost exclusively on the supplies of the country immediately around Herat and Ghorian, leaving the still more productive districts of Subzar and Furrah untouched.

"In short, I can state from personal observation that there is absolutely no impediment to the march of an army to Herat; and that, from all the information I have received, the country between that city and Kandahar not only presents no difficulty, but affords remarkable facilities for the passage of armies.

"There is therefore, my lord, no security for India in the nature of the country through which an army would have to pass to invade it from this side.

"On the contrary, the whole line is peculiarly favourable for such an enterprise; and I am the more anxious to state this opinion clearly, because it is at variance with my previous belief, and with statements which I may have previously hazarded, relying on more imperfect information.

"Under such circumstances, it appears to me that it would be a most hazardous policy to allow Persia to act as the pioneer of Russia, and under protection of the article of the treaty, to break down the main defence of Afghanistan, and thereby make the country untenable to us, at a moment when the concert between Persia and Russia in these operations is avowed." * * * * *

"It is currently reported and believed here, though I cannot say on what grounds, that there is a secret arrangement between Persia and Russia to exchange Herat for some of the districts beyond the Arras which formerly belonged to Persia.

"This report was first mentioned to me at Teheran, in March last; but I then paid no attention to it, because I could not see how Russia was to get at Herat, and I still am inclined to regard it as probably unfounded, though Count Simonich certainly threatened Mahommed Ameen, a servant of Yar Mahommed Khan (who was sent with a message from his master to the Persian camp), that if Herat did not surrender to the Shah, he would march a Russian army against it."—See Blue Book, pp. 131, 132.—ED.

CHAPTER XII.

Excursion in the environs — Uzbeks from Kundooz — Descendants of Alexander the Great — The Greeks — Of the Asiatic Dynasties — The sites of ancient cities — Artakoana, Aria Metropolis, and Sous — The seven sieges of Herat — Tooli Khan — Massacre by Ghengis Khan — Tamerlane — Obeid Khan — Herat sacked by the Uzbeks — Fortified by Shah Rokh Mirza — The actual position of Herat — The fortifications — The citadel — Improvements by the English engineers — Population before the siege and after — Yar Mohamed's acts at this time — His subsequent conduct — Persian cities as readily rebuilt as destroyed — Devastation at the siege of 1838 — The bazaars — The architect and the cupola — Public buildings at Herat.

THE day after I had made my round of visits to the distinguished persons mentioned in the last chapter I took a long walk in the environs of the town, and continued my excursion as far as the foot of the mountains and the royal residences of the Takht-sefer and Gazergah. Ascending the ridge of these hills, on the look-out for partridges, which I expected but did not find there, I entered a ravine, and came upon two enormous wolves and their three wolverines—most of them were quietly seated on their haunches, and seemed not the least concerned at my presence; nor did they retire until I had fired one barrel at them, though without effect.

On reaching Gazergah I was much surprised to find there a small encampment of persons in the dress of Uzbeks, but whose configuration of features clearly indicated quite another origin. Enquiring from whence they were, I was informed that they had come from Hazarat Imaum, a small town situated to the north of Kundooz, and were on a pilgrimage to Meshed, to propitiate the Mollahs in their favour with the Imaum Reza. Their language was a bastard Persian, which increased my astonishment; for the primitive Turk or Tartar is the language of the country in which they live. The singularity of this circumstance awakened my curiosity; and with a view to further and more positive information, I approached their encampment and conversed with them myself. They stated that they were the descendants of the Yoonanes (Greeks) that Alexander the Great, *Iskander Roomi*, had left in these countries; and when I heard this I recollected that Marco Polo, and after him Burnes, as well as other writers on Oriental history, mentioned the existence of Macedonian tribes which had settled on the north-west frontier of Chinese Tartary. I wished to convince myself that they had not been led into error on this subject; and, from the replies I received to the numerous questions I put to these people, I was convinced of the existence of the real descendants of the ancient Greeks in those countries.* These Younanes are not isolated and dispersed here and there, but united in tribes, occupying a considerable tract of country; nothing, however, either in their language or their habits, betrays their origin. They are Mussulmans, and have the reputation of being somewhat fanatical, and are not held in much consideration by the Tartars, amongst whom they are settled; but they are respected, for, like their ancestors, they are brave, and the consequences of their hatred are terrible to those who are the object of it. Burnes, while admitting the existence of the descendants of these Greeks in Central Asia, appears to doubt whether some of their chiefs are, as they affirm, the descendants of Alexander, for the historians of the son of Philip assure us that he left no heir to reap the fruits of his immense conquests.†

This may be true as to legitimate heirs; but the same historians mention several circumstances which lead to the conclusion that the great warrior bowed his plumed helmet to Venus, and he probably left several of his race in various provinces of the countries west of the Indus. The following quotation from Quintus Curtius confirms this supposition:—"After the Macedonians had laid siege to, and reduced to the last extremity, the town of Massaga, the queen of that country, named Cleophe, made her submission to Alexander, and came herself with a large train, accompanied by a numerous retinue of ladies, to meet the king. With her was an only son, whom she led to the conqueror's feet; Alexander raised him from the ground, and reinstated her in full possession of her kingdom. It is said that it was rather to the beauty of the queen than to the

* On the Kaffirs, see Appendices.

† The descendants of the Greeks mentioned by Burnes are not Mohammedans—they are called "Siah Posht Kaffirs," and live in the valleys of the Hindoo Koosh, to the north of the Caubul river. The persons here mentioned may have been "Taujiks," from the neighbourhood of Koondooz.—L.

merciful disposition of her conqueror that this happy result was to be attributed—the child she had by him was called by his name." As the son of Philip had these relations with Cleophe, it is perfectly possible that he was not insensible to the charms of several other great ladies in those countries, and that the offspring resulting from these irregular and itinerant rencontres perpetuated his race, who were looked up to with veneration and respect by the Macedonians that remained in Tartary. For my own part I see nothing in this supposition but what is very natural; for Asiatics in this country make no difference between the children of different women by the same father; they are equally entitled to his support and protection; all are legitimate, and there is little difference in their rights, whatever may have been the nature of the tie that has existed between the father and mother.

Herat is at the present time the asylum of all the fallen greatness of past centuries. Here are to be seen the descendants of Ghengis Khan, of Tamerlane, and Nadir Shah. I was introduced to a great-grandson of the latter, Agha Ahmed Mirza, who, possessed of large landed property, superintended it himself, and preferred a peaceful and retired life to one surrounded by the dangers attendant upon power. The English, who have a happy knack of making a profitable use of princes on half-pay, were so considerate as to give him a pension when they occupied Afghanistan. Since their evacuation of that country the pension has been withdrawn.*

The territory of Herat corresponds pretty nearly with the territory called Aria by the historians of Alexander, the principal cities of which were, according to them, Artakoana, Aria Metropolis, Sousia, Akhala, and Candace. I must confess that in spite of every possible effort of imagination I could never comprehend how Artakoana could be any other than the city of Aria Metropolis spoken of by Ptolemy. The more I reflected the less I could account for the separate existence of these two capitals, and I am led to the belief that the one was only a continuation of the other. If we suppose that Artakoana was really a distinctt city

---

* Among those who received advances for cultivation of his lands, or other allowances, was a chief from the borders of the Seistan desert, who was said to have traced his descent from *Darius*.—L.

from Aria Metropolis, it could only have been a town or locality of inferior importance, at which the princes of Aria generally passed the summer months, and this may have led historians to suppose it was a capital. This was, however, but another repetition of the custom of the Persian kings, who retired from Persepolis, the ruins of which are still to be seen near Istakhr, to pass the summer months in another town of the same name, situated in the cool and verdant valley of the Moroghab, fifteen parasangs more to the north. Were there not also two Ecbatanas, the summer and the winter one? If this supposition with reference to Artakoana and Aria Metropolis is not correct, then the town of Kussan, whose ancient ruins, beautiful climate, and charming situation on the banks of the Heri-rood, indicate the spot on which once stood this ancient city.

But in advancing this supposition I do it with some reservation, and for this reason: the admirable position occupied by Herat must at all times have attracted the attention of the sovereigns of Persia—there is not a position of more importance in a strategical and commercial point of view, and the fertility of the soil is great. On this plain, in the centre of which the city stands, the great roads from all the principal countries of Asia meet; the numerous streams of water that furrow the sides of the adjoining mountains would flow uselessly through the plain, and lose their fertilizing powers in the Heri-rood, if Herat and its suburbs did not intercept them. The benefits arising from the presence of these abundant streams have been much too greatly appreciated at all times by the inhabitants for them to have ever thought of removing to a district less favoured by nature. There will be, I am aware, a difference on this point between myself and other authors who have written upon the same subject; but I have met with few amongst them whose opinions agree even among themselves as to many things connected with the ancient history of Central Asia. The impressions taken from the writings of travellers often differ sensibly from those formed on seeing the localities themselves. I believe we are all more or less alike when we endeavour to fix the sites of ancient cities; we are like the etymologists—the mind plunges into an infinity of suppositions equally vague and problematical, and without producing any very enlightened results; nevertheless, as we are all agreed in thinking that these cannot exist except by the contact of various opinions, I will mention a few of mine, even at the risk of entangling the question a little more than it was before.

Why, for example, call Zeuzan, a little locality in which not the faintest traces of ancient ruins are found, the site of the ancient Sousia of Aria? It seems to me that the resemblance existing between the name of this ancient city and that of Tous (the modern Meshed),* a name which, except the first letter, is identical with it, and the difference in the orthography of which is sufficiently explained by the alterations in the language, ought rather to make us conclude that this latter city is the Sous mentioned by Arrian, who places it on the borders of the Arian territory. All my reflections and researches did not enable me to fix even approximatively the position of the city of Khandak.

But to return to Aria Metropolis. Persian authors, whose works merit some attention, mention only one capital of Aria, which they designate by the name of Heri. This no doubt gave it to the principality, as in our days Ispahan and Yezd give their names to the governments of which they are the chief places. The city of Heri is said by the Persians to have been founded by Lohrasp, to have been increased by Gustasp, and to have been greatly ornamented and embellished by Bahman. They add that it was finished by Alexander the Great, who ordered his lieutenant Haree, perhaps Aræus, to fortify it. It would be difficult to contest the truth of this narrative, so far as Alexander is concerned, as it entirely agrees on every point with those of the Greek historians. It was indeed impossible that a city of such importance, both with reference to its position and the fertility of the soil in its neighbourhood, should not be turned to a useful account by the Macedonian conqueror, who must have made it the principal depôt for his supplies of every kind before he advanced to the Indian frontier.

What, however, is less likely, is the conviction the Heratians entertain, that their city has never undergone any change since the time of Alexander. They pretend, and what is more, ask you to believe, that the fortifications which now protect them are the very same that were erected by that monarch. Their own history is there to prove to them the contrary; and in consulting its pages,

* The ruins of Tous are, however, situated thirty miles N.W. of Meshed, and the name still remains.—ED.

which can be done for the last nine centuries, there are to be found at least seven occasions in which Herat, if not completely destroyed, was so laid waste as to necessitate its entire reconstruction.

The first catastrophe which befell Herat occurred in the twelfth century. In the reign of the Sultan Sanjar, and about the year 1157 (Hejira 544), it fell into the hands of the Turcomans, who committed the most frightful ravages, and left not one stone upon another.

The second ordeal was equally deplorable, as the following brief account will testify. "This town," says Herbelot, "was the largest of the three capitals of Khorassan (the other two were Merv and Neshapoor) which were besieged by Tooli Khan;* the city was defended by Mohamed Goorgani, governor of the province, who had under his command a considerable army; and, accordingly, during the first seven days of the siege, Mohamed made such frequent and vigorous sorties that the Mongols were soon made aware that they were not likely to finish this enterprise so easily as they had done the preceding ones; but it happened shortly after that the intelligent and gallant governor was unfortunately killed by an arrow. After his death the besieged gradually lost courage, and already talked of surrendering. When Tooli Khan heard this, which he did from his spies, he advanced with only two hundred horse to one of the gates, to confer with those citizens who were the most inclined for peace. To them he declared that if they would voluntarily surrender—and he was in a condition to force them—he would respect their lives and property; also, that he would be satisfied if they paid him half the tribute which they had hitherto given to the Sultan of Khooarezm. The Khan having pledged his word, and confirmed by a solemn oath the terms of the capitulation, the citizens of Herat opened their gates and received him with every honour. Tooli Khan religiously observed the conditions of the treaty, and would not permit the Mongols to commit the least excess; the garrison, however, with whom he had not capitulated, was put to death; and naming as their future governor Malek Aboo Bekr, he hastened to rejoin his father at the siege of Thaleh, Khan Talighàn. But the destruction of this noble city having, says Khondemir, been

* Tooli means "a mirror" in Mongol. Tooli Khan received his name because of his great likeness to his father, Gengis Khan. See D'Herbelot.—ED.

decreed by the Divine will, it soon came to pass; for a rumour having spread through the country that the Mongols had been defeated by Jellal Eddin near the town of Ghuzni, the inhabitants of the cities of Khorassan in which Tooli Khan had left governors rose simultaneously, and put all the Mongols to death who fell into their hands. The people of Herat were no exception; they massacred the governor Malek Aboo Bekr and his small force, and placed the defence of the city in the hands of Mobarek Eddin, of the town of Subzawar. Ghengis Khan, having been apprised of these reverses, roughly reprimanded his son Tooli for having by a false clemency spared the lives of his enemies and put it in their power to play him this trick, sent 80,000 horse to Herat, to take their revenge. The siege lasted six months, during which time the inhabitants fought with all the energy of despair, and made most extraordinary efforts in conducting the defence; but, being at length overcome, they were all put to death without mercy, to the number of 1,600,000.* The Emir Khovend Shah states that the physician Sharf Eddin Khatib, with fifteen of the inhabitants, who had concealed themselves in some grottoes and remained there undiscovered, and were afterwards joined by twenty-four other persons, were the only individuals that escaped, as if by a miracle, the general massacre. These forty persons resided in Herat for fifteen years before there was any increase in the number of inhabitants, so complete had been the destruction. This deplorable event took place in the year 1232 (Hejira 619).

Tamerlane, another devastator and scourge of the human race, closely imitated the example of Ghengis Khan by carrying fire and sword into every part of Khorassan.† Ghyaz Eddin, then sovereign prince of Herat, was the first who attempted to withstand the Tartar conqueror, but the danger increased with the length of the contest, and he surrendered at discretion. Tamerlane, to punish him for having thought of arresting his course, dismantled the fortifications of Herat and the citadel, and levied so large a contribution upon the inhabitants, that they were reduced to utter

* If these numbers apply to the city of Herat only, it is incontestable that it must have been much larger than it is now, for it could at the utmost contain only 100,000 persons.

† The Orientals say that three millions of souls were destroyed in this massacre, being the people of Balkh, Nishapoor, Merve, and Herat.—ED.

misery. He also seized the territory and the immense riches of Ghyaz Eddin. The governor, who under the protection of Tamerlane succeeded this chief, dying in 1398 (Hejira 785), a revolt ensued, when the inhabitants declared in favour of his predecessor, and the extermination of the Mongol garrison was the result. At the time this occurrence took place, Mirane Shah, a son of Tamerlane, happened to be at three days' march from Herat, on the banks of the Moorghab, and, hearing of the disaster, entered the city with a large force, laid it waste, decimated the inhabitants, and nearly destroyed the place.

The same fate awaited it in the reign of Olong Beg, the grandson of Tamerlane. This prince was at war with his nephews, Mirza Baboor and Allah ed Doulet; and the Heratians, thinking the moment favourable, again revolted: a Tartar chief, Yar Ali, was placed at their head; but Olong Beg having arrived, the former was defeated, and the city once more became a heap of ruins; the citadel, which opened its gates, was spared.

In 1477 (Hejira 864), and in the reign of Aboo Seid, of the race of the Timorides, a Turcoman prince, named Jehan, Shah of the dynasty of the Black Sheep (a very appropriate designation), again ravaged Herat; and the famine which ensued from the destruction of the crops nearly depopulated the country.

In 1554 (Hejira 941) the same fate attended it at the hands of Obeid Khan, an Uzbek prince, who burnt and pillaged everything up to the very walls of the citadel, which alone remained.

Finally, on the occasion of the seventh and last destruction of Herat in 1607 (Hejira 994), and in the reign of Shah Abbas the Great, it was once more sacked by the Uzbeks, commanded by Abdul Moomeen Khan.

How, therefore, after having been so utterly destroyed on so many occasions, is it possible that the existing fortifications should be those raised by order of Alexander the Great? From careful observation of this city and its environs during my residence there, I feel convinced that its present enceinte extends only to the area of the ancient citadel, and that the fort now called by that name was the castle of Ekhtiar Eddin, and a mere outwork; the fortifications actually existing are probably those constructed by Shah Rokh Mirza, a son of Tamerlane. This prince was the viceroy of the territory of Herat, of which he continued to retain possession after the death of his father; this city, for which he had an especial predilection, became the capital of his kingdom, and he spent immense sums in raising it from its ruins. In 1431 (Hejira 818) the ramparts which his father had thrown down were rebuilt, and he employed 7000 men in this great work.

The area on which the city of Herat now stands is about a parasang square, the sides facing east and west being longer than those on the north and south; it owes its strength to the enormous earthwork that surrounds it.* Tradition says that this was formed by the débris of the high and massive walls that were thrown down by the Macedonians, with a view of building new ones in their place. This continuous embankment is formed of excessively hard earth, heaped up, and it is easy to see that a great part of it was dug out of the interior of the town and to a great depth, as well as a little from the exterior. It is supported on the interior by a counterfort of sun-dried bricks, and on the exterior has a slope at a considerable angle, the base of which rests in a large and deep ditch, that can be filled with water or laid dry at pleasure. The height of this earthen rampart is not the same in every part, but, on an average, it may be considered as measuring about ninety feet. There are on it a great number of towers, distant about fifty feet from one another, connected by curtains and loopholed for musketry; the towers at the angles are massive, and on these only can guns be mounted: two covered ways, cut out of the thickness of the rampart, contribute very much to the strength of the place.

The citadel, that is to say, the Castle of Ikhtiar Eddin,† is situated to the north and within the enceinte of the city. This fortress is square, with large towers at the angles, and built of burnt brick; it stands on an artificial mound of higher elevation than the walls of the city, and is surrounded, like the exterior rampart, by a large and deep ditch, which is crossed by a drawbridge, and can be flooded at will. This work commands the town and the road from Meshed, and it would be difficult, if not impossible, to attack it with success, even with batteries on the heights of Thaleh-bengy, the only point where they could be placed with advantage.‡

* The area of Herat within the ditch is as near as possible a mile square; the extent of the ditch will therefore be about a parasang, as stated. Accurate plans of the city and fortifications were sent to the Military Board in India by the late Colonel Edward Sanders.—L.

† Ikhtiar means "power—authority," in Turkish.

‡ See Kaye's Affghanistan.

After the siege of Herat by the Persians in 1838, some English officers of Engineers,* under the directions of Major Todd, the British Resident at the Court of the Shah Kamran, restored a part of the fortifications; the line of the ditch of the enceinte appearing to them weak, they filled it up at several points, and dug another more in advance. This has given a greater elevation to the rampart, and a better and more plunging fire to the guns enfilading the ditch, in which they likewise placed several *caponnierès.*† The towers at the angles were also made more salient, and the gates to some extent altered, so that an attack would be much more difficult than it was during the siege of 1838. These alterations have unfortunately been carried out on two sides only; the other two are in bad repair, and attackable, if not accessible, on several points. If the improvements effected in the fortifications of Herat by these officers had been completed, they would have proved an efficient protection from the attacks of the Afghans, Uzbeks, and Persians; but were an European army to lay siege to it, the defence could not last twenty days, for it is, after all, but an immense redoubt, and, like all works of the kind, has the defect of four dead angles and a ditch difficult to defend. Herat cannot really be strong until works are erected which will flank those that now exist, and these are not likely to be made by Persians, still less by Afghans. The nature of the soil would offer considerable difficulties to any mining operations, for water rises freely at from nine to twelve feet, and the troops of Mohamed Shah had to make incredible efforts to drain their trenches and communications; the besieged did not experience the same difficulty, because they were enabled to carry down their mines from the first covered way by cutting though the thickness of the rampart: the two parties more frequently encountered each other in the ditch than elsewhere; here there were some bloody encounters, and several thousand men perished in them.

Herat contained a population of at least 70,000 souls before this siege, and when it was raised there were at the outside not more than six or seven thousand persons. This extraordinary decrease is to be accounted for by the great emigration that took

---

* Major Sanders, of the Bengal Engineers, an officer of first-rate professional ability, with the assistance of Captain North of the Bombay army, planned and executed these defences. Major Sanders was killed at the battle of Maharajpore.—ED.

† *i.e.* Flanking defences for the ditch.

place, the casualties during the siege, and the deaths by famine. The mortality continued long after it was over, and was of a most fearful and heartrending character; many of the unfortunate Heratians, to escape its terrors, sold themselves to the Turcomans as slaves, to provide food for their wives and children. Yar Mohamed was then in as great a difficulty as any one else during this frightful visitation, and he met the difficulty in the most pitiless manner; for the least fault, probably without any, he sold the Parsivans to procure provisions, and bartered four or five against a horse or a few quarters of wheat. His officers and agents traversed the city, and endeavoured to excite the people that he might have an excuse for selling them in a greater number to the Turcomans; the inhabitants, however, perceived the snare, and remained quietly in their houses: but Yar Mohamed was not, however, to be foiled; he closed all the outlets of the bazaars at an hour of the day when they were the most crowded, drew up his troops at these points, seized indiscriminately all he could lay his hands on, and sold them to obtain funds.

Since these sad episodes took place, the Vezir has usurped the sovereign authority and enriched himself with English gold, and under his altered circumstances has given up a horrible traffic, which he justified by the necessities of the times. Since the year 1842 he has endeavoured to repeople Herat with several thousand nomads, Hazarahs, Jumshidies, and Taymoonees, whom he made prisoners in the expeditions he has at various times successfully undertaken against these tribes. At the period of my visit every one enjoyed the most complete security, and commerce and agriculture had greatly developed themselves during the last few years. An amnesty had been granted to the Heratians who fled to Persia or the English territories, and they have returned to their native city in considerable numbers. The population in 1845 amounted to from 20,000 to 22,000 souls, and ten years hence there will scarcely be any traces left of the disasters of the great siege.

It is easy to understand how Eastern cities built almost entirely of earth, and inhabited by half-nomadic tribes, are so readily destroyed and deserted, and for the same reasons the facility and rapidity with which they again rise to importance: the materials, earth and a little plaster, are found on the spot and cost nothing, and, generally speaking, the members of each family, men and women, construct their houses with their own hands. The doors and windows, the only carpenter's work required, cost but a trifle in this country; the rooms are vaulted. It is easy, therefore, to understand how Alexander the Great was enabled to build so many large towns in Central Asia. With his army he could in ten or fifteen days construct several thousand dwellings; and, considering that the walls were of straw and clay only, it is not very singular that no traces of them should now be left; for when these houses fell, either from the effects of time or by the hands of the enemy, they again mingled with the soil from which they were raised.

Though the population of Herat has continually increased during the last three years, it will be a long time before the ruins are all cleared away, for only one house in five at the utmost is inhabited, or in a condition to be so. Buildings of all kinds, caravansarais, bazaars, baths, &c. were nearly all destroyed by the Persian shells or fell to the earth from being abandoned by their owners. The besieged also pulled down many of those nearest to the walls to repair the breaches made by the enemies' guns. Nothing can be imagined more desolate than the appearance of the city in 1845; the traces of the wanton destruction of gardens and houses in the environs, originally so picturesque and fertile, was still apparent; villages and handsome esplanades, shaded by beautiful trees, have completely disappeared. The Persian troops during the ten months' siege, one of the most memorable in the annals of Eastern history, made greater havoc and devastation than if the country had been a prey to civil wars for a hundred years. Not one of the splendid trees which were the pride of the inhabitants and ornament of the suburbs was spared, everything was levelled to the ground by these Vandals, and on their departure the town and country round was one scene of desolation and ruin.

The greater number of the bazaars at the period of my visit were in a dilapidated state; a portion of those of the *Char Sook*, the four streets, were the only ones in good repair. The houses in these four streets are built of burnt bricks, and vaulted; there are shops on either side, and the four extremities of the streets unite at one end in a circular building, from the top of the cupola of which there is a panoramic view of the whole city. Close to it is a vast reservoir of water, the dome of which is of bold and excellent proportions—a chef d'œuvre of its kind.

This dome, according to tradition, was constructed by command of Shah Abbas the Great, and after it was partially built the governor of the town, a violent, overbearing man, commanded the architect to finish it within a very brief space of time. In vain the artist expostulated and informed him that it was impossible to do this in the time specified; the despot would listen to no reason or explanation, and the unfortunate man, to avert the consequences that might be perhaps fatal to his life, took the first opportunity of leaving Herat. A year elapsed, the building remained unfinished, for no other person could be found who had the talent to complete the work; at length the architect reappeared, and the governor, finding himself in a difficulty and anxious to have the edifice finished, consented, though unwillingly, to remit the sentence of death, but ordered him to be bastinadoed. Before, however, the punishment was inflicted, the governor, at his earnest request, accompanied him to the reservoir, and the architect, directing his attention to the walls, which were a considerable height above the earth, said, "Do you not see that the foundations of this building have sunk at least a foot in the ground since I left the city? If at that period I had refused to erect the cupola you would have cut my head off, or the same fate would have probably awaited me had it fallen down after it was finished. You refused to hear me, and I ran away to save my life. The time has arrived when I can successfully terminate my labours, and I have returned to do so." A free pardon followed this explanation, and the architect, filling the reservoir with chopped straw pressed into sacks, and heaping them up to the requisite height and form to make his centre, constructed over them one of the most elegant cupolas ever built.*

The great mosque of Herat is the only remarkable edifice which remains in the interior of the town; but it sadly requires repairs, which no one thinks of making. It was built towards the end of the fifteenth century, in the reign of the Sultan Hussein, a Timouride prince, by his relative Prince Shibali, to whom this country was much indebted for many other handsome structures now in ruins. The palace of Char-bagh, originally the winter residence of the chiefs of Herat, is of mean proportions; its garden, the only one in the town, is small, and closed up by houses on either side.

---

* The size of the dome here mentioned may have required this arrangement, but in general it is dispensed with by architects in those countries; and I have seen the most beautiful and lofty arches and domes erected by the Heratees without any support of the kind.—L.

Major Todd, who lived here during his stay in the city, added several convenient buildings to it, and repaired the main edifice. Four years only have elapsed since his departure, and it is nearly destroyed; the walls are cracked and covered with dirt and scribbling, the doors and windows have been removed, and no one is left in charge of it. The Persians allow their monuments and public buildings to perish by the effects of time; but the Afghans are not gifted with so much patience: they seem to hasten in every possible way the destruction of theirs. A ruined mosque or bath is never repaired, and the materials are soon used for building purposes by those who are in want of them; the only exception I ever saw to this apathetic feeling against repairs, is in favour of reservoirs. These are numerous and in excellent condition at Herat, and the water is remarkable for being fresh and cool.*

* Many of these reservoirs, and all the principal (jooees) canals, were repaired under superintendence of English officers during the stay of the mission at Herat, and it was very pleasing to have it in our power to confer such benefits on the people, and to see how highly they were appreciated.—L.

CHAPTER XIII.

The palace of Bagh-shah — Beautiful view from thence — Gazer-gah — Tomb of Khojah Abdullah Insah — The advantage of being buried within its precincts — Column of white marble — Mausoleum of a Mongol princess — Probably executed by an artist in the time of Tamerlane — Arabesques of Geraldi, an Italian, employed by Abbas Mirza — The mosque at Musella — Sultan Hussein and Shah Rokh great patrons of architecture — Mausoleum of the latter — Ruins at the foot of the mountains near Herat — Religious customs — The value of them — The cunning of the Mollahs — Thaleh-bengy — Ancient temple of the fire-worshippers — Site of the ancient city of Herat — Yar Mohamed's English garden — Rouzbagh — Climate — Productions — Men capable of bearing arms — Afghan ideas of European history — The author's imprisonment — Opinions of the people — The author released.

THE principal edifices of Herat are in the suburbs, which at one time were included in the city. Amongst these was the royal residence of Bagh-shah, situated about two cannon-shots north-west from the present town, now in ruins. The approach to it was by an avenue of fine trees, very few of which are left; the gardens, orchards, and avenue were, as already, destroyed by the Persian troops, and nothing remains but the four walls of the palace. A little further on is Takt Sefer, another summer residence of the chiefs of Herat. The view from the pavilions, shaded by splendid plane-trees on the terraced gardens, formed on a slope of the mountain, is beautiful; but the place shared the same fate as Bagh-shah.

If Gazer-gah,* another royal abode situated not far from hence, has not been so completely ravaged, it is owing to the precautions taken by Yar Mohamed, who garrisoned it with some nomad Taymoonees devoted to his cause. This spot is held in great veneration, for in the mosque is the tomb of a holy person, by name Khojah Abdullah Insah, who was interred here nearly five hundred years ago; his dust is still an object of pious regard, and pilgrims come to his shrine from all the country round—the

* This means in very old Persian "the fighting place."—ED.

mosque as well as his tomb were magnificent, and built by Shah Rokh Mirza. The court of the principal building, in shape an oblong and of burnt bricks, is entered by a superb portico, the sides of which are glazed and covered with an infinity of patterns in very good taste. In the interior are thirty cellular compartments, which occupy the four sides, and in them are two to three tombs, covering the remains of the princes of Herat, principally of the Timouride dynasty. The tombs of the great personages of the province take up nearly the whole area of the court; but those only who have a lively faith in the merits of the holy Insah are allowed to lay their bones here, in the somewhat apocryphal but consolatory belief that at the last judgment he will take them in his suite to Paradise. This faith is rather an expensive one, so that persons of more moderate means are obliged to place themselves under the patronage of some other saint, who will be their pioneer to Heaven on less onerous terms.

The only remnant of the original tomb of the Imaum now remaining is a column of white marble, thirteen feet high and about eighteen inches in circumference, the pedestal, capital, and cornice of which are admirably sculptured. There is also a head-stone of the same material, covered with Arabic inscriptions, setting forth the virtues of the holy gentleman beneath: the execution and finish prove it to have been the work of an accomplished artist. The people believe that this column and monumental stone came down from Heaven all ready sculptured, as they could not have been made by human hands. Though certainly beautiful specimens of art, their merit was diminished in my eyes when I was shown a mausoleum occupying one of the mortuary cells. It covered the remains of a Mongol princess, and consisted of one single block of black marble, six feet and a half in length, one and a half in breadth, and two in height. Numberless flowers, interlaced one with another in a very complicated design, evincing great taste, covered three sides of this stone, but cut so deeply and with such delicacy that it was almost impossible to imagine how the chisel could have executed anything so exquisite and minute. Sculpture was never carried to such perfection by the natives of these countries. Tamerlane informs us that he employed foreign artists. We read in his Institutes:* "The workmen who were spared at the sack of Damascus, and brought to Tartary, were ordered to

* Edition of 1787, p. 103.

build a palace at Samarcand, which they did with much intelligence." I think it not improbable that we are indebted to them for these beautiful monuments; at the death of Tamerlane they might have gone to Herat and been employed by Shah Rokh, who was a great patron of architecture. The marble of the tombs at Gazer-gah come from the quarries in the district of Obeh, distant a few parasangs east of that city.

This mosque is surrouuded by ruins; but amongst them is a small building in pretty good preservation, in which the sovereigns of Herat reside when they pay a visit to this holy place. The walls and cupola of the principal room are covered with gilt arabesques on a blue ground, so exquisitely drawn that they would do honour to the best artist of our day. These designs are from the pencil of an Italian painter that Shah Abbas the Great had attached to his service. His name, Geraldi, is inscribed in an angle of the wall. Yar Mohamed has turned the course of some mountain-streams in a gorge near here, and made them flow through Gazer-gah.* They are fresh and transparent, and pleasing to the eyes, as well as acceptable to the way-worn pilgrim who lies down on its banks to quench his ardent thirst. A few trees of great age are to be seen here, respected by man and time, which is rarely the case.

There is another mosque of about the same period, or, indeed, more ancient, at Musella, on the Meshed road, and on the highest point of some ground rising from the plain. The construction of this edifice, to which a college was attached, was commenced as early as the year 1192 (Héjira 588), by Ghyaz Eddin, the third Sultan of the Gauride dynasty. His son Mahmood finished it in 1212 (Héjira 609); and here he was interred, as well as his father and his uncle Shahab Eddin. This mosque, which was materially injured at the time the Mongols destroyed Herat under Ghengis Khan, was restored, or, more correctly speaking,

* The credit of having opened the canal of the Gazer-gah is due to Major Todd and the English officers rather than to Yar Mohamed. The Vezir, although ready to give his permission to open such canals, was always more anxious to procure advances for the payment of his "*sir bazes*," and for carrying on the repairs of the fortifications, than to see money expended for other purposes. I had the satisfaction of being present at the Gazer-gah, on the occasion on which the canal supplying the garden was opened (Shah Kamran having ridden out with a small escort to see the place, indeed, as he politely said, to show it to me), and I can well recollect the pleasure I derived from hearing those present express their obligations to the "Doulut Englees."—L.

was rebuilt by Shah Sultan Hussein, a Timouride prince, who reigned at Herat towards the end of the fifteenth century, and to whom, as well as to Shah Rokh, the city owes many of the remarkable monuments of antiquity which it possesses. The memory of these two excellent princes is still revered, and their names remembered even in the humblest cottage, are never mentioned but with respect and veneration. The mosque of Musella, which is of colossal proportions, was intended by the Shah Sultan Hussein for the sepulchre of the Imaum Reza, whose remains he wished to remove from Meshed to Herat. The works had been carried on for twenty-five years, when this prince died, and, though nearly terminated, were not completely finished. None of his successors had the pride to perfect the design; nevertheless, such as it is at the present day, it is still the most imposing and elegant structure that I saw in Asia. The mosque is completely covered with a mosaic of glazed bricks, in varied and beautiful patterns, and the cupola is of amazing dimensions. Several arcades, supported by pillars in brick, equal the proportions of the arch of Ctesiphon; and the seven magnificent minarets that surround it may be said to be intact, for the upper part of them only is slightly injured. Shah Hussein had commenced a smaller mosque close to this, which he had intended for his own mausoleum; of the walls, about ten feet in height alone remain; for the cupola has fallen in. A tomb of black marble, and similar to the one I had so much admired at Gazer-gah, in the centre of the ruins, is supposed to be the last resting-place of this magnificent patron of architecture. Springs of excellent water are abundant on the plateau of Musella, and the canals which formerly supplied the ancient city are still to be seen; many of these are dry, they were crossed by small bridges of burnt brick, but though some remain, the greater proportion are broken down.*

From Musella extensive ruins stretch away for a considerable distance to the N.W., skirting the foot of the mountains,—the remains of mosques, sepulchres, baths, and other public edifices.

* A Mohamedan Fakeer, a native of Delhi, had taken up his abode at the entrance to the great mosque of the Musella. He was a very intelligent man, had travelled much, and was greatly respected. Shah Kamran, when passing the Musella, was accustomed frequently to alight from his horse and pass half an hour in conversation with him, and, when riding with the King, I was on all such occasions invited to sit with them, and join in the conversation. We generally had a cup of tea prepared by one of the King's attendants.—L.

The tombs, which are in great numbers, are held in much veneration by the Heratians. Some of them are of immense proportions; others are only great heaps of stones, or rough masonry, at the top of which a long pole is fixed surmounted by a ragged piece of linen for a flag, a signal that some sainted mollah is there interred. Sometimes the heap is completely covered with rags, which the faithful have from time to time hoisted as an offering to the departed, in the hope of obtaining his good offices; sometimes they are strewed with the large horns of wild goats, in honour of his memory, and this is the greatest mark of respect which in Afghanistan can be shown to the dead.

But the people of this country are mighty accommodating in matters of sanctity and religion; and the facility with which they publish that fact to the world by the thousand external forms of it, proves the extent of the indulgence they require to meet and whitewash the iniquities they commit at every instant. It is sufficient for an Afghan devotee to see a small heap of stones, a few rags, or some ruined tomb—something, in short, upon which a tale can be invented—to imagine at once that some saint is buried there. This idea conceived, he throws some more stones on the heap, and sticks up a pole and rag; those who come after follow the leader; more stones and more rags are added, at last its dimensions are so considerable that it becomes the vogue. A mollah is always at hand with a legend, which he makes, or has had revealed to him in a dream; all the village believe it; a few pilgrims come, crowds follow; miracles are wrought; and the game goes on much to the satisfaction of the holy speculator, who drives a good trade by it, until some other mollah more cunning than himself starts a saint of more recent date or greater miraculous powers, when the traffic changes hands. The mausoleum of a chief, if of larger dimensions than another, is in itself a sufficient reason to attract to it the steps of the faithful, though the mouldering bones beneath may have been those of the greatest villain; but what of that?—he had power, and had the right to use it, and death sanctified him in the eyes of his subjects. It is thus that Shah Mahmood and Shah Kamran, who were monsters of cruelty, are now as honoured by the Heratians as the most revered saints of Islam; and crowds may be seen at their tombs demanding their intercession with the Almighty.

Between Musella and the city, from north to east, and about a cannon-shot from the town, is an artificial elevation of ground, called Thaleh-bengy, about forty feet in height, and 650 yards in length; this is crescent-shaped, the horns inclining towards the city, while the centre sensibly recedes: from the nature of the materials mixed with the earth, it is evident that this mass was once the site of extensive buildings. There is a tradition that Nadir Shah erected his batteries on this eminence when he besieged Herat, and that the embankment was made by that prince for this purpose, which is most unlikely, for he would have thrown it up nearer to the town.

The opinion of Afghans acquainted with the history of the Principality appears more reasonable. They affirm that a mosque which stood here was destroyed by Ghengis Khan. It was built in the reign of Abdullah, second prince of the Taharides, on the ruins of a temple of the Ghebers, which had been burnt by the Mussulmans. Herbelot speaks of this edifice as follows. He says, "it was a magnificent structure, to preserve which the Magi paid every year a considerable contribution. The temple attracted a great many Ghebers to Herat; and its splendour created considerable jealousy, exciting especially the zeal of an Imaum, who officiated in a mosque of much more humble exterior close to it. One day, in the height of his enthusiasm, he pointed to the idolatrous edifice, and said it was not extraordinary that the true religion languished in the city of Herat when such a temple so near to that of the faithful was allowed to stand. The hint was not thrown away; and on the following night the fire of the incendiary consumed them both. The Ghebers failed not to lay their complaints before Abdullah, who ordered an investigation of the circumstances, and commanded 4000 inhabitants of the town to appear before him; but not one amongst them would admit that he had ever seen a Gheber temple on the spot; they had only seen the mosque. Such authentic evidence was not to be set aside; and the fire-worshippers were never allowed to have another place of worship. The mosque was subsequently rebuilt, and on a far handsomer scale than the old one."

From the inquiries I made, I have little doubt that all the ground between the town and the mountains, on the slopes of which are Gazer-gah, Takt-sefer, Thaleh-bengy, Musella, and the vast ruins that extend to the north-west, on each side of the road to Mushed, were originally the site of the ancient city, and that the present city, as I have before said, was in reality at that time only the citadel.

Yar Mohamed has laid out a new and beautiful garden south-east of Herat, after a plan furnished him by the English.* Its shape is oblong; and in it is a great variety of the fruits and flowers of Europe and Asia. At one hour to the south, and on the left of the road to Kandahar, is another regal residence, Roouz-bagh. Here Shah Mahmood, and his son Shah Kamran, are buried. Independently of the royal gardens, the environs of the city are embellished by numerous private gardens, orchards, and villages; and their appearance in 1845 was very flourishing, the soil being exceedingly fertile—they were laid out by Yar Mohamed after the siege. The north-west wind blows with great violence at Herat from the commencement of June to the end of August; sometimes unroofing houses, uprooting trees, and carrying everything before it. The climate is nevertheless one of the most delightful in Asia, the average heat in summer being about 28° of centigrade in the shade; in winter the thermometer is rarely as low as 2° above zero.

Herat is one of the most ancient cities in Asia, and its inhabitants mention only Balkh, Maragha, and Naketchiván, as of equally ancient origin. Its central situation, as I have before remarked, must ever render it a place of great importance. The merchants of Persia, Turkistan, Afghanistan, India, and the Seistan come here to exchange the various commodities of their several countries. The productions of the province are much the same as those of Persia, and consist of wheat, barley, rice, assa-

* The garden alluded to is one which I believe originally belonged to Hajee Ferozeoodeen (grandfather of the present ruler). It is situated on the Candahar road, within a short distance of the Heri-rood. Like all the other gardens in the neighbourhood, it had been destroyed by the Persians during the siege, but after the retreat of Mohamed Shah's army, it was made over to Major Eldred Pottinger, who expended a small sum of money in restoring it, and repairing the garden-house. Major D'Arcy Todd continued to keep it up and embellish it, and all our party, especially Major James Abbott, while he remained at Herat, took more or less interest in putting it in order. Seeds and plants of various kinds were procured for it by Major Todd from India and England, with a view to make it useful as a nursery for the improvement and restoration of other gardens. Besides this garden, which was made over to the mission, a farm, at some distance up the valley, of about 200 acres, was presented to me by Shah Kamran, but at my request assigned for the support of a Dispensary and Poor-House which had been established in the city during our stay there. The farm was remarkable for its fertility, especially for the quality of the melons which it produced.—L.

fœtida, saffron, tobacco, silk, and fine cloths. The localities in which the rice-plant is cultivated are very unhealthy; the inhabitants are afflicted with cataract in both eyes before they attain the age of thirty, and have a bilious complexion and sickly look.

The following is the result of the census which has been taken of the male population of the province capable of bearing arms at the time I arived at Herat. It was given me by the minister Nejef Khan:—

District of Gorian	12,000	
,, Subzawar	10,000	
,, Furrah	15,000	
,, Bakooa	4,000	45,000
,, Kooruk	2,500	
,, Obeh	1,500	
Tribes in alliance with Herat, and obliged to furnish a contingent:—		
Hazarahs-zeidnat of Kaleh-rooh	12,000	
Taymoonees of Goor	8,000	25,000
Belooches of Seistan	5,000	
General Total		70,000

These numbers could, if any emergency arose, be increased by a levy *en masse*—a third of this may be considered as the effective force under ordinary circumstances. Eight battalions of regular infantry are permanently on duty; these are a kind of militia recruited in Herat and its suburbs, and taken principally from the tribes that Yar Mohamed has recently settled there: their organization is exceedingly bad, and they are drilled but very indifferently by an Indian Mussulman who had been a sergeant in the Company's service.* The soldiers are all married, and live in their own houses.

The great deeds of Napoleon have penetrated even into Central Asia, though, it is true, somewhat exaggerated. The Afghans look upon him as a kind of demigod: but as they confound one European country with another, and speak of their inhabitants under one name, that is, *Feringhees*, the confusion is great. For instance, they think Napoleon reigned over the English, who are almost the only Europeans with whom they have had any intercourse, and I had great difficulty in making the Afghan chiefs comprehend the truth on this point.

---

* The Indian soldier here alluded to was one of the golundauzes (artillerymen) who accompanied the mission to Herat. He deserted and joined Yar Mohamed's service about the time of our departure.—L.

From the first day of my arrival at Herat, Yar Mohamed had shown me great kindness, and I had to thank him at every moment for some fresh attention; nevertheless, as his politeness increased, my liberty diminished in a corresponding ratio, more especially after the day on which I had paid him my visit. I never was allowed to be alone for an instant, and an interpretation was put upon my words occasionally so absurd, that it was enough to drive one crazy. My escort, which at first consisted of six servants of the Sertip, was reinforced by ten soldiers: and every time I left the house they prevented any one from approaching me; even my servant, who was an Heratian, was always accompanied by a soldier when he went to execute a commission; and I rarely received a visit. At night my door was fastened; two *serbas* slept in the passage, while two more stood sentry on the terrace from sunset to sunrise; not only to prevent my escape but also from holding communication with the conspirators, with whose assistance I was expected to revolutionize the town, for such they supposed was my intention. The Vezir, though treating me with every consideration, wished to worry me into admitting that which he believed,—namely, that I really was an *employé* of the English government. Though this opinion might be complimentary, and was amusing enough, it did not make up for the ennui I experienced in being thus narrowly watched. As to the gossip of the people in the town respecting me it was endless; some said that I was imprisoned and put to the torture to make me disclose my secret intentions; others, that I had only purchased my life by having given or promised millions to the Vezir; and those who professed to be the best informed were of opinion that I should be well treated as long as I was in Herat for fear of giving offence to the English government, but that once out of the town my death would take place in some quiet corner, my body secretly buried, and there would be an end of me. I cannot but admit that this last version triumphed for a moment over my better judgment, for Afghans are capable of anything.

The Sertip and his friends represented these reports as calumnious; but, amidst them all, the prospect from any point of view was not agreeable. When I walked out a host of persons crowded round me—one of whom would exclaim in an under tone of voice, "Poor fellow! how thin he has become!" "How sad to die so young!" said another. "The scoundrels," murmured a third, "have robbed him of ten bags of gold, and kept it for themselves instead of distributing it amongst the poor who are so much in want of it."* At length, quite worn out, I insisted upon being allowed to depart, and in language so explicit that the Vezir, though he could not see his way perfectly clear, began to understand he was mistaken in his views respecting me, and that the hope he had indulged of my being an individual who had come to renew his relations with the English was not likely to be realised.

The result was a permission to continue my journey: and now that there was no chance of getting anything out of me, the Sertip's servants no longer treated me with attention, and at last ate my provisions under my very beard. Twenty-five centuries have not altered the customs and habits of the people of these countries; eunuchs and favourites have as much influence now as they had in the days of Darius and Xerxes, and I had a proof of this

---

* This is very much in accordance with the experience of the officers of the mission at Herat. Reports were constantly brought to us of Yar Mohamed's intention to assassinate us, or to imprison us, in the dungeons of the Char-soo, evidently trying to work on our fears; and on one occasion, so far did the threat proceed, that it became necessary to let Yar Mohamed know that we had no cause to fear him, and that "to pluck a few hairs from a lion's tail was somewhat dangerous."

I have written the name of the palace "Char-soo," but I observe the word spelt Kartchoo by M. Ferrier in another place. The latter may be the more correct way. There is some excuse for this irregularity in spelling Afghan words, the Pushtoo being merely a colloquial language.

Strange to say, the first book in the Pushtoo language ever seen by Shah Kamran and his family, or by any other person, I believe, at Herat, was *a New Testament*, which I had brought from India, and which had been published by the missionaries at Serampore, in the Persian characters. It excited great interest among them, and was read by some of their learned men. It was, if my memory serves me right, in possession of Shah-zadeh Mohamed Yussuff, the present ruler of Herat, at the time of the departure of the mission. At all events, he had got it from me a short time before, and it was not among the books brought away with me. May I hope that it has been equally useful as the Hebrew transcript alluded to in page 123. After the siege, Eldred Pottinger commenced a translation into Pushtoo of a part of the Holy Scriptures, but discontinued it on finding that I had brought a copy. In connexion with this I may mention, that I gave away several copies of Martin's New Testament in Persian to people of influence at Herat, and a Testament in Toorkie to the Kalifah of Merve, a man of considerable sanctity among the Turcomans. With the latter I had, perhaps, more intercourse than any other member of the mission, from the circumstance of almost every one of those who came in with kafilâs from Khiva and Bokhara being anxious to consult the "Feringee Hakeem" at the dispensary, for their own maladies, or those of their relations; and few of them went away without asking to see the "hikmut" by which the blind were taught to work in the poor-house.

I must confess that it was not a little gratifying to me to learn from Wolfe's Journal that kind inquiries were afterwards made at Merve for a gentleman of the name of "Luggun," with whom Dr. Wolfe said that he had not the pleasure of being acquainted!—L.

in the conduct of these menials, one of whom took every opportunity of endeavouring to prejudice the Sertip against me, because I had not given him as handsome a present as he expected. An European just arrived in Asia would have lost his temper, but I knew the people with whom I had to deal too well to do so; I cajoled the servant, and flattered the Sertip, and but for this the consequences might have been as unpleasant as those which befe Captain Eldred Pottinger five years before.* I could only escape from Afghan suspicions and rapacity by paying them off in their own coin; that is to say, adopting their crafty phraseology and deceit. The English failed in carrying out their views, because they approached them with that stiffness, punctilious etiquette, and domineering tone,† which they adopt everywhere; and this does not fall in with the off-hand and easy habits of Asiatics; the French are naturally more pliant and conciliating, and they conform more readily to the various circumstances in which they may be placed in a foreign country. For instance, I thought there was no great impropriety in eating with my fingers, my modesty was not put to the blush by their coarse expressions; and, though I never allowed them to think that I intended to knuckle down, I made no pretension of being superior to them.

Yar Mohamed Khan would not allow me to depart without giving me a dinner; at this he entertained me handsomely, and in-

* Major Pottinger, notwithstanding his great services during the siege of Herat, was treated by Yar Mohamed in the sequel with great indignity. On one occasion, indeed, when the chief sent his brother to deliver an impertinent message, and Major Pottinger, whose patience was exhausted, ordered his servant to turn him out of the room, the servant was immediately afterwards seized, and lost his right hand by Yar Mohamed's sentence. The poor man now enjoys a small pension from the British Government.—ED.

† I hope that the circumstances which led to the failure of the Herat mission can be more satisfactorily accounted for. M. Ferrier is mistaken in supposing that the most friendly personal intercourse did not exist between the chiefs of Herat and the members of the mission up to the time of its departure. The envoy kept an excellent Persian cook, to whose abilities Englishmen and Afghans, at our morning meals, did ample justice, with such knives and forks as may have been used by Abraham; but we generally dined alone in the English style, and I think the prudence of this arrangement cannot be doubted, after the description given of an evening party in the text. During the Ramazan, the public Afghan breakfast gave place to private English ones; but we were then honoured with the presence of Sirdar Sheer Mohamed Khan, the brother of the Vezir, who, to entitle him to the privileges of a traveller, had, while the fast lasted, pitched his tent outside the gate of the city, and came to learn the European mode of eating with knife, fork, and spoon! Travellers are exempted from the necessity of observing fasts in Musselman countries.—L.

vited some of the principal chiefs on the occasion; and, notwithstanding the injunctions of the Prophet, these gentlemen passed the wine so freely that they became completely intoxicated. Under the influence of these potations they talked amazing nonsense, and mightily amused me. It was curious to hear them dabble in politics: at first, and not to wound my feelings, they began by praising the English a little, but finished by thoroughly abusing them. They then spoke of Russia as threatening their independence; and of Persia as a worn-out field-piece. All agreed that they did not know the French, but they thought their sovereign Napoleon, of whom I spoke much, was almost as great a man as Nadir Shah; adding, "What a pity that he was not a Mussulman!" Such a sentiment expressed by these sectarians of Islamism was significant; in short, praise for the greatest hero not of their faith—no matter what splendid deeds he might have done—would have little merit in their eyes. At the close of the repast the guests were incapable of even sitting upright, and at two in the morning I left these worthy Mussulmans rolling on the carpet. The following day I prepared for my departure.

CHAPTER XIV.

General Ferrier leaves Herat — Advice of Yar Mohamed — Execution of a Taymoonee chief — Horrible scene in the bazaar at Herat — Afghan morality — Purwana — Kooshk-robat — Kooshk-assaib — Chingoorek — Turchikh — Encampment of Hazarah Zeidnats — Their origin and history — District of Kalehnooh — Kerim-dad Khan — Defeated by Yar Mohamed — Cloth made from the wool of the camel and goat — Hazareh horses — Intrigues of Kerim-dad Khan — His contingent — The Jumshidies — Murder of Yar Mohamed's envoy — Mingal — Origin of the Tajiks — Physical characteristics of the Hazarahs — Their women soldiers — Village of Moorghab — Abdul Aziz Khan — Friendly reception by him — The Moorghab river — Fever — The Firooz-Kohis — Their chiefs — Kaleh-Weli — The Kapchaks — Eïmaks — Their military strength — Charchembeh — Kaissar — Khanat of Meimăna — Military force — Departure of Feiz Mohamed — Opinion of him.

I HAD been long undecided by which road I should travel to Kabul, but the Vezir Sahib having determined to send his chamberlain, Feiz Mohamed Khan, with a message to the Wali of Meimăna, I resolved to accompany him, and take advantage of that functionary's protection so far on my way. Yar Mohamed, though he warned me of danger even on that road, did not recommend any other as safer, but refused to give me the letters of recommendation, for which I had asked him, to the chiefs through whose territories I must pass, assigning as his reason that they would do me more harm than good; and urged me, after I had quitted the protection of Feiz Mohamed Khan, carefully to conceal the fact that I was an European, and travel with the utmost secresy and expedition, visiting no one until I reached Kabul.

Purwana, June 22nd—three parasangs—across the mountains; soil sometimes clayey, sometimes flinty. At this halt is a group of about forty houses, inhabited by some Eïmaks. In conformity with the orders of the Vezir Sahib, Feiz Mohamed Khan furnished me with the horses necessary for the transport of myself and my baggage. We quitted Herat after breakfast; and I had during my stay in that town acquired so much of the language and manners of the Afghans, and was so admirably dressed in the native costume, that it would have been very difficult to detect me in my disguise. Crossing the large square of the citadel and bazaar, we witnessed two executions. The first was that of a petty chief of the Taymoonees, who had been three times brought prisoner into Herat and three times made his escape, in spite of the oath he had taken never to leave the town. Hearing that he was captured once more, the Vezir sentenced him to be blown from the mouth of a gun. It was a scene that I shall never forget—a horrid spectacle, and touched me to the very heart. The broken limbs of the unfortunate man were scattered in all directions, while his bowels, which had not been thrown to so great a distance, were in an instant devoured by the dogs that were loitering about the spot.

The story of the second was as follows. A lieutenant of artillery, much esteemed by Yar Mohamed, had been assassinated in his sleep on the terrace of his house, in a walled village about a mile from the city, and the murderer, who escaped, could not be discovered ; but the nature of the locality was such that there were good grounds for supposing that the villain must be one of the inhabitants. Twenty persons were arrested by order of the Vezir, with some of whom the murdered man was known to have had some difference ; others were his nearest neighbours. His wife, who was suspected of having a lover, was also seized and put to the torture, but without being able to elicit from her a confession that she had any knowledge of the criminal. The Vezir then fined these twenty individuals one thousand tomauns, and ordered them to receive as many blows of the bastinado until they were *in extremis.* Still no discovery followed. The Vezir then ordered them all to be scalped ; and under this species of torture some little information was obtained, which put the police on the scent of the real murderer, who was well known to the accused, but they had preferred suffering these dreadful tortures to denouncing him. There is a sort of tacit understanding between Afghans not to inform against one another ; they feel how much they stand in need of discretion for their own misdeeds, and therefore preserve a profound silence on those of others. An informer is in this country considered as bad as an assassin, and if found out would certainly share a like fate at the hands of some one of the relatives of the homicide. The murderer of the lieutenant was a neighbour ; and, though he was only suspected, Yar Mohamed ordered his belly to be ripped up, the body to be afterwards hung by the chin to a hook, placed for that purpose in one of the most public places in the bazaar, and there left until he was dead. The man hearing his sentence, confessed the crime; and the details of his confession left no doubt as to the truth of that avowal. It was unfortunate that these acccusations took place the very day I left the town; for, surrounded by the crowd, which blocked up every street leading to the place of execution, I was, much against my inclination, obliged to witness such horrid scenes.* It is deplorable to be forced to acknowledge that these atrocious punishments are almost necessary in Afghanistan to prevent crime; but this is nevertheless the case, for nowhere else is it committed for such trifling reasons and with so much impunity. I could not rejoin Feiz Mohammed for an hour after this.

Kooshk-robat, June 23rd—three parasangs—across a plain on an even easy road, the soil of clay. We made but short journeys the first two days, by way of getting our horses into good wind. If they have not been previously in exercise it takes two days to reach Kooshk-robat; but if they are in condition it may be done in one. The traveller must take his provisions with him, for the place is uninhabited, and nothing is to be found but a scanty streamlet of muddy water, which trickles slowly past the ruined caravanserai-shah.

Kooshk-assaib, June 24th—seven parasangs. I shall not mention the time occupied in each stage, for the chamberlain's horses travelled much faster than those of a caravan. We went usually one parasang an hour. The road was stony, and lay across mountains and valleys, and was frequently cut up by torrents very dangerous to pass after heavy rains. At this uninhabited spot we encamped by a ruined mill that stood near a stream of pretty good water.

Chingoorek, June 25th—seven parasangs—a clayey road over hill and dale. Again an uninhabited resting-place; we pitched our tents near a stream of good water. I pressed on to the end of this day's journey because, having left my face, feet, and hands

* A similar execution took place while the mission was at Herat, but was not, I believe, witnessed by any of our party, who purposely avoided it. Such executions had been very frequent before our arrival, and the atrocious cruelties practised by Yar Mohamed, not only on criminals, but on his "political opponents," are beyond belief. He is said to have flayed a chief of the Barooranees alive, and afterwards stewed him in a large caldron, not long before Pottinger arrived at Herat!—L.

uncovered to allow them to be well tanned and get the native tint, I received a sun-stroke, which caused me much suffering, and made me so exceedingly feverish that I could not swallow a mouthful of bread. Eastern travelling affects me quite differently from what it does the majority of Europeans. When I reach a halt I rarely feel hungry or sleepy, and can seldom eat or sleep before I have rested a couple of hours on my carpet.

Turchikh, June 26th—seven parasangs—with the exception of one rugged hill, on a plain clay soil, the road running through well-watered meadows. The halt at an encampment of two hundred nomad tents. Here commences the territory of the Hazarah Zeïdnat, renowned for their courage, and belonging to the Mussulman sect of Sunnites. The tribe takes the title of Ser Khaneh, head of the house, that is to say, the most noble branch of the Hazarahs. This nation was formed from a single tribe, not exceeding 15,000 families, broken up into camps of one hundred and one thousand tents; the Persian words *Sed* and *Hazar* mean respectively hundred and thousand, and the camps were accordingly named Sed Ejak and Hazarah: the former were soon absorbed in the latter, and only the name of Hazarah remains. Their subsequent increase has obliged them to take possession of the Paropamisus, and divide into different tribes, which I shall notice as I pass through their countries.

The original tribe, that of the Hazarahs Zeïdnat, inhabit the district of Kaleh-nooh—the name also of a small town which has replaced Badkees; the advantageous position it occupies, on the spot at which the principal roads of Turkistan and Afghanistan meet, cannot fail to render it, in the course of time, a flourishing place. The chief, Serdar Kerim-dad Khan, can at any moment have under arms 5000 excellent horsemen and 3000 foot; in case of need the cavalry can be trebled. His jurisdiction extends over 28,000 tents, and his brothers, Abdul Aziz Khan and Ahmed Kooli Khan, govern the districts of Mourghab and Pinjdeh, inhabited by Zeïdnats. The youngest, Mohamed Hussein Khan, resides at Herat with five-and-twenty chiefs of rank, where they remain as hostages for the fidelity of their relatives to Yar Mohamed Khan.

It is only five or six years since Kerim-dad Khan followed the noble profession of pillager; he plundered caravans, and extended his forays to the south of Persia in the district of Ghaïn, where he sacked the villages and carried off the people to sell them to the Usbeks. His depredations were so frequent, and gave rise to so many complaints, that Assaf Doulet sent to Yar Mohamed Khan and informed him that, as he seemed unable to keep his own vassal in order, he should chastise him himself at the head of an army. The Vezir Sahib, who had everything to fear from the violation of his territory by the Persians, marched in person against Kerim-dad Khan, vanquished him, and obliged him to acknowledge the sovereignty of Herat, which he had thrown off.

Since then the Sirdar has contented himself with the large profits arising from his stud, his numerous flocks, and the manufacture of a cloth called *kourk* or *barek*, woven of an exceedingly fine and silky wool which grows on the belly of the camel; nothing can be softer or warmer than these *bareks*, but unluckily they are badly woven—if they were better made, they would be preferable to every other kind of cloth. As the nomads never dye the raw material, the *barek* is of the same colour as the camel; the price varies from ten shillings to four pounds a piece, and one is sufficient to make an Afghan robe. The Afghan and Persian nobles, even the sovereign, always wear it in the winter. The wool, a kind of down on the other parts of the animal, is used for kourks of an inferior quality; this down is preserved from the effects of the weather by the wool that covers it, which is used for kourks of the coarsest description; a down similar to that which grows on the camel, but infinitely superior in quality, grows under the hair of the goat, and cloth of incomparable beauty and quality is made of it.

The Zeïdnats rear a great number of excellent horses of the Turcoman breed. They are smaller and not so well formed as those of the Tekies, but they are steadier, and their powers of endurance are unequalled; it is a pity that light bay should be the predominant colour amongst these animals, for I have observed that in Persia and Central Asia their skin is always finer and more delicate than that of the dark bay, grey, or black. A good many of them are very long-eared; but in the East that is not considered a defect. From their large flocks and herds of sheep, goats, buffaloes, and camels, the Zeïdnats derive immense wealth; these are reared in the splendid pastures of Kaleh-nooh, which are not equalled in Asia.

The yoke imposed on the Sirdar Kerim-dad by Yar Mohamed is not very heavy to bear; nevertheless, he submits to it with repugnance. He keeps up a secret correspondence with Assaf Doulet, and promises to assist him if the Persians should once more lay siege to Herat; but it is probable that, if his aid on such an occasion was ever accepted, he would, as soon as they were victorious, turn against them; for, in common with all other Asiatic chiefs, he cares far less for independence than for agitation, intrigue, and the indulgence of his predatory habits. His subjection to Herat is entirely to his advantage, as he pays no tribute; for a few choice horses that he annually sends to Yar Mohamed Khan, who returns the compliment with more than their value in beautiful Kashmir shawls and European goods, cannot be considered in that light. His brother, Mohamed Hussein Khan, and the twenty-five nobles who reside at Herat, have good appointments; his vassalage, therefore, costs the Sirdar only the contingent of troops that he is bound to furnish to the Vezir Sahib in case of war, and for this he is amply compensated in the benefit he receives from the Vezir's protection against his neighbours and old enemies the Usbek Khans.

The tenacity with which the nomadic tribes live in perpetual excitement is inconceivable—the most solid advantages will not tempt them to renounce it; though the result of the forced tranquillity in which the Zeïdnats have lived for some years has been the development of their industry in the manufacture of *kourks*, with which they supply all this part of Asia, and their wealth, and consequently their power, have augmented to an extent that they never would have done had they continued to live a life of pillage. A portion of them, amounting to 4000 tents, have established themselves in a valley formerly occupied by the Jumshidis, who had then 10,000 tents; this valley was as fertile as that of Kalehnooh, but it was depopulated by a very unhappy event, not uncommon in these countries. Taking advantage of the troubles at Herat during the siege by the Persians in 1838, they declared themselves independent of Shah Kamran, and the next year murdered an envoy who had been sent by Yar Mohamed to induce them to return to their allegiance. When the news of this reached the Khan he took the field, defeated the Jumshidis, and forced 5000 families of the tribe to live in Herat, which he wished to repeople, and which served also as hostages for the future obedience of the 5000 remaining in their camp; but these subsequently met with a much worse fate than their brethren in Herat, for a few days after the departure of the Vezir a body of Khivians suddenly appeared in the valley, and carried off men, women, and children into slavery in Turkistan.*

Mingal, June 27th—four parasangs—road through a plain, pasture, and water-courses, with one very rugged mountain to cross. Two hundred and twenty tents of Hazarahs at this halt, surrounded by a considerable extent of cultivation; this tribe intermarried with the Tajik population, descended from the ancient inhabitants and possessors of the country, Persian or Tartar. These Tajiks are subdivided into two very distinct classes:—the Parsivans or Parsi-zeban, who speak the Persian language, and inhabit towns and villages; and the wandering Eïmaks, who live under canvas. The Hazarahs are Eïmaks, though they pretend they are of Afghan race; the Afghans deny this, because they speak corrupt Persian, whereas the Afghan always speaks his mother tongue the Pushtoo. By their general appearance it is easy to see that they are of Tartar origin. A Hazarah's face is square, flat, and angular, the eyes are small, and obliquely placed; complexion pale and sallow, and beard scanty: they are rather undersized, but their proportions indicate great personal strength; their bravery amounts to rashness, and the Afghans dread them—there are no better horsemen in all Asia. Their duplicity is not so great as that of their neighbours; on the contrary, a certain simplicity may be observed amongst them, which contrasts strangely with their ferocious manners. The women are proud of being able, when necessity requires, to mount a horse and use a firelock or sword with an intrepidity equal to that of their warlike brothers and husbands. In time of peace they do all the house-work, cultivate the fields, and, with their children, weave the *bareks* that are the source of so much wealth to their tribe. They cannot be called pretty, but they are well made; and enjoy perfect liberty—a rare thing indeed

* After this was written, Yar Mohamed Khan also destroyed the power of the magnificent tribe of the Hazarahs Zeïdnats. Perceiving that his patience and forbearance were unavailing, and that Kerim-dad Khan persisted in his intrigues and depredations, he took up arms against him in 1847, and, after having completely defeated him in a bloody engagement, removed 10,000 families into the town of Herat. This event deprived the district of Kaleh-nooh of more than half its inhabitants; but such is its extreme fertility, that a few years hence the tribe will probably be as numerous and prosperous as ever. Kerim-dad Khan took refuge in Persia.

Kerim-dad Khan afterwards returned to his native country, and gave Yar Mohamed's son much trouble up to the time of the recent revolution at the end of 1855.—ED.

amongst Asiatics; their husbands are not jealous, though their Afghan enemies pretend that they profit largely by their indifference.

Mourghab, June 27th—four parasangs—along a fertile valley leading to the river Mourghab, on which is this village of two hundred and fifty houses; it is surrounded by a wall of earth, and outside the hamlet were encamped a thousand families of Hazarahs. The country for five parasangs round is cultivated, and rich pasturage extends ten more. This place is governed by Abdul Aziz Khan, brother of the Sirdar Kerim-dad Khan. I had heard a great deal about him, especially of his bravery, and certainly, if it equalled his boasting, there are few who could be compared with him; his manner is unprepossessing, but he was very hospitable. His dependents are well off, for he has an immense tract of land, the revenues of which are amply sufficient to meet his expenses, and he levies but a trifling tax. Disregarding my injunctions, Feiz Mohamed Khan told him that I was an European; and I had no reason to repent this indiscretion, though at first I dreaded the consequences; he saved me from many a false step, as will be seen hereafter, when I returned to Herat by this road. I could not have done so without the help of two Hazarahs, whom he now confided to my care to conduct them to Kabul, where their presence was necessary to settle a dispute about some property. The arrangement for their travelling with me was both useful and agreeable, as beyond Meimana I should have had to proceed alone through a difficult and dangerous country.

The Mourghab is a small but rather rapid river, and full of fish; amongst them are found excellent barbel, the Epardus or Margus of the Greeks. It waters a flat and marshy country, in which fever is very prevalent; but it is so fertile that, notwithstanding the mortality, the nomadic population frequent it in great numbers, especially the Hazarahs. This tract is nearly the limit of their territory, and they there unite with various other insignificant tribes of Eïmaks, who join and submit to them for the benefit of their protection. One of these might well dispense with an alliance on that score, as it numbers twelve or fifteen thousand families, and was under no necessity to exchange its real name, Firooz Kohi, for Hazarah; this union has been the consequence of repeated intermarriages.

The Firooz-Kohis are of Persian origin, and their forefathers fought Tamerlane bravely when that conqueror subjugated their country. After they were driven by him into the mountains south of Mazenderan, they there defended themselves most desperately; but they were eventually defeated and carried by him into Herat, where their descendants exist at the present time. Although this body of men belonged to several different tribes, from their being involved in one common misfortune, they were all included in the name of Firooz-Kohi, from the village in the neighbourhood of which they were surrounded and captured. They are thus subdivided:—

Five thousand families, commanded by the Sirdar Mooudood Khan, but who acknowledge the authority of Kerim-dad Khan, are established about ten parasangs N.E. of Kaleh-nooh. Each tent of this subdivision can, in case of necessity, furnish one soldier—3000 horse and 2000 foot.

Four other chiefs of the Firooz-Kohis are perfectly independent in their respective districts.

1st. Shah Pesend Khan, living in the fortress of Derzi, fifteen parasangs S.E. of Kaleh-nooh. He commands two thousand families, capable of furnishing 200 horse and 800 foot.*

2nd. The Sirdar Ibrahim Khan, son-in-law of Shah Pesend Khan. He inhabits the fortress of Kootcheh, S.E. of Derzi, in the midst of the mountains, and commands two thousand families, his armed retainers consist of 50 horsemen and 600 foot-soldiers.

3rd. The Sirdar Mohamed Azim Khan, Attalek, whose residence is the fortress of Chekcheran, S.W. of Derzi and S. of Kaleh-nooh. His tribe amounts to four thousand families, and can arm 2000 infantry.

4th. The Sirdar Hassan Khan, established at Doulet Yar, a fortress a little E. of the sources of the Heri-rood. His small command of two thousand five hundred families provides a force of 500 foot and 1000 horse.

Kaleh-Weli, June 28th—seven parasangs—over plain, valley, and mountain. At this halt we entered the district of the Wali of Meimana. Kaleh-weli contains two hundred and thirty houses, some inhabited by Usbeks, the rest by Kapchaks; a little river passes through it, flowing northwards. This tribe of Kapchaks

* Since I travelled through the country he has been assassinated by his dependents, upon whom he practised every description of wanton cruelty. His son has succeeded him.

has been decimated by many bloody engagements, and there remain only about eight hundred tents, furnishing 400 foot-soldiers. They are under the command of two sirdars, Tooram Khan and Tokhtemish Khan, under the Wali of Méimana, in whose territory they live.

The effective force of the Eïmaks can only be estimated approximately, and by report; but I found their country far better populated than I expected to see it, or than Europeans generally imagine.

Charchembeh, June 29th—three parasangs—across splendid meadows—a village of three hundred and eighty houses, inhabited by Afshars, Jumshidis, and Kapchaks, dependent on the Wali of Méimana: it is surrounded by gardens and capital cultivation. We only breakfasted at this halt, and proceeded to Kaissar, where we slept.

Kaissar, June 29th—three parasangs of plain—well cultivated all the way. This is a fine village, giving its name to a district, which includes ten others, each cultivating its own territory up to the boundary of its neighbour. They are inhabited by Kapchaks and Firooz Koohis, who have separated from their own tribes.

Méimana, June 30th—eight parasangs. An hour's ride was consumed in passing a rugged mountain, and at the expiration of that time we reached Nareen, a camp of a thousand tents, pitched in the midst of luxuriant pasture, watered by beautiful streams. After four hours' more travelling on this plain, covered with an Usbek population, we came to Elmar, from which village we could discern an infinity of others. The population is of a warlike character, and furnishes the best soldiers of this country. After travelling three parasangs further amongst the mountains, we came out upon a plain, on which stands the town of Méimana. It is fortified by a wall, with towers, and four gates, but no moat: its extent is about two miles; the Usbek population amounts to from fifteen to eighteen thousand, but there is a small proportion of Parsivan families also.

The Khanat of which this town is the capital was governed a few months before my arrival by the Sirdar Misrab Khan, who had been poisoned by one of his wives, and when I passed through it his sons Eukmet Khan and Shir Khan were still disputing the succession. Eukmet, the eldest, much preferring wine to business, seemed at first disposed to resign his claim in favour of his brother; but ambitious people about him, finding they could not obtain the direction of affairs unless in his name, diverted him from his peaceable intentions. Much misery to the town ensued, and eventually Yar Mohamed, nominal suzerain of the Khanat, interfered to settle the dispute. Through Kerim-dad Khan, who acted as his negotiator, he induced Eukmet to take the authority over the mercantile and agricultural population, and leave Shir Khan to reside in the citadel in command of the army. This in appearance was fair enough, but in reality placed the Khanat in the power of Shir Khan. Nevertheless, it was for the purpose of carrying out his determination to support the agreement made between the two brothers, that Yar Mohamed Khan had sent to Méimana Feiz Mohamed Khan, with whom I had travelled. I apprehend he had also secret instructions to establish more absolutely the rule of the Vezir Sahib; and in order to effect this object Feiz Mohamed was instructed to form two battalions drawn from the Tajik population, who detest the Usbeks, to the Ming tribe of which Eukmet and Shir belong. The army of this Khanat generally stands at 1500 horse and 1000 foot, but in case of war it could in a few days be raised to eight or ten thousand men. The revenue of Méimana is valued at about 20,000*l.*

At this town I was to part company from Feiz Mohamed, and I was very glad of it: for as he detested the English, and believed me to be an Englishman, he behaved accordingly, and we had become completely indifferent to each other, and rarely exchanged a remark, excepting in discussion, if not dispute. He was constantly, through one or other of his suite, asking me to give him something. At one time he would pretend he was short of money, at another he wanted my arms, or my watch, or anything else that he fancied—all of which, be it understood, I refused; but that was of no consequence to him, and he tried again and again, without the least shame or scruple, though with no better success. At Meimana, however, he took his revenge, as he thought; and, instead of taking me with him, according to the Vezir's order, to the Khan's residence, he represented that it was quite impossible for him to do so, and sent me to a caravanserai, saying I should be "more at my ease there." He little thought he was speaking the truth, and that he could not have done anything more agreeable to me; for, in consequence, I could start when I pleased, and with far more secrecy than would have been possible from under the

Khan's roof, where my proposed journey through Bokhara—the land in which poor Stoddart and Conolly had recently perished, under such horrible circumstances, the greatest precautions were therefore necessary. With the two Hazarahs recommended to me by Abdul Aziz Khan, I required neither protector nor guide, for they had friends or relations all along the road; I was sure of not being recognised as an European, and had nothing to fear if I were not betrayed. A few words that I overheard amongst Feiz Mohamed's servants were not reassuring, and from them I suspected that by some underhand means he would try to arrest me; I therefore left the town suddenly, without taking formal leave of the two Khans.

CHAPTER XV.

Kaffir Kaleh — Precautions — Rabat Abdullah Khan — Gipsies — Shibberghan — Irrigation and cultivation — Rustem Khan — A sketch of this chief — Siege of Andekhooye — Local politics — Rivalry and intrigues of the chiefs of Turkistan — Andekhooye — Akhcheh — Meilik — Cholera there — Balkh — Advice of the two Hazarahs — The author continues with them — Cuneiform inscriptions — History of Balkh — Fidelity of the two Hazarahs — The Emir of Bokhara — Mazar — Mosque there held in great reverence — Khulm — Uzbek politics — Army of Khulm — The river of that name — Report of Englishmen being in prison at Mazar and Khulm — Sepoys of the Kabul army — An unpleasant dose — The Mir Wali and Dost Mohamed — The war between these two chiefs — Cause of it — Akbar Khan and the slave girl — Asiatic curiosity — Heibak — Kanjeli Usbeks — Korram — Advice and discretion of the two Hazarahs.

THE Hazarahs had their own horses, and at the caravanserai in which I had put up I purchased three for five pounds, for myself, my servant, and my baggage. Previously to our departure I said nothing respecting my intentions, and desired the porter of the caravanserai to reply to any inquiry about the four strangers, who arrived with the *chik agassi*, by saying that we had left it to avoid the cholera that had appeared in the town, and were encamped under some trees outside the walls. We took the road without a moment's unnecessary delay, and had a long and harassing march of thirteen hours; the latter part over a mountain, and then along a beautiful, well-cultivated plain to—

Kaffir Kaleh, arriving at ten at night. This halt is on a mountain top, inhabited by Usbeks, and surrounded by their tents for some distance. From the time I left Meimana I was never a moment unarmed. I slept booted and spurred, with my sword at my side, and my hand on a pistol—indispensable precautions in this country of pillagers. I also travelled double stages whenever it was possible, which answered equally the purpose of keeping me ahead of any intelligence of my journey, and carrying me out of the way of the cholera, then ravaging the district. During my journey from Meimana, and until I reached Herat again, I was worn with low fever produced by the anxiety and watchfulness in which I lived, and the little sleep that I could get in consequence. I always avoided pitching my tent near an inhabited spot, and never accompanied my Hazarahs when they went for provisions; frequently a piece of black bread was all they could procure.

Rabat Abdullah Khan, July 1st—ten parasangs—the three first over a cultivated plain, forming the district of Khairabad. This village belongs to the Usbeks; the road goes through it, and it is surrounded by gardens, and enclosed by a wall and ditch. Another village called Jan Jumeh is close to it, on the top of a low hill. The rest of the way lay across arid steppes, with the exception of one small mountain—which we had passed over, and were just entering the gorge that was to bring us into an open valley, when we were assailed by a score of large dogs, against which we had some difficulty in defending ourselves. They sprang savagely at the horses, and lacerated them severely, in consequence of which the poor animals became utterly uncontrollable from pain and their exertions to shake off or kick them away: if either of us had had the misfortune to be thrown, which might easily have happened, his fate would have been fearful indeed, for the others would have been powerless to assist him.

These dogs were the vigilant guardians of a camp of Kalbirbend gipsies, near which we had passed, and the moment they perceived us they called off their dogs, who were replaced by the women and children, vociferous for alms. It was impossible to proceed a step, for they hung on our legs, clothes, and bridles, and completely hampered us; we were absolutely forced to comply with their clamorous demands, and, if they had not seen we were well armed, they would probably have taken the affair far more decidedly into their own hands. It would be exceedingly imprudent for any one to venture alone within reach of these harpies, for they would infallibly strip and plunder him. The women had sunburnt complexions, they were tall, with finely-developed forms, which they cared as little to conceal as they did their faces. The men were seated at a little distance, making sieves, and apparently quite unconcerned about the proceedings of their wives. I found these gipsies like all others I met with in Asia; they had the same wandering instincts, the same pride of race, were extremely dirty, and, living on very little, perfectly unscrupulous as to how they might obtain that little.

We encamped in the evening near a ruined caravanseraishah; there was no other habitation, nor any inhabitant, neither was there a drop of water, and we were compelled to use some of that we brought with us; the unfortunate horses were obliged to go without till morning.

Shibberghan, July 3rd—three parasangs—along a plain, three-fourths of the way steppe; the rest is richly cultivated. Shibberghan is a town containing 12,000 souls, Usbeks and Parsivans, the former being in a great majority. The town has a citadel, in which the governor Rustem Khan resides, but there are no other fortifications. It is surrounded by good gardens and excellent cultivation. The population of Shibberghan has a high character for bravery, and I may safely say it is one of the finest towns in Turkistan on this side of the Oxus, enjoying, besides its other advantages, an excellent climate. It is, however, subject to one very serious inconvenience: the supply of water, on which all this prosperity depends, comes from the mountains in the Khanat of Sirpool; and as there are frequent disputes between the tribes inhabiting it and those living in this town, a complete interruption of the supply is often threatened, and a war follows, to the very great injury of the place. Shibberghan maintains permanently a force of 2000 horse and 500 foot, but, in case of necessity, the town can arm 6000 men.

Rustem Khan, who was governor when I went through, was driven out for a short time the next year. The following is the story of his temporary removal:—

He had married the daughter of Misrab Khan Wali of Méimana, and, proud of the accession to his power by this connexion, fancied he could with impunity brave the Emir of Bokhara, Nusser Ullah Khan, by turning his vassal Kezemfer Khan Afshar out of the town of Andekhooye, of which he was governor. Kezemfer Khan, after he had been defeated and plundered, fled to Bokhara, and demanded the protection of his suzerain, promising not only to acknowledge his suzerainty as he ever had done, but to pay him an annual tribute besides. The Emir having then on his hands a war with the chief of Kokan, took advantage of an ununusually good understanding between himself and Mir Wali, governor of Khulm, to request him to act for him, and re-establish

Kezemfer Khan in his command at Andekhooye; Mir Wali acceded to the proposal with all the more satisfaction that he intended to turn it to his own advantage. With this view he sent Kezemfer Khan, with suitable recommendations to his son-in-law Mahmood Khan of Sirpool, who immediately set to work, formed a league with the governors of Mazar, Balkh, and Akhcheh, and, having united their troops with his own, marched to the siege of Andekhooye and Shibberghan. Rustem Khan had confided the defence of Andekhooye to Soofi Khan Afshar, nephew and enemy of the displaced Kezemfer; but a party was formed against him in the town, and he was seized and given up to the besiegers. As to Rustem Khan, who had shut himself up in Shibberghan, he might perhaps have been victorious in the end if he had not been betrayed by his allies, and given up to his adversaries. As long as Mizrab Khan of Méimana lived he afforded his son-in-law constant support; but, after his death, his sons Eukmet and Shir did not keep up the same loyal feeling, and instead of assisting their brother-in-law, as they promised to do, sent a large body of cavalry to join the besieging force. The inhabitants of Shibberghan, having lost all their crops, and seen their district completely ravaged, and being in a state of great suffering from the want of water, of which the supply had been entirely stopped, forced Rustem to surrender himself. Kezemfer, having regained possession of his government of Andekhooye by the active intervention of Mir Wali, declared himself his vassal in testimony of his gratitude, quite regardless of the Emir of Bokhara. Shibberghan remained in the power of Mahmood of Sirpool, who appointed his brother, Hussein Khan, governor; and Rustem Khan and Soofi Khan were sent prisoners to Bokhara, their presence in his capital being all the benefit the Emir obtained by espousing the cause of his vassal Kezemfer Khan, who evaded his authority.

But he could not submit to be duped. Some months after he confided the command of a body of picked troops to Rustem Khan, who repossessed himself of Shibberghan, and forced Kezemfer to perform all his promises to the Emir. At the expiration of one year, however, nothing remained of all these notable intrigues and combinations; for Yar Mohamed Khan arrived from Herat at the head of twenty thousand men. He reduced Méimana, Andekhooye, Akhcheh, and Shibberghan to submission to his own power, and returned, leaving in them strong garrisons under governors of his own choice.*

The amount of rivalry and intrigue that exist amongst the petty Khans of Turkistan is perfectly incredible to any one who has not been in the country; and, instead of trying to decrease or modify either, they exert their intelligence to the utmost to complicate and carry out their paltry schemes. The certain consequence is a permanent state of warfare, in which it is impossible for the people to attempt the development of the resources of the country, or undertake any enterprise with a view to its future improvement. The people of these little Khanats are ever thus the sufferers from the barbarous and ignorant ambition of their chiefs, who are the most absolute sovereigns in the world. They recognise the suzerainty of the princes of Herat, Bokhara, or Khulm, only because they have not sufficient power to throw it off; or, that occasionally it happens to be to their interest to acknowledge it. They will change their protectors as often as it suits them; for fear and the greed of gain are the only motives which influence their conduct, but they rarely pay their tribute to whichever suzerain they attach themselves for the time, and he is generally obliged to present them with khalats, or in other ways propitiate their transient good-will. If they furnish him a contingent for a war they receive an indemnity from him, and are otherwise repaid by a portion of the plunder taken. This continuous struggle of agitation, intrigue, perfidy, and dominion seems to be an innate necessity to a Khan; it has existed from the earliest times, and will certainly be the same a thousand years hence.

Andekhooye.—I did not visit this place, which is five parasangs N.W. of Shibberghan; but I learned that three-fourths of its population are of the Parsivan tribe of Afshars, and that they were established there by the Shah Abbas the Great—the remaining fourth are Usbeks. The government is in the hands of an Afshar chief; and the population has risen to 15,000. The force usually maintained is 1800 horse and 600 foot, which, in case of need, can be trebled in twenty-four hours.

Akhcheh, July 3rd—five parasangs from Shibberghan—over

* On Yar Mohamed's death in 1853, these places became again independent, and remain so to the present day.—ED.

a splendidly cultivated plain, reaching also to Andekhooye. It is one immense garden, and a most animated and picturesque scene. Besides having a wall and ditch round it, the town of Akhcheh is protected by a citadel, the residence of the governor. It contains seven or eight thousand souls, Usbeks; and its ordinary armed force is only 200 horsemen to protect its small but well-populated territory: these can, of course, be at once raised to 1000 or 1200; for in such small Khanats nearly every adult male is capable of bearing arms. The Khans never pay a larger force than is sufficient for the purpose of carrying on the government, well knowing that, in case of an attack, volunteers of every description, agricultural or commercial, would be immediately forthcoming, mounted and armed at their own expense, to defend their property against their neighbours, with the additional incitement of the chances of booty, if they prove the victors. The present governor is Ishan Oorak, vassal of the Emir of Bokhara, and brother of the governor of Balkh. The word Ishan is an Usbek title, corresponding to Syud, descendant of the Prophet. I did not enter the town of Akhcheh. After breakfasting under a tree at a little distance from it we continued our journey to sleep at—

Meïlik, July 3rd—five parasangs—over a marshy plain, full of reeds and trees, amongst the latter were enormous tamarisks. This place, containing about 2500 souls, is a dependency of the government of Balkh. The cholera, which I had at first met with at Méimana, and was much worse at Shibberghan and Akhcheh, was here at its maximum of intensity, raging fearfully; and the wretched inhabitants, decimated by this scourge, took not the least notice of me, a circumstance that contributed much to my comfort while here; for in Meïlik there is always a crowd of spies in the interests of the various princes and chiefs of Afghanistan and Turkistan, who keep them perfectly well informed of all that happens in the country. The place is particularly well situated for the purpose, for a great many roads meet there, by which travellers arrive from all parts. The extent of ruins round it indicates that it has risen on the site of a Bactrian town. They are of burnt brick, and apparently very ancient; but it would be difficult to say to what class of buildings they belong.

Balkh, July 4th—seven parasangs—along a plain, closed in on the left by not very high mountains, from which streams of water flow; these had broken up the road at every few paces, and sometimes formed marshes of mud, from which our horses had the utmost difficulty in extricating themselves.

About two parasangs from Balkh the Hazarahs turned out of the high road, taking an oblique line across the country to the left, and recommended me to follow them. I naturally asked the reason of this manœuvre. "If you wish to go to Bokhara, the road lies before you," was the answer. "Why, we have left Bokhara a fortnight's journey behind us!" I exclaimed. "True," continued my fellow-traveller, "but the revenues of Mir Suddour, the governor of Balkh, are scanty, and he tries to improve them by levying a tax for himself on the horses and baggage, as well as a personal toll upon every traveller he can catch. To accomplish this purpose the town is strictly guarded on the south, and every one is closely examined, in order that his luggage may be taxed to its utmost value. If you have no objection to the officials seeing your European books, clothes, &c., that I have observed within these few days, well and good,—go on; but you will surely be stopped and despatched to Bokhara; therefore we warn you not to proceed, for we certainly have no wish to share that fate, as we inevitably should. Come with us round the town, and we shall reach the ruins on the north, amongst which we can shelter ourselves unperceived. We have provisions sufficient for all three; and the horses will help themselves to the grass. Thus we shall all rest well, and proceed safely to the more hospitable government of Khulm. Travel with us, and we will not leave you for a moment; but if you persist in running into unnecessary danger, go; and may God protect you!"

It was impossible to resist this reasoning, so I adopted the advice, though I sadly regretted the disappointment of not seeing, as I had hoped, at my ease, this exceedingly ancient place, the Mother of Cities, *Oumme el belâd*, as the Asiatics call it. Having made the circuit, we reached the ruins alluded to, and established ourselves in the remains of an immense mosque, where nothing disturbed us; a stream of water flowed through it, and the horses browsed upon its banks. After our homely breakfast we lay down and slept, in order to be able to accomplish during the night the ten parasangs that would take us into Khulm. Towards evening I ventured to ramble over a portion of the ruins round us; they were built of equal parts of burnt and dried bricks: the former were of uncommon size; I took up some that measured about 20 inches by 15. On some, but they were very scarce, of which the quality was exceedingly fine and hard, almost equalling stone, I observed cuneiform characters.* The citadel, near which we had rested, is a square inclosure, with a turret at each corner, erected upon an artificial eminence; and this fortress, entirely abandoned, is as well as the mosques, colleges, and a long bazaar, in very fair condition. It is easy to distinguish buildings of very different ages in this town; and the Hazarahs assured me that the southern part of it contains a population of 3000 or 4000 souls, an enormous mosque, a large bazaar, and several caravanserais. Twenty years ago there remained amongst the ruins many good houses: but some of them having fallen down, from the effects of the rains, and exposed vases full of gold which had been concealed in the walls, the inhabitants of the southern part proceeded to demolish everything that was left standing, in the hope of finding more treasure; in any case, however, their trouble is not thrown away, for they sell the bricks to those who are building in the new town. This is open; the citadel is in the centre, and situated an hour further north than the ancient one. It is the residence of Ishane Suddour, the governor. The population consists of 10,000 Afghans, and 5000 Usbeks of the tribes of Kapchak and Yaboo; these proportions are the same as in the population of the old town.

Balkh was the first capital of the Persian monarchs, but all traces of its origin are lost in the obscurity of ages. Oriental authors in general ascribe its foundation to Kaïamur, the first Prince of the Pishdadian dynasty; there are but two or three who attribute it to Tahmurats. Alexander the Great found it in a flourishing state, and it was reckoned amongst the great cities of Asia through the long interval between the days of the Macedonian hero and those of Ghengis Khan, who exterminated its population. It had scarcely begun to recover from this fearful event, when it was again reduced by the devastating policy of Tamerlane, and the interminable wars of his successors gave the final blow to

* The existence of bricks with cuneiform characters among the ruins of Balkh has been remarked by previous travellers, and is of much interest, as no other similar relics are known so far to the east. Sir Henry Rawlinson suggests that they may belong to the Kushan (a famous Scythian race), who held Balkh in remote antiquity, and whose bricks, stamped with cuneiform Scythic legends, are also found at Susa, and on the shores of the Persian Gulf. —ED.

the last remnants of its struggling prosperity; it will be very difficult for it to regain its former importance. The territory of Balkh has been noticed for its fertility; water is abundant, and it only requires a numerous population to render it the most fertile in Asia. Even in its present state it is one of the most productive parts of Turkistan, of which it furnishes several provinces with grain, when their own crops are insufficient for their consumption. Many well-peopled villages are included in the government of Balkh, which is bounded by the Oxus on the north, and on the south by the chain of mountains running east and west, five parasangs from the town; in the other directions it extends from Mazar to Akhcheh. This last town, though recognising the sovereignty of the Emir of Bokhara, obeys also the Governor of Balkh, who is a vassal of Mir Wali of Khulm! This is certainly a singular amalgamation of politics—a political mystification, but in perfect conformity with the untruthful and intriguing habits of these chiefs—to outwit and deceive each other is the delight of their lives.

The lovely and advantageous position of the Mother of Cities, in the midst of a rich plain, though favourable to any agricultural or commercial undertaking, has rendered it liable to the sad misfortune of being a constant bone of contention between the Emirs of Khulm and Bokhara, whose ruthless armies almost annually dispute the suzerainty of the place. Ishan Suddour acknowledged that of the Mir Wali of Khulm in 1845. He maintains 2500 horsemen, and 1000 foot; the cavalry is excellent, for the horses of Balkh are of the best Turcoman breed.*

At eight in the evening, feeling ourselves sufficiently refreshed, we mounted, and rode quietly out of these interesting ruins, not having met a soul to notice our proceedings. I cannot find words to express the joy that I felt at thus happily finding myself outside the territories of the Emir of Bokhara. I had performed the journey towards his principality with the pitiless murders of Stoddart, Conolly, and Nasseli ever in my mind, and could not help feeling great anxiety. My safe passage through it was considerably facilitated by the presence of the cholera, which occupied every one's thoughts, and my manners and disguise further protected me. Notwithstanding all this it would have been almost

---

* In 1850 Balkh fell into the power of the Emir of Kabul.

impossible for me to accomplish my purpose without discovery, had it not been for the two Hazarahs sent with me by Abdul Aziz Khan. Unlike their countrymen, amongst whom fidelity is so rare, they earnestly exerted themselves to preserve me from every danger with which I might be threatened, and scrupled not to encounter every inconvenience that might tend to ensure my safety. In Bokhara an European is tracked like a wild beast; and as the Emir had at the time two wars on his hands, my assassination would assuredly have followed my discovery; for he would not have failed to attribute the hostility of his neighbours to my intrigues, as he had done in Conolly's case. The Khan of Shersebz, Khoja Murad, and the Khan of Kokan, Musulman Tchelak, Kirghiz, had agreed to organise an expedition against him; and it was also said that they were in alliance with the Wali of Khulm. Never had the Emir of Bokhara been in greater danger; but I learned afterwards that, after a little fighting, matters were arranged amongst them, and each returned to his home. We had scarcely got clear of the ruins when we found ourselves on cultivated ground, over which we had an hour's ride to reach the high road; it was intersected by large water-courses, which, the evening being dark, we found very troublesome to cross. The plain was cultivated as far as Mazar, and even beyond.

Mazar, July 5th—two parasangs—a walled village, containing at the utmost two hundred houses; but in the neighbourhood there were the tents of thousands of Usbeks and Eïmaks. The Afghans inhabit the village of wooden huts outside the wall. Ishan Shudja Eddin is independent governor of this place; nevertheless he shows much deference to the chiefs of Khulm and Balkh, and would not be more obedient if he were their vassal. The force that he keeps up is small—only 250 cavalry; but he can arm 1000 if requisite.

The mosque of Mazar* is held in great veneration by Mussulmans in general, and especially by the sect of Shiahs; because it was revealed in a dream to some Tartar prince, whose name I have forgotten, that Ali, son-in-law of Mahomet, was buried there. It is almost certain that the tomb of this caliph is at Nejef, near Bagdad; but the faith of a Shiah Mussulman is not staggered by

* Mazar merely means a place of pilgrimage, and is applied to this town in consequence of the sanctity of the famous mosque which it contains.—ED.

such a trifling difficulty: the power of Ali in their eyes is quite sufficient to increase or multiply his mortal remains, and even more than that. This mosque was built by Timouride Ali, Shah of Herat. It incloses the tomb of Shah Murdan,* and possesses immense revenues, the legacies of pious votaries, and the gifts of pilgrims; they are employed to feed crowds of poor who travel there from the various khanats of Central Asia to live on the bounty of Ali.

We stopped at Mazar an hour, near a caravanserai. From this place the traveller might reach Bamian without passing through Khulm and Heïbak, by taking the road through the small town Tash-gourgan, a dependency of Khulm, seven parasangs south of Mazar; this is much the shortest way to Kabul; but a stranger rarely escapes being plundered; the one through Khulm is always preferred, although that is not safe; for the defile of Abdou, beyond that town and Mazar, is the haunt of thieves, who generally attack caravans—we were fortunate enough to pass without interruption. The road is desert up to Khulm.

Khulm, July 5th—eight parasangs—over an arid plain. On the road between Mazar and this place were some clay hills, amongst which anciently stood the village and caravanserai of Abdou. Both are now uninhabited, and in ruins.

Khulm is improperly called by geographers Khullum. The first of these names is the only one by which it is known in Asia. It stands on the plain, and consists of four or five villages, now become quarters of the town, united with each other by gardens; there are bazaars, caravanserais, and baths; and the population may amount to fifteen thousand inhabitants. The citadel, erected on an eminence, is the residence of Mohamed Emin Khan, a sovereign chief, who takes the title of Mir Wali; this chief only attained his present position in 1836. Previously to that period he was simply Wali, that is to say, governor, of the town of Khulm, in the name of the Usbek Khan, Murad Beg; that Khan was then sovereign of the principality, and his power extended over the country, reaching north and south, from the river of Badakhshan to the mountains of Hindoo Kush, contiguous to Kabul. Balkh on the east and Badakhshan on the west form the other boundaries of his dominions. Murad Beg was a soldier

* Shah Murdan, or the King of Men, is the title given to Ali generally in Khorassan, and especially at this place. —ED.

of fortune, who conquered the Khanat for himself. At his death Emin Khan took possession of it; his administration is praised by his dependents, and as he is less of a rascal than the other chiefs, his good faith has become proverbial in those countries.

The state of Khulm exercises a certain influence on those around it, and its preponderance is not inferior to that of Kabul, Herat, or Bokhara; a great majority of the inhabitants are of the Tajik race, but the Mir Wali is an Usbek. The population is reckoned at 700,000 souls; the revenues of the principality amount to 24,000*l.* in silver and nearly 50,000*l.* in cereal produce, which is considerable for such a country. The standing army consists of 8000 cavalry and 3000 infantry. Of these last 800 form a battalion of so-called regulars, though no troops can be worse trained; amongst them are embodied the remains of a few companies of Eïmaks to whom the English had given some instruction when they occupied Kabul. The insurrection in this last town in 1841 obliged them to retire to Khulm, in company with a few sepoys who had formed part of the British army, and who serve the artillery of the Mir Wali; this consists of ten pieces, two are of very large calibre. The four best are those that Mohamed Akbar Khan brought with him after he had been defeated by the English at Butkhak; the six others, old and bad, were brought there by Nadir Shah and Ahmed Shah, Suddozye. Gendj Ali Beg, son of the Mir Wali, is Governor of Badakhshan; and Rustem Khan, son of Mir Murad Beg, the former sovereign of the Khanat, is Governor of Kunduz in the name of the Mir Wali. The river which passes by Khulm bears the name of the town, and is consumed for the purposes of irrigation before it reaches the Oxus. In conformity with my usually prudent habits, I encamped outside the town, in a retired spot, to avoid the inexhaustible queries of the inhabitants; but we had scarcely installed ourselves under the shade of a mulberry-tree when we were accosted by an Afshar, who thought he recognised me from having seen me three weeks before at Herat. Though both I and my companions denied this he remained doubtful, and persisted in his investigations; he talked to me of an European doctor, who, he said, had turned Mussulman, and lived at Mazar, but was of a different tribe from twenty-five or thirty Englishmen whom he pretended were also in exile in that town, and fed at the expense of the mosque. He assured me that other Englishmen were detained at Yajgar, at

Hezret Imaum, and other places. I had only one opportunity of testing the truth of his information, and that was with respect to those who, according to his statement, were in Khulm; I saw there only the Indians who had entered the Mir Wali's service; nevertheless, it was possible there might be some Englishmen with them. I dared not pursue the investigation energetically lest I should, without being of any use to these unfortunate men, if such they were, incur the danger of sharing their fate. This man offered to communicate with them for me; but I dared not trust him, as he was an entire stranger, and might easily have betrayed me for a trifling reward; I therefore declined his intervention, saying that a good Mussulman like me could not concern himself about infidels. He retired nearly convinced (at least I thought so), that he had never seen me, and that I came from Bokhara, and was returning to my family at Peshawur. However, he had excited my curiosity; and, in spite of the evils that might result to me, I went into the town, certain that if I saw any Englishmen I should at once distinguish them by their physiognomy, so different from that of the Indians, Afghans, or Usbeks. I was on foot, and, accompanied by one of the Hazarahs, went into the bazaars; but I watched in vain for anything that could indicate the objects of my search, though I have since seen many inhabitants of Khulm, Herat, and Meshed who assured me the information was correct.

After having rambled here and there for an hour or more, I thought I would refresh myself with a cup of tea, and entered one of the numerous shops in which that agreeable beverage is sold; here, at the request of the Hazarah, the master of the house showed us into a back room, and quickly returned with two enormous bowls full to the brim; the sight of which awakened the spirit of the gourmand within me. In delightful anticipation, I raised mine to my lips, when, lo! the moment I swallowed the first mouthful, so hastily taken, I believed myself poisoned. The wretched grocer had made it of equal parts of tea and rancid butter, which stood in the place of sugar. What a horrible treat the fellow had prepared for me! It was, however, imperatively necessary to conceal my disgust; for an exclamation of surprise at what I afterwards learned was a favourite beverage in Turkistan would infallibly have betrayed me to the bystanders. Taking courage, therefore, I held my breath, and proceeded with my disgusting dose as best I could. But this was not all; a ball of tea-leaves soaked and mixed with the same grease, was also placed before me, and this I was obliged to swallow with a gulp by way of a concluding relish. As to Rabi, my companion, he had as much pleasure in imbibing the detestable liquid as I had misery, and sipped it with leisurely contentment, while large drops of perspiration stood on my forehead from the exertion and self-control I had to exercise to enable me to drink it off without exposing my feelings. But I was then, as the Persians say, *bed sahat*, in an unlucky hour; and to this annoyance was soon added some alarm occasioned by the conversation of a man with his arm in a sling, who formed one of a group of guests beside us, and had been wounded in a late encounter that had taken place between the troops of Khulm and Kabul; he talked of nothing but the dangers on the road to the latter city, and was endeavouring to dissuade one of the party from going there. The least he must expect, he said, is that he would be stripped and plundered, even by his countrymen, who, once let loose, stop for nothing, and pillage and kill friends or enemies without mercy. Rabi, who was as much interested as I was, joined in the conversation, and, to our infinite regret, we obtained the following unsatisfactory information.

The war between the Mir Wali and Dost Mohamed, Emir of Kabul, had commenced from a trifling cause, though it was made to assume the most serious aspect. When Dost Mohamed declared war upon the Emir of Bokhara, against whom he had very great cause of complaint, he requested the permission of the Mir Wali to march through his territory, and received a sharp refusal; upon which he remarked, that what was refused to friendship he should take by force. The Mir Wali replied, and with reason, that to grant his demand was to give up the sovereignty of his state—for that the Afghans would ravage the country and keep it if they were strong enough.

This was the ostensible cause of the war; but, according to the best-informed persons, the Dost was pressed on by his son and Vezir, Akbar Khan, who, during his exile at Khulm, became deeply enamoured of a female slave belonging to the Mir Wali, whom he carried off when he returned to Kabul. But the young beauty found means to escape and return to her master, who afterwards scarcely ever allowed his recovered treasure to leave his presence. Akbar Khan was clamorous to regain her, and the inexorable refusal of the Mir Wali brought on the war. The two armies had already fought several engagements with various success; that of Kabul, commanded by the Sirdar Akrem Khan, another son of the Dost, occupied the hilly country in front of Bamian, and the forces of Khulm were stationed in the district beyond Sighan, in strong positions and passes very difficult to carry. This news annoyed me exceedingly, and we returned to our camp to consult as to the best course to adopt under these adverse circumstances.

The war had broken out so suddenly that we never heard of it till we reached Meïlik; but we were told at the same time that peace would be made, and the troops had not been moved. Great, therefore, was our disappointment at hearing the real state of affairs. I thought for a moment of trying to gain Kashmir by Kaffiristan, which is inhabited by the tribe of Siah-poush; but then the Hazarahs would not have accompanied me—indeed, they did not know that road, and their ultimate object was to reach Kabul. To adopt that plan I must also have thrown off my disguise at Khulm, and found a guide through an almost unknown country, and it remained to be proved whether I could do so or not; it was certainly very doubtful. In the end the opinion of all was to hold on our course till it became impossible to do so any longer. Having decided, we made no useless delay, but at once took our weary way across a country desolated by war and the cholera, determining to set out at nightfall to avoid the curiosity of the people. The marvellous intensity of this passion in Asiatics is incredible to those who do not know them. Every one in the street conceives he has a right to ask you anything he pleases; and not that only, but to expect an answer, and to set you down for an intriguing rascal, a spy or a thief, or whatever else he may fancy, if you do not give him one. Happily, favoured by the darkness, we departed without attracting observation; the Hazarah having prepared a reply for inquisitive persons that we belonged to an Usbek Khan beyond Sighan, and were travelling to rejoin him.

Heibak,* July 6th—ten parasangs—the first three-quarters of an

* Heibak was the extreme point to which our troops penetrated during the Afghan war. A party of Captain Hopkins's regiment, detached from Bamian, held Sighan and Heibak for some months, and thus threatened Khulm, where Dost Mohamed had first fixed his head-quarters on escaping from Bokhara.—ED.

hour in a plain which slopes gently towards and terminates abruptly in a chain of high mountains, rising almost to a peak, of great elevation; we entered them by a narrow pass, after which the valley opened a little, with here and there a few villages and gardens, and, as far as we could see in the night, this gorge was well watered and fertile Having started at sunset, we did not reach our halt till mid-day on the morrow, having rested only a couple of hours half-way, for all, man and beast, were much fatigued with the mountain journey. Heibak, where we now dismounted, is inhabited by Usbeks of the tribe of Kangelis, governed by a chief of their own tribe, who calls himself independent, but who nevertheless is in all things subservient to the Wali of Khulm; he even pays him dues, which he qualifies by the appellation of presents. This chief resides in a little fortress that commands the whole valley; his rapacity is amazing, and he levies a tax upon all caravans and travellers. Luckily he was at the camp at Sighan when we arrived, and his deputy allowed us to pursue our way untaxed and unmolested, perfectly indifferent as to my identity—I fancied they took us for some of the Emir's people going to Sighan. The soil here is of uncommon fertility, and the vegetation luxuriant; the gardens are numerous, and produce some of the best fruit in Turkistan. Agriculture is little attended to; and some extent of grain sown this spring had been torn up by the wild boars, which are very numerous in the mountains. The river of Khulm flows by Heibak, and its banks are shaded all the way by wild fruit-trees.

Korram, July 7th—five parasangs—across steep mountains, in a dark ravine, between high rocks some hundreds of yards in elevation; the road is execrable, covered with rounded stones, and broken up by water and brushwood. Occasionally the gorge widened, and we saw orchards and gardens around small villages, of which I was told the climate was exceedingly good, and favourable to the cultivation of fruit. We then passed through the village of Serbagh, arriving at Korram at midnight; here we found a crowd of wounded soldiers returning from the war; but under cover of the uncertain light, we thought we could without inconvenience encamp near them, for it was highly unfavourable for their conducting the usual investigations upon new arrivals, and they quite believed that we belonged to them and were going to join the chief. Their information, however, demonstrated the impossibility of our ever getting beyond the

Usbek camp, in which nothing would have induced me to remain. It was, however, necessary to determine upon some plan, and I inclined to return nearly to Heibak, and take the road to the east across the mountains to the little town of Tcharikar, whence we could reach Kabul. But Rabi told me that the mountains were inhabited by the most savage of the Afghan tribes; that the Emir could send his own people there only at the risk of their lives, and that it would be impossible for me to get through without misfortune. When I insisted upon taking that direction, my companions, including my servant, told me that if I pleased I was certainly at liberty to do so, but that it would be alone, as assuredly neither of them would accompany me; they advised instead, that we should make our way to a camp of Hazarah Tartars a few parasangs on our right, in which they had relations, where we could wait in perfect safety till the squabble was over and then go on to Kabul. This was undoubtedly an acceptable proposition; but so little confidence did I then feel even in Rabi and Roostem, that I feared some secret snare. Up to that time they had, it is true, acted with great fidelity, but it is impossible to trust implicitly to a native of Central Asia—perfidy is the basis of their character; but I hesitated the less when I reflected that in every way I was in their hands, and ended by acceding to the arrangement.

CHAPTER XVI.

Kartchoo — Mountains of the Paropamisus — Alayar Beg — Receives the author in his tent — Assassination of Saduk Khan— Despair of the author — The Hazarah Tartars — Kaissar Beg — Hazarahs of the East — The principal chiefs of this tribe — Military force of each — The Sirdar Hassan Khan ben Zorab — Strength of his army — Description of the country — Afghan inroads — Tamerlane and the Hazarahs — Quintus Curtius — The Berbers — Dehas — Beautiful carpets — Tracts of grass — Sirpool — Mahmood Khan the Governor — Military force — Monsieur Ferrier well received by this chief — Mahmood Khan desirous of an alliance with the British government — Description of the country through which the author is going — Quick travelling — Eimak dogs — Fertile valley — Rock inscriptions and bas-reliefs — Mountains — Description of Boodhi — Div Hissar — Defile — Steppe — The Seherai — Their habits — Idol temple — Timour Beg — Delicate attentions.

KARTCHOO,* July 7th—four parasangs. On quitting Korram we followed for an hour the great road to Kabul, and then turned into the steep mountains on our right, where we found the path so narrow and enclosed with rocks overhanging our heads that we lost the starlight and were obliged to trust to the instinct of our horses, and followed in file. At break of day we crossed the highest summits, covered with snow, and the cold was as great as in the plains in January. Here the mountains of the Paropamisus lay before us, and intersected the country in all directions over a very great extent of surface; the smaller chains were all ramifications of two principal ranges, one running from W. to E., the other from S.W. to N.W. Some few gigantic peaks stood here and there, wrapped in robes of snow that were perfectly dazzling in the morning light. It would certainly be impossible for any army having baggage with it to pass the mountain we had just come over; though I think it would be otherwise with those between Khulm and Korram, where artillery would not find any great obstacles.† From what I heard, I imagined the difficulties would be more serious on the Bamian road;

* Kartchoo is Afghani for "a market."—ED.

† See Masson, in 'Asiatic Journal.'

but whatever they may be, I do not suppose they are insurmountable, as we find a precedent to the contrary in the history of times past: for, on his return from India to the conquest of Bokhara, Nadir Shah took all his heavy artillery with him; and one of the guns, of which probably the carriage was broken, may still be observed half-buried in the sand between Serbagh and Korram.*

The descent from the summit of the mountain was not by any means difficult; it was certainly steep, but the ground was good and even, and no obstructions presented themselves. By nine o'clock we were on the plain, and could discern in the distance a few tents of the Hazarah Tartars, where Rabi afterwards went to make inquiries as to the direction of the road; he returned with a nomad, who accompanied us on our way to show us the encampment of Kartchoo, which we reached a little after midday. The chief of this horde, Alayar Beg, was a relative of Roostem, and at his tent we dismounted. He immediately ordered a sheep to be killed, and in every way fulfilled towards us the duties of hospitality. It was not, however, till the repast was over that Roostem explained the circumstances of our journey and the cause of our visit to the encampment; and, as he never spoke of my being an European, I passed as a merchant of Meshed travelling on business to Kabul: Alayar Beg listened attentively to the recital of our misadventures, and gave us his advice.

"The war," he said, "is by no means finished, indeed it is only just begun, and in my opinion will last till the winter snows make our mountain passes impracticable. If you like to wait till the spring under my tent, consider it as your own—settle yourselves at your ease; but I hardly think so long a delay would suit you, as you say yourselves that you desire nothing so much as to arrive quickly at Kabul. The only way now open to you is to go either to Ghuzni or to Kandahar, and then safely enough to Kabul; the road by Ghuzni is the shortest, and in ordinary times would be the best and easiest; but the chief of the Deh Zingy Hazarahs, Mohamed Saduk Khan, was assassinated about a month ago by Bahadoor Beg, who set himself in his place and now plunders the whole country. Moreover he is at war with Mir Muhi Beg, chief of the Hazarahs

* The British engineer officers sufficiently proved that there is no difficulty in conveying artillery from Bamian to Khulm. When it was thought possible that an advance on Bokhara might take place, Captains Sturt and Broadfoot were sent on to survey and report on the passes of the Paropamisus.—ED.

of Yekoo Oling, who intended to take the place of the murdered Saduk in the command of the tribe; it will therefore be as impossible for you to traverse that district, now contended for by those two chiefs, as the road you have abandoned; and you cannot do better than go to Kandahar by Gour. It is not a perfectly safe road, but is at any rate more so than the other. The great point for you is to reach Hassan Khan Zorab of the Pusht Koh Hazarahs;* with his help you have nothing to fear." This fresh incident plunged me into a perfect stupor of grief and disappointment. Had I then suffered and borne up against so much, to be stopped within a few days' march of the Indus? I was truly in despair, and wanted at all risks to attempt at least to make our way to Bamian through the Afghan camp; but my companions were as inexorable as ever, and informed me that they had no intention of going to certain death, and though they were as anxious as I was to get to Kabul, they wished to do so in safety.

Being alone in my opinion, I was as before obliged to adopt theirs; and it was decided that, instead of proceeding straight to Kandahar, we should first go to Sirpool, of which the Governor, Mahmood Khan, was the ally and friend of Hassan Khan Zorab, to whom we were to ask him for a letter of recommendation. Rabi had in his youth been in the service of the father of Mahmood, and entertained no doubt that he would give him this letter. I acceded to the plan like a man condemned, who has no will of his own, but I insisted that we ought to proceed immediately. However it was of no use my endeavouring to hurry them; we did not move the sooner on that account, for the Hazarahs were amongst their kith and kin. I was obliged to remain that day and night in the encampment of Kartchoo, and I must certainly acknowledge that Alayar Beg exerted himself to make it as agreeable or at least as little wearisome as possible.

The Hazarah Tartars with whom we were staying are a small tribe settled amongst the mountains intersected by the river of Khulm and the river of Balkh. Although the Mir Wali sets up a right of suzerainty over them, it is not possible for him to exercise it, the population is ungovernable, and has no occupation but pillage; they will pillage and pillage only, if it be but each other, and plunder from camp to camp. Their chief,

* Conolly's route went through the country of these Hazarahs.—ED.

Kaissar Beg, surnamed Delaver, courageous, is dreaded throughout the country, but his subordinates scarcely recognise his authority, unless when he leads them on a foray—excepting on those occasions each camp acknowledges only the chief of its choice. This tribe pretends to be a branch of the Hazarah Zeïdnats established at Kaleh-nooh, from which they assert that it separated only eighty or ninety years ago; although the distance is great between them, intercourse is constantly kept up, and the chiefs frequently contract matrimonial alliances. The Hazarahs know not the number of families they amount to, nor how many armed men they can furnish: the latter is a census which is only made in each encampment; moreover, they arm only for pillage, and no sovereign can reckon upon their following him into the field. South of this camp is the great tribe of the Hazarahs of the East, which extends N. and S. from the Hindoo Kush to the frontiers of Kandahar. It is known by the name of Hazarah Pus Koh, or Pusht Koh (Hazarahs of the other side of the mountain), and is subdivided into several branches, of which the principal are Yekoo Olingy, Deh Zingy, Ser Jingeli, Deh Kondi, Bolgor, and Kudelane. The three first are governed by independent chiefs, and the remaining three united under one more powerful one. The following is the state of their respective forces:—

The Sirdar Mir Muhi Beg, who resides in the fortress of Yekeuholing—2000 horsemen and 300 foot.

The Sirdar Bahadoor Beg, who commands the Deh Zingy, can arm 1200 foot and 400 horse.

The Sirdar Mir Saduk Beg, possessing the fortress and territory of Ser Jingel, can arm 900 horse and 800 foot.

The tribes under these three chiefs are Mussulmans of the sect of Shiah, but very lax in the practice of their faith and forms of worship.

The Sirdar Hassan Khan ben Zorab is recognised as their supreme chief by the other three tribes of the Hazarah Pusht Koh, though they are broken up into many separate camps, and each chooses a commander to be confirmed in his authority by Hassan Khan. This chief can assemble in arms 5000 horse and 3000 foot, and even double the number in a case of pressing necessity. It is not astonishing that these tribes should furnish so many soldiers, because, the armed force simply signifies every adult male, for they are always capable of bearing arms. In time of war no one remains in the camp but the old men, women, and children.

The Pusht Koh Hazarahs of Hassan Khan ben Zorab are constantly divided amongst themselves, either by the intrigues of subaltern chiefs, or by family quarrels; they are always scheming and plotting one against the other, and thus are ever exhausting that strength to their own detriment, which, if consolidated and well directed, would render them terrible to the Afghans, with whom they are constantly at war. Their country is difficult to invade, its natural defences being excellent; they could emerge when they pleased, ravage the plains of Kandahar and Ghuzni and retreat to their inaccessible haunts, if they would but act together. Such, however, is their disunion, that the Afghans always contrive to get through their passes and attack them on their own ground, though they cannot occupy it permanently, and they content themselves with straining every nerve to get a good booty and be off again. By this constant hostility is maintained such a lively hatred between the Afghans and the Hazarahs, that it is scarcely possible for the latter to venture singly in the Paropamisus—a lonely traveller would assuredly be assassinated. He is obliged, therefore, to make a considerable circuit to go from Kabul to Herat, or vice versâ, to accomplish a journey which would be so short if the country of the Hazarahs were safe. The caravans generally go by Balkh or Kandahar, and it requires more than a month to perform that distance, while the direct road between the two towns could be travelled in a fortnight easily. Yar Mohamed Khan assured me that the Emir Dost Mohamed sent him a letter in 1844 by a Ser Jingel Hazarah he had in his service, and that going straight through the country on his own horse, the man had been only eight days on the journey.

Tamerlane seems to have been the last sovereign who subjugated the Hazarahs; they shook off the yoke at his death, and have remained free in their mountains ever since. The Sufaveans, the Grand Mogul, Nadir Shah, and Ahmed Shah, Suddozye, have never been able to subjugate them again. It appears that they have been the same from time immemorial;* for Quintus Curtius,

* The Hazarahs are not, however, the descendants of the old inhabitants of the Parapamisus, but are Tartar tribes, first settled in the country by Gengis

one of the historians of Alexander, speaks of them in these terms:—

"Alexander advanced into a region imperfectly known to the bordering nations, as it cultivates no interchange by commerce. Designated Paropamisadæ, the wild inhabitants are the most uncivilized amongst the barbarians: the bare aspect of the local scenery has petrified their minds. Seated for the most part on the northern side of the frozen ridge, they touch Bactriana on the west. That portion of their territory which is enlivened by the sun stretches towards the Indian Sea. Their cottages are built, the lower part of brick and the upper of tile; for no timber grows in the sterile fields, nor on the naked mountains: their form, broadest at bottom, gradually contracts as the structure rises, till it terminates in the fashion of a ship's keel, with an aperture in the centre to admit the light. Such vines and trees as can endure the rigour of such a climate the inhabitants press down and cover with earth during the winter, and when the snow is dissolved, they dig them out and restore them to the air and sun. So deep are the snows which shroud the ground, and so bound up by ice and almost perpetual frost, that the vestige of a bird or beast is not perceptible. The light is rather an obscuration of the sky resembling darkness, in which the nearest objects are with difficulty seen.

"In this uncultivated wild the destitute army had every variety of ill to endure—scarcity, cold, weariness, despair. The blast of the snow extinguished life in many, and caused the feet of others to mortify; its white glare perniciously affected the eyes of the majority. Some, having stretched on a bed of ice their exhausted frames, through want of motion were so stiffened by the activity of the frost, that when they essayed to rise they were unable. The torpid were lifted up by their comrades; there was no better remedy than compelling them to walk: the vital heat being thus excited, the use of their limbs in part returned. Such as could reach a cottage were restored quickly; but through the density of the atmosphere, huts could be traced out only by the smoke. The inhabitants had never seen a foreigner in their territory; and as their armed visitants suddenly presented themselves, their hearts

---

Khan. It is very remarkable that they should have entirely lost their original language, and adopted an old dialect of the Persian. Their Tartar physiognomy remains, however, unchanged, so that it is impossible to mistake them.—ED.

died with fear: petitioning to have their lives spared, they produced what their hovels afforded."—Vol. ii. ch. iii.

This recital appears to indicate that the Macedonians crossed the Paropamisus in the winter, and I have no difficulty in believing the sufferings they endured; but had they gone in the summer they would have found as much pleasure as they did misery: for the soil of the valleys, nourished by the melting of the snow, becomes in the spring exceedingly fertile, streams intersect it in all directions, and the heat which is so intense in the Afghan plains is tempered by the mountain breezes, fresh from their contact with the snowy summits. This explains at once the difference between my narrative and that of Quintus Curtius.

Amongst the Hazarahs there is a tribe called Berber, like the inhabitants of Algeria.* The former disown these latter, and do not admit their common origin, but it is incontestably true that the Algerian race is Eïmak, and the corrupt or rather the primitive Persian is the only language in use amongst them. The Berbers of Africa are Mussulmans of the sect of the Shiahs, as are a small number of the Pusht Koh Hazarah: the majority of the latter, however, belong to the sect of Ali-illáhi, who believe in the divinity of Ali.

Dehás, July 8th—eight parasangs—along plains and valleys tolerably fertile; the supply of water near the road was deficient, but supposed to be more abundant at a distance, because we saw there many nomadic tents, which would hardly have been the case had the plain been perfectly arid. We avoided them all, and travelled entirely across country under the guidance of a Hazarah, sent with us by Alayar Beg to see us safe to Sirpool. After having ridden six parasangs, we crossed a range of thinly-wooded hills which branched from a mountain skirted at the base by the Balkh river. This was the only village that we saw on the journey, and its position was at once picturesque and startling: it appeared actually hung up on the side of the rock; our guide told us that the way to it was on the other side of the mountain, by an exceedingly difficult road cut in the solid rock. The inhabitants of this place make extremely beautiful carpets, which sell very well at Khulm and Kabul. This manufacture

* The tribes of Berbers are to be met with in every part of the East.—ED.

would procure them not only a livelihood, but an honest one; the latter, however, is apparently of no particular value to them, for they are the cleverest and most daring thieves in the country. They assert that they are descended from the aborigines, and have never submitted to any conqueror; their language, as well as that spoken by the Hazarahs, is the most ancient Persian, and their religion a species of idolatry mingled with Islamism.

In approaching the river of Balkh, we crossed immense tracts, the long grass of which reached the horses' bellies, and made riding very disagreeable; this pasture was intersected by an infinity of trenches, which lead the water of the river through the lands of the nomads, whose tents we had avoided as much as possible.

It was night when we reached Dehás (the name of the river), a very small Hazarah encampment of two-and-twenty tents, commanded by Chopan Ali, a cousin of Alayar Beg. We did not see him, for he remained in his tent, but ordered that one next to him should be prepared for our reception, and at midnight sent us for supper a side of grilled venison, Jerán * deer, which he had killed the day before, and some very black bread. To my great satisfaction, we had no visit from any one, and at daybreak were again in the saddle for Sirpool.

Sirpool, July 9th—ten parasangs. After having crossed the Dehás (which is rather rapid just here) by a ford, we travelled an hour and a half through fields, and then entered a chain of mountains of moderate height. The path was stony and ran near the edge of an abrupt precipice, and at the bottom of the ravine flowed a torrent, at which we saw troops of deer and wild boar come to slake their thirst, and lave and refresh their limbs; of the latter there were hundreds, and they especially splashed about and disported themselves in the water with peculiar delight. We lost the pleasure of watching them when we reached the top of the mountain, to which the latter part of the road was smooth and easy. The other side was slightly wooded, and the brushwood afforded capital cover for the red-legged partridge which abound here; at the foot of the mountain I remarked, for the first time in Central Asia, patches of the oleander† on the borders of the streamlets.

* Jerán means an antelope.—ED.

† The oleander, "khur-záhreh," or "ass-poison," is, however, very common all over the East.—ED.

Thence to Sirpool the road is over a plain or slightly undulating ground; the country is uninhabited to about a couple of parasangs from the town, but there the tents become numerous, and the flocks also. We had a good deal of trouble to reach it, for Roostem's horse and the one my servant rode were completely beat. Poor creatures! they were all of them reduced to skin and bone, and had suffered terribly from the forced marches which our difficulties and disappointments—not to mention danger—had driven us to make. If there had been another day's work between us and Sirpool, I really believe they could not have done it; we must have stopped on the road.

Sirpool is an agglomeration of houses utterly devoid of regularity, and built on the slope of an eminence crowned by a fortress in which the Governor resides. Numerous tents are grouped round the houses, and, including their inhabitants, the place contains 18,000 souls: the population of the Khanat does not amount to more than four times that number; most of them are Usbeks, a third only being Ser Jingel Hazarahs. Sirpool occupies a position greatly favoured by nature, for the valley is abundantly watered by streams from the mountains, which unite there and form a river that flows on to Shibbergan; the inhabitants were gathering in the harvest when we arrived, and the breadth of cultivated land and orchards of various fruits appeared to me considerable.

Mahmood Khan, the governor, is the son-in-law of the Mir Wali of Khulm, and is one of his best and most faithful allies. The influence of this chief extends far amongst the Eïmaks of the Paropamisus, and he is dreaded by them on account of his great daring and bravery: he is not less feared by his neighbours the Usbeks, and a letter from him carries as much weight with it as if he sent an army. He is about forty years of age, of middle height, and powerfully made; his countenance is open, and his features have more the Persian than the Tartar character; for although he is of Usbek race, I was told that for three or four generations his ancestors had allied themselves with Persian women of Kabul. Mahmood Khan keeps up a standing force of 2000 superior horsemen and 2000 foot, which number can be trebled in case of necessity.

All that I had heard of the character of Mahmood Khan determined me to take a perfectly open course with him, and to put him in possession of my real position and history. As soon, therefore, as we had encamped, I sent my guide and Roostem to the citadel to inform him of my arrival, when he immediately sent his Naïb to escort me to his presence, and we were at once installed in the fortress. He came down into the court to receive me, and, in the unceremonious Tartar fashion, make himself sure that the room which had been given to us was clean and well provided with carpets. His welcome was rough, but warm and frank, and prepossessed me in his favour; and after he had seen that everything was properly arranged for our comfort, he led the way to his own room. This apartment was furnished in the simplest style, utterly devoid of the least appearance of luxury, and he took his seat by the corner of the window, retaining, according to his custom from his earliest youth, his sword and pistols in his belt. After inviting me to be seated also, he inquired the object of my journey to Sirpool.

My reply was a short but exact account of the troubles and vexations that overtook me after I left Meshed, adding a request that he would grant me his protection to enable me to reach Kandahar in safety. Mahmood Khan's instant reply was couched in such kind terms that I felt at once that I had neither overrated his character, nor presumed upon it too far; and after a few words of consolation, he added, "They have however been fortunate for me, for I have thus the unlooked-for opportunity of showing you hospitality, and the presence of a stranger always draws down a blessing from Heaven on the roof under which he reposes."

The conversation then turned upon his quarrels and disputes with his neighbours, particularly Roostem Khan of Shibberghan; afterwards he made many inquiries about the military art, and desired me to explain to him the European system of attack and defence—endeavouring to fix it clearly in his mind with a view to its being of use to him at some future time. With him Feringhee meant an Englishman, but he had never quarrelled with them during their occupation of Kabul, and he had heard much of their generosity; therefore, as they were now out of reach of his country, he had no objection to make an alliance with them. "It would," he said, "give him great pleasure if I would act as his mediator;" only he begged I would not do so after the Asiatic fashion, and keep half the subsidy that he expected from the liberality of the

Government of Calcutta; in return he promised me all sorts of good offices. Of course I was lavish of fine promises, for my position rendered it necessary I should do all in my power to please him, and the best way to do so was by flattering his cupidity. I succeeded, it appears, in convincing him of my sincerity, for he promised that I should arrive at Kandahar without finding out that I had been travelling; "you shall be wafted there as if in your bed — the journey will seem like a delightful dream." Though I did not anticipate the enjoyment of all the sweets that his metaphorical language held out to me, I nevertheless congratulated myself on having removed all the scruples that he might have had.

In spite of the great fatigue I felt, I was anxious to set off the next morning; but the Khan would not hear of my doing so; he said I must absolutely remain his guest for one day more; besides there were eight or ten letters that he was to write for me, and that could not be done at night. He advised me to sell my poor broken-down horses, and the Hazarahs to do the same. We consented, and in order to compensate my travelling companions, I gave them the price which my own three fetched, and had the satisfaction of seeing them contented.

"The country you will pass through," said Mahmood Khan, "contains more horses than men, and with the letters that I shall give you, if you wanted twenty horses at every encampment between here and the fortress of Lar (the residence of Hassan Khan ben Zorab), they would be given to you in ten minutes without the cost of a *poul*. The camps are very near each other, and you will always be well mounted; so with these fresh and vigorous horses you can if you like ride twenty parasangs a-day. Nothing will impede your course, only conceal carefully that you are a Feringhee; not because they are disliked in this country, where they have never done any harm, but because they are supposed to be great alchemists, and some of them would believe your flesh is gold. Say everywhere that you are a Persian in my service, as I shall write in the letters you will take with you, and that I have sent you to confer on matters of importance with Hassan Khan. Be sure you will get to his encampment safe and sound, and, if you take my advice, you will not go to Kandahar; the Sirdars there are bad fellows. With the aid of Hassan Khan, and travelling as rapidly as you have done, you will take but five days to go from Lar to Kabul, and thus shorten your journey and avoid the suspicion which the Hazarah chief, who hates him of Kandahar, will not fail to entertain if you persist in going to that town after having traversed his country, with which the Afghans are very imperfectly acquainted. I shall write to him that you are a merchant of Meshed, so mind you behave accordingly."

It was impossible to make kinder arrangements for my comfort and security, and I presented the Khan with a pair of pistols in testimony of my gratitude. If the proverb that "small presents preserve friendship" be true in Europe, it applies in no country so forcibly as in Asia. Mahmood Khan had never seen any like them; he admired and caressed them as if they had been alive, and I had made him the happiest of men.

July 10th, I spent in rest and quiet in the fortress of Sirpool, and left it on the 11th. In the morning six horses were brought into the court-yard—four for riding and two for baggage. When the Khan saw my trunks, he advised me to leave them, for they would excite thievish propensities more than anything else. This was true, for, seeing them always padlocked, they fancy they are full of gold, and are always endeavouring to do some mischief to their owner, in order to get possession of them; and a large sack which it is the custom to throw across the horse does not attract half so much the attention of the evil-disposed. I therefore transferred my effects into two of these sacks, and one was put on each horse; thus divided the baggage was much lighter, and the animals so laden were either led or driven before us.

This was the most agreeable way in which I had as yet travelled in Asia, but such accommodation cannot always be procured. Up to my return to Herat, I travelled ten or fifteen parasangs a-day with horses that were fresh from every camp on the road; the firman of Mahmood Khan sufficed to bring them out at a moment's notice. A guide accompanied us to return with the horses, and was charged to smooth every difficulty. Never did I cross a more dangerous country, and never was I less uneasy. I avoided, it is true, putting myself forward, left it to Roostem and Rabi to procure what I wanted, and when I arrived at a halt lay down immediately, pretending to have a bad sore throat.

If, however, we were free from the suspicious investigations of the Eïmaks, I cannot say the same for their dogs; they were the most morose, ill-disciplined brutes that it has ever fallen to my lot to meet with. The moment we arrived in an encampment we were so surrounded and assailed that we could scarcely get off our horses. At last they gradually quitted my companions, satisfied with having smelt their legs and feet, and fastened themselves more savagely on me, as if they wanted to point me out to the whole camp as an intruder.

Boodhi, July 11th—ten parasangs. The country that we crossed in this stage was very varied in character; the most vigorous vegetation was to be seen close to the most arid sterility. The sides of the mountains on our left were abruptly broken and rocky, and utterly bare, while those on the right had many trees on them, and in some places patches of cultivation which indicated the presence of a village.

The valley through which we rode was remarkably fruitful, but the heat was concentrated in it like a furnace; the nomadic population was numerous, and their camps prettily situated amongst groves of trees, through which flowed streams of water. This scenery lasted about six hours when the valley began to rise, and contracted gradually into a narrow defile, the sides of which were nearly perpendicular and much broken; on the summits we distinguished pieces of wall indicating clearly the existence of fortifications in times past, which must have made the passage of the defile exceedingly difficult if not impossible.

It brought us out upon an enclosed space of which the centre had been occupied by a small square fortress with towers at the corners, under the murderous fire from which it would be absolutely necessary to pass to reach the other side of the mountain. On the most elevated point I remarked an enormous block of rock, turned to the sun, on the smooth surface of which were sculptured several figures and inscriptions. The former were in a group; one represented a king on his throne administering justice before his assembled court; a warrior stretched on the ground in chains had been executed, as the monarch's attitude and extended right arm appeared to indicate, by his order; another captive, liberated from his chains, has fallen at the prince's knee, and with terror depicted on his countenance seems to implore his mercy. The Arab inscription, which I could not read, seemed to me much more recent than the bas-relief, and appears to have replaced another which once existed a little higher up, where a hollowed part of the rock indicates that it has been cut or scraped to efface something.

My guide could not tell me anything about the sculptures, excepting that the people of the country attributed them to Sultan Mahmood the Ghuznehvide. He added that on the plain, two parasangs to the right, there were the ruins of a large town, amongst which lived some herdsmen of the tribe Mongol,* subject to the Khan of Sirpool. The descent of the mountain occupied only half an hour, and we continued to advance over a rather extensive steppe, on which an immense number of hares were enjoying themselves. Having travelled ten parasangs in seven hours, we stopped at the fortified village of Boodhi, situated just at the entrance of the first gorges of a chain of high mountains, and perched on a conical hill; the walls are of burnt brick, and loop-holed. The importance of this town in times past when the Mongols held sway in Central Asia, must have been very different from what it is now; for this fort guarded on the north the Paropamisus. The fortifications and nearly all the houses are in ruins; and there are but two hundred and fifty, or at the utmost three hundred, inhabited. Murad Beg Usbek, who commands there for Mahmood Khan of Sirpool, made us welcome to his house after having read the letter of his chief. The next morning he gave us a new guide, with our rested horses, and we started for

Div Hissar, July 12th—ten parasangs. After an hour's ride along a deep gorge we began to ascend a mountain, and found at each parasang a small stone fort, situated in the best position for defence; a detachment of a few resolute men could hold it a long time against an invading army. We worked up for four hours, with large blocks of detached stone obstructing the very narrow and winding road all the way to the top.

We descended the other side by a deep defile, at the bottom of which ran a torrent formed by the melting snows from the surrounding summits; in this defile we were frequently obliged to get off our horses, so utterly impracticable was the road any way but on foot—it was the worst I had yet seen. We were two hours amongst the gradually decreasing mountains reaching the plain

* It is an important fact to have found Mongols in this place, as before they were only known to exist in a small colony on the skirts of the mountains of Gour, far to the south-west of Sirpool.—ED.

into which they, as it were, subside: this is a space of thirty-six parasangs in circumference, entirely enclosed by mountains, from which there is only one other exit, and by that we were to leave the next morning.

The vegetation in this basin was magnificent; every part of the surface was cultivated in fields or gardens in every direction; there were trees also, and water from the mountains. These were indeed a contrast to the plain, being exceedingly rocky, but where there happened to be a little vegetable earth, a few shrubs would sprout up, which the inhabitants dignified by the term *jangal* (jungle). Many wild beasts infest these hill sides, and are much dreaded by the woodcutters, who are sometimes killed by them. The inhabitants of this plain call themselves Mongols, but they are known only by the name of Seherai, inhabitants of the plain; they form a small republic, which is in some degree subservient to the Khan of Sirpool, the lion of the country. They pretend to have been settled there by Ghengis Khan, and to have braved the efforts of every conqueror since the days of that grand exterminator; having seen how difficult is the access to their country, I could believe it, the more so as their plain produces everything necessary for their maintenance. They are not obliged to have dealings with or in any way concern themselves about their neighbours. The Seherai have a vague idea of Islamism, and sometimes swear by Ali and the Prophet; but these words are, I apprehend, mere relics of their former intercourse with the Mohamedan world, for, as far as I could discover, their worship is real idolatry. Like the ancient Persians, they recognise a principle of good and a principle of evil, but under the modern names of Khoda and Shaïtan, signifying God and Devil—they are uncircumcised, never pray, and condemn no animal as unclean.

Their habits are quite patriarchal: living far from the din of cities, and ignorant of their refinements as well as their superfluities, their manners have something wild and savage that at first shocks a stranger; but the feeling of dislike soon wears off when you find that, ignorant as they are of all that in our eyes contributes to social well-being, they are not the less content, and are exempt from many tribulations which we inflict upon ourselves in search of happiness. The largest collection of tents and houses on this plain was at the foot of the mountains which enclosed it on the south, exactly opposite the point at which we had entered this extraordinary basin. It stood on a little plateau, thickly covered with trees, which almost entirely concealed from view the fortress of Div Hissar, of the giant: a high tower rising on the north from the left angle alone indicates its presence.

We saw at the foot of the rise before going into the village a building that appeared to be a temple, with three sides closed, and open on the east; within were coarsely carved wooden idols, on which were hung many skins of wild beasts—the offerings of hunters. In conformity with the custom of the country, I bent seven times before the gigantic Jupiter, and then proceeded direct to the house of Timour Beg, chief of this secluded little domain. Roostem gave him the letter from the Khan of Sirpool, which he kissed three times and carried to his forehead four, before unsealing it; after having read it, he sent us a message of invitation to enter the fort by a pretty young slave, which surprised me much, as I was not aware of the freedom enjoyed by the fair sex at Div Hissar. I had, it is true, observed that the women we passed on the road were unveiled, and as this was the custom in Turkistan, I thought it might obtain here, but I did not expect to receive any invitation to be sent by one of the fair sex.

Timour Beg welcomed me with the rough and simple cordiality natural to the Tartars. He was between thirty-five and forty years of age, almost beardless, short, and built like a Hercules; a kind smile animated his countenance, and his features were far less ugly than those of Mongols in general. He received us with great cordiality, and immediately ordered a repast which would have sufficed for at least thirty persons; the beverage at this meal was a description of cider, with which he finished by intoxicating himself, and when we heard him snore we requested permission to retire; this was granted, and the Seherai ladies who had waited during dinner conducted us to our apartments. Their subsequent attentions were remarkable, for they not only assisted at our toilette, but washed our feet, and to my great astonishment subsequently shampooed me from head to foot, and this too in the most free and easy manner possible. I did not think it necessary to refuse to receive attentions which they thought it a duty to pay me under the sacred name of hospitality, for it has always been my habit to respect the customs of those countries through which I travel; but having a long ride before me on the morrow, I ventured to request the lady who had charge of me to moderate her exertions, and leave me to take some repose. Such is the invariable custom practised towards strangers at Div Hissar. At first I flattered myself that mine was an exceptional case, and intended as a special mark of honour on the part of Timour Beg, but I subsequently ascertained that my fellow-travellers and even my servant were equally the objects of these ladies' care, and that the chief's daughter is not exempt from the duties attendant upon this singular custom.

Timour Beg insisted upon my remaining the following day, and accompanying him on a bear and tiger hunt,—an invitation I, to his great annoyance, declined, accepting, however, an excellent horse to carry me to the next halt.

CHAPTER XVII.

Singlak — Singular excavations in the rocks — The legend connected with them — Quarrel between the Hazarahs and Firooz Kohis — Unsuccessful attack by the latter — Courage of the Tartar women — Their military capabilities — Alteration in the author's route — Kohistani-baba — Highest elevation of the mountain range — Magnificent view — Valley commencing at the sources of the Dehas — The Ser Jingelab and Tingelab — The Siah Koh and Sufeid Koh — Course of the Heri-rood — Coins found in the ruins of Karabagh — Hassan ben Zorab — Encampment of Kohistani-baba — The silent Agha — Deria-derré — Picturesque scene near a lake — The province of Gour — The tribe of the Taymoonis — Their military force — Wily policy of Yar Mohamed Khan — Ibrahim Khan — The value of seven Korans — Spirited conduct of this Khan — The author in a difficulty — Osman Khan.

SINGLAK, July 13th—ten parasangs. We had as much trouble to cross the mountains south of Div Hissar as we had in passing those by which we reached it on the previous day, and saw on our road some more small forts. Emerging from the gorges we came upon a steppe abounding with game; the wild boars fled at our approach to hide themselves in the reeds on the marshy ground. An encampment of Firooz Kohis were upon this plain and I once more had a narrow escape of being despatched by their detestable dogs. Thence we struck into another mountain on which are three ancient fortresses in ruins and deserted; the walls of a fourth enclosed a considerable space of ground full of trees; some cultivation and huts built of reeds and plastered with mud and straw proved the existence of a few inhabitants.

A parasang further the mountain had a sombre appearance, the scarped but smooth rocks on either side of the road being divided into the most whimsical forms possible, and at about sixty feet from their base pierced with oblong holes open towards the east. I could not account for these holes, and an observation made by my guide having increased my curiosity, I dismounted and climbed up to one by a steep fissure which appeared to have once been a staircase. Here I came to an excavation, which I entered and found that it led to a vast number of chambers cut in the living rock, the loopholes visible on the outside being intended to admit the light and air. These chambers led into a corridor one hundred and fifty yards long and ten wide; in the centre is an open cutting with basins at intervals, which seemed to warrant the supposition that a stream of water once flowed through it; the mountain has been excavated in the interior, and contained several stories of apartments one above the other, the access to them being by a spiral path round the cavity. I asked the guide whether he could give me any information respecting the origin of these singular and interesting habitations, but he knew nothing of their history; nor had he even a legend, excepting that they had been seized by genii, who had turned out the first occupants, and he offered up a prayer for my benefit that no misfortune might happen to me for having been so audacious as to intrude upon their abode.*

After this unusually interesting interruption to our journey we proceeded for five parasangs through valleys and in the mountains where many Hazarahs and Firooz Kohis dependent on the Sirdar Hassan Khan commanding at Doulet-yar were encamped. This chief married the sister of Mahmood Khan of Sirpool, and I had a letter for him from the latter that I was to have given him; but as I must have gone four or five parasangs out of my way to reach Doulet-yar, I preferred sending it by Rabi, which I did, giving him a guide from the camp at which we changed horses and desiring him to rejoin us at Singlak where I intended to sleep. But I much regretted this afterwards, for on arriving at Singlak I found the place perfectly deserted, with evident traces of recent devastation; not a tent was to be seen and nearly all the huts had been knocked down; a few snarling dogs were prowling about them, and alone in the midst of this mournful scene was one old man, who was evidently dying. At first we had not perceived him, but his moaning attracted our attention to the small hut in which he lay, and which we had taken for a hen-house. It was with much pain and difficulty that he turned towards us, and though incapable of uttering a word, he replied to our inquiries by raising his hand towards the neighbouring mountain, whither we directed our steps almost in despair. A nomad that we met told us the Hazarahs of Singlak had been

* Rocks similarly honeycombed occur in many parts of Afghanistan, and are probably of Buddhist origin. The small chambers were intended for the abode of the ascetics of the sect. There are some fine remains of this class in the Upper Valley of the Urgandâb.—ED.

suddenly obliged to decamp, for fear of the vengeance of the Firooz Kohis, some of whom were only two parasangs on the right. The Hazarahs had in a scuffle recently killed two of this tribe, and refused either to give up the murderers or pay the price of blood. Knowing themselves however to be the weaker party, they moved for their better security from the open plain on which they were usually encamped, to the mountains; the ravines and rocky caves of which would afford shelter for their families and flocks. Though we followed with precision the directions this man gave us, we rode a considerable distance up the ascent without seeing anything of the Hazarahs: so after having sought them in vain, I fired a pistol the report of which, a thousand times repeated, was borne far away by the mountain echoes, and in an instant every rock above our heads was alive with armed men who started to their feet from every cleft and ravine, imagining we had intended to challenge or attack them. Their reply came sharp enough, for before we could make them understand us they gave us a rattling volley, from which we were fortunately sheltered by the ground or must have suffered some casualties. Seeing we were so few in number they accepted our shouts as of a friendly character, and listened to our explanation that we were unoffending travellers seeking their hospitality. We then approached, and my guide informed them that we wished to remain with them till we could receive the answer to a letter I had sent to the chief at Doulet-yar, when they made no further difficulty about receiving us, a lamb was killed for our supper, and we were soon sleeping as soundly as men might be expected to do after so long a day's journey. But not so the Hazarahs, who kept on the *qui vive*—which was indeed necessary, for towards three o'clock in the morning an alarm was given that aroused us all. The enemy had hoped to surprise the hare on her form, and endeavoured to seize the heights which commanded our retreat, but the Hazarahs were on the alert and prepared to receive them. Our hosts, posted behind the rocks, preserved a profound silence; we ranged ourselves near them and waited with impatience the signal for the attack. A white streak on the horizon ushered in the dawn and just permitted us to distinguish the enemy advancing silently, and creeping stealthily towards us. The wary Hazarahs stood calmly to their arms, and when they were near enough, rolled down upon them large stones that had been previously collected for the purpose. This manœuvre brought them upon their feet, when a general discharge was poured in upon them which speedily made them retire. The women showed themselves as daring as the men in this affray, and were in the foremost rank, replying to the shots of the retreating foe like true heroines. No one was killed or wounded on our side, but at broad daylight, when the Hazarahs went over the ground occupied by the Firooz Kohis, they found traces of blood, clearly proving that some of our shots had taken effect. It was a remarkable sight to see brave and energetic Tartar women under fire amongst and as forward as the men; they fight also on horseback, and ride or act under any circumstances as well as the other sex: more than one of them would, I have no doubt, meet any European horseman on more than equal terms; the dexterity with which they manage their horses is extraordinary, and their courage is not less great—they take part in every war, and the vanquished dread their cruelty more than that of the men.

During this anxious night, I had been uneasy at the non-appearance of Rabi; he ought to have joined me on the previous evening, and the disordered state into which the country had been thrown by the quarrel between these two camps gave me much ground for uneasiness. This was however dissipated, for at six o'clock in the morning Rabi arrived in company with the *Naïb* of the Khan of Doulet-yar, who had been sent to settle the differences in question. The Naïb gave me letters to the chiefs of several encampments, charging them to provide me with horses; and he warned me that the Sirdar of Doulet-yar had altered my route because Hassan Khan ben Zorab, of the Pusht Koh Hazarah, to whom I was to pay a visit, had left his usual residence at Lar, and was gone with a body of troops to the mountains of Jevedge, fearing that the army from Herat which had invaded the province of Gour would cross the border and pillage his territories also; but the Naïb assured me this would make no difference as to the safety of the two roads. The Sirdar of Doulet-yar no doubt intended for the best, but this alteration did me no service. I had been represented to him as a dependent of the Chief of Sirpool on my way to transact some business with the Chief of the Hazarahs, and he thought himself quite right in directing me to where he was to be found; but as I foresaw that this incident would create fresh difficulties and complications, I grumbled heartily at my protector. In any case my best plan was to get on, which we did, and proceeded with the same horses we had ridden the day before, our hosts in this instance not having any to lend us. We were now three parasangs beyond Singlak, and had therefore eight remaining for our day's journey to—

Kohistani-baba, July 14th—eleven parasangs from Singlak. On leaving the hiding-place of the Hazarahs, we continued to ascend the mountain, and, passing crest after crest, at last found ourselves on the summit, and at the highest elevation I had reached in this country. The soil varied a good deal in this range, and we saw the oak, pine, and barbery shrub; many streams were crossed which, on the authority of my guide, are the sources of the Moorghab.

During the last hour occupied in the ascent, the ground was covered with snow; and although the sun's rays darted full upon us, the cold was so bitter that I was obliged to wrap my cloak close about me. Standing actually on the highest point of the ridge, I felt an indefinable sensation of admiration at the splendid sight thrown in bold relief at my feet. There was much variety in this magnificent view, and it was possible to see clearly the details of it. In the horizon, and at thirty parasangs from us, was the grand peak of Tchalap, which, capped with its eternal and unchanging snows, seemed to reach the heavens. The high mountains we had crossed in our ascent looked mere hillocks, compared with the distant giant. The district we had traversed between us and Sirpool was but a spot on the surface of the country spread out before us; and the chain on which we stood, stretched E. and W. to a distance that exceeded the powers of vision to measure. An infinity of lower chains diverged from the principal, and, I may say, imperial range, decreasing gradually in height towards the N., leaving lovely and productive valleys between them, with here and there an encampment of the black tents of the nomadic inhabitants, and luxuriant verdure intersected by streams of water shining in the sun like threads of silver. All this had such animation about it, that I felt charmed and riveted to the spot by the entrancing pleasure of contemplating it.

We were but two hours descending to the valley beneath, which was three or four parasangs wide and of considerable length. According to the inhabitants, it commences at the sources of the Dehás, the river of Balkh, at the foot of the Hindoo Koosh, and stretches without interruption beyond Herat, being in its whole length fertile and well populated. This valley, as appears by the course of the waters, inclines from E. to W. Two small rivers, the Ser Jingelab and the Tingelab take their rise in the chain of mountains which separates them from the Dehás, and after having kept an independent course of about twenty-five parasangs each, they join at Dowlet-yar, pursuing, under the name of Heri-rood, their course through the countries of Sheherek, Obeh, and Herat. The valley through which this river, the Heri-rood, runs, is bounded on the S. by a chain of mountains called Koh Siah, black mountains, from the dark colour of the rocks. It is a little lower though as extensive from E. to W. as the one we had crossed which borders this valley on the north; and which, from the snowy drapery that always hangs in dazzling folds over the summits, are called the Sufeid Koh, white mountains. The waters which descend on the northern side of the Sufeid Koh are lost in the steppes or join the Oxus; of those flowing from the southern side of the Siah Koh some join the Helmund—(the Etymander of the Greeks)—and some flow into the Lake Seistan. The Heri-rood is the intermediate line which marks the division of the waters that flow from the mountains on either side of it.

The first part of its course, as far as the village of Jaor, is many thousand feet above the level of the sea; and it is only between this village and the town of Obeh that it begins to increase its fall; from here its course is rapid, and there are several cataracts many feet in height. The compact character of the Siah Koh range, which borders it on the south, forbids the supposition that this river could have taken any other course even in remote ages.

The point at which we crossed it was six parasangs S.W. of Sheherek, once a populous and flourishing town, now much reduced and inhabited by Eïmaks. The Prince Saadet Muluk, who had been governor of this district, said that he believed this city was in ancient times the capital of the kingdom of Gour. But admitting this, it could have been the case for a short period only, for all the traditions and written history of the country mention Zerni as the usual residence of the Gooride princes of the dynasty of Malek Gour, corrupted into Malek Kurt.

The Prince also told me that Karabagh, another very ancient town situated beyond Lar, is surrounded by a great extent of ruins, and is even now well inhabited. Gold and silver coins are found there of dimensions rarely seen in our days, for, according to his description, they are nearly three and a half inches in diameter. Major Todd, to whom the Prince showed one, informed him that it bore the effigy of Alexander the Great. The position of the ruins in the centre of a fertile country leads to the conjecture that Karabagh was the town of Nysa. It is now known only for the excellent quality of the Kourk *bareks** woven there, second only in reputation to those of Derzi.

In the valley of the Heri-rood we found a succession of camps and villages and cultivation of all kinds, with cattle, horses, and camels in vast numbers on the pastures. The point at which we crossed this river was in the possession of the Sirdar of Dowlet-yar, who had declared himself the ally of Hassan Khan ben Zorab, the chief of the Pusht Koh Hazarahs, and who, in consequence of this act, would in all probability expect to receive an early visit from the troops of the Vezir Sahib of Herat. He was, they said, endeavouring to avert the storm by recognising his suzerainty. Two hours after passing the Heri-rood, we reached the base of the Siah Koh, the summit of which we reached without difficulty in two hours, and descended by the bed of a small stream that tumbled from rock to rock with beautiful and picturesque effect. As we advanced the descent became more difficult, and we were at last obliged to proceed with the utmost caution. At one spot the ground was almost precipitous; a powerful torrent rolled in the gorge beneath it, and the path, sometimes cut in the rock by manual labour, sometimes worn by the travelling of ages, was just wide enough for the passage of a laden horse. To look down into the gulf beneath us was impossible without feeling giddy; and I was just rejoicing in the idea that we had passed the worst part, when, on emerging from a deep hollow, we saw some horsemen coming towards us at full speed. Happily they were only half-way up a low hill from which a small valley separated us, and being well mounted we increased our distance in spite of their exertions, and before they could come within gunshot we arrived at Kohistani-baba, an encampment of Hazarahs situated on a high plain covered with pasture in the midst of the Siah Koh.

---

* A coarse brown cloth, half woven and half felted, forming the ordinary winter dress of the Afghans. During the English occupation, it was a favourite article of dress both with officers and men.—ED.

Agha Ali, the chief of this encampment, received us in his tent, treated us handsomely, and was discreet in his conversation to an extent that I should have been very glad to find in some of our former hosts. He spoke but three times while we were under his roof: "Good morning," when we arrived; "All right," when he had read the letter from the Sirdar of Doulet-yar; and "Good bye," when we departed. To make amends, however, for this extraordinary silence, he smoked his *tchilim*, water pipe, without quitting his hold all the time; his gurgle was the last thing I heard when I fell asleep, and the first when I awoke in the morning. This place was a dependency of the Sirdar's, who was Governor of the district Dagha-rejeb.

Deria-dereh, also called *Dereh Mustapha Khan*, July 15th—thirteen parasangs. We travelled three hours before we got clear of the Siah Koh, at the foot of which we found a large encampment of Mongols, who gave us a good remount. We had then five hours of a plain to cross, on which were some low hills; the plain was pretty well peopled with Eïmaks and Taymoonis, and was partly steppe and pasture, but without wood. Two hours more amongst a chain of not very high mountains brought us to their summits, from which we saw a most lovely landscape at our feet. In a small oblong valley, entirely enclosed by the mountains, was a little lake of azure colour and transparent clearness, which lay like a vast gem embedded in the surrounding verdure; there was no stream from this beautiful natural reservoir, and its surplus water therefore must be consumed by evaporation. From this chain of hills we descended by a gentle slope to the borders of the lake, round which were somewhat irregularly pitched a number of Taymooni tents, separated from each other by little patches of cultivation and gardens enclosed by stone walls breast high. The prodigious height of the grass particularly attracted my attention, for it almost concealed the cattle that were grazing there. The luxuriance of the vegetation in this valley might compare with any that I had ever seen in Europe. On the summits of the surrounding mountains were several ruins, and the inhabitants on the borders of the beautiful little lake had a legend to tell of each. The north side, by which we had arrived, was the least elevated, and pastures stretched half-way up the mountain; on the west were projecting rocks of most capricious form, under which were a few copses of ash and oak; and the east was covered from the summit to the base with a forest of small trees. The southern side, quite a contrast to the others, presented a chaotic mass of naked rocks, broken up into ravines, whence gushed abundant waters and completed the circle round this oasis of the mountains. Fishermen were dragging the lake; the women, unveiled, were leading the flocks to water; and young girls sat outside the tents weaving bareks, with the most simple machinery—health, cheerfulness, and contentment were depicted on every face. The inhabitants of this isolated and romantic valley would surely be the losers were they transported to the sumptuous cities of civilised countries, of which perhaps they have heard something without desiring in the least to change their lot; their desires are limited by what they possess—what more is necessary to happiness?

Our arrival excited to the highest pitch the curiosity of these people, who reiterated their questions until we were fairly stupefied; and we refused to gratify their curiosity before we had seen their chief, Mustapha Khan, for whom I had a letter. As he lived on the opposite shore of the lake, we were conveyed across it in two little boats, made of reed and plastered on the inside with a whitish cement. Mustapha Khan's dwelling stood in the middle of a very pretty garden, in which we were hospitably received, though, as he was engaged when we arrived, we did not see him till supper time. We found with him an Afghan from Herat, who had arrived a few days before us, and I at once recognized him as one of my most obtrusive visitors there. His name was Osman Khan, and he appeared as much astonished to see me as I was to find him there; but, independently of the surprise, I was not at all pleased to meet him, for his presence was a fresh source of difficulty for me. Before, however, I speak of my personal vexations, I must say a few words on the local politics of the country in which I was, and which, influencing to a considerable extent the conduct of Mustapha Khan respecting me, was the cause of much fatigue and many annoyances.

The province of Gour, south-east of Herat, is the inheritance of the Gouride Princes, who raised their throne on the ruins of the kingdom founded by Sebek-Taghi and his son Mahmood the Ghuznivide. This part of the Paropamisus was then inhabited by a tribe called Soor, of which there still remain four or five thousand families in the north-west of the province. In proportion as the civil wars reduced the power and prosperity of this tribe, the star of the Taymoonis rose in the ascendant; they peopled the country vacated by the Sooris, and soon found themselves strong enough to form an independent government under the protection of the sovereigns of Herat; but after the death of the Timouride prince Sultan Hussein Ghazi, at the commencement of the sixteenth century, they looked upon their vassalage to that power as merely a nominal affair. When the principality of Herat was at peace and in possession of an army capable of invading them, they quietly paid a small tribute in kind, of grain, cattle, or horses; but these were exceptional cases, for Herat was almost always in a state of violent agitation when the Taymoonis dispensed with the duty of paying the tribute. This tribe was, in short, either an excellent ally or a powerful enemy to its suzerain. In latter years it has been divided into three branches, viz.—

1st. That under the orders of the Sirdar Ibrahim Khan, who resided at Teivereh. This was the nearest to Herat, and the most powerful, and in great emergencies could bring into the field 1000 horse and 700 foot, effective men.

2nd. That commanded by Mustapha Khan of Deria-dereh, whose force consisted of 200 horse and 3000 foot.

3rd. That whose chief was Mahmood Khan, encamped in the valley of Jevedge, who had at the utmost 1000 foot.

The chief, Ibrahim, was devoted to the Shah Kamran, the last of the Suddozye monarchs of Herat, from whom he had received many favours, and who refused at his death to recognise the usurped authority of Yar Mohamed Khan. He gave an asylum to the two sons of Kamran and other exiles from Herat, who took refuge with him. But the Vezir Sahib, who was not a man to put up with his opposition patiently, attacked him and for a couple of years failed to subdue him; for he had the support of the two other branches of the Taymooni tribe, and Hassan Khan ben Zorab of the Pusht Koh Hazarah. The wily policy, however, of Yar Mohamed Khan having detached them from the common cause, gave him at length an advantage over the Sirdar; and at the close of 1844 he had carried off half his population, men, women, and children, and settled them in Herat, where he made all the men capable of bearing arms *serbas*,* militia. After this

* "Serbas" properly means playing with your head, or risking your life, and is the name applied in Persia and the adjoining countries to the regular troops. "Janbas," playing with your life, is applied in Afghanistan to the irregular cavalry, similar to the Bashi-bouzouks of Turkey.—ED.

severe reverse, Ibrahim Khan shut himself up in the impregnable fortress of Chalap-dalan, and here he held out stoutly against every effort of the Vezir, and when his provisions were exhausted endeavoured to cut his way, sword in hand, through the Afghan army; unhappily his horse fell at the very moment he was fiercely engaged in the midst of his enemies, and the gallant and spirited chief had the grief and mortification of being taken prisoner: but he did not remain so long, for in a few days he made his escape and reached Chalap, when he was again surrounded by the troops; and famine, which had in the first instance forced him to quit his stronghold, now drove him to ask a truce of the commander, Sirdar Habib Ullah Khan, the terms of his submission being a promise to surrender if he were allowed to retire to Kabul. On this the Afghan chief sent for seven Korans, in which Yar Mohamed had written with his own hand, and sealed with his own seal, a solemn promise to grant his demand; but the confidence of the Khan was betrayed, for as he came out of the fortress he was seized, and his captors fully intended to carry him to Herat, had he not escaped from their hands; two of his sons, also at the time captives in the citadel of that town, found means to regain their liberty and rejoin him. With a handful of Taymoonis they attacked and pillaged a Mongol encampment, subject to Yar Mohamed, and then retired to Kandahar, the sovereign of which was his most powerful antagonist, and without doubt well pleased to have in his hands a man who might cause much embarrassment to the Chief of Herat. To revenge himself for the escape of these important prisoners, the Vezir Sahib seized three thousand families of Taymoonis, and with them he peopled the new villages in the neighbourhood of Herat. An equal number of these wretched people managed to escape and gain the territory of Hassan Khan ben Zorab, who, finding a part of his frontier exposed by the discomfiture and exile of Ibrahim Khan, had moved over to that side. Yar Mohamed did not let this pass without observation, and gave strict orders to his lieutenants respecting him.

As to my host, the Sirdar Mustapha, who, to gain favour with Yar Mohamed, had betrayed his own cousin, Ibrahim Khan, into his hands, he might have had to regret this base conduct and cruel complaisance had not his rugged mountains presented natural obstacles to an invasion of his country. There was indeed very little chance of this, for I heard him declare before Osman Khan that he acknowledged himself the vassal of the Vezir Sahib, and would pay him tribute for the future.

It is easy, therefore, to understand that my presence at Deria-dereh would excite the suspicions of Mustapha and Osman. The latter, who was not in all his master's secrets, could not tell whether his opinions respecting me were or were not satisfactory. He had seen me a prisoner at Herat, vowing by all that was sacred I was going to Lahore, and having put faith in my representations, believed I was on my way through Turkistan to Kabul, to which place I had not gone. On the contrary, he finds me at Deria-dereh, introduced to Mustapha Khan as a Persian in the service of the Khan of Sirpool, and going to the Vezir's declared enemy, Hassan Khan ben Zorab. It was useless my stating to these Khans the real truth, and the reasons that forced me to change my route and take a false name; for they would not listen to anything, and telling me it was impossible to allow me to go about the country intriguing with the Pusht Koh Hazarahs against the Khan of Herat, informed me that I should be sent the next morning to the camp of Sirdar Habib Ullah Khan, to whom I must account for my presence in a district where no European had anything to do, and through which I had no authority from the Vezir to travel. This appeared to me the best course I could have taken had I been at liberty to choose, and the most likely one to extricate me at once from my difficulties, so I announced my perfect acquiescence in the decision. I reflected that from Zerni, where the Khan then was, I could by Zemindavar reach Kandahar in five days, and a trifling delay would be the only unpleasant result; this hope consoled me, for I was far from foreseeing the misery in store for me.

CHAPTER XVIII.

The author leaves for Zerni — Storm in the mountains — Afghan faith — Ancient capital of Gour — History of the province — The Sirdar Habib Ullah Khan — The author detained — The mountain of Chalap-dalan — The ancient towns of Kaleh Kaissar, Kaleh Sigeri, and Fakhrabad — Destruction committed by Yar Mohamed's troops — Inhabitants of the Paropamisus — The Eïmaks — Admirable horsemanship of their women — The necessary qualification before they marry — Eïmak women dreaded by the Afghans —Mineral riches — Geographical features — Difficulty in describing this country — Its inhabitants — Abinevane — Author obliged to separate from the faithful Hazarahs — Bad traits of Afghan character—Narbend — Tarsi — Herat — Kind reception by Yar Mohamed — Preparations for departure to Kandahar — Interesting account of Captain Conolly's servant — Letters of Yar Mohamed to Dost Mohamed and Akbar Khan.

ZERNI, July 16th—fourteen parasangs. A stormy sky replaced the brilliant sun of yesterday, and the whole valley was overshadowed in gloom and darkness. Mustapha Khan did not like the appearance of the weather, and endeavoured to detain me a couple of hours by relating many fearful accidents that had occurred in such hurricanes as the one which now threatened us; but the distance to be travelled this day was long, I was not afraid of a little rain, and was very impatient to see the Sirdar Habib Ullah Khan, from whom I expected a decision favourable to my wishes and intentions. I paid therefore no attention to the advice of the chief of Deria-dereh, and he ceased to press it, especially when Osman Khan gave it as his opinion that I had better start at once. This double-dealing Afghan wished the proof of his zeal to arrive at Herat as quickly as possible, and he wrote to the Vezir Sahib the most absurd letter about me: in this I was described as a dangerous intriguer, and himself as an example of penetration, ability, and devotion.

It was soon evident that Mustapha Khan's advice had been sincere, for a few minutes after I had left the shelter of his tent the certain approach of such a convulsion of nature as we look for before the Day of Judgment was apparent. The granite masses, scantily covered with brown, scrubby, and almost leafless trees looked dark and wild, and as we entered a gorge between them, a cloud hid the valley from our sight. We had heard distant thunder since daybreak, but at this height we were in the midst of it; here it rolled in loud detonations over and around us—crash after crash, echo after echo—as if the very heavens would be rent asunder. There was something in it so sublime, that I could not help feeling admiration, at least equal to the sense of terror that I could not repress. To the roar of heaven's artillery succeeded the wind, at first in gusts, but finally in a hurricane, which tore the trees up by the roots and carried them to a considerable distance; blocks of granite were hurled down the mountain-side, and clouds of dust, of earth and stones mingled with moss and leaves, were whirled into the air, and formed every now and then a cloud which added to the darkness. A deluge of rain followed the other fearful features of this furious storm: the clouds looked like the agitated waves of the sea, and every loose or earthy particle of the mountain-side was mingled with the waters and washed away by the torrents that gushed forth on every side.

Happily for us we were able to shelter ourselves in a cave, and in this we watched, in silence, the awful tempest which lasted three-quarters of an hour. The sky then began to clear, the clouds dispersed, and it was then only we could see the effects of this convulsion of the atmosphere. The valley at the base of the mountain had not suffered from it, the tents were all standing on their verdant carpet, and the cattle grazing tranquilly just as they were when we lost sight of them. My guide said that these fearful visitations were usually confined to the mountain, and that they rarely occurred in the winter or spring.

The storm over, we proceeded on our road, and ascending passed from one table-land to another, until we reached a steep descent which took us into a fertile valley well peopled with Taymoonis, whose tents we did not gain without difficulty, in consequence of the swollen torrents. Here we entered another chain of mountains of very singular formation, presenting difficulties of all sorts to the traveller, and occasioning much delay. Our vexation was not a little aggravated by the people on the opposite side of the valley, who, taking us for Afghans by the form of our turbans, were far from polite, calling out as we passed, "Fine country this to invade; fine roads, smooth as the faith of an Afghan." "Go and tell your countrymen we shall be delighted to receive them." "We will meet them handsomely sword in hand. Go, and God be with you." The rascals always finished their perorations with a giggle in no way flattering to our pride, and had it not been for the presence of Mustapha Khan's people, I doubt whether they would have waited the arrival of our supposed countrymen to compliment us with the swords they talked about. These sallies were not surprising, for they were, and not without reason, irritated at the conduct of the troops of Herat, who had laid waste the most fertile part of the province of Gour, cut down the trees, turned the water-courses, destroyed the houses, and driven the population from the country. These reasons were, it must be admitted, more than sufficient to exasperate the Taymoonis against them. The storm and the difficulty of the road prevented our reaching Zerni before two in the morning. The Sirdar was up, but half inebriated with his nocturnal libations, so I postponed my visit to the next day, and went to seek the repose I so much needed.

Zerni was, as I have before remarked, the ancient capital of the country of Gour; ruins lie upon ruin: the town is small and enclosed by a wall of stone and burnt brick, which has in many places fallen in. Its position—in a valley—is happily chosen, the hills around are covered with trees, and the vigorous shoots of the vine have interlaced their branches with them in such luxuriant festoons, that they appear to form one mass of foliage. Beautiful streams, in which are vast quantities of trout, wind through this delightful spot. Zerni is forty parasangs from Herat, the population does not exceed twelve hundred, Sooris and Taymoonis; there are also a few Gheber families, the only ones I met with in Afghanistan.*

The principality of Gour occupies its own little niche in Asiatic history. It formed, in the twelfth century, an independent sovereignty, the princes of which made themselves celebrated by the taking and sack of Ghuznee, and extending their dominion over all the countries known in these days as Afghanistan and the Seistan. The Gooride dynasty commenced in A.D. 1150 (Hejira 528), and lasted sixty-four years. There were five sovereigns, viz.:—

* If the information on this point given to M. Ferrier be correct, the circumstance is very curious, as no other Ghebers are known to exist between Kirman and India.—ED.

Allal-eddin-djehan-sooz,	who reigned	6	years.
Seif-eddin Mohamed	,,	7	,,
Ghyaz-eddin-abool-fetah	,,	40	,,
Shehab-eddin-abool Moozaffer	,,	4	,,
Mahmood	,,	7	,,

July 17th.—The astonishment of the Sirdar Habib Ullah Khan was great when he heard of my arrival in his camp. I went to him at daybreak, and he received me with a politeness which I thought augured well. We talked much about the journey I had just made, and he seemed surprised that I should have accomplished it without any misadventure, and in a country in which an Afghan could not travel three or four parasangs without risking his life. At last he drew from his pocket the letter of Osman Khan containing one, unsealed, which the rascal had written to Yar Mohamed, and read to me the contents of both. It was not difficult to refute his stupid allegations against me, indeed the Sirdar appeared not to give them credence; but he would not allow me to go on to Kandahar, observing that the chief of that province was the declared enemy of his master, and that if the Vezir had intended me to pass by that town he would not have sent me by way of Balkh. It was in vain that I protested he had given me my choice, and that I had taken the northern route entirely of my own accord; he thought it would be committing himself too far to let me proceed by the road I wished, and I was obliged to resign myself to the necessity of wasting three or four days in his camp while he despatched a courier to Herat, with whom he intended subsequently to send me back to that town. This fresh annoyance nearly cost me a fit of illness. Were all my cares, fatigues, and exertions during the three last months to be thrown away? Was all the fine weather to pass before I could reach Kabul, where the winter is so severe as to put a stop to all communication? My position was not an enviable one; I dreaded to be sent before Yar Mohamed—that prince might believe all the foolish tales against me and keep me an indefinite time a prisoner, or, what would distress me just as much, send me back to Persia. However I could only submit.

In the interval I was obliged to accompany the Sirdar in his devastating excursions. The peak of Chalap-dalan, one of the highest in the world, commanded this part of the country, rising before us in imposing majesty, and developing beneath its elevated and snow-capped cone a variety of graceful and picturesque outlines. The circumference at half its height is twelve parasangs; the sides are covered with forests and pastures, villages and tents, and also some naturally impregnable positions, where successive chiefs have built strongholds to which they might retire in stormy times. That so lately the refuge of Ibrahim Khan was only three parasangs from us, and plainly visible from the camp of the Herat army. In winding round the mountain to the S.E., I saw three ancient towns, large and fortified, which must in former times have been of some importance in the principality :—*

1st, Kaleh-kaissar, built by Ghyaz-eddin-Abool-fetah.

2nd, Kaleh-sengy, built by Shah Sultan Hussein Ghazi.

3rd, Fakhrabad, built by the Emir Fakhreddin.

These three fortresses are situated only a few parasangs N.E. of Teivereh and in the most fertile and picturesque part of the province. Unhappily the scourge of war had driven away the people, who retreated into the mountains and ravines, from which they could see, without being able to prevent them, the ravages committed in the plain by the troops of Yar Mohamed; and whatever the inhabitants could not carry away was pitilessly destroyed—harvest, trees, houses, nothing was spared.

July 17th.—We encamped in a funnel-shaped hollow, the sides of which were covered with trees and brushwood, in the centre of which was a small lake about a parasang in circumference, and from it I saw some fine trout taken. In a brook that fell into the lake I found some delicate little craw-fish, the only ones I had seen in Central Asia. There is a small island in this lake, and on it are many pines and tamarisks shading the ruins called by the inhabitants Butguiah, the place of the idol.

The town of Kaissar is not far from this, but nothing remains of it but the citadel, built of burnt brick, and situated on the top of a small hill, the side of which is so steep that there would be little chance of taking it by escalade. On the N. was an aqueduct now in ruins, which conveyed the water from the Chalap-dalan

* Although the mountains between Herat and Kabul have been traversed in some directions by previous travellers, this particular portion of the range, forming the ancient kingdom of Gour, has never before been visited by an European. A memoir on the adjoining district to the north, called Gharshistán, by Baron Von Hammer, is to be found in the 4th volume of the 'Mines de l'Orient.'—ED.

into the town; a few of the arches are still standing; there were two rows, one upon the other.

Kaleh-sengy is very near Kaleh-kaissar, and is so called from the materials of which it is constructed, *sengy*, meaning, *of stone*. This fortress also crowns an eminence level at the top. The wall which surrounds it is built of large and roughly cut stones, piled upon each other without any cement; it is nevertheless very solid, for it has resisted the effects of time and the destructive tendencies of the Afghans. Portions of these ruins are covered with climbing plants; there are no inhabitants, and wild beasts lurk about the fallen débris. It was once supplied with water by two aqueducts similar to those of Kaleh-kaissar, which led it into an immense tank in the centre of the fortress. On its sides were some broken columns, which lead to the supposition that it was once surrounded by a colonnade, of which these are the only traces left. On the N.E. is seen a road paved with pieces of rock in pretty good preservation; it is said it reached as far as Ghuzni. A paved road is an unusual thing to see in Central Asia, for the roads are generally traced out at random by successive travellers, and are never kept up or repaired. Yar Mohamed, fearing these ruins might be made available by the rebels, had just ordered the Sirdar to raze them to the ground.

Fakhrabad, situated about two hours more to the S., and inhabited by Mongols, is now only a large village. There is also a great extent of ruins here, and it is said that many gold and silver coins have been from time to time found in them. Mongols are also encamped round Kaleh-sengy and Kaleh-kaissar.

It would be a useless endeavour to make any researches with a view of ascertaining what are the races of men known under the name Eïmak, inhabiting the Paropamisus, for they are so intermingled, their origin is so uncertain, and their own ignorance on the subject so great, that all investigation must be renounced as a hopeless task. The conjectures that have been formed with regard to their history much resemble the far-fetched ideas which are so frequently and readily brought forward in support of some theoretical subject. I have already said that under the name of Eïmaks are comprehended all the tribes descended from the ancient conquerors of the Paropamisus speaking the Persian language. There is amongst them such a conformity of manners and language, such a physical resemblance, and also such a decided tendency to unite against the Usbeks and Afghans who endeavour to subdue them, that it is allowable to suppose they are one great nation subdivided into small governments or republics, which are frequently obliged to unite and act together by the force of circumstances and for their mutual interests. The Eïmaks live a comparatively savage life, passing from a state of animal repose to the activity of a soldier as the occasion requires, without suspecting it to be possible to adopt a middle course, which would be more beneficial to their welfare and their health. The Usbeks and the Afghans are civilized people compared with them. The Persian they speak appears to be exceedingly ancient, and there is but little Arabic mixed with it; they only recur to the latter on occasions—and they are rare—when their own language does not afford a word by which they can express any particular idea. I think the fact of the Koran being very imperfectly known amongst them is the cause of this. However, ignorant as they are, they are not the less happy, and wish for nothing beyond a tent, a horse, a wife, and plunder. They are very hospitable, and to each other faithful and devoted. Well organised, they would make excellent soldiers, especially cavalry; their arms are the lance and bow, and they have very few fire-arms.

Their women do all the work, domestic and agricultural, and, like the Hazarahs, take part in the combat; the Afghans dread them as much as they do the men. A girl does not marry until she has performed some feat of arms; they never cover the face, even in the presence of strangers; their forms are large and robust, and well developed, but their beauty is mediocre, and at forty they are frequently decrepid. Though the winters in the Paropamisus are very severe, the inhabitants prefer a tent to a house because they can more easily gratify their love of frequent change, or even comply with the necessity for it, without being obliged to leave anything behind them. Their tents, made of felts woven of camels wool, are thick and impervious, and when carefully closed the cold rarely penetrates them. The remarks I have made in connection with the fertility of their country when describing my journey are, if not complete, at least sufficient: there are few populations in Asia more favoured in this respect. They are shepherds rather than cultivators of the soil, nevertheless they have some crops of corn, barley, maize, and a kind of millet which they consider a great delicacy. I have seen but little rice; they keep what they have for feasts and when they receive a guest. The fruits are as abundant as they are delicious, and all articles of first necessity are exceedingly cheap. They procure everything by barter, caring very little for silver or gold, and copper has no currency amongst them. The Eïmaks encamp in the plains during the winter, and on the table-lands of the mountains in the summer and autumn. They are intrepid sportsmen, and frequently neglect the small game to pursue the wild beasts which abound in their country. Ruins are frequently met with, but no inscriptions are found that can lead to any explanation of their origin. I could not at first comprehend why there were so many camels in such a mountainous country, these animals being of no service for transport excepting on a plain. I found afterwards that the tribes keep them expressly for their wool, which is so valuable to them for bareks and tents; they told me they could use them for travelling provided they kept in the valleys, though to gain the principalities near them this would involve a considerable circuit. Judging by the form of the highest peaks of the Paropamisus,* their origin must have been volcanic, and warm springs frequently issue from their sides. The mineral riches of this district are very great—gold, silver, copper, iron, lead, sulphur, coal, rubies,† and emeralds; but no mines have ever been worked.

The country that imitating the ancients I have called Paropamisus, is not known to its inhabitants by this denomination, who have no name for it that comprises its whole extent; they never speak of it but by the name of the tribe inhabiting it or the chief who commands it, as for example, Velayet Firooz Kohi, country of the Firooz Kohis, Mulk Hassan Khan ben Zorab, the territory of Hassan Khan ben Zorab. I have included in the term Paropamisus all the mountain country enclosed by the circle formed by Herat, Meimoona, Balkh, Bamian, Ghuzni, Kilat i Ghiljie, Kandahar, Zemindávar, and Sakhir;‡ it may be looked upon as a vast natural fortress thrown on to the centre, and on the culminating

* This name first occurs in the trilingual tablets of Darius, where the mountain range of Gandara is termed Paru-Parisanna. Paru merely means a mountain, in Sanscrit.—ED.

† This requires explanation. The well-known Balass ruby is so called from Badakshan, which is N.E. of Badakshan, and emeralds are found still farther to the E., but in that part of the range which intervenes between Kabul and Herat precious stones are unknown.—ED.

‡ This place is on the frontiers between Gour and Herat.

point of the great Asiatic table-land. From whatever side, it must be approached by rugged and high mountains, and it is also intersected by others in various directions, particularly E. and W. Successive travellers will in vain endeavour, by their observations and researches in the Mohamedan districts of Central Asia, to give exact ideas of that country and population that will be correct for any length of time. They will never be able to do more than describe with precision the state in which they find it, on account of the multiplicity of political changes, followed by the displacements of whole tribes, the turning of rivers and destruction of towns, near the ruins of which others will rise in an incredibly short space of time—the very existence of either the old or the new being unknown beyond the province. How is it possible to establish any system for the future student or traveller where everything is perpetually changing, or even to relate distinctly what has happened? What I have said of the movements of the Jemshidees, the Hazarahs, Zeïdnats, Taymoonis, &c., will make the difficulty, if not impossibility, perfectly evident.

Abireván,* July 19th—fourteen parasangs. The Sirdar having finished his despatches for Herat, we left for that town on the evening of this day. It was, I acknowledge, the most painful moment of my whole journey, for Habib Ullah Khan pushed his ideas of zeal and prudence to the extent of separating me from my excellent fellow-travellers, Roostem and Rabi, under the pretext of not finding horses enough at the different camps at which we were to change on the road. I offered to pay for the hire of them, but he would not grant my request, and in the order specified six — two for me and my servant, two for the messenger and one of his own servants, and two for the baggage. I had to pay for all six, and that in advance, as he wished to appropriate the cash to himself. It was little, it is true, but anything is a windfall to an Afghan, and well they know the necessity of taking care of the brooks to feed the rivers. My heart was heavy indeed when I parted with my friends, who had gone through so much for my sake—a lengthened circuitous journey and many troubles, and all now fruitless, and they had reaped only discomfort, vexation, and danger from having linked their fortunes with mine. At parting I slipped some pieces of gold into the hand of each,

* This name means running water.

and after we were at some distance I still heard them calling for the blessing of Heaven upon my journey.

The road as far as Gour lay among mountains, the forms of which were scarcely distinguishable in the pale starlight, and at sunrise we came out upon a plain, and after two hours' travelling, reached an encampment of Noorzyes of Abireván, where we found a crowd of Afghans, come from I know not where to quarter themselves upon the unfortunate nomads. The hospitality in the tents of these wanderers is often basely taken advantage of by the idlers of the tribes, who avail themselves of every opportunity of living entirely upon the bounty of others; they go from camp to camp, and having practised upon good nature in one, proceed to the next, where, on the score of their claim upon the virtue of hospitality, they continually eat the bread of those who have gained it by the sweat of their brow. But an Afghan is always a bird of prey, and so low is his standard of morals, that it is impossible ever to trust him. If, from the force of habit or prejudice, he respects a stranger while in his tent, he loses sight of his own character of host directly his guest has left it, and considers it perfectly legitimate to overtake and despoil him, to whom two hours before he had given food and shelter.

*Narbend,** July 20th—twelve parasangs—in a desert where water is scarce. Here was a small mill, standing on a brackish water-course. We passed two or three villages and a few tents on the road, and rested at Narbend for two hours.

Tarsi, July 20th—four parasangs. A large encampment of Eïmaks, with a few mud-houses and a great many modern ruins near it.

HERAT, July 21st.—We travelled nearly all night amongst low mountains, and had some difficulty in crossing the Adreskan river. At dawn, and in the distance, a forest was seen on the plain, and a cupola and minarets rising from it indicated the position of Herat. We reached the city about seven in the morning. The servant of the Sirdar, who had gone on an hour or two in advance of us to inform the Vezir Sahib of my arrival, met us at the gate and conducted me to the house of my old acquaintance the Sertip, as he had been ordered to do. Lal Mohamed was not at home, but he soon came and appeared very

* Narbend, or Narwund, is the name of a species of tree resembling the dwarf elm of England.—ED.

kindly disposed towards me. He was accompanied by a mirza who took notes of all the incidents of my journey, and having done so, hurried off with them to Yar Mohamed. I waited in much anxiety for the Vezir's decision, for all the precautionary measures which had been observed when I was here before were renewed. It was only towards evening that the Sertip returned and brought me the agreeable news that Yar Mohamed, knowing war had broken out between the chiefs of Khulm and Kabul, admitted the truth of my statements, and authorized me to continue my journey to India. The Sertip then withdrew the guard which had been placed over me, informed me that I was free to go where I pleased, that the Vezir Sahib would look upon me as a friend; and this Yar Mohamed repeated to me when I saw him an hour afterwards. He approved of my determination to go by Kandahar and Kabul, promising me letters of recommendation to the sovereigns of these principalities, but, he added, "leave them in ignorance of the journey you have made in Turkistan and the Paropamisus; it might awaken their suspicions. I shall write to them to say that I have advised you to take the road by Kandahar, and I think that whatever may be the differences between me and those chiefs, they will in this instance pay respect to my wishes." I was surprised at this treatment, especially when I remembered how different it was from that I received at my first visit. The Sertip attributed this change to the answers the Vezir had received to inquiries he had made respecting me when he heard of my departure from Meshed for Herat. It seems the replies had been completely satisfactory, and Osman Khan's missive, from which so much was expected, was treated as a joke.

The preparations for my journey detained me three or four days in Herat, and at one time I thought I should be obliged to give it up altogether, for I had great difficulty in finding any one who would accompany me as my guide to Kandahar. Many persons endeavoured to dissuade me from going there, representing the province as full of fanatics, exceedingly hostile to Europeans, and prophesying much trouble and danger from the attempt. I found only one person who offered his services, but, apprehensive that some misfortune might happen to him in the course of the journey, he would only engage himself at so exorbitant a price for the hire of his camels, that I relinquished the idea of taking him. However after a wonderful deal of talking, bargaining, and trouble of all sorts, I succeeded in obtaining three yaboos, baggage horses, from the same Sultan Mohamed, the brother of the Sertip who had charge of me on my first visit to Herat. This gentleman had at that time the coolness to ask me for a present, to recompense him for the trouble imposed on him in being my jailer. To this request I never condescended to reply; but he had a hold upon me now that I wanted to hire his horses, and although the affair was entirely one of business and under the orders of the Vezir, I was obliged to pay three times the usual price for them. He also provided me with a servant, by name Ali, a *serbas* under his command.

My own servant, a young Heratian, the only Asiatic whom I had ever found faithful, had fallen ill, and I sadly regretted being obliged to leave him, for that was the only reason for our separation. About ten years before his family had, for some peccadillo, fallen under the displeasure of the Shah Kamran; some of them were put to death, others sought safety in flight, and he, then but a child, was sold by Yar Mohamed Khan to the Turcomans, and carried to Khiva. Many years after, and while still a captive, he had the good fortune to find a purse containing twenty tellahs.* This was about the time that Captain Conolly arrived in Khiva, and that officer added sixteen to them, enabling him to purchase his freedom, and took him into his service. From that period Mohamed shared the misfortunes of his master, and remained with him up to the day of his assassination by the Emir of Bokhara. After he regained his liberty, he returned to India, where he served successively Captain Conolly's brother, Sir Richmond Shakspear, and Major Rawlinson; the latter brought him to Bagdad, which place he left at the same time as myself, but he did not enter my service till after the theft and flight of the rascal Sadeuk at Meshed.

In addition to this Ali, there was a man in charge of the horses, a Parsivan named Ahmed, and Yar Mohamed ordered the Major, Habib Ullah Khan, to give me a subaltern as an honorary escort. The gallant Major ought to have provided this officer with the necessary funds; but under the pretence of buying a robe and boots for Mr. Jubbur Khan, he cheated me out of thirty-six shillings. This was simply a falsehood, as the latter never had either the one or the other, and was started with the odd six shillings to keep

* A tellah is a gold coin worth about ten shillings.—ED.

him on the journey to Kandahar and back. Before leaving Herat I made an unlucky outlay in buying two trunks for the better preservation of my luggage, which had fared but indifferently in the bags that I used when on my journey to Sirpool. I had reason to regret the purchase, for they were nearly stolen several times, it being supposed, as the Khan had warned me, that they were full of gold or silver. The letters that Yar Mohamed Khan gave me for the Emir Dost Mohamed and his son, but which I never had the opportunity of presenting, were admirable specimens of the flowery and bombastic style adopted in Eastern courts. The following is a translation :—

Letter from Yar Mohamed Khan to the Emir Dost Mohamed Khan.

"By the Divine protection, and to the affectionate person of my most happy brother, the dispenser of the clemency, of the power, and of the force of the state; the glory of the standard of the kingdom, of its strength and its fortune; the ornament of the throne of magnificence, grandeur, and glory; the conservator of renown and the inaccessible fortresses; the setter up and embellisher of the crown of prosperity and splendour; the founder of great things and great ideas: May you be on the carpet of wealth and of fortune; in the sanctuary of the Creator preserved from all accident and every mischance of this world! May you in short further augment the splendour of the seat of magnificence and power!

"The rules of sincerity and intimacy having been set forth, the testimonies of sympathy and friendship presented, I will communicate to your high wisdom that, as the laws and friendship of the union that exists between us require that I should, as a matter obligatory upon me, inform you of any circumstance affording me the opportunity of testifying my sincerity, I shall by this page of rejoicing increase the sensibilities of your generous heart. I profit by this opportunity of informing you that one of the great Lords of the Kingdom of France, the General Ferrier, on his way from Persia, came to the holy city of Meshed, and from thence arrived in the capital of Herat, where he has sojourned some days. After having seen him, and after many inquiries regarding the object of his journey, it is proved that he has none other than to reach

Lahore. In consequence, and as observing the laws of hospitality is a duty, especially when they apply to a government, I have, while he remained at Herat for the purpose of determining the route by which he would proceed to the place of his destination, rendered him all the services and performed all the duties that the most perfect hospitality could require at my hands. I have thought it desirable for the security of his person, and for the honour of us both, to recommend to him as the safest road, combining the greatest ease and advantages, that which goes by Kandahar and Kabul.

"The very sublime above-named Lord having appreciated my advice, I immediately undertook to provide him with all that he could possibly require to transport himself and his baggage to Kandahar. I have also sent a person charged with his safe conduct to that city in all security and convenience. I have also written on the same subject a letter to the (Sirdar Kohendil) Khan of Kandahar, the all-powerful and my generous and very noble brother. I trust in the Divine power that out of regard to my letter he will order the sublime aforesaid Lord to be accompanied by one of his servants who will conduct him with all propriety to the presence of my well-beloved, very indulgent, and very clement brother the Emir Dost Mohamed, that he may have the honour of being presented to him. I have a profound conviction that the sublime above-named will travel under good protection to his destination, and that in every way my very generous and very clement brother will acquire renown by his cordial reception of him. As it was urgent and necessary, I have increased your trouble with this letter. I am always ready to receive your orders and recommendations.—Salutation, &c."

Letter of Yar Mohamed Khan to his Son-in-Law, Mohamed Akbar Khan.

"By the grace Divine, the sublime and joyous person of my very generous and very happy son, the light of my eyes, whose presence is the presage of a good augury ; the star of the zodiac of the kingdom, of power, and of fortune ; the pearl of the treasure of grandeur, of magnificence and munificence, the morning light of dignity and prosperity ; the true source of a noble and valorous origin : May God prolong his days ! may he be preserved here below from every snare and deceit, from all trouble and all affliction, that the course of the object of his desires and wishes should be subject to him; And, lastly, that his cup should overflow with the nectar of joy and felicity!

"The rules of friendship, and all that depends upon them being set forth, I announce to my most generous son, whose wisdom is an object of rejoicing and satisfaction, that, as his intentions, which flow from clemency, are and have always been to be kept by me informed of all affairs and events, I fulfil this task in writing this sheet of rejoicing, and profiting by the opportunity of telling him that at this time a Lord of the Kingdom of France, General Ferrier, coming from Persia, has been at the holy city of Meshed, whence he came to the capital of Herat. After his arrival there he remained several days, and it was clearly established and demonstrated, after many inquiries, that he had no intention but that of travelling to Lahore, and that that was the only object he had in coming to this country. As under all circumstances it is a duty to honour and respect a guest, above all when he is admitted to be one of a government, I observed towards him, during the time that he remained at Herat, all the laws of hospitality; and I considered it my duty to advise him for the security of his person to take the road by Kandahar and Kabul, that he might so arrive in safety at his destination, and that the honour resulting therefrom should be upon him as well as upon us. The very sublime abovementioned having approved and appreciated my counsels, I sent with him a person charged to serve him as guide and protector to Kandahar, who will return after having reached that town. I have the conviction that my most generous son as well as the Sirdars and Grandees of Kandahar will take my letter into consideration, and exert themselves to testify their friendship to the sublime abovementioned Lord, and that they will make every effort to satisfy his wishes; that on his arrival the admirable laws of friendship and hospitality will be observed with regard to him; and that after this he will proceed to his destination loaded with attentions and benefits, which will be honourable to both of us.

"As it is urgent and necessary that you should be instructed in this matter, I have addressed you this present letter, and I beg you to inform me constantly of the state of your health.—Salutation."

CHAPTER XIX.

The author leaves Herat — Shabith — Inundations of the Heri-rood — Mode of preventing them — Continuation of the Siah Koh — Steppes between Herat and Kandahar — Adreskan — Caravanserais built by the English — River of Adreskan — Called by various names — Description of it — Route of an army going to Kandahar — Kash-jabaran — Irruption of Afghans into the author's tent — Scene there in consequence — The friend of man in Afghanistan — A nice specimen of this country — Diplomacy of the author — Rascality of Mons. Ferrier's escort — The *Meseh* — Ab-Kourmeh — Cool impudence of Jubbur Khan — Necessity for submission — Scarcity of water — Fever and thirst — Thermometer in the shade — Military position — Rascally exactions — Afghan character — Miserable condition of the author — Gurm-ab — The hot wind — Jubbur Khan again — The plain of Bukwa.

Shabith, July 24th.—Having completed my preparations, I set out this evening with my guide Jubbur Khan, my groom Ahmed, and the serbas Ali, who was to unite the functions of valet and cook. At one hour's distance from the town we crossed the Heri-rood by a bridge of twenty-six arches, called Pûl Malan; it is built of burnt brick, and has been recently restored by Yar Mohamed. In Europe it would have been an ordinary work; but at Herat it was an object of general admiration. At this place the bed of the river is hollowed out of the sand, and the waters flow through fifteen canals, twelve feet wide and very deep, enclosed between two embankments, formed of the earth taken out of the excavations. They have been made as a precautionary measure against the overflowing of the river, from which the country had often suffered; and however great be the volume of water in future, there are now channels sufficient for it to flow in. The rise of the Heri-rood in the spring is considerable; but such is the number of outlets cut from it to carry on the irrigation of the country between Obeh and Herat, that it was nearly dry when we crossed it at Pûl Malan. The cultivation extends for two miles south of Herat, and scattered in various directions are the remains of houses, aqueducts, and other monuments of antiquity, which even now give an idea of what the environs were in former times. The royal residence of Rozeh Bagh closes the long series of country-houses in this neighbourhood. Hence we ought to have taken the direct road to the caravanserai of Mir Davood, four parasangs distant; but Jubbur Khan having to receive the orders of Major Habib Ullah Khan, whose residence was at Ziaretgah, we were obliged to go a parasang out of our way. I passed in making this détour the ruins of a beautiful mosque; within is the tomb of some holy personage, to which many a Mussulman makes his pilgrimage. At the caravanserai of Mir Davood, half way to this halt, is a well. It is dry during the summer and autumn, and the land for a couple of parasangs all round it is arid and desert.

After having passed this spot we struck into a chain of mountains, decreasing in height as it approached to the town of Kaffrooge. It is a continuation of the Siah Koh which I had crossed near Doulet-yar, and I now saw it was impossible that this high mountain should ever have been anywhere intersected by the Heri-rood; the waters which descend from it, instead of taking a southern course, fall on the contrary into that river on the north, as I have already stated. The similarity between the names Heri-rood and Haroot-rood must have given rise to these erroneous conjectures. The uninhabited caravanserai-shah at Shabith, that we reached at midnight, is close to a torrent, the banks of which are covered with reeds and a little grass, the only forage to be found for the horses. The surrounding country is perfectly uncultivated and uninhabited; red and grey partridges abound there. Between Herat and Kandahar there are a hundred and twenty parasangs of steppe, often destitute of accommodation for the traveller, who must frequently pitch his tent in nameless spots, depending only on the resources he may have with him for refreshment, and to enable him to encounter the great heat of the sun. The length of the day's march must, therefore, always depend upon such circumstances as the weather, means of locomotion, supply of provisions, water, &c. These often obliged me to make long stages, or sometimes to travel a little by day and a little by night, in an irregular manner, and therefore, as I give my dates from memory, the specified distances only are to be depended on: from them the time requisite for the journey must be calculated.

Adreskan, July 25th—nine parasangs—across mountains and a little plain. The streams, which at Shabith flowed to the north, here take the opposite direction, down the southern side of the mountain. Occasionally we could descry the tent of a nomad in the horizon; but the track was destitute of inhabitants and water, though tolerably wooded. It was the same thing all the way to Kandahar, and I might have concluded that the tamarisk and mimosa, of which there were thick copses, were trees that never required any water, as they would here have only three months' rain to support them through nine of excessive drought. I could not reconcile this fact with the one that I had previously noticed, that there are almost always forests of these trees along the banks of the Euphrates, Tigris, Helmund, and other rivers.

Almost all over Afghanistan a dwarf kind of reed grows freely, and on this, as it is tender, the horses will graze readily. So far, therefore, as their food is concerned, the traveller need only carry a supply of barley; but it is quite otherwise for himself. He might die of hunger in these steppes if he did not take provisions for the whole journey, and from many places the party must carry sufficient water to last them to the next supply—perhaps far distant. This is not difficult to manage in the small skins, called *meseks*, generally used for the purpose, which are slung behind the baggage. Without this precaution, one would infallibly die of thirst in these burning regions.

From Herat to Shabith is a distance of eight parasangs, and six from the caravanserai at Shabith to the river Roodi-gez, so named because it has formed its bed across a forest of tamarisks, which much encumber it.* Three parasangs farther is Adreskan, a small caravanserai built of mud, and a dry well, both the work of the English.†

* The tamarisk in Persian is called *Gez*.

† Between the Khash-rood and Herat, caravanserais were found at distances varying from thirty to fifty miles. They were in a most dilapidated condition, and had evidently for many years been more the resort of Belooche and Afghan robbers than of peaceable travellers and caravans. They were said to have been built by Shah Abbas, and were at some places evidently designed on a large and commodious scale, though apparently left unfinished.

As it was necessary for the Herat mission to keep up communication with Kandahar, horsemen were posted along the road at convenient distances, averaging about twenty miles; and wherever any of these caravanserais could be made available for their accommodation, and the reception of passing travellers, they were temporarily repaired and suited to the purpose. At intermediate stations, where water was procurable, convenient buildings (chupper khanas) were erected of sun-dried bricks for a similar object.

By means of these horsemen the mission at Herat was generally able to communicate with Kandahar in shorter time than was taken between Cabul and Kandahar, although the distance was greater by 100 miles; and so efficient was the protection of the road, that, if I rightly recollect, only two or three robberies, and those of trifling extent, occurred during the eighteen months that the mission remained at Herat after their establishment. The employment of two or more Afghan foot-soldiers at each station, *on the security of the "Sir i Khail"* (chief of the tribe) of greatest influence in the neighbourhood, to assist the horsemen in protecting travellers, contributed *no doubt greatly* to our success.—L.

A large river, bearing the same name, passes Adreskan a little above the caravanserai; it receives the waters of the Roodi-gez, and thus increased directs its course through the districts of Subzawar, Jedge, and Kaleika, of which it takes the name, in crossing this territory. A little lower down it is called the Haroot-rood, and that seems to have been the name it anciently bore through its whole course, which is closed by its falling into the Lake Seistan on the south. Near its mouth it receives the Khashek-rood, which is dry in the summer and fed in winter and spring by the rains and melted snows which descend from the Siah Koh. The multiplicity of names by which this river is known is caused by the custom of each government dividing a river into as many parts as it crosses districts, each of which pays a rather heavy tax for the use of that part of it within its own boundaries for the purposes of irrigation and agriculture. It follows that the inhabitants consider it as their own within these limits, and give their portion the name of their own district. The Adreskan-rood, which in the upper part of its course is incorrectly marked on the maps of Asia, takes its rise near Jaor, above Obeh, and debouches in the plains of the district of Adreskan, following to the south the Sefid Koh.

The bed of this river, like that of the Roodi-gez, is partially dry during the hottest part of the year; but there is always enough water for the purposes of irrigation. In the winter and spring the Adreskan river is as large as the Heri-rood, and flows without interruption from its source to the Lake Seistan

An army marching in the summer months from Herat to Kandahar, or *vice versâ*, ought to follow the course of this river, for it would be the best route, and the movement might afterwards be prolonged by the banks of the Helmund to avoid suffering from the want of water. On this account it is not surprising that the English, who up to the present time are nearly the only people who have had the privilege of visiting this country, should have left the Russians in ignorance of its topography and resources, as at their hands they expect, and with reason, an invasion of India.

Kash-jaberan and *Shah-jehan*, July 26th—thirteen parasangs—alternately plain and mountain, but always descending towards the south. The country uninhabited and uncultivated, but covered with tamarisks up to Kash-jaberan, a village enclosed by a wall of earth, and distant six parasangs from Adreskan:

it contains seventy-six houses. A water-course passes near it. The heat during this stage was intense, and not a drop of water could be procured to quench our burning thirst. Two parasangs further west is the small fortress of Subzawar,* or Sebzar, which must not be confounded with Subzawar in Khorassan, of which I made mention when I passed through it. Subzawar is situated at the extremity of a large oblong plain, ten or twelve leagues in circumference, on which are seen here and there a few tents and villages of nomads. The ruins of large buildings, houses, and dried up wells, give an air of desolation to the whole plain. It was formerly well peopled and fertile; but the wars between Herat, of which it is a dependency, and Kandahar have reduced it to its present wretched condition.

From the morning of my departure I found it was impossible to place any confidence either in my guide Jubbur Khan, or the servants, and on my reaching Jaberan they immediately published to the village the arrival of a Feringhee. The little tent given to me by Lal Mohamed Khan was, of course, rapidly filled with Afghans, crowding one upon another as if they came to look at a wild beast, and wished to know whether my eyes, nose, and mouth answered the same purposes as their own, and in fact I was subjected to a repetition of the impertinences I experienced elsewhere. I believe, too, they were by no means guiltless of an intention to pilfer had anything been lying about, or a favourable opportunity presented itself of putting their hands into a trunk—for thieving is the principal subject of their thoughts, and how and where they can lay their fingers upon other people's property is a constant topic of conversation with them, indeed I may almost say the only one. I was not, as the reader may imagine, very much flattered by their presence, or at all pleased with their usual effrontery and curiosity. I was pestered with questions which, to avoid annoying them, I was obliged to answer; besides, it was as well to be on good terms with them. Some of these vagabonds, finding every corner of the tent occupied, were almost upon my back and in my lap watching how I ate, so that I was obliged to keep my plate on a level with my chin, lest they should put their noses into it. Some of them who had taken off their shirts and seated themselves upon my felts, hunted

* The proper name of this place is Isphizar (old Persian for the horse-pasture), of which Subzavar or Sebzar is a modern corruption.—ED.

the vermin with which they were covered; while one fellow, who had caught one of these loathsome creatures of unusual size, brought it to me with an exclamation of delight, in order that I might myself judge of its proportions and the beauty of the species. Disgusted at this proceeding, I requested my visitors to leave the tent, which they seemed in no hurry to do. "What business have you to be offended?" said one fellow; "the louse is the friend of man—an Afghan has always at least a hundred about him. You don't suppose we catch them because, as you are pleased to say, they are impure; but because they make one itch, which is disagreeable. The fact is they are so fond of us, they will never leave us." This peroration was followed by a furious diatribe against all Feringhees, with an announcement that it was fortunate that I was accompanied by Yar Mohamed's people, or they would have made mince-meat of me.

This rascal had a villanous expression of countenance, and looked as if he would willingly have made his words good; and then, with all the bravado and impudence of an Afghan, he favoured me, and in the most meaning manner, with a recital of all his deeds of blood—how many Englishmen he had killed, and how many more he intended should share the same fate—concluding that flourish by saying that if they had not opposed them with cannon, "the Afghans would have made but a mouthful of India, and then gone on to Franghistan (Europe), and brought all the people away bound like children, and sold them for slaves. *Shemsheeri adam hestim!*" we are all swordsmen! And this was the climax, for when an Afghan has said that, he considers he has said and proved everything. There was, of course, no use in my keeping up a war of words with this scoundrel, so I listened patiently to his bravado, telling him that it was really of no consequence, for I was a Frenchman, and that there was as much difference between us and the English as between him and a Persian; therefore that the hatred he bestowed upon me as an European, because his nation had had to complain of the British Government, was in no way deserved by me; and as I had carefully avoided wounding his pride, he left me, perfectly satisfied that I had formed a high estimate of his bravery.

A little diplomacy had dissipated the storm the unlucky insect had raised; but I thought that if some Europeans could have heard me make such a liberal use of flowery Persian metaphorical praises and compliments to soften these obdurate and pitiless brutes, they would have conceived a very poor opinion of my character. Nevertheless, I only acted as circumstances obliged me to do, and conformably to my knowledge of the prejudices and ignorance of the people with whom I had to deal and at whose mercy I was. To speak of humanity, personal liberty, loyalty, laws, or honour to such a set, would be like addressing oneself to so many buffaloes. The Afghans are to be met only in two ways—by force or by the hope of gain: chance flattery may occasionally help, but it must be administered with dexterity. I had been tolerably successful, and my antagonist retired pretty well content with me, but not so much so as if I had been an Englishman and he could have brought me acquainted with his sword or his matchlock.

I was rejoicing in the tact with which I had avoided a conflict when a fresh incident occurred to augment the *désagrémens* of my stay at Jaberan. The three rascals sent with me had during this scene sided more with the Afghans than with me; and when they were gone began to annoy me themselves. Although I had given Sultan Mohamed three times the tarif price for the use of his horses, Ahmed his groom endeavoured to make me pay for their forage, and that at four times its value. Jubbur Khan, and the serbas Ali supported him in this attempt at extortion, adding to it a demand that I should feed all three of them, which would have been impossible had my store been ten times larger than it was. On my refusal Ahmed threatened to return to Herat with his beasts and leave me in the middle of the road; I had, therefore, no choice but to compromise the matter with the villains, and we left our camping-ground in the afternoon.

Our little caravan was joined at Jaberan by a young Afghan merchant of Kandahar, making his annual journey to Teheran, where I had known him. This was no small comfort, as, doubtless, his presence was a restraint upon the evil designs of my rascally escort upon me—or, at all events, my baggage and the immense sums of money they fancied I had in my portmanteaus.

We travelled till midnight—for three hours on a plain, and the rest through low mountains, arid, rocky, but of picturesque and varied forms. Our last skin of water had been consumed at sunset, and our intense thirst was aggravated by the suffocating state of the atmosphere and the blasts of the hot wind, which every now and then dried up the mouth till it felt like a piece of parchment.

To aggravate the misery there was no water in the marsh near the caravanserai at Shah Jehan, or, indeed, moisture; and I suffered tortures impossible to describe from the stings of the mosquitoes and the bites of the vermin that had fallen on me from my Afghan visitors. Guided only by accident in choosing the site of our halt we pitched our tents near some brushwood, uneasy enough as to what might befal us during the night, for the road was one of ill repute for robbers.

I have remarked that foot-passengers never travel this road without a *mesek* filled with water attached to the body like a cartouche-box; the water even when exposed to the sun is kept very cool in it by the evaporation effected by the slightest breeze, while in a jug it soon becomes heated. I have also found that mastication alleviated the sufferings occasioned by thirst.

Ab-Kourmeh and *Giraneh*, July 27th—fourteen parasangs—at first in the mountains, then on the plain; the country, uncultivated and almost uninhabited, was well wooded, and abounded in game, notwithstanding the want of water.

Before we left Shah Jehan I had had another altercation with Ahmed. This rascal, finding that I gave in on the previous evening about their food, declared the next morning that he would not go a step further if I did not give him the Afghan robe I wore. It was in vain I told him I had none other, and invoked the protection of Jubbur Khan, my guide and protector. The rascal replied by demanding my boots for himself, and Ali, the serbas, my turban! For an instant I thought of bringing the matter to a crisis with the scoundrels. I was well armed, and, though they were the same, by taking the initiative I might kill them—treat them, in fact, as I should have done bandits who demanded my money or my life. But that would not have forwarded me in any way. How could I present myself in the midst of a hostile population? how explain my reasons for having shot them? Would they have been believed? So I finished by compounding with them, as I did at Jaberan; there was nothing else to be done, and I gave them the value in money instead of stripping the clothes off my back. After this new scene I was so exhausted by excitement and thirst that I could not have gone one step farther, if, by God's mercy, a traveller on foot had not come up at the time, and given me a draught of water from his *mesek*, for which I paid a franc. Despite the price, the bargain was a most advantageous one for me, for that water probably saved my life, and certainly enabled me to travel five parasangs farther across the scantily wooded mountains that separated us from Ab-kourmeh, a deserted English caravanserai. Near it was a camp of thievish nomads, from which we considered it best to keep at some distance, and we therefore took shelter amongst the tamarisks on the borders of a stinking marsh, at which man and beast were obliged to quench their thirst. After resting a couple of hours we mounted our horses, though I was suffering from burning fever aggravated by twelve hours of the hot wind. We travelled all the afternoon and all night, over a vast salt plain, on which we lost our way, and after riding ten parasangs instead of seven, arrived as the day broke, perfectly worn out, at Giraneh.

Very near here was a custom-house, on the bank of a river nearly as rapid as the Heri-rood, bearing the name of the place; it falls into the Furruh-rood. The heat this day was 46° of Centigrade in the shade.* Giraneh is an open village of forty houses and two hundred tents; there are many others not very far off, as well as a fortress of burnt brick, apparently very ancient and falling to pieces—on one side it rises abruptly out of the water, and on the three others the base of its thick walls can only be reached by climbing up a steep slope about thirty or thirty-five feet high.

This position is important; it commands the passage of the river and the defiles in the mountains on the South. A small force quartered there might maintain its authority in the districts of Subzawar, Furrah, Laush, Bukwa, Gulistan, Gour, and Sukkur, Giraneh being the central point round which converge these localities—information for the English and the Russians. Here, as at the halt of the night before, my servants made further extortionate demands, which I was content to pacify with ten francs. I resisted as well as I could, for I could afford no more; but, had I been richer, I should have done the same, for making one present to an Afghan is only creating a claim for a second: he looks upon the first as an acquired right, and acts accordingly. It is therefore necessary, as a matter of policy and

* This equals about 135° Fahrenheit. Major Sanders' thermometer, on the Furrah-rood in 1840, rose to 175° in the sun, a heat which enabled him to poach eggs in the burning sand.—ED.

security, to prevent an Oriental from having the idea that you possess any superfluities, but most especially an Afghan; that idea always excites their cupidity, and renders them capable of every crime. To live amongst them it is requisite to be pre-convinced that, even if they are treated with the utmost kindness possible, it will never ensure their gratitude, or render their affection any more constant than their enmity; their sole incitement to action, the sole influence over their conduct at all times is—the love of gain.

The grand argument which the cut-throats who formed my escort always threw in my teeth when I refused them anything, was, that they were wearing themselves out and ruining their health in my service; but, as they were well paid, I had good reason to complain of their conduct. At every halt they would throw themselves down to sleep, and leave me to help myself and watch the baggage, which, for any care they took of it, would have been stolen at the first stage; indeed, in all probability they would themselves have commenced the pillage. Three-fourths of the time I had to cook for all of us, and they invariably ate by far the greater part of the provisions I had purchased for myself.*

---

* It appears very evident that the men who accompanied M. Ferrier from Herat had taken their instructions from the Vezir as to the manner in which he was to be treated, and that it was not Yar Mohamed's wish that he should find the journey a pleasant one. Had not his Herat attendants encouraged the Afghans in their impertinence, they would never have presumed so much.

The bravado regarding the number of English they had killed I believe to have been merely assumed. Some of these Noorzyes of the Adreskunde may have taken part in the attack on the English at Kandahar, 300 miles distant; but the greater number had probably seen no other Feringees than those attached to the Herat mission, against whom they had no enmity whatever.

The circumstances under which Dr. L. travelled between Herat and Kandahar, when detached from the mission, were very different. The objects of his journey were to convey despatches and presents to Kandahar, for transmission to England, and to bring back money (in sovereigns) to Herat, for the use of the mission; inspecting the line of horse and foot men, and the arrangements for protection of travellers, and conciliating, as far as he could, the chiefs of the various khails of nomade Afghans on his way. In effecting all this he was very successful; his control over the guards on the road, and a well-armed party of ten or twelve men, being not more useful to him in one way, than his reputation as a "Feringhee hakim" in the other; and the consequence was that he met with the utmost civility and kindness, in their rough way, at every khail he passed through. The Afghan nomads are certainly as dirty a race as can be imagined; but they were quite on their good behaviour when he travelled among them, and he saw nothing of the disgusting insolence which M. Ferrier experienced. He has no doubt, however, of the correctness of M. Ferrier's statement; indeed the whole account of his journey in those countries appears eminently truthful and graphic, and evinces his high qualifications as a traveller.—L.

At last my spirits, as well as my strength, began to fail under the combined effects of fever, anxiety, vexation, and fatigue, crowned by frequent and overpowering distress from the want of water. I grew melancholy; I yearned for my own country; I thought of those dear to me that I had left there, and began to feel as if courage would forsake me. It would indeed be difficult to imagine the horrors of my position in the company of such villains, in the midst of this vast and burning plain, in which often a quart of water and a black loaf was all the sustenance I had for a whole day. When I succeeded in overcoming one obstacle another and a greater rose before me, and when I put up with any privation it was only a warning that I must submit in everything.

In this country the difficulty of procuring what you want is much increased by the circumstance I have before alluded to,— that the nomads know not the value of money, and it is sometimes impossible to purchase anything with it. Whatever articles they let you have they insist upon being paid for with something that they can wear, such as sashes, turbans, trowsers, or a piece of cotton cloth, called kerbas, for a shirt; or tea, coffee, sugar, or tobacco: and I have often suffered the pangs of hunger for hours, because I had not had the forethought to bring a packet of such articles with me for the purpose.

Gurm-ab and *Shahguz*, July 28th — thirteen parasangs — in narrow valleys between high mountains, quite uncultivated and covered with brushwood of tamarisk; a few tents now and then appeared in the distance. We arrived here after a march of six parasangs in the night. The place is named after a so-called warm-spring, but its heat is not more than four or five degrees above zero. It has no particular metallic flavour, nevertheless it seemed to me scarcely probable that it should always have been so tasteless. I think it likely that, for want of being preserved, it may have become mixed with others and deteriorated. One thing, however, is certain,—that in former times the place was frequented, for there are the ruins of an edifice which might have been princely, and they are still shaded by trees centuries old; the heat was, in the shade, 45° of Centigrade. Close to it is an unfinished English caravanserai.

I had purchased a small supply of provisions at Giraneh—all that they would sell me, but my honest companions had eaten them during the night's march; when, therefore, I expected to breakfast, nothing was to be found but a little rice. Exceedingly savage at this, I determined, in spite of hunger, fatigue, and the heat, to shoot some of the immense number of partridges that with other game abounded near the halt, and in the course of an hour I returned with three birds and a larger appetite; but how can I paint my disappointment, my grief, my rage, when I saw that the rice, which was such an important ingredient in my repast, had been eaten—eaten, as Ali told me, by four sepoys on their way from Herat to Kandahar! They pounced upon it, said he, without the least ceremony. I could not avoid being his victim, but I was not his dupe, for his beard being full of rice and grease, clearly showed he had been a participator in the theft, if he had not instigated it. The same proofs convicted Ahmed and Jubbur Khan: they had not even done masticating. What could I do? To be angry was useless, perhaps dangerous; so when my strange guests departed, ironically complimenting my eatables and my cook, I answered in the same tone that I quite regretted that a supper intended for four only had to serve for seven, and, without manifesting further discomposure, sat down to pluck my partridges. When they were roasted, I ate two, and, to the great disgust of my three villains, put the other into my pocket to eat alone at sunset.

At three o'clock in the afternoon we were again in the saddle and continued our way along a deep valley; but in about two hours the horses absolutely refused to advance further against the burning wind. This terrible hot blast, which inflicts upon animals the same tortures as on the human race, is called *sirocco* in the south of Europe, *khamsine* in Egypt, and *saum* and *simoom* in Arabia and Persia.* In Egypt, Damascus, Arabia, and Bagdad, it blows by sudden squalls, the approach of which is indicated by a certain perturbed state of the atmosphere. It is filled with masses of livid opaque vapour, which

* M. Ferrier here alludes to the ordinary hot blast of the desert, and not the real saum or simoom. The latter is a poisonous current of air, probably electric, of rare occurrence, and causing instant death, and peculiar, I believe, to the deserts of Arabia. It has no injurious effect on vegetation, perhaps because it does not come in contact with it, as it rarely approaches within one or two feet of the ground. The camel, instinctively being aware of its approach, kneels down, and lays its head close to the ground, thus escaping its deadly effects.—ED.

conceal the horizon, and not unfrequently objects that are at no great distance from the traveller: the light of the sun comes through it tinted red, and causes visible alarm to the animals, who drive their noses into the sand, or turn their backs to the squall till it has passed, and men are almost suffocated by it; perspiration is suddenly arrested, an impalpable sand fills up every pore—eyes, nose, ears, and mouth; the pulse beats violently, and the sufferer sometimes falls down suddenly, as if struck by apoplexy. Decomposition always rapidly follows death under these awful circumstances, and at the slightest touch the corpse becomes dismembered—everything attending the prevalence of this death-charged blast is singular, exceptional, startling. In the vast southern steppes of Central Asia it rarely blows in squalls, it is only in the deserts of the Seistan that it exhibits that characteristic; but here it blows about three days in moderate force, in which one suffers much, though death rarely ensues. There is no protection against it, except a house hermetically closed on the side from which it comes.

We had suffered sadly during the seven parasangs between Gurm-ab and Shahguz, because our *mesek* had been torn, and much of the water had escaped; nevertheless, by turning it, I had contrived to save about a small basinful, of which I took the greatest care, in case, as might very possibly happen, one or other of us should be struck by the simoom; but Jubbur Khan, seizing the opportunity, while I was rolling on the ground in agonies from a kick I had received from one of the horses, drank the precious liquid. I perceived that he had done so the moment I asked him for some to recover me a little; and to my reproaches he only answered that he could see no necessity for my being angry at his taking a little mud that hardly served to wet his moustache. "Water," he added, jeeringly, "is the drink of Mussulmen—infidels, like you, drink wine. We must each take our chance; I have not encroached upon yours, so let me hear no more about it.' I had no resource, so suffered without complaining.

Four hours before daylight we came out of the defile of Dervazeh, upon the immense plain of Bukwa, bounded only by the horizon. All the mountains were left behind us; and the vast level, naked surface was modified only by two or three small and isolated hills, at great distances from each other.

The exceedingly steep and high mountains bordering this plain on the north are doubtless the southern limits of the country known to the ancients by the name of Paropamisus; those we had traversed in coming from Herat were its boundary on the west. Extensive plains are spread immediately at their base. That of Bukwa may be considered the largest, but it is not the most populated. A few villages, or camps of nomads, are met with in the northern part, others more numerous are ranged on the banks of the Helmund or the Khash-rood; all the central part is uninhabited, not because it is sterile, but from the want of water to irrigate the cultivation. Anciently it was well supplied with water from the mountain by numerous wells, and then contained many villages; but during the last century it has been the theatre of the almost constant wars between the states of Kandahar and Herat; and the result has been that the inhabitants have fled from the perpetual miseries entailed upon them by their frontier position between the two countries. In the plain of Bukwa the heat is excessive, though the air is healthy, and nothing grows there except scanty brushwood of tamarisk and mimosa; were it peopled and cultivated to the extent that it might be, it would become an abundant granary for Afghanistan.

We stopped at Shahguz, near a well of brackish water, by the side of which were a few nomadic tents. Bukwa is not the name of a place, but of the district embracing the whole plain.

CHAPTER XX.

Tax upon travellers — Camp of Noorzyes — Another scene in a tent — Curiosity and questions — Why the European's skin is white — The limits of Iliate hospitality — Haji-Ibrahimi — A night with the nomads — Their dish called kooroot — The Persian Kesht — Attack of the Noorzyes — Hatred existing between Afghan tribes — Character of the Afghan — Incapable of amelioration — Habits of the Eïmaks — Washeer — Afghan instincts — Mode of calculating time — The Persian talker — The author enters the territory of Kandahar — Crosses the Khash-rood — The Wali of Washeer — The advantages of hospitality — More troubles — What a European is in the eyes of an Afghan — The author turns cook — Imprudence of travelling with trunks — Treachery of the new guide —Attack upon Mons. Ferrier and his servants — Character of the Parsivans — Biabának.

HAJI-IBRAHIMI, July 29th — six parasangs — a few tents and a little cultivation appearing on the horizon. In the middle of the plain, by the road-side, is the village of Kassem-abad, containing about one hundred and fifty hearths, and enclosed by a wall of earth. The governor of the district resides in it, and also the contractor for the toll upon travellers.

This tax is frequently renewed in Afghanistan, and is very onerous, for it must be paid every three or four stages. In Herat the contractors are generally rich Indian merchants, and pretty easily satisfied; but their deputies, usually Afghans, are much less so, and always claim more than is fixed by the tariff. It is certainly possible to complain to their superiors, but the traveller would gain nothing by so doing: he would only protract indefinitely the vexatious examination of his effects; and in revenge the official would probably find the opportunity, during the process, of slipping some little article into his own pocket. I therefore always paid at once what they demanded. Kassem-abad is the last inhabited spot in the principality of Herat, towards the frontier of Kandahar.

We stopped to breakfast near a camp of nomadic Noorzyes, and found the men armed to the teeth, and ready for any surprise that might be attempted against them by the tribe of Haji-Ibrahimi, whose camp lay a few parasangs farther east. The two tribes had been at war for the last few days, about the turning of a water-course, and several men had lost their lives.

Scarcely had I succeeded in settling myself in my tent when these ragged warriors crowded in upon me, close as herrings in a tub, to my no small discomfort, for the mercury stood at 48° of Centigrade in the shade. The rascal Jubbur Khan, instead of preserving me from this intrusion, amused himself by pressing them to come in and inquire after my health; this the fellows did most pertinaciously, and with the most unpleasant familiarity. Some had their itchy, filthy children on their knees; and these wretched little monkeys screamed and cried most frightfully. In short, it was a repetition of Jaberan; each one, great and small, seemed bent upon trying which could make the most noise; and I was persecuted by a continuous cross-fire of the most stupid and impertinent questions. "What are you?" "Where are you going?" "Where do you come from?" "What is your rank?" "What do you want to do?" "Are you rich?" "Is your country more fertile than ours?" "Have you as good melons there?" "Are the men as clever and brave as we are?" This last was characteristic; for they are exceedingly conceited, and look upon themselves as in every respect the first people in the world.

They touched upon every subject; would be told everything, and applied everything to themselves; they inquired about the smallest details, and with endless repetitions—nothing could be more irritating, more tormenting. If I took up my kalioon, they walked off with it before I had drawn two puffs; passed it from hand to hand, and sucked the pipe till it was consumed. They pounced upon my meals, leaving me only the scraps; and scrupled not to ask me for sugar, tea, coffee, and tobacco, in tones that made it clear they had no intention of submitting to a refusal, which it would have been dangerous as well as useless to give.

These fellows never for a moment considered they were annoying me. It was a duty of hospitality to keep me company. It would have been the same to give as well as to receive; but covetousness, that thoroughly Afghan vice, drove them, in spite of themselves, to trespass upon the laws of hospitality, or, even as other nations would consider, ordinary civility. They did not leave me five minutes' peace in which to change my shirt, but pleased themselves with ascertaining whether I was of the same shape as themselves or not; feeling by turns my face, hands, feet, and body; and, above all, holding long discussions upon the whiteness of my skin. They could not account for the difference between us on this point, each offering some most ridiculous conjecture about it, till the mollah brought them all to one mind by telling them,—"His condemned faith forbids the European women to suckle their children, and they supply the mother's place by an ewe. This, therefore," he added, "preserves the natural whiteness of the skin; but they are not the less half-beast, half-man; and that is the reason they cannot understand the sublime religion of our venerated Prophet." What I suffered from these investigations exceeds belief; for similar scenes were enacted in various places. I found, however, exceptions to the multitude in several Afghan chiefs, who possessed both good manners and strong good sense under a rough exterior, and who were in some degree educated; but the middle and lower classes were all unintelligent brutes, in the most degraded state of ignorance.

When I visited the plain of Bukwa two years only had elapsed since it had been replaced under the dominion of the Khan of Herat; and the iron hand of Yar Mohamed pressed heavily upon the people. They dared no longer live by pillage, formerly their best resource. They now cultivate the ground, and rear flocks, by which they realise larger profits; but that sort of life is odious to them, and they cease not to curse the Vezir, by whom the change has been forced upon them. One of these Iliates frankly told me that but for the awe in which he stood of Yar Mohamed he should have followed me a couple of parasangs beyond the prescribed limits of hospitality, and then rifled my trunks, which he was persuaded were filled with gold, and undisguisedly expressed his vexation at not being able to appropriate the contents. The confession of my avaricious visitor no way increased my confidence in him: I much doubted whether the temptation might not overcome his fears even of the Vezir Sahib, and therefore, setting out immediately, after five hours' journey I arrived before nightfall at Haji-Ibrahimi. The encampment is watered by a kariz,* near which there is an English caravanserai, and the tomb of the Imaum from whom the place takes its name.†

* A kariz is an underground watercourse or aqueduct, with shafts at intervals for the convenience of repairing it. They are met with in great numbers in all the plain country of Persia and Afghanistan.—ED.

† In illustration of M. Ferrier's remark in the text, an incident may be

The inhabitants of Haji-Ibrahimi were armed and on their guard, like the tribe with whom I had breakfasted, and they only received us because it was night, and there was neither water nor inhabited spot within ten hours' march. Had it been daytime they would not have considered it imperative upon their hospitality to receive us, and we must have pushed on. My companions, weary and longing for repose after the fatigues of the day, thought to obtain it sooner by carefully concealing the fact of my being an European, for fear of exciting their curiosity; they therefore gave out that I was a Parsivan, in the service of Yar Mohamed, thus procuring me the tranquillity which I required even more than themselves. We were soon provided with supper—"for the love of God"—*ez bérayé Khoda*—no payment being asked for in any

---

mentioned in Dr. Login's journey from Herat to Kandahar in 1840. He had been received, with all his party, by an Afghan chief in the neighbourhood of Washeer, in a most courteous and hospitable manner; for he had been honoured with an "Istigbal" in the Afghan style—the eldest son of the Khan, with several horsemen, having been sent out to meet him, and to display their feats of horsemanship as he approached. The chief had also invited all the principal men of his tribe to a feast on the occasion.

It was arranged before they parted for the night that the Khan, with some of his people, were to accompany Dr. Login next morning for a short distance on his way to Girishk. It happened, however, that he awoke very early (the Afghan pilau may have been indigestible!), and could not again fall asleep; and finding that the moon was very bright, and the weather most favourable, he left his little tent, which was pitched in the court-yard of the caravanserai, and walked outside the gate, where he found a Pharsivan awake, holding the horse of a sleeping Afghan, who was supposed to be on duty as sentinel. After a little conversation with this man, during which he was enlightened as to the character of his host and his people in general, and their treatment of Pharsivans in particular, he determined, being anxious to get on to Girishk as soon as possible, to wake up his men and proceed on his journey. He accordingly did so, sending a message to the Khan apologising for starting so early, and a small present in acknowledgment of his kindness. On hearing, however, of his intention to depart sooner than had been arranged by fully two hours, the Khan came out to dissuade him; but failing in this, he ordered his horses out to accompany him. Dr. Login very civilly declined his escort. After rather a trying march, nearly fifty miles, he reached Ghirishk in safety, and was cordially welcomed by Captain E——, then in charge of the district.

On the day after his arrival there information was brought in by some of Captain E——'s police agents that Dr. Login's host of the preceding day had, while he was enjoying his hospitality, sent notice to a Dooranee chief named Akhtar Khan, who had for some time been in arms against us, and who was encamped with his followers not far from Sadaat, that Dr. Login would pass that place at a certain time, urging him to intercept him, as he might prove a valuable prize!

Had Dr. Login not providentially been induced to start so early, and to decline the proffered escort, he might not have got into Girishk so safely; and a valuable copy of the "Shahnameh," presented by Shah Kamran to her most gracious Majesty, of which he was the bearer, and which he has since had the happiness of seeing in the Royal Library at Windsor, might have passed through the hands of a few more Afghan murderers before reaching those of her Majesty's librarian.—L.

form. It consisted of black bread, sour milk, and an uneatable ragout—grains of maize cooked and crushed, with small pieces of bread, floating in boiling and rancid grease. Despite my voracious hunger, I contented myself with the bread and milk, and left the kouroot to a score of fellows, also at supper, amongst whom it disappeared in the twinkling of an eye. When this dish is well made it is excellent, though I believe unknown in Europe—in Persia it is called *kesht*, and is thus prepared. Some butter-milk is boiled in a very large saucepan, by which means the watery particles escape in the form of steam, and the solid ones are deposited at the bottom of the vessel; when sufficiently thickened the mass is divided and made into little balls about the size of a pigeon's egg, which are dried in the sun, and will keep for years. When required, these balls of concentrated grease are continuously stirred in hot water, and in a metal dish, till completely dissolved: the epicures add a quarter of a pound of fresh butter, which gives the sauce an exquisite flavour. It is poured over the bread, maize, or meat which it is intended to season, just at the moment it is to be served. Kesht is used with meat, but more particularly with black cucumbers and fish.

To return from this culinary digression. After the repast was finished our hosts pressed us to go to rest immediately, and proceeded to do the same themselves around us, charging our party not to pass beyond the circle, lest we should receive a shot or two from their matchlocks, which were on the ground beside them ready for the anticipated attack of the Noorzyes should they present themselves. The precaution was not altogether useless, for in the middle of the night we were awoke by the noise of firing. Our hosts, who rose at the first shot, put us in safety in the caravanserai, and then marched resolutely to meet their enemies, of whom they wounded several, and put them to flight. Not caring to remain longer than we could help in this place, we were as early on the road as possible.

The mutual hatred existing between the various Afghan tribes and their subdivisions, each of which might almost be called a separate nation, will for a long time impede the establishment amongst them of any combined action or form of government. The smouldering fire of old grudges and quarrels is not to be extinguished; the most trifling motives will revive the flame and arm them against each other, and the consequences of the conflicts are deplorable for the country and the population: but for this the Afghan cares little; nothing can exceed his patience under misfortune—it is only equalled by his turbulence, ferocity, and love of vengeance. An energetic man, just, generous, and brave, might perhaps soften their character a little, but such a man is rarely to be found amongst them; and I believe that even he would fail to arouse them from the idleness in which they love to indulge; once in possession of a paltry little mud cabin, a tent, a wife, a horse, and arms, their ambition is satisfied, and they will only rouse themselves from their torpid existence to fight and pillage. Their ideas rarely take an industrious or mercantile turn; those amongst them, and they are few in number, who have a little property are obliged to apply to a Parsivan to tell them even the value of it, or how to turn it to account. It is to the industry and activity of these people that the country is indebted for all it possesses, but they derive only a small profit from their exertions, and but few of them ever attain a position which is not in some degree subservient to their tyrants. Amongst the nomadic Eïmaks I have seen many old men who have never tasted meat, though their whole lives have been devoted to the rearing of flocks; they have never been able to afford to buy any: a coarse loaf, fruit, and a few grains of maize, are their only subsistence.

Although the severity of Yar Mohamed Khan has repressed the thievish tendencies of the Afghans in the plain of Bukwa, a traveller cannot feel himself perfectly safe in the district, because it is constantly scoured by the independent Belooches inhabiting the banks of the Helmund. Mounted on their fast dromedaries, they make frequent incursions upon the territory of Herat, and, when in sufficient force, attack the encampments and villages, which they utterly ruin. It is to these raids, as frequent as those of the Kandaharians, that the desolation and depopulation of this fine plain is to be attributed; and the few inhabitants living between the alternatives of pillaging or being pillaged have acquired a courage, daring, and ferocity beyond what it is easy to imagine any people to possess, which, however, does not prevent them from being very hospitable. As under the sovereignty of Yar Mohamed they dare not carry on their skirmishes in Herat, they exercise their predatory talents upon the Belooches subject to or in Kandahar. They always go out at night, and when they have learned from their spies the position of an encampment they advance stealthily to surprise the sleeping travellers, arranging themselves in parties of three to attack each person. One throws himself on the body of a victim and ties his hands with cords, while the other two seize his head and feet, and pin him to the ground—every man carrying a short chain, with a large nail attached to each end of it, to be used for the purpose. Having by this manœuvre deprived the unfortunate man of the power of moving, they proceed to strip him quite at their ease; retiring with their chains, satisfied with leaving his hands tied. But when these thieves are too few in number to follow their usual plan, two of them creep together in silence to the unhappy object of their cruelty and avarice; one approaches his head, the other in the opposite direction, and while the latter draws a well-sharpened knife across the soles of his feet, to disable him entirely, the former simultaneously slips his havresack, which generally contains all he possesses, from under his head, and both escape at full speed.

Washeer, July 30th—thirteen parasangs—over fields; the road followed the base of the mountains, but as that was a long round out of my way, I preferred taking a direct line for the Kohi-duzdan, the Robbers' Mountain, which stands, like a detached sentinel, in the middle of the plain, and in front of the river Khash-rood. Between Haji-Ibrahimi and Khash-rood there is not a drop of water; and he who journeys through these arid plains must endure the lively torments of burning heat and thirst that I have before mentioned. All his strength is consumed by fever, taking from him almost the sense of existence; the only relief is in mastication, which creates saliva, and so far alleviates the feeling of intense thirst as to render it bearable. The facility of travelling straight across the country, from one point to another, renders strategy a very useless science in Afghanistan; and an army is seldom uneasy about securing its communications, being sure of always finding an open passage by which to retreat. For the same reason it always marches straight on, without any uneasiness as to the enemies that may swarm on its flank or rear. I have never seen a people so clever in judging of the direction in which they ought to travel, be the place they want to go to at ever so great a distance. In crossing the steppes they always strike the point they intend to reach.

The country which separates Haji-Ibrahimi from Washeer is

covered with briars and brambles; and amongst them were scattered groups of tamarisk, serving for the shelter of scores of wild asses, *goor khur*, and every variety of antelope; there were also a great many partridges and bustards.*

* The road by which M. Ferrier travelled is not the most direct one from Bukwa to Girishk. That by Dilaram to the south of the Kohi-Duzdan is considerably shorter than by Washeer; but the distance between the halting-places, from the scarcity of water, and the dread of Belooche robbers, have caused it to be less frequented.

Perhaps an incident or two in the journey of the mission from Herat to the Helmund may serve to illustrate M. Ferrier's text.

Our party, under Major D'Arcy Todd, consisting (with the escort commanded by Sirdar Futteh Khan, our Mehmandar) of about 300 persons, had passed through the Herat territories by the ordinary kafilah marches, and without the least molestation, receiving indeed marks of goodwill at several places where we halted; but on reaching the frontier of the Kandahar state we were more doubtful as to our reception, as Akhtar Khan, a Dooranee chief already mentioned in a former note, was known to be on the watch to intercept us, with a considerable force, at no great distance to the left of the Washeer road. It was therefore determined to conceal the route by which we were to travel until we had passed through Bukwa, and we proceeded by the lower road to Dilaram.

On arriving at the latter place in the afternoon, after leaving Hagee Ibrahim, our people prepared their encampment for the night in the usual way, and, to avoid suspicion, were not prevented; but after having had their meals, and a very short sleep, the whole party were quietly turned out, and prepared for the march as quickly as possible.

Accompanied by Sirdar Futteh Khan, who was in the secret of our councils, and whose conduct had always given us cause to trust him, Dr. Login proceeded during the night, with an advanced party of well-mounted horsemen, a little in front of the main body under charge of Major Todd, until early dawn, when the advance pushed on rapidly to take possession of the first set of wells, which they were apprehensive might be held by a party of Akhtar Khan's men.

Finding these, however, unoccupied, the advanced party halted there until the main body came up within a sufficient distance to secure them, when it again pushed on to occupy another small pool in a similar way, and thence reached the appointed halting-place, a distance of upwards of fifty miles from Dilaram, where it waited the arrival of the main body.

Halting only a sufficient time for a slight refreshment to men and animals, the order of march was again formed as on the previous evening; but as it was considered dangerous to show any lights, for fear of attracting the notice of the Afghans, much difficulty was experienced in finding the proper pathway; and heavy clouds having for a time obscured the stars, by which he guided us, our one-handed Cossid—a man well known in these parts for his wonderful intelligence as a guide—actually had to *feel* for the trodden path on the hard surface of the desert, and found it. By occasionally sending back a horseman from the advanced party, communication was kept up with the main body during the night; but as soon as the morning dawned our advance was pushed more rapidly onwards.

On approaching some broken ground near the "Houz," said to be a favourite rendezvous of Belooche marauders, and likely to be occupied by a party of Akhtar Khan's men, our advance was made with much precaution, covered by files of horsemen in front and on our flanks; and on a signal being made from our right flank, and a horseman riding in to report that a large number of saddled horses were seen in a ravine near the Houz, we immediately prepared for action in Afghan style. Chogas (cloaks) were put in saddle bags, kummer-bunds tightened, turbans firmly bound, loose sleeves turned up, arms bared to the shoulders, and matchlocks and bucklers unslung. The signal of the horseman had been seen from the main body, about a mile distant, and the effect of his report observed; and we were

One of the greatest annoyances in travelling over these immense solitudes is the complete uncertainty which always exists as to the distance that must be accomplished before the next halt. The inhabitants have no clocks or watches; many of them are ignorant of the divisions of time in use in Europe; and some do not know even the length of a parasang. They divide the time in their own manner; from one prayer to another; from one meal to another; till time to sleep, or time to rise; and as every one calculates distance by the power of his own legs, or the speed of his own horse, it follows that there exists no fixed idea either of time or distance. I have often travelled five or six parasangs when the Afghans had assured me that it was only a short gallop, *yek meïdane asp*, to the place to which I proposed to go.

Our little party was increased at Haji-Ibrahimi by a Persian merchant, who joined us. He was a native of Meshed, and, like all his countrymen, boaster, gossip, and buffoon; he perfectly stupefied me with his perpetual talking, from the time we left the halt, being, according to his own statement, on his twelfth journey to India. He related a thousand adventures, of which he was, of course, the hero. On one occasion he threw himself, alone, sword in hand, upon three hundred Belooches, and massacred them fearfully. At another, he had ridden a hundred and sixty parasangs without drawing bridle; and in fact, let the subject be what it might, in the boasting line he kept the conversation to himself for eight hours, and always in the same strain, till we had reached the top of the Kohi-duzdan. There a score or so of horsemen suddenly appeared upon the road, and came towards us at a gallop; the moment he perceived them he was silent. Our

---

shortly joined by a large party whom Major Todd detached in support. They came up at full gallop, similarly prepared, each man wishing to appear a very Roostum. Thinking it strange that no horsemen from the front had fallen back, the ground becoming more broken preventing our seeing them, Dr. Login proposed to the Sirdar to ride on with him to ascertain the cause; and on losing sight of their party, and descending into a ravine, they came suddenly in view of a kafila of asses, laden with corn and butter from the Helmund, on its way to Bukwa, escorted by a good many Afghans on foot! They had just been laden and prepared to start when seen by our vedette, and in the haze of the morning were mistaken for horses! After passing through the broken ground, and again emerging on the level desert, our main body closed up, and we proceeded together to Girishk, having safely accomplished a distance of upwards of 100 miles, with camels and other slow-travelling animals, with only a few hours' halt. It was reported to us afterwards that we had got over our difficulties just in time, and that a detachment of Akhtar Khan's men had been sent to Houz to intercept us, but arrived too late.—L.

valiant Mirza Zein Allah Bedin was seized with a complete panic; his face became ashy white, and his tongue clove to the roof of his mouth. I felt uneasy myself, but endeavoured to rouse my companions to show a firm front; a point in which they were quite as much interested as I was, for the Belooches never give quarter to the Afghans. But the Persian considered what I had said exceedingly imprudent, and in an instant, turning from white to black, declared the defensive attitude that I had recommended perfectly ridiculous. "Just like the Feringhees," he said, "always ready to quarrel for the slightest reason; for my part, I have managed twenty times to get out of such a difficulty. Imitate me and all will be well." Quickly endeavouring to assume a composed and jovial countenance, under which, however, he could scarcely conceal his alarm, he advanced towards the two leading horsemen, who, detached from the group, had come forward to reconnoitre, whom he took for granted were a couple of real robbers. In the most pressing manner he presented to them his Cashmir sash and his muslin turban, accompanying the offer with a most charmingly flowery address: "May the hour be propitious; may you be most welcome," he said; "my eyes have been enlightened since your illustrious shadows have been projected before me; may Allah never diminish them! Blessed be the fortunate constellation that brought you to this spot; but you were really too good to take the trouble to come to meet us—we poor folks, who have nothing, who were going to find you, to kiss the dust of your feet, and offer you as a present these wretched rags, so unworthy of you; but God is merciful; he will permit me to meet you again, and satisfy the wishes of my heart, in offering you presents that shall be worthy of you." The good man accompanied his truly Persian oration by an infinity of bowing and scraping, and seemed not in the least affronted at the roars of laughter which the horsemen could not repress at his ill-dissembled fear, and his naked shaven skull shining in the sun. When, however, he found his presents were not accepted, he tried to make up a new tale, to save his *amour-propre* from our ridicule; but clever as he thought himself, he became so completely entangled in his own rhodomontade that even we joined in the laugh against him. Mirza Zein Allah Bedin, now rendered furious, declared we were all Jangeli, inhabitants of the forest, incapable of appreciating the resources of his intellect.

The horsemen who had so startled us on their first appearance belonged to the Khan of Washeer. Having been informed that the Belooches were prowling about this part of the country, their chief had sent them on a reconnaissance beyond the Khash-rood, to render assistance to those who might be in need of it; but not having found the dreaded Belooches, they were going home, and we took advantage of their escort to enter the territory of Kandahar. After nine hours' march from Haji-Ibrahimi we reached the Khash-rood, the boundary between Herat and Kandahar. At the spot where we crossed its banks were deep, and covered with tamarisk brushwood. We continued our way along a defile, in which we observed some nomads, and then arrived at Washeer, a district composed of four villages, almost touching each other, though each is separately enclosed with a wall of earth. They stand on a plain stretching on the left to a chain of mountains, the torrents from which provide water for the irrigation of the surrounding cultivation. After having pitched my tent under the shade of some trees, near a wall breast-high, I sent Jubbur Khan to Sultan Khan Wali of the district, with a letter of introduction from the Sertip Lal Mohamed Khan. The Wali came to see me immediately, bringing some cakes of black bread, and a jug of milk, which he offered me in the name of hospitality; a trifling offering, indeed, in itself, but very precious as a mark of his feeling towards me. It is really most difficult to understand why one of these nomads, so hospitable in his tent, should pillage the traveller without mercy, if he meets him a hundred paces from it. Sultan Khan told me, laughing, "You are my guest; may Allah shed his blessings upon you, and may your shadow never be less! But it would have been a fine piece of good luck to meet you half a parasang from this place. Those pistols, that gun, and that sword that you always have your hand upon, would soon have been hung up in my *divan khaneh*;" and he closed his teeth upon his lower lip, as a man would do who felt vexed at having lost a good chance. However, I heard something of this sort at every halt; and the danger was generally the greatest in an inhabited place. To prevent the miscreants from taking my baggage, I was obliged to sleep upon it, scarce daring to cease watch even then. I was never less anxious than when I encamped in the middle of the wide steppe in a desert spot; my felt spread upon the ground, I rested for a time before

I cooked my food, if Ali, whose duty it was, did not choose to do so, and I had nothing further to think of.

On entering the principality of Kandahar, I foresaw many difficulties, of a nature different from those I had encountered in Herat, where the protection of Yar Mohamed had restrained the actions of those whose feelings were hostile to me. But now, before I could find another protector, I had forty parasangs to travel through a country recently occupied by the English, and where any one supposed to be English could look for nothing but persecution; I was therefore most anxious to reach Kandahar, and present myself to Kohendil Khan, the sovereign of that country. To accomplish this as quickly as possible, I determined to proceed by forced marches; and therefore at sunset, after six hours' rest, proposed to my companions to load the horses and depart. But I had not yet calculated the extent of their avarice. Though I had already paid Ahmed and Ali the value of the clothes they asked for, actually from my back, at Kash Jaberan, they renewed their demand at Washeer, and, on my second refusal, declined to accompany me further, and prepared to return to Herat. Jubbur Khan was not less exacting; and though before setting out from Herat I had paid his master three tomauns for the express purpose of securing his services as far as Kandahar, he declared that he would not go beyond Washeer, and stated his intention of supplying his place by a new guide, a servant of the Wali Sultan Khan, for whom I was to pay an additional sum, forming, of course, no part of my agreement.

This knavery irritated me to the last degree; and I decisively refused the demands of all three. "Return without my certificate to Herat," I said, "and see how the Vezir Sahib Yar Mohamed Khan will receive you. I shall write to him." This threat frightened them sufficiently to prevent them from deserting their duty so far as to return; but as they knew it was impossible for me to replace them with Afghans taken at random from amongst the bandits of Washeer, they insisted on stopping there till I had satisfied their other demands. Perhaps I should have given way so far as to change my new robe for Ali's tattered and filthy dress, had I not been well convinced that any concession would only induce them to make fresh demands. I resisted, therefore, and remained at Washeer that night, much against my wish; for delay might seriously aggravate the dangers of my journey. Up to this time I had, by the rapidity of my movements, kept in front of the caravans that started from Herat at the same time I did; and the fanatical population through which I had to pass, though they might have learned that a Feringhee was expected, would not be able to fix the precise moment, and could not recognise me in my disguise, unless I were betrayed by my escort, or pointed out by travellers who knew me. What I had so much endeavoured to avoid, however, resulted from my stay at Washeer; five or six persons who overtook us, and continued their journey to Kandahar, would, without doubt, mention the fact of my being on the road—a circumstance that caused me great uneasiness.

At nightfall the Wali bid me look out for myself, because his officials would not hesitate to plunder me when it became dark; and his warning was in no way superfluous, for I found some days afterwards that I had really been in danger. At the instigation of a mollah and two syuds several persons assembled and unanimously agreed to rob me, the only question being whether they should not also take my life. This came to the ears of the Wali, who dreading lest their villany should compromise him, suddenly appeared in the midst of the group and conjured them to renounce their project. In this he with some difficulty succeeded, and subsequently imparted information of it to me.

July 31st.—This day was also passed at Washeer, surrounded by a crowd of Afghans, whose proceedings were simply a *da capo* of what I have already described at Kash-Jabaran. To their curiosity, impertinence, and rhodomontade I showed the patience of a martyr, and was careful not to betray any symptoms of fear or anxiety, as that would only have increased the annoyance and the evil. With Orientals of all classes it is the wisest plan to assume a Mussulman imperturbability, to evince neither timidity nor bravado, to be apparently incapable of any demonstration of feeling,—for emotion of any kind is sure to bring on some complications which lead to disastrous results. These Afghans were curious to know why we eat pigs and frogs, in their eyes unclean animals, which they imagine are, with rats and serpents, our only articles of food.

One of their favourite subjects of conversation with an European is religion. They are generally better informed than we suppose upon the dogmas of the Christian faith, and will discuss each article of it with wonderful tenacity: but not choosing to give them the satisfaction of obtaining a triumph over me, which their power and my fear of annoying them would, under the circumstances, have rendered easy, I declared myself a Deist, believing neither Trinity, Miracle, nor Prophet, but simply a natural law ordaining good and rejecting evil. Their amazement was great; but as they were not prepared to dispute that ground, and their intellects were not fertile in resources, they left me alone, satisfied that I spoke of their religion and their Prophet with deference. I mention this anecdote in the interest of future travellers in Afghanistan who may find themselves in a similar difficulty.

My compulsory stay at Washeer was useful to me as an opportunity of studying Afghan manners; but I should have been driven mad had it lasted one day longer—my mind being ever on the strain to watch, to converse, diplomatize, and suffer with patience. My servants had evidently come to an understanding with the inhabitants to torment me in every way, and if possible drive me from this war of endurance to some composition of the matters in dispute between us. Ali ate and drank under my very beard the small store of tea, coffee, and sugar I had kept back in case of illness, and yet it was droll enough to see him doing the honours to the bystanders with my property, without even offering me a share. Sometimes, as I have said, he refused to cook my dinner, and I then performed that important operation myself: when it was ready I had the gratification of seeing this rascal come and plunge his filthy unwashed hand into my pilau and eat his share. On one occasion, when the meal was over, he took two copper plates of mine and changed them away for some articles he fancied and kept for himself.

I think I never felt such concentrated rage in my life as when I saw the insolent provocations of these miscreants; but prudence imposed silence, and I adopted the shortest and only course, namely, to compound with them. In the first place I came to an understanding with Jubbur Khan, the least hostile of the three, consenting to let him leave, and to engage another guide, whom I was to pay: I then made him a present of my boots, which secured his services as mediator between me and the other two, who were for the time satisfied with a tomaun each and the promise of my Afghan dress the day I should arrive at Kandahar. Urgent necessity drove me to this, for small as my baggage was the cut-throats at Washeer were bent upon getting possession of it. As they believed the trunks contained gold and silver I knew not how long the protection of the Wali would have availed me.

As a general rule it is the height of imprudence to travel with trunks or boxes that are locked, for in Afghanistan the sight of them is sure to generate in the minds of the natives the most rapacious ideas. They immediately believe they are full of specie or other valuables, and cannot conceive that any one would take so much care of his clothes. Their cupidity is greater than their fear of danger, and they will not stop at the commission of any crime to attain their object. *Khourjines*, a kind of sack, is the best and most convenient thing to carry one's baggage in this country.

Mahmoodabad, August 1st — twelve parasangs — the first half in the mountains, the rest on a plain. I started at daybreak from Washeer, accompanied by a man on foot, the successor of Jubbur Khan; but, instead of taking the direct road to Biabának,* my new guide followed that to the right, a very difficult and stony one across the mountains. To justify this proceeding he told me the report of my arrival had spread, and that robbers would probably be lying in wait for me on the other. I had the simplicity to believe this, which I ought not to have done, having seen a caravan take the ordinary road at the very moment that we were leaving Washeer, and by joining that I should have had nothing to fear, but, unfortunately, to do so never occurred to me till a couple of hours afterwards. At this time we were in a narrow pass, where the road was exceedingly bad; and I noticed that my guide was wonderfully perturbed and disconcerted, or on the watch for something. Suddenly he made off over the rocks and ravines with the rapidly of a gazelle, while on our left arose ferocious cries from a dozen rascals, who soon appeared with lances, swords, and shields. I glanced instantly at Ali and Ahmed to see if their countenances indicated any expectation of this attack, but their alarm convinced me of their ignorance; they evidently feared as much for their lives as I for mine.

This point cleared up, I looked about me, and espying, fifty paces in advance, a rocky eminence, I ran to it, followed by my two servants, determined to sell my life as dearly as I could.

* *i. e.* The little desert. The English had a post both here and at Washeer during the Afghan war.—R.

Fortune favoured us, for we found the position could be gained only along the road by which we reached it. A few minutes later our adversaries came near enough for us to see they had no fire-arms, while we, on the contrary, were well provided. Ali had a gun, I gave my double-barrel to Ahmed, and reserved for myself a pair of six-barrelled pistols: sixteen balls therefore were at the service of these cavaliers. However, on they came, and steadily, for Ali's first shot did not take effect; but Ahmed's having told, seeing that I was ready to follow it up, they halted, and, as we rapidly reloaded, kept their distance. Our blockade lasted an hour and a half; to every summons to surrender we replied with a volley, when suddenly, to our great amazement, they fled and left us. At the moment we could not see the reason, but were soon enlightened; five or six Afghan horsemen, on their way to Herat, hearing the firing, came up at a rapid pace. For a trifling sum they consented to turn back and ride with us a couple of hours. When they left we proceeded at a sharp trot, and soon reached Karakan, a small village of fifteen hearths, surrounded with gardens, watered from a kariz, and inhabited by Parsivans.

I always found that I could at once distinguish this race of people from the Afghans; their reserve, politeness, and respectful bearing indicating a conquered and oppressed people. I remarked also that the laws of hospitality were not observed amongst them in the same degree as amongst the Afghans; they sell everything very dear, are active, but greedy of gain, and deceitful. I stopped at Karakan only for breakfast, and an hour after reached Biabának, a village surrounded by a wall of earth, containing sixty hearths: its numerous gardens are irrigated by abundant water-courses. It lies at the base of the mountains, at the commencement of a vast plain. I remained here only four hours, having learnt that the Sirdar Mohamed Sedik Khan, commandant of the fortress of Girishk, to whom Yar Mohamed had given me a letter of recommendation, was not at his usual residence, but at another, called Mahmoodabad, nearer to Biabának. Taking a new guide, I pressed on, and arrived under the walls of the former village three hours after midnight. At that unseasonable hour I would not, of course, disturb the Sirdar, and encamped in a field for the night. Mahmoodabad is five parasangs from Biabának.

CHAPTER XXI.

Arrival at Mahmoodabad — The Moonshee Feiz Mohamed — Interview with Mohamed Sedik Khan — The scene at his house — His personal appearance — Ferrier's spirited conversation with him — The Englishman with green eyes — Sedik Khan demands the author's notes — The Khan's specious arguments — His cunning conduct when alone with the author — Places Ferrier in confinement — Character of Sedik Khan — His administration — Englishmen arrested in Kandahar — English prisoners sold to the Turcomans — Attempt of one at Girishk to communicate with the author — The messenger returns from Kandahar — Ferrier still detained — Journal — Vile conduct of the Khans — The Moonshee's opinion of Ferrier's position — Singular termination of a marriage — Visit from an Afghan Khan — He proposes a plan of escape — Brutality of the guard — Unpleasant reflections — Erroneous opinion respecting the Afghans — Sir Alexander Burnes — Insults of the soldiers — The author leaves Mahmoodabad — Arrives at Girishk — Occupied by the English in 1841 — Courage overcomes prudence — The author in prison here.

I WAS far from expecting the annoyances that befel me in the morning. I had scarcely awoke when I was surrounded by a crowd of sepoys and farrashes* belonging to the Sirdar, who hailed me with bad jokes and insults. The proverb, "Like master like man," came into my mind, and from that moment I felt a presentiment of the tribulations that were to be my fate here. I had been for upwards of an hour the butt of these scamps when I was accosted by a young man dressed entirely in black, whose manners contrasted singularly with those of the other individuals around me, and the moment he appeared my persecutors retired to a distance and remained silent. It was the Moonshee secretary, Feiz Mohamed, who, having heard of my arrival, had come to offer me his services.

This young man had been employed by the English when they occupied Afghanistan, and having been well treated remembered them with gratitude and secretly sighed for their return. His father was an Afghan, and his mother an Indian; and after the disasters of Kabul, and its evacuation by the British army, he had

* Literally "carpet-spreaders," but applied to under-servants generally in Persia and Afghanistan.—ED.

much difficulty to escape from the barbarity of his countrymen, who reproached him with having allied himself with the oppressors of his country. He had, however, acquired a little knowledge of English, and, as the Sirdar Mohamed Sedik wished to learn that language, he attached him to his service, and the Moonshee was thus placed under his protection. At my request he immediately carried to his master the letter I brought from Yar Mohamed Khan. About a quarter of an hour afterwards he returned with a huge shabby-looking fellow, named Sadullah Jan, the Sirdar's man of business, who seized me roughly by the hand and desired I would follow him. I did so, and we entered the *kaleh.** Several courts through which we passed were filled with scowling soldiers; the last was that of the harem, and from this we descended immediately into a *serdab*,† or cave, to which the Asiatics usually retire during the heat of the day. The stairs were narrow, dark, and winding, and I could hardly persuade myself that he was taking me to an inhabited place: it seemed rather as if I were being led to secret execution or imprisonment. The darkness concealed my discomfort from my guide, but it was dissipated only when I found myself in the presence of the Sirdar and his numerous court. Opposite to him was Akhter Khan, the irreconcilable enemy of the English, and at his side Rahimdil Khan, brother of the famous Sirdar Abdullah Khan,‡ who instigated the revolt against them at Kabul; there were besides in the *serdab*, Mohamed Azim Khan, the Sirdar Mohamed, Sedik's own uncle; lastly, Berkhordar Khan and five or six Mollahs and Syuds—all hostile to Europeans, who gave me an icy-cold reception; the Sirdar acknowledged my *salam alek* by only a slight inclination of his head, and made me a sign to seat myself in the last place, near the door of entrance. His countenance was dark and severe, and produced the most unpleasant impression upon me. His false look, abrupt questions, wounding remarks, and haughty and contemptuous manner, indicated a predetermina-

* A name given to everything — town, village, or private residence—surrounded by a wall of earth.

† Most houses in the East are provided with subterranean chambers, called serdabs (literally cold water), to which the family retire during the heat of the day. They are often furnished with the greatest luxury, and their refreshing coolness is increased by the play of fountains, and punkahs or large fans hung from the ceiling. This is the favourite place for the ladies' afternoon siesta.—ED.

‡ The head of the Achikzyes, and a man of great influence. He died of wounds received at the fatal battle of Bimaroo.—ED.

tion in his mind against me. To ascertain the purpose of my journey was his first object, and his interrogations respecting it were exceedingly pinching. He also attempted to prove that I contradicted myself; wherefore I subsequently limited my replies entirely to the following :—

"I am a Frenchman; and not, as you suppose, an Englishman. I am going to Lahore entirely on my own account, to take service with the Maharajah of the Punjab. I have no political mission, either for Afghanistan or any other country or government. The Vezir Sahib Yar Mohamed Khan tells you so in his letter; and here are other firmans of Mohamed Shah, your ally, whom I have served, testifying the truth of what I state."

"These firmans," he replied, "may have been made out for some other person; and as to your confidence in Yar Mohamed, it might have been better placed; that chief was wrong to send you into this country—his orders are of no effect in Kandahar."

"But that is not an order," I remonstrated; "it is a friendly introduction from an ally, which I did not think would be thus received."

To my objections he replied, "You were quite wrong to come this way. Do you know," he added, "the Englishman who came last year from Persia to Kandahar?"

I answered in the negative. "Well," he said, "then I am better informed than you are. He was an officer of rank, with green eyes and a red beard, and having been in garrison at Kandahar during the time it was in possession of the English, one of my people knew him, and we seized him, and he is now in a safe place—*der jah-i-qaïem*—from which he will not escape to trouble Afghanistan again. There is another besides him, who, also an Englishman, passed by Candahar about seven months ago; may God pardon him!—*Khoda biy amurzed esh*," meaning that he was dead. "All these visits of the Feringhees in our country are very extraordinary, and we mean to put a stop to them. I know you have written every day all you have seen from one stage to the next. Who gave you leave to act thus? Where are your notes? Give them to me this instant, or I shall order you the bastinado, which will surely make you do so."

"But what mischief can my notes do?" I represented. "You are spoken of as one of the most enlightened Afghan chiefs; you love the sciences, and are not ignorant that the Europeans endeavour to extend them. I have noted, it is true, the direction of the mountains and the rivers, the positions of the towns, villages, and tribes; but that is a work which the English, your enemies, have done before me, and better than I have. They have occupied your country, and know it, beyond a doubt, topographically better than you do yourself." To this he sharply answered,—

"Never mind, I will have the notes."

There was no refusing this formidable demand, but I partly eluded it by sending for a small case, and taking therefrom a copybook with the notes of my journey from Constantinople to Bassora, which I regretted the less because I had sent a copy of them to France before I quitted Bagdad; unhappily it contained also my route in Turkistan and the Paropamisus—this I had forgotten, and it was now too late to hope to withdraw it from beneath his searching glance. Giving up the manuscript appeared to satisfy him, and, after he had turned it over, without understanding a word, for he knew nothing of French, he made renewed attempts to force me to acknowledge that I was an Englishman. My denial was of no use in correcting his false impression, for this reason.

During the first part of my stay at Herat, before Yar Mohamed's suspicions of me were dissipated, he wrote as follows to Kohendil Khan: "An English agitator, calling himself a Frenchman, has just arrived at Herat. He wants to go by Kabul to Turkistan, but I will not let him, and will only leave open to him the road by Kandahar. When he reaches you, you will deal with him according as you think fit." Besides this, two messengers from Kabul to Herat had, on their way back, assured the Sirdar that they knew me perfectly, by having seen me at Ghuzni in 1840.

It was, therefore, perfectly useless to endeavour to convince him to the contrary, and he told me that he intended to write to his father Kohendil Khan for instructions as to what he should do with me. He did not conceal that the letter of Yar Mohamed only added one more to his preconceived opinions, because there was enmity between that chief and his family; and that, after having been pointed out as an agitator, he could not understand my being so warmly recommended by him. In his opinion it could only be the result of machination between me and the chief of Herat, to the injury of his father the sovereign of Kandahar. I could not help secretly thinking he was right. He judged his neighbour of Herat as he knew he should be judged himself,—that is, by supposing him capable of every species of disloyalty and dark intrigue which forms the foundation of Afghan policy, and I could not impute it to him as a crime that he put my sentiments on a level with his own. Had he not had for thirty years before his eyes the English system of invasion in India? And could he not cite me a hundred examples of the audacious policy which subdued by turns Moguls, Nawabs, Emirs, and Rajahs? All that I could do was to affect a tranquil indifference, which, however it might impose upon the Sirdar, was far indeed from reflecting my own feelings. After an examination and cross-questioning of two hours the Sirdar ordered breakfast, which the farrashes brought on several trays, and placed before the guests, and of this I was desired to partake with some persons who were present, but of the less elevated ranks.

The repast over, the visitors retired, and I was going to do the same, when the Sirdar made me a sign to be seated. Directly we were alone he dropped his surly manners, and seemed desirous of showing himself to me in more favourable colours. "Forget," he said, "the severities I have shown you; it was impossible for me to act otherwise in the presence of the fanatics who were about me. You see in me now a friend who will preserve you from every danger; but, in return, I have one service to ask of you. You are English, I am certain, and your denials will not affect my opinion on that point; listen, then, and do me the service I am going to ask of you. At the death of my father Kohendil Khan there will be twenty pretenders to the sovereignty of Kandahar, and he whom the English favour will be sure to succeed: therefore, to obtain their support, there is no sacrifice that I am not ready to make; I would take up arms against my father, my brothers, my uncles; I would do it without hesitation; I would be the devoted slave of the English, and ask nothing in return but their influence to assist me in maintaining my hold upon the sovereign power."

Possibly I might have been beguiled by the air of sincerity assumed by this miserable wretch, if I had not detected something in his expression which warned me to put no faith in him. I also saw that, being in the hands of an ambitious villain, I must make use of his vices to secure my own safety. I assured him that, though positively a Frenchman, it was not out of my power for me to make known his wishes to the British Government of India. After a long discussion on that subject, therefore, he assured me it was impossible for him to treat me publicly with the respect he was disposed to show me, but he promised faithfully that no harm should happen to me. "If they are harsh to you, shut your eyes to the brutality of my people; they look upon you with distrust and hatred, and would not forgive me if I manifested any consideration for you."

Before I left his presence he despatched a messenger to Kandahar to demand his father's instructions respecting me, and the Sirdar then conducted me to a small building covered with straw, near the post of the sepoys who were to be my guard. Rahimdil Khan was ordered to watch me, and my friend the Moonshee to establish himself in my den, and not to leave me for an instant, even in the night; moreover he dismissed the Heratians, Ahmed and Ali, saying he should provide me with servants himself, if I went to Kandahar at all.

Although I had serious grounds of complaint against Ahmed and Ali, I forgave them on account of their brave and energetic conduct when we were attacked by the brigands near Washeer; and besides an attestation that I was satisfied with them, I gave them my long-coveted robe and turban, and added a small sum of money: and so they went away contented.

Mohamed Sedik Khan, the eldest son of the Sirdar Kohendil Khan, is about thirty-two years of age; his person is small, and his regular features are not wanting in expression. His deep-set black eyes are three parts covered by the eyelids, and indicative of a treacherous character. Ferocious and intractable, he has a heart of bronze; his ambition is insatiable, and I have known but one Afghan more covetous or more vain. Knowing no law but his own will, governing by fear only, his rule is heavy indeed to bear, for he tyrannizes and tortures with or without reason. His heart is incapable of friendship; he has no affections, and would without remorse sacrifice his nearest relations to gratify his ambition or his pride. With respect to religion, he is the worst Mussulman in Afghanistan. For years he has never said a prayer, fasted in Rhamazan, or observed any other precept ordained by the Koran; his scepticism is extreme, and in that respect it is certain that his equal is not to be found in the whole country.

But the character of this Sirdar is a strange compound; for, combined with the lowest vices, he possesses some superior intellectual qualifications. It is impossible to deny that he has an inexhaustible imagination and amazing intelligence, and that possessing a powerful memory, and earnestly desiring to acquire knowledge, he has learnt much from Europeans, and classed his desultory information in his own mind in a very remarkable manner. He can perceive the salutary influence of science and the arts on the regeneration of nations, and if ever he attains the supreme power, though his reign will be that of a bloody and avaricious tyrant, it may also be that of a reformer. In his youth he had an Italian drawing-master, and profited exceedingly by his instruction; his talent for the art would be appreciated even in Europe. It is truly deplorable to see the manner in which this chief misuses all the gifts bestowed upon him by nature. His mind is ever bent towards evil, but this perhaps is less owing to his own organization than to the manner in which he was brought up, for he was made governor of Girishk in his childhood, and confided to the care of strangers, who found their own account in flattering all his passions and caprices. They therefore left him to the intoxicating enjoyment of absolute power, without ever seeking to give him the slightest insight into the difference between good and evil, or directing him in the good course. All his relations, including even his father, cordially detest him, and he possesses not a friend in all Afghanistan. He has not contrived to retain even the alliances most necessary to the attainment of the great object of his desires—the sovereign power. In 1844 he was secretly connected with Yar Mohamed Khan and Mohamed Akbar Khan of Kabul, with the intention of assisting each other to secure the immediate possession, or ultimate succession to the three Afghan principalities. But the dealings of Mohamed Sedik were so tortuous, his outbursts of overbearing pride so absurd and so frequent, that, when I was at Girishk, he had alienated even these allies; and now all he can hope for is to hold the government of his own fortress and the territory connected with it, from which he draws a very large revenue. Complaints, however, of his violent and deceitful conduct have been so often carried to his father that he has taken from him his jurisdiction over the villages from which he drew the largest portion of his revenues.

In the immense steppes extending over the south of Afghanistan roads are rare, and caravans are necessarily obliged to follow those on which they find provisions and inhabited places. Girishk is, with reason, considered one of the principal points, and they cannot avoid it, for, besides the custom-house, the ferry by which they must cross the Helmund is there; and as the Sirdar has posted guards in all directions to oblige them to pass at this place, they are always exposed to extortions of some kind. Besides the duties fixed by his father, he has imposed another very high one on his own account, and sometimes seizes on a particular bale of choice merchandise, or a remarkably fine horse, and sends it to India to be sold to the English for his own exclusive benefit.

It must, however, be added that the severe measures taken by Mohamed Sedik have greatly reduced the number of robbers in the country, though he has done so only by monopolising the trade, not annihilating it, and the caravaneers have gained little by this transition of interests. He is so detested by his countrymen that he can only recruit his army from the very dregs of the people; every man in his service has committed a murder or a crime of some description. Living, like their master, by continual depredations, they do anything but protect their countrymen; they are like so many pirates wandering over the country and committing every sort of iniquity: master and dependents equally worthy of each other.

As soon as I was installed in my hut, Rahimdil Khan and the Moonshee Feiz Mohamed took charge of and remained with me. The former was a pretty good fellow in his way, and gave me no annoyance; but the Moonshee was my guardian angel during my captivity, and I certainly owe my life to him. If his efforts to preserve me from the insults of the subordinates did not always succeed entirely, they at least softened many an aggravated insult, and he constantly endeavoured to make my keepers more tractable. Clearly foreseeing that my baggage would not escape the cupidity of the Sirdar, he concealed the articles most precious to me in his own lodging, and I kept with me little more than was actually necessary for present use.

What the Sirdar told me of the two Englishmen who had been travelling in Kandahar occupied my thoughts much, and the first time I was alone with the Moonshee I begged him to tell me what he knew of their history, and from him I learnt that the one first mentioned by the Sirdar had been recognised and arrested in Girishk, and then transported to the district of Zumeendawer, and confided to the keeping of the Sirdar Akhter Khan. The second, who spoke Persian perfectly, wore the costume of a Syud, and passed for such, calling himself a native of Samarcand, and replying to all questions that he was on a pilgrimage to Mecca. He was accompanied by two servants, and all three were perfectly well mounted, armed, and equipped. They had been eight days at Kandahar when he was first suspected, and the Moonshee Feiz Mohamed was the person who gave him the earliest intelligence of the fact, immediately on receiving which he mounted his horse and secretly left the town. Kohendil Khan did not know of his flight till the following day, when he despatched horsemen after him in all directions; but they preserved so strict a silence on their return that no one in Kandahar ever knew whether he had been taken or not. However that may have been, the Moonshee told me that he had acknowledged to him that he was an Englishman, and had assured him that many of his countrymen, who had formed part of the army of occupation in Kabul, had been sold into slavery in Turkistan, where, less fortunate than himself, they still dragged on a mournful existence.

In 1846, when I returned to Teheran, I communicated this fact to Colonel Sheil, who exerted himself much to rescue his suffering countrymen, and sent an Afghan, Akhond-zadeh Saleh Mohammed,* to find them out. I placed some faith in the sincerity of the Moonshee, because, as I have already said, when I passed through Khulm, an Afshar told me that these unfortunate people were still in captivity.

The following circumstance, however, which occurred very few days after my arrival at Mahmoodabad, would have removed every doubt from my mind, had any existed, of the fact of there being an Englishman at Zumeendawer. A sepoy of the governor of that district, Akhter Khan, kept hovering about my prison, but dared not approach me too closely for fear of exciting the suspicion of the guards. I had observed his manner, and also detected that

* This is the Moonshee who saved Captain Abbott's life on the shores of the Caspian, when he was in the hands of the Turcomans, and who furnished the only trustworthy reports ever received of the execution of Stodart and Conolly. See p. 458, where M. Ferrier again mentions him.—R.

he made signs to me, but I abstained from acknowledging them, fearful of compromising him. After a time a momentary opportunity presented itself for his speaking to me unobserved, and he seized it with alacrity.

"Sahib," said he, "I bring you news of your countryman: he has been very ill, but is better to-day. Having heard of your stay at Herat and arrival in Kandahar, he gave me this letter for you, knowing that about the time I should arrive here you also would have reached Mahmoodabad." With these words he slipped into my hand a sheet of coarse grey paper, folded in the form of a letter, and in fact containing one, but without any address. I opened it with impatience, thinking to learn the story of the unhappy writer's sufferings, and to prepare to bear with resignation those which were probably reserved for myself; but what was my vexation, my grief, at finding that I could not read a single word! It was written in English!

While endeavouring earnestly to make out the sense, a pichkhid-met of the Sirdar's came up, and seeing the paper in my hand, and the sepoy near me, suspected some mystery, and informed his master. Mohamed Sedik questioned me most severely, and my denials were useless; for the unfortunate letter was found under my felt carpet. As he could read and understand a little English, he proceeded to do so, and therefore learned more or less what unhappily it could not reveal to me. Then ensued a most violent scene. He accused me of coming into Kandahar to revolutionize it, and overwhelmed me with invectives. I believed my last hour was come; but nothing happened beyond remanding me to my prison, to be more carefully watched. The unhappy soldier was seized, bound, and bastinadoed in a fearful manner; and though he fainted, the executioners did not leave off until his feet were reduced to a bruised and bleeding mass.

From this moment I was incessantly the object of insults from my guards, despite the representations that I made to the Sirdar. The wretch endeavoured, indeed, to make me believe he felt kindly towards me, by showing me occasionally, though at rare intervals, some little civilities, such as sending me a dish from his table, or some other refreshment; but I was not deceived, for more frequently he allowed me nearly to die of hunger, and my daily fare seldom exceeded three or four ounces of coarse bread.

The messenger, who had been sent by this villain to his father to demand instructions as to how to dispose of me, returned in five days; and Kohendil Khan informed his son that in his opinion I was an Englishman; nevertheless he commanded him to treat me well, till he had further orders, and to send the courier back with an exact description of my person. "Was I a man of capacity and a certain rank? Could I serve him as a negotiator with the English?" That was the point it was most important to know. In communicating these details the Sirdar informed me that his father, confiding but little in the Court of Persia, and wishing to ensure himself protection against his neighbours, Yar Mohamed Khan and Dost Mohamed Khan, had the most anxious desire to ally himself with the English, but had hitherto been restrained from making his friendly overtures by the dread of the vengeance that this alliance would bring upon him on the part of his nephew Akbar Khan. He added that my presence would strengthen his resolves, and determine him to break with his dangerous relative, if I would undertake to procure him the alliance and support of the English.

Was all this told me in good faith, or was it a snare to induce me to confess that I was an Englishman? I could not satisfy myself on this point; but in any case I could only repeat that I was a Frenchman, and had no connexion whatever with the British Government; but that if such was the pleasure of the Sirdar of Kandahar, there was nothing to prevent me from carrying his propositions of amity to his neighbours, without in any way answering for the success of my endeavours. My reply was given to the messenger; and Mohamed Sedik bid me hope that he would return with permission for me to proceed to Kandahar.

The behaviour of Mohamed Sedik Khan to me during my imprisonment was always a puzzling problem. He hoped through me to render the English favourable to his cause, and yet did nothing to induce me to interest myself in his favour; he kept me in a place not fit to be a stable; the dogs of his hunt were better fed than I was; and the Pariahs in India do not submit to outrages greater than I endured from his ill-conditioned and savage soldiers. In fact, his protestations of friendship were never followed up by any act that could induce me to believe in them. He always looked upon me with the eyes of an Afghan, and always fancied he had to deal with a countryman. It is scarcely possible to conceive the facility with which an Afghan is deceived.

With the facts before them to deny what they are told, they are always to be caught with fine words.

Various motives induced the Sirdar to allow his people to maltreat me; but the most important was to impress me with the belief that the Afghans had a violent hatred to the English. Another was, the desire of satisfying his covetousness at my expense; to compass which purpose he excited them to abuse and ill-treat me, and then would appear just at the appropriate moment for putting a stop to their proceedings, and seeming very angry; thus, as he flattered himself, establishing a claim upon my gratitude, and making use of it to despoil me, one by one, of the few things I possessed. During fifteen days that I was in his custody at Mahmoodabad he took all my arms, and many other things; afterwards he stole all my money. I will now give the reader an opportunity of perusing a few notes that I made secretly and in haste during my imprisonment here; sometimes almost in the dark, and often by moonlight, when the Argus for the time was asleep.

August 6th.—Seized with ennui, depression, and a violent desire of vengeance against my tormentors; I feel also a lively dread of reaching Lahore too late, where events might take a turn very unfavourable for me, and all my exertions, sufferings, and dangers would then prove useless. My sepoy guard are the vilest of the Afghan race, and daily circumscribe my remaining liberty. I am not now allowed to leave my den.

A rather rare occurrence varied the monotony of to-day. Some Afghans, with the permission of the Sirdar, came to visit me. I know neither their names nor their rank; and I was to them only as a curious animal. I bent to circumstances, and answered their as usual disagreeable questions with a tolerably good grace. On my part I turned their loquacity to account, in obtaining easily, though cautiously, information that I was very glad to have. They are so talkative that only a word thrown in at the right moment—a compliment dexterously administered—will make an Afghan talk for an hour, quite unconscious he has only fallen into your trap. He will tell you all you want to know, and a great deal more than the best of memories would care to remember. I could not help thinking how ridiculous is the whole affair of my imprisonment. They shut me up to prevent me from knowing their country, and then come and tell me more than I should have found out about many things, which, if I were an Englishman, as they believe I am, it would be doubly their interest to conceal.

In the evening the Sirdar took me into the country with him. I had before been thankful to him for this pleasure, though in taking me he had an object of his own. Preserving some appearance of dignity, he wanted to cajole me out of my pair of pistols, six-barrelled, and my dress uniform. He promised to pay me for them, but has never done so.

August 7th.—To-day the Sirdar sent me a melon, with a message, to the effect that he should thank me to send him my double-barrelled gun as a present in return, for he wished to present it to his cousin Akbar Khan of Kabul. To refuse would not have forwarded my interests, and in any case he would have taken it, so I acceded. The rascally Afghans! Moonshee Feiz Mohamed did his utmost to console me. In his opinion I ought to consider myself fortunate in being alive. "The stranger who ventures into Afghanistan," said he, "may look upon himself as a man specially protected by Heaven, if he gets out of it safe and sound, with his head on his shoulders. You ought to see that yours is wonderfully shaky. Have patience, then, and do not compromise yourself by any violent recriminations." This was wise advice; but I could not profit by it; I could not remain silent. I wanted to assure these villains that my energy and courage were not failing me under all the infamies they heaped upon me, or the bodily privations they had inflicted. If this violence caused me an increase of persecution on the part of these ruffians, it served at least to elevate my character in their eyes, as I found out afterwards.

Yesterday the Sirdar extorted my pistols from me; to-day he takes my maps and my telescope, thermometer and compass, and twenty other things, which were exceedingly precious to me, and impossible to replace. When shall I escape from the hands of this cut-throat?

An unlucky incident that occurred this day made me more anxious for that much-wished-for moment. Attended by a soldier on all occasions, I one day, when outside the kaleh, tore up two leaves of a book written in Arabic characters, which I found on the ground. I had scarcely left the spot when the tutor to the children of the Sirdar happening to pass that way and see the leaves, immediately raised a yell which brought half the population of the village about him. "There," said the mollah, "there is the work of an infidel; 'tis thus he desecrates the holy Koran; death to the impious dog!" and he and the crowd, some with drawn knives, were soon round my hut and shouting in chorus, "To the death! to the death!" It was with difficulty that Rahimdil Khan and the Moonshee prevented them from entering my room; for the soldiers, excited by the mollah, were on the point of doing so, and probably drilling a hole in my jacket, when Sedik Khan appeared, and seizing a musket from one of his adherents, vowed by the head of the Prophet he would shoot the first person who entered my apartment. There seemed to me to be a good deal of acting in this; for I had seen the Sirdar at a distance, and he did not attempt to appease the tumult, of the cause of which I was then in complete ignorance; but, be this as it may, the rioters left in apparent indignation at the protection I obtained from Sedik Khan, who endeavoured to impress upon me the obligation I was under to him, for having thus saved my life. As to the mollah, who had, it appears, been hunting for the missing leaves all the morning, he was, there being no other Koran in the village, obliged to re-copy them, and, we may conclude, not much to his gratification, which, I confess, did not particularly grieve me.

August 9th.—Some Afghan merchants arrived to-day from Meshed, and having seen me when I passed through that town two months before, went to the Sirdar and swore to him by the beard of the Prophet I was a real live Englishman, and perfectly well known to them. This declaration convinced him more than ever that my firmans from Mohamed Shah are false, and that my journey is positively undertaken with the intention of intriguing against the peace of the country. Confusion to all impostors! I thought.

This afternoon, hearing a great noise outside my prison, and seeing the last soldier of my guard disappear in a great hurry, I seized this moment of freedom, and rushed up to the terrace, to learn whence the tumult proceeded. It arose near some tents pitched towards the south, about a gunshot off, and I saw distinctly six corpses, around which were several armed men. I returned to my prison, and heard from the Moonshee what had happened. Two persons, each having a son and a daughter, had projected a double marriage, and the celebration of the event was at hand, when the fathers quarrelled about a stream of water that one of them had allowed to run upon his land half an hour longer than he had a right, to the detriment of the opposite party. According to Afghan custom, but few words had passed when the daggers were called into play, the friends on either side took part in the fray, and the wedding was soon converted into a funeral.

Shortly after this catastrophe I received a visit, authorised by the Sirdar, from an Afghan Khan of the Ghilzee tribe. He was chief of a branch composed of twelve or fifteen hundred tents, which had been for nearly a century in the province of Kirman in Persia. These were all that remained of a much larger number who had taken part with Nadir Shah at the period when he became sufficiently powerful to destroy the Afghan monarchy in Persia. These Afghans remained faithful to the Persian warrior, who made them some concessions of territory on the frontiers of Seistan, which they were to guard against their countrymen of Kandahar, and prevent them from gaining a fresh position in Persia. They had not modified their habits in their last residence, and were accounted the greatest bandits in the country. The Persians fled from their neighbourhood, and their presence was scarcely tolerated in that of Boom and Burpoor. This state of exclusion had disgusted them with Persia, and their chief had come to Kandahar to obtain the authority of Kohendil Khan to settle in his dominions; but he had been unable to reach the sovereign, as his son had arrested him at Mahmoodabad, and transmitted his request to Kandahar. Some days after an answer was received from Kohendil Khan, refusing his consent to the proposal of the Ghilzee chief. The Sirdar well knew the intrepidity of this migratory colony, and was not inclined to receive them, lest they should at some time prove a powerful accession to the discontented amongst his population, who were very numerous. The language of the Ghilzee convinced me that Kohendil Khan had acted prudently in rejecting his offer; for, before he knew whether it would be accepted or not, he did not disguise from me his smothered hostility to him whose generosity he was supplicating, or his intention to injure him as soon as he might have it in his power. When he heard, therefore, that he had no chance of re-establishing himself and his people in his dominions, he proposed that I should escape with him, promising to take me safely to Shikarpoor, by Beloochistan, where he said he was known to the chiefs of all the tribes. I did not think it wise to trust a man who had shown himself capable of so much duplicity; and there the affair ended.

August 10th and 11th.—These two days were passed in the most gloomy reflections, in a state of ravenous hunger, for I had had scarcely half a pound of bread for the last thirty-six hours. Up to that time I had forborne to buy provisions, the greatest portion of which would most certainly have been eaten by the sepoys; moreover, they would then have known that I had a little money, and acted accordingly—as Afghans; but my prudence could hold out no longer against my sufferings, and I gave a rupee to one who had appeared to me somewhat less of a brute than the rest, to buy me something to eat. He soon returned with an ass-load of melons, but I could only judge of them by their beautiful appearance, for they were eaten by my guards, who afterwards brought me some of the rind on a plate, begging me ironically often to purchase the annoyance of a similar offering—they almost crazed me. The Moonshee at last told me plainly that they would not dare to act thus if they were not authorised by the Sirdar; he told me also that it was entirely his planning that prevented my now being at Kandahar, for he had requested his father to leave me with him till he had made his determination respecting me. By acting thus he had secured the opportunity of pilfering me at his leisure, intending to keep what he stole under the name of presents if I were allowed to go on, and to strip me of everything in case of the reverse.

This confidential information determined me to speak categorically to the Sirdar on the subject, let the consequences be what they might. The next time, therefore, that he passed before my prison on his way into the country I asked him what he meant to do with me; and why he did not send me to his father, to whom I could explain myself much better than through his correspondence. I accused him of cruelty in allowing me to perish with hunger, and exciting his satellites against me. Perfectly confounded as the villain looked by this apostrophe, he nevertheless contrived to elude all serious explanation, and only gave me a few words of reply. "Never mind," he said, "my apparent coldness; it is caused by the force of circumstances. I suffer more than you suppose at seeing the brutal conduct of my people; but what can I do with low-born Afghans, devoid of reason? They are already more irritated with me than enough for having taken you out of their hands the day before yesterday. They would never forgive me for too much kindness to you. Nevertheless, do not be alarmed, I will see to your safety; I will write again to my father, and request him to order you to Kandahar. If he does not, do not be uneasy, I will send you safely and honourably back to Herat; and you shall be protected from all insult."

After this hasty speech he left me, without waiting for a reply, and I remained in as uncertain and painful a position as ever, a prey to the most distressing and mournful anxiety. I called to mind the words of my companions from Teheran to Meshed, and their unceasing endeavours to dissuade me from "going amongst those barbarians, those anthropophagi; if they do not eat you, they will not fail to cut your throat." I could not conceal from myself that to all appearance there was every chance of their predictions being verified; but from frequently reflecting upon it I accustomed myself to meet that awful moment. I remembered the proud and heroic deaths of Stoddart and Conolly, and I would not have had it said that a Frenchman died with less courage. I was therefore fully armed against the bitter reflections suggested by the prospect of my approaching end: but, strange to say, that was not my greatest trouble; I actually suffered more from the mortal weariness of the long unoccupied days, and the total privation of intercourse with civilised beings. I felt the loneliness far more acutely than the danger.

August 12th.—My detention, cruel as it is, is less painful to me than the behaviour of my guards is aggravating and exasperating. These brutes stand at my door immovable as logs, and stare in and giggle for half a morning at a time. In the countenances of one or two I sometimes fancied I could read this reflection,—"Poor fellow! what induced you to come here, where there is nothing but death to hope for?" The many never come near me but with an insult on their lips or in their gestures, and in time make way for their neighbours to do the same; they look upon my presence among them as an event, and never leave me alone or quiet. All the strangers who arrive in the town come as a matter of course to look at the Feringhee Kaffir, European infidel, as a curiosity; and, then, am I not a prisoner? Can they not outrage me at their pleasure, without fear of reprisals? They hold the most ridiculous discussions upon my shape, my features, manners, and religion; the extent and absurdity of the rude and vile things they say is not to be imagined, nor my sufferings at hearing them; but patience again is my only refuge.

August 13th to 16th.—Before 1840 so little had Afghanistan been visited by Europeans that they could not possibly form any just ideas of the character of its inhabitants. I will explain, therefore, how previously to that date they had almost generally been looked upon in a favourable light by those who wrote about them. The unfortunate Sir Alexander Burnes himself, who may be looked upon as an incontrovertible authority upon a multitude of facts relating to these people, on the point of character fell into the errors of his predecessors. He believed the Afghans to be honest, well educated, devoid of religious prejudices, and capable of great things. I conceive that he took this impression on his first journey to Kabul, in 1832, because the English had then in that country a great reputation for ability, justice, power, and, above all, generosity. The Afghan princes all ardently desired the alliance, and the sympathies of the people flowed from theirs.

Sultan Mahmood Khan of Peshawur, and the Emir Dost Mohamed his brother, having an interest in impressing Burnes in their favour, received him with the greatest consideration; it was natural therefore that he should form a favourable opinion of them, and the Chiefs of their courts. But the upper classes alone do not exhibit the character of a nation. In Asia, as everywhere else, they are more civilized than the masses. It might be supposed that Burnes, travelling as he did in the Afghan dress, and in an unostentatious manner, would have mixed enough with the people to see them as they are, and appreciate them at their just value; but this would only be the case if his expenses were consistent with his appearance of an Afghan in moderate circumstances: by paying as he did generously every one about him, and for everything he wanted, he deprived himself of the best means of judging them, for if gold will soften the habits or manners anywhere, it is most assuredly in Afghanistan. If, instead of having only to pay them, he had been obliged to ask of them, or to make them feel his power, as happened after he had printed his Travels and was Resident at Kabul, I am convinced he would not have praised them so much. After all, the Afghans, to do them justice, never pretend to the possession of great virtues—they never praise themselves for any thing but their courage; and if they hear of a bad action or a great crime, they exclaim at once, with the consciousness of their own sentiments, "*In kar Afghan est,*" that is Afghan work. But, notwithstanding this sincerity, it will always be difficult for a traveller, however keen his penetration, to estimate them as they really are, unless he allows them to express their own feelings before he satisfies their avarice. Neither must he fear to degrade himself by adopting the Asiatic costume or mixing freely with the people; it is only by so doing that he can acquire an insight into their real nature.

I cannot believe that so fine an intellect as Burnes's could not see what I advance, but perhaps he preferred avoiding annoyances, and even dangers, by disposing freely of the Company's gold. His opinion of the Afghan character is, with one or two exceptions, almost the only subject on which any one can differ from him in what he has written respecting Afghanistan.* His work, taken as a whole, is one of the greatest merit, and will long be the surest guide on that country. I should not probably have fallen into so many troubles if I had consulted it before I undertook my journey; but, unhappily, it was not until I returned to Teheran, and I could not profit by the information it contains, that I first had the opportunity of reading it.

Nearly sixteen days have passed, and Kohendil Khan has not yet come to any decision: this delay is more depressing than captivity itself. The society of Moonshee Feiz Mohamed, who seeks to cheer me by every means in his power, is my only con-

---

* "The Afghans are a sober, simple, steady people. They always interrogated me closely regarding Europe, the nations of which they divide into twelve 'koollahs,' or crowns—literally, hats. It was delightful to see the curiosity of even the oldest men. The greatest evil of Mohamedanism consists in its keeping those who profess it within a certain circle of civilization; their manners do not appear ever to alter. They have learning, but it is of another age; and anything like philosophy in their history is unknown. The language of the Afghans is Persian, but it is not the smooth and elegant tongue of Iran. Pushtoo is the dialect of the common people; but some of the higher classes cannot even speak it. The Afghans are a nation of children; in their quarrels they fight, and become friends without any ceremony. They cannot conceal their feelings from one another, and a person with any discrimination may at all times pierce their designs. If they themselves are to be believed, their ruling vice is envy, which besets even the nearest and dearest relations. No people are more incapable of managing an intrigue. I was particularly struck with their idleness; they seem to sit listlessly for the whole day staring at each other: how they live it would be difficult to discover, yet they dress well, and are healthy and happy. I imbibed a very favourable impression of their national character."—*Extract from Burnes's Travels into Bokhara,* vol. i. pp. 143 and 144.

solation; he has, however, little enough of comfort to impart, for he tells me that the Sirdars persist in believing I am an Englishman, and only spare my life for their own interest. The English army, having its advanced posts in the Bolan pass, might return any day in a few marches to Kandahar, and in that case I might be a hostage, through whom they could make advantageous terms. In the meanwhile, no alteration of my condition; the rascally guards, by most unmistakeable signs, give me to understand that I shall have my throat cut, and call out to the passers by to "come in, come in, and look at the Ingleez Kaffir." "He is thirsty, and wants to drink," said one, and he flung a jug of dirty water over me; others say that I am hungry, and throw rinds of melon at my head, with other varieties of annoyance; and to all my complaints the Sirdar always replies, "Have patience, for I cannot alter these brutes."

August 16th.—At last I am informed that we set out to-morrow for Girishk. One prison was not more likely to please me than another, but the unhappy cling to the smallest hope, and I did hope to find in change of place some relief from my misery. This thought afforded me comfort, when another source of satisfaction arose. During the day the Moonshee found an opportunity of getting a friend of his, whose handwriting was unknown to Mohamed Sedik, secretly to write a letter in my name to Kohendil Khan, in which I loudly complained of the treatment I had been subjected to, and entreated him to grant me my liberty, or terminate my sufferings by a speedy death.

Girishk, August 17th — five parasangs — eight hours — on a plain, broken, undulating, and covered with brambles, which shelter multitudes of partridges, deer, hares, and gazelles. At three in the morning I mounted a camel, to the pitching pace of which I found it difficult enough to accustom myself. The fortress of Girishk is situated on an eminence, a short distance from the Helmund; the village near it and the district bear the same name; the latter is populous and very productive. The castle of Girishk is very ancient, but has been enlarged and repaired by the present sovereign; it is of oblong form, with towers at the angles, and could not be taken without artillery. Some English sepoys, supported by Afghans attached to the British interests, and commanded by the Sirdar Mohamed Kooli Khan (son of the Vezir-Futteh Khan, who was assassinated by order of Shah Mahmood), resisted all the attempts made by the insurgents in 1841 to possess themselves of it. The English had a small body of troops here during their occupation of Afghanistan, and the ruts made by their guns were perfectly visible in 1845.*

On both sides of the Helmund, above and below Girishk, may be seen immense ruins and mounds, indicating that large towns once existed there. The inhabitants of the country believe that these flourished in the time of Alexander, particularly the one on the northern side of the fortress, at the foot of the mountains of the Paropamisus.

At Girishk I was put in a prison scarcely more habitable than the one I had left; it possessed, however, one advantage, for which I was thankful—it was at a distance from the sepoy post, and

* During the English occupation of Afghanistan, the maintenance of Girishk was always considered an important object, as it not only defended the high road, and offered security to travellers, but presented a good military point against Herat. When the Afghan troubles broke out in November, 1841, the governor of Herat being at that time unfriendly to us, it was of particular importance to maintain Girishk, and with this view Major Rawlinson, then political agent at Kandahar, was anxious not only to retain on the Helmund the regiment to whose care the fortress was entrusted, but to strengthen the position with reinforcements from the Kandahar garrison. General Nott, however, insisted that the retention of the fortress of Girishk was under the circumstances a false position, and moreover impracticable; he accordingly insisted on withdrawing the regiment and guns to Kandahar before the country became generally disturbed, and their retreat impossible. In this juncture Major Rawlinson determined on sending out Mohamed Kooli Khan to assume the government of Girishk. He allowed him a small party of Barukzye horse, and further placed under his orders a body of 200 musketeers, Sindis, Belooches, Punjabis, and Indians, who were led by a fine Indian soldier named Bulwunt Singh. This small garrison, supported by a couple of guns furnished by the Afghan government, successfully held Girishk throughout the whole period of the Afghan troubles, from November, 1841, to August, 1842, notwithstanding that the Dooranees, to the number of 10,000 or 15,000 men, were in arms around them, sometimes assaulting and besieging the fortress, sometimes cutting off the communications with Kandahar, and at other times engaging General Nott's army in the field. This defence of Girishk, difficult of course as it was to furnish the garrison with food and ammunition, and to communicate to them orders from Kandahar, was one of the most brilliant exploits of the war, and reflects the greatest credit on the leaders Mohamed Kooli Khan and Bulwunt Singh. At one period the Dooranees besieged Girishk closely for three successive months, and made repeated assaults. It may be added, that it was mainly owing to Mohamed Kooli Khan's influence in the Helmund, where the ooloos[a] were principally of his own tribe, that we were mainly indebted for the supply of provisions to the garrison. Immediately before our evacuation of Kandahar, Major Rawlinson withdrew the Girishk garrison unmolested to the city of Kandahar, settled their arrears of pay, and transferred them to the service of Suftur Jung, who was left in the government when the two columns of the English army marched respectively for Kabul and Sinde.—ED.

[a] The Afghan tribesmen, as distinguished from the Parsivan cultivators.—ED.

I indulged some hope of quiet. This was soon dissipated, for the Naib, lieutenant of the Sirdar, Gul Mohamed Khan, had never seen me, and therefore proceeded to gratify his curiosity the moment he heard that I had arrived. He burst into my room, out of breath with haste, and then stood still and mute to stare at me. After having scanned me from head to foot with a savage and ironical look, he broke silence thus: "If I were not afraid of the Sirdar, I should have cut your throat by this time." Regardless of all prudential considerations, I obeyed the sudden impulse to chastise his insolence, and, springing at his throat, threw him down. I then rated him soundly, and pitching him him out of the door, had the satisfaction of hearing him roll down the staircase, while I barricaded myself inside in the best way I could with two tent-poles which happened to be in my prison. His cries soon brought five or six sepoys to his assistance; they broke open my door, and beat me till I was covered with blood, and I hardly know what the result might have been, but for the timely arrival of Rahimdil Khan and the Moonshee, quickly followed by the Sirdar. Though abusing me all the time, he had the two soldiers beaten who had been most forward in injuring me, and severely reprimanded Rahimdil Khan and the Moonshee for having left me even for a moment. He ordered them to occupy the room next to mine, and my door was locked and a sentry ordered to remain constantly seated against it. Whether from forgetfulness, or from an intention to punish me, the rascals left me the next four-and-twenty hours without anything to eat.

I remained in close confinement for eight days, seeing only the Moonshee, who brought me each morning a few ounces of black bread and some sour milk. My prison was in the highest tower of the fort, amongst the rubbish, about twenty or twenty-five feet above the ditch, and on one side open to the country, for the external wall had to a certain extent fallen down. On the other side of this, the sentry, who was on guard there night and day, ready to seize me should I be so rash as to try the leap, was posted. I had thought of it more than once, to escape the sufferings I endured in this loft: a burning sun shone into it the whole day, and I was pestered unremittingly by flies, gnats, and humble-bees; but my worst misfortune was, that I was obliged to sit almost constantly in the corner they particularly fancied, for, if I stood or sat where the passers by could see me, I was sure to be insulted. During the first few days the more humane amongst them would give me words of kindness and consolation, but they were sometimes beaten by the fanatical party in consequence, so that I subsequently received nothing but abuse. In keeping from the open side to avoid this, I lost my only pleasure, that of looking at the country, and following the broad waters of the Helmund winding through the smiling plain, covered with plantations, cultivation, and beautiful green pastures. Notwithstanding my helpless position, I loved to let my imagination run riot: sometimes I fancied I was free; sometimes that I was in France again amongst my family and friends. The romance, however, did not last long, for the vermin that I could not prevent from getting into my clothes, and the rattling of my inside from the scantiness of my daily ration, quickly dispelled these day-dreams, and dragged me roughly back to the sad reality of my position.

CHAPTER XXII.

Return of the messenger from Kandahar — Further delay — The Khan turns thief — Khak-i-choupan — Khoosk-i-Nakood — Tomb of the Imaum zadeh— Haouz — Sufferings of the author — Takht Sinjavi — The Urgund-ab river — The old town of Kandahar — The climate and productions — The present town — Inhabitants — Trade of Kandahar — Population — History of the city — Alexander the Great — Anecdote of its Arab conquerors —Yacoub ben Leis — Mahmood the Ghuznehvide — The Tartar conquests — Kandahar taken by Baber —By the Persians — Sultan Hussein Mirza — Kandahar taken by Shah Abbas — Afterwards by Jehanghir — By the Uzbeks — By Nadir Shah — Kandahar becomes the capital of Afghanistan —The family of the Mohamedzye — Ferrier enters Kandahar — Lal Khan sends him a pilau — Description of the author's abode — Fate of Mirza Mohamed Wali — Villanous act of Sedik Khan — Liberality of the English — The author in better quarters — Interview with Kohendil Khan — Description of the Sirdar — Afghan politics — The Sirdar's opinion of the Russians and the English — Of the Persians — Persists in thinking the author an Englishman — Opinions on European Governments — The Sirdar's advice to the author.

At last, on the evening of the 25th of August, Berkhordar Khan returned with orders from Kohendil Khan to send me under escort to Kandahar. Thank God! I was then on the point of leaving the hands of these brigands. Perhaps, it is true, I might fall amongst others as bad; but at least it was one step in the right direction, and that fact gave me the liveliest sensations of pleasure.

My departure ought to have taken place on the 26th, but, on divers pretexts, the Sirdar delayed it till the following day, and that also passed without my starting. On sending to him to inquire the motives of this conduct, he came to me himself, begged me to be patient, and assured me that I should set out the next night. After he was gone, the Moonshee explained the reason. Mohamed Sedik had discovered that one of my trunks had escaped his vigilance, and he wanted to examine it. He had written about me to his father, in a tone which he hoped would induce him to send me back to Herat, or by Shikarpoor to Kelat, when he could have plundered me without any danger of my complaints reaching Kandahar. But Kohendil Khan's last letter destroyed his plan, and he was undecided for a day or two what to do. Eventually he sent two porters to my prison with the trunk I had concealed at the Moonshee's, and arrived a few minutes after, to take an inventory of its contents; having affirmed that Kohendil Khan had charged him to examine my papers strictly, to see that I was not the bearer of any letters for his enemies that might be injurious to him. After having closely examined every article, he quietly put aside those that he thought he should like to keep, and then said, that in consideration of the services he had rendered me, the food I had consumed, and his having at different times saved my life, he hoped I would make him a present of the trifles he had selected. Although so entirely in his power I refused, and reproached him in the bitterest terms for his barbarous conduct; but the villain was in no way moved, and only remarked that he should have been willing to obtain my consent, but could do very well without it, and then retired, carrying off two-thirds of my things and all my money, for fear, he said, that I should use it to his father's detriment, and promised to restore it at Kandahar.

Khak-i-choupan, August 28th—seven parasangs—over a barren plain. I was very early on horseback, with my escort of eight soldiers, and left Girishk with a heart full of hatred for its inhabitants and lively joy at my departure. We forded the Helmund a quarter of an hour from the fortress. This can only be done in the three summer months; for the rest of the year it is so much swollen by the rains and the melting of the snows in the mountains of the Paropamisus that it can only be crossed in a ferryboat which the Sirdar lets to the highest bidder. After seven hours' travelling we came to a muddy and offensive marsh, near which we made our halt. There was a village about half an hour further on the right; but as a bad fever was raging there, my escort would not go into it. They dined in a few minutes off bread and cheese and raw onions, and threw me the fragments when they had finished. I was obliged to be content, all insufficient as the meal was to satisfy my ravenous hunger.

Khoosk-i-Nakood and *Haouz*, August 29th—eight parasangs—through a plain destitute of water, and covered with brambles. When I awoke in the morning I found my escort had been increased by two soldiers, who had been sent after me by the Sirdar. He had taken from me the first volume of Bianchi's Turkish and French Dictionary, but I had succeeded in concealing the second by sliding it under me unperceived, as I hoped, by any one; but his rogue of a naib had noticed me and told the Sirdar after I was gone. Immediately on receiving this information he sent these two satellites on my track, with orders to overtake me and bring it back; and they performed their mission with their usual brutality.

We remounted when they had left, and stopped again, after two hours' riding, near a caravanserai of mud built by the English, named Khoosk-i-Nakood; close to which we found one or two inhabited houses, with gardens, supplied with water from a kariz. Vast ruins surround this place; the most remarkable is an immense artificial mound, anciently crowned by a fortress said to have been destroyed by Nadir Shah. This had undoubtedly been the citadel of the town, of which there are traces all round, but of which nothing habitable remains except an Imaumzadeh, where a dervish lives in charge of the tomb.

It was here that Ahmed Shah Suddozye was elected king of the Afghans by the united Sirdars. I do not know why the inhabitants of this place call it also Kaleh Nadir. Besides the Imaumzadeh there are several other tombs in pretty good preservation, and about twenty cypresses, the perpetual verdure of which is in singular contrast to the aridity of the place. We waited here through the four hottest hours of the day, and then rode on to Haouz, leaving a little on our right the river Urgund-ab, and having mountains of dark rocks, most capriciously tossed about, on our left. The moving sands, of the reddish tint of the desert south of the river, are brought by the south wind as far as the base of the mountains. By night we had very nearly reached Haouz, so named from the vast reservoir of water there. The Prince Sufder Jung, the governor left by the English in 1842, was here defeated by Kohendil Khan.

A league to the right, a short distance before arriving at Haouz, is seen an artificial mound, similar to that at Khoosk-i-Nakood, named Sungusur. Several large villages surround it; and in one near the road, beyond Haouz, we halted. I arrived at this place so exhausted by heat, hunger, and thirst, that I could not dismount by myself; and when I had been lifted from my horse I fell down. The guards did on this occasion show me some compassion, for they gave me a larger allowance of bread than usual, and added to it some cheese and a jug of milk.

Kandahar, August 30th—six parasangs of plain. After having travelled three hours across a desert, we sheltered ourselves from the mid-day heat under a plantation of trees on the borders of a branch of the Urgund-ab, in a place called Takht-i-Sunjuree; thence to Kandahar it is three parasangs, and the country all the way is covered with houses, trees, and cultivation, on both sides. We crossed the Urgund-ab an hour and a half before we reached the town. The bed was nearly dry, and contained only a few pools of water in the deepest parts; for all that the heat had left was consumed in artificial irrigation. Beyond the river the country contracts, and rocks are scattered here and there over it; it is intersected by streams, watering large gardens and orchards.

The old town of Kandahar was situated halfway between the Urgund-ab and the present town. It occupied an exceedingly strong position upon a very high mountain of abrupt rocks, and was divided into three distinct parts, each on a separate eminence, and capable of mutual defence. The highest crests of these mountains are crowned with many towers, united by curtains; the one on the culminating point may be called impregnable. It commanded the citadel which stood lower down on the second eminence, and this in turn commanded the town, which was on a table-land elevated above the plain. The triple walls surrounding the city were at a considerable distance from it, and enclosed a space between them and the town to admit of the encampment of a garrison in time of war; it was used as garden-ground in time of peace. Close to the road I observed the remains, in pretty good preservation, of a formidable bastion that had been built by the troops of Nadir Shah, to breach the walls.

Above this bastion may be seen a flight of sixty steps cut in the side of the rock, leading to a small chamber also cut in the rock; the walls of the inside are decorated with sculptures, amongst which two chained lions attract particular attention from the grandeur of their dimensions.

The ramparts of the old town were principally constructed of pieces of rock, cemented together by a mixture of clay and chopped straw; and thus constructed they resist much longer than would be expected the attacks of artillery. That of Nadir Shah was numerous and well served, and yet he was a long time under the walls before he made a practicable breach. It was from the heights, and by the heroic gallantry of the Baktiyaris, that the place was taken and subsequently entirely ruined. Nadir Shah rebuilt it a cannon-shot lower down, on the plain, and called it Nadirabad; but it was not long before the new city underwent the same misfortunes as its predecessor.* Ahmed Shah Suddozye depopulated it when he obtained the Afghan throne, after the death of Nadir, and installed its inhabitants in another new town which he built on the same plain, three quarters of an hour more to the east. This he surrounded with a ditch, and flanked with a citadel. The whole is now in existence, and may be approached in all security to within forty or fifty yards of the walls, under cover of the numerous gardens and orchards. It is commanded on several points by the rocky hills, the last slopes of which come almost up to the ditch of the fortification. The place could be easily reduced; and nothing can compensate for the security of the fine position that Kandahar originally occupied.† The environs

* "The ancient city is sometimes said to have been founded by Lohrasp, a Persian king, who flourished in times of very remote antiquity, and to whom also the founding of Herat is attributed. It is asserted by others, with far greater probability, to have been built by Secunder Zoolkurnyne; that is, by Alexander the Great. The traditions of the Persians here agree with the conjectures of European geographers, who fix on this site for one of the cities called Alexandria.

"The ancient city stood till the reign of the Ghiljies, when Shah Hoossein founded a new city, under the name of Hussein-abad. Nadir Shah attempted again to alter the site of the town, and built Nadirabad; at last, Ahmed Shah founded the present city,[a] to which he gave the name of Ahmed Shauhee, and the title of Ashrefool Belaád, or the noblest of cities; by that name and title it is still mentioned in public papers, and in the language of the court; but the old name of Kandahar still prevails among the people, though it has lost its rhyming addition of Daurool Kurrar, or the abode of quiet. Ahmed Shah himself marked out the limits of the present city, and laid down the regular plan which is still so remarkable in its execution. He surrounded it with a wall, and proposed to have added a ditch; but the Dooranees are said to have objected to his fortifications, and to have declared that their ditch was the Chemen of Bistan (a meadow near Bistan, in the most western part of Persian Khorassan). Kandahar was the capital of the Dooranee empire in Ahmed Shah's time, but Timour changed the seat of government to Kabul."—*Extract from Elphinstone's Kabul*, vol. ii. p. 129.—Ed.

At the foot of the ruins of the old town of Kandahar is one of the most celebrated reliques of antiquity belonging to the Eastern world. It is neither more nor less than the water-pot of Fo or Buddha. It was carried to Kandahar by the tribes who fled in the fourth century from Gendharra on the Indus to escape an invasion of the Yutchi, who made the irruption from Chinese Tatary with the express purpose of obtaining the pot. It is the holiest relique of the Buddhist world, and still retains among the Mahometans of Kandahar a sacred and miraculous character. It is called the Kash-guli-Ali, or Ali's pot. It is formed of stone, and may contain about twenty gallons.—Ed.

† According to the ordinary military

[a] In 1753 or 1754.

are exceedingly picturesque. The town may be said to be buried amongst gardens, orchards, and plantations of beautiful shrubs, through which flow streams of the clearest water. In these gardens are many little hillocks and rocks, on the slopes of which the inhabitants have cut slides, on which they amuse themselves on gala days. Fruits and vegetables grow here luxuriantly, better than anywhere else in Afghanistan; the pomegranates have not their equal in the world. The sweetmeats and grapes also deserve to be noticed; and the tobacco, which is produced in abundance, is much esteemed. The cereal produce is of superior quality, most especially the wheat: its whiteness and beauty are rare. All the necessaries of life are sold here surprisingly cheap; and with these advantages it has that most valuable one, an agreeable climate.*

---

opinion, a position on the plain is always stronger than a position on the side of a hill, and it is difficult to say why this should not apply as much to Kandahar as to other places. Kandahar is weak, because, in the first place, it has no glacis, nor has it any ravelins or flanking defences to defend the long line of curtain. The ditch, moreover, on the southern side is very shallow, and the water might be cut off from the city, the streams which supply the city being diverted by an enemy on the Urgund-ab. It may be remembered, however, in speaking of the weakness of Kandahar, that it was strong enough to resist the whole Afghan army of 10,000 men, when held by a very weak garrison, on the memorable night of the 29th March, 1842.—ED.

* The following is Burnes's account of Kabul, the other capital of Afghanistan:—

"Kabul is a most bustling and populous city. Such is the noise in the afternoon, that in the streets one cannot make an attendant hear. The great bazaar or 'chouchut,' is an elegant arcade, nearly 600 feet long, and about 30 broad: it is divided into four equal parts. Its roof is painted, and over the shops are the houses of some of the citizens. The plan is judicious, but it has been left unfinished; and the fountains and cisterns that formed a part of it lie neglected. Still there are few such bazaars in the East, and one wonders at the silks, cloths, and goods which are arrayed under its piazzas. In the evening it presents a very interesting sight; each shop is lighted up by a lamp suspended in front, which gives the city an appearance of being illuminated. The number of shops for the sale of dried fruits is remarkable, and their arrangement tasteful. In May one may purchase the grapes, pears, apples, quinces, and even melons of the bygone season, then ten months old. There are poulterers' shops, at which snipes, ducks, partridges, and plovers, with other game, may be purchased. The shops of the shoemakers and hardware retailers are also arranged with singular neatness. Every trade has its separate bazaar, and all of them seem busy. There are booksellers and venders of paper, much of which is Russian, and of a blue colour. The month of May is the season of the 'falodeh,' which is a white jelly strained from wheat, and drunk with sherbet and snow. The people are very fond of it, and the shopkeepers in all parts of the town seem constantly at work with their customers. A pillar of snow stands on one side of them, and a fountain plays near it, which gives these places a cool and clean appearance. Around the bakers' shops crowds of people may be seen waiting for their bread. I observed that they baked it by plastering it to the sides of the oven.

"Kabul is famed for its kabobs, or cooked meats, which are in great re-

The great heats of summer are tempered by the north-east wind which comes fresh from the snowy regions of the Paropamisus mountains. Snow does not fall on the plain every winter; and when it does it melts almost as soon as it touches the ground. The mildness of the temperature in that season attracted the Suddozye sovereigns from Kabul, where they resided in the summer; and thus both towns were equally looked upon as capitals. But Kandahar lost the title in the reign of Timour Shah, for having supported the pretensions of his brother Suleiman Mirza to the Afghan throne, on the death of their father Ahmed Shah.

The town of Kandahar is an oblong, with nearly a parasang of area. It is surrounded by a high and thick wall of earth, protected by a deep but not very wide ditch. The citadel is situated on the north of the town, and contains a very good residence, which Kohendil Khan inhabits. The fortifications were put into a good state by the English, and are capable of resisting the attacks of an Afghan army; they also built large barracks on a great space situated outside the Herat gate; these were uninhabited, but in good condition, in 1845.

The interior of Kandahar is in no way remarkable. The water circulates abundantly through all parts of it, and would be of infinite value to the inhabitants if they did not deprive themselves of it in a thousand stupid or careless ways. A swarm of women

---

quest. Few cook at home. 'Rhuwash' was the dainty of the May season in Kabul. It is merely blanched rhubarb, which is reared under a careful protection of the sun, and grows up rankly under the hills in the neighbourhood. Its flavour is delicious. 'Shabash rhuwash! Bravo rhuwash!' is the cry in the streets, and every one buys it. In the most crowded parts of the city there are story-tellers amusing the idlers, or dervises proclaiming the glories and deeds of the prophets. If a baker makes his appearance before these worthies, they demand a cake in the name of some prophet; and to judge by the number who follow their occupation, it must be a profitable one. There are no wheeled carriages in Kabul. The streets are not very narrow; they are kept in a good state during dry weather, and are intersected by small covered aqueducts of clean water, which is a great convenience to the people. We passed along them without observation and even without an attendant. To me the appearance of the people was more novel than the bazaars. They sauntered about dressed in sheepskin cloaks, and seemed huge from the quantity of clothes they wore. All the children have ruby-red cheeks, which I at first took for an artificial colour, till I found it to be the gay bloom of youth. The older people seem to lose it. Kabul is a compactly-built city, but its houses have no pretension to elegance. They are constructed of sun-dried bricks and wood, and few of them are more than two stories high. It is thickly peopled, and has a population of about 60,000 souls. The river of Kabul passes through the city, and tradition says it has three times carried it away or inundated it. In rain there is not a dirtier place than Kabul."—*Extract from Burnes's Travels into Bokhara*, vol. i. pp. 144, 145, 146, 147.

are always washing their clothes in it; the men go in with their clothes on to get rid of the vermin in them; and every species of impurity from the houses and shambles is thrown into it—nevertheless, the population feel no repugnance to using it with their food!

The mosque, which contains the tomb of Ahmed Shah Suddozye, is the only fine monument existing in the town. The bazars are composed of four covered streets, which meet at a round point called Charsook, where the chief judge resides, and where his sentences are executed. The town is divided into many mohullas, or quarters, each of which belongs to one of the numerous tribes and nations which form the inhabitants of the city. The population of Kandahar is composed as follows:—

1. One-fourth, Afghans of the tribe of Barukzyes.
2. An eighth, Afghans of the tribe of Ghiljees.
3. An eighth, Afghans, various other tribes, Dooranee.
4. Half, Parsivans and Hindoos.*

There are neither Jews nor Armenians there.

The trade of the place is almost entirely in the hands of the Parsivans and Hindoos, and was considerable till 1841. The merchandise came from India, and was dispersed amongst the Hazarahs and Belooches in Kabul, Herat, Bokhara, and even Khiva. But since Kohendil Khan regained the reins of government in 1843, after the retreat of the English, his tyranny and spoliations, for his own benefit and to provide himself a store against reverses of fortune, have driven away the principal merchants, or obliged them to realize their property and bury it in the earth, awaiting the return of security.

The population of Kandahar amounted, eight years ago, to 60,000 inhabitants: it is now reduced to half that number, and diminishes every year, on account of the inflictions and insults which weigh upon the people. Kohendil Khan has given, in vain, the most severe orders for the unhappy emigrants to be arrested at the frontiers; the greater number always escape, and seek security in Herat or in India. But woe to those who are caught! they suffer piteously indeed. Brought back bound to Kandahar, they are not only stripped of the property they may have upon them, but are put to the torture to make them disclose

* One large quarter of the town, however, the N.E., is entirely inhabited by the Berdorani tribe.—ED.

where, if they have any more, they have hidden it; and they are afterwards employed on public works, where they earn nothing but an insufficient subsistence, their small pay being seized by the sovereign—who, by exactions of every description, alienates more and more the good-will of his subjects. Up to the year 1844 he confined his cruelties to the industrious classes only, the Parsivans and Hindoos; but since that period he has persecuted the Afghans equally, and that may eventually cost him dear.

From the remotest times Kandahar must have been a town of much importance in Asia, as its geographical position sufficiently indicates, it being the central point at which the roads from Herat, Seistan, Gour, India, and Kabul unite, and the commercial mart of these localities.

Some authors consider Kandahar as an Indian, others as a Persian town; the Afghans themselves include it in Khorassan, to which province they assign the Indus (called also the Attok and the Scinde) as the limit. According to them *India* commences only on the other side, and to the south of this river, from the point at which it receives the Sutlej; that is to say, north of the territory of the Mahrattas and Moguls.

The Punjab, comprehending Kashmir and the country of the Sikhs, and Zablestan, comprehending Ghuzni and Kabul, form another country called by them *Hindostan.*

The inhabitants of India they call Hindees, and those of Hindostan Hindostanees. This arrangement apppears to be a very ancient one; and it is not astonishing that Kandahar, being so near both these countries, and frequently added to one or the other by conquest, should have been considered as alternately belonging to either by the ancient authors, whose ideas have been adopted by some geographers of our own days. They consider Kandahar to have been one of the seven cities built in the interior of Asia by Alexander the Great, resting their opinion on the slight supposition that Kandar or Kandahar* is only an abbreviation of the name Iskandar, by which Alexander is known in the East; and in this there is nothing improbable, for it must be the point to which the Macedonian conqueror advanced when he quitted Furrah to go

---

* Kandahar is said to have been called so from the Gandharras (Greek Gandaridæ), who migrated to the westward from the Gandharra of the Indus in the fourth century. See Appendices for further account.—ED.

to Arachosia,* whence he turned northward. Finding the country rich, and a desirable site existing on the southern point of the mountains, from which the various roads could be commanded, he could not select a better for the purpose, and there he erected a fortress, destined to shelter his troops and contain the population.

From the hands of Alexander Kandahar passed into the power of the Seleukides, whose history is involved in obscurity. It is scarcely possible to determine what its condition was under the dominion of the Parthians and Sassanides, for the history of Kandahar at that time is enveloped in darkness, which lasted nearly to the period when the successors of Mahomet invaded Persia; but it appears certain that the Arabs penetrated into it in the first age of the Hegira. That is the opinion of Herbelot, who founded it upon that of Kawan el Moolk. These are his words:—"In the year of the Hegira 304 (A.D. 916), in the Caliphat of Mocktader, in digging for the foundation of a tower at Kandahar, a subterranean cave was discovered, in which were a thousand Arab heads, all attached to the same chain, which had evidently remained in good preservation since the year Heg. 70 (A.D. 689), for a paper with this date upon it was found attached by a silken thread to the ears of the twenty-nine most important skulls, with their proper names." This would indicate that the Arabs at first met with no great success in their enterprise against this town: nevertheless they eventually became masters of it.†

In Heg. 252 (A.D. 865), Yacoob ben Leis, founder of the dynasty of the Soffarides,‡ possessed himself of Kandahar; the Sassanides drove out his successors, and it was taken from them by the famous Mahmood Ghuznevi, whose dynasty was overthrown by that of the Gaurides. Under these last Kandahar fell by turns into the hands of petty ambitious chiefs, who all succumbed to the Seljookides. These possessed it till Sanjar, a prince of that dynasty, was overthrown by the Turkomans.

* Arachosia can be distinctly shown, by the Greek measurements, to have been at the ruins of Shehr-Zohauk, or Olan Robat, between Kilaat-i-Ghiljie and Mokoor.—ED.

† The early campaigns of the Arabs against Kandahar are given at length from the work of Beladeri, in M. Renaud's 'Fragments of Arab History,' Paris, about 1843.—ED.

‡ Soffar means a worker in copper. The Soffaride dynasty began, according to some, Heg. 259, according to others, 248, and lasted for three generations, till it was replaced by that of the Sapanides, about the end of the same century of the Hegira. See D'Herbelot.—ED.

The last were established in the town in Heg. 540 (A.D. 1153), and a few years after it fell under the power of Ghyaz eddin Mohamed, a Gauride prince. Allah eddin Mohamed, Sultan of Khaurism, took it, Heg. 597 (A.D. 1210); and his son was dispossessed by the famous Ghengis Khan, Heg. 609 (A.D. 1222).

The descendants of that conqueror allowed it to be wrenched from them by the prince of the dynasty of Malek-Kurt, who were succeeded by the chiefs of the country till the period at which Tamerlane invaded and took possession of it, Heg. 776 (A.D. 1389); at his death it became part of the dominions of his son, Shah Rokh. The Timourides retained it till Heg. 855 (A.D. 1468), at which epoch the death of the Sultan Aboo Seid caused the dismemberment of the empire: after this time Kandahar and some surrounding districts soon formed an independent state. In Heg. 899 (A.D. 1512) it was in the power of a chief called Shah Beg, who was dispossessed by the famous Baber, founder of the dynasty of the Moguls in India, to whose dominions it was annexed.

Not long afterwards Kandahar was seized by the Persians, and became from that moment the cause of perpetual wars between the two empires. In Heg. 922 (A.D. 1535) it was taken, and for some time after held, by Sam Mirza, a revolted prince of the dynasty of the Seferiges; but it was retaken by Thamasp Shah, and the government of it confided to Pir Boodak Khan, Kajar, who, having been besieged the following year by Kamran Mirza, son of Baber, gave him up the place, which fell therefore for a short time into the power of Thamasp. At the death of that prince one of his nephews, Sultan Hussein Mirza, had himself proclaimed king, and declared himself independent of the Shah Ismael, son and successor of Thamasp to the throne of Persia.

This prince, wishing to take the life of one of his officers whom he distrusted, laid a plan for having him poisoned at a banquet to which he invited him; but his intended victim, being warned of Hussein's treachery, dexterously managed that the cup intended for him should be presented to the Sultan, who unsuspiciously quaffed the contents, and died, as he deserved to do, the victim of his own perfidy.

After this event, Humayoon, son and successor of Baber, seized upon Kandahar; but having been dethroned in a revolt, he rewarded Thamasp, who aided him in regaining his power, by the cession of this town, Heg. 932 (A.D. 1545). Akbar, son of Humayoon, took it by stratagem from the Persians; but Shah Abbas the Great retook it, Heg. 996 (A.D. 1609), and it soon after fell under the power of Jehanghir, Emperor of the Moguls.

It fell to the Persians again Heg. 1007 (A.D. 1620); but at the death of Shah Abbas, the Usbeks, thinking they could recommence their depredations with impunity, invaded Khorassan; beaten however by the Persian troops who held this province, they marched upon Kandahar, of which they possessed themselves by means of the defection of the Persian governor, Ali Murdan Khan, who, conceiving he would be condemned to death by Shah Sefi, grandson and successor of Shah Abbas, evacuated the town, and at the head of his troops arrived at the court of the Great Mogul, to whom he rendered homage.

The Usbeks were not driven from the place till Heg. 1021 (A.D. 1634), by the Emperor Shah Jehanghir, from whom the Persians took it, Heg. 1037 (A.D. 1650), under the reign of Shah Abbas the Second. After this epoch, although frequently besieged by the Moguls—once commanded by the famous Aurungzebe in person, Heg. 1096 (A.D. 1709)—they were never able to retake it, and it continued Persian up to the time of the revolt of the famous Mir Veis, an Afghan chief of the Ghiljee tribe, who was succeeded, first, by his brother, Mir Abdullah, and afterwards by his two sons, Mir Mahmood and Mir Hussein.

The last was dispossessed by Nadir Shah, at whose death Kandahar became the capital of the new kingdom of Afghanistan, of which Ahmed Shah Suddozye was the founder; his dynasty was overthrown by the Barukzyes, Heg. 1203 (A.D. 1816). The family of the Mohamedzyes possessed itself of the various provinces of Afghanistan, from which it was expelled by the English, Heg. 1226 to 1228 (A.D. 1839 to 1841); but after their retreat, Kohendil Khan returned to Kandahar, and reigned there absolute, [until his death in 1855. Kandahar is now said to be in the possession of Dost Mohamed.]—ED.

To return from this historical sketch to my own journey. One of my escort went on in advance from Tekie Sindjavi to give Kohendil Khan notice of my approach, and at nightfall I met him near the English barracks returning for me, accompanied by ten ferocious-looking rascals, by whom I was surrounded to prevent the possibility of any person coming near me. The sun was setting, and the voice of the muezzin from the tall minarets summoned all good Mussulmans to prayer; my guards immediately formed up in line and went through their various genuflexions with a precision worthy of a picked company. In one instant after they proceeded to satisfy the most voracious appetites it was ever my lot to witness amongst all the hungry men I have seen. They fell upon a pile of melons exposed for sale in the open air, and having thrown two or three pieces of small coin to the owner, who knew better than to grumble at the price offered by the soldiers of the great Sirdar, a score of them disappeared in a moment of time. I had at first thought them savage, but they seemed to me absolutely kind, when, after they had finished, they threw a melon to me, calling out "*bigir*," catch. I did so with the dexterity of the most practised monkey, and in an instant the delicious fruit had disappeared, for I was famished, and it was a long time since I had tasted anything so nice.

After this short halt we entered the town, but the captain of the escort not having found at the gate the man who was to take us to a lodging, set about looking for him in a labyrinth of tortuous streets, the kiabane,* and the bazaars, where I was carefully scrutinised by the people; we rode to and fro for an hour without finding him, and at last stood still, waiting for the return of a messenger that my guard had sent to look for him. Surrounded and, as usual, questioned by the crowd, and my escort being completely puzzled what to do with me, they at last decided upon taking me to the Char-sook, where I was provisionally placed in the public prison, from which some criminals were turned out to make room for me. Happily Lal Khan, an Afghan Barukzye, came about half an hour after, and took me from there to a house that had been prepared for me.

The darkness prevented me from seeing much of its details, but it appeared tolerably comfortable. What, however, I enjoyed exceedingly was an excellent pilau that the Khan sent me from his own kitchen. I ate it with avidity, and, feeling greatly refreshed and renovated by such a meal, threw myself down to rest, and slept profoundly, under the happy impression that my reception at Kandahar augured better treatment for me than I had met with at Girishk.

---

* *i.e.* The avenue.

August 31st.—When I awoke this morning I was struck with the beauty of my dwelling; it was worthy of a prince. This palace contained various blocks of building, and I occupied the one destined for the harem. My guard amounted to fifty, and their orders were neither to let me go out of it, nor to let any one come in to see me; the commander Lal Khan was not to lose sight of me for a moment, and to sleep across my door at night. As, however, every avenue to the harem was well secured, I was allowed my liberty within the building; the portion next to me contained another prisoner who had also come to wander in this dangerous country; it was Saadet Mulook, son of Shah Kamran, the enemy of the Mohamedzye then reigning. The room which I occupied was spacious, and the walls were covered with many and various ornaments, beautifully executed in relief in a species of plaster hard as stucco and shining as quartz, in which one might fancy spangles of silver had been mixed; this plaster is found in abundance in the plains of Kandahar on the very surface of the earth, but, instead of being compact and in lumps like that which we use in France, it resembles when found a bank of coral, is brittle, and crumbles under the slightest pressure; sometimes it is found of the consistency of raw honey coming from the comb, but the colour is always of silvery whiteness.

Besides its beauty, my apartment had the charm of a shady aspect in the daytime, and at night, by opening the upper part of the blinds, it could be kept cooler than the terraces on which the inhabitants of Kandahar sleep in the summer; the court was large, well-aired, and ornamented with two little gardens, separated by a very large basin, the water in which was frightfully filthy, but the soldiers would not take the trouble to change it, and even bathed in it morning and evening. Whatever might be my sensations of disgust at the thoughts of this water, I was nevertheless obliged to drink it all the time I was at Kandahar. My guards would not take the trouble to bring me any other; why should they? They drank it themselves: it was their only drink.

Continuing my inspection of this elegant prison, and congratulating myself on the selection that had been made for me, I wandered, accompanied by Lal Khan, into a small garden, o which the alleys were paved with tiles, but as I approached the point where they met, which was occupied by a small dry basin, my breath was almost taken away by a dreadfully fetid smell that proceeded from a mass of corruption alive with millions of worms and flies. Supposing it to have been the carcase of a sheep, I asked my companion, in some astonishment, how they could possibly use such a place as a butcher's shambles? He replied to my question with so strange a smile that I repeated it, and he answered sharply, "This house belonged, some months ago, to the Mirza Mohamed Wali, during the time that he received the taxes for the English, and the blood you see there is his. Kohendil Khan had him killed for a traitor. God recompense him in this world and in the next." This sally was accompanied by a grin so ferocious that I felt almost alarmed by it, and my heart sank within me at the fearful scene and recital. Wishing, however, to hear more details of the wretched story, I inquired of one of my guards, whose answer was an ironical laugh that might be thus translated, "Take care they do not do as much for you."

I could not learn the history of the Mirza Mohamed Wali till after my return to Girishk, when the Moonshee Feiz Mohamed told me that he had lost his life simply because Mohamed Sedik Khan coveted the house that I inhabited. This most rapacious and cruel Sirdar had not one of his own at Kandahar in which to spend the winter season; he was tired of living in a hired domicile, and to build one would cost more money than he could make up his mind to part with, so he preferred appropriating to himself, by the crime of murder, the beautiful residence belonging to the unfortunate Mirza.

The first step towards the attainment of his object was the writing of a false letter in the name of the English governor of Shikarpoor, in which he informed Mohamed Wali that the English, not having given up the intention of taking Kandahar, would arrive almost immediately in great force, and charged him to purchase a large quantity of corn, barley, and straw for the army, and also to keep the partisans of the English cause together in the town, ready to seize the Sirdars on the first signal.

This precious missive once fabricated, the villain informed his father of the unwary Mirza's pretended treachery, and advised him to set spies round his house to seize his correspondence; this was done, and of course it was not long before the malignant forgery was intercepted, and taken to Kohendil Khan, who commanded the unhappy victim of his odious son to be killed immediately. Mohamed Sedik then begged his father to give him the house as a reward for his shrewdness and zeal in his interests, and, as he expected, his request was granted.

The English are, it must be acknowledged, great and generous, and reward handsomely those who serve them well or suffer in their cause. When the news of this atrocious assassination reached Calcutta the Directors ordered a pension of 1200*l.* a-year, and a present in ready money of 2000*l.*, to be paid to the surviving nephew of Mirza Mohamed Wali; the other had been killed with his uncle.*

September 1st, 2nd, 3rd.—However beautiful the residence in which I was now kept, it was quite impossible for me to forget that it served me only as a prison, and the consciousness of that fact, with the remembrance of the tragical end of the proprietor, was well calculated to make a mournful impression even on the firmest mind. The delay also in obtaining an audience of Kohendil Khan made me profoundly sad, though excepting that delay and my seclusion I had nothing to complain of at Kandahar. A good meal was brought to me daily, morning and evening, from the Sirdar's own kitchen; my guards, though neither better brought up nor more sociable than those of his son, were far less coarse; they were content to keep their watch in my room, and sometimes laugh at me, but they never insulted me by word or deed, and that was an amazing amelioration of my condition. As I was continually supplicating Lal Khan to try to induce the sovereign to receive me, he at last consented, and his intercession was crowned with success. About two hours after sunset on the 3rd, I was conducted to the presence of this prince, who has the reputation of being one of the most valiant sons of Payendeh Khan. I went on horseback, in an Afghan dress, and with a good escort, though the citadel was only ten minutes' ride from my prison; a large space in front of the fortress was crowded with booths, wood, bricks, and camels.

* Another chief of the Parsivan party, Jan Mohamed, cotival, or chief of the police of Kandahar during the English occupation, was of the utmost service to our government throughout the war. After our retirement he succeeded in maintaining himself in favour with the Sirdars longer than others of his party. In 1854, however, having been pillaged of his last farthing, and lost several members of his family from the hardships to which he was subjected, he effected his escape, and came through Persia to Bagdad. Hence he was sent on by Colonel Rawlinson to Bombay, and Lord Elphinstone, the governor, in consideration of his services, nominated him to the police mastership of the town of Shikarpore. He died on his way up, but his family are still in the receipt of a small pension from the British government.—Ed.

Kohendil Khan gave me audience in the garden, and when I was ushered into his presence he was seated on a carpet near a fountain; several mollahs, who were in attendance, retired at my approach, and left us alone. The expression of his countenance, lighted by the moon, was entirely different from the character of the man. It was serious, gentle, and kind, and though his complexion, pale and sickly, contrasted strangely with his beard dyed black, I should have taken a favourable impression of him, if his eyes, like those of his eldest son, had not warned me of falsehood and perfidy. His age was about fifty-eight or sixty, and his figure short and stout. His dress was perfectly simple; a thick white cotton robe, and a white muslin turban; round his waist was a rich Kashmir shawl; the only article that could be called an ornament was a Persian knife, with a jewelled handle.

He invited me to take a seat near him; and as I did so he politely rose on his knees, and we exchanged the usual compliments. After the preamble, always sufficiently long amongst the Afghans, he asked what business had brought me to Afghanistan. My reply was the simple truth, that I desired to take service at Lahore. He then insisted upon knowing if that was the only motive that had induced me to traverse the country, and seemed to doubt it, giving as a reason that the Sikhs had seen Europeans leave them who had been twenty years in their service, without feeling any regret at their doing so, and he thought it very unlikely that my offer would be accepted.

"From having been our enemies," he said, "the Sikhs have become our allies. I have to-day received the news of the cession of Peshawur and Attok, made by them to my brother Dost Mohamed Khan. His son, Mohamed Akbar Khan, ought soon to take possession of the country at the head of a large body of troops, who are assembling at this moment, and, Inshallah! please God, we will soon join Kashmir to those two places. The concessions they make prove how the Sikhs value our alliance. They do not want Europeans,—their enemies and ours. You must know that, and vainly seek to deceive me. You can only have come to this country to ascertain the feelings of the people, and to raise them a second time against us. The firmans of the Sultan of Istambul and the Shah of Persia that you have shown to my son, do not prove to us that you are not English; for you may have stolen them from a Frenchman; and that, in my opinion, is the truth. Own it now." This speech, made in a very calm and distinct tone, and with an appearance of its being his profound conviction, really embarrassed me, as my agitation might have been visible to the Sirdar. In reply, I assured him "that the character of Englishman was quite honourable enough for me to have no wish to throw it off, if it had really belonged to me; but that I was a Frenchman, which was equally good, and that so I presented myself to him without any mental reservation." Kohendil Khan did not seem convinced, but suddenly abandoned his investigations concerning me and my intentions, and commenced a long oration, in which he threw a retrospective glance over the history of the few previous years.

He complained in equally strong terms of the English, the Russians, and the Persians. He reproached the first bitterly with having violated the conventions made by Burnes in the name of the government with him and his brother Dost Mohamed, with having disloyally invaded the country, turned out and set aside all persons of rank or importance from public appointments, and replaced them by upstarts.

He held the Russian government, he said, to be no less disloyal, because they had not fulfilled a fourth part of the engagements that Vitkevich had made for them. "The Czar has allowed you English to invade us, and abandoned Mohamed Shah at the moment that he would have taken Herat; just when my son had started with four thousand horsemen to make a diversion in his favour on the Furrah side of the country."

"Thus," said he, "the two nations of whom we had the highest opinion, whose truth and loyalty were proverbial among us, have proved this reputation to be groundless; they are second to none in duplicity. But the Afghans now are fully aware of the value of their promises, and their protestations of friendship; they know they have but one object, the subjugation of their country, and have ceased to listen to perfidious advice, tending only to arm them one against the other. It is in vain to try to do that now; you ought to have found that out since you arrived in the principality; for there is everywhere the same cry:—War to the death with the Feringhees and the Infidels!"

After that he discussed the Persians with no less bitterness, recriminating against the Shah and his minister Haji Mirza Aghassi, laying to their incapacity the failure of the siege of Herat, and, besides, accusing them of having tampered with the negotiations that brought on his ruin; but the point on which he felt the greatest indignation against them, was the manner in which they treated him when he took refuge in their country.

He considered that the estate, appointed him by the Shah for the support of himself and his family, was unequal to the maintenance of his dignity. This fief was the district of Shehribabek, lying between Kirman and Shiraz; the revenue was estimated by the Persian government at 12,000 tomauns, but its real value is nearer 20,000, and Kohendil Khan, putting in practice the system of oppression that made him so hated in Kandahar, had raised it to close upon 30,000. I could, therefore, with justice, have appeared astonished at his unreasonable discontent, had I not long been aware that gratitude is a virtue unknown in the breast of a Mussulman. He sees only the finger of God in everything that happens to him; therefore, whoever does a man a kindness, stands simply in the position of an instrument, and as such has no claim upon the feelings of him whom he has benefited when nothing more can be expected through his agency. However, I did not think it incumbent upon me to defend the governments the Sirdar chose to abuse, and contented myself by replying, that the facts of which he complained had taken place without the knowledge of the other European states, who blamed the successive aggressions of the Russians and the English, though they could not prevent them.

The conversation then turned on a variety of subjects; the Sirdar took much interest in the details that I gave him respecting the different countries of Europe, and their respective riches and power. He had heard much of France, and talked a long time about it, making me specially repeat all that concerned her commerce, manufactures, and modern inventions worked by steam. The Asiatics believe everything; they imagine that in an hour they can be made to understand arts and sciences of the most complicated character, and which it has required ages to bring to their present perfection. He was also quite surprised that I could not make easy to him the political economy of the nations of the West, nor enable him clearly to understand by what means the population had been brought under obedience to the laws without coercion by physical force.

"I have confiscated, bastinadoed, tortured, and cut heads off," said the wise and merciful Kohendil Khan, "but I have never yet been able to bring my savage Afghans to obey my decrees; and there is not a Sirdar in my principality, not excepting even my brothers, my sons, or my nephews, who would not seize with joy a chance of wrenching the sovereign power from my grasp, if they thought it at all probable they should succeed in the attempt. Here might is right; why is it otherwise in Europe?"

"It is," I answered, "because with us the governments act for the benefit of the people, without regard to their personal interest. All the acts of a government are subordinate to the law, while yours are regulated only by your good pleasure."

"But," he replied, "what is the use of power if it is not to enable one to get rich? What is a government without absolute power? What is a king who cannot, when he pleases, bastinado one of his subjects and cut off his head? It is turning the world upside down, the most terrible thing that can be seen; it must be permanent anarchy—I know it; I can judge by my Afghans. They are like other men, but they respect me because they fear me: and it is by constant oppression that I succeed in inspiring this fear. If God had not inspired men with terror, by pointing out the torments with which they would be punished, would they obey the dictates of his holy book the Koran? I think despotism, therefore, appears the best form of government for doing good; nevertheless, if you can teach me a better, I will hasten to put it in practice."

"The system," I said, "was shown you by the English when they were in your country: do as they did; regulate everything according to justice and equity, encourage commerce and agriculture, carry out works of public utility, make your roads safe from robbers, repress the tyranny of subordinate agents, let the people know what they owe to the state, and be exempt from extortion when they have paid it; fear not then that your country will be rich and prosperous, the population will increase instead of emigrating, and venerate the prince who shall first teach them the value of order, justice, and abundance, and their gratitude to him will be the best security for the endurance of his power." Kohendil Khan listened, but it was plain that he thought me a short-sighted Utopian visionary, devoid of any real idea of the science of good government.

As in fact I had no interest in it, I was glad to drop this irritating subject for the immediate object of my visit, and I begged him most earnestly to allow me to continue my journey. With some embarrassment in his manner, he at first replied evasively, but as I pressed my cause with earnestness, he at last replied: " Although I am the absolute and independent sovereign of Kandahar, my position as younger brother of the Emir Dost Mohamed of Kabul imposes upon me the duty of consulting the head of the family on every affair of importance that may arise. Your arrival here is one of which I could not do otherwise than inform him, since your intention is to go through his states; I therefore wrote to him the day I received the letter from my son announcing to me your arrival at Mahmoodabad, but his answer has not yet arrived, and it is he who will decide your fate. Be assured, however, his desire will be like mine, that no harm shall happen to you, and whether he orders me to send you to Kabul or Shikarpoor, I promise to take every precaution necessary to your safety on the journey. Do not be alarmed at my refusal to let you go out of your house; prudence alone dictates that order, for, in walking about the bazaars, you might easily come to misfortune—some fanatic might perhaps assassinate you. I could not bring you to life again by killing him; and how could I answer to the English, who would come to demand the price of your blood? Believe me then, and do not insist upon having more liberty than you now enjoy."

" But," I said, " there is not the same difficulty about people coming to see me."

" True;" and he smiled as he spoke, " but you are best alone—be content."

Seeing that, in spite of all my denials, he still thought I was an Englishman, I insisted no more, and retired sufficiently disappointed. He saw it, and told me to keep up my spirits; that Dost Mohamed knew the English and valued them as they deserved, and recommended him to enter into alliance with them, in which case my assistance would be useful to both of them.

CHAPTER XXIII.

Sikhs and Afghans — Intended league against the English — The result of it — English policy in the north of India — The power of Russia and England — The political morals of Asiatics — English government advantageous to the natives — The fruits attendant upon Russian conquests — Sketch of them — Her conduct in Poland — Encroachments in Asia — Universal dominion — Peter the Great — Russian interference at Herat — Attempt to make the Turks their vassals — Administration of the Russians in their colonies — Christian population in the province of Erivan — Contrast between England and Russia — Reflections on the conduct of these Governments — Imprudence of the English at Kabul — The Afghan opinions of the English after the occupation — The author's opinion on British administration of India — Tabular statement of the English possessions — The conquests of Russia.

THE morning after my interview with Kohendil Khan was one of happier presage for me than I had expected; and as I looked round my beautiful prison I felt more at ease concerning my life, but very anxious to know how much longer my captivity would last. What Kohendil Khan had told me about the alliance between the Sikhs and the Afghans seemed to me incomprehensible; for from the remotest times these two nations, though forming one kingdom, had always been irreconcilable enemies. A great political change, therefore, must have taken place since my departure from Bagdad. When I left it I knew there was some disturbance in the Punjab, and that the English were watching it closely; but I had not thought that the conflict between them and the troops of the Maharajah was so near at hand; I thought I should arrive at Lahore at a propitious time, and obtain suitable employment, with the rank that I held in the Persian army; but all that I heard in Kandahar singularly diminished my hopes. Mohamed Sedik Khan had frequently spoken of the imminent danger of a rupture between the Sikhs and the English, and had seized the opportunity of expressing his great wish to take part with the latter, if his services would be accepted by them. But according to the Afghan habit of divulging everything, even matters it is most important to conceal, he did not dissimulate that he and his father were ready to profit by another alliance, if the English refused their co-operation, and, adding proofs to his assertions, he showed me several letters from Sikh, Belooch, and Mahratta chiefs, which he was charged to send to his cousin Mohamed Akbar Khan of Kabul, establishing in the most positive manner evidence of the existence of a formidable league between them and the Afghan princes. These chiefs had mutually sworn on the Koran to strike in concert a decisive blow in the northern provinces of India, subject to the English, and the Sikhs especially claimed immediate aid from their allies, to support an offensive movement which they were preparing to make with the least possible delay against the army of the Company. I had looked upon Mohamed Sedik's confidence as merely a scheme for frightening me, without any object, by a false correspondence about the danger incurred by those whom he supposed to be my countrymen. The subsequent revelations of his father induced me to give some credit to what he had said, and I began at last to think that the English were likely to have a serious struggle with their antagonists. Nevertheless I doubted not for a moment of their success, knowing well that a lasting union amongst the coalesced Asiatic chieftains was a thing impossible; they were different in nation and religion, and, above all, in interests, submitting to no species of subordination, and each aspiring to sovereign power.

[The result was just what I expected; for the Sikhs, having attacked the English four months after, gave way at Sobraon, notwithstanding the courage of which they gave proof, without having been assisted by those who were as much interested as themselves in their not being beaten by the Indo-British army.

The Belooches of Scinde, Kelat, and Kharran, who had shown themselves the most furious in their correspondence, never raised a hand when the time came to take up arms; and a part of the force under Sir Charles Napier was enabled to quit this country, and effect a diversion useful to the Bengal army, by moving towards Multan.

The corps of 800 horsemen sent by Dost Mohamed to help the Sikhs did not arrive at Peshawur before the English had beaten them at Sobraon and crossed the Sutlej. It was the same with the thousand cavalry that went out of Kandahar under the orders of Mohamed Omar Khan, second son of Kohendil

Khan; they heard of the rout of the Sikhs on the second day of their march; and he was so frightened at anticipated punishment that he forbad the soldiers on pain of death saying that they had set out to fight the English, and had it reported that they were simply in search of brigands amongst the Belooches dependent on Kandahar.

Every progressive step of the British in India has been marked by similar events; there have always been leagues against them, but of materials too heterogeneous to offer any effectual opposition. The superiority of their policy and arms has insured them their colossal dominions; and whatever may be said in Europe, their firmly-seated power is less odious than that of the tyrants they have dispossessed, and will last for ages, if not attacked by any European nation.

The public press protests daily against the grasping tendency of England and Russia; and it is, I own, reasonable for less-favoured nations to be alarmed at it. But is it not the fault of those who allowed them to act upon it? What can the papers hope to do by vain and sterile words? When a flood is not restrained by dykes it sweeps all before it. It is the same with the politics of Russia and of England, which have for a long time destroyed the equilibrium which the treaties of 1815 were intended to secure in Europe. The fortunate possessors of India and the Caucasus have reaped the benefit of these possessions, and now give laws to empires more vast than either the Roman or the Macedonian, and whose fate is in the one case in the hands of the most absolute, the most severe, and the most ambitious of sovereigns; and in the other in those of the too selfish, egotistical, and calculating Company of London Merchants, who, tranquilly seated behind their counters, enjoy without trouble the revenues of opulent Asia.

These immense empires have now attained limits which might content the most unbridled ambition; but there is an unseen power, stronger than their will, which impels Russia and England to seize upon the countries that lie between them. They obey this impulse in spite of themselves, in spite of reason, in spite of their conviction of the danger to themselves in augmenting their territories. They cannot resist it, much as they may endeavour to do so. Once entered on the path of conquest, it became impossible for them to maintain the limits they had proposed to themselves, and within which wisdom dictated they should remain.

Let us take a glance at the necessity for these invasions, and begin with the English in this retrospective sketch.

The obstacles which they encountered and wished to vanquish arose more especially from the petty independent princes their neighbours, who passed their whole lives in intrigues, and unceasingly maintained an underhand war, of which it was impossible for them to unravel the policy or prove its hostility, so as to meet the enemy fairly in the field. They have been obliged to meet him with his own weapons: in that manner only could they consolidate their power over their early conquests. Then, to put an end to Indian duplicity, which kept them in continual uncertainty, they threw off all reserve, and openly acknowledged a policy which, however much in accordance with oriental practice, could not be sanctioned by moral and international laws, to subdue these faithless princes, who, in truth, were lawless depredators. It is far from my intention to applaud the means by which the English became possessed of some of these principalities; but it is impossible not to admit that, to possess them,* they could not act otherwise. Our ideas of morals and politics do not coincide with those of Asiatics; and it is just because we judge of circumstances which concern them from our point of view, and never from theirs, that we make such frequent mistakes. They simply make a joke of all loyalty and treaties and the most sacred oaths; and all these dispossessed Rajahs and Emirs were so many tyrants, oppressing those whom they ruled with a rod of iron, and the traveller who witnesses the effects of their tyranny and cruelty, or who has lived under their laws, feels little pity for them.

It may be regretted that on the English only devolves the mission of succeeding them, on account of the frightful expansion of the British power, the weight of which is already felt in every part of the world. I do not contest the point; but then the question must be looked at with regard to that only, and not as a matter of compassion for these sanguinary and avaricious princes, and we must refrain from raising a hue and cry in favour of these perfect scourges of humanity, exercising, for the most part, a usurped authority, and always maintaining it by a series of crimes. To say that the English might have done more than they have done for the material amelioration of their Asiatic subjects would be

* Rather, with justice, say, "*to secure their own possessions* they could not," &c.—L.

risking very little; but the moral transformation of them would be quite another thing—this is a question which involves a careful review of many important circumstances. Before any other would come the consideration of the consequences resulting from changes made too suddenly, without allowing time for gradual transition. Amongst so many native populations, whose origin and habits are so various, hasty changes—such as some well-meaning people have thought would insure their happiness—would very probably only astonish them, and provoke irregularities, the sad consequences of which might be avoided by awaiting the effects of time, patience, and the judicious and persevering application of the principles of mixed government; causing the rational and vivifying European system progressively to succeed the enervating and anarchical governments of the native sovereigns.

By founding entirely European governments the English would not at once amalgamate the various elements of which their Indian empire is composed. It would take many years to bring about unity of administration; and they would have to use force to surmount many difficulties, it being the sole means in that country of completely developing its resources, and destroying the rivalry of existing races. But the power of England is much too solidly settled on the banks of the Indus for her to dread the disasters with which the press threatens her by means of the conquered nations. So true has that been, that every revolt, every attack that she has had to repress for the last fifty years, has only given her the opportunity of a fresh triumph.

If there has been one instance to the contrary, of which in 1841 Afghanistan was the theatre, its existence may be traced to circumstances perfectly exceptional; above all to the imprudence of the English Government, in sending their troops so far from the base of their operations, and yielding a sense of security which there was nothing to justify. Enlightened by their misfortunes at Kabul, their vigilance has not failed them a second time; and the revolt of the Sikhs in 1848 proved once more that India belongs to the English, and cannot be taken from them by any of the native powers. An European nation only could wrench it from them. Their power is too firmly rooted to be shaken by any Indian conspiracies. I shall not, as most authors who have written upon this country, indulge in sterile declamation against the unmeasured and insatiable ambition of the English; first, because with them conquest is a question of their existence in India until it is completely absorbed; and, secondly, because I should like to know what state would abstain from increasing its well-being, prosperity, and grandeur, when it had the power of so doing.

What I heard and saw in Afghanistan gave me the most profound conviction that the moment the British flag is seen in an Asiatic state the shameless government in force under the native ruler is replaced, if not by abundance, certainly by security and justice. However burdensome the taxation of the English may be, it is always far less so than that extorted by Native princes, who add persecution to rapacity. I have naturally adopted these opinions from hearing the Afghans, so hostile to the English, sigh for the loss of their administrative system. The Sirdars, Mollahs, Syuds, and soldiers, classes who live by plundering the industrious portion of the inhabitants, were always declaiming against the English, because under them they could not practise their iniquities. The people were irritated, it is true, because their prejudices had been shocked, and rose to shake off their yoke; but now they regret them; and I have twenty times heard Afghans speak in terms of just appreciation of what they had done for their good.*

They remembered with gratitude their justice, their gratuitous care of the sick in the hospitals; the presents of money and clothes they received when they left them cured; the repairs of their public works, and the extension of commerce and agriculture owing to their encouragement. These, it is true, were the expressions of a newly-conquered people. They were brave; and it was good policy to tame them with kindness; and they were certainly less taxed than other parts of the British dominions in India, though what I relate is not the less true; and after exhausting all their praises of their unfortunate conquerors, they would finish up by—"What a pity they were not Mussulmans like us; we

* It is satisfactory, to Englishmen generally, to observe the manner in which an intelligent French traveller alludes to their rule in Afghanistan; but, to the few surviving officers of the mission to Herat, it is especially gratifying, as M. Ferrier's impressions are derived from what he witnessed and heard in that quarter. Although the mission to Herat failed in its immediate object, from circumstances by no means discreditable to the officers who composed it, and Major Todd was severely censured for a time, there can be little doubt that, of all our transactions in Afghanistan, there are none on which we can look back with greater pleasure—certainly none more honourable to our creed and country, than our proceedings at Herat.—L.

would never have had any other masters!" After hearing such observations, is it not allowable to regret, in the name of humanity and civilisation, that the British power was not consolidated in Afghanistan, whatever means might have been employed to attain that end? For my part, I should much have preferred it to the melancholy perspective of seeing the country consigned to lasting barbarism, either in the government of its own chiefs, and the continuance of ancient circumstances, or under the influence of Russia, whose civilising tendencies are small indeed.

The Czars have never had any inclination to civilise the masses. The ancient barbarism of the Muscovite empire is modified only in the upper classes. The middle classes and the *mujiks* are just where they were when Ghengis Khan and his Tartars appeared amongst them. How is it, then, that with everything to be done at home, the Emperor of Russia should have the presumption in these days to aspire to be arbiter of the destinies of the Old World? Constantinople, towards which he extends his right hand, appears insufficient for the gratification of his ambition, for the left is at the same time seeking to grasp India. How is it that this empire, that scarcely two centuries ago was almost unknown—certainly had scarcely emerged from the regions of the icy pole—has acquired such preponderance in Europe? Russia has continued to extend the radius of her power from the hour when the Western nations permitted the dismemberment of Poland. The wars at the commencement of that century brought out in relief the real valour of her soldiers; but the fatal disaster of 1812—disaster of which the elements were the principal cause—was wanting to give her the influence that she has possessed ever since. From that epoch must be dated the real importance of Russia. She has never since then neglected an opportunity of throwing her weight into Europe; and her acute foresight is especially observable, when, favoured by events, she co-operated in the reconstruction of the kingdom of Greece. After this she subdued the Tartars.

Since the treaty of Adrianople her influence at the Porte has become almost sovereign: the treaty of Turkmantchai confirmed it equally in Persia. She had nothing then to fear in Asia, and turned towards the West, and threatened to arrest the course of events in France in 1830. Poland, however, her advanced guard, faced about, and, attacking her with vigour, for some months held the sword of Damocles suspended over her head. Thanks to this generous diversion, Europe may yet be called free. Poland, however, has been sacrificed; for, left to her own resources, she sank under the pitiless dominion that she sought so earnestly to shake off. The Russian government, powerless this time to subjugate Europe, threw itself afresh upon Asia, and pushed its encroachments on that side with greater ardour than ever. It approached at the same time Constantinople and Herat. It seeks not impregnable frontiers for itself, for Russia is covered on the south by tremendous natural obstacles; this movement is only the persevering and consistent carrying out of the will of Peter the Great. It is the craving for universal dominion he bequeathed to his successors, and each has endeavoured, so far as in him lay, to accomplish it triumphantly.

The Emperor Nicholas has staked his honour upon it, and he will not rest till he has extended his empire to the Indus in Asia, and to the Dardanelles in Europe. This ambitious project is revealed in all his transactions with the Sultan, and in the pressure that he exerted in 1836 and in 1837 on the Shah of Persia, by obliging him to besiege Herat. The checks that he encountered did not repulse him; they only rendered him more tenacious and more vigilant than ever: but in order that we may be perfectly fair, let us at once acknowledge that the Emperor Nicholas has made but trifling use of the cunning and address so often employed by the English, who are always anxious to keep up appearances on the score of rectitude. He has justified his course by the power of his armies, and cared but little for what the world's opinion of it might be. Taking advantage with much judgment of the opportunity left him of subjugating Turkey and Persia, he made them his vassals. The occupation of the Moldo-Wallachian provinces, which he reserved to himself in the treaty of Adrianople, has enabled him to throw all his weight upon the Divan whenever he wished to alarm the Sultan; and under the same treaty, and that of Turkmantchai, he has enticed into the Transcaucasian provinces the Armenian population subject to the Turks and Persians: in fact, he has neglected no opportunity of placing himself in the position of arbitrator between the Sultan and his subjects. He has been, perhaps, even more exacting with the Shah of Persia, who now governs his own empire only by the prompting of the Czar's will, leaving him the upper hand in the administration of his finest provinces.

If complaint is sometimes made, and with reason, of the little interest manifested by the Indo-British government on certain questions respecting the welfare and moral amelioration of its provinces, what will be said if the veil were removed from the secrets, not very well kept either, of the administration of the Russians in their new conquests? The venality of the public functionaries passes all that the force of imagination can depict; peculations and depredations are permanent; and they so crushed the Christian population (who moved from the Pashalik of Erzeroum and Azerbijan into the province of Erivan), and made them so wretched, that they bitterly regret their migration, and are not deterred from attempts to escape and return to the Mussulman dominions by any severity employed against them if detected.* Such is not the fate of the Christians of the south of Turkey and Persia. Those who emigrate to India find with the English liberty and security, and may always, with a little intelligence, realise a small fortune, which is in no danger from the functionaries of that government—under the Russians all hopes are prematurely blighted.

This contrast between the extension of the Russian empire and its internal disorder shows that the Czar has much to do before he can justify the pretensions he has set up to universal dominion. I repeat, therefore, that the point to be regretted in the conquests of the Russians and the English is, that it will destroy the equilibrium between these nations and other European states, and throw into their hands an amount of power and riches but little encouraging for the political independence of their neighbours. I frankly acknowledge that I look with terror on the success of Russia, for her rule will set barbarism in array against civilisation, and from that antagonism there would be nothing good to hope.

The English nation, in all ages, have prominently shown the love of wealth, and that has induced them to commit many actions not justifiable by European morality; it is not my object to defend those actions, but England has in my eyes partly redeemed the wrongs she has committed by introducing unquestionable ameliorations in the

* The Russian administration has been much improved since this account of it was written, and that of Turkey remains weak and oppressive. The sympathies of the Christians in Turkey are consequently to a great degree with the Russians, but if Turkey improves they will not remain so.—ED.

countries where she has established her power. As it is impossible for me to say the same of Russia, it is easy to understand why my sympathies are not engaged on her side. In conclusion, the other powers of Europe will only have themselves to thank for the misfortunes that these two countries may one day inflict upon them at home—Europe to one, Asia to the other; it will only be the just reward of the indifference with which they have seen their encroachments. Not that I think that the other states ought to have opposed them entirely, but they ought to have co-operated each in due proportion. It would only have required a better understanding amongst themselves; but that was too much trouble! What matter to them these unknown and distant countries? Rather than take the trouble to become acquainted with them, they thought no more about them. England and Russia could desire no better; for while others slept in delusive security they acquired territories which doubled their power. The great European governments will not discover the evil of their want of vigilance till it is past remedy—too late for them to arrest the disastrous consequences.

The foregoing ought naturally to interest the reader in all that concerns India, and he will no doubt be glad to examine the following tabular statement of the extent and population of the British empire in that country, its tributary states and allies, and the independent states on the frontiers. This will show at one glance the immense importance of the interests attached to the safety of the Anglo-Indian possessions.

BRITISH TERRITORY.	Square Miles.	Population.
Presidency of Bengal	328,000	57,500,000
,, Madras	154,000	15,000,000
,, Bombay	11,000	2,500,000
Territory of the Deccan, acquired since 1815, and forming part of the Presidency of Bombay	60,000	8,000,000
	553,000	83,000,000
ALLIES AND NATIONS TRIBUTARY TO THE ENGLISH.		
1. The Rajah of Mysore	27,000	3,000,000
2. The Nizam	96,000	10,000,000
3. The Rajah of Nagpore	70,000	3,000,000
4. The King of Oude	20,000	3,000,000
5. The Guicowar	18,000	2,000,000
6. Bhopal, 5000; Kotah, 6500; Boondi, 2500	14,000	1,500,000
7. The Rajah of Sattara	14,000	1,500,000
8. The Rajah of Travancore, 6000; Cochin, 2000	8,000	1,000,000
9. The Rajah of Jyepore, Odeypore, Bikaneer, and other Chiefs of Rajpootana 10. Holkar 11. Sikhs—Gonds, Bheels, Koolis, and Kattis	288,000	15,000,000
	1,108,000	123,000,000
INDEPENDENT STATES.		
1. Scinde	30,000	4,000,000
2. Rajah of Nepaul	53,000	2,000,000
3. Rajah of Lahore	50,000	3,000,000
4. The Emirs of Scinde	24,000	1,000,000
5. Afghanistan	18,000	1,000,000
General Total	1,283,000	134,000,000

The conquests of Russia during the same period have been as follows :—

	Square Miles.	Population.
Provinces conquered from Poland	10,498	11,950,000
German provinces conquered from Poland and Sweden	735,000	2,715,000
Provinces conquered in European Turkey	4,517,000	1,902,000
Provinces conquered from the Cossacks and Tartars in Europe	4,893,000	3,289,000
Provinces conquered in Asia	115,000	1,500,000
	10,270,498	21,356,000

CHAPTER XXIV.

Remarks on the annexation of the Punjab to the British possessions — Shere Sing, the predecessor of Runjeet — Origin of the Sikh kingdom — The army disciplined by foreign officers — Their advice to Runjeet — Policy of the British Government towards him — Karrack Sing — Nahal Sing — Murders at Lahore — Peshora Sing — Treaty with Dost Mohamed of Kabul — The Maharanee Chanda — Murder of Peshora Sing — Revolt of the Troops — The Maharanee proceeds to the camp — Her brother's just punishment — The Maharanee returns to the palace — Gholab Sing refuses the throne — The Maharanee again in power — Sketch of the campaign in the Punjab — Murder of Messrs. Vans Agnew and Anderson — Fight at the ford of Ramnuggur — Battle of Chillianwallah — Battle of Goojerat — Reflections.

IT will be seen by the foregoing statement that the extension of territory by the Russians is in square miles upwards of ten millions, while that acquired by the English in Asia has been little beyond one million. With the exception of Nepaul and Afghanistan, the powers that are mentioned as independent in the preceding Table (1842) have been brought within the list of conquered countries. Scinde has been annexed, and if we turn our eyes to the Punjab, we shall there find that another fragment of the Afghan kingdom passed under the dominion of the English, apparently without the least wish in the world on the part of the Company.

To persons who look no further back than the events that have happened since the death of Shere Sing, the last king of Lahore but one, it cannot be doubted that the Sikhs were the aggressors, and voluntarily brought upon themselves the hostility of the English; but that is only because the latter, knowing perfectly well the former would some day furnish them with legitimate grounds for an invasion, persevered quietly in a system of ostensible inaction, though it had been their secret policy for years to add the district of the Punjab, or the Five Rivers, to their possessions. It is now theirs; and it is only necessary to say a few words as to the manner in which they succeeded.

The province of the Punjab was raised to the rank of one of the most flourishing kingdoms of Hindostan by the genius of a man of humble birth and without education. Runjeet Singh was originally only a petty chief, and appointed governor of Lahore by the King of the Afghans, Zeman Shah. Favoured by the dissensions between this prince and his brothers, he made himself entirely independent, and soon* added to the province confided to his care Kashmir, Peshawur, Kohat, Dereh Ismael Khan, and Mooltan, which accessions of territory rendered his power equal, if not superior, to that of his former master.

The English, his southern neighbours, did not see without jealousy a state rising into power close to them, which might prevent their encroachments towards the north; and they endeavoured, therefore, secretly to undermine it from the commencement, leaving the Maharajah to believe that they sincerely desired his alliance.†

Runjeet, however, penetrated their designs, and to prepare himself the better to resist them successfully, should a war break out between them, engaged the services of several officers who

---

* Runjeet did not extend his conquests to Kashmir, Mooltan, Peshawur, or even beyond the Jelum, until he was assured of the pacific intentions of the English. It is very doubtful whether he ever required the advice of the French officers in his service to restrain him from attacking us. The characters of the several French officers in the Sikh service have been very well described in the 'Adventurer in the Punjab,' already alluded to.—L.

† A more correct impression of the policy of the English Government may be obtained from Kaye's 'Life of Lord Metcalfe.' A note at page 131 of Lawrence's 'Adventurer in the Punjab,' also describes the circumstances under which Lord Metcalfe made known to Runjeet our wish to restrict him to the Sutlej as a boundary. Kaye has found nothing in Lord Metcalfe's papers referring to the circumstance, and discredits it; but Lawrence's informant had it from Lord Metcalfe's own lips at Agra, in 1837, about the time General Ventura waited on him there by order of Runjeet Singh, and, to the best of his recollection, Lord Metcalfe stated that it occurred at Kussoor.

On taking charge of the Maharajah's treasury at Lahore, in 1849, a small miniature of Lord Metcalfe was found, bearing an inscription, probably in the handwriting of Fakeer Azeezoodeen:—"Mister Charles Metcalfe, Sahib Bahadoor, Dost-Kudeem," (an old friend).

We are indebted to Lord Metcalfe and to Fakeer Azeezoodeen—Runjeet's confidential adviser—for the favourable impression which the old Lion entertained of us, and which he continued to have up to his death, notwithstanding many attempts to arouse his suspicions against us.

It was told the writer of this note at Lahore, in 1849, that when our Government had, through the agent at Loodianah, on one occasion, asked permission of Runjeet Singh for an English traveller to visit Cashmere, Gholab Singh strongly dissuaded the Maharajah from granting it, and expressed his suspicions as to our motives in asking for it. Whereupon Runjeet immediately ordered him away from the Durbar; declared his high confidence in our Government, and his readiness to meet their wishes in every way; and did not permit Gholab Singh to make his appearance again at the Court until he had paid a heavy fine. The person who related this anecdote was the late Fakir Nooroodeen, to whom Englishmen have also been much indebted for many kind offices at Lahore.—L.

had served the Emperor Napoleon—Messrs. Allard, Court, Ventura, and Avitabile (the two first Frenchmen, the third a Milanese, and the fourth a Neapolitan), whose honourable reputation is sufficiently established in Europe for me to dispense with an eulogium here, that has been already so much better made by others. But I cannot refrain from saying that they not only became his right hand in organising the Sikh army on the French system, but by their judicious advice restrained his impetuosity for war when it might have perilled his reputation for ability, and endangered his rising power. This was not the least of the services they rendered him, and those who think differently in Europe know neither Asia nor the character of its inhabitants, and still less the resources of every description possessed by the East India Company.

However that may be, Runjeet Singh always avoided compromising himself with the English; and, without ceasing to mistrust them, he constantly kept up friendly relations with their government, which was eager to support him, with the view of confirming him in the possession of the Afghan provinces which he had seized without right or excuse. It should be added, that if the Directors gave their support on this occasion to Runjeet Singh, it was less from sympathy with that prince than with the intention of preparing the way to gaining eventually for themselves the provinces of which he despoiled the Afghans, and which they had long since destined to be their own, though they had the prudence not to attempt the conquest during the life-time of Runjeet Singh.* If,

* M. Ferrier has misunderstood the policy of the English Government; for, although they occupied Afghanistan for a defensive purpose, which they now know to have been unnecessary, they have had no wish, for many years, to enlarge their territories. They were perfectly satisfied with the Sutlej as a frontier, and it was considered by no means a bad one. Had Runjeet Singh's successors shown equal confidence in our policy, it might have continued our boundary until the present day; but then it is doubtful whether, for years to come, we could have seen railroads in India, or even the completion of the Ganges canal.

When asked, by one of Runjeet Singh's successors, why railroads had not been laid down in India, as well as in England, it was not difficult to make him understand, that while a large insubordinate army occupied the Punjab, threatening our north-western frontier, and talking, freely, of what they were to do at Delhi, Benares, and Calcutta, Government found use for all the spare revenues of India, in keeping up a sufficient force to protect its subjects against such an invasion; but now that this danger no longer exists, and this drain on their resources has been removed, they can afford to pay interest on large advances for railways, and convert their "iradas" (lines of roads marked out—literally "good intentions") into metalled roads. As if to make amends, so far as he could, for having been in any way an obstacle to so great an improvement, he expressed his readiness to take shares in the East India Railway.—L.

after the death of that sovereign in 1839, his kingdom fell rapidly to decay, it was the fault of his heirs and successors, who could not continue his intelligent policy.

His son, Karrack Sing, was a hopeless nobody, poisoned at the end of the first year of his reign, just when his folly had engaged him in a war with the Company, whose army was marching against him 25,000 strong, and stopped on its way only on hearing of his death. His son, Nahal Sing, of whose character some hopes were entertained, was crushed the morning after his accession by the falling of a beam upon his head as he was passing under one of the town gates. The death of these two princes extinguished, according to the opinion of the Sikhs, the legitimate succession from Runjeet Singh; for the old Maharajah had always, right or wrong, disowned his third son, Shere Sing, whose father was said to have been one of the officers of his court.*

He was, however, none the less elevated to the sovereign power at the death of Nahal Sing, and succeeded in suppressing, though not without some trouble, the partial revolts by which he was opposed. This prince possessed sufficient intellect and decision of character to have consolidated his kingdom on the basis established by his father; but his excesses, and particularly the immoderate use of spirituous liquors, turned him from the worthy course on which he had entered.

From that time the Sikhs relaxed in their obedience; there were conspiracies in every town in the Punjab; and, after three years' reign, Shere Sing came, like his predecessors, to a premature death by assassination. It was a general of his own army who committed the treacherous deed on the 15th of September, 1843. Having pretended to the Maharajah that he wished to show him an improvement in the equipment of his dragoons, Ajit Sing brought into the palace court six troopers in the altered uniforms, and drew them up in line for inspection, when, in compliance with his request, Shere Sing placed himself on a balcony to look at them; but the unsuspecting prince had scarcely done so when he received a volley from the villains, one of whose balls struck him on the forehead and laid him dead on the floor.† His unfortunate

* For a correct account of all these events, see 'Cunningham's Sikhs.' Consult also Carmichael's 'Reigning Family in the Punjab.'—ED.

† Ajeet Singh shot the Maharajah with his own hand with a double-barrelled rifle, which he asked the Prince to examine, to throw him off his guard.—L.

young son, Pretab Sing, only ten years of age, who was with him at the time, was murdered with swords while kneeling at his prayers by other remorseless wretches, who had rushed into the palace.

After this atrocious villany, Ajit Sing and his brother, also a general in the army of the murdered king, possessed themselves of the fortress of Lahore, and succeeded in attracting to it the Rajah Dyan Sing, first minister of Shere Sing; they put him to death also, and then appealed to the people in the name of liberty, taking for their motto, "No more masters; death to the English:" for one of the most prominent of the motives for which these insensate men had murdered their sovereign, and summoned their countrymen to arms, was the cordial understanding that existed between him and the East India Company.

To this they attributed all the evils, real or imaginary, that weighed upon the kingdom; but the people showed themselves very little inclined to support them, and the troops, cantoned within a couple of hours' march of Lahore, responded to the harangue of Heera Sing, son of the murdered minister. They declared against his assassins, and arrived in the town the next morning, commanded by General Ventura, when a cannonade of a few hours, and an assault, sufficed to reduce the fortress and place it in the power of the assailants. Ajit Sing and his brother were taken and put to death; but this did not repair the evil they had done, for the difficulty still remained of finding a man capable of holding the reins of government.

The first person thought of was Gholab Singh, the brother of Dyan Singh, a very influential man in the country; but he declined the proffered honour, for his accepting it might have created new difficulties; the Sikhs refused his conditions, and the revolted soldiery threatened his life. In his place therefore was substituted a child, Duleep Singh, whose mother, the Maharanee Chanda, was charged to exercise the ruling power during her son's minority, and she associated with her in quality of regent her brother Jovaher Singh, a man disgraced by more than one crime.

Duleep Singh, the youngest acknowledged son of Runjeet Singh, born about ten months before the old Lion's death, was placed on the throne by the Sikhs. The two first years of his reign were troubled by incessant disasters and crimes provoked by the Sirdars, and an undisciplined soldiery gave the law to the government. The result was general confusion, and the appearance of many pretenders to the throne, of whom Peshora Singh, a prince of the family of Runjeet, supported by Gholab Sing, had succeeded in possessing himself of Sealkote, Attok, and Peshawur, and in drawing to his standard a great part of the army. After these successes he entered into a negotiation with Dost Mohamed of Kabul, promising to cede Peshawur to him if he would assist him in dethroning Duleep Singh. Dost Mohamed readily accepted this advantageous proposition, which would replace under his power the province that had cost so much blood between the Sikhs and Afghans; and that was the arrangement of which Kohendil Khan had spoken to me, concealing at the same time that the alliance of his brother was with the party aspiring to power, and not the party who possessed it. Thus stood the affairs of these two countries when I left Afghanistan, after Dost Mohamed Khan had altered his plan of alliance with the Sikhs on account of the death of Peshora Singh, and some other sanguinary incidents, of which the following is a short summary.

Maharanee Chanda and her brother the regent, Jovaher Sing, seeing the cause of Duleep Singh deserted by the army for that of his competitor, resolved upon putting Peshora Singh out of their way, and for this purpose despatched Chuttur Singh, furnished with a royal firman, countersigned by the queen and her brother, promising to secure the regency to him if he would come to Lahore to take the reins of government, and thus put an end to the dissensions that enfeebled the state. Peshora Singh, to whom the envoy had also remitted a false letter with the pretended sign and seal of Gholab Singh at the bottom of it, begging him to accept the regency, acted under the advice which he supposed emanated from his protectors, and imprudently started with Chuttur Singh for the capital, accompanied only by a few servants, and leaving at Attok the troops that were devoted to him.*

This was a most unfortunate determination, for on the journey, in the night of the 13th of September, 1845, Chuttur Singh entered his tent and beheaded the prince as he lay asleep. The ill-fated

* For a correct account of the murder of Peshora Singh, see Cunningham's 'Hist. of the Sikhs.' Cunningham's facts may be generally depended upon, although his inferences are not always correct. Chuttur Singh was a chief of rank and influence in the time of Runjeet; Peshora Singh was murdered at Attok.—L.

victim was then only a few leagues from Lahore, and a vague rumour of the crime reached the garrison; the soldiers rose in the utmost indignation against the authors of it, and devoted three whole days to the most minute investigation as to what had befallen Peshora Singh, but the search was entirely fruitless.

On the 16th of September they presented themselves tumultuously before the residence of Jovaher Singh, and imperatively demanded his acknowledgment of the crime and the details respecting it, or the immediate liberation of the prince if he were still alive and a prisoner. The regent swore to them that he was alive and would be in Lahore in a few days; and sought by a thousand subterfuges to calm their just irritation. His reply not having satisfied any one, on the morning of the 17th a deputation of officers claimed an audience of the queen, to obtain authentic information; threatening, in case of refusal, to put her to death, with the rest of the royal family. Maharanee Chanda ordered three of her ministers to accompany this deputation back to the camp, charged, she said, to give explanations to the troops; but they, instead of satisfying them, gave evasive replies to their most searching questions, and attempted to appease them with valuable presents, which were indignantly refused. The ministers saved their lives only by declaring that the prince was still alive; and pacified for a short space by this reiterated assurance, the soldiers waited the return of Peshora Singh till the morrow, when, as he did not arrive, they broke out in the most fearful tumult.

The queen, perceiving the imminence of the danger, resolved to tell the truth to the negotiators of the previous day, and desire them to inform the troops of the prince's death; to represent the inutility of their menaces and lamentations, as they could not recall him to life; and to recommend them to resign themselves, and resume their tranquillity, as the only rational course in such a case. This advice procured the envoys very bad treatment; and, having given them in charge to the camp-guard, the troops went in a body to the palace, and, with terrific shouts and howlings, commanded the queen and her brother to show themselves, and justify their conduct, on pain of immediate death. They also informed them of their intention of replacing Duleep Singh by a son of Shere Sing's, yet alive.

The negotiations lasted till the 20th of September; Jovaher Singh strongly advised that the palace should be defended to the last, and, as a prelude to the defence, to commit another murder. The son of the unfortunate Shere Sing was in the palace, and Jovaher Singh wanted to throw this young prince's head at the insurgents.* Happily one of the ministers, sent from the guard at the camp by the troops with a truce, arrived at this juncture, and persuaded the Queen of the utter uselessness of this new crime, and the perfect security in which she might place her own life and that of her son. The Maharanee was for once convinced, and, besides, seeing herself abandoned by her servants, she no longer refused to surrender to the troops. In the evening of the 21st she took her way towards the camp situated on the plain of Miyan Mir, carried in a palanquin, and followed by the Regent and the King Duleep Singh, mounted on the same elephant; a very scanty escort of women and devoted servants accompanied them. Half way to their destination the royal party met several battalions of infantry coming from the camp in a state of great irritation to assault the palace, under the impression that the Maharanee still refused to come out to them and justify herself; but seeing her on her way, accompanied by her son and brother, they ranged themselves in silence on each side of the cortege of degraded royalty, and escorted them into the camp, where the Queen was at once made prisoner, and placed in a soldier's tent.

They then ordered the man who drove the elephant, on which were seated the youthful King and his guilty regent, to make the animal kneel, to enable them to remove Duleep Singh from the howdah. While the boy was being lifted out, the soldiers fired a volley at Jovaher Singh, which caused the elephant to swerve, and the child, bespattered with his uncle's blood, to fall forward into his servant's arms. Jovaher Singh fell dead in the howdah. Duleep Singh was then placed under a guard in the same tent as his mother. With the wretch Jovaher, whose life was stained with so many crimes, died two of his principal officers, who had advised and participated in all his villanies; this execution having satisfied the troops, the Queen and her son were kept in the camp all night. On the following morning they were allowed to return to the palace; being warned, for the hundredth time, not to treat with the English, as she valued her own life and that of her son, for the

* The circumstances here stated may be true, but have not been mentioned by any previous writer.—L.

most frightful deaths awaited them if she should transgress the injunction.

Maharanee Chanda, overwhelmed by the death of her brother, at first refused to direct the affairs of the government; and as a report of the advance of the English to invade the Punjab was then very generally credited by the Sikhs, the position appeared sufficiently critical to some of the chiefs; for they decided upon writing to Gholab Sing, who had retired to Jamboo, to put himself at their head, promising to bring the troops to passive obedience, to renounce all augmentation of pay, and the settlement of their arrears. The old Rajah had once before been taken in the same snare, had trusted to the same false promises; his life had been in great jeopardy in the midst of the undisciplined troops, and was preserved only by a species of miracle. He refused therefore to respond to the appeal of the Sirdars; he sent them, however, one of his lieutenants, named Miyan Perthi Singh, charged to make known to them the conditions on which he would act, of which the following is the tenor:—

1st. To place absolute power in his hands.

2nd. To give him the right of life and death over the nobles, the people, and the army.

3rd. The pay of the soldiers to be reduced to what it was in the reign of Runjeet Singh.

Such was then the state of anarchy, and the necessity of a strong government at Lahore, that these hard conditions were accepted almost without an exception; Gholab Sing had hoped the contrary; and finding himself at a difficulty for an excuse for not accepting the responsibility, pretended that ill health detained him in the mountains, and never went to Lahore. The Sirdars, therefore, were driven to ask the Queen to assume once more the royal authority, and she consented, not, however, without expressing her resentment at the death of her brother, and her determination to punish the assassins. She also made known her disapprobation of the application to Gholab Sing, promising, however, to think no more of it if his lieutenant was sent to a safe retreat, and sharply watched, to prevent his interfering with the government. The Sirdars having given up these points, she resumed her power with truly masculine spirit; but she was feebly seconded by the ambitious chiefs. It was impossible for her to re-establish order in the country; and, unable to oppose a contest with the

English, for which the troops were clamorous, she was obliged to permit it to save her own life and her son's. The time had arrived when the fate of the Punjab was to be accomplished.

[The Sikhs having crossed the Sutlej in the following December, to attack the English, were beaten by them, and driven back to the river, near Sobraon, making their retreat in great disorder, after very heavy losses, and the Indo-British army entered Lahore without further opposition. Then came the first phase of subjection in this nation, so proud and so hostile to the English, who, in order to carry out to the last the appearance of moderation, hitherto so well maintained, placed themselves simply in the position of the protectors of royalty and the pacificators of the country. Duleep Singh was maintained in the sovereign power, and provided with ministers of his own nation; but their nomination being subordinate to the good pleasure of the English, the British resident was, in fact, the supreme governmental power at Lahore. The army, re-organised, was commanded by British officers exclusively;* and as the old Sirdar, Gholab Singh, had had the dexterity to preserve the friendship of the protectors, he was provided with the independent government of Kashmir, on condition of paying annually, and only for the purpose of constituting a species of vassalage, the tribute of a shawl and a goat. This province was as difficult for them to invade as to preserve; and the English had quite enough work on their hands in the Punjab without going to Kashmir to seek for more. The appointment of Gholab Sing, therefore, was a very good means of establishing the rights of sovereignty over it, until an opportunity offered of rendering its subjection as complete as that of the Punjab.

It was evident that a people so irritated against the English as the Sikhs were sure to turn against them the little liberty they had left; and consequently the British agents passed the first two years in the midst of continual agitation, at which in secret they were not altogether displeased—they, therefore, allowed them to continue without slackening the vigilance necessary in such cases. However, not to exhibit weakness, the Maharanee being actually

* In this M. Ferrier is incorrect. The French officers had certainly left or been removed from the Sikh army, but no British officers were substituted in command of brigades or battalions. The army was officered by natives of the Punjab in whom the Durbar had confidence.—L.

detected in the act of conspiring against them, was exiled. Her firmness had been a great obstacle to the completion of their object, and the obstacle was thrown down; but they were careful not to calm the turbulence of the Sikhs, and the system soon bore its fruit.

In 1848, one of their chiefs, Diwan Moolraj, governor of Mooltan, preceded a revolt by the murder of two British officers, Messrs. Vans Agnew and Anderson, excited, it is said, thereto, by the native ministers of Duleep Singh, installed in power by the English. At this signal the whole of the west of the kingdom rose in arms, from Mooltan northwards to the province of the Hazarahs. Various circumstances at first authorized the supposition, and there was soon no doubt of the fact, that Gholab Sing favoured the insurrection. The Sirdar Chuttur Singh, and his son Shere Sing, after having quitted the English party, held the country against them with very considerable forces, while Moolraj kept a portion of their army in check under the walls of Mooltan, into which he had retired. On the other side, the Afghans, with Dost Mohamed at their head, appeared to interfere and complicate the business. The English had heavy work on their hands there; at first their military operations were far from flourishing, and several checks which they received from the Sikhs warned them of the danger of their position. Fresh forces were brought up from Lahore to the points on which they were required, and General Sir H. Gough, Commander-in-chief of the British forces in India, joined them, to direct in person the military operations in the Punjab. On the 22nd of November, 1848, they came up with one of the insurgent chiefs, the Sirdar Shere Sing, encamped with his army on the borders of the Chenab, near a ford known by the name of Ramnuggur; there they attacked him without any beneficial result, and the loss of the English was great, especially in officers. But this unfortunate engagement was soon followed by a brilliant victory.

On the 21st of January, 1849, General Whish, charged with the siege of Mooltan, had reduced the fort, and made Moolraj, the prime mover in the revolt, his prisoner. This advantage ought to, and would, have been sufficient to bring the war to a satisfactory conclusion for the English, if, nearly at the same time, a check of a very different character from that at Ramnuggur, and which caused the liveliest uneasiness as to the pacification of the Punjab, had not occurred. In an ill-fated moment, General Gough, without having made himself sufficiently acquainted with the ground, and perfected his combinations, decided on offering battle to Shere Sing in his encampment at Chillianwallah.

It was the 13th of January, 1849; the battle was bloody, and the English, charging the well-chosen position of their enemies, had the misery of seeing their best troops, three regiments of European cavalry, take flight before the Sikhs, with such precipitation, that neither death nor wounds took place in their ranks; and they rode with such impetuosity through their own guns, that they involuntarily killed and wounded many of the gunners, upset the pieces and caissons, and threw the whole park of artillery into the utmost confusion.*

This affair cost them six guns, eight flags, and 2500 men, amongst whom were 97 officers of various grades. When the news arrived in England, there was an universal cry of anathema against the unhappy general, who had so imprudently compromised the reputation of the British arms, and, in the panic which seized them, the Directors of the Company, managing the affairs from their counting-house in London, sent two officers to succeed him in the command; first, Sir William Gomm from the Mauritius, and a few days afterwards, Sir Charles Napier; but, in their anxiety, they forgot to revoke the authority of General Gough, and consequently, some time after, three Commanders-in-chief met at Calcutta!†

As the commission of Sir Charles Napier bore the latest date, the government there decided in his favour, but in any case he arrived too late to revenge the disaster suffered by the British at Chillianwallah. General Gough did not leave him the opportunity, for, on the 15th of February, he gave battle again to Shere Sing at Goojerat, completely routed him, and took all his artillery. The victory was decisive; the vanquished were hotly pursued, and chiefs and soldiers

* M. Ferrier is mistaken; there was only one regiment of Europeans.—L.

† The appointment of the commander-in-chief, like that of all important functionaries in India, rests with the English Cabinet; and in this case Sir W. Gomm, who was then at the Mauritius, was first appointed. Subsquently, when the intelligence arrived of the reverse of Chillianwallah, the expression of public opinion was so strong in favour of Sir Charles Napier, as the man for the crisis, that the Government were obliged to send him out. The war, however, was concluded before he arrived. He shortly afterwards had a difference with Lord Dalhousie, threw up his command in disgust, and was succeeded by Sir William Gomm.—ED.

ended by making unqualified submission to the British army. This event entirely removed the tarnish that had for a moment shadowed the reputation of General Gough, and changed his failure into a brilliant triumph, which the Queen rewarded by raising him to the rank of Viscount. The precipitation with which he had been condemned in London was absurd, for it was evident that the English army, placed as it was in a plain country, and mistress of the mouths and course of the Indus up to its highest ramifications, which come close upon the province of Lahore, whence it drew supplies of men, money, provisions, and munition of every sort, could have but little to fear from the conspiracy. The same may be said of all the states on the north and west of the great stream,—they must, as in this instance, yield to the superiority of European tactics. England took possession of the countries which the revolt of Mooltan had been intended to snatch from her army, and converted them into English provinces; and her wise policy in government in the course of a few years will double the million and a half of revenue it had hitherto produced. It is not only in a financial point of view that this conquest will be profitable to the East India Company, who will henceforth derive from it the greatest advantages, statistical, military, and geographical, as well as commercial.

If this simple summary of the events that led to the entire subjugation of the Punjab should induce the reader to consult the more ample documents respecting it, published by the British press, he will soon see that England had for many years previously anticipated and prepared the annexation of these provinces. It was at first under the most friendly appearances that her diplomacy was accepted in the time of Runjeet. She caressed and flattered him, supported him in his quarrels with the Afghans, and, under the name of ally, took root in his dominions, to prepare secretly for the future invasion.

If the East India Company's army did not take possession of the Punjab at the death of the Maharajah, it was because its services were required in China and Afghanistan. But the English are not wanting in patience, and they know how to wait in order the better to assure themselves of ultimate success.

While the accomplishment of the conquest of Lahore was in abeyance, the British resident, with much talent, let the weight of his unseen influence be felt, and quietly excited on the one hand,

and suppressed on the other; he divided the chiefs, and brought them into his views without appearing to interfere in their affairs, till at last the furious hatred of the Sikhs against the English was abated; he turned their passions with dexterity against the successive Maharajahs instead, by apparently giving to each his interest and support. Acting thus, by the mediation of their agent, the Company well knew itself to be in the best position for exciting a contest with the Sikhs, and from that would arise, as they were well aware, its mediation and protection in the Punjab, taking with it a brave and numerous army, well practised in European tactics, to control as a sovereign all the actions of the native government, and to banish the Queen Chanda to Benares when she opposed them. When the irritation of the people increased and they conspired, the Company never interfered; for they knew they had time enough to make their preparations for converting their protection into permanent invasion. At last the revolt took place; the English battalions arrived to put it down, and, beaten at first, they finished by a victory that put them in possession of the country; there was no farther difficulty, for everything comes to an end for him who knows how to wait for it, and England has proved that she does.* It is, above all, by that virtue patience, and the Roman maxim—"Divide and conquer"—that she has subjugated in turn Moguls, Mahrattas, Belooches, and so many other Indian nations, whose wealth she has carried to her island home.

---

* M. Ferrier's idea is very natural, though by no means correct. There are Englishmen in India who act from higher motives than those for which he gives them credit. The Resident at Lahore was not a man to use his influence in the way M. Ferrier supposes. He acted in the best faith for the interests of both Governments; and so far from desiring the annexation of the country, on finding that it could not be avoided, and that all his efforts to uphold the native Government were unavailing, Sir H. Lawrence was only prevented from resigning his high position, and returning to his regiment, as a captain of artillery, at the earnest entreaty of his friends. He remained at Lahore almost with the sole object of exerting his influence to conciliate the chiefs and people of the Punjab to our rule. In the same good faith did our soldiers at Mooltan, Ramnugger, and Chillianwallah, give their lives in support of the authority of the existing Government, but—in the inscrutable wisdom of Divine Providence—not with their usual success; and it was not until after every man of influence in the Punjab, *except two*, (as Shere Sing said) had made overtures to him, and the utter impossibility of carrying on a native Government with such instruments became apparent, that the battle of Goojerat was fought, and the annexation of the Punjab forced upon Lord Dalhousie. That the result has been beneficial to the Punjab and to India, and may yet, with God's blessing, be still more so, who can doubt?—L.

The conquest of the Punjab has admirably completed the succession of invasions, and secured to her the finest empire in the world. It would perhaps be wise were she to stop here, and be content with her present power: but can she? Does the thundering torrent arrest itself in a course where it meets with no obstacles; or even where it does? Such is the British torrent. Descending from the snow-clad summits of the Himalaya, it will yet submerge Nepaul, Birmah, China, and its dependencies; turning to the East, it will once more inundate Afghanistan, and overturn the citadel of Herat. Little does this vast extension of territory by the British Empire appear to signify to the other European states; they seem perfectly indifferent, and the prophecy that it would crumble of itself, either by the effects of revolt or bankruptcy, has been so constantly repeated that the world has finished by believing it. Well, I predict that indifference will cost you, if not your liberty—because England loves liberty and practises it—at least your political independence, and you will submit to the law that you have not dared to give to this gigantic invader. She will divide the world with the other Colossus.] *

* General Ferrier appears altogether to have overlooked America in this prospective view of future history.—ED.

CHAPTER XXV.

The Author taken ill — His sufferings at this time — Singular disease of Mohamed Azim Khan — Visit of his brother to the author — Monsieur Ferrier's dinners improve—Murder of one of his guards—The Author's reflections on his own fate —Attacked with Cholera — The knowing soldier-priest — Dreadful mortality in the town — Fanaticism of the Mollahs — Protection afforded to Monsieur Ferrier by Kohendil Khan — Attack upon the Author's house — Gallant conduct of the soldiers — Advance of the troops sent by the Sirdar — Defeat of the mob — Monsieur Ferrier escorted from the town — Arrives at Girishk — Lal Khan's explanation of the riot at Kandahar — The author again confined — Rascally conduct of Sedik Khan — Monsieur Ferrier leaves Girishk — Boundaries of the Belooches — Nigiari — Mian-pushteh — Benader Kalan — Hazar-juft — Affray with the villagers there — The author returns to Girishk — Zirok — Biabanak and Paiwak — Washeer — Koh i Duzdan — Ibrahimi and Shiaguz — Short commons — The escort and the shepherd — Morality of an Afghan horseman — Their gossip when travelling — Treatment of their horses — A cool hand — Khoormalek — Crypts at Shiaguz.

BUT to return from this political digression. On September 4th and 5th, ennui, the intense heat, privations and bad food—for it had been good only the first few days – threw me into a violent inflammatory fever. I raved all night, became prostrated by weakness, and found it impossible to stand up; my guards stood stupidly by looking at me, and saw my sufferings without taking the slightest care of me. I was destitute of medicine, for Mohamed Sedik Khan had stolen mine with my other things, and my sole resource was the filthy water of the tank in the garden. Kohendil Khan had not authorized me to hire a servant, so that I was in a fearful state of combined suffering and helplessness, which I felt most acutely. At one time the blood rushed so violently to my head, that I feared it would suffocate me; no barber would bleed me lest he should be defiled by the blood of an infidel, and it was necessary to procure a positive order to oblige one of them to perform the operation, that I might have this most necessary relief. Great God! what misery!

September 6th.—The bleeding did me so much good that, though still weak, I could accept the invitation to go on horseback to the house of the Sirdar Rahimdil Khan; the Asiatics look upon all Europeans as doctors, and he had sent for me to see his eldest son, Mohamed Azim Khan, who was dangerously ill. He was a fine young man, about four-and-twenty years of age, who had been stretched on the bed of sickness and pain for fifteen months, from a periodical hemorrhage by which he lost ten or twelve pounds of blood at each attack; it was accompanied by dryness of the skin, and he looked like a skeleton. He spoke a few words, but with the utmost difficulty, and was nearly deaf; his left eye was covered with a thick film, the glands round his throat were enormously swollen, and his life evidently hung upon a thread. The cholera shortly after probably hastened his death by a few days only. When I left him, I visited his father and uncle Mirdil Khan (both younger brothers of Kohendil Khan),* who were surrounded by personages of rank and importance. They were very polite to me, but very reserved, and their conversation concerned only the condition of the sick man; they carefully abstained from touching upon any other subject, and their brother's susceptibilities on the subject of government, no doubt, impressed this caution upon them. I implored them in vain to intercede for me for a little less rigorous treatment, but I could get neither promise nor even answer, and I returned desolate to my prison.

September 7th.—Nevertheless to-day there was some relaxation of the measures taken respecting me, and Mohamed Alem, the second son of Rahimdil Khan, obtained permission of his uncle to visit me: I was the more pleased at this as the young noble appeared more highly gifted than his countrymen: he was about seventeen years of age, with a countenance expressive of rare intelligence, and appeared at once to take the part of a friend towards me. I tried a thousand devices to ascertain the real object of his visit, without success, and I could come to no precise conclusion; the extent to which Asiatics can practise dissimulation is incredible, even in children. It is more easy to penetrate the designs of the Afghans than any others; but this young man seemed to me to place himself out of that category, for he said the only object of his visit to me was to improve himself in the English language by conversation. With a few books and the help of a Moonshee, who could barely spell, he had succeeded in acquiring some knowledge of it, and could write and speak it a little; he had a surprising organization. Indeed he belonged to the

* Mirdil means, in Persian, "the friendly hearted;" kohendil "the strong hearted;" "rahimdil, "the merciful hearted."—ED.

Mohamedzyes, who form a remarkable exception to other Afghans. Their intelligence is as extensive and developed as the generality of their countrymen are usually contracted and brutal. This young man's visit was the only agreeable hour I passed in Kandahar.

September 8th.—Since my audience with Kohendil Khan I had had most wretched fare, and it was very difficult for me to reconcile this treatment with his almost kind reception. Why not treat me as before my visit? I could not find out. Boiled rice or maize, or a water melon, had been my diet for two days; but as even that was very superior to what I had had at Girishk I did not complain, and only begged for some tea or broth, of which being so ill I much felt the want, but my request was refused. Mohamed Alem, to whom I related my grievances on his next visit, assured me his uncle had ordered that I should have everything that I wished for; and I was the more inclined to believe it because I saw the enormous pilau, with other meats and fruits, that was brought every day and set aside till evening by the guards because it was the period of some fast, which lasted several days, and they could not eat them till night came on, when they devoured them without offering me a morsel. Unluckily for them my complaints to the young Sirdar caused a change in their capital regime; and the same day I was provided with most comfortable meals brought by one of the kitchen attendants, who waited till I had eaten what I liked and carried away the remainder, not leaving them the opportunity to touch a single dish.

September 9th.—The same scene was repeated; Lal Khan and his acolytes were furious at my having deprived them of such good rations, and they took their revenge by insulting me in every way; their glances were daggers, and I saw they were looking out for an opportunity to pay me off. But former suffering had hardened me, and caring little to annoy myself about them I slept soundly without fancying what their evil designs might be. One night when fast asleep I felt myself roughly seized by the arm, and on opening my eyes they met the savage face of Lal Khan foaming with rage, while he pointed to some wretched verses that, deploring my fate in a moment of great depression, I had scribbled with a pencil on the wall. In these lines Lal Khan saw a complete conspiracy, a project of invasion, I know not what—a thousand fooleries, of which he made a lamentable history to the

Sirdar. Kohendil Khan immediately sent his nephew, Mohamed Alem, to ascertain the truth of the crime imputed to me. I had no difficulty in making my young friend understand the cause of the exaggerated fears of the captain of my guard, and was soon relieved from the persecutions that he had hoped to bring down upon me. Finding this plan had failed, Lal Khan became furious, and wreaked his vengeance on a poor wretch who could not help himself; but it was the only means left him of adding to the bitterness of my position, and he failed not to use it.

The greater number of soldiers forming my guard were Sunnite Mussulmans; three or four only being Shiahs, one of whom had been in the service of the English and well treated by them. This man had at different times done me little services, in acknowledgment of which I had made him some trifling presents; for these he had shown himself grateful, and therefore Lal Khan sought to pick a quarrel with him, and did so on a sufficiently frivolous pretence. Mohamed Ali, for that was his name, replied with all the curtness of manner habitual to the Afghans. The Khan grew angry, and by degrees the reprimand relating to the service assumed the character of a religious discussion; he overwhelmed the Shiah with epithets insulting to his faith, and the other retaliated upon the characters of Omar, Osman, and Aboubekr, but the unhappy being had scarcely pronounced the maledictions against the three caliphs condemned by his sect, when twenty daggers were plunged in his breast. Attracted by his cries, I rushed into the court just in time to see him fall dead, in the midst of a band of villains, who hacked his corpse with their sabres, dragged it to the middle of the bazaars, and finally hung it on a hook where every one cursed and spat upon it. To curse Omar and his two successors is a crime deserving of a thousand deaths in the eyes of the Sunnites, and before so many witnesses as Lal Khan could have furnished of the guilt of Mohamed Ali, Kohendil Khan himself dared not have blamed his people for having committed the murder. I was shocked at the sight, and could not help looking at my own position in the worst possible light—it was frightful.

For three months I had been in Afghanistan, subject to dangers of every description, and nothing seemed to indicate the probability of a termination to my captivity. Perfectly isolated from every living being that took the slightest interest in me, my reflections grew more and more gloomy, and I knew not whether to wish for liberty or death; the former would only leave me utterly without protection amongst the ferocious Afghans, the latter would terminate all my troubles at once. Not a friend was near me, and those who showed me the smallest sympathy paid for it with their lives like Mohamed Ali. Guards, jailers, and perhaps executioners,—these were the people constantly before my eyes: at last I renounced the hope of seeing my country again, and resigned myself to my fate—to die, far from my relations and friends, and lay my bones in some corner which no one would ever suppose to be the grave of a poor and adventurous French soldier. Sleep, which I courted in the hope of forgetting my misery, proved only a continuance of it, for it was ever harassed and broken by some fearful dream; to the anxieties of the mind were added very acute physical sufferings; I endured torture. My trials were too much for my resignation, and I felt myself sinking under them.

September 10th.—The next morning one of my guards, seeing me absorbed in sad reflections, said to me, "Have patience; in three days you will be off, *Murakhas*." * This news slightly raised my hopes, but the same evening a communication from Mohamed Alem Khan revived all my anxiety. He had been at his uncle's on the previous evening and heard him say that I was certainly an Englishman, that my Persian firmans had been written for some other person and not for me, and that I was sent into Afghanistan by the Indo-British Government to raise the people against their legitimate sovereigns. "It is," he said, "Mohamed Sedik Khan who has sent this information, with the proofs, to his father."

September 11th.—After having passed a most anxious and feverish night, I was at daybreak seized with cramps and vomiting, and dysentery left me no rest. I felt as if I were dying. At all risks I insisted on being bled again, from which I derived great benefit in my last attack, and by the evening the bad symptoms had entirely disappeared. Mohamed Alem came to see me in the evening, and from him I learned that the cholera had been in Kandahar seven or eight days, and it was the cholera that I had had; the deaths had begun at 15 to 20 per day, but on the previous one they had been quadrupled.

The society of this young noble continued to be a great pleasure

* This is what a superior says to an inferior in dismissing him.—ED.

for me, and in some degree alleviated the miseries of my captivity; he was really amiable and kind, and had all the frank and open manner natural to his age. Still I perceived that he lent some credence to the notion that I entertained the hostile intentions towards his uncle that were attributed to me. He tried an infinity of ways to penetrate my supposed secret and bring me to confess that I knew English, which he so much wished me to help him to learn; that would, he thought, have been a conclusive proof of my nationality, and I was most fortunate in concealing that I knew the elementary part of that language. The perseverance of my young friend was such that I was at last sharp with him, and he retired angry; I never saw him again, and regretted it, for his natural disposition was excellent; living however amongst Afghans, it must of necessity be soon modified.

September 12th.—Twelve of my guard died to-day of cholera. Having seen me set up by bleeding they adopted the remedy; but, as if Providence intended to punish their brutality to me, it did not succeed with any one of them, and they were terribly decimated afterwards. I saw them frequently thumping and rubbing each other most vigorously, and I believe that such treatment might be useful as a preservative by keeping up the circulation and drawing it to the surface.

September 13th.—The intensity of the scourge reached its climax: upwards of four hundred persons died yesterday. The soldiers of my guard tried all kinds of extravagant remedies which their superstitious countrymen suggested. One of them was the son of a mollah, and he, pretty well versed in ecclesiastical lore, indulged them with sermons recommending the most inconceivable absurdities; his stupid brethren in arms looked upon his words as divine, and after having collected fifty more comrades they all marched in procession round the court, he having placed himself in one corner. There he held the Koran above his head wrapped in a sash, of which two persons held each an end. Each soldier on arriving opposite the holy book, kissed it upon the sash, carried it to his forehead in sign of his respect, and at the same time slipped a few sous into the hand of their knowing comrade, who for this contribution recited some short prayers which he said would infallibly preserve them from the malady. This ceremony was renewed after every prescribed prayer, five times in the day. I looked on with an apathy that provoked glances the malevolence of which could not be misunderstood. Lal Khan was offended at my indifference, and said savagely, "As you do not approve of our proceedings get back into your room, you infidel dog; you have not the blessing of being a Mussulman; you will never kiss the holy Koran, and if you die it will be all reprobate as you are." The same ceremony was performed in every part of the town; many families, whether happily spared or not, purchased as many oxen, sheep, horses, and camels as they could afford, killed them, and distributed the meat to appease the wrath of Heaven. When night came, crowds of people went upon the terraces of their houses and filled the air with mournful cries, invoking Allah, Mohamed, Omar, and company; and these lugubrious noises probably determined many cases of cholera that perhaps might have been saved had they preserved silence and quiet as religiously as they made these prolonged and terrifying howlings.

September 14th.—Seven or eight hundred persons died in Kandahar this day. Consternation was visible on every face; the plague was terrible in the villages also, and the people from the country came into the town in the hope of reaching a place of safety; on the contrary, the poor people only found it worse, and aggravated the evils in that dense population. The doctors and the mollahs had been assembled for three days consecutively, consulting as to the means of putting an end to the misery at once, as they had promised the people they would do. But their faithful believers had waited in vain, and began to murmur and threaten violence; reports of poisoned wells and bread spread amongst the masses, and it became dangerous to allow the discussions of an ignorant populace to continue any longer. The position was a perilous one, and the puzzle amongst the Ulemas great, when one whose wits were rather sharper than the rest, exclaimed on a sudden, "Mussulmans, it is in vain that you search the depths of science, fast and mortify yourselves, to ascertain the cause of the evil: the decrees of Providence are inscrutable. But the great God sometimes allows his creatures, especially the faithful, to see in a dream the reasons of his wrath against them. Believe me, illustrious and learned brothers, it is not far from us. It was revealed to me in a dream last night by the angel Gabriel. While Ahmed Shahi (Kandahar, from the name of its founder) is sullied by the presence of an infidel, the enemy of God and man," said he, in a voice of thunder, "there will be no cessation of your affliction." The sally was too direct to be mistaken. I was the infidel pointed out to their vengeance. A council was held instantly as to the best course to pursue, and eight of the principal mollahs proceeded to Kohendil Khan and demanded my head. This the Sirdar decisively refused; there was a long discussion, but he braved their menaces, and to prevent them from executing their purpose locked them up in a room, while he sent a strong guard to my residence. He also sent in the utmost haste provisions and ammunition, enjoined us to barricade ourselves and carefully watch for the event that he anticipated. The cries of the populace obliged him at the expiration of a few hours to release the mollahs; they were furious, and followed by a dense crowd proceeded to the mosque; it would not contain them all, so they removed to the public square, where they harangued the crowd in a manner to increase their fanaticism and excite them to revenge upon me the injury they had received from the Sirdar. A messenger appeared soon after from Kohendil Khan; he followed them there, being charged to address them in the opposite strain, and remind them that the duties of hospitality were sacred; he alleged that I was not come amongst them as an enemy or a spy, but trusting entirely to their good faith. The mollahs replied that all laws and usages might be broken towards an infidel. The masses took this up immediately and proceeded to my prison to exterminate me, but having been received with a sharp volley of musketry, they fled, crying out "To arms." The mollahs, of whom one was wounded, returned to the square, where they set up a pole and the Koran on the top of it, which was reverently saluted by every Mussulman that passed, as in former times Gessler's hat had been in Switzerland. The crowd took an oath on this venerated symbol, neither to eat, drink, nor bathe until they had cut me to pieces and thrown my body to the dogs of the bazaars. This demonstration against me took place about eleven in the forenoon, and at five in the evening a sharp file-firing was opened on the house from the ramparts on which the insurgents had placed themselves; but finding they were too far off, they advanced into the houses in my neighbourhood. As the one I inhabited commanded nearly all the others, we had a great advantage over our assailants. I had a few moments of anxiety lest the soldiers intended for my guard should join the rioters, but it was soon dispelled, and those who had the most ill-used me fought as zealously as the men who had reinforced them. They were all men devoted to Kohendil Khan, who had followed him into exile in Persia, from 1839 to 1841, and their hatred of me vanished before their devotion to a positive order from him to defend me. Seeing their excellent feeling, I roused myself from the torpor that had crept over me and joined in the defence, and as the Afghans have a high opinion of European officers, they, with an abnegation of self-love which I was far from expecting in them, accepted my advice. In consequence, I distributed my little party on the terrace in the manner that seemed to me most suitable to defend the point most likely to be attacked; I also placed two sections of reserve in the court to defend the entrance. For seven hours we were regularly besieged; three men were wounded on our side, and it was impossible to ascertain the loss of our adversaries: after fourteen hours' rest, hostilities recommenced, the insurgents having employed the interval in parleying with Kohendil Khan, who had removed to the citadel, where he was free from danger; but the Sirdar rejected all their demands, and tried to put them off with promises instead, with which they were in no way satisfied.

September 15th.—At two o'clock in the afternoon they opened fire upon us again; it was like that of the previous evening, continual, but causing little loss of life. At night, under cover of the darkness, many of these fanatics, following the windings of the small stream which flowed by the walls of the house, reached the entrance door, which they soon forced; we let them alone, because there was an inner door which would prove a fresh obstacle more difficult to overcome. As soon as they had succeeded in getting into the vestibule and thought they had us quite safe, they were saluted with a point-blank fire from loop-holes which we had made in the walls, and immediately after we forced away the props of the worm-eaten ceiling and it came down upon their heads; those who were not crushed or suffocated by the rubbish, retreated wonderfully knocked about into the crowd that filled the street. The reflux caused by this movement created a panic amongst the people, which, from the inside, and owing to the darkness, we could not see; we could only judge by the cries of distress raised by this sanguinary mob. Our continuous fire completely ploughed them up, and the clearance became general; by nine in the evening the place was perfectly swept and our enemies retired to a respectful distance out of our reach. Their loss was great in the last encounter.

September 16th.—Part of this day we were left quiet, but at five in the evening we were attacked the third time, and with a vigour from which I boded no good. The surrounding terraces were covered with rioters, the projectiles beat like hail on our house, and in a twinkling we had seven men killed and more than double that number wounded; in vain the reserves from the terraces came down to our aid, they only added to the evil, for the more numerous we were the worse their fire told upon us. At nine I saw that our position was desperate; we could not have held out another half-hour, when to our great astonishment the enemy suddenly disappeared on hearing the report of sharp firing towards the citadel. There Kohendil Khan had temporised and amused the people for the two first days, it being quite impossible for him to repress these fanatics with the two or three hundred sepoys that he had at that time with him; but at the commencement of the riots he had sent orders to the cavalry dispersed in the neighbourhood to come into Kandahar, and uniting at a given spot, to enter the town and charge the mob in the rear; this diversion obliged them to face about; they sustained the unexpected shock but for a moment, and were completely put to the rout. The principal mollahs having been arrested, tranquillity was restored—to our great satisfaction, for we had been watching and fighting for two nights.

The excitement of the last forty-eight hours had been great, I therefore slept soundly, and should probably have continued to do so had I not been suddenly and roughly awakened by Lal Khan, who desired me to dress quickly and come with him. My first fear was that I was betrayed; but a moment after, remembering the energy with which I had been protected, I rejected the idea, and rejoiced in the thought of being once more comparatively at liberty. "Where are you taking me?" I asked; "You shall see," he replied; and we left the house and at last the town (where my presence made Kohendil Khan fear more disturbances) by a hole in the wall to prevent my being seen in any part of it again. By a postern gate I found a horse, on whose back I quickly vaulted, and rode away, an escort of twelve soldiers travelling with me.

Girishk, September 17th.—By sunrise we had reached Achogan, a village on the left bank of the Urgund-ab opposite to

Takht Sunjuree; this road is shorter than the one on the right bank by which I had arrived, but not so well defined, being less frequented. My escort baited for an hour, and told the villagers that I was the Feringhee who had brought so much misfortune upon Kandahar. This absurd gossiping might have put me once more in a most disagreeable position; however I escaped with a little abuse, a few stones from the children, and a desperate barking from the dogs, upon which the Afghans remarked that they did not understand why *between dogs* there should be such a disagreement. I had reached that point at which I could not be offended at anything, and besides, of what use would it be to me to be angry? We continued our road at a more rapid pace, and I lost sight of the inhospitable town, where, but for the firmness of Kohendil Khan, or more correctly his fear of the English, of whom he persisted in thinking me the countryman—I should most certainly have found my grave. As we rode on, Lal Khan described to me the various phases of the revolt, and to those I have related he added the following. The answer respecting me sent by Dost Mohamed arrived at Kandahar after the 11th of September; he had informed his brother that he would willingly have consented to send me on a mission to the English if he had not had to contend with the violent dislike to them expressed by his son Mohamed Akbar and his other relations. They had given this opinion in a council met to deliberate on the measures to be taken respecting me, adding that Yar Mohamed, after having spoken of me as an intriguer, had only recommended me to them in consequence of a plot of his own hostile to the Mohamedzyes. He therefore advised sending me back to Herat, and suggested that I should be well treated, though all my actions were to be closely watched, and any attempt at agitation on my part repressed without transgressing the laws of hospitality. Kohendil Khan annoyed at a decision which destroyed his project of an alliance with the English, at first paid no attention to these injunctions, and supporting his own views by the individual opinions expressed by the Dost, had determined upon sending me to Shikarpoor with his propositions to the British Government. But according to the incredible habit of his countrymen, he could not keep his own secret, and showed his brother's letter to four different persons, whom he acquainted with his projects. The Sirdars and mollahs, secretly warned, opposed his intentions, and not having succeeded in shaking his determination, they turned the fury of the people upon me—I have already related the results.

Kohendil Khan and several influential chiefs who took his part had vainly represented that by remaining in hostility to the English, or by cutting my throat as they wished, they would at once draw a British invasion upon Kandahar; but they would listen to nothing, and adopted for their motto that passage of the Koran which says that "Mussulmans shall not ally themselves with infidels;" to this they added, "to give a passage through our territory to this one, is to encourage other travellers whose intrigues might be fatal. Our intentions are irrevocable—he shall die!" The fear of losing their privileges rendered the mollahs audacious; they had seen their power taken from them under the British rule, which had also annihilated their influence, and they wished at any cost to avert the return of such an injury.

The report was generally believed amongst them that the English had been completely beaten by the Sikhs and the Beloochees; "India," said they, "has risen from one end to the other;" they believed a thousand other reports which harmonized with their secret wishes, and all these circumstances stimulated them to resistance. Kohendil Khan, better informed than they were, defended my life; far more, however, to gain himself credit in the eyes of those whose countryman he believed me to be, than for any real interest that he felt in my fate personally, which was probably perfectly indifferent to him. Nevertheless he dared not send me to Shikarpoor for fear of the indignation of Mohamed Akbar Khan, for he knew that if his savage and ambitious nephew had not been at different times restrained by his father, he would before then have invaded Kandahar, to join it to Kabul. It was therefore prudent on his part to do nothing that could give him an excuse for dispossessing him, for the rupture with the mollahs was an incident which went quite sufficiently against him, without its being necessary for him to persevere in his original project of sending me to Shikarpoor, which he would probably have had to regret afterwards. This was all that Lal Khan could tell me on the subject.

We went on to Girishk by the banks of the Urgund-ab, which in several places crossed the desert of shifting sand. The heat was intense, the atmosphere heavy, and the water brackish, even that of the river, of which most unfortunately, I drank heartily; for instead of calming, it excited my thirst. There are several flourishing villages on the borders of this river, and we passed in succession Demrazi, Penjwai,* Spirvàn, Tulookh, Moochan, Kaleh-pirabad, Kaleh-shamir, Chesh-meh, and Bend-i-Timour, where the chief of my escort had some orders to deliver. Thence we turned obliquely to the right, and traversed the desert to Girishk, where we arrived, having travelled twenty parasangs since our leaving Kandahar.

September 18th.—I fell again into the hands of the Sirdar Mohamed Sedik Khan. He had me incarcerated again in the turret-room, where I had previously passed so many unhappy days, with a sentinel at my door. I was to be kept in close confinement; the worthy Moonshee Feiz Mohamed was not allowed to visit me. However, during my short stay we contrived to communicate with each other by the terrace, but our means of intercourse were rare; he would sometimes pass under my window and make me signs, and his gestures or the expression of his face were the thermometer by which I regulated my hopes and fears; these occasions were the only circumstances that cheered my imprisonment. The road to Herat, it is true, passed under my turret, and when the travellers went by, oh! how I longed for wings to follow them! Informed that I was there, they almost always looked up to see me; and often, if I did not appear at their call, they would throw stones into the room—which was, as I have said, open to the road on account of the falling of the wall—to force me to appear and receive their taunts. Ah! how many unhappy hours I passed there!

September 19th.—I had hoped to leave Girishk for Herat the same day I arrived, for that was the strict order of Kohendil Khan; but I was mistaken—Mohamed Sedik Khan had not quite done with me. He pretended at first to take an interest in me, and proposed to send me to India with his own people, passing through Seistan and Shikarpoor; and for this he demanded from me the simple declaration that, in asking him to send me that way, I accepted the responsibility and perils of the journey and relieved him of them completely. Never suspecting the double design that lurked in this offer, I accepted it

* In the early Mahometan period, here stood the chief city of the district, considerable ruins of which are still to be seen. Near this place, in March, 1841, General Nott met the Dooranees, and after a skirmish obliged them to retreat. They immediately returned to Kandahar and made their night attack on the city, which so nearly succeeded.—ED.

with joy, and thought him the more sincere, because, immediately after he took his leave, I received a portion of the things he had taken from me the first time I was in his town. But my joy was of short duration, for when the Moonshee Feiz Mohamed came in the evening with the required declaration for me to sign, he told me in confidence that Mohamed Sedik had only returned my things because he knew that he should get them back with the addition of a few others, for he had instructed the escort he intended to send with me to rob me when we arrived in the deserts of Seistan.

September 20th.—The next morning the Moonshee, at my desire, informed the Sirdar that I refused to sign the declaration, and had determined to travel by the route indicated by his father, that is to say, to Herat; this induced him to send for me. He spoke to me in the most friendly terms, and insisted that I ought to decide for Seistan, but I decidedly refused and was replaced in my prison. An hour after, he came to me accompanied by three of his rascally servants, and delared that my refusal now to go by the road I had chosen implied a distrust very injurious to his character. He then ordered me to give up the things he had restored to me the evening before, and, without waiting for my consent, his villains opened my trunk and rifled it. I had become too much used to this kind of thing to be at all affected by it, and saw them proceed with perfect indifference; but my anger knew no bounds when this titled thief wanted to force me to write him, in the presence of witnesses, a request that he would accept the things he had thus impudently stolen. When he saw me so resolved, he assembled a sort of council, composed of a dozen rogues like himself, before whom I was brought; here I was asked to set a price upon the articles he had taken, and the value was immediately paid to me, partly in shawls and partly in precious stones. The ready money that he had taken was made good to me by a letter of exchange on a merchant of Herat named Syud Mehine Shah. Though much injured by this forced agreement I should have been satisfied, had not Mohamed Sedik come privately in the night and carried off the articles which he had publicly exchanged with me in the morning, leaving me only what probably he had forgotten, the bill upon the merchant; this I subsequently found was not payable when presented. After having accomplished this robbery, the Sirdar left me in triumph with these words, "Go now by the road you like best; I will send you and your baggage gratis; do not regret these trifles so useless for a traveller. God is merciful, and you will no doubt get safe to your journey's end." "Admit then," I said, "that his mercy is not shown at this moment in leaving me in the hands of such an inhuman chief as you are." "Blaspheme not," he replied, "it will bring you to misfortune. The mercy of God is infinite, and you should not complain, since, after your intense folly in coming into Afghanistan, you have still your head upon your shoulders." In spite of this indirect warning, I cursed him heartily as he went out, calling up all the imprecations that are current amongst Asiatics.

September 21st.—The hateful Sirdar came to me again very early this morning, and demanded a written attestation of my good-will, and the receipt for the articles with which he had paid me in presence of the witnesses. This proposition only added to the irritation that the altercation of the previous evening had caused me, and I rejected it energetically, overwhelming him with reproaches, to which he appeared very little sensitive. Seeing that he could not intimidate by words, he took me to an isolated court and tied me to a post with the burning rays of the sun falling on my uncovered head; here the soldiers came up by turns to insult me, and threw filth in my face. This torment lasted five hours, when the Sirdar came himself to ascertain if I was immoveable in my resolution to resist his base demands; seeing that I was in the same mind he menaced me with his dagger, of which I felt the cold point at my throat. It was a terrible moment, and I never shall forget it; but having resolved to die, I could not bring myself to obey him. The miserable wretch spared me, much more from fear of the vengeance of his father and uncle than from pity for me. He remained, however, threatening me with death for nearly two hours, and in my presence gave an order for heated irons and boiling oil to be prepared to torture me into compliance. Enraged as I was, this exasperated me a thousand times more, and at last he left me without having gained his point. The soldiers remained all night to torment me and prevent me from sleeping.

September 22nd and 23rd.—At eight in the morning the Sirdar came again accompanied by a mollah, his son's tutor, the same who would have had me killed at Mahmoodabad. This fellow assured me in the blandest tone that he had pacified the

Sirdar, and he could promise me honourable treatment if I would only be circumcised and become a Mussulman; but he exerted his eloquence and arguments in vain. I remained perfectly silent, for I saw at once there was a snare in this proposition which he knew I should not accept. If I had done so I should have renounced all my European rights, to place myself absolutely under Mussulman law; and taking advantage of my abjuration of my faith they would reply by that fact only to all the remonstrance of the English, my supposed countrymen. But it was not upon that probably that they had reckoned. Seeing me so irritated, they had hoped that I should blaspheme Islamism, and then, according to their creed, they would have been justified in murdering me on the spot, and Kohendil Khan and Dost Mohamed could not have blamed them in any way for so doing; but finding that I avoided the snare, Mohamed Sedik recommenced the scenes of the previous evening, and exhausted all the resources of his cruel imagination to reduce me, till my physical strength could support me no longer: two days and nights passed without food, drink, or sleep, had entirely worn me out; my mind alone had been my support; and I at length gave way to the demands of this infamous villain. I gave him a receipt for the things he had stolen, and wrote on the first leaf of one of the books the attestation of friendship that he wanted. He gave me a similar declaration written in the Persian language but in European characters, of which the following is a translation:—

"As the very dear lord, General Ferrier and I have made friendship, and that in whatever place we may be we shall remain friends all our lives—I give this written declaration in proof of this friendship for the lord General Ferrier. It is agreed that when I shall become Sovereign Governor, General Ferrier shall serve in Afghanistan. Dated the month of Rhamazan 1223 (Sept. 24, 1845). This is written by the Sirdar Mohamed Sedik Khan of Girishk."

PERSIAN ORIGINAL.

"Tchun mehirban general Ferrier Saheb ve bendeh baham dosti Kerdim ki madame ki zindeh veder hayat bashim baham dost ve yek jehat bashim. Ve in khatti dosti namera bercanki nishan dosti bached, be general Ferrier Saheb dadem. Qarar shud ki her vaqt ki men hakim kull shude bashem general Ferrier beraye nokeri der Afghanistan biyayed. Ba tarikh 20 September, sani Aïsai 1845. 24 Rhamazan, sani Mohamedi 1223—.

"In Khatt ez Sirdar Mohamed Sedik Khan, Girishk."

[The seal of the Khan was attached to this document.]

At the same time I made a declaration, stating that I desired to change my route and go to Persia by Seistan.

September 24th.—I had scarcely slept four hours when I was roused, and told I might start; I was very tired and could hardly stand, but to leave Girishk was my most ardent desire, and seeing it about to be realized I did not keep the guard waiting. In place of my European clothes which had been taken from me, I hardly know for what purpose, the Sirdar sent me by the Moonshee Feiz Mohamed a complete Afghan dress, new and clean, which I put on with inexpressible pleasure, for the one that I wore was alive with vermin in every seam, notwithstanding the efforts I made to keep myself clean. I could not tell exactly why, as I was returning to Persia, the Sirdar should so greatly object to my going by Herat: the Moonshee told me the reason. Mohamed Sedik wanted to prevent me from seeing Yar Mohamed, who might have been offended that in my person so little respect had been shown to his recommendation, and he was a dangerous neighbour to displease. To avoid this difficulty, the Sirdar put me in charge of seven soldiers to take me as far as Banader, following the course of the Helmund, and to place me in the hands of the chief of that locality, whence I was to be forwarded to Laush-Jowaine, a fortress belonging to the Sirdar Shah Pesend Khan, his ally, who was in his turn to send me on to Persia.

Everything was ready for my departure; besides the seven men of my escort, four Afghans and five Belooches joined our detachment. In spite of the friendship plastered up between me and the Sirdar, he threw a degree of irony into his farewell, and as I climbed on to my dromedary, he said, "I hope you have nothing to complain of; I saved your life by telling my father that you are a man devoid of bad intentions; I have fed and lodged you gratis; hospitality made it a duty for me so to do, gratitude ought to induce you to speak favourably of me to the English, and to elevate my reputation: depart then, and God be with you! *Khoda humra!*" Our little cavalcade then set off. We were mounted on Belooch dromedaries, whose pace is very rapid. I did not at first like the motion, but soon became used to it, and never wished for any other animal to use in crossing the deserts. The one on which I was mounted had both his nostrils pierced and a ring in each, to which was attached a rope bridle, and by that the animal was very easily guided. I remarked that it was the only female in the detachment, and my escort did not conceal that she was chosen on purpose, because having neither the speed nor powers of endurance of the male, my being so mounted was an effectual precaution against any attempt at escape. The dromedary is called *onti* * in the Belooch language. These animals are meagre in appearance and very small, but remarkably strong; they can travel twenty-five or thirty parasangs a-day for a week together, and will go fifty or sixty hours without drinking. They are used much more for riding than as beasts of burden, and it is their speed which gives the Beloochess such advantages in their forays to long distances from their camps, when the horses sent in pursuit of them perish from fatigue and thirst. The ontis of the banks of the Helmund are almost all of a pale brown colour, and, as in the case of the camel, food that will suit them is easily found. They are particularly fond of a kind of thorn, *khar-i-shutar*,† which grows in great abundance on the Asiatic steppes, so that on arriving at a halt, it is only necessary to turn them loose and they help themselves. Sometimes the drivers will give them once in the day a ball of barley flour as large as a man's fist, but it is not always done, and they get on without it very well. Camels with two humps are also seen in Seistan, but they are difficult to acclimatise and the third generation generally degenerates; they become lean, sickly, and stunted. They exist in a healthy state in those countries only where it is not so hot—above 32 degrees of north latitude. In Bactria especially they attain a strength and development perfectly extraordinary. They are used only as beasts of burden, and carry from 6 to 8 cwt.; but it is an animal that can only be used with advantage in a level country where the soil is dry. The foot not being protected by a hoof these animals cannot step with the necessary firmness in a rugged, hilly country; they frequently fall, and never to rise again, for they easily dislocate or even break their limbs, which are very

* Probably a corruption of the Hindostani word "ont'h."—ED.

† This means camel's thorn. In Arabic it is called "agûl," and all the deserts of the East are covered with it.—ED.

brittle. In such a case there is no remedy, the animal must be killed on the spot, and Asiatics often eat the flesh.

Nigiari, September 24th—fourteen parasangs. Our dromedaries were strong and fresh, nevertheless we spared them on the first three days, reserving their best efforts for the following, in which we were to cross a nearly desert and very difficult country. We slept the first night at this place and passed the following places on the right bank of the Helmund:—Malgeerk, Baba-haji, Bolan, Ahmak, Kaleh-i-Bist, Kosrabad, and Giovregi. Kaleh-i-Bist is an old fortress picturesquely situated on an island in the middle of the stream. *

Mianpushteh, September 25th—fourteen parasangs. We departed at daylight and passed by Kalach, Iarest, Sarkdooz, and Shemalan; there we crossed the river at a ford, and continued our journey along the left bank through Hazar-juft, Khar Akoo, Joui-gooroom, Basabad, Dervishanser, Dervishanpain, Kuscheh, and Mianpushteh, where we stopped opposite to a large village on the right bank, named Kirlaka.

Benader Kalan,† September 26th—nine parasangs. On the left bank of the Helmund passing Jooijaneh Khan, Lani-Sapar, Jooijaneh, and Benader-reis to Benader Kalan, where we slept. I arrived at the halt feverish and went to bed immediately; but I could not sleep, for an animated discussion arose between the soldiers of my escort and the inhabitants of the place, who crowded into the mosque of reeds in which we had established ourselves. I could understand nothing of the motives or merits of this quarrel, for they spoke only Pushtou, ‡ or the Belooch language, of which I knew not a word; it lasted all night. Fatigued and unwell as I was, I paid little attention to this incident; but a great noise which roused me the following morning, proved that the differences were serious and might lead to a catastrophe.

Hazar-juft, § September 27th.—I opened my eyes at the moment when the chief of my guides was demeaning himself like

* This city was known to the ancients by the name of Abeste, or Beste, and to the Arabs by that of Bost. It was formerly a place of great consequence, and was only reduced to ruins in the time of Timour Leng. The remains of the city are still very considerable.—ED.

† Kalan, a word almost unused in Persia, is Afghan for "great."—ED.

Benader, or Bender, means a port on the sea-shore, or an emporium on a river.—ED.

‡ Pushtou is the name of the Afghan language. Two languages are spoken in Beloochistan, the Brahui and the Beloochi; Mr. Ferrier probably means the former.—ED.

§ *i.e.* "The thousand yoke of oxen."—ED.

one possessed, and with a stick in his hand defending himself against a score of peasants who were showering blows upon him with their utmost strength; the uproar attracted six more men who had been sleeping elsewhere and arrived at the scene of the conflict, and the combat would have become general if a mollah who came in with them had not pacified the combatants. A few minutes after, we were mounted, but instead of continuing our road to Laush, as I had hoped, I saw with astonishment that our little caravan retrograded towards Girishk, by the same road that we had travelled the previous evening. As we rode I asked one of the sepoys the reason of this; he replied that the Khetkhoda and the inhabitants of Benader Kalan were "dogs, the sons of dogs, grandsons of dogs," worthy of a berth in the lower regions; he hoped he should soon put the cord round their necks. I could obtain no further information from this brute, but in the evening, at the halt of Hazar-juft, as the chief of my sepoys conversed in Persian with the mayor of the place, I discovered by degrees what had been the cause of the commotion.

The Sirdar Mohamed Sedik Khan being in want of money had sent our detachment to anticipate the levy of the year's taxes of Benader; but the rayahs had not yet sold their harvest, and as they were already six months in advance with the Sirdar, had refused to make the desired payment still further in anticipation, and they threatened to appeal to Kohendil Khan. This resistance did not suit the sepoys, who had hoped that the order to get it would give them the opportunity of recruiting their own exhausted finances by means of a little exaction; they did their utmost to render the inhabitants of Benader more tractable, but finding themselves beaten they feared that worse might happen, and decamped as quick as possible, taking me with them, as they found the rayahs refused to send me to Laush for nothing, solely to please the Sirdar Mohamed Sedik.

Girishk, September 28th.—We arrived at this town again five days after we left it, to the great disgust of the Sirdar, who ordered the unlucky party to be bastinadoed for having failed in executing their orders. The rogues made me testify to the efforts they had made to get the money, and the dangers they had braved. But I took good care not to say much for them; I was too well pleased to see them suffer a little as a set-off to the annoyances and indignities they had put upon me, to intercede for the diminution of their punishment by one blow, and it was not till the beating was over, when their feet were bleeding, and they began to look deplorable, that I told the Sirdar what I had seen and heard. His anger, however, did not fall upon me. I was again lodged in the tower it is true, but I had the liberty of walking in the court during the day, and I was allowed to talk to the inhabitants of the fortress. I made use of the permission to communicate with Moonshee Feiz Mohamed on many points that concerned me which I had never been able to clear up.

September 29th.—Waiting at Girishk for the escort that was to accompany me to the frontier of Persia.

Zirek, September 30th—five parasangs. The four soldiers ordered for my escort having called for me at daylight, I mounted and we set off. The chief was a good fellow named Mirza Khan, whose physiognomy pleased me at first sight. It was the first time that a being with human sentiments had had custody of me since I came into the Kandahar territory. The orders he received from the Sirdar were that he should avoid Herat and take me direct to Furrah, a town belonging to Yar Mohamed Khan and governed by a mollah by whose co-operation he hoped to get me passed on to Ghayn in Persia. After having travelled through a plain we arrived at Zireh, a small village situated at the foot of the mountains on the right of the road to Herat and opposite to Mahmood-abad, where I had stopped on my journey to Kandahar.

Biabanak and *Paiwuk*, October 1st.—After four parasangs of plain we reached Biabanak, a halt already described, where we stopped for the heat of the day to pass over; in the evening we resumed our journey, crossed the mountains by rough roads, and slept five parasangs and a half further on at Painek.

Washeer, October 2nd—two parasangs. By sunrise we had ridden this distance. Sultan Khan, chief of the district, was much surprised to see me again; he had fancied me dead long since. The Sirdar Mohamed Sedik had written to him to provide me with two sepoys and a horse to replace those that had come with me from Girishk, who were to return. Sultan Khan peremptorily refused to do so, asserting that the Sirdar ruined him by all sorts of means, disposing of his goods according to his own pleasure, and it required all Mirza Khan's perseverance and entreaty to induce him to obey his rapacious chief.

Koh i Duzdan, October 3rd.—This morning my horse and the

two fresh sepoys were brought to me. The strongly marked countenance of one struck me forcibly, and I thought I must have seen him somewhere, though I could not call to mind on what occasion; he observed that I looked at him attentively, and very soon in the most shameless manner, being perfectly sure of impunity, told me that he was one of the gang who, two months before, had attacked me on the road to Karakan. He expatiated much upon the affair, and the resistance we had made: "What good was it to you to refuse your things to us poor devils, who, three parts of our time, have no bread to eat, when a month after you had to give them all up to the Sirdar, who wants for nothing? He gives you no good will for them, while I, in going upon your escort to-day, should have been delighted to do it out of gratitude; that would have been far better—Khoda kerim!" After four hours' march we crossed the Khash-rood, the boundary between Kandahar and Herat; and, after three hours more, we encamped in the middle of a desert steppe, in sight of Koh i Duzdan, Mountain of the Thief, where there was not a drop of water. Happily we had two skins-full with us. We gave the greatest part to the horses, keeping only what was strictly necessary for ourselves to moisten a small ration of black bread, all that we had with us. It was a scanty supper after such a ride, but I soon fell asleep, and that overcame the gnawings of an ill-satisfied stomach.

Ibrahimi and *Shiaguz*, October 8th.—At daybreak we saw large herds of deer, to which the sepoys gave chase in vain; they only exhausted their ill-fed horses, that were sufficiently tired with the journey. To repay themselves for their trouble they seized upon a goat and a sheep from the first flock we came to. Astonished at this barefaced robbery, I was surprised to see that the shepherd, instead of resenting it, complimented them and gave them his blessing. I asked Mirza Khan what that could mean? "That is the way of the Afghans—in kar Afghan est," he said, "we always do so when we find a flock on our road; it is our right." "But who gave you the right; would you do thus under the walls of Kandahar?" His answer was characteristic, like the Lamb and the Wolf in the fable. "There, there are authorities, it would be dangerous; but their power reaches not thus far. The soldier is king of the steppes. As to those ragamuffin shepherds, do you think they would go to Kandahar to complain of our borrowing twenty or thirty of their animals in a year? his loss is not worth his journey; and besides, if any of them complained, we should settle him the next time,—that is all. There is therefore a great advantage in keeping friends with us."

This reasoning of Mirza Khan's did not convince me of his justice, but I noted it as a specimen of the received ideas of the Afghans; when they are not restrained by the fear of power, and have the slightest chance of impunity, they are capable of committing the most frightful excesses. As to this sheep-stealing I have seen it often. They kill one, take out the inside and tie it under the horse's belly in no time, and at the next halt they eat it if it is fat and good; if lean they throw it to the dogs, and rail at the shepherd as if he were a traitor and had cheated them. If the flock is not very far off they will go back for another, and the shepherd may think himself fortunate, if on this second visit he escapes maltreatment; so he is generally careful that they should have good sheep at once. They consider that tainted meat gives the dysentery. One of the greatest vexations that I met with in travelling with the Afghans is their habit of dawdling on the road. If necessary, no one can get on faster than they will, but if they have time before them they will stop at every twenty paces for the most trifling reasons; when they know any place near the road where perhaps a relative or acquaintance may live who will regale them with a kooroot,* nothing will induce them to pass without stopping, and whatever may prevent them from so doing is a great vexation to them.

The Afghans, accustomed as they are to a camp life, cannot endure fatigue and privation so well as Europeans. They will want some though very little food, when the latter will do without; on the road they are always stopping to gossip, to drink, to smoke, or to pray, and could never understand how I could go from one halt to another with just a crust for breakfast. They seldom travel without their *chilim*, or waterpipe, at their saddle, for it is a punishment to them to pass a single hour without smoking. If they have not this indispensable article with them, they will make two little holes in the earth communicating subterraneously, fill one with water and one with tobacco, put a reed in the former, and, lying on their stomachs, smoke this primitive apparatus with as much pleasure as if it were

* Sour milk.

the hooka of a nawab. When they meet on the road, whether known to each other or not, they stop to talk and exchange the news of their respective countries; each tells his name, where he lives, what he is, and the object of his journey; and it is thus that public news is spread over all Asia sometimes almost as quickly as in Europe by newspaper. Etiquette and ceremony are quite unknown to them, and they address each other as old acquaintances: if they are in a hurry the conversation does not flag, they tell the news in a minute and part; but if they have time to spare they dismount, seat themselves under the shade of a tree, or by the waterside if there is any, and repose for ten minutes looking at each other without saying a word. Silence is then broken by a reciprocal salutation, repeated twenty times on either side, then comes the news, repeated as often; it may be the health of a thoroughbred horse, or mare and foal, the flocks, the harvest, the children, the relations, and they finish up with the last political news. The querist has in his turn to reply to a similar series of questions, and it is long before the polite ceremonials on both sides are exhausted. I could never understand how they could preserve their composure, repeating these commonplaces so often, and I have many times laughed in my sleeve at this strange ceremonial; I remarked that they prolonged these repetitions when they perceived me attentive to what was going on, probably to give me a great idea of their urbanity, compared to which our mutual civilities are only the counterfeits of real politeness. Their treatment of their horses on the road made me observe that the poor beasts have but inconsiderate masters.

The first quality an Afghan thinks of in a horse is a rapid gallop, to enable him to overtake his enemy when he retreats, or to escape himself if he should be the beaten party: a thin horse is worth nothing in their eyes, and yet they feed them in a manner that renders it impossible they should ever grow fat. At home they give them chopped straw, and 6 lbs. of barley a-day; on the road they hobble them, and turn them loose in the steppe to find their own forage, and give them half the quantity of barley in the evening in one feed: they let them have green food whenever they can find it, but the barley is then taken away as superfluous: and when they are ill, a diet, or gross superstitions, are the only remedies to which they have recourse. Like the Turcomans they make their horses gallop after drinking, as they say, to warm the water in the stomach of the animal; were this neglected, they affirm that the hide would swell after the saddle is taken off, and in a short time fall away from the flesh at this spot. It is this belief that induces them to keep their horses saddled and without food for four or five hours after a journey, if only of half an hour, and they will leave the saddle on all night if they have travelled a day's journey; they only take it off in the morning to clear the sweat and hair from the lining, scrape the horse's back with a knife, and the grooming is over. They take the shoes off the horses that are not in use, as a matter of economy, and, in fact, in all that concerns these animals they think only of saving trouble and expense.

After travelling seven hours under a fiery sun, on a steppe where there was no water, with the hot wind blowing, from which we suffered much, we arrived at Ibrahimi, a halt that I have already described, and put up with some nomadic friends of Mirza Khan. They killed a sheep to make us welcome, and we were comfortably refreshed in this hospitable tent. Here we remained three hours and then travelled five to our halt at Shiaguz, in a large encampment of nomads. One of the horsemen of my escort, as he took my sack off his horse, here declared he should go no further; "for," said he, "I have killed three people in Furrah, and I am still *khooni*' (that is, guilty of blood that he had not paid the price for); to go there would be to expose myself to the law of retaliation, which I care not to do." He therefore announced his intention of going back to Washeer. "As you mean to go," said Mirza Khan, "you shall be off,—shall I tie you on your horse?" for it was necessary to make some remark upon his proceeding. To this he quietly replied, "If you attempt it I will find a joint between your ribs with the point of my sword." Much discussion ensued, and at last it was settled that we should replace him by a man of the village, but then he wanted to be paid a ducat for his pains and I had not a sou left. Mirza Khan therefore cut the business short; assisted by the other three sepoys, he seized the deserter's horse, which we required, and gave the man such a drubbing as determined his *locum tenens* to do our bidding without further delay or any expectation of payment.

Khoormalek, October 5th—six parasangs—the first and last parts of this stage through plains, fields, and marshes, and the intermediate part intersected by stony mountains, steeply scarped at the sides. Going out of Shiaguz we left the road to Herat, by which I had come, on the right, and proceeded straight on. The sides of the mountains on that side were pierced with excavations in high, and in these days inaccessible, positions; anciently they were used as habitations by the people of the country, and they doubtless reached them by fissures in the rock, which have caused large masses to fall away. In the middle of the plain of Khoormalek, on the other side of the mountains, are two kalehs, about a mile from each other: the first was called Kariz-belal, the second Kariz-makoo; at the first we stopped, and it was impossible here to get anything to eat, so we were obliged to be content with some small pieces of bread that we had brought from Khoormalek; the horses browsed upon the reeds in the neighbouring marsh.

CHAPTER XXVI.

The author leaves Khoormalek — Arrives at Furrah — Wretched quarters — Visit of the Governor Mollah Mahmood Akhond-zadeh — His kindness to Mons. Ferrier — Departure of Mirza Khan — Marvellous heat at Furrah — The Governor's fear of the cholera — The fortifications of Furrah — Ancient history of that town — The modern town — Siege by Nadir Shah — Removal of the population by Sedik Khan — Remarkable changes in the cities of Central Asia — State of the country — Aversion to taxation — Banks of the Furrah-rood — Military position of Furrah — Letters of Yar Mohamed to Mons. Ferrier — Preparations for departure — The author and his escort leave the town — Kariz-makoo — Description of the escort —Khoospas — Description of the country — The fetid marsh — Khash — Geographical errors — The Khash-rood — The wild ass — A nice dish for a hungry man — Shâh-aziz-Khan — Shâh-aboo-thaleb.

FURRAH—seven parasangs. The road was over a plain totally devoid of drinkable water. On leaving Khoormalek we wound round the last spur of a chain of mountains, which, running towards the south, is detached from the range of the Siah-bend. When distant from these mountains we had on our left the boundless plains of Seistan. Numerous ruins near the road seemed to indicate that the country was once well inhabited, it is now arid and desert; two salt and offensive marshes are situated halfway and a few palms may be seen near them. At last we reached Furrah, and it was time. Exhausted by the fatigues, privations, and cruel mental anxiety of two months, this last journey from Kandahar had destroyed my physical strength, and I was sustained only by the moral power of hope in the heart of man. On arriving at the town we retired under the shade of an immense cupola that formerly served the governor for an ice-house, and Mirza Khan went alone to present the letter of the Sirdar to the Mollah Mahmood Akhond-zadeh, commandant of the fortress. Two hours elapsed before he returned. At first he had a very bad reception from the mollah, who would not see me, and recommended him to take me back to Girishk; however he was softened by the recital of the sufferings and dangers that I had gone through in Kandahar, and determined to receive me. Furrah is only half the size of Herat, but built exactly on the same plan. I was lodged in a hole over the north gate of the town. This building was in a state of decay, difficult to describe, and open to all the winds that blow with violence at this season; they rushed into it at eight enormous holes, through which also came the rays of the sun. It had been taken possession of before my arrival by wasps and other insects that were domiciled in the interstices formed by the falling plaster; their continual buzzing round my head, against which they beat every few minutes, excited in me a most nervous irritability, from which I suffered sadly. It was an annoyance that hitherto I had not met with; and I had infinite trouble to preserve myself from being stung by them in the day, and by the scorpions at night—that was the great occupation of my stay at Furrah. By way of compensation, I had the companionship of a dozen tiny mice, who played about me without evincing the slightest fear; they had doubtless been caressed by my predecessors in the room, for they would take crumbs out of my hand. Their society was actually an agreeable relaxation, and I was thankful to let them divert my thoughts from my misfortunes; I felt sorry when I left them.

October 7th.—At noon I received a visit from the governor. He was a short, fat man, with a kind and jovial face, filling his nose with snuff every moment. Six persons accompanied him, and, by their clear brown skins and expressive eyes, I recognised them as Belooches; two of them had beards and long hair, as white as snow. After having seated themselves, and examined me for ten minutes, Afghan fashion, he saluted me with—

"Khosh amedid," you are welcome; "you are no stranger to me," he continued, "for we have already met at Herat, where I was when you first passed through. I am sorry to hear of the sad treatment you have suffered. The recommendations that our excellent Vezir Sahib—may his shadow never be less!—had given you to the Sirdars ought to have smoothed every difficulty; but be assured he will avenge you a hundredfold."

I replied by giving him an account of my imprisonment and the treatment I had met with. He appeared indignant, and after many reflections, little favourable to the Sirdars of Kandahar, he added,—

"The reasons that you assign for your return into Herat were not the only ones that determined it. The insurrection of the

Ulemas was, I am informed, serious; but if, instead of declaring to Kohendil Khan that you were in penury, you had made him a present of five hundred ducats, he would have sent you safe and sound to Shikarpoor, in spite of the insurrection."

"I cannot," I replied, "believe in such avidity on the part of a sovereign. How could so small a sum affect the decisions of so rich a prince?"

"Avidity!" he exclaimed; "it seems to me only natural. It is by small streams that the sea is fed. Each takes advantage of his position to improve his interests; and you Feringhees—possessors of so much gold—you can well spare a little to the poor but brave Afghans, so worthy of being rich. I have never yet seen an Englishman so avaricious as you are; when they were in our country they gave us money of their own accord: they are noble, generous, polite; their praises were in every mouth, and you are wrong, by your avarice, to spoil so fine a reputation."

This pompous eulogy of my supposed countrymen touched me very little, and I persevered in endeavouring to make him believe that it was impossible for me to spend much money; besides, it was clear to me that he wished, by flattering the English, to pique me into confessing that I had money concealed, and induce me to give to him the sum that he taunted me with not having given to Kohendil Khan.

My answer was, that "it might suit the English to give money to the inhabitants of the country in which they wished to establish their dominion; it was the best means of making partisans; and, nevertheless, you have very little valued their generosity, for you massacred them all, even to the last man, in Kabul. But I am a Frenchman, and, consequently, not an Englishman, and cannot do as they did. First, because my government does not want to possess Afghanistan; and, secondly, because I have neither the power nor the money. I paid for all I wanted, at four or five times its value, up to the moment that I was robbed of everything I possessed: will not that content you?"

"I agree in a good deal that you say about the English," was his reply; "but what is past is past. Let us think only of the present. I do not like you, a Feringhee of elevated rank, and one of the principal ornaments of Christianity, to go about with such a miserable equipage. Amongst us the lowest officer never moves without six or eight horses and as many servants; and for you to do otherwise is to compromise your dignity."

"Do as you please," I said, with some temper and tired of the discussion, "and leave me to do the same. I had not much money when I came into your country; now I do not possess a sou, and all your discourse is superfluous."

This outbreak seemed to convince the mollah; he concluded his self-interested observations, and, seeing that he had only a distressed person to help, his goodnature resumed the ascendant, and he asked me if I was willing to go to Shikarpoor.

"With all my heart; but, having been stripped of everything, I cannot undertake such a journey.

"What!" he exclaimed, with warmth, "have you no faith in the mercy of God? Do you believe that all men are like Mohamed Sedik Khan? and no one has a feeling and humane heart? You have not the means to go to Shikarpoor, you say? Well, I will provide you with them. If at first I did not like to receive you, it was because I could not lodge you worthily in these ruins, and I feared the disapprobation of Yar Mohamed Khan; but now that I have heard all you have suffered at Girishk, at the price of my blood I would not have you return. Fear nothing. Mohamed Sedik commands not here; and I shall not send you to Ghayn, as he desires. I am neither Khan nor Sirdar; but I have the heart of a man, and I love to be kind to my fellow men. You owe me no gratitude; for in that I obey the commands of God, the master of us all. If you are the friend of the Afghans, so much the better for you. May the blessing of Heaven rest on you and on your descendants! If you are their enemy, may God forgive you, and remove the bad thoughts from your heart! In either case, I shall write to-night to Yar Mohamed for permission to send you to India. Those who are seated by me now are inhabitants of Seistan, driven from their lands by Mohamed Sedik, your persecutor. One of them, Assad Khan, well known by the Belooches, shall conduct you to Kelat; Nassir Khan, Emir of that town, is my friend; I shall write to him to send you on to Shikarpoor, and be sure you will arrive there all right. If, as a recompense, you will tell me how to make gold—a science in which the Europeans are very learned—you can do so, and I shall be grateful to you; but I make no conditions for my assistance. God be with you!"

Knowing how little Afghan promises could be depended upon, I could scarcely believe all this; but there was so much frankness in the mollah's manner, and so much feeling in his accents, that I was more than half-convinced, and thanked him heartily for his kindness. When he left he told me that, while waiting for Yar Mohamed's answer, I must remain in the room where I was, and have a guard of four serbas, as I had at Herat. But, he added,—

"It is only for form's sake, and to cover my responsibility. You will go out and visit the environs as you like, attended by your guard. Ask for all you want, and they will give it you; for I consider you more as my guest than my prisoner, and you shall have proof of it."

My first impression of Mollah Mahmood was favourable; his cheerful countenance, and the heartiness of his manner, pleased me much; but as he gradually allowed his covetousness to show itself, that impression wore off, and I looked upon him as I did his countrymen; for in offering his services an Afghan always means that he should be substantially recompensed for them.

Mollah Mahmood was, it is true, a little avaricious by education, but not by nature, and he redeemed this fault in my eyes by his evident and sincere desire to help me; I have ever cherished the remembrance of his good offices, and his humanity and generous attentions have, in some degree, softened my horror of the Afghan race.

Mirza Khan soon came to take leave of me, and ask me for—a receipt of—my person! He was muffled up in a khelat, an Afghan robe of honour, of English cotton, which had been given to him by Mollah Mahmood. He was wonderfully proud of this distinction, though it was not worth more than three shillings. I gave him also a certificate of my satisfaction with his conduct, though he had allowed his people to steal my kalioun, and other trifles; but I attached no importance to those little pilferings, which are an Afghan's supreme delight. I only thought of the kindness of this venerable old man. My heart felt at parting from him as if he had been twenty years my friend; and this sudden sympathy was easy to understand, for he was nearly the only creature with human feelings that I had met with since I left Herat: however, the thought that he was leaving me in the hands of one no less generous soothed the pain I felt at seeing him depart. The same day the mollah wrote to Yar Mohamed, and

I sent a letter also, relating the vicissitudes I had suffered in Kandahar, and explaining to that prince my reasons for returning to his dominions.

October 8th to 13th.—The next day a change as violent as it was sudden took place in the atmosphere of Furrah. At this time of year I was assured that the heat is usually so great up to the 15th of November that an egg exposed to it will get quite hard in an hour; and a ball of lead will become malleable by the middle of the day; but this autumn was perfectly exceptional, the north wind blew violently on the 8th of October, and produced a degree of cold hitherto unknown to the inhabitants of Furrah. It was impossible to protect myself from it in an apartment so exposed as mine, and I felt it severely. The following days I had a return of the symptoms of cholerine, and remained stationary in my room. Mollah Mahmood was very kind, and gave me all that the extreme poverty of the country would allow him to do; his daily visits and cheerful, instructive conversation formed an agreeable relaxation from my ever-present cares, and alleviated my illness.

The cholera was then raging in Furrah, and the exaggerated manner in which he expressed his fears amused me very much. Every day he had an ox killed, and distributed the meat in charity, to propitiate Heaven in his favour; and he entreated me to ransack my memory or imagination for some remedy that might preserve him from the scourge. I was delighted at his confidence in my medical skill; for it enabled me to recommend him to remove from his neck a little bag, containing a few drops of garlic, camphor, and assafœtida, of which the combined odours nearly suffocated me, and replaced them by some sweet-smelling drugs, which he felt satisfied would be a complete preservative from the evil that he so much dreaded.

Two towns about an hour's distance from each other have borne the name of Furrah. The most ancient was built before the expedition of Alexander, and situated half an hour south of Furrah-rood, in the middle of a plain surrounded on three sides by the last spurs of the mountains of the Paropamisus, of which it commands the entrance. Towards the south the prospect is open, and melts into the horizon, over the plain of Seistan, where two or three isolated peaks thrown up in front of the Helmund and the lake Roostem, just break the monotony of the view.

The modern town is a parallelogram, lying north and south; its area is half a parasang. Except in the difference of size, it is similar to Herat, and, like that, surrounded by an enormous embankment of earth mixed with chopped straw. A covered way entirely surrounds it on the outside. This embankment is from 35 to 40 feet in height; on the top are many towers connected by curtains, and the rampart has become so hard that a pick will not take effect upon it. Several governors have tried to excavate it, and never succeeded, not even by watering the ground; two things only would affect it—vinegar and melting snow, but Saadat Mulook, son of Shah Kamran, formerly governor of Furrah, assured me that snow rarely falls there. When it melts, the earthwork becomes soft, but the first sunshine dries it harder than ever; tradition brought this fact to the knowledge of the inhabitants, and once only in this century have they been able to verify it.

A wide and deep ditch, which can be flooded at pleasure, defends the approaches to the embankment. The citadel occupies the north angle of the place; and the town has but two gates, that of Herat, in the centre of the northern face, and that of Kandahar, exactly opposite, on the southern side.

The ancient chronicles and traditions preserved in the country unite in considering Furrah as a very ancient town, and, till it was sacked by Ghengis Khan, a very flourishing one. He destroyed all the houses; but the fortifications, as strong then as now, resisted all his efforts to annihilate them. The conqueror gave quarter to many hundred families, and transported them an hour further north, on the right bank, and half an hour from Furrah-rood; and to judge by the extensive ruins still existing at that spot, the new town which arose there must have been of considerable extent. The citadel, and many other fortifications and dependencies, are still standing, and crown an artificial eminence; but the houses are all in ruins, and the ground is covered with thick bushes and brambles, which afford good cover to a great quantity of game, particularly hares, heath-cock, and partridges. Great numbers of baked bricks, nearly three feet long and four inches thick, were scattered about the citadel. That their origin was certainly anterior to that of the town was plainly indicated by the inscriptions upon them, in the Cuneiform character;* and

* The existence of bricks with Cuneiform characters at Furrah is very im-

without doubt they once belonged to the monuments of the ancient town of which the remains were used by Ghengis Khan in the construction of the fortress for his new one; the latter increased rapidly, and was one of the most important in Seistan, till Shah Abbas the Great laid siege to it. The resistance of the inhabitants was long and determined; but eventually it was taken by assault and dismantled. The population then retired to the fortification of the old town; and the misfortunes of war were soon effaced by the presence of wealth and abundance. It prospered to the close of the Suffavian dynasty.

Before even Nadir Shah had completely destroyed it he brought the town under his dominion. The siege was long and bloody, and Furrah lost two-thirds of its inhabitants; and there may still be seen at the interior base of the embankment some smoky niches, made by the besieged with infinite trouble, in which to shelter themselves from the artillery of Nadir Shah. On the exterior of the town, a little distance from the two northern angles of the place, may be seen also two enormous cavaliers, constructed at that time to batter a breach in the walls. It is observable that these are constructed more scientifically than would have been the case had they been the work of Persian engineers; they were probably thrown up under the directions of the French artillery-officers who served Nadir Shah. From this period, being frequently taken, retaken, and pillaged by Tartars, Persians, and Afghans, the devoted town of Furrah gradually declined in power and prosperity; still, in 1837, the population amounted to 6000; but they were seized and carried off into Kandahar the year after by the Sirdar Mohamed Sedik Khan, who, by order of his father, invaded it with a corps of cavalry, to make a diversion in aid of Mohamed Shah, then besieging Herat. When this sovereign retired into Persia, after having failed before that place, the troops of Kandahar retired to Girishk, and Furrah, deprived of its population, fell once more under the dominion of the prince of Herat. There are not now more than sixty houses in the interior of the place, which would easily contain four thousand five

portant, and is not mentioned by any other traveller.[a] The size of the bricks is also remarkable. The only place where bricks of this large size have been found is in the kitchen of Sardanapalus, at Calah or Nimrood.—ED.

[a] Dr. Gerard visited Furrah in 1831-2.—*Journal of Asiatic Society, Calcutta.*

hundred; they are all partially concealed by the ruins, and the scattered jets of smoke rising from them were the only indications of the presence of animated beings in this desolate scene: the bazaars that cross the town from one gate to the other may be traced by the foundations of the shops. Large pools, which dry in the summer and produce excellent saltpetre, surround the interior of the town; this Yar Mohamed uses in the manufacture of his gunpowder. Furrah is one example of the difficulty of stating anything certain about the geography of Central Asia; a place may to-day be the centre of a flourishing population, and in four-and-twenty hours a desert. The Afghans have become so used to sudden and forced displacements, that they never attach themselves to the soil; their tent is their country. In two days a family will build themselves a good house of earth, roofed, with the door only made of wood; and the facility with which they do this explains, as I have already said, how so many towns appear and disappear without leaving a trace behind them, and how others of which the existence is not suspected are suddenly mentioned by successive travellers: it would not be surprising if the European who first follows me to Furrah should find it either utterly deserted or in a state of unlooked-for prosperity. This mania of the chiefs for removing whole populations renders it so difficult to ascertain their numbers with accuracy that the statistics we have on the subject of Central Asia can never be depended upon; for a successful chapaoul may any one day alter the figures by many thousands: nothing there is certain; nothing is durable; everything is liable to impromptu changes,—men as well as things. There is neither liberty nor civil estate, nor the least notion of the rights of people, in that country; the law of might is supreme. With them liberty, justice, moral influence, and government are in direct opposition to the received ideas in Europe. The liberty of these people is disorder, anarchy, pillage, and murder: the policy of the great is to deceive both friends and enemies, and to swallow up the property of those they govern. After all, they are worthy the one of the other; for if those in power carry off all the revenues, the nation would value them none the more for regulating the taxation in just proportion. They prefer revolt, expatriation, and the risking their lives and goods, and the liberty of their wives and children, to consenting to pay to the state what is legitimately due to it. Taxation in Afghanistan is regulated by a struggle between fraud and power; it is always the result of a forced transaction, and never, on the most moderate scale, is willingly paid.

All ruined as it is, the town of Furrah is, in a military point of view, of great importance, and the tenacity of the Afghan princes in disputing its possession proves the fact. Whoever holds it has one foot in Kandahar and the other in Herat, and commands the northern entrance to Seistan. This position would become of extreme importance to the Persians and the Russians, if they ever determined on an offensive alliance to invade the British possessions in India.

The banks of the Furrah-rood, which traverses all this district, are like those of the Helmund, the Haroot-rood, and the Khash-rood, covered with forests of tamarisk and mimosa. The river is deep and full, except in the heat of the summer, when an immense quantity of water is withdrawn from its bed to supply the irrigation, and this lays it nearly dry on the greater part of its course. In the deeper parts long pools remain stagnant, and the water creates fever in those who use it; nevertheless the flocks, goats, and sheep drink it without repugnance.

October 15th.—The reply of Yar Mohamed Khan reached Mollah Mahmood in the night of the 14th-15th; and it was favourable,—ordering that every road should be open to me, and that I should be furnished with an escort sufficient to insure my safety. The kind-hearted governor came to communicate the happy news to me immediately, manifesting great pleasure in it, but he went away again directly, not wishing, he said, to delay for a moment the preparations for my departure to Shikarpoor, for which I was so impatient. He also placed in my hands a letter, written to me by Yar Mohamed himself, replying to the one that I sent to him, of which the following is a translation:—

"May the very noble, very exalted, the companion of honour, of fortune, and of happiness, my kind friend General Ferrier, ever be under the protecting arm of the Almighty God, preserved from all vicissitudes of fate and all sorts of misfortunes in this world, and may he attain the object of his desires in the next! In a happy hour we received the honour of your letter, so full of friendship, arrived to honour us with its presence, the reading of which procured me perfect joy and most agreeable moments. I had been much distressed at hearing of the conduct and actions of the people of Kandahar towards you; but it has consoled me that you have arrived safe and sound in the province of Furrah, and that the exalted commander of the frontier has not neglected to show you every customary honour ; on the contrary, that he has followed the dictates of the laws of hospitality. As to your departure from the province of Furrah, you are at liberty to do exactly as you like best ; but the road to Shikarpoor is extremely dangerous, and it would be grievous if, which God forbid, any deplorable accident should happen to you. However, should that be your determination, may you prosper in it ! I shall recommend the very exalted governor of the frontier to place at your disposal a mounted guard, to accompany you to whatever place you please, and give them orders not to leave you till you dismiss them. In case you should return to Herat, I beg you to regard this town as your house, and to return with an escort of horsemen, that the very exalted commandant of the frontier will command to attend you. God willing, after your return to Herat, by taking the road to Turkistan, you will this time arrive safely at Kabul. I have given orders respecting your arrival to the very exalted commanders of the frontiers, to assist you in either case in every way that you may wish or require. You are therefore entirely your own master. I have nothing more to say than that I request you to let me hear of your health, and to write to me on any occasion on which you may require my assistance. I wish you honour and prosperity."

October 16th to the 19th.—Assad Khan Ishakzye, who offered the first day of my arrival to conduct me to Shikarpoor, was selected by Mollah Mahmood to escort me with twelve horsemen. I could not be accompanied by a better person, for Assad Khan had passed his life on the banks of the Helmund near Kernasheen. He had been recently driven out of that country by Kohendil Khan, who was not sufficiently sure of his fidelity to leave him in a position that would make that Khan the arbiter of his fate, in case the English should again drive him out of the sovereignty of Kandahar. In such a case his only refuge would be Persia; therefore the road to it should be open, or in the hands of chiefs devoted to his person : if only one barred the passage, his liberty would be compromised. Assad Khan might be the man to oppose him, and his enmity would be the more dangerous because he possessed the small but strong place of Mula-Khan, situated on an eminence commanding the road. The Sirdar had many times called upon him to recognise his suzerainty, but he always received a negative reply, and Mohamed Sedik Khan was ordered to besiege and reduce his stronghold. A hundred men resisted all his efforts for many weeks, and he would have come out of the struggle victorious had not the credulity of Assad Khan involved them with himself in ruin. Mohamed Sedik Khan succeeded in tempting him into his camp, swearing upon twenty Korans, placed on a tray, that he would not do him the slightest harm; that he wished to meet him only to spare the effusion of blood, and that in case no arrangement should result from their interview, he would be at liberty to return to his fortress. Assad Khan, relying upon an oath taken with such extreme solemnity, trusted himself in the traitor's power, was arrested, and dispossessed of Mula-Khan. Happily he found an opportunity of escaping, after a year's captivity, and took refuge in Furrah, where Yar Mohamed granted him a piece of ground, on which he settled himself with those who had followed his fortunes. The hope of pleasing the Vezir and obtaining a good recompense induced him to volunteer for the duty of escorting me to Shikarpoor.

In any other country two hours would have sufficed to prepare for our journey, but in a town so destitute of everything as Furrah, it required three days to collect six water skins, ten bags of barley, and shoes and cloaks for the men of my escort. My utmost endeavours to get away sooner were futile, and at last the fourth day was absolutely fixed for our setting out; but some astronomer in the town, I knew not who, discovered by an unpropitious conjunction of stars in the sky that it would be an unlucky one, and the event that I so ardently longed for was again put off.

Kariz-makoo, October 20th.—This morning, at noon, Assad Khan had not arrived, and I sent him most heartily to all the devils; at last he appeared, and I thought we were going, but I had reckoned too much upon the Afghans: the horses had not a single shoe amongst them, and they had to be found—no easy matter. This was the result of my entreaties to the Mollah for the last six days to hasten the simple preliminaries for my journey; his constant answer was "everything is ready," and then he laughed with so much good humour, that I could not find it in my heart to be angry. This time, however, I showed that I was vexed, and said I would change my road and go to Herat. I thought the poor fellow would have gone crazy, for he fancied that, if I went to Herat, I should certainly complain of him to

Yar Mohamed Khan; so he ran about from one person to another, praying, swearing, threatening, beating, tearing his beard, and giving evidence of a despair that I would most willingly have spared him, could I possibly have anticipated such a crisis. He got salt from one, flour from another, horseshoes from two or three more, and etceteras from anybody he happened to meet, and returned to me two hours after, streaming with perspiration, and informed me that everything was ready. I immediately mounted my horse, and he, accompanied by twenty horsemen, rode with me an hour from the town. Here he took leave of me with a thousand protestations of friendship, and begged me to take great care of a dozen indifferent horses—wretched hacks, which I was to have, and exchange for some small dromedaries at an encampment of nomads on the banks of the Khash-rood. These animals were better adapted for travelling in the deserts than horses; my baggage, however, consisted only of a *havresac*, which was slung behind and on the crupper of one of my escort. This was composed of twelve solid and determined fellows, well armed, though dressed in rags; they looked just what they were—regular plunderers and scouts, and as I looked at them, I augured well for my journey; but this time I was mistaken, I had yet to make my acquaintance with the Belooches, and it was a serious affair. In the evening we arrived at Kariz-makoo, near which I had already passed when returning from Girishk.

Khoospas, October 21st—seven parasangs—through a plain. Instead of following the road to the left by which I had come from Furrah, we moved on leaving Kariz-makoo in a south-easterly direction and to the right, and crossed a defile which intersects the last spur of the mountains of the Paropamisus, which here advance like a promontory into the plain of Bukwa and separate it from that of Furrah. We marched eleven parasangs, through an arid and uninhabited country, and in advancing towards the south, and away from Furrah, the soil was, if possible, more arid; scarcely a trace of vegetation was to be seen, except a few scattered tufts of the tamarisk, which gave these desert solitudes a still greater air of desolation; even the wild beasts fly from these sterile steppes, and the wild ass was the only living creature that we saw. The travelling days are long in this part of Seistan, and there is no possibility of shortening them, for it is absolutely necessary to halt at some well or spring, where alone water can be found; between the two stages not a drop is to be obtained, there is nothing but the burning sun overhead, and the fiery sands beneath the feet. As the Belooches know that travellers must stop at these wells, they frequently lie in wait for them there, and, if they are not in force, rifle them without mercy; every one, therefore, is on the *qui vive*, and ready for them with loaded arms.

In debouching from the defile I have just mentioned, we moved, as if by hazard, over an immense sandy plain; my guides, however, who had traversed it at least twenty times before, with native instinct evidently knew their road, and by signs which an European would never have noticed; the colour of the ground, a little mound, &c., were the marks by which they recognised the route. The heat was intense, the hot wind blew from sunrise to sunset, and the great god of the Ghebers darted upon our heads its scorching rays, while the sands beneath our feet reflected others scarcely less hot; our very throats seemed on fire, and as for the poor horses, I thought they must drop at every step. On arriving at Khoospas, they immediately lay down as if never to rise again. This was a complete desert, with a small marshy pond of fetid water concealed amongst some reeds. By the side of that muddy and tainted water, however, I threw myself down, drank eagerly and with bated breath one long continuous draught, and blessed heaven for having sent it me; as to the taste, I never noticed that, but half an hour after my stomach rejected the water, and for the future I repressed my burning thirst until I had boiled it with some wild mint, and subsequently filtered it. Our guides prepared the repast, such as it was; it consisted of barley-cakes baked on some round stones, heated with the dry reeds; these were not famous, but we fared admirably with a lamb which Mollah Mahmood had provided for us: this, cut into pieces and wrapped in its skin, was put into a hole with red-hot stones at the bottom; other stones also heated were put on the top and covered up with earth. Four hours after we sat down to a roast which it would be useless to ask any Paris or London *restaurateur* to give you,—nothing can equal the delicacy and flavour of a kid dressed in this manner by an Afghan.

Khash, October 22nd—seven parasangs—still through an arid desert, on which, and about halfway, we came to a place called Basruig, a wretched village of Parsivans who had been exterminated by the Belooches at the beginning of the year. Here we obtained with great difficulty a little water from a well; it was as heretofore very bad, but it alleviated my thirst, which was intense, for the hot wind had blown with violence all day, and it was with inexpressible joy that in the evening we arrived on the banks of the Khash-rood; the course of this river is inaccurately laid down on the majority of maps of Central Asia, not excepting that of Burnes. The geographers describe it as taking its rise in the mountains of Siahbend, and trace its course from north to south until it falls into the Helmund at Kernasheen; whereas it flows in this direction only as far as Koh-i-duzdan, a village situated between Washeer and Ibrahimi; there it forms an elbow turning suddenly south-west, and runs from that point straight to the Seistan lake. At this season of the year its bed is generally dry and full of reeds, in which are numbers of wild fowl. On its banks are tamarisk bushes, the mimosa and dwarf palms, under the shade of which there is sometimes a little scanty herbage, on which the sheep find a bare subsistence. Its banks in the upper part of its course are rather high, and at the spot where it is crossed to go to Washeer there is a descent of half an hour on either side to reach it, but, after leaving Koh-i-duzdan, the river is exhausted by irrigation. There is a little cultivation near the few isolated villages on its banks inhabited by Afghans and Belooches. The tents of the nomads are found in much greater numbers, especially in summer, and they have with them large troops of dromedaries, sheep, and goats; horses are bad and rare. Morning and evening we saw several herds of wild asses, numbering some hundreds, come down at full gallop and rush into the river to cool themselves. The natives hunt and eat them; the flesh is considered inferior to that of a camel or a horse, but superior to the ox. If a wild ass is taken alive—which is rarely done, for they are as fleet as a deer—it is sent to the chief as a curiosity, or killed at once and devoured. The form of the animal is elegant, even delicate; the head very small, the eye quick, the coat fine, colour a light yellow and slightly striped, the ears short, and the limbs of great beauty; their pace is as good as that of the best Arab horse; their skin is so remarkably thin and so easily chafed that they are quite useless for work. We arrived at Khash at nightfall, and remained only a quarter of an hour; it was here that we were to exchange the horses lent us by Mollah Mahmood for the dromedaries. To conceal as much as possible the passage of so large a party, Assad Khan, with only one of his men, went to the village, and in about two hours after returned to us accompanied by a Belooche friend of his, with the pleasant information that all the dromedaries had left the evening before to fetch a load of English goods from Khelat, that were to be smuggled into Kandahar and Herat. On hearing this bad news every one gave his opinion; mine was to return to Furrah, for I felt thoroughly upset and out of spirits, more so indeed than on any journey I had taken; but Assad Khan was hurt at the proposition, and insisted upon our proceeding as far as the Helmund with Mollah Mahmood's horses. I gave way with regret to his wish, and the result proved that my fears were well founded. The dangers and privations which we had before us were not to be avoided unless we could get rapidly over the ground, and dromedaries were indispensable for the purpose; I knew this, and so did Assad Khan, but here was an opportunity to show his zeal for Yar Mohamed Khan, and such a chance was so unlikely to occur again that he determined not to lose it. The advice of Assad Khan having prevailed, we next thought of our supper, for we were nearly famished, but our provisions being all consumed, the Belooche friend of the Khan was despatched to the village for something to eat ready cooked. The messenger was not long away, and on his return produced a wooden bowl full of *kooroot* and covered with *keshk;* into this I plunged my fingers with the rest of the company and withdrew some of the mess, which I quickly conveyed to my mouth and more quickly spat out again: I thought I was poisoned, but it was only the green stalks of assafœtida preserved in salt water, to be sure not quite to my taste, and yet the inhabitants of Seistan think it a great delicacy. This ragout, and the tea of Khulm with rancid grease, are two things which I hold to be diabolical.

Shah-aziz-Khan, or *Shindeh*, October 23rd—eight parasangs—through the most arid and monotonous plain we had yet traversed, without shrub, without the least vegetation. The first half was not, however, positively sterile, for after the rains of spring the surface of the soil is usually covered with grass, and in some quantity, which the heat of the June sun shrivels up; water here, as in so many other places in Central Asia, is wanting; without artificial irrigation nothing will grow. The second half of our journey was over shifting sands, whereas on the preceding days the ground was solid and mixed with clay. No stage was ever more fatiguing than this. There are few sandy deserts in Central Asia beyond Bokhara and Seistan, but they are much more vast in the former than in the latter country. In Seistan they are divided at short distances by steppes covered with vegetation in the spring, and particularly of tamarisk bushes. These oases are inhabited in winter, for the rains accumulate in the low grounds, and afford sufficient pasture to the flocks of the nomads whose tents are pitched here in this season. If these fail them, they find water at a depth of from three to six feet. This fact demonstrates the possibility of this country being permanently inhabited, and establishing halts pretty near to one another, and thus facilitating the communications between Herat or Kandahar to Shikarpoor and Khelat Nasser Khan.* We arrived at Shah-aziz a little before sunset, and found in the dry bed of a river only a putrid pool of water surrounded by tamarisks, and in this was the carcass of a wild ass, which, not having been able to climb its steep sides, had been drowned.

Shah-aboo-thaleb, or *Derwazeh*, October 24th—six parasangs—through a plain similar to that of yesterday, melancholy and monotonous. The sand raised by the hot wind blew into and irritated our eyes so that we could not see two yards before us; sometimes no trace of a road could be observed; at others, but they were of rare occurrence and in the middle of a little oasis, a few ruins and stunted bushes relieved the arid uniformity of the desert. The saline incrustations are of as frequent occurrence as in Persia, and are seen on a great extent of surface in the low grounds, where the water has dried up; the want of this blessed liquid during this day's journey was severely felt, and we arrived at Shah-aboo-thaleb very exhausted, where we found the water drinkable.

---

* The difficulty of this line would be to the south of Seistan, along the skirts of Shirawuk. It is, however, occasionally traversed.—Ed.

CHAPTER XXVII.

Helmund — Belooche encampment — Imprudent conduct of Assad Khan — Serious consequences resulting from this — Flight of the Afghans — Attacked by the Belooches — The Author and his party cross the river — Fight amongst the tamarisk bushes — The Author in the mêlée — The party conceal themselves in some ruins — A council of war — The result not agreeable to Assaf Doulet — Night march on the banks of the Helmund — Rondebar — Guljeh — Rafts on the river — Halt at Poolkee — Difficulty of ascertaining distances — The bread of Seistan — Value of wheat in that country — Jehanabad — The tower of Alemdar — Canals on the Helmund — Extraordinary musquitos — Mohamed Reza Khan — Ali Khan, the murderer of Dr. Forbes — Amazing superstition of this scoundrel — Hospitality of Reza Khan — Descendants of the ancient Persians — Jelalabad — Curious forage for horses — Sekooha — Duration of things in Seistan — Ser Jadda — Zerdabad — Laush Jowaine — Shah Pesend Khan — Strategical point between Persia and Kandahar — Local politics — Fortress of Laush — Military force of this district.

HELMUND, October 25th—six parasangs—and through a plain to the river here. The more we advanced the more the country became wild and difficult, by reason of the moving sands; the soil changed for the better when about half an hour from this place; the vegetation was here abundant and in singular contrast to the hot parched ground we had travelled over. At first we halted by a stream in the middle of a tamarisk wood, and not far from a large encampment of nomads, called Noonabad, situated near Kernasheen; here we awaited the night before showing ourselves, which on several accounts was a prudent measure. After a frugal repast, we remounted our horses and went forward to meet Assad Khan, at about a gunshot from the encampment: he had preceded us with one of his men to try and hire some camels from the tribe, without which we could not have advanced another step. In half an hour the Khan returned with the news that it was impossible to hire the animals at the exorbitant price they asked, and requested us to accompany him to Kernasheen, from which place we were half a parasang, and could there obtain them on moderate terms. His people represented the danger he ran in going to a locality dependent on Kandahar, from which country he was banished, and at this time inhabited by Belooches

Mamessani, one of the smallest but bravest of the tribes of Seistan —also one of the most savage; the men lead a wild, disorderly life, and are very frequently at feud with their neighbours. When Assad Khan was in possession of the kaleh of Mula-Khan,* situated at ten parasangs south-west of Kernasheen, he lived for a long time on very good terms with these Belooches; but in the year 1840, having during a friendly meeting had some dispute with one of their chiefs, a quarrel and blows ensued between the Afghans and the former, in which two of the Belooches were killed. From this moment the populations of Kernasheen and Mula-Khan became irreconcilable enemies, and a month rarely passed without hearing of some victim having lost his life in some fresh fray; for in these countries, where the *lex talionis* is in force, the man who does not obey that law is, as in Corsica, dishonoured; blood wills blood. Assad Khan knew this better than any one else, for his life had been twenty times at stake in many an ambush prepared for him by the Mamessani; nevertheless, regardless of the earnest representations of his own people and mine, he persisted in going to them to hire the camels. Seeing how obstinate he was, I followed him, but with regret, and his men did the same.

When we arrived at the encampment at Kernasheen the greater part of the tribe were stretched outside their tents, and nearly asleep, but here and there a few men were seen surrounding some cholera patients in the last stage of that frightful disease, then raging on the banks of the Helmund. Our party approached the encampment, and Rahim, a cousin of the Khan, asked one of the first groups he came to whether he could have any camels. A demand of this kind, so unusual and at so late an hour, was naturally calculated to awaken the suspicions and distrust of the Belooches; we were at once pestered with questions as to who we were, where we were going, and what we wanted: it was impossible not to admire the prudence and presence of mind displayed by Rahim in his replies, and if he alone had been the spokesman we might not perhaps have succeeded in getting the camels, but he would at least have got us out of the false step of going there at all. The impatience and violence,

* This was the furthest point south that was occupied by the English during the Afghan war. A detachment of irregulars were maintained at Mula-Khan under an European officer for a considerable period, and relations were kept up through this party with the Belooche and other chiefs of Seistan. —ED.

however, of Assad Khan led to one of those episodes so frequent in Afghanistan and not at all to my fancy, which spoilt everything. The Khan uneasy at the opposition made to our wishes, and probably annoyed at the various difficulties we had encountered, became in his turn the speaker, in a tone of defiance and authority, which had no effect upon the Belooches, who were on their own ground and in force. At last Assad completely forgot himself, abused them, and would, if they had not recognised him, I believe, have gone so far as to throw his name in their teeth as a defiance. The Khan once identified, the Mamessani were furious; a burst of indignation followed, and then loud cries. The alarm spread from one end of the encampment to the other, the women and children vociferated in shrill accents and threw stones at us, the greater part of the men seized their arms, and some the bridles of our horses; our case was critical—the crowd of Belooches increased like a tempest on every side.

It was time to act. A few vigorous sabre-cuts well dealt kept back the crowd, and turning our horses' heads we profited by the hesitation of the Belooches and scampered off. The animals though fatigued by a six days' march seemed to scent the danger and galloped like lightning; but two hours of this pace was more than enough for the poor brutes, and whip and oaths were necessary to get them along. This was not reassuring, for the Belooches having collected some dromedaries were in full pursuit, and seeing it was impossible to escape, we dismounted to give our horses breathing time and await their attack, determined to sell our lives at a high price. We had scarcely done this, when several of our pursuers imprudently advanced without being supported by their main force. We remounted and charged with impetuosity upon them; the Khan shot the first man he closed with, but received a sabre wound on the shoulder, and in consequence we again beat a rapid retreat. An undulation in the ground now hid us from the Belooches, and to more effectually prevent their tracking us, we forded the Helmund near Kaleh-i-Sebz, where the river was tolerably deep. But this scheme did not succeed; for three quarters of an hour we counted from twenty to twenty-five of the fellows at our heels, and were obliged to face about and meet them once more, this time with the desperation of men whose time seemed to be not worth a few minutes' purchase: luckily the dromedaries moved with difficulty amongst the brushwood, whereas our horses were active and easily handled, which gave us a great advantage. We were also armed with good guns and swords, and they with their matchlocks and spears. The mêlée became general and obstinate, lighted by the bright starlight and our dropping fire. One of the rascals attacked me with a boar-spear, and wounded my horse in the neck, but I got in at him, and with one blow laid him on the ground. I then flew to the Khan's assistance, who, partially helpless from his wound and attacked on all sides, had more upon his hands than he knew what to do with; his men, however, fought like good ones, and made head against the foe, killing and wounding twelve: we had on our side four killed and three wounded; amongst the former we had to regret the loss of Assad's cousin, the brave and prudent Rahim. As reinforcements were continually arriving for the Belooches, and our numbers decreased every minute, we again took to flight, and about half an hour after we had to support another onslaught, and here by the light of the moon which had just risen we charged once more with vigour.

This time we left one of our men, who was wounded and entangled with a hook, in the hands of the Belooches; and while they were occupied with cutting him to pieces we resumed our flight, for there was no use remaining to share the same fate, and passing in front of Kheir-abad, Kaleh-i-Sebz, Taghaz, and Siah Koh, situated on the other side of the river, we happily reached some low ground near it thickly covered with tamarisk bushes, through which, as our horses were quicker and more manageable than the dromedaries, we greatly increased our distance: but this advantage left us very little hope of escaping from the rascals, for our gallant steeds were dead-beat, and would not move even for blows. It was then that a fortunate sudden inspiration of Assad's saved our lives: he ordered the party to incline to the left in front of his old fortress of Mula-Khan, the environs of which he was perfectly acquainted with, and led us into some ruins, in the centre of which was a deep excavation, and round them the débris of what had once been baths; into this we with great difficulty got our horses, and waited in great anxiety the issue of this unfortunate business. Overcome with heat, thirst, and fatigue, both animals and men were *hors de combat*, and had our enemy come up we must have been massacred here without resistance. Those only who have been in such an extremity can understand the joy we felt when Assad Khan, who was perched in a tamarisk bush above us and on the watch, said the Belooches had passed wide of our retreat, and were moving in an opposite direction: they were moments of anguish until we heard this, for every one thought his hour was come. In this hole, however, we remained for fear they should return, and lucky it was for us we did, for two hours after we again heard their cries as they passed along the opposite side of the Helmund in the direction of Mula-Khan. Having lost all trace of us, they remained in that fortress the rest of the night, and finally disappeared altogether about two hours before day-light.

A council was now called as to future measures. We were ten parasangs beyond the direct road to Khelat, and our intention to reach that place was known: it would have been therefore the height of folly to persevere in that enterprise. Besides, my escort was now reduced from twelve to seven, two out of which were wounded, and the Belooche that Assad had taken as our guide to Khash; and we were quite unable to show a front to any further misfortunes which might arise. Nevertheless Assad, in spite of what had occurred, considering that he was bound in honour to conduct me to Shikarpoor, persisted in his attempt to reach that town with the limping animals of Mollah Mahmood. What will the Vezir Sahib say? what will the Afghans think—or the Belooches? my reputation is gone if we return, better to die than be dishonoured. These were his arguments, and they were sincere; but his men having no hope of receiving any favour from the Vezir, were less inclined to proceed, especially as I warned them that I could not reward their services as the English had done. On hearing this they were still less disposed for any more disasters or the chance of them, and insisted on retracing our steps. I might possibly have again given way to Assad's wishes, had I seen his men as well disposed as himself; but I felt they might abandon me in the moment of danger, and the fear of this determined me to take a decided course. Accordingly I informed the Khan, in the most positive manner, that I intended to return to Furrah, and gave him a written order to obey me. This done our measures for a retreat were soon taken.

The danger was as great in following the line of route we had come, as in taking a direct course to that town; in the latter case we should not have found either food or provisions: we determined therefore to keep close to the river, the sides of which being wooded offered us greater security. Concealed by the underwood, we could see without being seen by the Belooches, whose encampments we carefully avoided, and sometimes made a considerable circuit to do so. When a faint streak of light in the horizon announced the approach of day we mounted our horses, advancing cautiously amongst the willows, tamarisks, and mimosas, having the Helmund on our right, and leaving on our left the silent and sterile deserts of Seistan; the waning moon's reflected light was shed over its red and shining sands, which seemed like one immense furnace, and the noise of our horses' feet was lost in the sound of the gurgling river, or the gush of waters against some rock, which with several wooded islets obstructed the rapid current, or where at some shallower part it rippled over the gravelly bed beneath. But for the broken waters a profound stillness reigned around, no sound was heard, and no signs of an enemy being discernible, our anxieties had almost ceased, when on a sudden a covey of partridges comfortably ensconced in the bushes for the night rose with their loud whirr, and gave a slight and not agreeable sensation to our nerves. For the moment we thought the Belooches were before us, and crack, crack, went the guns, the report of which roused the jackals and deer from their retreats, and started a troop of wild asses that were in front of us off across the country at their best speed. This was the sum total of our alarms for the present.

About ten o'clock on the morning of the 26th we halted in a hollow, sending forward an Afghan and a Belooche to a place called Dishoo, about half an hour from the spot, to get provisions; they soon returned with some barley and two loaves, and the encouraging intelligence that our whereabouts was not suspected; the supply was soon devoured, and again mounting our horses we continued our march till nightfall, still skirting the Helmund. Here, near the village of Pul-alek, we saw several bodies in the river; they were those of some Belooches who had died of cholera, and had therefore been refused burial, on the ground that persons dying of this disease must be hardened and obdurate sinners: such was the reason assigned—the fear of infection might have been the real one.

Having passed this village and crossed the Helmund, we halted, near the small town of Roodbar, in a grove of trees—being there concealed from the inhabitants but in a position to see everything about us when the moon rose. Here again we sent on our Belooche, who brought back only some flour, and being afraid to light a fire for fear of discovery we moistened it with water and ate it raw—lying down to sleep after the meagre repast. Rest was indeed necessary, for we had travelled eight parasangs during the night, and nearly always at a canter or gallop, and eleven during the day. The course of the Helmund in the territory of Kandahar terminates at Roodbar. As far as I could see in a moonlight night, this is a large place for the country, and at any rate very ancient. Near the spot on which we were encamped there was an old dyke, the bottom of which was in the stream; it was constructed of bricks having the same form and size—a yard square—as those of Furrah. A little behind this dyke, and on each side of the Helmund, are high and ancient walls, also of brick, connected with some mounds, on which formerly there were in all probability fortifications; of these there are now scarcely any remains. In searching about the ruins I found a brass coin of the Seleucian era.

Gooljin, October 26th.—We marched twelve hours again this day, and skirting the river, the brushwood in the neighbourhood of which pointed out the sinuosities of the stream, and to shorten the distance we crossed from one turn to the next. In the morning we passed near Kheir-abad, a little fort of promising appearance—at noon we avoided a place called Trakoo, and crossed, at a quarter of an hour's distance from thence, to the right bank of the river on a raft of reeds floated by inflated skins, holding our horses, which swam in the rear and at the sides, by the bridles. The Helmund flows south-west from its source to this spot, but here, arrested by some sand-hills, it takes a sudden turn to the north-west, and runs for fifteen or twenty parasangs in that direction, divided into various branches, which fall into the Seistan Lake by several mouths. In the afternoon we passed in succession in front of Seinabad, Kaleï-pat,* and Poolka.† The latter town stands in the middle of ruins, which extend for a considerable distance along the left bank of the Helmund, and inwards as far as the moving sands, which have covered a portion of them. A shepherd whom

* The ruins of Kaleï-pat are the most extensive of any in Seistan, and probably mark the site of the ancient city of Zarenj.—ED.

† Poolka, or Pulaki, was the point where Captain Christie came upon the Helmund in his journey from Kelat to Herat in 1808. See Pottinger's Travels. London, 4to., 1816.

we questioned said that they were the site of the ancient city of Homedin *—might not the ruins be those of Ram, Prophtasia, or Zarangæ? The immense bricks I remarked at Furrah and Roodbar are also to be seen here, and amongst the ruined buildings are found the remains of mosques and other public edifices, fragments of vases, enamelled tiles, &c. The founder of the city, said the honest shepherd, was the Pehlevane Roostem, to whom as I have before observed the Persians refer as the architect of nearly all the ruins in the country. Tamerlane was the destroyer of Homedin.

Our horses being incapable of proceeding further without rest, we remained at Poolka some hours, and allowed them to browze on the young reeds and tamarisk leaves, which in the absence of better forage they managed to put up with; and thus they were in the evening able to carry us to Gooljin, a village likewise standing amongst vast ruins, and at which are a great number of tunnels for conducting water, but now dry; also large reservoirs, aqueducts, and towers, but all more or less destroyed. The inhabitants of this village are half Norvui Belooches and half Noorzyes Afghans. The Ket-khoda was a friend of Assad Khan, and of Afghan origin; he received us well, and showed us the greatest hospitality—all he knew of the ruins was, that they formed part of the ancient capital of the country destroyed by Ghengis Khan: the name he was ignorant of. The ruins around Poolka, at three hours' distance from the last we traversed, are no doubt those of the city which was built after the destruction of the former by the Tartar hero, and which was in its turn destroyed by Tamerlane. We were in hopes of being able to take a direct line from Gool in to Furrah, but to my great regret the Ket-khoda informed us that it was impossible. The country was infested by the Belooches Serbendee of Sheikh-Nassoor, who were at war with Shah Pesend Khan, an independent chief of the district of Laush-jowaine, situated to the north of the lake.

No sooner was this known than the fighting qualities of Assad Khan were at once roused,—he liked the adventure, would I not accompany him? I at once declined the honour, and the Ket-khoda completely dissuaded him by promising to lend him some

* All the local traditions of Seistan refer to the old romances of Rustum, Zal, Zohrab, Afrasiab, &c. The Shepherd probably meant Khamdan, the fabulous capital of the Shahnameh. —ED.

camels to make the tour of the lake, and by this means reach our destination in safety. As to our horses they were incapable of making a step, and it was arranged that they should remain at Gooljin for a fortnight, and then be sent on to Furrah. Assad Khan consented to this, but stipulated that we should push on to Jehanabad, and see if we could not avoid the belligerent parties by traversing the strait which is formed to the north by the Lake of Seistan, which is dry in summer; as this would save us a long march round it, and I agreed willingly to the plan. Unfortunately the upshot of this was that we increased our journey by two days, which we should have avoided had we reached by a direct line the southern extremity of the lake. It should be stated that from Gooljin I found it impossible to ascertain the distances from each stage with any degree of precision; because the horses being lame and harassed with fatigue did not go at a regular pace, and having to make long and frequent halts, there was no possibility of calculating them even approximately. A Belooche is perfectly ignorant of what a parasang is, and has no other mode of calculating distance excepting by the day's journey, and that depends again upon whether the pace of the dromedary, horse, or man, is quick or slow.

On the 28th of October we remained at Gooljin, to repose a little after our great fatigues, and the Ket-khoda treated us as well as the somewhat indifferent resources of the neighbourhood would permit him. He ordered a young camel and four lambs to be slaughtered for us, and they were served up in several highly seasoned *ragouts*, which my escort licked up to the very last morsel. On this occasion they made what the Afghans call a *kharabi-singiri*, an enormous destruction. In witnessing the privations which they support for several months, it is wonderful when the day of abundance arrives how they can eat such quantities without bursting. The greatest hardship in this way to an European in these countries, is the bad quality of the bread: that made of rye, which is eaten by the peasants of the Morvan and the Charollais, is a hundred times superior to that made of wheat which the Afghans and Belooches live upon; it is black, doughy, not half baked, mixed with bits of straw and grains of sand, and at the very sight of it one's stomach turns: when it is thoroughly dry it looks like the oilcake on which in Europe beasts are fattened. In spite of this description we thought ourselves lucky when we could get any, for the villagers only have it on fête-days; generally speaking they eat maize or assafœtida seasoned with *kourout.* But this is not because wheat is scarce in Seistan, or that the consumption is small; there is, on the contrary, a very fair breadth of it sown, but the inhabitants sell their corn at Herat, Kandahar, and Kerman, and an idea of the value of specie in this country may be imagined, when I state that the year I travelled through it, the *kharvar* or between six and seven cwts. of wheat could be bought for three *sahibkrans*, or three shillings English money, and one of barley for two shillings.

Jehanabad, October 29th.—We left at midnight, and, hearing that the right bank was infested by Belooche Serbendees, we crossed on a raft to the opposite one, which, though not so bountifully supplied with thieves, was full of game and wild beasts, that we turned up at every few hundred yards. The few tents of nomads that we saw were at a great distance. Our dromedaries got over the ground at a good pace, and by noon we reached the Tower of Alemdar, where we recrossed the river to the right bank. The banks of the Helmund from Dishoo are less cultivated and inhabited than in the middle part of its course—that is to say, between Girishk and Mula-Khan; this cannot be in consequence of any inferiority in the soil, for the pasture and arable land is equally good and productive, the banks are covered with meadows, and the land is more or less adapted for cultivation for a distance of a mile and a quarter from the river, where it meets the moving sands of the desert. Strange to say the neglected state of this tract is owing to its fertility; for when it was inhabited by a rich and industrious population, now decimated or disgusted with the insecurity which prevails, its prosperity was sure to attract the cupidity of those who lived by violence and rapine: many of its former inhabitants have since settled themselves in more secure positions, and under the protection of chiefs who can protect them; or they have concentrated themselves in and around two or three points, such as Pul-alek, Roodbar, Kheir-abad, Trakoo, &c. This system of concentration affords a better chance of making a successful resistance.

From May to December, a great number of Belooches, driven from the oases amongst the parched deserts of Seistan south of the river, find abundant pasture and water in this abandoned belt of country; but they are always on the alert, and sufficiently near to support one another against the attacks of the little Afghan chiefs who claim from them a tribute for the right of pasturage in a district of which they arrogate to themselves the possession. When the rains of December set in, the Belooches return to their own less accessible territory in the desert, where they can remain unmolested. The peculiar circumstances and the precarious life which these people lead are the chief cause of their being so cruel and savage, and enemies even to the humblest form of civilisation.

The Tower of Alemdar, constructed of earth, and standing in the centre of some modern buildings, must anciently have been a fortress of some consequence, and the residence of a chieftain of rank and authority. When we passed it there were from twenty to twenty-five tents of Afghan Noorzyes pitched round it. From this point the Helmund diverges into several streams of water, at some distance from one another; three of the largest of these in the rainy season overflow their banks before their waters fall into the upper part of the lake, and leave in their course a considerable detritus of vegetable matter, which contributes to the natural fertility of the soil. The land thus inundated forms a delta of several parasangs in circumference, and is naturally protected by the streams that surround it. It is planted on all sides by thick hedges of tamarisk, by which the cultivated lands are enclosed. The mass of the population of Seistan is here agglomerated in about twenty rich and prosperous villages: tents are unknown, and brick and stone are rejected for building purposes. The houses are constructed of reeds and branches of the tamarisk, covered with a thick layer of mud, and placed upon the most elevated points to avoid the inundations. The inhabitants of this delta suffer greatly from myriads of musquitos of a prodigious size, which torture both man and beast during eight months of the year; their sting will pierce the thickest quilt, and the skin through the clothes; for this reason the inhabitants cannot keep either sheep or goats. If an ox or a cow is stung by several of these gnats they rub the wounds with the juice of an herb found in t e neighbourhood; but, in spite of the application of this remedy, death frequently ensues. A coarse kind of linen, called *kerbas*, is made here; this is used for clothes, and occasionally sold at Herat and Kandahar, where, as I have before said, the Belooches sell their wheat and barley, of which they obtain large crops.

When we were here the weather was still hot, and the musquitos no doubt thought us a great treat. At four o'clock in the afternoon our party arrived at the little kaleh of Jehanabad, in the district of Sekooha, governed by a chief of the name of Mohamed Reza Khan, of the tribe of Sharegi,* the most powerful in Seistan. He was going the round of his villages to collect the tax upon the crops, and was here to receive us. The Khan's position had been recently considerably strengthened by the marriage of Yar Mohamed's son with his daughter. The letters of the Vezir, which I showed him and the escort which accompanied me, procured me the best reception; and it was as well I had them, for without these credentials I should probably have found myself at the end of my journey, the Belooches would certainly have treated me as an enemy if I had entered their country on the faith of their hospitality. We found here Ali Khan, of the Serbendee tribe, chief of the district of Sheikh Nassoor, situated on the banks of the Khash-rood, who had arrived here an hour before us. The Khan was at war with the chief of Laush-jowaine, whose people were plundering the country. Hearing me speak Persian fluently, he at first thought I was a native of that country; but when he heard I was an European, his countenance assumed a singular expression. He looked so astonished that I was prepared for the following: "What, have you a talisman from God, or a compact with the devil, that you dare to trust yourself amongst Belooches?" "Ah! Mohamed Reza Khan," addressing my host, "may you be preserved, since Heaven sends you such a windfall!" The Khan Reza, observing my countenance change a little, reprimanded his neighbour for making such a brutal remark; and assured me that the rights and duties of hospitality would be scrupulously respected. Ali, however, seemed unable to understand why the chief of Sekooha should take any interest in me, or why I was under his roof; and continued to make various insinuations by no means of a friendly character. After making several observations which proved the cruelty and perfidious nature of his disposition, he gave us an account of a most malignant and cowardly assassination in which he was himself concerned.

The Belooches have the most singular ideas of an European that can well be conceived: struck with all they have heard and seen of their power, intelligence, and riches, they think not only that

* So called from Shahrek, the residence of this chief's family, and one of the principal places in Seistan.—ED.

they can make gold, but also that their bodies and everything belonging to or in contact with them contains the precious metal. A few years before the date at which I am writing, Ali Khan received a visit at Sheikh Nassoor from an English doctor of the name of Forbes. He had been warned of the consequences which would assuredly befall him if he ventured within the clutches of this monster, but it was of no use—he was bent upon undertaking the journey, and paid the penalty of his curiosity with his life. Ali Khan murdered him in his sleep, and hung poor Forbes' body up in front of his own tent, which he ordered to be deluged with water during fifteen days consecutively. "You will see," he said to his people, "that this dog of an infidel will at last be transformed into good ducats." Finding, however, to his great amazement, that this proceeding did not produce the expected result, he thought he would boil the water with which the corpse had been washed, but with no better effect. It then occurred to him that the doctor, to play him a trick, had before his death made the gold pass from his body into the clothes and books which filled his trunks. Instead of burning these impurities, which had been his original intention, he had them cut and torn up into little bits, and mixed with the mortar destined to plaster his house. He had not yet had occasion to use it, but he informed us, as he related the details of this disgusting tragedy, that when he did he expected to see his house covered with a layer of the precious metal. Nothing would ever have induced him to forego this belief, and he did not disguise from me that he would have been happy if he could have added my poor corpse to the mortar in question.*

I confess I did not feel very comfortable at Jehanabad between this monster and his ally, and I urged our immediate departure from this nest of vultures. Assad, however, reassured me on the good intentions of my host, and we agreed to go with him on the following day to his own residence at Sekooha, from whence he promised to provide us with the necessary assistance and an escort to protect us in our journey round the lake; for the hostility and vile disposition openly manifested by Ali Khan rendered the idea of returning to Furrah by the north even more impracticable than

* A brief account of Dr. Forbes's visit to Seistan, and of his murder by the Belooches, will be found in the Journal of the Royal Geographical Society for 1842, transmitted by Sir H. Rawlinson from the deposition of the servant who accompanied the traveller in this his last fatal journey.—ED.

it had hitherto appeared, as we should inevitably have fallen in with some of his people in that direction.

Ali Khan is, after Mohamed Reza Khan, the most powerful Belooche chief in Seistan; the territory which he governs is bordered on the north by the rapid stream of the Khoospas, which flows from the north-east of the lake almost as far as the Helmund in a southerly direction; to the west it is bounded by the first canal which leaving that river falls into the lake. Sheikh Nassoor, the capital of this small state, is an old fortress surrounded by mud walls, and containing between fifteen and eighteen hundred houses, a bazaar, five public baths, two caravanserais, and a mosque. Some geographers have it on their maps under the name of Kedda, by which it was formerly known, at two parasangs to the north of Khash-rood and Peer Kisri: it is the first town in Seistan on the north.

The territory of Mohamed Reza Khan is comprised in the triangle marked out by the Lake of Seistan to the north and west, and the Helmund river in the elbow which it makes from Trakoo as far as the junction with its first canal to the north and at the southern point of the lake. Jehanabad, as I stated before, forms part of this district; this village is fortified, and contains about one hundred and fifty houses, and is inhabited by people who are known in the country as *Pehlevan*, or heroes, warriors, athletæ, and descendants of the famous Roostem. Whether this tradition adds to their courage, or they are naturally very brave and their neighbours are awed by it, I cannot say; but they have the reputation of never turning their backs upon any danger, and of attacking without calculating the force opposed to them, were the odds a hundred to one. They understand the Belooche language, but do not speak it. I detected many Persian words in their own, which they pretend is the *Pehlevi*, the language of the ancient Persians. An old man showed me a book that was written in a character which was in use before the Mahometan era; this might be the key to many dialects now forgotten.*

Jelalabad, October 30th.—At noon this day the two Be-

* If this be a true Pehlevi MS., it must be regarded as one of the greatest literary treasures of the East. There are traditions of ancient MSS. said to be possessed by Ghebers, who resided in an island of the Lake of Seistan; but modern research has led to the belief that this is a mere fable. Edward Conolly carefully examined the island and found nothing.—ED.

looche chiefs took leave of one another: Ali Khan, after having obtained a promise from his neighbour to remain neutral in the war he was waging with the chief of the Laush-jowaine, to return to Sheikh Nassoor; while Mohamed Reza, with ourselves, took our way to Jelalabad—also called Beharami, after its founder Behram Khan, Kayanee.

This little fortalice in earth contains about one hundred reed houses, and is commanded by Abdullah Khan, Norvui; it is situated south-west of Jehanabad, and at four parasangs from the lake. The ruins by which it is surrounded prove that it was at some period or other much greater in extent; but it is difficult to believe that it was ever the large city which it is represented to be on the various maps of Asia. The same may be said of the tower designated as Iloomdar; this represents, perhaps, the Tower of Alemdar, already mentioned. Dooshakh, again, is not a town but a mountain with two peaks, from which it derives its name *Doo-shakh*, two horns. A stream runs from this, and on its banks are scattered some excellent reed huts. There were also a few ruins here, the *débris* of some fifty or sixty houses, quite out of character with those which are supposed to have existed here, and which in imagination only have hitherto passed as the site of the capital of Seistan.

After a halt of a hour at Jelalabad, or Beharami, to enable Reza Khan to transact his matters of revenue, we left for Shelling, a little village, the reed houses of which surround a large tower. This might at pleasure be turned into a fortress: and within its walls we slept. The place is a very short distance from the lake; and here I saw horses fed on dry fish reduced to powder.

Sekooha, November 1st.—We arrived here in three hours from Shelling, taking across the country to the fortress of Deshtak. Reza Khan's lieutenant here was Dost Mahomed Khan, Norvui, a brother of Abdullah Khan of Jelalabad. There are about six hundred reed houses within the walls, and twelve hundred without. It is not improbable that this is the locality which has been described by geographers as Dooshakh—the names, as will be seen, are very similar. Deshtak is situated on the banks of the Helmund, which is at this point very deep and three hundred yards in breadth. We remained here till noon. Remounting our dromedaries, after having crossed the river on a raft, we made our way through the brushwood and cultivation, and entered the desert;

when about halfway the village of Dowlat-abad was seen on the right, and continuing we arrived at Sekooha, our friend's capital, in the evening.

This fortress is the strongest and most important of Seistan, because, being at five parasangs from the lake, water is to be obtained only in the wells which have been dug within its *enceinte*. The intermediate and surrounding country being an arid parched waste, devoid not only of water but of everything else, the besiegers could not subsist themselves, and would, even if provisioned, inevitably die of thirst. It contains about twelve hundred houses, each of which would furnish one and in some cases two fighting men. I have called it the capital of Seistan, but it is impossible to say how long it may enjoy that title—no doubt until some chief, more powerful or more fortunate than Reza Khan, obtains the upper hand, which may happen at any time, for in this country no one can tell what the morrow may bring forth. It is impossible to calculate upon the duration of anything—neither the power of a family nor the existence of a town: the first may be feared, may have great authority—the second may be rich, populous, and the best fortified—but both may disappear in a moment; may be laid low by those elements of strife and selfishness which pervade all classes, but more especially the chiefs, so that scarcely a trace of either can be seen. The existing generation will alone preserve any remembrance of the past, and that only for a few years; here everything is in a state of change, and it is almost impossible for the geography of the country to be accurately described; general information may be given, but details will ever vary, and they can only be furnished from time to time by the few travellers who wander through these uncivilized parts of the earth. These remarks apply more especially to the territory of Seistan.

Ser Jadda, November 3rd—twelve parasangs. We left Sekooha at daybreak, most truly thankful to Mohamed Reza Khan for the great kindness and hospitality he had shown us. He undertook to send back the dromedaries we had hired of the Ket-khoda of Gooljin, and let us have others in their place; one of these was loaded with rice, flour, dried fish, water, and other things for our consumption between this and Laush-jowaine. A relative of the Khan accompanied us halfway to the village of Koondoor, and there gave us an escort of four men. We lost some time here, and did not in consequence arrive at Ser Jadda, situated at the most southern extremity of the lake, till nightfall. The Khan's people had some difficulty in affording us protection, and were obliged to keep watch and ward all night to prevent the villagers from robbing us; two of our dromedaries were nearly taken, and but for their leg-couplings would have been so, and we should never have seen them again.

Zerdabad, November 4th — fourteen parasangs — nine hours. This day we were accompanied by eight Arabs on their way to Laush, who served us as guides and knew the country well. There is no road actually traced on the western side of the lake; in the summer and autumn, when the water is low, travellers skirt the lake, though there is some difficulty in doing so, by reason of the pools and the tamarisk woods, which in many places obstruct the way and oblige him to make a circuit. These obstacles may be avoided by following the track at the foot of a chain of mountains a short distance from the lake, which run north and south, and parallel with its length. Zerdabad, where we encamped, consists of two ruined towers, round which were half a dozen tents; the inmates were nomads of Arab origin.

Noorroozabad, November 5th—twelve parasangs—eight hours. We kept a little more from the lake to reach our halt. The moving sands were succeeded by a firmer soil, though still sand, amongst which were some fine tamarisk shrubs and a little grass, yellow, and long since dried up by the scorching sun. We met a party of ten Belooches early in the morning, evidently out on the watch for the helpless, but our numbers and appearance did not promise an easy adventure, and they contented themselves with asking if we had seen anything of a caravan that was near us, and which, as we learnt afterwards, they plundered nearly in the same spot where we met them.

Laush-jowaine, November 6th — about ten parasangs — seven hours—following the lake and turning round it a little to the north, at the spot where it receives the waters of the Haroot-rood. This river we crossed at Kogha, at about a quarter of an hour from its mouth; the water was not higher than the bellies of our dromedaries, for it was at that period of the year when the stream was at the lowest by reason of the long drought and the great quantities of water removed from it for the purposes of irrigation. On our right, but at a considerable distance, we left the vast ruins of Peshaveran and those of Lukh, both probably of the same city—

the second constructed after the destruction of the first, but at a little distance from it. Assad Khan assured me that there is a sulphur spring between Lukh and Peshaveran, and the tomb of Syud Ibkal. Beyond this is the district, now deserted, of Shoorab. We arrived very early at Laush-jowaine; a fortress situated on the right bank of the Furrah-rood, and about seven or eight parasangs above the place at which it falls into the lake. We were received at the house of Saloo Khan, an Afghan of the tribe of Ishakzye, and chief of this district. The Khan is more generally known by the name of Shah Pesend Khan—he with whom the king is pleased—a title which he received from Shah Kamran. This Sirdar, as I have already said, was at war with the Belooche chief Ali Khan of Sheikh Nassoor, but he had other difficulties to surmount. Laush had always been a dependence of the principality of Herat; nevertheless, Shah Pesend Khan refused to acknowledge the complete sovereignty of Yar Mohamed, and he was secretly encouraged in this rebellious spirit by the Persian Court and Kohendil Khan, who, both one and the other allied against the chief of Herat, had the greatest interest in making the chief of Laush independent, inasmuch as it furnished them with the means of mutual communication without being obliged to send their envoys or correspondence through Herat, where there was every chance of their being seized or examined. Besides this, the fort of Laush is the key to the position, and the road from Persia to Kandahar by the rivers; and Kohendil Khan, as well as Mohamed Shah, with that duplicity so common in Eastern nations, each thought to deceive the other, and obtain the support of Saloo Khan for his own particular interest: but Saloo had married his daughter to Mir dil Khan, the brother of the Kandahar chief, and seemed therefore to be devoted to that personage; his eldest son, Rassool Khan, had also married a niece of Kohendil Khan.*

* Shah Pesend Khan, from his position between Persia and Afghanistan, has always been possessed of much political influence. He was equally courted by the court of Persia on one side, and the chiefs of Cabul and Kandahar on the other. Nominally dependant on Herat, he was seldom trusted either by Shah Kamran or Yar Mohamed; but from the moment the English came into the country, he studiously attached himself to their cause, doing good service on several occasions. One of his sons, Ressool Khan, always resided in Kandahar, in attendance on the prince governor during our occupation; and this chief was most useful as a medium of communication between the British authorities and the heads of the different Dooranee tribes. Ressool Khan is the chief referred to in Kaye's 'Afghanistan,' as having accompanied Sufder Jung to the Dooranee camp, when that

These circumstances, and the somewhat rebellious spirit shown by Saloo Khan, were not agreeable to Yar Mohamed, who frequently menaced his disobedient and crafty vassal; but He-with-whom-the-king-is-pleased, while protesting his great devotion for the chief of Herat, always turned a deaf ear to his demands for tribute, and declined to pay, alleging as an excuse, either that the crops were bad, the harvest was bad, or he was at war with a neighbour, or had some fort to build, &c. I was aware of these details before I arrived at Laush, and was careful not to speak of Yar Mohamed's friendship for me as a means of obtaining the good offices of the former. I left Assad Khan to arrange this for me in any way he chose; and as he was Saloo's cousin, we were received as of the family, and sheep and poultry were roasted in honour of our visit. Being told that I had the intention of returning to Teheran, my host was still more pressing in his attentions, in the hope that I should give the Shah a favourable opinion of him. As a promise was not expensive, and he was most hospitable, I assured him that I should be very glad if there was any way in which I could be of use to him.

The fortress of Laush is situated at fourteen parasangs south of that of Furrah, on the summit of a sugar-loaf eminence. There are three lines of defence, connected by towers and protected by ditches. It would be difficult to take it even with a European army, unless they had a siege-train. There are not more than seventy or eighty houses within its *enceinte;* but there are several thousand tents of nomads encamped in its environs. The fortress of Jowaine, situated at half an hour from Laush, on the right bank of the river, is a dependence of Shah Pesend Khan; and his uncle resides and commands here under him. The canton of Kalehi-kah is also under the chief of Laush; and these three strips of territory are designated as the country of Ho-kat, or Beled Ho-kat. The population may be estimated by the number of houses and tents; of the former there are about 2400; and of tents 4500, of nomadic Afghans, Belooches, and Eïmaks: these would furnish 500 horsemen, and from 3500 to 5000 infantry. They have a good reputation as soldiers. The contingents which the chief of Laush would receive from several Arab, Afghan, and

---

prince in a moment of ill-humour fled from Kandahar to join the rebels. Shah Pesend Khan is still living (1856) in the enjoyment of all his honours.—ED.

Belooche chiefs in the neighbourhood, with whom he is allied, would double this force. This fact somewhat explains the moderation of Yar Mohammed towards a vassal so little disposed to be submissive. Besides the Haroot-rood, the Khashak-rood, and the Furrah-rood, which flow through the Ho-kat district, it is also watered by seven canals, which are fed by these rivers: these are the Jowaine, the Penj-deh, the Darg, the Soh-moor, the Kogha, the Khair-abad, and the Sherki-av,* which give their names to as many villages; the gardens and cultivation about which are irrigated by means of wheels, which raise the water and serve at the same time to grind the corn.

* Sherki-av means the Eastern stream.

CHAPTER XXVIII.

The district of Laush — Ancient inhabitants of Seistan — Arrian's mention of this country — The state of it in the days of Alexander — Geographical description of it at the present time — Origin of the word Seistan — Course of the Helmund river — Inhabitants on its banks — The cultivation and pastures on them — Navigable from Girishk to its mouth — Rafts on this and other Eastern rivers — The Aria Palus — Description of the Seistan lake — The affluents of this lake — Language of the Belooches — Characteristics of that tribe — Their religious faith — The Peer Kisri — Gross superstitions of the Belooches — Their love of thieving — Their excuse for this vice — Etymology of their name — Description of their life when encamped — Number of armed men they could bring into the field — Their courage superior to that of the Afghans — Their singular mode of keeping touch when fighting — The Author arrives at Furrah — Surprise of the Mollah Akhond-zadeh — Itineraries to several parts of Persia—Furrah to Nishapoor by Toon — Furrah to Semnoon by Tubbus—Description of the latter town—Beerjoon to Kerman by Khubhes—The city of Ghayn — The Author leaves Furrah — Khosh-ava — Jeja — Singular request of a lady of this place — Subzawur — Ruins at Subzawur — Legend of the inhabitants — The fort of Subzawur an important military post — Position attributed to Subzawur erroneous — The Shah Thamasp put to death here by Nadir Shah — Adreskan — Shabith — Roozbagh.

THE district of Laush is at the extreme northern limit of Seistan, and some geographers have included Furrah in this last country, but the inhabitants reject this arrangement; I will mention here the observations which I was enabled to make, and the information I obtained relative to the history of this country, the Helmund, the Seistan Lake, and the Belooches.

In reading the histories of Alexander, and comparing their statements with the geographical data we now possess, it is almost impossible to reconcile them one with the other. The difficulty of determining the portion of territory inhabited by this or that people of such a remote period is the greater, because nothing has remained—no vestige of an edifice, no sculptured stone—to support the proof; it is only by induction that we can arrive at a result which is often doubtful. Seistan is no exception to this rule; and there, perhaps, more than anywhere else, we are reduced to accept vague suppositions respecting the original inhabitants, as well as the country. One half the population is now of the Belooche race; the other half is composed principally of Afghan tribes and Arabs, with a few Turkish families, and even Kurds, which have been thrown here by the waves of revolution and intestine feuds. A mixed race has been the result; but we may certainly, without fear of error, consider the three last races as not having inhabited Seistan in the days of Alexander. The Afghans and Belooches, therefore, remain; and it would be, indeed, difficult to say positively which of these two nations were the Zarangæ or Dranghes, the Agriaspes or the Arrachoti. Arrian states "that in leaving Artacoana (Herat), to which town he had gone to suppress the revolt of Satibarzanes, he rejoined his army, then commanded by Craterus, and came direct to the capital of the Zarangæ." That is the only remark made by this historian on this most important town. Amongst modern authors, Herbelot is a little less obscure. Speaking of Zarangæ, he calls it a commercial town, well inhabited, of the province of Seistan. Yacoob ben Leith constructed several canals; so that the city and its environs were, by means of these waters, well supplied with all kinds of grain and merchandise, although the soil was bad and sterile. Arrian's account indicates that the country of the Zarangæ was contiguous to that of the Arii, and consequently south of the town of Furrah; but nothing that he states can fix the position of their capital. We may, therefore, look for it in that extensive circle of ruins which I have already mentioned, or in those localities which are still of some importance, such as Sheikh-Nassoor, Laush, Jehanabad, Deshtak, and Sekooha. In accordance with Herbelot's opinion, this capital must have been at a distance from the rivers. If not, it would have been unnecessary to construct canals there, to conduct the water which could not be obtained from its arid soil. From these latter words it is impossible to suppose that it could have been situated in the centre of the delta formed by the several branches of the Helmund, where it falls into the lake. No town corresponds so well with Herbelot's description as the fortress of Sekooha. As to the other ancient cities, such as Ram, Prophtasia, and others, it is still more difficult to affirm that they were cities distinct from Zarangæ, or simply a continuation of it. All the ruins scattered round the lake, and on the borders of the river, may equally represent their sites.

Alexander passed from the country of the Zarangæ to that of the Agriaspæ, in which, says Quintus Curtius, he remained two months; and, for him to have resided so long in this country, it must have been sufficiently fertile, and adapted to meet the requirements of his army. The deserts of Seistan have extended themselves, rather than been reduced, since that period; we may, therefore, conclude that the only district the resources of which have not diminished since the time they sufficed to supply the wants of the Grecian army, is to be found on the banks of the Helmund, between Mula-Khan and Girishk. This, then, would be the country of the Agriaspæ; and that of the Arrachoti the continuation of the same, running towards the south and east, as far as the Sea of Oman and the Indus. With reference to the Drangæ, it must be admitted that their position will be more difficult to determine; perhaps we may assign to them the districts of Bukwa, Gulistan, and Washeer, with some degree of probability. As to the Agriaspæ, it may be said that if they were the ancestors of the Belooches that now occupy the territory they inhabited, there is no country in which time has so completely transformed the habits and customs of a people. Arrian remarks that they were surnamed the Euergetes, or Benefactors, because they assisted Cyrus, the son of Cambyses, in his expedition against the Scythians; and that Alexander treated them with distinction, in commemoration of the conduct of their ancestors, and out of regard for their institutions. "In fact, these people," he adds, "do not live like barbarians, but, like the civilised Greeks, they understand what justice is. Alexander gave them their liberty, and the territory, of little extent, which they requested to have." The facts are far otherwise in our day. Here, where justice had her seat, and civilisation reigned, there is nothing but anarchy; and every one lives according to his own barbarous, ignorant, and perverse instincts.

Seistan is a flat country, with here and there some low hills. One-third of the surface of the soil is composed of moving-sands, and the two other thirds of a compact sand, mixed with a little clay, but very rich in vegetable matter, and covered with woods of the tamarisk, *saghes*, *tag*, and reeds; in the midst of which there is abundant pasture. These woods are more especially met with in the central part of the province, through which the Helmund and its affluents flow. The detritus and slimy soil which is deposited on the land after the annual inundations fertilize it in a remarkable manner, and this has probably been the case from time immemorial; at any rate, the number of ruins on the banks would lead one to suppose so. The banks of the Helmund are cultivated to the extent of a mile and a half on either side, from Girishk as far as Mula-Khan; but from thence to the Tower of Alemdar they consist principally of grass land, and are more wooded than cultivated.

The Sirdar of Kandahar has subjected to his rule that part of Seistan comprehended between Kaleh-i-Bist and Roodbar. The portion that lies between this and Alemdar is an object of perpetual discord between this sovereign and the nomadic Belooches, who, as I have before remarked, pitch their tents here during the eight months of the year, when the scorching sun has dried up every vestige of moisture in their own oases of the desert, where the wells and cisterns are only filled by the rains of spring and winter during the other four months. Two Belooches and one Afghan chief divide the rest of Seistan. To the south is Mohamed Reza Khan of Sekooha; in the centre is Ali Khan of Sheikh Nassoor; and to the north, Shah Pesend Khan of Laush Jowaine. Houses of earth and reeds are seen only on the banks of the Helmund; in every other part the inhabitants are encamped under their felt tents, or those made of goats' or camels' hair. The heat is always excessive in Seistan, and the hot wind blows with violence, frequently raising whirlwinds of impalpable dust, which obscures everything and is very injurious to the sight; of the enormous musquitoes that infest the district I have already spoken. The history of this province is intimately connected with that of Persia; and the inhabitants are very proud of belonging to the country in which King Jemshid and the heroes Zal and Roostem, of whom Eastern authors have written such extravagant fictions, first saw the light.

The word Seistan, the present name of this province, came originally from the word *Saghis*, the name of a wood much used in Persia for burning at this time, and considered very much superior to any other wood for the same purpose. It is frequently found in the steppes of Central Asia, but in much greater quantities near the Helmund, and it is this that has given to the country in which it grows so abundantly the appellation of Saghistan, the place of the saghis, which by time and degrees has been successively corrupted into Sedjistan, Seïstan, and at last Sistan, by which it is now generally called. This was given me as the most correct etymology by the learned Mohamed Hassan, Kazi of Herat.*

The Helmund of the Afghans, the Etymander of the ancients, is a fine river, the only one to which these words can be applied between the Tigris and the Indus. After the junction of several small streams coming from Koh-i-baba, situated at a short distance west of Kabul, it runs from north-east to south-west a length of two hundred parasangs, at first in a deep channel through scarped rocks and obstructed by enormous blocks of the same, and across the mountainous country of the Paropamisus, inhabited by Hazarahs Pusht-Koh, but at ten or twelve parasangs above Girishk it begins to flow over a sandy and gravelly bed, and through a flat country within a channel less confined: it is then turned to account, and irrigates by artificial means the meadows and arable land in its vicinity, until, nearly exhausted by the soil, it reaches at its extreme limit on the south the Meshila-Seistan,† or Lake of Seistan. Several inhabited islands, and some of them, like Kalehi Bist, fortified, are in the middle of the stream, the aspect of which from one extremity to the other is picturesque and sometimes majestic. The Helmund is also at several points prevented from overflowing by embankments of very ancient construction, which, for want of necessary repairs, have fallen into decay. The vegetation on its banks is as luxuriant as in the tropics—but with all these advantages they are unfortunately inhabited by the greatest plunderers and the most cruel race to be found in all Asia. The water of the Helmund is cold, clear, fresh, and sweet, and though a considerable portion is turned off for the purposes of irrigation, there is at all times sufficient for navigating it from Girishk to its mouth, but it would in such case be necessary to repair the old embankments and construct a few others. In the spring and winter the volume of water is doubled, it then overflows and inundates the surrounding country which it thereby vivifies.

---

* This may serve as a specimen of the eastern Kazis. The good man had probably never heard of the Sakæ and their migrations, but it is perfectly well known to geographers that the Seghistan of the Arabs, whence Sistan, is the same as the Sakestané, or country of the Sakæ, of the Greeks. See Isodore Char. in Hudson's 'Geog. Minores,' vol. ii.—ED.

† Meshila merely means, in Arabic, a muddy swamp. The ordinary name of the lake is Hamûn, or the expanse.—ED.

If this river was in the possession of Europeans, steamboats would soon navigate it, and the supply of wood on its banks would remedy the want of coal. The course of the Helmund is very rapid, especially in winter after the floods, and the Hazarahs say the width varies a good deal in the upper part of its course. At Girishk it is from sixty to ninety yards wide, but from its point of junction with the Urgund-ab it attains a breadth of from three hundred to three hundred and eighty yards; the average depth is from one and a-half to two fathoms. The fords are few in number, nevertheless boats are rarely seen, and these are roughly and clumsily built; rafts made with reeds and branches, supported with inflated skins, are the most common. The historians of Alexander have perhaps erred in stating that the rafts on which this hero crossed the rivers of Central Asia were buoyed up with skins stuffed with straw;* they were then, no doubt as now, inflated with air; and it is thus that the Euphrates, the Tigris, the Karoon, the Indus, the Oxus, and other rivers in this quarter of the globe, are still navigated. It is probable that when Craterus left Alexander, and returned to Persia with the sick and the heavy baggage, he followed the course of the Helmund.

The *Aria palus* of the ancients, a lake formed by the accumulation of the waters of the Helmund at the southern extremity of its course, is called the Lake of Zurreh† by Europeans; this name is not known by the great majority of Asiatics, it is found only in some old Persian books, in which it also bears the appellation of Deria-reza; both of these words signify the little sea; the present inhabitants of Seistan call it the Mechila Seistan, Lake of Seistan, or Mechila Roostem, Lake of Roostem, in honour of the Persian hero of Firdousi. According to this author this extraordinary warrior resided on an island, situated on the eastern side of the lake; several geographers have erroneously given the lake the name of Deria Hamoon—this designates the Sea of Oman, which washes the shores of Arabia and Mekran.‡

The form and position of the Lake of Seistan are not accurately

* On the Cabul river, and on the Upper Indus, it is still the custom to stuff the skins with reeds or straw. The writer of this note descended the Cabul river from Jelalabad to Attock on a raft so constructed.—L.

† Zurrah, by which name the lake is usually known, is a mere contraction of Zerenj, the ancient capital; and this name again represents the Zarangi or Drangæ of the Greeks.—ED.

‡ M. Ferrier has probably forgotten that Hamûn is an old Persian word signifying expanse.—ED.

given on the generality of maps; it is neither a circle nor an oval, but a kind of trefoil without a stalk, having the head very long. Its length from north to south is twenty-five parasangs. It extends from about the thirty-first to the thirty-second degree of north latitude, and follows an oblique line, starting at the north from the sixtieth degree of longitude, terminating at the south at the fifty-ninth degree. Its greatest width in the north is about twelve parasangs, and in every other direction from six to seven at the outside. The water of this lake, though not salt, is black and of bad taste. Fish live with difficulty in it, and are always very small; the large ones ascend the clear waters of the rivers, in which are enormous barbel. The lake is only from four to five feet in depth, and the bottom has a constant tendency to rise higher, while the beds of its affluents become on the contrary deeper every year; we must perhaps seek in this last fact for the explanation of the first. The winter floods carry with them a great quantity of detritus and sand from the beds of the rivers, and deposit them in one common reservoir, which must of necessity finish by being filled up, and it is quite possible that in a few years its waters may be displaced—perhaps they may occupy again a dried-up spot more to the south, where it is affirmed the lake once existed.

The general appearance of Mechila Seistan is rather picturesque; it is surrounded on all sides by the tamarisk and other trees, the branches of which, always verdant, rise above its waters; the bottom of the lake is composed of a moving sand which absorbs its waters with such astonishing rapidity that if it were not so it would be difficult to say what would become of those conveyed here in such abundance by the Helmund and its other affluents. The evaporation could never be so great as to dissipate them, particularly during the winter and spring. It is true that in these seasons the lake is amenable to the same laws as the rivers—it overflows its banks and inundates the country to some distance; but by the end of April it has resumed its original proportions, and three months after it is so exceedingly dry to the north that the inhabitants of Sekooha, Deshtak, Jehanabad, and other neighbouring places, go direct to Laush by crossing dryfoot the strait between Berungi-Kefter and Peshaveran. There are several buildings, and many ruins, situated on the island in this lake; the northern end terminates in a high hill called Koh Khojeh, the Hill of the Eunuch.

A few words of emendation of the generally received opinions may be said with reference to the small affluents of this lake. The Khash-rood does not fall into the Helmund near to Koonesheen, as indicated by Arrowsmith's copy of Burnes's map; the Seistan Lake receives the waters of that river on the north-east, a little lower down than the Khoospas, a dry torrent in summer, but always much swollen in winter. On the other side of the lake, but still also to the north, the Furrah-rood and Haroot-rood add their waters to it at about three parasangs distance from each other,—the latter, after having received the Khashak-rood, which flows between them. Ptolemy in ancient times and some modern geographers have confounded the Heri-rood, which, passing Herat, flows into Turcomania, with the Haroot-rood just mentioned. I have stated elsewhere, when speaking of the Adreskan-rood, why these two rivers are distinct one from the other, and could never have formed one stream. With the exception of the Helmund all the foregoing rivers are dry in the summer, their waters being turned and employed in the irrigation of the land.

There is every reason for supposing that the Belooches of Seistan are descended from the original inhabitants of this country, for this race has become very little altered; their ideas respecting their origin are various, and of the most extravagant kind, and nothing is to be gleaned from this source; their language has nothing in common with those of their neighbours, and it would require deep and careful study to obtain any satisfactory proof of that from which it was derived: all that can be said of it is, that it is Belooche, and nothing but Belooche, augmented no doubt by many Arab, Persian, Pushtoo, and Indian words. Each tribe has its peculiar dialect, but they are all from the common stock, and the actual difference between them is trifling.*

The Belooche tribes are generally subdivided into several hundred branches, but they are better known under the three great divisions, which form as it were three distinct people—the Nervuis, the Rinds, and the Meksis. The majority of the inhabitants of Seistan, especially those on the banks of the Helmund and the shores of the lake, are of the first of these divisions. It is difficult to estimate even approximately the total

* Grammars of the Belooche and Brahui dialects have been lately published, which clearly show that the former is of the Arian or Sanscrit, and the latter of the Scythic or Turanian family.—ED.

number of the population of this province, because being partly nomadic, independent, and always on the move, even speculation becomes fruitless; inquiry of themselves is absurd, as they are in the habit of grossly and ridiculously exaggerating everything. These Belooches have no written laws, but are governed by ancient usages and traditions. The authority of the chiefs is slight, and consists solely in settling the quarrels and misunderstandings that continually occur between the members of the same *kheil*, village, or encampment; in fixing the camping ground, and other matters of the same nature; also, what is of much importance, the relations which are to exist between the tribe and their neighbours.

With these exceptions every Belooche is absolute in his own family. The life led by these nomads is as savage as that of the wild beasts, which like them rove through their deserts. To observe laws like other nations, to work, or traffic, or obey a master, are things to them impossible. The most complete liberty of action is an imperious necessity of their nature, they are as proud of their crimes as we of our good actions, and the law of revenge is the only one which is invariably observed. When blood has been spilt, eternal hatred, which outlives generations in the families in which the deed was done, is the result; a reconciliation even cemented by a marriage, or the good offices and intervention of a *Peer*, holy man, will not be permanent; the *vendetta* alone is always remembered. To gratify this, they will track their enemy with a quiet perseverance perfectly wonderful, and either openly or secretly, frequently in ambush or laying some snare, will cut his throat with a savage barbarity really inconceivable. Two Belooches of adverse tribes, or who have a family feud, and never saw one another, have a marvellous instinct in divining the fact; they scent it like a pointer: when they find themselves in presence of each other, there is no burst of furious outbreak, they regard one another for a moment in silence, but this calm is the sure forerunner of the death of one, and sometimes of both—I might say, often. They are without pity, and if unarmed they will tear each other like tigers with their nails, bite with their teeth, or strangle one another without making the least cry. I here speak only of those who inhabit Seistan.

The Belooches call themselves Mussulmans, but they do not observe the precepts of the Koran; their religious ideas are a mixture of Islamism, Christianity, and idolatry, the whole seasoned with the grossest superstitions. The greater part are not circumcised, do not fast, do not pray, and, although acknowledging that Mahomet is a prophet, there is another they consider of much greater importance than he, and as second only to God, with whom they sometimes confound him. The power of this being is unlimited, he is called the Peer Kisri,* and when they swear by him they may be trusted, but only then. The Belooches are ardent, impulsive, well-formed, and nervous; their complexion is olive, like that of the Arab, and these two races have more than one analogous point between them; their features express astuteness and ferocity, they are insensible to privations, and support them and fatigue in the most admirable manner; no matter how painful and long the journey may be, they are always ready for the march. A Persian and Afghan travels at night to avoid the great heats; the Belooche, on the contrary, is not only not afraid of them, but seeks that which these nations as much as possible avoid; they march only between sunrise and sunset, and before or after will never move a yard; if the great luminary disappears before they have arrived at their intended halt, they encamp on the spot they happen to be at, at the time. Their most extraordinary physical characteristic is the facility with which, camel-like, they can for so long a time go without drink in their burning country—a draught of water once in the twenty-four hours is sufficient for them, even on a journey; they have also a particular instinct for ascertaining the spot at which water is nearest the surface of the soil, and they rarely dig further than three feet without coming to it.

They march with a rapidity which it is impossible to conceive, and will walk faster than the best horse; there are instances amongst them of men who will tire out three horses, one after another, in this manner. They eat very little, and believe most implicitly in auguries; the cry of a wild beast, the sight of a serpent, a bird on the wing, a flight of birds, or a troop of wild asses which separate into two divisions, is sufficient to stop them short suddenly in the midst of their journey. They will never leave the place they are in before the sun, under which they were warned by this augury, has set and risen again; this delay is to allow Fate time to alter her intentions, should they happen to be adverse. When the opportunity for pillage arrives their activity is amazing, their

* The word *peer* signifies literally *old,* but figuratively it has the same meaning with them that *holy* has with us.

plans are undertaken and executed with great promptitude, and courage, and wonderful address; life is as nothing to them, and they will expose it for the least trifle; theft is an irresistible habit. They sit back to back on a dromedary, that they may have a perfect view in every direction, and on these beasts they will cover in a short time immense distances. They scour the southern roads of Afghanistan, and sometimes carry their raids into the centre of Persia; they kill all prisoners they cannot carry away with them, and will sometimes ride a race of several score miles for the chance of getting a handkerchief or a rag—the smallest trifle in short will excite their avidity. They know so thoroughly how strong is their predilection for thieving, how inveterate the habit, that two friends, two brothers, aye, even a father and a son, travelling together, will take good care not to sleep close to one another. When the time for rest arrives, one will point out to the other a spot one hundred yards off where he had better sleep, and they both swear by Peer-Kisri not to approach each other until the hour of departure. They have a remarkably quick sense of hearing, and the least noise or movement made by one will be sure to awake the other, who reminds him of the Peer-Kisri. Sometimes a Belooche will kill another for his dress, the value of which may be about three shillings.

They justify their passion for plunder by the following singular reasoning. "Some thousand years ago," they say, "God divided the good things of this life in a manner far from equitable. Whether from forgetfulness, or at the instigation of some bad genii, the Belooches received nothing from him beyond an arid, ungrateful, and unproductive soil. This was unjust, and it is very natural that we should try and take from others that which has been so unjustly withheld from ourselves." The etymology of their name, they say, is a proof of the justifiable character of this argument, or as it were a kind of corollary to it; *bé* in Persia signifies without; *leuct*, naked, stripped. This by corruption is pronounced by them and the Afghans *leucht* or *loucht*, thus the two words united make bé-loucht, which denotes that they came into the world naked and despoiled of their share in this world's goods, and upon these grounds alone are authorized to lay their hands upon everything that comes in their way or out of their way. The Belooches detest Mussulmans more, perhaps, than the people of any other religion; they are not so hospitable to strangers as other nomadic tribes, and as I have before said, except under the protection of the Peer-Kisri, it is dangerous to put any faith in them. They look upon Europeans as castaways, deriving their origin from genii, being in league with the devil, who has taught them how to make gold, and as having the power of the evil eye, and of being able to find hidden treasures; the ardour with which they see us examining and groping amongst old ruins confirms them in this last opinion.

When encamped they lead a life of complete idleness; the women and children only are occupied in tilling the ground and looking after the flocks, from which they make considerable profits. They sell the wool of the sheep, and spin the goats' and camels' hair to make clothes and tents; the cloth from these materials is so closely woven, that they make bags of it in which they carry milk, water, and other liquids, without losing a drop; their clothes made of this material are worn in the rainy season. In summer they wear a cotton tunic, drawn in at the waist, and large pantaloons; the turban is twisted and tied like that of the Arabs, and not like that of the Afghans; the front of their heads is shaved, the remainder of the hair being allowed to fall loosely over their shoulders. If all the Belooches of Seistan, capable of bearing arms, were united in one *corps d'armée*, they would certainly present an effective force of from 30,000 to 35,000 men, all excellent infantry. There is no cavalry, for horses in Seistan are few in number. The Belooches are armed with a lance and sabre; fire-arms are rarely seen—a few matchlocks and some bad pistols are the extent of their armoury in this way; they carry the Indian buckler, covered with a thin plate of copper, or with the skin of the elephant or rhinoceros. Of their courage they boast and swagger as much as the Afghans, but perhaps with more reason; the latter are good for a rush, but they do not meet the shock of an attack, or stand under the fire of artillery. The Belooches, on the contrary, though as ignorant as the latter of the art of war, surpass them in tenacity and bravery; they remain firm under the fire of the enemy, and are bold in their advance. They attack in small parties of ten or twelve, and to prevent any one from running away and ensure the immediate removal of their wounded, they tie their tunics together; in the latter case four files in rear of these little detachments, untie the tunic of the wounded man, and having fastened the party together again remove him to the rear. On many occasions they hold firm, and die on the ground like real heroes; there are no better soldiers in Asia than these Belooches.*

Furrah, November 7th.—Fourteen parasangs—ten hours—through a plain, and following the left bank of the Furrah-rood, amongst brushwood of tamarisk and *tag* underwood, the ground always rising in front of us. We saw only one single village, but numerous ruins and the tents of nomads, and arrived at Furrah at nightfall. Nothing can picture the stupefaction of Mollah Mahmood Akhond-zadeh on seeing me; he was so disappointed that he stared at me without the power of saying a word. He listened in silence to the statement of Assad Khan, and when it was finished, accused him of being a rascal, a brigand, who wished to dishonour him by making it appear that he had not taken the necessary measures and sufficient precautions to ensure the success of my journey. "What will the Vezir say?" said the Mollah at every pause; "I am a lost and ruined man." At length, after being an hour in a state of complete prostration of mind, he suddenly exclaimed, "I am saved; in five days you shall leave again; I know where to find some dromedaries." Unfortunately for him, however, I did not intend to take advantage of the resources of his imagination, having quite determined, after what had happened, not to attempt any new adventures. To this he was obliged to resign himself, and remain satisfied with receiving my certificate, setting forth the good services he had rendered me. I did the same for Assad Khan, but as he thought this might not be quite sufficient to cover the responsibilities he conceived himself under towards me, he determined upon accompanying me to Herat, though his wound was still open, and he suffered much from it.

I remained at Furrah the 8th and 9th, and rested myself after the fatigues and dangers I had encountered in Seistan, and to prepare myself for my journey to Herat. During my first stay at Furrah, and previously to my receiving Yar Mohamed's reply, authorizing me to go to Shikarpoor, I had an idea, in case of his refusing, of entering Persia by way of Toon and Tubbus, and taking the road through Yezd and Kerman to Bunder-Busheer. With this in view, I had obtained every information from a certain Meshedi Hadi, a camel-driver of Furrah, who during thirty-five

* It may be remembered that the army of the Ameers of Scinde, which fought so gallantly at Meeani, was composed almost entirely of Belooches.—ED.

years had been continually passing to and fro through these vast and solitary regions; he also furnished me with an exact list of all the halts, and I give them a place here, without completely accepting the responsibility of the details, though I believe them to be accurate: they may be useful to the geographer, or to subsequent travellers. It should be remembered that it is impossible to give the exact distances on the map, by compass, or as the crow flies, for it will be necessary here, as much as in every other case, to allow for the great circuit which it is frequently necessary to make, to avoid the obstacles and difficulties of ground, and to obtain water.

Direct Road from Furrah to Nishapoor.

From Furrah to—

Killah-Khan—10 parasangs—a walled village, 400 houses; inhabited by Persians.

Daroo—14 parasangs—walled village, 300 houses; inhabited by an agricultural population and shepherds of the Arab race.

Shehrbisha—12 parasangs—walled village, 400 houses; inhabited by cultivators of the soil, shepherds, and caravaniers of the Persian race.

Mood—5 parasangs—an open village, 400 houses; the inhabitants Persians.

Boodj—5 parasangs—walled village, 300 houses; the inhabitants Persians.

Beerjoon—2 parasangs—a walled town, 1000 houses; population Arab and Persian. 1000 houses surround the fortress.

Shah-hag—9 parasangs—walled village, 60 houses, and 100 tents of nomads round it; an Arab population.

Mohamed-abad—5 parasangs—walled village, 100 houses, 200 tents in the environs; Arab population.

Doost-abad—2 parasangs—an open village, 100 houses. The inhabitants Persians.

Serayoon—4 parasangs—walled town, 2000 houses. This is a very large place, but half destroyed: water is in abundance, and comes from the neighbouring mountains; two hundred and sixty reservoirs are fed by these streams. Serayoon is surrounded by numerous gardens, and there are great numbers of excellent camels. The majority of the inhabitants are camel caravaniers; it has a manufactory of small arms and one of felt carpets, called *remed*. In the environs are many prosperous and handsome villages.

Ayask—2 parasangs—500 houses, a small walled town; the inhabitants are Persians.

Toon—3 parasangs—a walled town, the *enceinte* recently repaired; 3500 houses; population Persian. There are handsome bazars, mosques, and caravanserais, built of burnt brick; the gardens are large and numerous. There is a considerable commercial movement here; the productions are opium, silk, cotton, tobacco, and fruits. Water is scarce, and the corn-crops are consequently light; in years of drought wheat for consumption is obliged to be imported. Camels and sheep are numerous; horses scarce.

Booroo—2 parasangs—a walled village, 150 houses; a Persian population.

Ser-i-deh—3 parasangs—a walled village, 300 houses; a Persian population.

Bejistan—2 parasangs—a small town, walled; 700 houses within the *enceinte*, 300 outside; a Persian population; abundance of fruit.

Ser-dagh—4 parasangs—a walled village, 100 houses; population, Persians. In a plain, where there is an abundance of salt; this forms a considerable article of commerce.

Sahadedi—5 parasangs, a walled village, 100 houses; a Persian population.

Kadoogan—3 parasangs—a walled village, 150 houses; a Persian population.

Kaboodan—4 parasangs—a walled village, 300 houses; a Persian population.

Kaleh-meidan—3 parasangs—a walled village, 70 houses; a Persian population.

Singird—4 parasangs—a walled village, 300 houses; inhabited by 100 Persians and 200 Belooches.

Pabaz—5 parasangs—400 houses; a Persian population.

Nishapoor—5 parasangs—a walled town, of which I have already made mention.

Route from Furrah to Semnoon.

From Furrah to *Beerjoon*, as in the preceding route.

Shah-zileh—4 parasangs—a walled village, 100 houses; an Arab population.

Shaneh—4 parasangs—a walled village, 100 houses; a Persian population.

Hooz-jinbek—5 parasangs—encampment of nomads; 10 tents tenanted by Belooches.

Khoor—5 parasangs—a walled village, 400 houses; a Persian population.

Mikh-Khoor—2 parasangs—a spring of water; without houses or inhabitants.

Talkh-ab—5 parasangs—a spring of water; without houses or inhabitants.

Haooz-firooz—4 parasangs—a spring of water; without houses or inhabitants.

Haooz-Mohamed-Kassem—8 parasangs—a spring of water; without houses or inhabitants.

Payistan—2 parasangs—a walled village, 100 houses; a Persian population.

Joriz—4 parasangs—a walled village, 200 houses; a Persian population. Here Khorassan terminates.

Tubbus—2 parasangs—a town surrounded by an enormous embankment of earth, on which are towers connected by curtains and protected by a ditch. Tubbus is in a plain, the soil of which is of a silicious character, and water is bad and scarce. There are, nevertheless, in the neighbourhood thirty villages inhabited by Arabs, who have managed to fertilize to a certain extent this ungrateful soil. The town contains about 5000 houses: the population is Arab and Persian; but in this number should be included those which are scattered amongst the cottages in the gardens outside. The citadel, situated within the town, is very strong; but that which protects it more than the fortifications are the deserts that surround the district of which it is the chief place, and which extend on all sides to a distance of at least 10 parasangs. Considerable quantities of silk are produced here; this is taken to Yezd, and then spun: also *tambaki*, which is as much esteemed as that of Shiraz. The exportation of this article is great. The dates are of inferior quality; grain and cotton are grown in sufficient quantities to meet the consumption on the spot. Camels and sheep are more numerous here than in any other part of Persia. A large number of the population of Tubbus are by occupation *caravaniers*. The gardens are very productive and well watered, and the orange-tree is cultivated. The province of Irak commences here.

Shardeh—4 parasangs—a walled village, 100 houses; population Persians.

Kalmoreh—8 parasangs—a spring of brackish water; uninhabited spot.

Kerbas-ao—8 parasangs—a spring of brackish water; uninhabited spot.

Girdab—6 parasangs—a spring of brackish water; uninhabited spot.

Chechmeh-aziz—8 parasangs—a spring of brackish water; uninhabited spot.

Majerad—8 parasangs—a spring of brackish water; uninhabited spot.

Chechmeh-kooh—6 parasangs—a spring of brackish water; uninhabited spot.

Rezeh—6 parasangs—open village, 100 houses; a well; population Persians.

Turood—5 parasangs—walled village, 500 houses; population Persians.

Hussein-noon—5 parasangs—walled village, 400 houses; population Persians.

Ab-gah—5 parasangs—a spring of fresh water; uninhabited.

Semnoon—5 parasangs—a town of which I have already made mention, at six days' journey from Teheran.

Route from Beerjoon to Kerman.

From Beerjoon to—

Rakat—4 parasangs—walled village, 100 houses; population Persians.

Zehr-abad—4 parasangs—walled village, 25 houses; population Persians.

Majan—4 parasangs—walled village, 400 houses; population Persians.

Ser-chah—4 parasangs—walled village, 100 houses; population Arabs.

Atesh-kedeh—5 parasangs—a spring of fresh water; uninhabited.

Kooh-Bakhtan—5 parasangs—a spring of brackish water; uninhabited. The towns of Neh-bindan are on the left of Kooh-Bakhtan, 7 parasangs distant.

Haooz—3 parasangs—a dried well; uninhabited spot.

Good-nimeh—5 parasangs—a dried well; uninhabited spot.

Kosrood—4 parasangs—a dried well; uninhabited spot.

Goojar—4 parasangs—a dried well; uninhabited spot.

Bagh-assad—5 parasangs—a small stream of bitter but not salt water; uninhabited spot.

Daood-evooak—3 parasangs—ruins; no water; uninhabited spot.

Chechmeh-Dehrief—6 parasangs—a walled village, 50 houses; population Persians.

Khubhes—4 parasangs—a town of 800 houses, surrounded by a wall of earth. The productions here are dates, lemons, oranges, henna, and rice. This place is much nearer to Kerman than it appears on the generality of maps; this error of the geographers has arisen from there being two Khubhes—the ancient one in ruins and uninhabited, of which they speak; and the modern one, of which they do not speak, and which is nearer to Kerman.

Paï-kotal—4 parasangs—a walled village, 100 houses; population Persians.

Dirakht-ingoor—5 parasangs—a walled village, 500 houses; population Persians.

Kerman—4 parasangs—a large town, and capital of the province of this name.

The city of Ghayn, of which I have made no mention, is an important fortress, being surrounded with a high embankment, above which is a wall of earth, the whole being protected by a ditch; there are not more than seven hundred houses within the *enceinte*, but the inhabitants of several villages close to the fortress, and which are dependent upon it, considerably augment the total of the population: this is composed of Arabs and Belooches, and they have the reputation of being a brave though turbulent set. There are large numbers of sheep, goats, and camels in this locality; the horses are good, and of Arabian blood; the carpets are considered the best and the dearest in Persia. Ghayn is in a plain, about twenty parasangs from Furrah, sixteen from Laush Jowaine, and twelve from Neh-Bindan. A man on horseback will require two days to go from Laush Jowaine to Neh-Bindan; the distance is about twenty-five parasangs.

I should likewise state that the routes and their prolongations, as far as the most western frontiers of Persia, which I have just given, are frequently scoured by the Bakhtiaris and Belooches; the first only rob the caravans, the second add to robbery murder, when they cannot carry their captives with them. Another danger awaits the traveller in the central parts of this country—he may be swallowed up in the shifting sands, which are undermined in consequence of the rains dissolving the salt, and the consequent filtration of the water.

During the two days I remained at Furrah, Mollah Mahmood did his best to persuade me to venture once more through the Seistan, and endeavour to reach India by that route; but the three trials I had made, once by the north and twice by the south, having cruelly tried my health and my courage, I positively refused, and persevered, under this feeling, in my determination to return again to Persia, the more so as I had failed in the original object I had in view.

Khosh-ava, November 10th—five parasangs, over a plain, on which were several villages, also many ruins, of which the inhabitants know nothing, not even the name. To any question that is put in reference to the ruins, one is pretty sure to have the same kind of reply all over Central Asia—it is always the story of some beautiful maid, two lovers, a barber, or some holy individual who is the founder of such remains; and, if there is no legend of the kind, they father them upon Roostem, Shah Abbas, and even Nadir Shah, or the genii. The land near Khosh-ava is rich and well-cultivated. A narrow foot-path only marks the first part of the route from Furrah to Khosh-ava; the second is through fields, and in the direction of the mountains, at the foot of which that village is situated, and consists of about 100 houses. The Ket-khoda happened to be at Furrah when I was there, and Mollah Mahmood, to propitiate him in my favour, had presented him with a *khelat* made of an English print; I expected, therefore, from him a large share of hospitality, but the rogue took all he could get, and charged me double for the loaf and some sour milk with which he supplied me.

Jeja, November 11th—seven parasangs—the two first across a plain; three canals, which are fed by the waters of the Khachek-rood are then crossed, and subsequently we entered some valleys enclosed by high mountains: the Sefid Koh is on the left. The country is but slightly populated; the vegetable world is, on the contrary, very flourishing, and the land covered with pasture and underwood. Meeting with a flock, Assad Khan and his people seized a sheep, and, contrary to what I had previously seen, the shepherd demurred to the theft, but an application of the stick subdued him considerably; he himself enacted the part of butcher without further delay, and when the animal was ready for the cook tied it under one of the horses of the escort. He then offered up many a prayer for our safety, and assured us how very fortunate he thought himself in having made the acquaintance of such highly distinguished and kind individuals.

Jeja, which we reached in the afternoon, is a little *kaleh,* inhabited by a chief, and surrounded by the tents of some Noorzye nomads, who are dependent on the chief of Herat. It gives its name to the river, which, running through the whole length of its district, is above it called the Subzawur-rood, and below it the Haroot-rood. The women of Jeja, hearing that a European was encamped in the river, came to me in a crowd to ask for medicine, and I could not get rid of them either with good reasons or fair speeches: they were sure the Feringhee doctor had some medicaments, and I was at length obliged to give them a dose of aperient pills all round.

Subzawur, also called *Sebzar*, November 12th—nine parasangs. Crossing the river of Jeja, we marched for the first hour through the mountains, and subsequently, for eight more, across a plain, nearly always following the course of the Jeja-rood. The country was less wooded than on the previous day, though not so populated; several villages were seen on the side of the road, and reservoirs of water, round which were many encampments of nomads.

Half an hour before arriving at Subzawur, at the extremity of the mountains running east and west, and on the last ridge stretching into the plain, are the remains, and some of them in pretty good preservation, of the large and ancient city of Sabah. The walls of the citadel, which crowned the highest eminence, are still standing: the city was below, and connected with the fort above it by thick walls, flanked by towers originally of stone, but subsequently repaired with sun-dried bricks; these walls descended to the river, and protected the town on the only side by which it could be approached. The appearance of these ruins points to a period of great antiquity as the time of their origin. Some of the people in the neighbourhood say that they are anterior to the conquests of Alexander; others, who probably prefer legends to history, are believers in the following ridiculous tale:—The city, say they, was built by women of gigantic stature, under the protection of genii; these ladies, after having obtained children from their husbands, sacrificed the latter to their sanguinary gods, whose appetite for blood was it appears not easily satisfied. The great Roostem, distressed at witnessing the male population thus decimated, put an end to these cruelties; he attacked them singly, put the genii to flight, made prisoners of the *softer* sex, and imprisoned them in his island on the Seistan lake, where they could do no further injury. Since then Sabah has never been permanently inhabited, and misfortune has always been the lot of those who endeavoured to establish themselves there.

The river has again to be crossed to reach the new town of

Subzawur, at an elbow of the stream, and at the foot of the mountains south of the plain on which it is situated. This little fortress is constructed on the same plan as Furrah, but is only half as large. Its circuit may be about a mile in extent; it contains a small bazaar and one hundred houses, and must in former times have been the citadel of a large city, now represented by extensive suburbs, partly in ruins. Gardens and cultivated ground, surrounding villages and encampments of nomads in all directions, are seen in its neighbourhood. Water is conducted to the town from the Subzawur-rood by numerous canals, that protect the approaches to the fortress, which is one point in the strategic position which a Russian or Persian army ought to take up as the base of their operations, if they intended to advance into Afghanistan; that is to say, if they hoped for any chance of success.

The town of Subzawur is often erroneously mentioned in history as that of Subzawur which is situated near Neshapoore in Khorassan. Shah Thamasp, the last of the kings of the Severige dynasty, was confined and put to death here by order of Nadir Shah. I did not enter the fortress because the cholera was raging; also because it would have been necessary to obtain an order from the commandant of the district. This precautionary measure is taken with all strangers, for surprise or treachery are of common occurrence amongst the people of these countries.

Adreshan, November 13th.—A halt already described.

Chabith, November 14th.—The same.

Roouz-bagh, November 15th.—This is a royal residence of the sovereigns of Herat, but now in ruins, and of a miserable appearance. Here we halted, and sent on a man of our escort to carry a letter to Yar Mohamed Khan, announcing our return. The night was exceedingly cold, and we heard that the cholera was making sad ravages at Herat and in its neighbourhood.

CHAPTER XXIX.

Arrival of Monsieur Ferrier at Yar Mohamed's residence near Herat — Is received by the Sirdar Habib Ullah Khan — The Author makes the acquaintance of Fethi Khan — Description of that nobleman — His liberal and kind conduct to the Author — Interview with Yar Mohamed — Asiatics arrested at Kabul for Europeans — Assad Khan rewarded by Yar Mohamed — Visitors at Ullah Khan's — The Author proceeds to Herat — Unfortunate accident to the Sirdar — A dear glass of vinegar — Scene at the Sirdar's house — The prayer over the broken leg — The doctors disagree at Herat as elsewhere — A singular plaster — The bone-setters — The Sertip Lal Mohamed Khan — The two physicians — Monsieur Ferrier's mistake — The dream of Goolam Kader Khan — The genii of cholera — Jew doctors of Herat — Merchants of India in that city — Remarkable effect of a pair of pantaloons — Statistics on the military forces of Central Asia — Geographical inaccuracies.

HERAT, November 15th—one parasang and a half—through cultivated land. After crossing the Heri-rood by the bridge of Malanne, we met the soldier whom we had on the previous evening despatched to the Vezir. Yar Mohamed had ordered him to return and prevent us from entering the town, in which the cholera was making such havoc, and conduct us to the gardens of Kartch, where he was for the moment residing; we turned our horses' heads therefore in that direction, and on our arrival found a complete encampment surrounding his house. I was taken to the tent of Sirdar Habib Ullah Khan, who had been appointed by the Vezir to receive me; this chief was a brother of Mollah Mahmood, governor of Furrah, and I had met him before in the district of Ghoor, where he was making war against the Taymoonis. The Khan gave me a very friendly reception; and with him at the moment of my arrival was the Sirdar Haji Fethi Khan, a cousin of Yar Mohamed, whom I had not seen during my two previous visits to that city, as he was at that time on a pilgrimage to Mecca. The Vezir had at first intended me to share his cousin's hospitality, but subsequently altered his plan, thinking it not impossible that he, being devoted to English interests, might concoct something with me which would militate against his own.

Fethi Khan was a handsome young fellow, with polite and distinguished manners, and had nothing of the rough and savage aspect of his countrymen about him; this agreeable contrast was owing probably to the frequent opportunities he had had of associating with Europeans. In the years 1836 and 1837 he had been charged by the Shah Kamran with a diplomatic mission to Teheran, and had passed a considerable portion of the time he was residing in that capital amongst the members of the foreign diplomatic corps; recently, also, in going to and returning from Mecca, he passed through India, and the highest functionaries there had received him with every honour. Some French merchantmen were at Bombay during his stay there, and the interviews he had with their officers had given him a high opinion of the character and power of our nation. He had made some purchases of them instead of the English, as he preferred our manufactures, more especially guns, watches, and silk goods, because he found these articles as good as those of our rivals, and cheaper. Napoleon and his companions in arms, with whose names and history he seemed perfectly acquainted, was a constant topic of conversation between us, and his remarks, which were clever and to the point, were exceedingly original, and being expressed in the highly figurative language of his country were the more striking. Having learnt through Assad Khan of the distress and penury into which I had been plunged by the conduct and cupidity of the Sirdar Mohamed Sedik Khan, he made me most obliging offers of assistance. As Asiatics are generally very lavish of propositions of this kind, without the least idea of carrying them into effect, I received those of Fethi Khan as simply the expression of a polite feeling: but I was in error, for a very short time after he had left he sent me 350 francs in gold, a complete Afghan dress, a gun, a watch, and three horses; and during the whole time I resided at Herat was of service to me in many other ways. "After the many civilities I received from the English in India," said he, "it is only a duty which I perform—they are Europeans, so are the French, so that it is all one and the same thing."

November 16th.—The day after my arrival I paid my respects to the Vezir, who received me with the same kindness as on former occasions. After listening with attention to the history of my adventures in Kandahar and in Seistan, his indignation broke forth against the Sirdars of that country; and his pride was especially wounded at the little consideration they had paid to his recommendation. "They are all infidels!" he exclaimed; "may their fathers be burnt! An envoy of Kohendil Khan's to Assaf Doulet arrived here yesterday on his way to Meshed; but as the Khan would not allow you to go farther than Kandahar, neither will I permit their envoy to pass Herat. He shall be sent back to Kussan, and he may go by way of Seistan, if that suits him, but he shall certainly not go through my territories; the precautions they took to prevent you from seeing and knowing what they are doing with them are absurd. Do they suppose that their public acts are not known to the English?—are they so stupid as to imagine that these people, who held possession of their country for two years, are not better acquainted with it than themselves?—and they are actually afraid that they will map it. If this does not sufficiently prove to you how wanting in intelligence they are, the following fact may. About fifteen months since, a young man, originally of Herat, and ten years in my son's service, received my permission to proceed to Kabul to arrange some private affairs. His beard and hair were light, and his eyes green, like the English—and woe betide the traveller who enters the states of the Mohamedzyes with these characteristic proofs of an European origin! Such, however, was the personal appearance of my Heratian, and such the reasons for his being denounced by Kohendil Khan to Dost Mohamed, who kept him in prison for three months, and subsequently sent him to me under an escort, with a request that I would forward him immediately to Persia, and never allow a Feringhee in future to enter Afghanistan on that side."

I could believe this, for during my stay at Girishk I had opportunities of observing the exaggerated fears entertained by the Sirdars of Kandahar, who arrested three or four Asiatics on similar grounds; and, in spite of my assurance that they were not Europeans, which was easy to see at the first glance, Mohamed Sedik Khan would not release them. Having informed the Vezir how much I had been indebted to Assad Khan for the great courage, fidelity, and assistance I had received from him, Yar Mohamed sent for the Khan, and complimented him in the most flattering terms:—"You have," said he, addressing him, "well understood and carried out my intentions; and to prove that I am perfectly satisfied with your conduct, I propose to accede to the wishes of this European and grant all that he has asked for you—I give you therefore the two horses which you lost recently in the war with the Taymoonis, the payment of one hundred and fifty ducats due on account of your arrears of pay, plus a present of fifty ducats, and a grant of water in the neighbourhood of Khash-rood, to enable you there to establish yourself with the rest of the tribe who have followed your fortunes; and, lastly, a silk robe of honour."

These gifts were bestowed at my request, and confirmed me in the opinion I had previously formed, that Yar Mohamed was secretly desirous of being on amicable terms with the English, and obtaining their good opinion and support in his misunderstandings or quarrels with Persia and Kandahar; for though I was a Frenchman, he hoped that I should mention the good treatment I had received, and thus give a favourable impression of his actions. The visitors at the Vezir's were rather numerous, those with whom I was acquainted were the Kazi Mohamed Osman, Mirza Nejef, the Ekim Bashi, Mirza Ibrahim Khan, and the Athar Bashi, the old confidential minister of the Shah Kamran. After returning to my tent and as night fell, the Vezir sent me an excellent dinner, which disappeared in an instant under the vigorous assaults of myself and the Sirdars—visitors who, attracted by the grateful smell, came in numbers to our tent.

November 17th.—Having obtained the permission of Yar Mohamed, and undeterred by the cholera, I went into the city. The Sirdar Habib Ullah Khan and Assad Khan accompanied me there with a large number of horsemen; the population having heard beforehand from their people of my arrival, had assembled to see me pass; the news of the bad treatment I had received in Kandahar had been brought back to them some time before by the caravans, and my return to their town was an event. Accompanied by the crowd, the cavalcade had just arrived at the Char-sook, in the centre of the bazaars, when a horse mounted by a servant, and placed at the head of the column to clear the road before us and open a passage through the mob, flung out with his hind legs and broke the Sirdar's left leg. He was quickly lifted from his horse and taken to a shop, and the people closed round in such numbers and so suddenly that they prevented me from getting to him; seeing me thus separated from the escort, a host of beggars quickly surrounded and almost stifled me, and with loud cries demanded alms. For more than a quarter of an hour I was at their mercy, and was at length only rescued by the police, leaving behind me a part of my clothes.

During this time my poor host had fainted away, and lay extended on the front of an old-iron shop, where instead of any one assisting him, the curious were making him suffer ten thousand tortures, by moving the limb to see where it was broken.

Every one gave his opinion, and no two agreed; the hubbub and confusion were at length so great, that there was no hearing oneself speak. I called for some vinegar, but though there was plenty in at least ten shops close at hand, none was brought. I went, therefore, to a grocer, who said, "Give me a rupee (two shillings), and I will let you have half a glass." "Rascal and ass," I replied, "your countrymen have robbed me, I have not a sou for you: besides the Sirdar is dying, and this is no time for bargaining;" but the rogue was of a different opinion, and replied, "When can I hope to have another opportunity of making such a bargain?" after which he showed me his back, and I supplied the place of the vinegar with the smoke of some burnt paper, which I placed under the Sirdar's nose, and in a few seconds he came to himself. At last a stretcher was brought, and, with the assistance of the police, and a continual application of the stick on the backs of the mob, we reached Ullah Khan's house.

Here was another scene and as much confusion. The women, though in the presence of the men, made an irruption from the harem into the room, sobbing and shrieking for at least an hour, before they thought of attending to their suffering master. The doctors and bonesetters who had been called in to set the leg, arrived one after the other, and two hours elapsed before they examined it; they were another hour discussing the mode of treatment, and, of course, without agreeing about it: one wanted to wash the wound made by the nails of the horseshoe, another proposed something else; at last the Vezir's surgeon arrived—he was for washing it; and the dresser who was fixing the splints stopped short, declaring that he would do nothing further unless a mollah came and said the prayer usually offered during an operation—a prayer beforehand constituting in his opinion at least three-fourths of the chances of a cure. A good hour again elapsed before the kazi arrived, who then recited a long orison; and as it finished, the leg was wretchedly and most unskilfully set, the horrible agony and loud cries of the patient being little regarded. The surgeons then put on a plaster made of barley-flour and yolks of eggs to facilitate the joining of the bone, but even at this point they had not done with the sufferer; a new dispute arose as to the general treatment, how he was to be dieted: one was for complete abstinence from food, another abstinence from liquids; one was for hot drinks, another for cold; and, as they could not agree, it was determined to have recourse to the *tesbih*, a chaplet with which Mussulmans consult fate. On this authority, and that of a constellation given by an astronomer who was present, it was at length settled that the patient was to have no drink at all, but as much as ever he could eat, while he, without the least appetite and nearly moribund, declined everything that was brought to him. As the Vezir's surgeon had some authority in the midst of such a mob, and was supported by the favourite wife of the Sirdar, the discussions, propositions, and arrangements were at length brought to a close; they had occupied four hours, and if it had not been for these two persons, they would not have terminated till the following day at the same hour; but it should be remembered, that to mend a leg is not a small thing at Herat, and for several reasons. It would be thought the height of imprudence to have only one surgeon, *jerrah*—the more there are the more they are worth; but his duty, under these circumstances, is only to dress the wound: it is the dresser, the *shikesti-bend*, to set the bone, and the *hakim* to prescribe the regimen, &c., and, as in this case there were three wiseacres of each class, the result to the patient can be readily imagined. This melodrame at an end, I was in great hopes that the poor man would be allowed a little quiet, and be left alone to obtain that repose of which he was so much in need; but instead of this, all his friends—and they were not a few—came in succession to see and condole with him; this lasted long into the night. On entering the room and leaving it every one of these acquaintances offered up a prayer for the speedy cure of the wounded limb, and as those who were stationary around the bed, and belonged to the house, repeated these in chorus, the effect was an uninterrupted litany, till by degrees every one retired to bed.

On the day succeeding this unfortunate affair, I called on my friend the Sertip Lal Mohamed Khan, who, under the influence of enormous doses of calomel, was swollen out to the size of a barrel; he could scarcely speak, and died three or four months afterwards. The ignorance and presumption of the medical empirics of these countries is beyond belief, and the faith which the inhabitants have in them is still more remarkable; I could relate a hundred anecdotes of their deplorable stupidity of which I myself was a witness, and sometimes, though rarely, the laughable result. Amongst them the following may be taken as an example, and of the blind belief the people have in dreams. The reader must not suppose there is any exaggeration; I have, on the contrary, withheld much that would assuredly have appeared untrue, and those who are acquainted with this country will be convinced that I have not overcharged the picture. During my previous *séjour* at Herat, I made the acquaintance of all the *hakims* in the city; two of the most noted—perhaps I ought to say, the most fashionable—Mirza Asker and Goolam Kader Khan had more especially made me numerous visits. I had always mistaken them, had called one by the name of the other, and *vice versâ.* Before I returned to Herat, Mirza Asker died of cholera: my astonishment, therefore, was very great when I saw him enter the Sirdar's apartment to assist in setting his leg. Convinced of my error, I testified to him the happiness I felt in seeing him still in the land of the living. "Ah!" replied the Hakim, "I was perfectly certain it must have been myself of whom you spoke to the Vezir, when you said that the wisest of the doctors of Herat was dead; you might mistake the name, never the person: no other individual but myself could be worthy of your admirable praises." Though of quite a different opinion I left Goolam Kader Khan in this delusion, and, turning the conversation to the cholera, requested to have some information on the subject. "Oh! with pleasure," said the doctor; "my ignorant colleagues find it no doubt a difficult disease to treat, but to me it is child's play; ask rather the whole population I have saved." Amongst the thousand ridiculous prescriptions he had given, he said the most effectual had been the ninety-nine attributes of God repeated in the presence of the patient by three old men, two young men, and one maid, twice out loud and once to themselves. After having confided this marvellous recipe to me, he added, "God is merciful, and has never ceased to be favourable to the most humble of his creatures. During the whole of this unfortunate time, I flatter myself that I was especially the object of the Divine solicitude; listen, and you will be convinced of the fact. Two days before the cholera appeared within our walls, I was warned in a dream of its approach; my sleep was heavy and oppressed, and I was in a kind of nightmare, when the chamberlain of our excellent Vezir entered my apartment, and requested me to make my daily visit to the palace. I rose immediately to obey the summons, when I was suddenly arrested by the sinister appearance of two strangers, dressed in red, of a pale and cadaverous aspect, who stood on the steps of the palace gate. They were the first to give me the *salam*, and it was with some difficulty that I returned it, so sad was the impression made upon me by their countenances. 'Oh! strangers,' said I, 'what kind of people are you? From whence do you come? What do you want?'

"'We are the Cholera, *Veba estim*,' said they, in a solemn voice; 'and we come by order of the Most High.'

"At these words I drew my *poostine* still closer round my chest, and held my breath to avoid the frightful infection which hung on theirs. After this precaution, having retreated a few steps and recommended my soul to God, I plucked up sufficient courage to ask them whom they wanted.

"'Neither you, nor the Vezir nor his family; but we have more than one account to settle with certain unbelievers who have abused the Divine goodness and ignored the laws of the Prophet.'

"'Dread messengers,' I replied, 'I am neither a drunkard, an opium nor a *bengy* eater; leave me therefore in peace.'

"'It is not with thee that we have to do, but with one of your colleagues, whose ignorance and incapacity have caused the death of so many people; his victims demand his life, and God, having taken their petition into consideration, has given us instructions to return with him.'

"At these words they disappeared and I awoke. Though completely occupied with my numerous engagements and my large practice, I could think of nothing but this dream for two whole days; on the third I was the first person in the town attacked by cholera. During fourteen hours I suffered the most intolerable agonies, but thanks to my *sang froid* and to science, I escaped death. These fourteen hours of suffering revealed to me which organs were particularly attacked; I discovered the causes of the disease, and at once comprehended what remedies should be applied. The day after my recovery, I made as usual my visit to the Vezir Saheb, and found that Mirza Asker, the most ignorant and decided rival I had, was there before me. I saw immediately by the hue of his countenance that he was already attacked by cholera. The ignorant fellow, however, did not know it, a humane feeling came over me, and I informed him how he should treat himself, offered to prescribe for him—but how can we escape from our destiny? Mirza Asker was the unbeliever described in my dream by the two strangers; and accordingly six hours after, he died, and had to give an account to God of all the assassinations—may God forgive him!—which, in his lifetime, he committed with the drugs of the infidels! My dream, its results, and my success in the treatment of this fearful malady were soon known to the population of Herat, and they blessed the name of him whom this scoundrel, this Asker had vilified; my reputation is now at its height, and I have so many patients that I cannot attend to them."

Having listened, and not without laughing, to this long tirade of the doctor Goolam Kader Khan's, given in a tone of buffoonery, which is not to be described with the pen, I congratulated him on his success, and again testified my satisfaction in seeing that he was still alive; but this verbal assurance was not sufficient: he must have a written certificate to show to the Vezir that he was really the very hakim whom, imagining to be dead, I had so much praised; and to this request he joined another, somewhat more ludicrous. He besought me to send him a pair of surgical scissors from Teheran, to operate with in cataract, a disease to which the Heratians are extremely subject; they were to have flat blades, and be very slender: I promised to execute the commission, but never did so, out of compassion for his patients. The certificate I gave him, and received his best *salam* in return.

Jews practise as doctors at Herat, and sometimes also as sorcerers. The Israelites are rather numerous there, more especially since their persecution at Meshed. Though their departure from that city is forbidden, and they are mulcted in very heavy fines if they are caught absconding, they nevertheless continually make the attempt, and arrive at Herat, where they are permitted to trade, and commerce through their means flourishes more than it otherwise would. They are also allowed the free exercise of their religion, and are thoroughly protected by the Vezir.

Some natives of India are also met with here, but in small

numbers; and these, though apparently of very humble exterior, are immensely rich, and enjoy great consideration. The commerce of India with this city may be said to be almost entirely in their hands; they are held in great estimation by Yar Mohamed, and farm nearly all the taxes. One of them, Chatroo by name, had previously to my first visit been assassinated; and the Vezir tried every means in his power to discover the murderer, and would certainly have put him to death if he had succeeded. The Indians I saw at Herat had been there for upwards of twenty years, without ever leaving it; but their wives, in almost every case, had never joined them. One of them had, however, a son of about fifteen years of age with him; and I was wondering how he came there, considering that his mother had lived at Shikarpoor for a score of years, and his father the same number at Herat, when I received a solution of the enigma from my acquaintance, Syud Elias, an Afghan merchant, who had made a good many journeys to India, and was familiar with the customs of the people of that country. According to his showing, an Indian, when he leaves his home, leaves also a pair of pantaloons with his wife, who puts them on when she is desirous of being in that condition so natural to, and, generally speaking, so much coveted by married women; no husband, it appears, would ever dream of repudiating a child obtained by this simple method: to do so would be a perfect scandal.

When speaking of my journey through the states of Afghanistan, I have given approximately the amount of the forces of the various chiefs. I will now recapitulate the total strength, so that they may be more readily referred to. (See Table, p. 455.)

To those who are ignorant of the fact that all Asiatics are born soldiers this total may appear high; but in the towns, as well as in the country, every house and every tent can, under pressing necessity, furnish a fighting man, and sometimes two. The Table has reference only to the *Defteris;* that is to say, those who are registered and receive pay, or instead an indemnity, an allowance, contribution in grain, freedom from taxation, or the gratuitous grant of a water-course; besides these, so to speak, regulars, there are always in time of war plenty of volunteers, who are attracted to the field by the hope of plunder. The Belooches of Seistan are not included in this statement, because they are not in Afghanistan; and I have only given in the infantry of Laush-jowaine those who are in the service of Shah Pesend Khan.

MILITARY STRENGTH OF THE STATES OF AFGHANISTAN.

Nations.	Principalities and Khanats.	Cavalry of each State.	Total Cavalry of each Nation.	Infantry of each State.	Total Infantry of each Nation.	General Total.
Afghans	Herat	8,000	41,500	10,000	31,000	72,500
	Kandahar	12,000		6,000		
	Kabul	21,000		10,000		
	Laush-jowaine	500		5,000		
Uzbeks	Khulm	8,000	18,000	3,000	8,100	26,100
	Balkh	2,500		1,000		
	Siripool	2,000		2,000		
	Akkehu	200		..		
	Andkhoo	1,800		600		
	Shibbergan	2,000		500		
	Meïmana	1,500		1,000		
Hazarahs	Zeidnats	4,000	10,900	..	5,300	16,200
	Poosht-kooh	5,000		3,000		
	Yekenholing	1,000		300		
	Deh-zingy	400		1,200		
	Sir-jingel	500		800		
Eïmaks	Firooz-koohi	3,750	4,950	6,400	16,800	21,750
	Kipchaks	..		400		
	Taymoonis	1,200		10,000		
		75,350	75,350	61,200	61,200	136,550

An enterprising and clever chief could in Afghanistan obtain from fifteen to eighteen thousand excellent Belooche infantry; but it would be difficult to keep so large a force under the same flag for any length of time, as long as Seistan is in their possession.

I have in this journal offered from time to time several remarks intended to rectify the errors which are to be found in the existing maps of the countries of Central Asia, they being all more or less incorrect. Some lakes and rivers have been altogether omitted; and the course of others of the latter improperly traced; entire districts thought to be deserts are, on the contrary, fertile and well inhabited; while such towns as Dooshakh and Iloomdar, the centres of a considerable population, are described as localities of very little importance, and not ranking with towns even of the third class. The English only are well acquainted with these countries; they thoroughly explored them from 1840 to 1842; and it is not difficult to comprehend why they have kept the information to themselves. Anxious on the subject of India, they have an interest in exaggerating the difficulties which must attend an attack on this side, and in withholding information regarding the roads, rivers, and territory which would prove useful to an invading army. I do not pretend to throw much light on this subject, or to add to any great extent to the amount of existing information; for during the period of my wanderings in these countries I had not sufficient time at my disposal, nor the tranquillity of mind necessary to establish a full and perfect judgment upon this important subject. My remarks, however, may enable others to form an approximate opinion on the advantages and disadvantages that will present themselves in the struggle so long foreseen between the Russians and the English. I will endeavour to enumerate them without a bias in favour of or against either party, and state them simply on the grounds of the interest attached to them.

CHAPTER XXX.

Invasion of India by a Russo-Persian army — Manuscript of Sir Alexander Burnes — Military colonies of the Russians between the Embah river and Lake Aral — Advance from the Oxus — Passage from the work of Sir A. Burnes — March of the Russian army by the Moorgaub and Merv — Opinion of General Mouraviev on a Russian invasion of India — Advance on the side of the Caspian, and march of the Russian army through Khorassan — Facility of provisioning their army — Advance from Herat by the Haroot-rood, the Helmund, and the Urgund-ab — Position on the Indus — Russian communications in their rear — Line of operations — Probabilities of a revolt in British India — European and Sepoy troops — Impedimenta of the English army — Qualifications and strength of the invading force — The opinions of authors on this subject — Reply to the Khan of Khiva — Recent battles in India — Tactics of the English in the event of an invasion of that country — Advance upon Kandahar —Effects of English diplomacy — State of the roads in the countries of the Hazarahs and Eïmaks — Facility in obtaining supplies — Routes through Central Asia to Kabul and Kandahar — Country near the Bolan Pass — Desert between Khelat and the Helmund — Afghan politics — Disputes for the throne of Kabul — Opinions respecting Dost Mohamed's children — Kohendil Khan — His apprehensions of the English — State of the Government at Kandahar — Succession to the throne — Children of the Sirdars — Yar Mohamed — Succession to the sovereign power at Herat — The probable results of Afghan politics — The policy of Sir A. Burnes — Conduct of the Directors of the East India Company — The Czar's motto — Advance of the Russians into Turcomania in 1852 — Author's opinions.

THE difficulties attending an invasion of British India by a Russo-Persian army, or Russian only, are, without doubt, serious; but they may be said to exist far more in the character of the people of Afghanistan and the Tartar states than in the scantiness of the resources of the countries through which the expedition would be obliged to pass—their poverty and the difficulties of the ground have been greatly exaggerated. The statements of Macdonald Kinnear and Sir Alexander Burnes have, it is true, generally served as the basis upon which public opinion has been formed. Both one and the other have taken pains to bring these difficulties very prominently forward, and this with considerable tact, though it must be admitted that Burnes only saw that road which presented the most unpromising features. Nevertheless his manuscript, which was for several years in my possession, in some things contradicted that which he printed; and he admitted in it, as I now do, the possibility of marching an invading army across the deserts and steppes of Turkistan and Afghanistan. This was not likely to escape his superior intellect; but it would not be easily accomplished, however possible at several points. Let me add, however, that the English have a chance of victoriously repulsing the attack, although to obtain this success, incessant vigilance is imperatively necessary, and an European war might endanger the whole question. In the meanwhile the Russians have not abandoned the long-cherished plan of extending their conquests in Southern Asia; and they seek to advance more and more every day towards the Oxus and Khiva.

The various military expeditions which they have organised having failed from privations and the effects of climate, they have for the last seven or eight years adopted a system, once that of the Roman tacticians,—namely, to proceed but little at a time, slowly and surely. After having descended the course of the Oural to the Caspian Sea, they reached the mouth of the Embah, situated a little lower down to the south-east, and ascended that river to the point at which, turning south, it approaches the Aral Sea. Here they have established a military colony, and dug wells at short distances in the desert, between the Embah and the sea; they have also placed around these wells settlements of Cossacks, who cultivate the soil in the neighbourhood, and create resources which never existed before; so that in a few years an army will be able to obtain sufficient food and forage in all their encampments, and will reach the Aral without serious difficulty.* Two other lines of wells have been also dug by the Russians; one on leaving the river Ourloo Irghiz, tending towards the northern end of the Aral Sea; the other commences from two points, Ming-kishlak† and Dash Killeh,‡ on the eastern shore of the Caspian, which unite in one line half-way, and is thence laid down in the direction of Khiva.

By means of these chains of posts the Russians intend to advance to that town and the Oxus, and when they shall have reached

* It is by this route that the Russians have recently (1853) reached Khiva. Ten years were occupied in preparing these arrangements, and a *corps d'armée* was employed to effect the object.

† *i. e.* The meadows-winter quarters.

‡ The other name of this place is Alexandropol. It was near here that Captain Abbott was so nearly murdered. —*See Abbott's Travels.*—ED.

that point it will be impossible to say where they will stop. The possession of that river is of as much importance to them as that of the Indus is to the English; it is the artery which vivifies the territories of the great Tartar hordes through which it flows, who are otherwise unapproachable on all sides by reason of the steppes and deserts of shifting sand. Once masters of this river it would be easy for the Russians to subjugate the tribes on its banks, from the Aral to Badakshan. The Russian army could readily ascend the Oxus in the boats of the country, within two parasangs of Balkh, where it first ceases to be navigable. Burnes is on this subject a competent authority, and the following is a passage from his work, very much to the point:—

"Facilities in the navigation of a river rest much on the supplies of the country through which it flows; in particular of the nature and quality of wood which is there procurable. The number of boats on the Oxus is certainly small, since they do not amount to two hundred, but there is every facility for building a fleet, the supply of wood being abundant, and fortunately found in single trees along the valley of the river, and not growing in forests in any particular spot. There are no cedar or pine trees brought down by the inundation, which I hold as conclusive proof that the mountains from which the Oxus and its tributaries flow are destitute of that wood. The only other trees which I saw on the river were mulberry and white poplar, which last is floated down in quantities from Hissar to Charjooee, and applied to purposes of house-building. In any increase of the tonnage on this river the immediate resources of the neighbouring country must therefore be called into action, but these are highly important. The nature of the build in the boats of the river requires no skill in naval architecture; the wood is not sawed, and it does not require seasoning, so that the utmost dispatch might be used at all times in forming a flotilla, whether it were desired to navigate, cross, or bridge it. I believe that one hundred and fifty men might be embarked on a boat of the size which I have described. The river could only be bridged by boats, for the wood is too small for an application of it in any other way; and furze and tamarisk which grow on its banks would supply the place of planks, and make it at once complete and practicable. . . . . . .

"The advantages of the Oxus both in a political and commercial point of view must then be regarded as very great: the many facilities which have been enumerated point it out either as the channel of merchandise or the route of a military expedition; nor is it from the features of the river itself that we form such a conclusion. It is to be remembered that its banks are peopled and cultivated; it must therefore be viewed as a navigable river, possessing great facilities for improving the extent of that navigation. This is a fact of great political and commercial importance, whether a hostile nation may turn it to the gratification of ambition, or a friendly power here seek the extension and improvement of its trade. In either case the Oxus presents many fair prospects, since it holds the most direct course, and connects, with the exception of a narrow desert, the nations of Europe with the remote regions of Central Asia." *

Burnes might have added that water carriage was not in this country the only available means of transporting an army, and that in following the course of the river by land, with its *matériel*, it would always be ready to meet an attack, and avoid many inconveniences. A Russian army might thus direct its march as it thought fit either to Khulm, or withdrawing from the river on its arrival at Charjooee, reach Merv by the desert, and marching along the fertile and populous banks of the Moorghab gain Herat. There would not be any obstacle of a serious nature to stop an army on its way to the river, and the desert situated between it and Merv offers no difficulties that cannot be surmounted; the Khans of Khiva and the Emirs of Bokhara have sufficiently proved this in their almost annual expeditions to seize upon Merv, some of which have been made at the head of ten to twelve thousand horse. Would they have exposed themselves to the dangers mentioned by Burnes, if they had been of his opinion?

Wherever it was impossible to skirt the Oxus the army might without inconvenience keep five or six parasangs from the river on either side, for here they would be sure to find enough water for the troops in the numerous wells dug by the shepherds for the use of their flocks; similar wells might also be made with little labour, and in a very short time; water is generally found at a depth of nine or twelve feet, and the soil is of a silicious nature, easy to work, but it must be supported by planks or wattles. Brushwood or brambles for fuel are readily met with, and in the winter and

* See Burnes's Travels into Bokhara, vol. ii. p. 197.

spring the steppes are covered with sufficient herbage to meet the requirements of an army. I mention these facts in reply to the opiniated arguments of some persons, who affirm that nothing is to be found in these deserts except sand, and if this were so the obstacles would not even then be insurmountable. The Russians themselves are well aware how and where they can obtain supplies. The following quotation from Mouraviev's work is evidence on this head:—"In our days, with the knowledge we have of these countries, the success of such an enterprise is certain. A corps of three thousand Russians, under a resolute and disinterested leader, could subdue and keep this country so necessary to Russia by reason of her commercial relations with the East. . . . Even at Khiva we might augment our force by the addition of the three thousand Russians who are in slavery there, and the thirty thousand Persians who suffer with the same impatience as the Russians the miseries which they are obliged to support. . . . . . As to supplies, where are they to be obtained? At Khiva itself, where they are in abundance."

Thus the Russians, as well as the English, admit the resources of this country, and yet the latter like to indulge the illusion that it is impossible for the former to cross the deserts of Tartary to get at them. They ought, however, to be well persuaded that when the Russians have made up their minds to attack India, *these* obstacles will not stop them; and, besides, their adversaries calculate upon avoiding them by interesting Persia in their enterprise; an expeditionary corps embarked at Badkooh and Astrakan would then land in perfect security south of the Caspian, and proceed to concentrate itself at Astrabad; Khorassan, which the Russian army would in consequence have to cross, is a fertile and populous country, and it would find a welcome everywhere if strict discipline was preserved. As far as Kandahar the difficulties would be no greater for them than for the English, who would have to advance beyond it to dispute the ground with them. With few exceptions the Russo-Persian army might always march through plains in which they would find water, food, and fuel; but if it was found more desirable not to draw the supplies for the whole army from one district only, they might march in three columns through this province.

The first, to the north, on leaving Astrabad would follow the course of the Goorghan,* cross the territory of the Kurdish colonies

* For an account of the Goorghan river, see Mouraviev's Travels, p. 33.

at Boojnoord and Koochan, and thence to that of the Seraks, and strike the Heri-rood at the spot where it loses itself in the steppes, following its banks up to Herat, through a well-cultivated country.

The second column would direct its march to the south on Shah-rood Bostan; there it would be formed into two divisions; the first would follow the direct road by Sebzevar, Nishapoor, Meshed, and Kussan; the second would keep more to the right by Turshiz,* Khaf, and Gorian, and the whole army uniting at one point by the routes we have indicated, would concentrate itself at Herat, where provisions of every kind abound or could be obtained from the rich districts of Meimana, Kaleh-now, and Obeh, &c.; here it might winter before advancing southward. The fortifications of this city should then be put into an efficient state, and the place properly provisioned and supplied with all kinds of military stores. Its central position within a line of fortresses, commencing at Balkh on the north, and passing by Akhcheh, Andekhooye, Shibberghan, Meimana, Kaleh-now, Sebzevar,† Ferrah, and Laush Jowaine, renders Herat a particularly suitable point for this concentration.

A glance at the map will clearly show that, adopting the routes I have mentioned, all the districts of Khorassan, and even some of Irak, such as Damghan and Tubbus, would contribute materially to supply the army. It would of course be necessary for the Russians to form their magazines beforehand; the Shah of Persia never troubled himself much on the subject, and yet he has frequently marched an army of from thirty to forty thousand men into Khorassan, and always found the means of feeding them by simply making a decree for a tax in kind. When they hear the Shah is coming the peasants expect these extortions, as well as being pillaged by the troops, who strip them of all they have; and yet they never try to evade them. On the great lines of communication the Shah's troops are never short of provisions. If the Persian peasant submits to this imposition so quietly, what might he not do from the Russians, who would pay punctually for what they took? If their army were to reach Kandahar by way of Jaberan, Giran, Bakooa, Washir, and Girishk, the road usually taken by the caravans, the end of winter or the commencement of

* This was the route followed by Sir J. MacNeil when he visited the camp of the Shah, before Herat, in 1838. It is, however, rarely attempted by troops, because of the scarcity of water and supplies.—ED.

† Properly Isfezar, the horse-pasture. —ED.

spring would be the most propitious time for them to leave Herat; water would be then everywhere plentiful in the steppes, the temperature mild and the air pure, and supplies could be drawn from Meimana, Kaleh-now, Shibberghan, and Andekhooye on the north, if those of Neh-bindan, Ghain, and Birjan, &c., on the south did not suffice. The certainty of a trifling profit would bring the people to the camp with their productions; they take them without as good a chance to that of Yar Mohamed's, and they would eagerly seek that security for themselves and their property which they could never hope to obtain from the native rulers of their country.

If unforeseen circumstances should not permit the army to move from Herat at the proper moment, the springs and streams would be dry on the road designated above; it would then have to lean more to its right by Sebzevar, and follow the Haroot-rood, the Helmund, and the Urghend-ab, which leads up to Kandahar. The army could be easily subsisted in these districts. From the last-mentioned city to Shikarpoor they would have to traverse some desert steppes and get through the Bolan Pass, but these ought not, I should think, to be serious difficulties, though I had no opportunity of judging of them myself. The victorious march of the English army upon Kandahar, in 1839, is a sufficient proof of this; they had to ascend the pass, the Russian army would merely have to descend it. The English consider, and with reason, the Indus their best line of defence on that side of their Indian possessions, but would it stop the enemy? It may be permitted to doubt that fact, nay, almost to prove a negative to the question. When the Russians had reached this river, it would, if not impossible, be at any rate very difficult to prevent them from crossing it. The attention of military men has been directed to two points, which alone offer the necessary facilities for the passage of an army—Attok to the north, and Bukkar to the south; if this be so, it would be sufficient to erect *têtes-de-pont* and other important fortifications at both these places.

But the Russians are as well aware as the English of the possibility of crossing the Indus at other eligible spots, and this in spite of the rapid current, the great width, and the precipitous banks of that stream. A pontoon train would not be required: with a few mule-loads of empty *mesek* skins, adapted to the purpose, a sufficient number of rafts might be constructed in twenty-four hours, and the whole army transported to the left bank. The points where such a passage might be effected are not rare, for there is ample choice on a length of upwards of two hundred miles. Two at once suggest themselves. One of these is to the south of Attok, on the line of road from Ghuznee and Kandahar, —namely, by the pass of Dera Ismael Khan, from whence Mooltan could be gained; but there would be a disadvantage in choosing this route, inasmuch as after the Russians had crossed the Indus, they would also have to cross the rivers of the Punjab: it would therefore be much better to take the Indus below their confluence with it by the pass of Dereh Ghazee Khan,* from whence they would descend into Scinde and Guzerat, and raise the discontented populations of those conquered provinces, who would eagerly seize the opportunity to revolt—and this with the secret determination of subsequently getting rid of their new allies also. Before undertaking such an enterprise, it would of course be very desirable that Russia should be in possession of Khiva, Bokhara, and Balkh; but it would not be necessary, as several writers have declared, to exterminate the Tartars before they could reach the Indus; their neutrality, which might be obtained, would be all that the Russians would require. If the neutrality were not observed, two small Persian divisions posted at Surraks and on the banks of the Moorghab would hold them in check.

The rear being thus covered and protected, the Russian army would unite and perfect its communications with Herat; that is to say, with its magazines and resources, by the important places of Ferrah and Sebzawar. This would be the right, *i. e.* the point on which would fall one of the extremities of the line of operations; nevertheless it would be well, in carrying it by Laush-Jowaine, that it should rest on the Seistan Lake, from which it would in running north extend as far as Khulm, having as intermediary points Balkh, Shibberghan, Meimana, Herat, and the before-mentioned places. This line is equally adapted for offensive and defensive operations, not only from the means of defence afforded by the fortresses of which we have just spoken, but because of the numerous roads which terminate on it, connecting it with the most fertile districts of the country, from which the army

* The only practical passes for artillery are the Bolan to the south, and the Bunnoo and Khyber to the north. The passes leading to Dereh Ismail Khan and Dereh Ghazee Khan, although followed by caravans, are impassable for an army.—ED.

could be supplied. It is intersected at several points by different rivers, which are never dry, a circumstance that cannot be sufficiently appreciated in a country where such an occurrence is rare. It can also only be attacked on the flanks,—the centre being protected by the largest ranges of the mountains of the Paropamisus, through which no army has penetrated for ages. This natural line of defence would give the greater part of the Russo-Persian army the power of withdrawing the troops from the centre, and thus strengthening the flanks in case they were attacked.

It may be affirmed that this line is the first parallel which ought to be opened in a Russian attack upon British India. Gold, the only means of securing the co-operation of the Afghans and Belooches, would be required, and would no doubt be forthcoming; and the march of the invading army on Kandahar would then be merely a military promenade. It would be difficult for the English to avert the danger of so easy a march, if they remained behind the Indus.

The two principal cities of Afghanistan once in the hands of the Russians, they would become the arbiters of the various and conflicting interests of Central Asia, and could unite them all in their own favour, by proclaiming that they march to the conquest of India, with a view of restoring the national dynasties, subverted by their enemies, some of whose princes are incarcerated in Indo-English prisons, where they languish in a confinement from which they can never expect under any other circumstances to be delivered.* The very presence of the Russians in that country would of itself immediately create a hostile feeling against their adversaries among the native population; many chiefs and their dependents would take arms; the English would then find their rear menaced and on their own territory, and it may be foreseen that, instead of their being able to bring forward the whole of their forces against the enemy, they would be obliged to detach and employ the best and most efficient part of it—that is to say, their European troops—in putting down the revolts which would probably take place in almost every direction, more especially amongst the Sikhs, Mahrattas, and Scindians.

* I am not aware of any state prisoners now in India, except the Sikh Sirdars at Calcutta. The Emperor of Delhi is not a prisoner, although he rarely moves out of the citadel of that town. Duleep Singh's mother is not a state

The sepoys when commanded and led by English officers are certainly superior to any Asiatic troops; but they would become demoralised at the approach of the Russians, and would not stand the shock of their attack five minutes.* Supposing war to be declared in Asia and Europe at the same time, the British government could send but a very small reinforcement of English troops to India, and in all probability three-fourths of these would fall by the climate two months after their arrival in the country. This fact has been established whenever European troops have been sent there direct from the northern country; and now they are partly acclimatised before going there, by being quartered during several years at Gibraltar, Malta, the Cape of Good Hope, Aden, or Ceylon: nevertheless the mortality is always very great, and though specious arguments are maintained to the contrary by the English medical men in favour of their system, this mortality may partly be attributed to the stimulating character of their food and drink.

The Russian soldiers, hardy and more sober, would it is true be also decimated, but not to so fearful an extent; more especially if they were recruited from the southern provinces of the Russian Empire. When we reflect that from sixty to eighty thousand mules, camels, and elephants, are required to carry the impedimenta of an Anglo-Indian army of from 25,000 to 30,000 men, the very thought of the superfluities they must carry with them is stupefying. Even a young ensign is obliged to adopt the style of a nawaub, or submit to unpleasant criticisms; the number of servants, mule and camel drivers, camp followers, and others, are always double the number of the fighting men, if indeed they are not more. The Russians are not in the habit of living like the English—even in war *avec le comfort Britannique;* they exist upon little, and do not overload themselves with unnecessary baggage or a long and useless train of servants. A soldier taken from the ranks, but who does not leave them either on the march or the field of battle, is sufficient for each officer—why do not the English adopt the same simple system? There would not be any necessity for the army of the Czar to bring

prisoner. The Ranee escaped from a state prison and now resides at Khatmandhoo, the capital of Nepaul.—ED.

* This however is not the opinion of military men in India, who have enjoyed opportunities which did not fall to the lot of M. Ferrier of testing the qualities of the native soldiery.—ED.

siege artillery with it, as the arsenal at Teheran is well supplied. To procure it there would save both time and money.*

Many persons, and amongst them Macdonald Kinnear, think that an army intended to invade India should consist of from 35,000 to 40,000 men at the least; I so far differ from him, that I think it would be most impolitic and dangerous if it exceeded that number; of which two-thirds should be Russians, and one-third Persians, and the latter ought to be convinced that the chances are in their favour, with this force. These should be picked troops, well disciplined, commanded by generals selected with judgment; the latter ought to be well versed in the details of Eastern administration, honest, capable of keeping a strict control over the Russian commissariat agents, reproached not without reason with being excessively venal. Marauding would produce great misfortunes, and it would be easy to suppress it, as the price of everything is exceedingly low in Central Asia, and the troops could be therefore abundantly supplied at a trifling cost. The inhabitants being well satisfied, the Russians, if they understood how to turn their avarice to account, would no doubt obtain their support; it is simply a money question, and as the English can play that game as well themselves, it would be the poorest against the most generous, and not the weak against the strong. But the Russians never having quarrelled with the Afghans would have the best chance of being listened to; the English, on the contrary, having been their conquerors and their enemy, would run the risk of giving their money, as they did on a previous occasion, to people who would fight against them after having received it to fight for them. The English could not oppose the Russians with more than 20,000 of their countrymen, for they would be obliged to have garrisons in those provinces where Russian gold and intrigue might excite revolt. It would be impossible to leave England without troops—she might be attacked herself; and then Ireland must be watched: might not revolts break out in other colonies? has not England to defend herself in all parts of the globe?—these possibilities must all be met. How are soldiers to be improvised in a country in which there is no conscription? How much time would be required to

* The Persian artillery is excellent, and really formidable. Under European management, and if money were provided, 500 guns, many of them of the largest calibre, might be equipped for the field in a very short time.—ED.

train them? Before this could be done the Russians would have reached the heart of India—for I cannot help thinking that the 40,000 or 50,000 sepoys who would be opposed to them, deduction made for the garrisons of those provinces the fidelity of which is doubtful, would not stand after the first discharge of their artillery.

All the important battles that have been fought by the English in India have demonstrated that the sepoys, who fight well against undisciplined Asiatics, have proved unequal to meet a determined enemy; and they would never have beaten the Mahrattas and the Sikhs if the British soldier had not been at their side and obtained the victory, often at a very heavy cost of life.* I have not here endeavoured to show whether Russia does or does not possess the necessary resources for such an invasion. Various authors, of whom the most recent is M. Hommaire de Hell, having seen the army of that country and examined the details connected with it more closely than I have, decide in the negative; founding this opinion upon the inefficient state of several of the departments of it—above all the confusion and venality which reign in the commissariat.

I do not propose to inquire whether Russia, by making certain reforms, could not obviate this state of things; I have only proposed to show the possibility of directing a military expedition upon India, because I believe such expedition to be very practicable. It belongs to the parties interested to estimate the value of my observations; but, not to incur the reproach that would certainly be thrown upon me of partiality for the Russians, by pointing out only the route that would be the easiest to them to take, it remains for me to point out to the English the steps I should adopt in their place,—happy if I can by that means avoid the criticisms of both parties.

In the first place it would be very difficult to find the English off their guard; they would always know the moves of Russia and Persia soon enough to make their own preparations to resist them. In the event of the enemy posting himself in the heart of Afghanistan to attack them, the means that have been indicated, and which would facilitate the march of the Russians in that country, would naturally, and in a great measure, be available to

* The British soldier would now also be at their side as on previous occasions.—ED.

their adversaries; the chances would, however, be in favour of the English, if they could during such a war rely upon the tranquillity of India, for they would have the enormous advantage of operating at a short distance from their possessions and supplies, upon which, in case of suffering a reverse, they could fall back and resume the offensive.

The Russians, if they could hope for the concurrent support of the discontented population of certain provinces under the British rule, would, even then, always be liable to the treachery of doubtful allies, and at a great distance from their own country, from which they would be separated by a sea in the hands of their enemies, and steppes or deserts difficult to cross without the aid of the native population. A reverse would easily alienate them, and a primary condition of success to them is, that it should be a permanent success. Sir R. Shakespear was right when he said to the Khan of Khiva, "We have a garden, which is India; the walls are the fortified towns of Tartary and Afghanistan. Let the Russians once seize them, and our garden is theirs." I am entirely of this officer's opinion. The Indus is a very sufficient barrier against the inroad of an Asiatic army, and the English may remain tranquilly behind it as long as they have to contend only with them; but what the event might be in the event of the Russians joining them I have elsewhere said.

The success of the English against the Rajahs, Emirs, Sirdars, and Nawaubs of India, has been owing far more to the cleverness of their policy and administration than to the force of their arms. It is only of late years that they have had hard battles to fight, especially against the Sikhs, who were organized and manœuvred upon the system of European tactics; but they had no enlightened head, they were divided into parties, and there was no unity of action and intention previous to and during the sanguinary struggle; nevertheless what difficulty the English had to reduce them! If they imagine they will have less with the Russians and their auxiliaries, they will make a serious mistake; and it is because we consider them more formidable that we recommend the English not to wait for their first attack behind the Indus if they manifest any aggressive intention. This river is a line of defence of which they ought to avail themselves only as a last resource, after they had been forced back upon it. It would be dangerous to hazard on its banks the issue of the first conflict, for the Indians, accustomed to look upon this splendid stream as an impregnable barrier, would be paralysed at seeing the Russians cross it, and the English might from that moment consider them as lost to their cause.

To avert such a misfortune they ought at once to establish themselves strongly on the right bank of the river at those excellent positions of Peshawur on the north, and Shikarpoor on the south, and establish their influence in the neighbouring provinces in such a manner that on a given day they could reckon upon the sincere and energetic co-operation of the chiefs, or be in a position to annihilate them in case they should refuse to come to their assistance.* This ought to be the prelude to vigorous offensive operations against the Russians; and in case they should attack them on the less accessible side, that is to say, by Balkh, Khulm, and the Hindoo Koosh, after having ascended the Oxus, the English should occupy Kabul in time, leave there a small corps of occupation, and advance with the mass of their forces in two divisions to receive the enemy. The first of these should march on Heibak and dispute the passage of the Hindoo Koosh; the second should take the route from Bamian to Yekkenholing, and from thence descend the fertile and populous banks of the Dehas, as far as Balkh, whence it would turn to the right towards Khulm, and fall upon the enemy's rear when he was well in amongst the mountains.

It would be difficult for the Russians to meet these combined attacks, especially if the English should succeed in interesting the warlike inhabitants of these countries in their cause, or awe them into observing a strict neutrality. Their adversaries would, it is true, be able to watch the valley of the Dehas with a *corps d'armée*, but it would weaken their force; this and other circumstances would make an attack from the Russians on this side less dangerous than on the south. Let us consider therefore what course the English would pursue if they were menaced on the south. They ought to march upon Kandahar without delay and defend the approaches to that city, which would be easy enough on the Herat road by reason of the mountains and the nature of the ground through which this road runs. In case of a defeat they could fall back on the Bolan Pass, taking care

* This course has been followed by the English since this book was written. —ED.

to lay waste the country behind them and destroy the roads; and then, should the fortune of war continue against them, they would still have the Indus to cover their retreat. But let them not depend too much upon that river as a barrier; let them bear in mind the opinion of the Lacedæmonians, who would not surround their town with a wall, because in their opinion the best rampart was a good army. Let the English prepare theirs. In either case, according to the direction of the attack, Kabul or Kandahar ought to be occupied and defended by them. They might possibly repent having neglected this means of safety; for the Russians, if they took either, might from thence reach the banks of the Indus at a point where they were not expected, and cross it without firing a shot.

The clever diplomacy of the English in Persia would also materially assist them and create a powerful diversion in their favour; they have attached to their cause the nomadic population of the south of the empire, who would rise at the first signal and excite a feeling in the country that might threaten the existence of the reigning dynasty, which so many princes pensioned by the British Government hope to overthrow; and the minimum result to the Shah would be the loss of a portion of his kingdom. It is probable therefore that potentate would look twice, and would require ample guarantees from the Russians before he engaged in an enterprise that might have such fatal consequences for him. An invasion of India with his assistance would be an advantage to Russia only, who would take the lion's share; and Persia would alienate a power which has on so many occasions prevented the Russians from seizing some of her finest provinces. Persia can have nothing to fear from the English until she sees them masters of Herat; having then one foot in Persia on this side, like the Russians in the north on the banks of the Araxes, they would show themselves equally exacting.

But to reckon upon the sympathies or the hatred which the people of Central Asia might entertain either for the English or Russians would be extremely hazardous; the stability of the sentiments of such a population could not be depended upon for any length of time, and, I repeat, that the success of an invasion of India by the Russians is above everything a question of money: nevertheless, supposing the Afghans to have been well bribed, it would still, as I have already remarked, be absurd to place confidence in them. However, it is for the English to be on the alert, if they are not already so, and prepare while they have the opportunity to meet events that might otherwise, at a period more or less distant, disturb their rule over a vast fertile and populous empire.

Before concluding these remarks it may be useful to say a few words respecting the roads which traverse the country inhabited by the Eïmaks and the Hazarahs of the Paropamisus. The Afghans, whether coming from Balkh, Kabul, Kandahar, or Herat, never venture into the mountainous district of those intrepid and hardy nomadic tribes; but the difficulties of the ground here are not so great as they have been hitherto represented, and whenever the Afghans in former times directed their steps that way, it was always to pillage and massacre the inhabitants; the result is, that in the present day the Hazarahs look upon them as wild beasts, and treat them accordingly; and the Afghans prefer making a long circuit from one town to the other to exposing themselves to the chance of meeting with certain death by taking the direct road. An European army, whose chief had the tact to ingratiate himself with the Khans and interest them in his favour, might, I think, advancing with prudence, march through their territory without meeting with any serious impediments; water can be procured at every step, and at all seasons sheep and fruit are to had in abundance, and a sufficient quantity of grain at a moderate cost; the pasturage is excellent, and the cavalry could, if necessary, complete its remounts with great facility from the splendid studs of the Hazarahs.

The mountains, which are the cause of so much alarm to the Afghans, might be avoided by following the course of the rivers and the valleys, and several positions fortified by nature would soon fall into the hands of the Europeans, for a few shells would inevitably dislodge the natives from these fastnesses. From the numerous details I received from persons who had travelled through these countries during a period of many years, as well as my own observations, I am of opinion that there are two easy roads on the north and centre to Kabul, and one to the south direct to Kandahar.

The first is from Herat by Chekcheran, Derzi, Ser Mourghab, Ganimet Hazaret, Deregez, Khorram, Bamian, and Kabul.

The second from Herat by Feiz-abad, Obeh, Khojachest, Sheherek, Doulet-yar, Hassanek, and Deh Zingy. Three roads diverge from the latter place; the first, and to the north, passes by Yekkenholing, Bamian, and Kabul; that in the centre by Dirazgul, Barek Khaneh, Kaleh-mirvalee, and Kabul; that on the east passes through the villages of Alayar-beg, Guzeristan, and Narvar, and rejoins the Kabul road at Ghuzni; no obstacles of any importance would be encountered on this road. Another route goes direct from Deh Zingy to Kandahar, by Meïdan, Deh Koodi, and Derevat.

With regard to the third, instead of reaching Kandahar by Giran and Washir, time might be saved by taking the road through Sakhar, Teirereh, Gulistan, and Goorek; but the mountains are rugged, the country unsettled, water is scarce in the neighbourhood of Kandahar, and caravans never go by this route.

It would be easy for the English to make a road from Shikarpoor to the Helmund. If what I heard during my residence at Kandahar was true, the English advanced posts are established to the north at Dadur, this side the Bolan Pass;* to the west Khelat Nassir Khan is subject to them, and a hundred sepoys suffice to maintain order in that country; the Emir of the town, in the pay of the Company, administers the judicial power under the *surveillance* of the British resident, who himself manages its finance. The distance between Khelat and the banks of the Helmund is not more than forty, or at the outside, forty-five parasangs; the route winds across steppes which in these days are almost a desert during eight months of the year, but anciently well-populated and provided with water at all seasons; the sandy desert encroaches but little, and in small patches along this road. Nothing therefore prevents the English from following the example of the Russians and digging wells at stated distances, and establishing around them small agricultural and military settlements; by this means they could quickly reach the Helmund, and then they would be only six or seven days' march from Herat. The continual passing to and fro of the caravans from Persia and Turkistan would soon make this tract of country very prosperous; the traffic to India at the present time makes a long circuit by Kandahar, and that road from being unprotected is very far from secure, so that the merchants would eagerly take advantage of this shorter and less dangerous one.†

* This is not the case.—ED.

† *See* Appendices.

For the information of those persons who take an interest in the affairs of Afghanistan I will now throw a rapid glance at the respective positions of the sovereigns amongst whom the three principalities of Kabul, Kandahar, and Herat are divided.

The Emir Dost Mohamed Khan, an Afghan chief, of the tribe of Barukzye, reigns over that of Kabul, and holds the first rank in Afghanistan. Circumstances, but more especially the influence which in his absence was obtained by his son Akbar Khan, considerably diminished that of the Dost himself; since his return from India his authority has paled before that of the heir-presumptive, who is all-powerful in political and other matters. This will probably continue until his father's decease, when difficulties will arise, of no ordinary kind, before he can consider himself firmly established as his successor; and if his courage is equal to the task, it is more than can with truth be said of any of his other qualifications. Dost Mohamed has appointed this prince his heir, only because his mother belonged to the noble tribe of Popolzyes. He has an elder brother, by name Mohamed Efzel Khan, who has been excluded from the throne because his mother was of low extraction—of the mountain-tribe of the Bengeshis. Everything leads to the belief that when the time arrives this chief will in all probability stoutly dispute Akbar's accession to power, and the other brothers are no less ambitious than he is.

Mohamed Efzel Khan.	Shir Jan Khan.
Mohamed Azim Khan.	Mohamed Akrem Khan.
Mohamed Akbar Khan.	Mohamed Sherif Khan.
Goolam Haïdar Khan.	Mohamed Emin Khan.

Sultan Jan Khan.

The three first are said to be the bravest of the Emir's sons, and Akrem Khan the most sensible and intelligent.* Goolam Haïdar Khan is Dost Mohamed's favourite; but the Afghans speak of his partiality for him with as much dissatisfaction as they were wont to do his preferencce for Akbar; and, in a spirit of opposition easy to be understood, they openly express their sympathies in favour of Efzel Khan, who on his mother's side represents the

* Both Akbar and Akrem have died since this was written, and Goolam Haidar, the eldest surviving son, is now the acknowledged heir of the Dost, but being notoriously of a weak and irresolute character, he will very poorly supply his father's place. Nawab Jubbar Khan is also dead.—ED.

people, and on his father's the chief. This prince, perfectly aware of the difficulties of his position, has taken a quiet line of his own, and no doubt bides his time. He is highly spoken of for his intelligence, courage, and noble sentiments.

These princes are not the only ones who will be ambitious to rule. Several brothers, nephews, and cousins of the Dost might be added to the list. The first that should be mentioned is his cousin Mohamed Zeman Khan, who, after the disasters of the English in 1841, held for a few months the supreme power in Kabul; secondly, his son Shoojah-ed-Dowlet, the murderer of Shah Shoojah-el-Moolk; thirdly, Shemseddin Khan, who has the reputation of being the bravest of the Mohamedzye chiefs; lastly, the Nawab Jubbar Khan,* the brother of the Dost. He is the most knowing and the cleverest man in Afghanistan. For twenty years before the English invaded his country he was their friend and correspondent; but after their arrival at Kabul they displeased him, and he joined the ranks of the insurgents. His son Abdul Ghyaz Khan is also in some repute; and these two are the kings of every intrigue at Kabul.

Such are the men whose schemes Mohamed Akbar Khan will have to contend with during his father's lifetime, and who at his death will probably meet him in arms. But who is to conjecture

* We had previously heard of the amiable character of our host, Nawab Jubbar Khan; and even found him, on personal acquaintance, to be quite a patriarch. He heals every difference among his many turbulent brothers: himself the eldest of his family, he has no ambitious views, though he once held the government of Cashmeer, and other provinces of the Dooranee empire. His brother, the present chief of Kabul, has requited many services by confiscating his estate; but he speaks not of his ingratitude. He tells you that God has given him abundance for his wants, and to reward those who serve him; and there are few pleasures equal to being able to give to those around, and to enjoy this world without being obliged to govern. I discovered, during my stay at Kabul, that the Nawab assumes no false character, but expresses himself as he feels, with sincerity. Never was a man more modest and more beloved: he will permit but a single attendant to follow him, and the people on the high and bye-ways stop to bless him; the politicians assail him at home to enter into intrigues, and yet he possesses the respect of the whole community, and has at the present moment a greater moral influence than any of the Barukzye family in Afghanistan. His manners are remarkably mild and pleasing; and from his dress one would not imagine him to be an influential member of a warlike family. It is delightful to be in his society, to witness his acts, and hear his conversation. He is particularly partial to Europeans, and makes every one of them his guest who enters Kabul. All the French officers in the Punjab lived with him, and keep up a friendly intercourse. Such is the patriarch of Kabul; he is now about fifty years of age; and such the master of the house in which we were so fortunate as to dwell.—*Extract from Burnes's Travels into Bokhara,* vol. i. pp. 134 and 135.—ED.

even the possibilities of an Afghan succession? The chief who is at the height of power one day may have his eyes put out or be in his grave the next. There is no stability, no fixed principles of government, no law of primogeniture, or other definitive rule which points out and establishes the succession to the throne. Every act of administration is a temporary expedient. There is no regard for the future; and authority, being neither the privilege of birth nor the reward of merit, is often, nay, almost always, wielded by the most clever, though perhaps most unprincipled, of these warlike chiefs who can seize it.

As far as regards the succession to the principality of Kandahar, it is quite as uncertain. Some months after its evacuation by the English, Kohendil Khan, brother of the Emir Dost Mohamed, having overcome Sefder Jung, son of Shah Shoojah-el-Moolk, who held it under the suzerainty of the English, seized the government; and if this chief has not had so much to contend with as his relative of Kabul, in re-establishing tranquillity in his dominions after his restoration, it is owing to the privileges which he conceded to the Sirdars and Mollahs. He makes such a point of conciliating the latter that they may, generally speaking, be considered as the real governors of Kandahar; the Khan is indeed but a mere intermediary between them and the people, and, short of being personally menaced, he takes care not to do anything without having first asked their advice. On the other hand he has a great deal of trouble with the Hazarahs of Pooshtkoh, in the north of his territory, and is obliged to maintain a force of 2000 cavalry to keep them in check. He is also obliged to abstain from taking any course which would be likely to affront his nephew Akbar Khan, and above all, from having any communication with the English, which would be the signal for an immediate attack upon Kandahar by his ambitious and dangerous relative.

Kohendil Khan is in some degree under the influence of Persia, where he was hospitably received during the three years of his exile; he seeks, in concert with her, to overthrow Yar Mohamed, and hopes to seize the principality of Herat, and give it to one of his own brothers.* Up to the present time he has simply

* It may be remembered that one of the principal causes of the Afghan war was the discovery of a treaty entered into by Kohendil Khan with Persia, under the guarantee of Russia, which had for its principal object the cession of Herat to the Kandahar chief. The original draft of this treaty, which was

intrigued with a view to this object; for an armed manifestation would bring down upon him the enemies he has most to dread: on the north, Mohamed Akbar, who would not probably remain an indifferent spectator of the ruin of his father-in-law; and on the south the English, who would scarcely permit the affairs of Herat to be altered in any way that would increase the power of Persia or the Barukzyes, until the latter are completely in their interests.* Kohendil Khan is so thoroughly persuaded that the English will again occupy Kandahar, that, in expectation of their return, he has 800 beasts of burden always ready in the neighbourhood of the city to transport himself, his treasures, and his family, to Persia. Even if these fears should not be realized, they may cause him serious inconvenience; for as he is always levying taxes on the community with the view of filling his coffers, in anticipation of his flight, and never pays any one but his treasurer and his mule-drivers, who are to help him off, he is far from popular.

When the English took Kandahar in 1839 they doubled the taxes; and Kohendil Khan on his return made no alteration, alleging that as the Afghans found no difficulty in satisfying the demands of the infidels, they ought to consider themselves fortunate not to have them still further increased by their legitimate sovereign.† The argument was specious; but the English paid with great punctuality the government officials, and the Khan does not. They doubled their pay; he reduced their salaries to the original rate.

---

never formally executed, may be seen in the Afghan Blue Book of 1838-39.—Ed.

* After the death of Yar Mohamed, Kohendil Khan sent two expeditions against Herat, and was only deterred from laying formal siege to the city by the interference of Persia in favour of the new ruler Syud Mohamed Khan. England has only so far exerted her power up to the present time with respect to this matter, that she has obtained a formal engagement from Persia not to send an army against Herat, unless the place be threatened from the eastward and assistance be demanded by the governor. At the present moment a very difficult question has arisen with regard to this place. Dost Mohamed occupied Kandahar on the death of Kohendil Khan, and afterwards advanced on Herat to avenge the murder of his son-in-law Syud Mohamed Khan, upon the present ruler Mohamed Youssouf Shah. Persia, considering this demonstration to absolve her from her engagements to England, has responded to the call of the present ruler for assistance, and is now (May, 1856) in possession of Herat, and marching on the road to Kandahar. A collision between them and Dost Mohamed's force is thus very likely to arise.—Ed.

† M. Ferrier was misinformed on this point, for the taxation under the English was considerably less than under the Sirdars. The actual assessment, half in money and half in kind, was maintained on the old footing established by Nadir Shah, but remissions were granted for fully one half the revenue to meet the expense of entertaining a body of 2000 Dooranee horse.—Ed.

Under the English rule extortion was unknown; with the Khan it has become permanent. The result of this will probably be a revolution, that will save the English the trouble of turning him out. Half the population of Kandahar has fled from his tyranny; and if it continues the town will be deserted. He has endeavoured to check this emigration at the frontier, by seizing the runaways and fining them heavily; but this was a short-sighted policy, for, withheld by force, they will be the first to revolt.

Kohendil Khan and the other Afghan chiefs, the Shah of Persia, the Belooches, Sikhs, and Mahrattas, are agreed on one point, namely, their hostility to the English; but they have never been able to originate and carry out any plan for acting in concert and striking a blow which would shake the power of the Feringhees. They have temporised and been false to each other, and when they have fought have been beaten in detail. This system has been fatal to them; for England is crushing at the moment I am writing the most important of the confederates on the banks of the Sutlej. The empire founded by Runjeet Singh will in a short time exist only in name; the power of the Mahrattas and the people of Scinde is gone; and if the Afghans are not on their guard, they will fall into the net which England will spread for them, or exhaust themselves in continual conflicts or intestine quarrels, which must eventually end in their complete subjection. Kohendil Khan is well aware of this, and would not be sorry to secure the sympathy of the English unknown to his own allies; but the chances of this double game might turn against himself; the English government could very well receive his advances without promising to entertain them, and abandon him when it was their interest to do so. The ties of blood would not prevent Akbar Khan from taking his revenge if he only suspected that his uncle had any treasonable inclinations, and the Shah of Persia, whose influence contributes greatly to keep him in power, would withdraw his support directly he appeared to abandon the common cause; if, contrary to these speculations, Kohendil Khan is not deprived of his throne in his lifetime, his death will be the signal for many a bloody episode amongst the various competitors for the principality. His sons, brothers, and nephews, are all resolute and determined characters, and each of them has a party devoted to his cause. In this country the right of succession is considered to rest rather in the brother than in the son, and this accounts for the fact that Kohendil

Khan reigned after his two half-brothers, Poor dil Khan and Shir dil Khan;* two others still survive, these are Rahim dil Khan and Mehr dil Khan, who aspire to the succession. The Kandaharians have the following opinion of their three principal Sirdars, viz.: that Kohendil Khan is a good general and has never been beaten; that his brother, Rahim dil Khan is loyal, eloquent, and persuasive; and that Mehr dil Khan is wise and a good counsellor. All these brothers have had tolerably large families, and the following is a list of their children:—

The sons of Poor dil Khan.	*The son of Shir dil Khan.*	*The sons of Kohendil Khan.*
Mir Efzel Khan.	Mir Ahmed Khan.	Mohamed Sedik Khan.
Abdool Waat Khan.		Mohamed Omar Khan.
Abdool Rassool Khan.	(This prince is insane.)	Mohamed Osman Khan.
		Sultan Ali Khan.
		Abdoolah Khan.
		Goolam Maheddin Khan.

The sons of Rahim dil Khan.	*The sons of Mir dil Khan.*
Mohamed Alem Khan.	Khoch dil Khan.
Goolam Mohamed Khan.	Shir Ali Khan.
Mohamed Sawar Khan.	Moonaver dil Khan.
Goolam Haïdar Khan.	Mohamed Hoossein Khan.
Mohamed Kooli Khan.	Ali Akbar Khan.
	Ali Asker Khan.
	Fethi Ali Khan.

To these princes must be added Mohamed Kooli Khan, son of Futhi Khan, vezir of Shah Mahmoud; he lives at Kandahar, and is highly respected; he served the English faithfully, and their support will probably not be found wanting to him. But if the succession comes, as the Afghans think it will, to the prince who is dear to them by reason of his many good qualities and straightforward conduct, it will, without doubt, be left to Rahim dil Khan,† and after him to his brother, Mehr dil Khan.

The dissensions in the family of the Suddozyes, of which the Mohamedzyes took advantage to raise themselves to power, contributed more than foreign wars to precipitate the downfall of the dynasty of the great Shah Ahmed. United at first, discord was introduced amongst the Mohamedzyes, when, after having conquered, they had to divide the kingdom amongst them; but their quarrels did not prevent them from forming a league against the

* Poor dil means "the full-hearted." Shir dil means "the lion-hearted."—ED.

† Rahim dil Khan is now the only surviving brother. He has been superseded in power by Dost Mohamed.—ED.

common enemy whenever they were menaced, and in this has consisted their strength up to this day. This was easy so long as there were only the nineteen sons of Payendeh Khan upon the scene, but their posterity in Kabul and Kandahar amount already to three hundred and seventy-two sons and grandsons, amongst whom a good understanding is more hopeless than amongst their fathers. They will fight desperately for power, and this will probably fall into the hands not of the bravest, but the most prodigal; for in Aghanistan, more than anywhere else, is the conscience swayed by gold. To gain partisans, all these princes by turns flatter and caress the Sirdars, and these individuals profit by the offers that are made them to secure their co-operation, raising their pretensions accordingly, and augmenting their price in proportion to the importance of the services required; but more than one of them, instead of supporting the chief who has paid him well beforehand, will perhaps become his most dangerous enemy, and raise himself to power over the bodies of the family of the very man to whom he has sworn fidelity.

The principality of Herat forms, with that of Kabul and Kandahar, what we call Afghanistan Proper; and there, in 1842, expired the Suddozye dynasty, for Shah Kamran, great-grandson of the Shah Ahmed, was strangled in prison by order of his Vezir Yar Mohamed Khan, who, as I have already observed, reigned in that principality till his death, under the title of Vezir Sahib. What I have stated elsewhere respecting him incontestably proves the administrative talent which he possessed. After the death of his master, order and tranquillity, which had not existed in Herat for many years, were re-established. His alliances with the Hazarahs and Usbeks, and still more the marriage of his daughter with Mohamed Akbar Khan of Kabul, gave him up to the time of his death a certain preponderating influence in the affairs of Central Asia; but such ties are so little respected that this marriage would weigh very little against the decisions of either party if any circumstance occurred detrimental or beneficial to his interests. If Kohendil Khan had not been for a long period the declared enemy of Yar Mohamed, his alliance with the princes of Kabul would have been sufficient to make him so. As to the Shah of Persia, there is very little sympathy between him and the chief of Herat; neither is he ostensibly hostile. Yar Mohamed acknowledges his suzerainty in a manner perfectly nominal, and nothing indicates the probability of a better understanding between them.

Of the three sons of Yar Mohamed Khan, only one, the Sirdar Syud Mohamed Khan, is old enough to govern; but he is wanting in the talent necessary to enable him to succeed his father. After the Vezir's death, therefore, it is not unlikely that one of the Sirdars of Kandahar will try and seize the reins of power; but this must be with the connivance, and possibly the assistance, of the Shah of Persia, who will never allow such a prize to fall into any hands inimical to his own influence. This policy would meet with the approbation of Russia, for that power would not certainly like to see Herat in the possession of any chief or party which could at any moment, by a little manœuvring on the part of the English, be induced to take an interest in their cause. It is, however, highly improbable that more than twenty years should elapse before the forces of the Company will again appear in Afghanistan: they will in all likelihood be called there by the Chiefs and Sirdars, who will from time to time be disputing and fighting for the supreme authority in one or other of the principalities, or the English will take advantage of some circumstance arising out of their own policy to invade it once more. They are clever in originating such opportunities, and when their flanks and rear are sufficiently protected, will not fail to take advantage of them; at the present moment the extension of the British frontier on this side would be useless so far as the security of India is concerned, but the English would without doubt prefer being ready to meet the eventualities of a Russian invasion. Taught by previous disasters, they will not, as in 1839, advance into these wild and unsettled countries unless their communications are secured: they have acted since then more cautiously and with more method; and if ever they invade the territories west of the Indus they must be governed by the laws of prudence as well as of courage. They have established *têtes-de-pont* at Peshawur and Shikarpoor, and this is the only measure which denotes any ulterior project on their part. But time will show if I am mistaken in my opinion of their intentions.

Since the occupation of Afghanistan by the English, the discussions that have arisen in consequence of that event in the periodicals and daily papers have proved that the real interests of England in Central Asia were perfectly understood by the unfortunate

Burnes. The advice which he gave of strengthening and firmly establishing the power of the Mohamedzyes was a measure of sound policy, and would have secured for ever the influence of the government of Calcutta over Afghanistan; we have indeed only to refer to the events of which that country was the theatre in 1838 to be convinced of the justice of this opinion. The armies of Kandahar and Kabul united might have easily seized Herat, which was stripped of everything after the retreat of the Persians; the imbecile Shah Kamran might then have been replaced by a brother of the Emir Dost Mohamed. The English would by this means have had, through their allies, an immediate and decided influence over Persia; but the Court of Directors were too avaricious to be satisfied with an extension of influence. They were anxious to appropriate the finances of Afghanistan, and this induced them to invade that country—a most unjust and impolitic act; but instead of its serving as a rampart to their Indian possessions, which they had erroneously hoped it would, it proved a gulf which swallowed up their soldiers and their treasures. This hard and unpleasant lesson has not made them renounce invasions for the future: it is true they protest that it is their intention to remain on the line of the Indus; but are they likely to stop short on such a tempting road? Nevertheless, the press of India state that the Afghan question, as it was conceived and understood by Burnes, is to be renewed; and that the government is to take advantage of the friendly feeling manifested by Dost Mohamed, and enter again into negotiations with their old antagonist.*

This may be possible; but should it be so, the Emir will not have with him the consent of the masses of the people. His leaning to the English has already lost him popularity; and too great a manifestation of that feeling would again endanger his throne.

However, be this opinion accurate or otherwise, Russia cannot but be alive to her position, and many persons are anxious to know what barrier she can oppose to the increasing influence which must flow from these negotiations amongst her neighbours in Asia. The answer to this is, that the Czar is in no respect

* Since this was written a general treaty of friendship was formed with Dost Mohamed in 1855, but no minister or agent has been sent to reside at Kabul.—ED.

behind his neighbours; his motto, like that of the Romans, is, "Conquer to avoid surrender:" let the English give him time, and we shall see whether his plans are well conceived or not. He only waits for the fall of the Caucasus, to strike his talons into Afghanistan. The repeated blows that he has inflicted on the former country sufficiently prove that he wishes to terminate the war there, and carry his arms into Turkistan, which he has already encircled with a chain of fortresses. The distance from thence to Herat is short and the road is easy. If the Persians are not masters of it, and do not open the way, the Russian army in ten days can do so, and, once at Herat, who can foresee where they will stop?*

---

* Since the above was written, matters have been modified in Afghanistan much as I had anticipated, excepting that the career of Mohamed Akbar was cut short when he was on the point of engaging in a war with the English: he was poisoned in 1848. His brother, Goolam Haïdar Khan, succeeded him as Vezir at Kabul, and he stands precisely in the same position with regard to his elder brother, Mohamed Efzel Khan, as Mohamed Akbar did. Less obnoxious, however, to the English than that chief, he has the opportunity of coming to some compromise with them, though he cannot make any great concessions, as the Afghans would not suffer it. The English, on their side, after passing the Indus at Peshawur, have advanced against the Momund mountaineers, and engaged in an irregular but sanguinary conflict. Their mountains are the bulwarks of Kabul, and the subjugation of the one would probably be followed by the invasion of the other.

In Kandahar, though Kohendil Khan is dead, affairs have remained very much as they were; and this is not surprising, for the English can advance with greater facility and promptitude upon this point of Afghanistan than upon any other. The Khan was succeeded in the government by his brother. Yar Mohamed Khan died in 1852, when the Persians immediately prepared to besiege Herat, notwithstanding the representations of England. Her attention was more especially excited by this demonstration as it was coincident with an inroad of 5000 Russians into Turcomania. This corps marched along the banks of the Attrak through the Goorghan to chastise the Turcoman hordes of the Yamouts, who had in the previous year, 1851, carried fire and sword into the Russian settlement of the Ashounadeh, situated at the entrance of the Bay of Astrabad. The English fearing, and with reason, that they might, in conjunction with the Persians, advance as far as Herat, gave their ultimatum, and upon this the Russian troops suspended their march; but this halt is only a temporary measure, and I have no doubt that, sooner or later, the ulterior events will one day be realized in the manner I have pointed out. In order that the reader may not suppose that I have prophesied after this fact was known, I must refer him to the *Journal de Constantinople* of the 6th and 11th of July, 1847, in which will be found two articles sent by me to the editor; they contain a summary of my opinions on Afghanistan, and are identical with those enunciated in these volumes.

CHAPTER XXXI.

Preparations upon departure — The Author receives his passport from Yar Mohamed — Leaves Herat — Shekwan — Kussan — Yar Mohamed's letter to Dad Khan — Turcomans on the road — Kariz — Toorbut Sheik Jam — Mahmoodabad — Hedireh — Herds of deer — Singbest — Arrival at Meshed — Reflections on the Author's journeys — Advice to travellers in Central Asia — Old acquaintances — Mollah Mehdi and Dr. Wolf — Hussein Khan Hashi — A Russian spy — The Author leaves Meshed — Conduct of a Persian official — Fidelity how looked upon in Persia — Sherifabad — Corpses on their way to Kerbelah — A preservative against every evil — Kadumgah — Persecutions of the Ghebers by the Imaum Reza — His foot-print on the rock — Nishapoor — Dreadful state of that town from cholera — Zaffourounee — Difficulties of the road from snow — Subzawar — Mehir — Muzeenoon — Abbasabad — Meyomeed — Shah-rood — Deh-mollah — Damghan — Grievances of the Serbas — Treatment by their colonel — Goosheh — Semnoon — The Author meets with the English *chargé d'affaires* — Lasgird — Quarrel with the Hazarahs — Deh-nemuck — Kishlak — Eywanee Key — Katoor-abad — Teheran.

I PASSED a few more days at Herat, occupied in making preparations for my journey, and without being in the least interfered with or watched as I had been during my first visit. When not thus engaged, I enjoyed the society of my friends the Sirdar, Hadji Futteh Khan, and Assad Khan, whose kindness was uninterrupted to the last moment of my stay. The former obtained for me an official letter to the commandant of the frontier, an escort of two horsemen, and a passport, in which Yar Mohamed set forth the vile conduct of the Sirdars of Kandahar, with a view of making it public. The following is a translation of the *vezirial* letter:—

"The object of this (*erz-i-rah*) passport is to inform you that the very exalted and high-placed Monsieur, the General Ferrier, the hero, the companion of bravery, is arrived at Herat, with the intention of going to Peshawur. After having visited this city on two different occasions, he took leave of us and directed his steps to Kandahar. We had heard with certainty that the above-named general arrived at his destination, when, after an absence of several months, he returned to the city of Herat, and then made serious complaints against the Sirdars of Kandahar. They took from him all his property, and prevented him from continuing his journey and he now returns to us, saying, 'Here I am, destitute of everything.' During the time of his stay at Herat the laws of hospitality have been observed towards him, and he, having requested permission to return to his own country, has chosen the route by Meshed. As the above-named general has requested to have two guides with him, I have acceded to his wish; and they have orders to conduct him to the district of Toorbut Sheik Jam, from which place they are to return to Herat. I have written these lines in order that all seeing them may remember me and obey. Salutation."

Shekwan, November 27th.—Already described; arrived in miserable weather.

Kussan, November 28th.—Already described. On the frontier of Herat. I went in search of the Sirdar Dad Khan the commandant of the fortress, and presented him with two letters of recommendation, one from his brother Shiran Khan, the other from the Vezir Sahib. The first runs thus:—

"May the very exalted Dad Mohammed Khan, the companion of honour, be joyful! This day the very elevated and very exalted General Ferrier, the hero, will leave Herat; God grant that on his arrival in the district of Kooh Sevieh you will pay the utmost respect to the exalted hero above mentioned, and will observe towards him the laws of hospitality, and, at his departure, you will send with him two men to accompany him to Kooh Sevieh, who shall see him safe and sound as far as Toorbut Sheik Jam, whence they shall return. Take care that in regard to this order nothing be neglected; as to the tolls of the roads and custom-houses, give orders that he is not to pay anything. He is to be allowed to pass on quietly to his destination."

The Turcomans were scouring the road that I was to travel the next day, and they had plundered several caravans in the course of the few preceding days; therefore, Dad Khan advised me to wait for a party of a dozen horsemen, expected from Moorgaub, on their way to Meshed, and travel in company with them. It proved fortunate that I did so, for a caravan that started from Kussan on the 29th, in defiance of his warning, was met two hours from the place, and all the travellers were carried off into captivity.

Kariz, November 30th.—A halt already described. The expected party not having arrived, I set out with the escort of two horsemen, and my servant Mohamed whom I left at Herat when I went to Kandahar, and engaged again when I returned. We got our arms ready, but had the good fortune not to meet any of the depredators.

Toorbut Sheik Jam, December 1st.—A place already described. It rained in floods at sunrise, when we mounted our horses. Dervish Ali and Rehmet Agha, the soldiers that were to escort me, at first refused to start, pretending that the rain was impure, and tried hard to persuade me to give them a good pilau and wait for fine weather; but as I paid no attention to their remonstrances, and started without them, it ended in their following me in a desperate passion, storming against Europeans and their eccentric habits; in truth it required some resolution to brave the storm, but it was just because I thought the Turcomans would remain under shelter somewhere, that I seized the opportunity of getting over the most dangerous part of the road. My conjectures proved correct; for after an hour's riding, we came to a place covered with fresh horsedung, indicating plainly that they had just been driven from the spot by the torrents of rain; when they saw this, my escort were as loud in their praises of me as they had previously been the reverse: but it was after all an interested move; they did not wish to lose, by carrying their perversity to extremes, the little present which they expected me to make them at Toorbut, where, according to orders, they were to leave me and return to the frontier. This was a very severe day's work, the weather continued deplorable, and we arrived at our halt as wet as if we had ridden through a river.

Mahmoodabad, December 2nd.—A halt already described. We found the gates of this small fortress closed; it is one of the best in Persia. The Turcomans had within the last eight days made several attempts to take it by surprise, and no doubt the inhabitants thought that we were in league with them, for they refused to open the gate, and threatened to fire upon us if we did not quickly retire; there was nothing to be done but obey the inhospitable mandate, so, though destitute of provisions for ourselves and horses, we took refuge in the tomb of the nephew of the Imaum Reza, situated near the road, and remained expecting the Turcomans, who luckily never came.

Hadeerah, December 3rd.—Caravanserai already described. I

never before saw such an immense number of deer as on leaving Mahmoodabad; the plain was covered with them, each herd consisting of several thousand head. Here we should have had to keep a forced fast, if a shepherd whom we met had not given us some of his black bread and a little milk, which sustained us till the next morning.

Sangbut, December 4th.—Already described; at this place we found the cholera.

Meshed, December 5th.—Described on my previous visit. We arrived just in time to escape the Turcomans, but were once more in the midst of the cholera;—it was worse than ever at Meshed. I thought little of it, as I had been the last five months in countries where it was common, but the population here was in a state of consternation, and to this cause of alarm was added the despair of a great many families from a very different one. A great many of their children and relatives had recently been carried off in a chapaoul, that the inhabitants of Khelat-nadir had committed almost under the town walls; these cruel marauders had pillaged all the neighbouring villages, and the desolation was general. It is true that in having reached the capital of Khorassan, I could not consider myself as out of danger, but I was fortunate to be very nearly in safety. When I determined to cross Afghanistan, I had not acted under any delusion as to the dangers or trials that awaited me; but then there was before me the chance of reaching Lahore, and that object sufficed to decide me. Unhappily the hostility to the English had not subsided in Afghanistan when I arrived there, and I still look upon it almost as a miracle that I escaped from the hands of the natives; I should infallibly have paid for my temerity with my life, if I had not been so much accustomed to Asiatic habits and character. I succeeded in dissembling my fears, and seeming to believe that the rights of hospitality were sufficiently sacred to guarantee my life and property; the fact of my being a Frenchman I never ceased to declare, though I could have concealed that fact, as well as the object of my journey to Lahore; but the least inconsistency in my story—and, once departing from the truth, it is easy to fall into one—would have been fatal to me. To the Afghans a subject must always be stated simply and without affectation; it is equally dangerous with them to appear too humble or to try to domineer. A certain manner must be preserved, which keeps them at a distance—a natural dignity devoid of presumption: they must be conversed with as suits their limited intelligence,—sensibly and firmly, without either arrogance or stiffness. Their plain, coarse good sense, delights in a conversation conducted clearly and in few words. Going amongst them with our French ideas of superiority in all and everything, if I had shown myself discontented, or even surprised, at their manners and ideas, I should have considerably augmented my difficulties, and probably lost my life. My inflexibility with the Sirdar Mohamed Sedik Khan very nearly did so, and it was a lesson by which I profited; a little humouring enabled me to retrieve the false step I had made, but it was not easily done. An European who has lived much with Asiatics and knows the Persian language thoroughly—who is not of a fair complexion, and whose eyes are neither blue nor green—might, I think, by dressing like the natives and conforming to their customs, travel amongst them as a Persian merchant, and conceal his nationality, especially if he took care to provide himself with a good supply of articles of small value for sale; but he who cannot unite all these requisites had better acknowledge what he really is.

When I returned to Meshed, I again saw my old acquaintances Mirza Mohamed, the Tajar Bashi, and the English agent Mollah Mehdi. The latter was furious against Dr. Wolf, who had published a letter in an Eastern paper, saying that he had converted the Mollah to Christianity. "How," he said, "could I, a Hebrew by birth, and by force a Mohamedan, how could I be converted by the mediation of that crazy man? It would be to expose myself to the resentment of the fanatical population of this town. May the head of Wolf be covered with cinders, *khakister bé ser-esh*, may he go blind, *koor sheved*, for having told such a falsehood!" I could only console him by promising to send a letter from him to Dr. Wolf, in which he would desire him to retract his statement. By the intervention of this worthy man I made the acquaintance of the learned Kazi of Herat, Mohamed Hassan, who furnished me with most valuable information on Afghanistan. His son, Akhond Zadeh Saleh Mohamed, was mixed up with almost every act of policy of the English in this country.

I saw also the envoy from Khulm, Mohamed Hussein Khan-Kashi; he was the only person in the house of Sir Alexander Burnes at Kabul who escaped the frightful massacre in it by the Afghans, in November, 1841. Lastly, Deen Mohamed Khan, cousin of Yar Mohamed, and renowned for his daring valour; but his political career seemed finished, though he was young, for when I saw him he was nearly blind. I also had great pleasure in conversing with Yoosoof Khan, son of the famous Sirdar Kalesh Khan, chief of the tribe of Taymoonis, who took so great a part in the events of the siege of Herat at the beginning of this century. I found at his house an original, who was called Pellatou, and said he was a doctor from Pegu, but nothing in his physical conformation denoted that nationality; he had the Georgian type strongly marked, spoke Turkish and Hindostanee with facility, and was going to Bokhara and Kokan; I always thought he was a Russian spy. The Imaum Jumeh of Meshed, the last person that I visited, is a learned and tolerant man—a rare thing amongst the Mussulman priesthood of Persia; he entertained me much with the eccentricities of Dr. Wolf, who was anxious to convert him. The Governor-General of Khorassan, Assaf Doulet, received me with as much kindness as he did at Nishapoor. One of his sons, the Salar, General-in-chief, had left a fortnight before with some troops to chastise the inhabitants of Khelat-nadir, and retake from them the captives of Meshed, whom they had carried off shortly before my arrival, and Assaf requested me to join him and assist him with my advice, for Khelat-nadir is one of the strongest positions in Persia. The camp of the Salar was then pitched a little beyond Koochan, and on the 9th of December I set off in that direction, accompanied by my servant and Islam Beg, servant of the Governor-General; the latter was provided with an order in obedience to which we were supplied with fresh horses at the different villages, and therefore travelled fast, crossing by turns hill and dale, cultivations, fallows, and desert, with many ruins in all directions, and a succession of fortified villages surrounded with orchards, watered by abundant streams, reaching into the distance. We passed Shinaran and Ameerabad,* but the rapidity with which we travelled day and night made it impossible to collect any information respecting them. In twenty-four hours we reached Koochan, where we learnt that the Salar had left

* There was a famous siege of this place in the Khorassan campaign of Abbas Mirza in 1832. An English sergeant, Hayward, under Colonel Shee, was killed here. The Persian troops were under the command of Colonel Shee and General Burowski. The latter was afterwards killed at the siege of Herat, on the ramparts, and his body exchanged for some sheep to Futteh Khan!—ED.

with his force the previous evening, and was then at Deregez—therefore there now lay between us and him a large tract of ground, which was in the possession of the insurgents, it was consequently impossible for a party of only three to undertake to cross it; having learnt also that Assaf's son intended to march thence direct upon Khelat without retracing his steps, I returned to Meshed, after a stay of four-and-twenty hours at Koochan. From Meshed I could get to Khelat more easily, and with greater safety; but Assaf Doulet was so ill with the gout that he could not receive me. Foreseeing that it would be a long blockade, and being very anxious to reach Teheran to rest and recruit my health before the winter, I wrote to him for his permission to go on, which he gave me with the greatest kindness.

December 18th.—A certain Mirza Ibrahim sent for me on the part of the Governor-General, and read to me a note from the latter, apologizing on the grounds of severe illness, for not receiving my farewell visit; he also informed me that Assaf Doulet had ordered two guards to accompany me to the borders of Khorassan, and had sent me a *talikeh*, or order, for provisions to be served to me at every village for five men and ten horses, as far as Teheran. That was all that the Mirza communicated to me, although he was desired to give me fifty tomaums for my journey to Koochan; but to execute that part of his instructions did not suit his book, he hoped to keep the greater part of the sum himself; nevertheless, his embarrassed manner and awkward insinuations led me to infer the generous intentions of Assaf Doulet. Mirza Ibrahim tried hard to persuade me to write to him, and ask him to grant me a sum of money, in addition to the order for provisions, but as I conceived that would be a dishonourable step to take, I decisively refused to do so, and he then said he should write for it in my name, whether I consented or not, and obtain the sum in question; I quitted the room, leaving to him the responsibility of doing as he pleased, but reserving to myself the right to protest against the proceeding. If he had induced me to act in accordance with his views, he would probably have given me half the sum sent, and kept the rest himself; thus cheating me of ten or twelve tomaums and laughing at me besides—such are the habits of Persians. In their country fidelity is looked upon as a want of common sense, and the grossest dishonesty as a proof of intelligence or capacity, *ziringi*. However, the rascal was disappointed, for he had forgotten that it was necessary to induce the treasurer to join in this knavery, and the latter arrived at my rooms with the money about sundown; he told me that the Mirza had tried several times that day to persuade him to trust him with the payment of the sum in question, but he suspected his intentions, and therefore chose to bring it himself. I presented him with ten tomaums as a recompense for his honesty. Mirza Ibrahim was furious that I made no present to him, and complained bitterly of my bad conduct towards one who had taken so much trouble in my affairs.

"What!" said he, "you have the face to present part of this gift to the treasurer, and give me nothing; me! who have taken so much trouble about your affairs. This ignorance of the usages of well-bred people, denotes that you have had a very bad education, and have very bad manners; and it is not astonishing that, with such a wretched intellect, you should have been robbed and plundered by the Afghans—that will be the case with you wherever you go;" and he finished by a shower of insults and maledictions, proving his excessive disappointment and prodigious want of money. I replied ironically in the most flowery style, and with the bombastic metaphors in which the Persian language abounds, that the resources of my intellect were in no way equal to his.

"I thank you," I concluded, "for sharpening my wits; you gave me a useful lesson, and, rest assured, I shall profit by it, to get you recompensed in the right quarter. The example of the Afghans is, I see, considered a good one for Persians to follow; I congratulate you upon having let me know that you are amongst the number of imitators." In execution of my threat, I sent his letter, and a copy of mine, to Assaf Doulet, from whom he received a severe reprimand, and it was only at my intercession that he escaped the bastinado. To revenge himself, he made out my talikeh without including the *dzireh*, or order for provisions; but I insisted, and he was obliged to add them. There is more possibility of disputing with the Persians than the Afghans, and provided you can reckon upon the protection of the Russian or the British ambassador at Teheran, they must always be firmly met, for, in a question of money, they will trample you underfoot the moment the least concession is made to them. I remained at Meshed till the 20th of December; on that day, everything being ready for my departure, I determined to leave on the morrow.

Sherifabad, December 21st—six parasangs. I left on the right the road to Derrood, by which I had come to Meshed, and took the one to the left. Two hours of plain and four in the mountains; it was very cold and the snow fell thick, but, nevertheless, several friends accompanied me to the foot of the mountains. After we had left them my escort lost the road, and we wandered over the fields till night, when we reached Sherifabad, a small village of about fifty hearths, with a caravanserai-shah, at which a caravan of pilgrims had arrived before us. They kept howling "Ya Ali!" all night, and we could not sleep. This caravan was conveying twenty corpses to interment in the holy ground of Kerbelah, and though the deal coffins were lined with cloth prepared with naphtha, the effluvium was pestilential; the pilgrims however appeared not to perceive it, and man and beast slept pell-mell amongst the miserable remnants of mortality. One old fellow having washed his face and greasy hands in a dish, was going to throw the water away, when a pilgrim came up to him, and, begging for it most humbly, drank it off with extraordinary relish. Not a soul there but myself saw anything surprising in the sickening action, which seemed to me most enormously filthy; but one of my guards told me that the old fellow was a highly venerated Syud, and that in swallowing his ablutions, a person would absolutely be preserved from every evil moral and physical. A few moments after, the dirty washing-dish was filled with an enormous pillau, with which a score of hungry fellows satisfied their hunger, without the slightest disinclination, much less disgust: these, however, are the people who consider as impure all those who are not Shiah Mussulmans like themselves, and shun all contact with them.

Kadum-gah, December 22nd—seven parasangs—in the mountains. We were in the saddle two hours before daybreak, and there being a thick fog, had scarcely left the gates when my guides lost their way again; two days in succession we were really the sport of fortune! we came round to the village again without suspecting it, and started once more. This day's journey was disagreeable enough, continual up and down hill. Kadum-gah, the halt for the evening, is a little village on the mountain-side, inhabited by Syuds, being, on account of the sanctity of their origin, exempt from taxes; they refused to give me the djireh to which my talikeh gave me a right, and even refused to admit me within the walls, because I was an infidel. I went, therefore, to a caravanserai-shah on the plain, where I was provided with all I wished for. This village is one of the places to which the Persians make pilgrimages, because, according to them, the Imaum Reza, compared with whose miracles those of Mahomet and Our Saviour are as nothing, here roasted a thousand Ghebers out of a population then amounting to fifteen hundred, and afterwards, by efficacious means, converted the remaining five hundred to the true faith. It would take up far too much time and space to relate all the Imaum's miracles here, but the two following are fair examples of the value of the rest. By simply raising the forefinger of his right hand, he arrested in its progress a huge stone, hurled at him down the mountain by the Ghebers in the hope of crushing him; the stone is at this day surrounded by a rail of silver gilt, and is much venerated by Mussulmans. Another enclosure contains the Imaum's footprint, three inches deep, *in the rock!* This was to perpetuate the remembrance of his passage there, and hence the name of the village—*Kadum*, step; *gah*, place. Shah Abbas embellished it, but there is nothing now but some magnificent sycamores and a ruined mosque.

Nishapoor, December 23rd—four parasangs in a sandy but very fertile plain. I never remember to have felt such a distressing impression as that which came over me on my arrival at Nishapoor. The cholera had not spared a single family, and it was desolate. The sky was dark, and on the mountains covered with snow was a most singular and gloomy effect of light and shade, and a sadness came over me which harmonised entirely with the mournful scene on which I gazed. In the middle of a cemetery near the eastern gate of the city, a hundred corpses lay, with their faces exposed, extended on the snow awaiting their burial; their unhappy relatives were weeping and wailing round them; and there were not gravediggers enough in the place, so the mournful work went on slowly. What a subject for a painter was there! I entered the splendid caravanserai as quickly as possible to escape from the dreadful spectacle, but there again was a scene of fearful affliction. The sufferers with the cholera, and the terrified creatures who were not yet stricken, were making heartrending supplications to deprecate the wrath of Heaven. I retired to the farthest corner of a stable, endeavouring to isolate myself from the misery, but there, as elsewhere, I found victims in tears and agony excited by terror. The deputy-governor of the town had transported his household into a *balakhaneh*, belvidere, of the caravanserai, where he thought the air might be pure; there he fasted, prayed, and performed mummeries of all kinds that the fear of death could suggest, and though at the time he lived in dread of his last moment he actually cheated me. After having asked for, and received the payment for the provisions to which my talikeh gave me a right, he suddenly disappeared, and I never received them.

Zaffourounee, December 24th.—As the governor did not show himself this morning, I could not obtain the escort to which I was entitled to replace the one that had returned to Meshed; I started, therefore, with two servants, as I had hired a second for the journey. It was late when we left, the weather very bad, the snow deep though melting, and the road so frightfully broken up that our horses had infinite difficulty in getting along. After riding three hours, we lost ourselves in the middle of a plain covered with snow that concealed every trace of the road. At last, as it ceased to fall quite so thick, I could distinguish several villages on our left, and to them we directed our steps. The gates were closed, and our shouts were answered by the appearance of about a dozen men on the walls, armed with firelocks, and threatening to shoot us; they ordered us to retire as quickly as possible, if we were not prepared to receive a disagreeable salute. These poor devils acted thus, first, from fear of the Turcomans and Kurds, who had been pillaging their territory for the last two months; and secondly, to preserve themselves from the cholera, with which they had not yet been attacked. Our position was critical, but we could not hesitate, and continued our road; a peasant whom we met an hour afterwards, warned us to make a circuit to avoid the Kurds, who were in ambuscade in a defile we were going to pass through. This piece of service deserved a reward, and I was on the point of giving it to him, when he foolishly said that he belonged to the village from which we had been driven away; thereupon, in spite of my reiterated orders to the contrary, my servants gave him a shower of blows, and then recommended him to take their compliments to his hospitable townsmen. We continued our road according to the directions that the poor fellow had given us, and at midnight I arrived, without any unlucky rencontre, at Zaffourounee, and established myself as best I could in the ruined caravanserai.

Subzawar, December 25th.—The cholera, though on either side of it, had not attacked this town.

Mehir, December 26th.—A halt already described.

Muzeenoon, December 27th.—This halt has also been described. Here I met Prince Shapoor Mirza. The cholera showed itself here in a very singular manner: out of one hundred and four deaths, two only were men, old and sickly; eight were children under six years of age; and all the rest women.

Abbasabad, December 28th.—I trusted myself to Prince Shapoor Mirza for this dangerous day's journey. We set off in the dark, and at first lost the road, but reached our halt in the evening without further accident.

Meyomeed, December 29th.—The prince wished to rest a day at Abbasabad, and, to my great regret, I started alone, for the road to Shah-rood is not safe; it is rarely that the Turcomans are not upon it. I reached the halt, Miyane-desht, without mischance, but the inhabitants having warned me that the Turcomans had been in the town in the morning, and were hanging about the neighbouring mountains, I did not think it wise to put up there, and pressed on to Miyameed much fatigued.

Shah-rood, December 30th and 31st.—We saw the Turcomans at a distance, but they appeared to have game in hand, and did not trouble us; it was a very long day from Meyomeed to Shah-rood, the horses were very tired, and I thought it prudent to give them the rest of a day, which we passed very uncomfortably. The animals were up to their bellies in water in the caravanserai, and our rooms were exceedingly damp and cold. An English courier came in in the course of the night, and from him I had the first European news that I had heard for eight months.

Deh Mollah, January 1st, 1846.—The year begins for me once more in the midst of the vicissitudes of fortune, and the fatigue and peril of Asiatic travelling.

Damghan, January 2nd.—The snow fell thick and fast, the horses stumbled at every step; it was necessary to reload them at every few paces, with the mud up to my knees. The trouble of getting along exceeded everything I had previously met with, especially near the town, where the road was worst cut up. Having by incredible exertion reached the citadel, I found an impediment of a very different sort under the walls. A crowd of the serbas of the battalion of Damghan, who were loitering there, learning from my servants that I was a Frenchman going to Teheran, tormented me with their entreaties to lay their grievances before the Shah. Their story was a sad one. Their pay was nine years in arrear, though their colonel, Reza Kooli Khan, had received it, and they refused to march for Khorassan unless they were paid half the amount. The colonel had refused to give them anything, and several had started for Teheran to lay their case before the Prime Minister. Pursued and brought back to Damghan by order of Reza Kooli Khan, they were tortured according to their various degrees of culpability in his eyes; some were bastinadoed, some had their beards cut or their mouths slit.

The colonel hearing of my arrival was terribly frightened, and sent his nephew to me with his compliments and an excellent dinner, to secure my neutrality. I acknowledge to my shame, the dinner tempted me and I ate it; nevertheless, to set my conscience at ease on my arrival at Teheran, I related the case to the minister, but it was one of very little importance in Persia, and the colonel remained in his command.

Goosheh, January 3rd.—Heavy snow, bitter cold, and nothing to eat.

Aheeiyon, January 3rd.—The same.

Semnoon, January 5th to 7th.—I had passed the mountains, and was about two hours' ride from the town, when I observed with inexpressible joy in the distance a horseman in the European dress. As I drew nearer I saw that it was Mr. Taylor Thompson, secretary to the British Legation at Teheran. I hailed him in French, and great was his surprise to hear that language so well spoken by a Turcoman; for, having assumed their habit in its minutest particular, beard and all, he did not at first recognise me in the least. We had a long chat and then continued our respective routes; he was going to Astrabad to watch the Russians and their intrigues. After being so long deprived of any intercourse with Europeans, it is easy to imagine the pleasure that I felt at hearing news of my country once more, and that from an acquaintance. I found Semnoon in the midst of the mourning of the Moharrem, and there was not a single caravan to join; my baggage-horse was quite broken down. At last I made an arrangement with some

Sunni Hazarahs, who were also going to Teheran, and I proceeded with them the next day.

Lasgird, January 8th.—Here I met with the last episode of my journey, and it very nearly proved tragical. An Hazarah wanted to take away the horse for which I had paid him the hire, because his pack hurt him; this my servants opposed, and a quarrel began. A score of Hazarahs soon came up to the assistance of their countryman, and blows fell like rain on the backs of my two servants; though an European I also was in no small danger of personal maltreatment from the brutes, who are men in name only, when I put a stop to their demonstration by levelling my gun at them; the remedy had a miraculous effect; they all slunk off, and I kept the horse all the way to Teheran.

Deh-nemuck, January 9th.—Plenty of mud on the road, and nothing to eat at the halt.

Kishlak, January 10th.—Torrents of rain had fallen here for four days, and so destroyed the usual road that it was impossible to travel upon it. I took the upper one, close by the foot of the mountains; it was very much sounder than the other, but flinty, and at the mouth of a narrow defile was broken by a foaming torrent, which we had great difficulty in crossing. We arrived at the halt with every thread dripping, and found it full of water.

Eywanee Keif, January 11th.—Two hours before I reached this place one of my horses fell down and died. He was still breathing when a flight of crows settled upon him.

Khatoorabad, January 12th.—A rather large village, situated opposite to Essan-Emir.

TEHERAN, January 13th.—I reached Teheran after having crossed one of the ranges of the Elburz. After such a long and perilous journey I felt much the necessity of rest, and occupied myself during the time I remained in the capital in arranging my notes. These pages are the result of my labours, and I trust that some portions of them may interest the reader.

END OF THE NARRATIVE.

APPENDIX (A).

ON LURISTAN.—*Extracts from* MAJOR RAWLINSON'*s Notes on a March from Zohab to Khuzistan.*

LURISTAN is divided into two provinces, Luri-Buzurg and Luri-Kuchúk, the greater and the less Luristán. The former is the mountainous country of the Bakhtiyárís, stretching from the frontiers of Fárs to the river Dizfúl; the latter is situated between the river and the plains of Assyria, being bounded to the N. and S. by Kirmánsháh and Susiana. This province of Luri-Kuchúk is again divided into two districts, Pish-kúh and Pushti-kúh, the country before and behind the mountains, referring, of course, to the great chain of Zagros; and Pushti-kúh thus represents the Másabadán of the geographers,* except that perhaps at present its northern frontier is somewhat curtailed. I entered this territory of Pushti-kúh at Chárdawer, a plain stretching N.W. and S.W. to an extent of about twelve miles in length and five in breadth, and alighted at the tent of Jemshíd Beg, the head of a tribe of Khizil † Kurds, who have been long located at Chárdawer, and incorporated into the extensive tribe of Failí. I was much pleased with the frank and open demeanour of my host, so strikingly at variance with the mean and cringing courtesy of the Persians, and even, though in a less degree, of the Kirmánsháh Kurds. He welcomed me to his tent with every evidence of disinterested kindness, and seemed to tax his powers to the utmost to do honour to his Firingi guest. These black goat's-hair tents are of all sizes, from the petty cabin of the ráyat to the spacious and commodious abode of the hákim. The size of the tent is computed according to the number of poles, which often extend to ten or twelve, at a distance of 20 feet from each other. A large apartment is thus formed, which is divided into a number of different chambers by means of matting; and the díwán-khánah, anderún,‡ place for servants, kitchen, stable, and sheepfold are thus all included under the same roof. Around the díwán-khánah are spread coarse carpets of I'liyát manufacture, and in the centre is dug a deep square hole for the fire. In the tent of Jemshíd Beg the hole was filled with chips and large logs of wood, and above were piled huge branches of trees to the height of several feet, and the mass of

* The name of Másabadán is now unknown in the country.

† A corruption, I fancy, from Khizr, the Muselman of Elias.

‡ The inner apartment for the women.

combustibles, when ignited, threw out, as may be supposed, such a heat that it was with difficulty I could remain in the tent.

Between the twelfth and seventeenth centuries the province of Luri-Kuchúk was governed by a race of independent princes, who were named Atábegs. The last prince of this last royal race, Shah-verdi Khan, was removed by Shah Abbás the Great, and the government was granted to the chief of a rival tribe, Husein Khán, with almost unlimited authority, and with the title of Wálí, in exchange for that of Atábeg; his descendants have retained the title, which in Persia is almost equivalent to royalty;* and though their power is now greatly weakened, they still affect a royal style in their manners and establishment. Owing to the intestine divisions of the family, Pish-kúh, which is by far the fairest portion of Luri-Kuchúk, has been wrested from them, and placed under the direct control of the Kirmánsháh government. Pushti-kúh, however, still acknowledges the sway of the Wálí; and since the death of Mohammed Alí-Mirzá, Hasan Khán, who had enjoyed this dignity, had yielded a mere nominal allegiance to the crown of Persia. Shortly before my visit, however, a breach had taken place in the family between Hasan Khán and his two eldest sons, and, the tribes being divided, the Kirmánsháh government had taken advantage of the moment to interfere, by supporting the sons against the father, and thus to establish a partial influence over the country. Hasan Khán, therefore, had been formally deposed, and Alí Khán and Ahmed Khán appointed joint Wális in his place. The old man, for he was upwards of ninety years of age, took refuge with a small body of adherents among the Arabs of the Assyrian plains, where, for some time, he baffled all the attacks of his enemies; and lately the I'liyát, finding that they alone were the party likely to suffer in the struggle between their rulers, and the consequent extension of the Persian authority over them, have obliged the father and sons to be reconciled, and Hasan Khán now again governs the territory of Púshti-kúh with the power and energy of an independent prince. When the whole of Luri-Kuchúk was under the dominion of the Wálís, all the tribes were included under the general denomination of Failí, the peculiar title of Huseín Khán's clan. At present, however, the inhabitants of Pish-kúh do not acknowledge the name in any way; they have a distinct classification of their own, and the title of Failí is applied alone to the tribes of Pushti-kúh, who are under the sway of the Wálí. The maps, therefore, are incorrect when they describe the whole of Luri-Kuchúk as "a mountainous country, inhabited by the Failí tribes." Luristán is divided, as I

* The title of Shahinsháh, or King of Kings, was assumed by the Persian monarch as lord paramount over four tributary princes, the Wális of Gurjistán (Georgia), Ardelan, Luristán, and Hawizah.

have stated, into two provinces,—Luri-Buzurg and Luri-Kuchúk. The inhabitants of Luri-Buzurg are now classed under the general title of Bakhtiyárís; but originally this name merely applied to a small tribe, one of the twenty-six district clans among whom the province was divided. The Bakhtiyárís, with their dependencies, number at present 28,000 families. They comprise, exclusive of dependencies, three divisions,—the Haft Lang, the Chahár Lang, and the Dínárúnís. Their assessment is fixed at 100 kátirs (mules), the term kátir, however, being merely conventional, and used to denote a sum of money, which is increased or diminished according to the prosperous state of the tribes and the power of the Persian Government to exercise authority over them. The institution of this assessment is very ancient, and in the time of the Atábegs, when the province was in its most flourishing state, a kátir seems to have been equivalent to 1000 tómáns; at present it is valued at 100 tomans, but the government, for many years, has been unable to realise this amount, or even, upon an average of twenty years, a moiety of it. The following table (see next page) describes the general distribution of the clans and their respective assessments.

The main power of the Bakhtiyárís, as will be seen by this table, lies in the hands of Mahommed Tákí Khan, the chief of Jánnikī, who is a lineal descendant of Ali Mardán Khán, the Bakhtiyárí King of Persia, in the times of anarchy that succeeded the death of Nádir. At the outset of his career he was the acknowledged chief of his own single tribe, and he owes his present powerful position to the distinguished ability with which he has steered his course amid the broils and conflicts of other tribes. He has done everything in his power to break the tribes of their nomadic habits, and, to a great extent, he has succeeded. In Feridún he has purchased very extensive lands, where he has founded several villages; and in the plain of Rām Hormuz, which he farms of the Shīrāz Government for 3000 tómáns annually, he has also settled a vast number of peaceful colonists. The Bakhtiyárís pursue a certain extent of traffic. They exclusively supply Khúrzistan with tobacco from Jánnikī; they also export a small quantity of grain, and the Isfahan market is furnished, during the summer, with mutton, almost entirely from the Bakhtiyárí flocks. The cherry-sticks, for (chibuk) pipes, which grow in profusion among their mountains, would also prove to them, if steadily pursued, a most lucrative line of traffic. Charcoal, gallnuts, gum mastic, and the sweetmeat named gaz, or gazú,* form the only exportable articles, I believe, which the

* The Gaz, or Gazú, which is much used for making sweetmeats in Persia, is a glutinous substance, like honey, deposited by a small green insect upon the leaves of the oak tree. See Diod. Sic., book xvii. chap. viii. (It is the manna of the chemists.—F. S.)

Great Divisions.	Tribes.	Number of Families.		Residence.		Assessment in Mules.		Assessment in Money; the Mule being valued at 100 Tomans.		REMARKS.
		Of each Tribe.	Of each Great Division.	Summer.	Winter.	Per Tribe.	Per Great Division.	Per Tribe.	Per Great Division.	
Haft Lang	Ulaki and Mál Ahmedí	400	. .	Jápalák and Siláhkhúr	Sar, Dasht, & Plains about Dizfúl	5		500		The famous hill-fort of Diz belongs to this tribe.
	Bukhtiyáríwand	600				10		1,000		
	Durakí	4,000		Chahár Mahal	. .	15		1,500		The tribe is under the government of Burújird.
	Sallakí	2,000		Burbúrúd	. .	10		1,000		
			7,000				40		4,000	
Chahár Lang	Kunúrsi	1,000		Ferídún and about Zardah Kúh	Rám Hormuz Jánnikī-Garmasír, and Plains about Shuster.	6		6,000		Mohammed Tákí Khán, who has all these other tribes under his sway, is a Kunursí.
	Suhúní	1,500				8		8,000		
	Mahmúd Sáleh	1,000				6		6,000		
	Mogúi	500				6		6,000		
	Menúwand, Zallakí	4,000				8 6		8,000 6,000		
			8,000				40		40,000	
Dínárúní	Báwáí*	3,000		Bázuft.	Súsan and Mál Amir	10		1,000		Dinárún contains a great number of villages, and a small party only of these tribes are nomadic.
	Urak and Sháluh	2,500				10		1,000		
			5,500				20		2,000	
Dependencies. Jánnikī Gamisīr	. . . . . .	. .	4,000	Hills of Mungasht	Bághi and about Tul	. .	. .	. .	2,400	In both these divisions half the numbers are Dih Nishíns, who do not emigrate at all. Lurdigán, in Jánnikī-Sadasír, is a very large village; perhaps even it may be called a town.
Jánnikī Sardasír	. . . . . .	. .	2,000	Gandeman & Lurdagan	Valley of Kuran	. .	. .	. .	800	
Gunduzíu	. . . . . .	. .	1,500	. .	Gulgír and Baitáwand	. .	. .	. .	1,700	This is an Afshār tribe, transplanted into this country by Nádir Sháh. They are notorious thieves.
			28,000	. .	. .	100	100	. .	50,900	

* These are probably the Silacenses of Strabo; they are one of the original tribes of Luri-Buzurg, and the name may be derived from Soloce, the ancient title of Seleucia or Manjanik.

country affords. The Haft Lang tribe, who formerly doubled the number of the Chahár Lang, have been the victims of their never-ending conflicts with each other. For many years during the reign of the late Sháh they were the terror of kafilahs, and at one time, indeed, threatened to put an end to the traffic between the south of Persia and the capital. They have not become in any way divested of predatory habits, but intestine quarrels have not of late left them leisure to indulge in them. The constitution of the Bakhtiyárí system of clanship is quite distinct from that of the tribes of Luri-Kuchúk: in the one, each tribe has its acknowledged chief, who rules over his particular subjects with despotic sway; in the other, the great tribes have no regular head, but each petty subdivision is governed by its own Tushmáh, and they all meet as equals on great occasions to discuss their common interests. It is true that Mohammed Tākī Khán has exerted himself much to break the control of these feudal dependants; but the tendency of his system is merely to merge the power that was before separately exercised into the consolidation of his own individual authority. The great wealth of the Bakhtiyárís, as is the case with all nomade tribes, consists in their flocks and herds. They are naturally most averse to agriculture, and, until the last fifteen or twenty years, they always migrated in a body to the warm pastures of Khúrzistan on the approach of winter, and at the return of spring again moved back to their Yaíláks around Zardah Kúh and along the northern skirts of the great range from Isfahán to Burújerd.

In matters of religion they are lax, but still they are outwardly Mahommedans, and neither respect nor understand the mystical tenets of the Ali I'láhis. Their language is a dialect of the Kurdish, but still differing in many respects, and more particularly in their method of pronunciation, from any of the other modifications of that tongue which are spoken by the different tribes extending along the range of Zagros. I believe them to be individually brave, but of a cruel and savage character; they pursue their blood-feuds with the most inveterate and exterminating spirit, and they consider no oath or obligation in any way binding when it interferes with their thirst for revenge; indeed, the dreadful stories of domestic tragedy that are related, in which whole families have fallen by each other's hands (a son, for instance, having slain his father, to obtain the chiefship; another brother having avenged the murder, and so on, till only one individual was left), are enough to freeze the blood with horror. It is proverbial in Persia that the Bakhtiyárís have been obliged to forego altogether the reading of the Fátihah,* or

* The first chapter of the Korán, used by the Mahommedans much as the Paternoster was anciently used by us. Most Turkish epitaphs end by the words "Fatihah ruhun ichun"—Say a Fatihah for his soul.—F. S.

prayer for the dead, for otherwise they would have no other occupation. They are also most dexterous and notorious thieves; indeed, I have myself seen instances of their dexterity in conveying a horse out of a stable in an inner court, which was particularly watched, and padlocked, moreover, with a chain for security, that, unless I had witnessed, I could not possibly have believed. Altogether they may be considered the most wild and barbarous of all the inhabitants of Persia; but, nevertheless, I have passed some pleasant days with their chiefs, and derived much curious information from them.

The tribes of Luri-Kuchúk are far more numerous than the Bakhtiyárís; with their dependencies they number 56,000 families. The assessment of the tribes of Pish-Kúh is fixed at 120 kátirs, or mules, but the distribution fluctuates at the discretion of the Persian governor. The tribes of Pushti-Kúh and the dependencies are not included in this arrangement, but have a separate amount of revenue assigned to them. The valuation of kátir varies, as with the Bakhtiyárís, according to the state of the province; but under the late Wazír, Mírzá Buzurg, who administered the revenues with eminent success for about ten years, it was raised to the rate of 200 old tómáns, or 333$\frac{1}{3}$ of the present currency; the 120 kátirs were, therefore, equivalent to 40,000 tómáns, and the amount annually realised from Písh-kúth alone rather exceeded than fell short of this sum. The following table (see next page) exhibits the classification of the tribes and the revenue system, as observed by Mírzá Buzurg.

The sum realized from the tribes thus amounted to 60,500 tómáns; but the government possessed another source of revenue in the town of Khorram-ábád and the crown lands scattered over the province, according to the following list:—

Names of Districts.		Taxation in Money.	Taxation in Grain.	Remarks.
		Tómáns.	Kharwars.	
Khorram-ábád	Revenue of town	5,000	. . .	This consists of the rent of shops, gardens, orchards, mills, and customs.
	Crown lands ..	2,000	2,000	
Seímarrah		2,000	2,000	
Jáídar		1,000	500	
Alishtar		. . .	1,000	
Kúh-dasht		230	200	
Terhán		500	700	
Kír-A'b		100	500	
		10,830	6,900	

Great Divisions.	Tribes.	Subdivisions.	Number of Families. Of each Tribe.	Number of Families. Of Great Division.	Residence. Summer.	Residence. Winter.	Assessment of Great Division.	REMARKS.
Písh-kúh	Dilfún	Kákáwand Yúvetíwand Múmináwand Raísáwand Bíjináwand Chuwárí	15,000	38,000	Khâwah Hárásim Khâwah	Hulílán Hulílán and Kúh Dasht Rúdbár Chárdawer Terhán	40,000	The Yuventiwande and Múminawands supply at present a body of 350 infantry to the crown.
	Sílásilá	Hasanáwand Kulíwand Yúsufáwand	15,000		Alíshtar and Khâwah	Jáídar Seímarrah Pushtí Kúh		
	Bálá. Giriwá	Reshnuh Sákí Pápí Dirikáwand	6,000		Táf, near Khorramábád Abistán Sar Hurú Kuhi Haftbád Pehlú	.. Kír A'b & plain of Lur Kerkí Mángerrah and plain of Rezá		The distribution of this sum of 40,000 Tómáns varies yearly, and it is impossible therefore to give the details. The Amalah tribe, however, who are offsets of all the other tribes, and were employed by the former Wálís as their immediate servants, are very lightly charged, the cultivation of the crown lands being accounted in lieu of taxation.
	Amalah	Kushkí Zíwahdár Umrái Mírákhúr Kátirjí Gholám Mótimad Rukruk Zulah	2,000		These tribes are Dih Níshins, who cultivate the Khálisah or crown lands at Khorramábád, Seímarrah, Terhán, and Kúhdasht: they do not migrate at all.			
Pushti-kúh	Faílí	Kurd Shauhún Mehakí Chahár Sítún Dínáríwand	12,000	12,000	Yailáks of the range of Kebir-kúh, both on the N.E. and S.W. faces	Sirwán, 'Iistán, Bádrái, and plains of Abládáni.	15,000	The Wálí of Push-tikúh has the sole direction of his own revenues, and claims to account personally with the Kirmanshah government for the assessment of his district.
Dependencies.	Bájilán	Dálwand Sagwand*	900 1,100 (2,000)	4,500	Húrú	Plains of Sús and beyond the Kerkhah to Deh Lurán	2,000	These tribes are the refugees of the last century, from the vicinity of Mosul: they are lightly taxed, having to furnish a body of 1200 horse to the crown.
	Bafránd-wand	Alíwand Dushíwand	1,500 1,000 (2,500)					
	Hulílání	Osmánáwand Jaláwand Dájiwand Báláwand Surkhámeri	500 500 200 100 200	1,500	Hills adjoining Hulílán	Plain of Hulílán	3,500	These tribes are now usually included in Kirmánsháh; they furnish 500 infantry.
			56,000	56,000	..	..	60,500	

* This is the only tribe of Luristan in whose name any similitude is to be detected to the Sagapeni of Strabo; but as the Sagwand is a stranger tribe, no weight can be attached to the resemblance of the titles.

If we reckon the kharwan of grain at one tómán, which is the usual valuation in Luristán, this will give an addition to the revenue of 17,700 tómáns, and raise the whole amount which may be annually realised from the province, to 78,200 tómáns. The system of revenue in Písh-kúh is very simple; when the 120 kátirs have been duly distributed among the tribes and their subdivisions, in a general council, and to the satisfaction of all, each subdivision determines the amount of share to be paid by the different camps of which it is composed, and the Rísh Safíd* of each encampment collects from the different families under his rule, according to his knowledge of their individual ability to contribute. But in a wild country like this, where many of the tribes live in a state of open rebellion, and will not attend to the distribution apportioned by the general council, the governor would certainly fail in his contract to the crown, unless he had indirect means of raising an extraordinary revenue to make up for many defalcations. Mírzá Buzurg, therefore, introduced an extensive system of fees and fines; and, where robberies and murder were of almost daily occurrence, he did not want opportunities of exaction; indeed he is said to have realized about 20,000 tómáns annually in this manner, and that, too, without cruelty or injustice. Luri-Kuchúk is far more capable of sustaining a heavy taxation than the Bakhtiyárís, for, though agriculture is equally neglected, it has other valuable sources of profit. The principal of these is its breed of mules, which are esteemed by far the best in Persia. It certainly exports on an average 1000 of these animals annually; and, taking the mean price at 20 tómáns, this alone will give a sum of 20,000 tómáns of yearly produce. The I'liyát drive a considerable traffic also, in carpets, hurs or packing-bags, and all descriptions of horse-furniture; they exclusively supply the towns of Hámádán, Niháwand and Burújird with charcoal, and their flocks and herds likewise afford them a considerable profit. The great tribes of Písh-kúh, as I have already mentioned, have no single chief like the Bakhtiyárís; neither, indeed have the subdivisions in general; some four or five Tushmáls are usually associated in the government of every subdivision; and on great occasions all these Tushmáls meet as equals, and consult; so that their internal constitution, which I believe to be very uncommon among the clan nations of Asia, more nearly assimilates to the spirit of a confederated republic than of a great feudal aristocracy. The Wálí of Pushti-Kúh alone retains the kingly power of his ancestors. Among the Lurs most of the offices of labour are performed by women; they tend the flocks, till the fields, store the grain, and tread out that which is required for use. The men content themselves with sowing and reaping, cutting wood for charcoal,

* Literally "grey-beard," the head of each petty encampment.

and defending their property against the attacks of others. The carpets, the black goat-hair tents, and the horse-furniture, for which Luristán is famous, are almost all the work of the women. The men seem to consider robbery and war their proper occupation, and are never so well pleased as when engaged in a foray. The language of the Lurs differs but slightly from that of the Kurds of Kirmánsháh, and a person conversant with one dialect will perfectly understand the other. These dialects of the mountaineers of Zagros have been hitherto assumed by all writers as remnants of the ancient Pehleví, but it appears to me on insufficient grounds; I regard them as derived from the old Fársí, the Fársí-Kadím, as it is called; which was a co-existent, but perfectly distinct language from the Pehleví, in the age of the Sásánian monarchs: certainly the Pehleví, as we read it at the present day, upon inscriptions and in books, does not possess any analogy with the Kurdish, and I doubt if any dialect of it now exists as a spoken language, except among the Gabr colonies, and in a few detached villages of Azerbáiján.* The religion of the tribes of Luri-Kuchúk is very curious, and well merits to be attentively observed; for, although the foundation of all Alī Ilāhism is the same, consisting in the belief of a series of successive incarnations, yet they have superinduced a number of local superstitions, apparently of remote antiquity. The Lurs do not affect the slightest veneration for Mahommed and the Koran; their only general object of worship is their great saint Bábá Buzurg; but there are also several holy men amongst them, who are considered the living representatives of the Divine Principle, and who are thus regarded by their particular disciples, with a reverence little short of adoration. Their sacrifices and their mystical meetings form a subject of much interest; for many of their observances are certainly to be traced to a source long anterior to the institution of Mohammedanism. Macdonald Kinnear has noticed the midnight orgies of the Charágh-Kushán.† I do not believe that any such rites are observed at the present day, but meetings of this nature were certainly held until within the last half century, and there cannot be a doubt but that we may recognise in them a relic of the worship of the principles of generation and fecundity, which had descended through the orgies of Mithra and Anaítis, from the time when Sesostris erected the emblems of the sexual‡ organs as objects of adoration, and Semiramis delivering herself to indiscriminate pleasure doubtless intended to fulfil a religious ceremony.§

* In the village of Dizmár, in particular, the vernacular dialect is certainly Pehleví.

† "The putters-out of lights,"—literally lamp-breakers.

‡ Diod. Sic., book i. chap. iv.; Herod., book ii. chap. cii. and cvi.

§ Diod. Sic., book ii. chap. i.

APPENDIX (B).

Extract of Letter from MR. McNEILL *to* VISCOUNT PALMERSTON. *Dated Camp before Herat, April* 11*th*, 1838. (From Blue-Book, p. 85.)

CAPTAIN VICOVICH continues to remain at Cabul, and I learn from Captain Burnes's communications that the success of his negotiations there will in a great measure depend on the failure of the Shah's enterprise against Herat. At Kandahar our position is even more precarious; and I have the honour to enclose a translation of a draft of a treaty between the Shah and the Chief of Kandahar, which it is proposed to conclude by the mediation and under the guarantee of Russia, and which has for its object to unite Herat and Kandahar under a chief, who shall be nominally subject to Persia, but actually under the protection of Russia. I am unable to inform your Lordship what progress has been made towards the conclusion of this treaty, or what view the Shah may have taken of the position, in respect to these countries, in which, by this arrangement, he would be placed; but the treaty is said to have been signed by Kohundil Khan, and I am not without very serious apprehensions that, even before the fall of Herat, Kohundil Khan may be induced to co-operate with the Shah; while, in the event of Herat's being reduced, I cannot doubt that the Chief of Kandahar will consider it to be for his advantage to connect himself with Persia and Russia rather than with England.

I therefore continue to be of opinion that the fall of Herat would destroy our position in Afghanistan, and place all, or nearly all, that country under the influence or authority of Russia and Persia.

I need not repeat to your Lordship my opinion as to the effect which such a state of things would necessarily have on the internal tranquillity and security of British India; and I cannot conceive that any treaty can bind us to permit the prosecution of schemes which threaten the stability of the British empire in the East. The evidence of concert between Persia and Russia for purposes injurious to British interests is unequivocal; and the magnitude of the evil with which we are threatened is in my estimation immense, and such as no Power in alliance with Great Britain can have a right to aid in producing. Our connexion with Persia has for its real and avowed original object to give additional security to India, and it has been maintained for the purpose of protecting us against designs of the only Power which threatened to disturb us in that quarter; but if the proceedings of Persia, in concert with that very Power, are directed to the destruction of the security and tranquillity which it was the sole object of the alliance with Persia to maintain, and if they obviously tend to promote and facilitate the designs which the alliance was intended to counteract, I confess I cannot believe that we are still bound to act up to the letter of a treaty, the spirit of which has been so flagrantly violated. I do not hesitate to repeat my conviction, that, if our only object were to preserve as long as possible the alliance of Persia, that object could best be effected by preventing her taking Herat.

Copy of the Draft of a Treaty sealed by Kohundil Khan.

Proposed terms of a Treaty between His Majesty Mahommed Shah and Kohundil Khan, Sirdar of Kandahar, under the sealed guarantee of the Russian Ambassador at Teheran.

I, as Minister Plenipotentiary of the Russian Government at the Court of Persia, guarantee the fulfilment of the following conditions of treaty between His Majesty Mahommed Shah and the Sirdar of Kandahar:—

1st. The Principality of Herat is to be bestowed by the Shah on the rulers of Kandahar, as a reward for their faithful services performed to him since his accession to the throne of Persia.

2nd. The territories and tribes at present subject to the Sirdars of Kandahar to be preserved to them free of violence, injury, or confiscation.

3rd. The Persian Government in no way to amalgamate with their own subjects any of the Afghan tribes, great or small, nor to employ them upon service unconnected with their own affairs; and all business relative to the Afghan states to be submitted by the Persian Government to the rulers of Kandahar.

4th. The Prince Kamaran and his Minister Yar Mahommed Khan to be excluded from all participation in the councils of Persia.

5th. Should any hostile movement be made against Kandahar by Shooja-ool-Molk, the English, or the Ameer of Cabul, aid to be afforded by the Shah to the Sirdars.

6th. In the event of the sons or brothers of Kohundil Khan coming with an auxiliary force to the royal camp, no violence or injury to be in any way offered to the persons or property of them or their followers, and none of them to be detained as hostages, with the exception of a single son of Kohundil Khan's, who will always remain in the service of the Shah.

7th. A contingent of twelve thousand horse and twelve guns to be supplied by the Kandaharees to garrison Herat, receiving pay and rations from them, and to assist the Shah on occasion of service.

8th. On the arrival of treaty duly ratified at Kandahar, Mahommed Omar Khan to be immediately dispatched to the royal presence.

9th. After the presentation of this prince, the necessary money for the outfit of the horse and artillery to be made over by the Persian Government to the Sirdars of Kandahar; Sirdar Mehrdil Khan to be then sent with a thousand horse to the royal camp.

This Prince being presented, and mutual confidence being established between the Shah and the Sirdars, no other demand to be made upon the Kandaharees by the Persian Government than that of military service.

Should Mahommed Shah fail to fulfil any of these several conditions, or depart in any way from the stipulations, I, as Minister Plenipotentiary of the Russian Government, becoming myself responsible, will oblige him, in whatever way may be necessary, to act fully up to the terms and conditions of the treaty.

This memorandum is framed as a draft of the proposed terms of treaty.

True Translation.

(Signed) H. C. RAWLINSON, Major.

APPENDIX (C).

SIR A. BURNES'S *Description of Balkh.*

WE continued at Balkh for three days to examine the remains of this once proud city. Its ruins extend for a circuit of about twenty miles, but present no symptoms of magnificence; they consist of fallen mosques and decayed tombs, which have been built of sun-dried brick; nor are any of these ruins of an age prior to Mahommedanism, though Balkh boasts an antiquity beyond most other cities in the globe. By the Asiatics it is named the "Mother of Cities," and is said to have been built by Kyamoors, or Cyrus, the founder of the Persian monarchy. After the conquest of Alexander the Great it flourished under the name of Bactria, with a dynasty of Grecian kings. In the third century of the Christian era "Artaxerxes had his authority solemnly acknowledged in a great assembly held at Balkh, in Khorasan." * It continued subject to the Persian empire, and the residence of the Archimagus, or head of the Magi, till the followers of Zoroaster were overthrown by the inroads of the caliphs. Its inhabitants were butchered in cold blood by Genghis Khan; and under the house of Timour it became a province of the Mogul empire. It formed the government of Aurungzebe in his youth, and was at last invaded by the great Nadir. On the establishment of the Dooranee monarchy, after his death, it fell into the hands of the Afghans, and within the last eight years has been seized by the king of Bokhara, whose deputy now governs it. Its present population does not amount to 2000 souls, who are chiefly natives of Cabul, and the remnant of the Karanoukur, a description of militia established here by the Afghans: there are also a few Arabs. The Koondooz chief has marched off a great portion of its population, and constantly threatens the city, which has driven the inhabitants to the neighbouring villages. In its wide area, the city appears to have enclosed innumerable gardens, which increased its size without adding to its population; and, from the frail materials of which its buildings are constructed, the foundations being only brick, I doubt if Balkh ever were a substantial city. There are three large colleges, of a handsome structure, now in a state of decay, with their cells empty. A mud wall surrounds a portion of the town, but it must be of a late age, since it excludes the ruins on

* Gibbon, c. viii.

every side for about two miles. The citadel, or ark, on the northern side, has been more solidly constructed; yet it is a place of no strength. There is a stone of white marble in it, which is yet pointed out as the throne of Kai Kaoos, or Cyrus. Balkh stands on a plain, about six miles from the hills, and not upon them, as is erroneously represented. There are many inequalities in the surrounding fields, which may arise from ruins and rubbish. The city itself, like Babylon, has become a perfect mine of bricks for the surrounding country. These are of an oblong shape, rather square. Most of the old gardens are now neglected and overgrown with weeds; the aqueducts are dried up; but there are clumps of trees in many directions. The people have a great veneration for the city, believing it was one of the earliest peopled portions of the earth, and that the re-occupation of it will be one of the signs of the approaching end of the world. The fruit of Balkh is most luscious, particularly the apricots, which are nearly as large as apples. They are almost below value, for 2000 of them were to be purchased for a rupee, and with iced water they are indeed luxuries, though dangerous ones. Snow is brought in quantities from the mountains south of Balkh, about twenty miles distant, and sold for a trifle throughout the year.

The climate of Balkh is very insalubrious, but it is not disagreeable. In June the thermometer did not rise above 80°, and the next month is the hottest in the year. The wheat ripens in that month, which makes the harvest fifty days later than at Peshawur. Its unhealthiness is ascribed to the water, which is so mixed up with earth and clay as to look like a puddle after rain. The soil is of a greyish colour, like pipe-clay, and very rich; when wet it is slimy. The crops are good; the wheat stalks grow as high as in England, and do not present the stubble of India. In Balkh, the water has been distributed, with great labour, by aqueducts from a river. Of these there are said to be no less than eighteen; but many are not now discoverable. They frequently overflow, and leave marshes, which are rapidly dried up under the sun's rays. This seems to account for the diseases of the place. All old cities and ruins are perhaps more or less unhealthy. It is not probable, however, that so many kings and princes would have patronised a site which was always unfavourable to the health of man; and Balkh itself is not situated in a country naturally marshy, but on a gentle slope, which sinks towards the Oxus, about 1800 feet above the level of the sea. All the water of its river is lost long before reaching that stream.—*Extract from Burnes's 'Travels into Bokhara,'* vol. i. pp. 237-241.

APPENDIX (D).

Accounts by MR. ELPHINSTONE *and* SIR A. BURNES *of the Kaffirs of the Hindoo Koosh.*

THE country of the Kaffirs occupies a great part of the range of Hindoo Coosh and a portion of Beloot Tagh. It is bounded on the north-east by Kashkar, on Budukhshan, and on the north-west by Koondooz in Balkh. On the west it has Inderab and Khost, also in Balkh, and the Kohistan of Cabul; and on the east it extends for a great distance towards the north of Cashmeer, where its boundary is not distinctly known. The whole of this alpine country is composed of snowy mountains, deep pine forests, and small but fertile valleys, which produce large quantities of grapes, wild and cultivated, and feed flocks of sheep and herds of cattle, while the hills are covered with goats. Grain is inferior both in importance and abundance. The common kinds are wheat and millet. The roads are only fit for men on foot, and are often crossed by rivers and torrents, which are passed by means of wooden bridges, or of swing-bridges made on ropes of withy or some other pliant tree. All the villages that I have heard described are built on the slopes of hills, so that the roof of one house forms the street leading to the one above it; and this is said to be the constant practice of the country. The valleys must be well peopled; that of the Camojee tribe, at least, contained ten villages, and the chief place, Caumdaish, consisted of 500 houses. The people have no general name for their nation. Each tribe has its peculiar name, for they are all divided into tribes, though not according to genealogy, but to geographical position, each valley being held by a separate tribe. The Mussulmans confound them all under the name of Kaffir or infidel, and call their country Kaffiristan. They also call one division of them Siaposh (black-vested), or Tor Kaffirs (black infidels), and another Speen Kaffirs (white infidels). Both epithets are taken from their dress, for the whole of the Kaffirs are remarkable for the fairness and beauty of their complexion; but those of the largest division wear a sort of vest of black goat-skins, while the other dresses in white cotton.*

* The following are the names of some of their tribes. The first set were given by the young Kaffir of Tsokooee, the second got by Moollah Nujeeb at Caumdaish, and the third by Dhunput Ray at Kuttaun, and on the borders of Bajour:—

1st. Traiguma, Gimeer, Kuttaur, Bai-

There are several languages among the Kaffirs, but they have all many words in common, and all have a near connexion with the Sanscrit. They have all one peculiarity, which is, that they count by scores instead of hundreds, and that their thousand (which they call by the Persian and Pushtoo name) consists of four hundred, or twenty score. All these observations apply also to the Lughmanee or Degganee language, which seems to be a Kaffir dialect, and gives reason to suppose the Lughmanees and Deggans to be Kaffirs converted to the Mahommedan religion. I imagine the inhabitants of the Cohistan of Cabul to have the same origin, particularly as the name of Cohistanee is that applied to all the lately converted Kaffirs. This derivation of their language seems fatal to the descent of the Kaffirs from the Greeks, and their traditions do not furnish us with any distinct account of their origin. The most general and the only credible story is, that they were expelled by the Mussulmans from the neighbourhood of Kandahar, and made several migrations from place to place before they reached their present abode. They allege that they consisted of four tribes, called Camoze, Hilar, Silar, and Camoje, of which the three former embraced the Mahommedan religion, but the fourth retained its ancient faith, and quitted its native country.

Their religion does not resemble any other with which I am acquainted. They believe in one God, whom the Kaffirs of Camdaish call Imra, and those of Tsokooee Dagun; but they also worship numerous idols, which they say represent great men of former days, who intercede with God in favour of their worshippers.

These idols are of stone or wood, and always represent men or women, sometimes mounted and sometimes on foot. Moollah Nujeeb had an opportunity of learning the arts which obtain an entrance to the Kaffir Pantheon. In the public apartment of the village of Camdaish was a high wooden pillow, on which sat a figure, with a spear in one hand and a staff in the other. This idol represented the father of one of the great men of the village, who had erected it himself in his life-time, having purchased the privilege by giving several

ragullee, Chainaish, Dimdeau, Waillee Wauee, Cauma Cooshteea, Dhaing, and Wauee, called Puneeta by the Mussulmans.

2nd. Caumojee, Kistojee (whose chief town is Muncheeashee), Moondeegul, Camtoze (half of whom are towards Budukhshan, and half towards Lughman), Puroonee (whose capital is Kishtokee), Tewnee, Poonooz, Ushkong, Umshee, Sunnoo, Koolumee, Roose Turkuma (to whom belong Kataur and Guinbeer), Nisha, Chumga, Wauee, Khoollum, Deemish, Eerait, &c. &c. I must observe that one of Moollah Nujeeb's list is Pusha, which is stated to live towards Cabul, and which, I doubt not, is the origin of the Pushawees mentioned by Baber, and still found in the Cohistan of Cabul.

3rd. Wauee Daiwuzee, Gumbeer, Kuttaur, Pundect, Khoostoze Caumozee Divine, Tsokooee, Hurunseea, and Chooneea.

feasts to the whole village; nor was this the only instance of men deified for such reasons, and worshipped as much as any other of the Gods. The Kaffirs appear indeed to attach the utmost importance to the virtues of liberality and hospitality. It is they which procure the easiest admission to their paradise, which they call Burry Le Boola; and the opposite vices are the most certain guides to Burry Duggur Boola, or Hell.

I can give but little account of the government of the Kaffirs. It is uncertain whether there are any acknowledged magistrates; if there are, they have very little power, everything being done by consultations among the rich men. They seem to practise retaliation like the Afghans, and I know of no other administration of justice. They have no titles of their own, but they have borrowed that of Khan from the Afghans for their rich men. Their property chiefly consists in cattle and slaves; a rich man at Camdaish had about eight hundred goats, near three hundred oxen, and eight families of slaves.

Those in good circumstances and those near the Afghans wear a shirt beneath their vest, and in summer the shirt forms the whole of their dress, as it always does with the women. The great do not wear goat-skins, but cotton cloth or black hair cloth. Some also wear the sort of white blanket woven in the neighbouring country of Kashkar. The blankets are put on like Highland plaids, come down to near the knee, and are fastened with a belt; they also wear cotton trowsers which, as well as their shirts, are worked all over with flowers in red and black worsted. The trowsers are slit at the bottom, so as to make a sort of fringe. They also wear worsted stockings, or perhaps worsted fillets, rolled round their legs; and the warriors wear half-boots of white goat-skin.

The houses of the Kaffirs are often of wood, and they have generally cellars where they keep their cheeses, clarified butter, wine and vinegar. In every house there is a wooden bench fixed to the wall with a low back to it. There are also stools shaped like drums, but smaller in the middle than at the ends, and tables of the same sort, but larger. The Kaffirs, partly from their dress and partly from habit, cannot sit like the other Asiatics; and if forced to sit down on the ground, stretch out their legs like Europeans. They have also beds, made of wood and thongs of neat's leather; the stools are made of wicker-work.

Their food is chiefly cheese, butter, and milk, with bread or a sort of suet pudding; they also eat flesh (which they like half raw); and the fruits they have, walnuts, grapes, apples, almonds, and a sort of indifferent apricot that grows wild. They wash their hands before eating, and generally begin by some kind of grace. They all, of both sexes, drink wine to a great excess; they have three kinds, red, white, and dark-coloured, besides a sort of the consistence of a jelly, and very strong. They drink wine both pure and diluted, out of large silver cups, which are the most precious of their possessions. They drink during their meals, and are elevated, but not made quarrelsome, by this indulgence. They are exceedingly hospitable; the people of a village come out to meet a stranger, take his baggage from those who are carrying it, and conduct him with many welcomes into their village. When there, he must visit every person of note, and at each house he is pressed to eat and drink. The Kaffirs have a great deal of idle time; they hunt a little, but not so much as the Afghans; their favourite amusement is dancing. Their dances are generally rapid, and they use many gesticulations, raising their shoulders, shaking their heads, and flourishing their battle-axes. All sexes and ages dance. They sometimes form a circle of men and women alternately, who move round the musicians for some time with joined hands, then all spring forward and mix together in a dance. They dance with great vehemence, and beat the ground with much force. Their only instruments are a tabor and pipe, but the dancers often accompany them with the voice. Their music is generally quick, but varied and wild.

One of their characteristic features is their constant war with the Mussulmans, whom they hold in detestation.

Though exasperated to such fury by the persecutions of the Mahommedans, the Kaffirs are in general a harmless, affectionate, and kind-hearted people. Though passionate, they are easily appeased: they are merry, playful, fond of laughter, and altogether of a sociable and joyous disposition. Even to Mussulmans they are kind when they admit them as guests, and though Moollah Nujeeb was once obliged to be kept by the other Kaffirs out of the way of a drunken man of their nation, he was never threatened or affronted on account of his religion by any man in possession of his faculties.—*Elphinstone's 'Cabul,'* vol. ii. p. 375–377.

I can offer no further addition to the notice of their religion and country than is to be found in Mr. Elphinstone's work, though I met the worthy and faithful man Moollah Nujeeb, who was sent into Kaffiristan for the purposes of inquiry. I had much conversation with people who had been brought into contact with them, and in Cabul was fortunate enough to see a Kaffir boy about ten years old, who had left his country for a period of two years; his complexion, hair, and features differed from those of Asiatics; his eyes

2 L 2

were of a bluish colour. The boy replied to many questions that were put to him about his country, and gave specimens of his language, which assimilated with the Indian dialects. The Kaffirs appear to be a most barbarous people, eaters of bears and monkeys, and scalping their enemies. The greatest intercourse which takes place between them and the Mahommedans is carried on from the country of Lughman, between Cabul and Peshawur, where a tribe of people reside who are called "Neemchu Moossulman," or half-Mahommedans. The Kaffir country is strong and mountainous. The people are much addicted to wine. Gold is found in its native state among their mountains, and formed by them into vessels and ornaments. These circumstances, with their appearance and complexion, have given rise to an opinion that they are the descendants of the Greeks. Both Baber and Abool Fuzzil have made mention of this supposition, but they have confounded the claims of the chiefs on the Oxus to a Macedonian descent with the Kaffirs, who have no such tradition of their origin. The great elevation of the country which they inhabit would appear to account satisfactorily for all their physical peculiarities; and I believe it will be found that this people are none other than the aborigines of the plains, who fled to their present abode on the conversion of the low countries to the religion of Mahommed; the Afghans, at least, tell you so, and the name of Kaffir, or Infidel, seems a strong corroboration of the opinion. The Kaffirs are a race of savages, and there is nothing either in their customs or religion which seems to be anywise remarkable among a people at their state of civilisation. The hill tribes in India have a religion which differs as much from Hindooism as that of the Kaffirs, and the reason is obvious—they inhabit remote regions that were not accessible to the manners and alterations which found their way into the more favoured plains. The Kaffir women do all the out-door work, and follow the plough; it is even said that they are sometimes yoked in it along with an ox.—*Extract from Burnes's 'Travels into Bokhara,'* vol. ii. p. 211.

APPENDIX (E).

Account of the Climate and Productions of Beloochistan, by the late Sir H. POTTINGER, G.C.B.

THE diversity of situation of the various provinces of Beloochistan, and the consequent irregularities of climate and soil, will, however, frequently induce me to revert to them, in order to discriminate with greater precision.

The seasons of the two mountainous provinces of Jhalawan and Sarawan are, like those of European countries, divided into spring, summer, autumn, and winter. The former is usually supposed to commence between the middle and end of February, and continues two months, or perhaps longer, a circumstance which rests entirely on the forwardness or otherwise of the season. The summer lasts till the beginning of August, and the autumn then follows, until the cold, or a fall of snow, announces the arrival of winter, an event that commonly happens in October; that portion of the year is consequently accounted much longer than any of the others.* The heat is at no time unpleasantly great, unless it may be a few days at the close of summer; but, on the other hand, the cold is intense during the winter, and attended by a north-easterly wind, that, blowing without intermission, and sometimes with extreme violence, not only throughout the season, but the spring months, brings with it heavy falls of snow, sleet, and rain; and it may also be remarked as a thing rather unusual in Europe, that here the very hardest frosts are experienced during the height of these winds, which appear to be the only periodically prevailing ones in these provinces.

Captain Christie and I were at Kelat from the 9th of February till the 6th of March, 1810, and to the latter end of our sojourn there the natives were in daily hopes of a fall of rain, which was to them

* None of the natives of Beloochistan seem to be aware that any unerring principle can be laid down to mark the commencement of the seasons, which they contend must depend upon the state of the weather, a mode of calculation that renders it an accident whether any two years correspond. In February, 1811, it snowed incessantly for fifteen days in the vicinity of Kelat, and the frost set in early in October following; so that, rejecting the winter, the other three seasons of that year, agreeable to the Belooche theory, did not include more than seven months and a few days.

the harbinger of spring, and expected to last for three weeks or a month; this is the only annual fall they have, but, in addition to it, the months of September and October are showery, and indeed the whole of the cold season is more or less so, four or five days seldom passing without either sleet or rain, save during frosty weather, when the air is keen and bracing. The salubrity of these provinces appears to be regulated by the seasons: the summer and autumn are said to be delightful, but in winter and spring, fogs, rain, snow, and cold are the origin of many diseases among the poorer classes, who have not means of protecting themselves against the effects of a climate that is equally fluctuating, and more severe than that of England.

In Mukran and Lus the seasons are likewise four in number, but they are not to be distinguished like those of the province just named, as they consist of two wet, one hot, and one cold one, the latter of which is very moderate, especially on the sea-coast. The wet seasons are in February or March, and June, July, and a part of August; the former comes from the north-west and only continues for three weeks, but the latter comprises all the fury of the south-west monsoon. The hot season begins in March, and lasts till October (the south-west monsoon intervening), and in it, occasionally, the heats are so excessive as to prevent even the inhabitants from venturing abroad during the days called the "Khoormu Puz," or date ripening, which take place in August. The months of November, December, January, and February are looked upon as the cold season, but even then it is much warmer than at any period of the year in the upper parts of Jhalawan and Sarawan.* North-west winds prevail at this time, and are particularly strong towards the close of the cold weather; during the remaining eight months the hot winds blow continually inland, and though they are seldom known to be fatal to life, they destroy every symptom of vegetation, and will, even after dusk, scorch the skin in a most painful manner. Mukran is considered by the people of the adjoining countries to be peculiarly unhealthy, except on the immediate coast, where the atmosphere is tempered by the sea breezes. To the European constitution it has, even there, been esteemed extremely prejudicial, as was proved (in the only instance I have heard of) by the late and much regretted Captain Grant, of the Bengal military service, who was about three months in this province, while acting

---

* Wherever two provinces lie contiguous to each other, as Jhalawan and Lus, it necessarily results that they must in some degree partake of the advantages and disadvantages of climate which prevail in each. Thus the southern districts of Jhalawan are not so cold as Kelat, and the part of Lus adjoining them is much colder in winter than the sea coast.

under the orders of Brigadier-General Malcolm, and quitted it in a state of extreme bad health. The small province of Lus is reputed to be an exception to the general insalubrity of this division of Beloochistan; and it is a very extraordinary fact, that the range of mountains that separate it from Mukran has also drawn a grand line of distinction between their natives, in manners, customs, and appearance. The Kohistan, or that division of Beloochistan lying to the westward of the sandy desert, being of a mountainous nature, resembles in climate the provinces of Sarawan and Jhalawan, except that it is much milder, and consequently healthier. The seasons here are like those of Mukran; but the rains in June and July, which are always regular in that province, are here often partial, and at other times so heavy as to destroy the crop: such was the case in 1809, and a famine succeeded, while in Sarawan the same calamity occurred from drought.

In Kutch Gundava the climate is oppressively hot throughout the summer, and during the winter it continues so warm that this province is resorted to by all the chiefs and inhabitants (who can afford the expense) of the provinces of Sarawan and Jhalawan.

I am not prepared to give any detailed observations on the soil of Beloochistan, which, in fact, is a subject peculiarly devoid of variety or interest. It generally appears to be exceedingly stony; and in the provinces of Sarawan, Jhalawan, Lus, and Mukran, this is evident to the most common observer, unless on the sea-coast of the two latter, where it is sandy and arid. The mountains of all these are chiefly composed of black or grey rock of a very hard nature, and the earth of the plains and vales, amongst them, is mixed with such a profusion of pebbles and small stones that there is often not the slightest appearance of mould; yet, in spite of this disadvantage, some of them produce plentiful crops of wheat and barley; and in others, where they are not tilled, grass grows luxuriantly and to a great height. The soil of the Kohistan is very diversified. In the valleys it is usually of a black loamy description, and even some of its loftiest mountains have fine earth to their very summits; whilst others are nothing else than a mass of black rock, destitute of verdure. Of Kutch Gundava the soil is rich and loamy, and so exceedingly productive that it is said, were it only properly cultivated, the crops would be more than sufficient for the consumption of the whole of Beloochistan; even as it is, they export great quantities of grain, beside cotton, indigo, and oil. The Badé Sumoom, of which I have made very particular mention in another place, blows in Kutch Gundava during the summer months, and many people lose their lives by it.

Gold, silver, lead, iron, copper, tin, antimony, brimstone, alum, sal-ammoniac, and many kinds of mineral salts and saltpetre, are found in various parts of Beloochistan. The precious metals have only been discovered, in working for iron and lead, at mines near the town of Nal, about 150 miles south-south-west of Kelat. The different other minerals I have enumerated are very plentiful. Rock-salt is very common to the westward, and saltpetre is likewise dug up in a native state; at Kelat they make the latter ingredient from the soil, and esteem it much the strongest.

On the high road from Kelat to Kutch Gundava there is a range of hills, from which a species of salt, perfectly red in its colour, is extracted, that possesses very great aperient qualities. Sulphur and alum are to be had at the same place. I saw quantities of white and grey marble in the mountains to the westward of Nooshky, but it does not seem to be at all prized by the Belooches.

* * * * * * *

The gardens of Kelat are planted with many sorts of fruit trees, of which all the finest were brought from Cabul during the government of Nusseer Khan, who paid vast attention to their rearing, and excited an emulation among his subjects by offering rewards for the best productions. The following, sold at a very moderate rate, in due season, in the bazar of Kelat, will show how far successful his endeavours have proved: apricots, peaches, grapes of various kinds, almonds, pistachio nuts, apples many different kinds, as also of pears, plums, currants, and cherries; quinces, figs, pomegranates, mulberries, plantains, melons,* guaivas, &c. &c.

At Shal and Mustoong, to the northward of Kelat, they have almonds of so delicate a quality, that they are blanched by simply rubbing them in a dry cloth.

All kinds of grain† known in India are cultivated in the different provinces of Beloochistan, and they have abundance of vegetables.‡ Madder, cotton, and indigo are also produced in Beloochistan, particularly to the northward and eastward of Kelat, and the latter is considered superior to that of Bengal, and sells for a higher price.

In the upper parts of Sarawan and Jhalawan, and the districts of

---

* Melons of all kinds are cultivated to an astonishing perfection, and some of the water-melons come to so large a size, that a man can hardly lift one. The Belooches pluck all the flowers except one or two off the stems, and nourish these with manure, alternately keeping the fruit above the earth or covered with it, which makes it sweet and juicy. The same plan is adopted for the musk-melons.

† The grains cultivated in Beloochistan are rice, wheat, barley, bajree (Holcus spicatus), jowaree (Holcus sorghum), moong (Phaseolus mungo), maize (Indian corn), dal (vetch), oorud mutter (a kind of pea), till (Sesamum), chunna (Cicer arietinum).

‡ Vegetables to be had at Kelat are turnips, carrots, cabbages, lettuces, cauliflowers, peas, beans, radishes, onions, celery, parsley, garlic, egg-fruit, cucumbers.

Shal and Mustoong, the wheat is sown in August or September, and reaped the June following; barley is put into the ground one month later, and the crop is gathered earlier, so that it comes to perfection in about eight months; maize in three or four, provided it be planted in the heat of summer, and in a sheltered place. Indigo will not thrive here at all, and rice only in low dales where there is a supply of water to keep it flooded.

* * * * * * *

The best timber the Belooches have is of the upoors* and tamarind trees, both of which are remarkably hard and durable, and the former resembles teak so greatly in grain, weight, and appearance, that Captain Christie and myself mistook it for that wood. Both these trees grow to a very large size, and to them may be added the babool, lye, and mulberry, as they are all used for building. To the westward the natives principally appropriate the palm tree to the same purpose. The neem, peepul, sissoo,† chinar, mango, walnut, and sycamore are also found in various divisions of the country, but the oak, ash, fir, &c., are unknown.—*Lieut. Pottinger's Travels in Beloochistan and Sinde.* London, 1816, p. 319-327.

---

* A species of the Zizyphus Jujuba.

† The babool, Farnesian mimosa; lye, tamarisk; neem, Melia azadirachta; peepul, Ficus religiosa; sissoo, Dalbergia sissoo (Roxburgh); chinar, Platanus orientalis.

APPENDIX (F).

Memorandum on the Political Relations of the English Mission with Herat, 1837 *to* 1841, *by* SIR JOHN LOGIN, *Knight, Surgeon to the Mission.*

THE position of Herat, on the line of advance from Persia and Toorkistân, towards the Indus, has made its possession essential to the success of any invasion of India from that quarter, and we accordingly find that, from the time of Darius to the present, its occupation has been a prelude to any attempts of the kind by successive conquerors.

As the city and province of Herat and its dependencies have been held by the Afghans under their Suddozye Princes* since the time of Nadir Shah; occasions of quarrel between them and their Persian neighbours have never been wanting; for, as in addition to the ordinary causes of strife between hostile races, their religious differences render it, in the opinion of a Soonee Afghan, as praiseworthy as it is profitable to despoil a Persian Shiah,† and sell him as a slave, it is only to be expected that offences must arise. When, therefore, it became the policy of the late Russian autocrat in 1836-37, to extend his influence to the countries bordering on the Indus, little difficulty was experienced in getting up a very just cause of war between the Persian King and the ruler of Herat; and as by the treaties which exist between the Russian Emperor and the Persian court, agents of the former are entitled to reside in all places in possession of Persian troops, it was thought that the object

* Since the murder of Kamran, Herat has been ruled by Yar Mahomed and his son, of the Alikozye tribe, but it is again in possession of a Suddozye Prince, of whom, from his antecedents, hopes may be entertained of a better government than that which had existed there for the last forty years.

† Of course they were not always very scrupulous as to creed, when the transaction appeared likely to be profitable. Unfortunate *Soonees* were often seized, and by torture made to declare themselves *Shiahs,* when they became legitimate merchandize. One of these miserable men, eluding his guards, crept up to Arthur Conolly's tent, near Merve, and told him how he had been entrapped, asking if ever a *Shiah* could claim *Pushtoo* (Afghanee) as his mother-tongue? as if to confirm his statement.

of the Emperor might in this way be attained without giving cause of offence to the British Government.

To assist the Persian army, however, in its operations against Herat, as far as practicable, without compromising the pacific character which the Emperor wished to retain, advances in money, and every encouragement were covertly given to the Afghan rulers of Kandahar and Cabul by the Russian ambassador at Teheran, and soldiers were permitted to desert from the troops in Georgia to form battalions under Russian officers attached to the Persian army.

During these preparations against Herat, the rulers of that little state, Shah Kamran and his able but unscrupulous minister, Yar Mahomed, might well have been dismayed at the prospect before them. They had, by their oppressive tyranny and exactions, rendered their most industrious subjects openly disaffected; the rulers of Cabul and Kandahar, with whom since the atrocious murder of Vizier Futteh Khan,* they had been at mortal enmity, had espoused the cause of the Persians; the neighbouring chiefs of Jumsheedies and Taymoonies had many old scores to settle with them, and seemed likely to avail themselves of so good an opportunity of doing so with advantage; and having only about 6000 men (composed of Sirbazes, Afghans, and Soonee Hazarahs), in whom they could place even the slightest confidence for the defence of their city, they must have been in great perplexity.

As they had been so much isolated for many years they knew little of the power and policy of the British Government. Some of them indeed remembered Mr. Elphinstone's embassy to Cabul, and almost all had heard of the influence of the English ambassadors at Teheran, over the Persian monarch, and of the names of Malcolm, Ouseley, Willock, Campbell, M'Neill, and others ('Sahibān Englees') connected with our mission there.

Two English travellers, Lieutenant Arthur Conolly and Dr. Gerard, had also passed through Herat at different times within the last few years, supposed to be the only ones who had ever visited the place—for Foster and Christie had escaped observation—and one of them (Conolly) had taken with him to Hindostan an intelligent native of Herat, as a personal servant; sent him for a time to a medical school in Calcutta, under Mr. Tytler, whence, after having been sufficiently instructed to practise among his countrymen as a Hakeem, he had returned to Herat shortly before these

* The elder brother of Dost Mahomed (and the other Barakeye chiefs), after having been blinded for some time, was cut to pieces in presence of Kamran, by the Afghan chiefs, who adhered to him, in order to establish blood-feuds between each of them and the Barakeye family.

events, supplied with the means of exercising his profession by the liberality of the East India Company, and full of laudation of the English Government in India.

In this emergency Yar Mahomed and Shah Kamran, seeing no hope of assistance from any other quarter, determined to apply to the ambassador of England at Teheran, to use his influence to avert the threatened danger.

Fortunately for them the gentleman who then held that distinguished post, Sir John McNeill, was fully alive to the necessity of preventing the Persian king and his Russian ally from extending their influence in Afghanistan and the frontiers of India. He warmly espoused their cause, and urged the Herat authorities, by timely concessions, and the suppression of slave-dealing and marauding, to deprecate the wrath of the Persian king, and ward off the threatened attack.

In this, however, he was not in the first instance successful, and Mahomed Shah's army advanced to lay siege to Herat, with every prospect of speedy success.

It happened, however, while these events were taking place, that a young English officer of the Bombay Artillery, Lieut. Eldred Pottinger, in that spirit of adventurous benevolence which had so distinguished Arthur Conolly, and which, it is to be hoped, may never be wanting among us, had, without any instructions from Government, merely on the grant of a few months general leave,* arrived at the city of Herat, by the route of Guzni, Cabul and the Hazarah country, in the disguise of a Mussulman from India. On passing through the bazaar he was recognised as an Englishman by the Hakeem above mentioned, who at once showed him every kindness in his power. He informed him also of the danger which threatened Herat, and urged him to make known his real character to the Vezir. Seeing clearly the importance of Herat to the independence of Afghanistan, and the prevention of Russian influence in those countries, Pottinger did not hesitate. He offered his services to Yar Mahomed, which were gladly accepted ; and how nobly

* It is to be hoped that the East India Company will give a more liberal interpretation to their orders regarding the grant of leave to officers *in India*, and that, in every case in which an officer can show that his leave has been employed advantageously for the public—by the production of a creditable journal of his travels, or of papers on useful subjects tending to advance our knowledge of the history and resources of our Indian empire—that the time so employed shall *not* be deducted from his period of service. Under such a regulation, and the establishment of good libraries of reference at each station, especially in the hills, "Billiards, beer, bacco and brandy sauce," may soon prove less attractive to our young officers.

he did his duty there, is well recorded in 'Kaye's History of the War in Afghanistan.'

Through his most gallant exertions Herat withstood the Persian army for upwards of nine months; and time was thus afforded to Sir John M'Neill to rouse the English Government to the imminency of the danger, and, by a threatened attack upon the southern provinces of Persia by a force from Bombay, to cause Mahomed Shah to raise the siege when Herat was almost in his hands. Its defenders and their families were thus saved (in September, 1838) from the indiscriminate massacre to which they had been doomed by the Persian king for their most obstinate resistance.

On the siege being raised, every effort was made by Lieutenant Pottinger and Colonel Stoddart, who had been sent by Sir John M'Neill to his assistance, to save the wretched inhabitants from starvation.

For several months some thousands of them had to be fed daily with such nourishment as these gentlemen could procure for them; * and grain-seeds of the most rapid growth † had to be obtained, to be sown for a small crop before winter.

As the trade in slaves had constituted a great part of the revenues of the state before the invasion of the Persians, and as no taxes could be raised for some time, it became necessary to grant an allowance from the Government of India for the support of the king and chiefs. A monthly sum was paid by Lieutenant Pottinger, under authority of the Governor-General, for this purpose, and to provide for the defence of the place.

As the habit of slave-selling had become almost irradicable, and the temptation to dispose of a few of his unfortunate Shiah subjects to the Turcomans, in exchange for horses,‡ and perhaps a little grain, was greater than the Vezir could withstand, the humane exertions of

* On the arrival of the Mission under Major Todd, from 600 to 700 of the 8000 inhabitants remaining in the city, had still to be fed daily by Lieutenant Pottinger. The only food which could be procured for them being iowaree and millet, boiled up with fat from tails of "Hoomba" sheep and a little salt, so as to form a very coarse broth, which they devoured greedily.

† Especially millet—of which three crops were raised yearly, in the rich ground near the city, under protection, at the time, of the "Jezails" on the ramparts; the frequent incursions of the Turcomans, after the siege, rendering the cultivation of their fields dangerous even at that short distance.

‡ The last source of revenue (slave dealing) was by no means so profitable as might at first be supposed. Although upwards of 12,000 slaves from Herat are stated to have been sold to Khiva, from 12 to 15 men and women were *frequently* given for a horse; and in one instance, of the truth of which I have no reason to doubt, for a horse presented to Major Todd, and sold at Girishk by auction, for, I think, Co.'s Rs. 500 (to a ressaldar of cavalry, for the Bhurtpore Rajah), 20 slaves had been given as the price, and one as a present to the servant who brought him.

Pottinger and Stoddart in suppressing the horrid traffic, and protecting the people against his oppression, exposed them to his ferocious enmity, so that, in the course of two months after the siege, they were insulted in the presence of the king, and ordered to leave the Herat territory; Colonel Stoddart accordingly left for Bokhara.

Lieutenant Pottinger having been requested to defer his departure, was again insulted, his house attacked by the Wuzír's retainers, and one of his servants seized, and publicly mutilated. This occurred in January 1839.

In the month of March, 1839, while the government and the people of Herat were receiving regular support from the British Government, overtures were made by the Wuzír to the Persian Court, and to the chiefs of Kandahar, to co-operate against Shah Shúja-úl-Múlk and his Majesty's British allies!

The rapid advance of our troops and the cautious policy of the Persian Court alone prevented this coalition. Kandahar was occupied, and Yar Mahomed Khan was among the first to congratulate his Majesty Shah Shúja on the occasion.

In return for these overtures from Herat, a mission * was sent

* The officers who served at Herat were as follow:—

1. Lieutenant Eldred Pottinger, of the Bombay Artillery, afterwards Major, C.B. He defended the city against the Persian army with determined gallantry.

He left Herat in August, 1839, after having been relieved of his duties there by Major Todd, and returned to India *via* Toorkistan and Cabul.

He was detained in Calcutta during 1840 in auditing the accounts of his expenditure during the siege, and returned to Cabul in 1841, to hold the appointment of political agent in the Kohistan. Of his subsequent history during the insurrection at Cabul, an account has been given by Kaye in his 'History of the War in Afghanistan.' His health had suffered so much from the anxieties, excitements, and privations he then underwent, and the treatment he experienced under the government of Lord Ellenborough on his return to India, that he found it necessary to visit China for the recovery of his health, and he *died* at Hong Kong in 1843.

2. Lieut.-Colonel Stoddart, of the Staff Corps of the British army, after leaving Herat, visited Bokhara, where he was thrown into prison, and afterwards cruelly *murdered* (along with Captain Arthur Conolly) by order of the Ameer.

3. Lieutenant Elliot D'Arcy Todd, of the Bengal Artillery, major in Persia, and K.L.S., K.D.E., &c., appointed Envoy to Herat in 1839, after having for some time held the appointments of Military Secretary to the Ambassador in Persia, and to the Envoy and Minister at Cabul, with distinguished credit.

His proceedings at Herat having been disapproved of by Lord Auckland's Government, he was remanded to his regiment, where, in the discharge of his duty in the command of a battery, he added to the respect in which his character was held by every upright man, and *fell* at Ferozeshah, at the head of his troop of horse artillery, while in action against the Sikh artillery.

4. Captain Edward Sanders, of the Bengal Engineers, afterwards Lieut.-Colonel, C.B., K.D.E., and Deputy-Secretary to Government, than whom the Indian army has never boasted a more gallant officer,—*killed* at the head of "the Kandahar Brigade," at the battle

under Major Todd for the purpose of negotiating a treaty of friendship and alliance between the British Government and Shah Kamran. By this treaty the independence of the Herat State was guaranteed, and the most substantial benefits were conferred upon it, on condition that slave-dealing should be abolished, and that no correspondence should be held with foreign powers without the knowledge and consent of the British agent at that Court.

This arrangement was completed in August, 1839, and a fixed monthly allowance, equal to the original revenues of the country, was granted by the British Government for the support of the State; the people were also exempted from all taxation until after the harvest of 1840; and advances for the purposes of cultivation, and for the restoration and support of trade, were most liberally made.

When pecuniary advances to the amount of not less than 60,000*l*. had been made for the benefit of the Herat State, and while every possible effort was employed by the British envoy to restore the country to prosperity,* Yar Mahomed Khan was detected in a treacherous

---

of Maharajpoor, in their successful charge on the Mahratta guns.

5. Lieutenant James Abbott, Bengal Artillery, since Major, and on the Ordnance Staff, after a service of some months with the Herat Mission as Assistant to the Envoy, proceeded on a political mission to Khiva for the release of Russian slaves, and in furtherance of this object travelled thence to St. Petersburgh, suffering the greatest privations. Of this journey he published an interesting account in 1843-44.

He was afterwards employed in civil and military charge of the Hazarah district in the Punjab in 1848-49, and most successfully defended it against Chuttur Singh and his Sikhs during the insurrection.

6. Lieutenant Richmond Campbell Shakespear, Bengal Artillery, since knighted, and Lieut.-Colonel, and in political employment in India, after serving at Herat under the Envoy, followed Lieut. Abbott to Khiva, and effected the release of a large number of Russian slaves, whom he made over to the Russian authorities at Orenburg. On his return to India *viâ* St. Petersburgh and England, he accompanied General Pollock's force to Cabul, and had the gratification of rescuing the English prisoners in that country. He has since been distinguished for his military services in Gwalior and the Punjab.

7. Assistant-Surgeon J. S. Login, Bengal Horse Artillery, since knighted, and guardian of the Maharajah Duleep Singh.

8. Lieutenant Chas. Fred. North, of the Bombay Engineers, distinguished for services in the advance of General Nott's force on Cabul in 1842, now Captain on the Staff in India.

Besides the above officers, who served for some time at Herat, the following accompanied the Mission, and left on other duties shortly after their arrival:—

Lieutenant Edward Conolly, of the Bengal Cavalry, Military-Assistant to the Envoy at Cabul, *killed* in a reconnaissance of the fort of Tootundurrah, in the Kohistan.

Assistant-Surgeon David Ritchie, of the Bombay Infantry, now Surgeon on the Staff, accompanied Major Eldred Pottinger on his return to Cabul through Toorkistan, surveying the greater part of that route, and by his professional services conciliating the good-will of the chiefs and people whom they visited.

Of the four European non-commissioned officers, serjeants in the Engineers and Artillery, who volunteered to accompany the Mission, only one now (1856) survives; two (Cameron and O'Gorman) were killed in Afghanistan.

* On the arrival of the Mission em-

correspondence with the Persian Assad-ed-Dowlah at Meshed, having for its object the expulsion of the infidel English from Afghanistan!

In the month of January, 1840, up to which time the advances to the Herat government and people exceeded the amount of 100,000*l*., and when king, chiefs, and people were equally saved from starvation by the exertions of our officers, a letter was addressed by Shah Kamran, at the instigation of the Wuzír, to Mahomed Shah of Persia, declaring himself to be the faithful servant of the Shah-in-Shah (Persian king), *that he merely tolerated the presence of the English envoy from expediency, although he was by no means niggardly in the expenditure of money, jewels, &c.*, and that his (Shah Kamran's) hopes were in the asylum of Islam!

This letter was, in March, 1840, sent by the Persian Minister to Lieut.-Colonel Sheil, her Britannic Majesty's Chargé d'Affaires at Erzeroom, in reply to the demand by the British Government for the restoration of Ghorian to Herat. Letters were at the same time addressed by the Wuzír, or his brother, to the Russian ambassador at Teheran, requesting that a Russian agent should be immediately sent to Herat.

Lord Auckland having been informed of the treacherous correspondence of Yar Mahomed Khan with the Persian Assad-ed-Dowlah (in October, 1839) was pleased to extend his forgiveness to the Wuzír for this breach of treaty, in consideration of his previous good

---

ployment was given, under the direction of Captain Sanders and Lieutenants Shakespear and North, to all the able-bodied men, in repairing the fortifications, and re-opening the numerous canals for irrigation which had been destroyed during the siege. Many families in the town, of persons unaccustomed to field labour, were employed in spinning thread for manufacturing into carpets (for which Herat had long been famous), receiving flour in exchange for their work; and advances were made to assist other tradesmen in procuring necessary materials for their business.

For the purchase of grain and seed-corn of different kinds from Seistan and Toorkistan considerable sums were expended, and arrangements were made with the chiefs of the neighbouring tribes to admit kafilas from all quarters free of duty.

One or two camp followers of the Mission had been picked up by marauders on our way to Herat, and sold as slaves to the Turcomans, but after a very short time it was made the interest of the chiefs on the frontier to stop the trade, and this was done effectually.

About thirty boys, rescued from slavery by Lieutenant Pottinger, whose parents could not in many cases be found, were supported by the Mission, employed half their time in learning trades in the city, and during the remainder under instruction at a school established for them. A dispensary and hospital were opened for the sick, at which numbers were daily under treatment; and for the numerous blind, lame, and infirm, a comfortable asylum was provided, in which all were to some extent made useful. These latter institutions were visited by almost every traveller who came to Herat from the most distant places; and it was as amusing as gratifying to witness their admiration of the hikmut by which the blind could weave "*mewar*" (coarse tape for tents, &c.), or make baskets.

services, in withstanding the Persians for so many months; and, in the hope that his lordship's leniency would have a good effect on the future conduct of Yar Mahomed, this forgiveness was extended to every such offence of which the Herat authorities might have been guilty previous to the receipt of his lordship's letter. As the Governor-General's order on the subject was received in February, 1840, the letters to Mahomed Shah and the Russian ambassador, which although unknown to the British Envoy until April or May, had been written in January, were consequently passed over without remark.

On being made acquainted with the lenient consideration with which he had been treated by the government of India, Yar Mahomed professed an extreme desire to give some convincing proof of his devotion to the British Government, and proposed immediately to re-take the fortress of Ghorian, then in the hands of the Persians. Trusting to his sincerity in this instance, he was some time afterwards permitted to make the attempt, and upwards of 20,000*l.* were advanced by the British Envoy, to enable the Wuzír to equip a force for the purpose. After every preparation had been made for surprising Ghorian, Yar Mahomed, on the most frivolous pretext, evaded doing so; and although no *direct* proof against him was obtained, the strongest circumstantial evidence supports the general belief that he, at the time, wrote to the governor of Ghorian, "that the English urged him (the Wuzír) to attack Ghorian, but that he (the Governor) need be under no apprehension"!! This occurred in the months of June and July, 1840, after advances to the amount of at least 190,000*l.* had been made for the benefit of the Herat government.

In consequence of this perfidious conduct on the part of the Wuzír, extra advances to the Herat government were no longer made, and their subsidy was limited to about 2500*l.* sterling per mensum.

When a sufficient time had elapsed for ascertaining the sentiments of the Governor-General on his conduct in the Ghorian affair, and no further notice having been taken of it than what I have above mentioned, Yar Mahomed, in September, 1840, renewed his intrigues with the Persians. An invitation was sent to the Persian minister for foreign affairs to meet the Herat authorities in conference, and the former accordingly left Meshed, en route to Ghorian, for that purpose. Believing, however, that by making this intrigue known to the British envoy, and attributing the blame of the transaction to his brother, he might reap a rich reward for his apparent sincerity, the Wuzír acquainted Major Todd with the circumstances, and urged very strongly his claims to further pecuniary advances.

In October, 1840, when intelligence reached Herat of the recapture of Khelat by Murab Khan's son, the advance of Dost Mahomed, and our reverses in Sindh, the Wuzír was only prevented from declaring against us by the occurrence of a feud in his family. He, however, made his involuntary forbearance a ground for further pecuniary demands, which were with difficulty refused to him.

Before information of the surrender of Dost Mahomed Khan had reached Herat, and when he found himself less embarrassed than he had expected by the seizure of his cousin (Sirdar Dín Mahomed Khan, who had been next in power and importance to himself), the Wuzír industriously circulated reports of his intention to march against Kandahar, and received emissaries from the disaffected in Shah Shúja's dominions. He at the same time, as usual, renewed his demands for money, which the British Envoy might, under the circumstances, have possibly been obliged to give him, had not the gratifying intelligence of Dost Mahomed's surrender, the re-occupation of Khelat, and the satisfactory result of our negotiations with Khiva, most opportunely reached him.

With regard to these negotiations, it may be mentioned that Yar Mahomed Khan had uniformly done the utmost in his power to thwart all the arrangements made by Captain Abbott and Lieutenant Shakespear, but fortunately without effect, as his character was well known and appreciated at Khiva. It may be also stated generally, that in this Memorandum notice has only been taken of acts of perfidy and treachery, of which there is direct and most convincing proof. To enumerate all the occasions on which, by spreading reports of our intended seizure, and of arrangements having been made with Persia, he endeavoured to intimidate the British Envoy into compliance with his demands, would be impossible. From August, 1839, to February, 1841, not a single week passed in which some rumour of the kind was not brought to us. On one occasion, in August, 1840, so general was the belief of our intended seizure, that in conversation with Shah Kamran, his Majesty took an opportunity to mention it to an officer of the Mission, and desired that we (Sahiban Inglís) should be under no apprehension, as he was our friend! but that, had he not protected us, not a Feringhí would have been left alive!! He pleased to conclude by asking, whether he did not deserve credit for behaving differently to us from what the Amír of Bokhara had done to Stoddard Sahib?

In reply, the English gentleman thanked his Majesty for his kindness, but said that we were under no apprehension; that we were conscious of having done only good to Herat, and feared no evil which could happen to us, especially as we knew that "to pluck a few hairs from a lion's tail was somewhat dangerous."

In January, 1841, when the disaffected Dúranís, in Zemindawar, had laid that district under contribution, and had sent exaggerated reports of their power and prowess to Yar Mahomed Khan, he again opened communication with the Persians, sent a large deputation under a confidential agent to the Persian Assad, at Meshed, and urged him to assist in an attack on Kandahar, while snow prevented communication between that city and Cabul.

As the opportunity appeared favourable to mark his opinion of this glaring breach of treaty,—the presence of a large force in Upper Sindh enabling him to do so with greater effect,—Major Todd determined to suspend the monthly allowances (2500*l.*) to the Herat authorities, until the pleasure of Government could be known, and he accordingly, on the 1st of February, notified this intention to the Wuzír.

Yar Mahomed having received, what he considered to be a very favourable account of the reception of his mission to Meshed, and intelligence having reached him of the re-assembling of the insurgent Dúranís in Zemindawar (after their dispersion in the previous month by our troops) by which he no doubt hoped that our communication with Kandahar would be cut off,*—trusting also to the continued forbearance of the British Government,—the patience with which they bore insults, and their evident extreme desire to retain the friendship of the Herat authorities, he determined to play a bolder game.

At an early period of our relations with Herat, and while he entertained some dread of punishment for his perfidy, Yar Mahomed had frequently proposed, as a test of his sincerity and of his devotion to British interests, that a contingent under British officers should be stationed at Herat. This proposal had at the time been favourably received by Major Todd, and by the envoy and minister at Cabul, but was disapproved by the Government of India. Knowing, however, Major Todd's sentiments on the subject, and believing that in this way only could he gain his end, the Wuzír again professed his acquiescence in the admission of a British brigade into the valley of Herat, on condition that a large sum of money,

* Yar Mahomed had, within the previous ten days, twice intercepted our letters to Kandahar. In the first instance, by employing Afghan thieves, he endeavoured to avoid the odium of the proceeding; but knowing that he was suspected, he, in the second case, gave orders to the horseman to stop the packet at a place (near Gurmal) where the Jummalzye Noorzyes were occasionally troublesome, and sent a horseman to feign having been robbed by them. On both occasions, it is to be remarked, that the intercepted despatches reported his treacherous proceedings, and of this, from previous occurrences, he must have been aware.

20,000*l.*, should be *immediately* paid to him, and the monthly allowances greatly increased. As a test of his sincerity in this instance, Major Todd required that the Wuzír's son, Sirdar Syud Mahomed Khan, should proceed in the first place to Girishk, there to await the orders of our Government, and to escort the troops to Herat, should the arrangement be approved of; and that, from the date of his arrival there, the advance of money should be paid, and the increased allowances commence. The Wuzír decidedly refused compliance with this counter demand, and by doing so showed, (however sincere he may have been when he first made the proposition for the admission of troops under British officers, — and that he was so while under dread of the vengeance of the British Government, there is no reason to doubt,) that the offer was now only made to serve his immediate purpose, viz., the obtaining of a large pecuniary advance. As this seemed to be the only available test of the Wuzír's sincerity, and as accommodation on the point seemed hopeless, Yar Mahomed brought forward what he considered his unfailing resource under the circumstances—the alternative of an immediate payment of the money, or the offer of a Mehmandar to conduct the British Mission from Herat.

Thinking it more dignified, in every respect, to submit no longer to the humiliating insults of an ungrateful miscreant, *whose very existence depended on our forbearance*, and whose arrogance and vanity were only increased by a continuance of our favours, Major Todd determined to accept the alternative offered him, and accordingly withdrew the Mission to Kandahar. To this proceeding he was further led, by his desire to leave Lord Auckland at full liberty to adopt any line of policy, which might afterwards be deemed expedient towards Yar Mahomed and the authorities of Herat, and to avoid the risk, which the daily increasing arrogance of the Wuzír's retainers augmented, of being left no alternative but the employment of force.

For having acted with these views and under these impressions, and for having failed in carrying out the conciliatory policy of our Government towards Herat, which Sir Alexander Burnes had, with his usual prudence, refused to attempt, Major Todd was, before the circumstances under which he had to leave Herat were known to Government, declared unfit for political employment, and remanded, with disgrace, to his regiment. * * * *

But to return to Herat,—Yar Mahomed Khan had by no means expected that the alternative he had offered would be accepted by the British Envoy. He consequently became greatly alarmed, and endeavoured, both by promises and indirect threats, to prevent the departure of the Mission from Herat. His attempts to effect this having been fruitless, he then entertained hopes of assistance from Persia, and meditated, in conjunction with the Dúranís of the Helmund, an immediate recourse to hostilities against us. With this view the Wuzír sent emissaries in all directions to rouse the disaffected in Shah Shújah's dominions, replenished his treasury by forced loans from the merchants (whom he had seized), by torturing all who had received advances for cultivation from the British Government, and by exacting fines from such as had been in the service of the "Feringhí kafirs," when at Herat. Doubtful nevertheless of the success of these proceedings, he, at the same time, thought it prudent to send letters fraught with friendship and devotion to the British Government, expressing his great regret that any misunderstanding should have taken place.

Of the failure of his hopes of assistance and co-operation from Persia he had not long to remain in doubt, and, as our negotiations with Khiva prevented aid from that quarter, as Sístan, Mymuna, the Hazarahs, Taymunnís, Jumsheedees, and Ferozekohís, were ready at a word to rise against him, and as of his own immediate adherents he had not 1500 men in whom he could confide, the Wuzír's hopes of resistance must have fled, and he must have prepared himself for any concession. Had a small * British force been at this time moved to the frontier, an *European* corps been sent from Quetta to Kandahar or the Helmund, and had the least display of offensive operations been made, Yar Mahomed must have *petitioned* for any terms which we might have chosen to impose upon him.

But in this extremity his proverbial good fortune did not forsake him : when he expected nothing less than the advance of a brigade of British troops across his frontier, he was delighted by the receipt of two friendly letters, assuring him of the high consideration of the British Government and of their deep regret that anything unpleasant should have for a time estranged their very faithful friend. To give him a better opportunity to explain his conduct, the Government disavowed all the late proceedings of Major Todd, and begged that the Wuzír would favour them with his own statement of the case; and greater effect was unintentionally given to these conciliatory letters, by our small force being withdrawn from the

* From the quantity of camp equipage which troops from India carry with them, the strength of any force in Afghanistan is always very greatly exaggerated, and the *moral* effect proportionate.

When the 38th Regiment Bengal Native Infantry arrived at Kandahar and encamped on the parade ground, it was reported at Herat that there were *eight* regiments; the tents of each company, according to Afghan ideas, being sufficient for a whole battalion. It may be useful sometimes to remember this.—L.

Helmund to Kandahar, leaving the Dooranees again at full liberty to renew their rebellious proceedings in Zemindawar.*

Satisfied, by these conciliatory overtures, that he had no immediate cause to apprehend an attack, and that the British Government were as anxious as ever to retain his friendship—satisfied also, that so long as the English did not attempt to molest him, he was free from any other attack—Yar Mahomed puts the letter from the British Government into his pocket, says that he can give no answer until, through his brother, whom he had sent to Teheran, he receives the commands of the "Imperatúr-i-Rús," continues to foment rebellion in Shah Shúja's territories, and torturing and enslaving his wretched subjects, whom the presence and protection of a British Mission at Herat had again tempted within his power!

---

* Of this they have not failed to avail themselves—Akhtar Khan, the Alizye chief, has ever since been in arms. Within the last month he, with, it is said, 6000 followers, has besieged the fort Girishk, which has only been saved by the advance of a small force under Captain Woodburn. The rebels have been defeated with great loss, in a night attack on Captain Woodburn's camp, but they have retreated to Zemindawar, and are still in force there. 1847.

THE END.